CRISIS OF THE HOUSE DIVIDED

CRISIS OF THE HOUSE DIVIDED

*An Interpretation
of the Issues in
the Lincoln-Douglas
Debates*

HARRY V. JAFFA

Doubleday & Company, Inc., Garden City, New York

1959

Library of Congress Catalog Card Number 59–10671
Copyright © 1959 by Harry V. Jaffa
All Rights Reserved
Printed in the United States of America
First Edition

To my Father and Mother

Acknowledgments

Two foundations contributed to the research and writing of this book. I was recipient of a Faculty Fellowship from the Fund for the Advancement of Education (Ford Foundation) in 1952–53, and of a grant from the Rockefeller Foundation, under its program in legal and political philosophy, during 1956–57. By the enlightened practices of these great foundations, they have had no prior knowledge of the results of my studies and can, therefore, have no responsibility for them.

I would like to express my gratitude to Mrs. James G. Randall for permission to quote from a letter by her husband to the author, and to the following publishers for permission to quote from books bearing their imprint: Dodd, Mead and Company; Harper and Brothers; Houghton Mifflin Company; Alfred A. Knopf; Princeton University Press; Rutgers University Press; Charles Scribner's Sons; University of Kentucky Press; University of New Mexico Press.

Preface

This volume is the first in what—it is hoped—will be a two-part study of Lincoln's political philosophy. Corresponding to *Crisis of the House Divided* would be (inevitably) *A New Birth of Freedom*. I would not so rashly give the name of a book not yet written had it had not been a convenient symbol of my conception of the axis upon which Lincoln's career and thought turned—an axis constituted by the House Divided speech and the Gettysburg Address.

Although it belongs to a larger whole, the present work is intended to have a unity of its own. I have attempted a thorough explication of the political principles by which Lincoln was guided from his re-entry into politics in 1854 until and through the Senate campaign against Douglas in 1858. To understand these principles, however, I have found it necessary to interpret the great occasional speeches of his early Whig period. This I have done in Part III, wherein I tacitly reject the prevailing view of Lincoln's slow growth to maturity: it is my conviction that he was extraordinarily precocious but that part of that precocity consisted in the self-control that compelled a supremely ambitious man to be a political follower when leadership could be seized only by irresponsibility. I have not, however—except by implication—dealt with Lincoln's position on political questions, as distinct from political principles, during his Whig period. Recent historiography has dealt harshly with him because of his partisan stand, both on internal improvements and on the Mexican War. The principles of this historiography are virtually identical with that revisionism which condemns him so bitterly for his opposition to Douglas in (and before) 1858. This latter condemnation is the subject of the critique with which this book begins and ends; and it is my hope, in still another study, to discuss critically the practical policies of Henry Clay's follower, as I have done those of the Republican leader.

Lincoln was elected to the presidency upon the issues and, largely, upon the speeches of the 1858 campaign. Although the secession crisis, as distinct from that concerning slavery in the territories, dominated the period after 1858, there is no sharp cleavage between the two. I have attempted to express herein the full meaning only of Lincoln's debate with Douglas from 1854 to 1858, yet I have not hesitated to borrow occasionally from Lincoln's 1859 and 1860 speeches when it was felt that such borrowing clarified the meaning of what he had said earlier. No endeavor has been made, however, to interpret with equal fullness that final phase of the debate between Lincoln and Douglas which merges into the election of 1860 and the secession crisis. This, I feel, belongs properly to the treatment of the war years.

The crisis of the house divided was the spiritual crisis which preceded secession and war. It is the thesis of this volume that, had not Lincoln challenged Douglas in 1858, there would probably have been no subsequent crisis, or at least none of the same nature. In 1858, by effectively destroying Douglas as the leader of a national political coalition, by dividing him both from the Republicans and from the South, Lincoln made morally certain that the nation would be constitutionally committed to his view of national political responsibility, a view which he well knew most of the South believed incompatible with its dearest interests. The crisis of the war years, with all its agony and possibility of failure, was yet in a profound sense less critical than the moment in which the commitment which produced it was being debated. The two crises differed as the defense of something differs from the decision to defend it. Or, to use the familiar metaphor which dominated Lincoln's own vision of America's experience, they differed as the Passion differed from the Temptation in the Wilderness. This study is meant to record, not without suggesting something of its passion, Lincoln's conception of the intellectual content of that moment of deliberation when the nation, as he believed, was tempted to abandon its "ancient faith."

Since Lincoln's thought emerges, in considerable measure, in dialectical fashion from the context of his continuing debate with Douglas, it can be understood only in the light of the contrasting policies and principles of his doughty antagonist. I have therefore attempted to re-create as fully as possible the moral and political horizon of the Little Giant. Douglas was a gallant as well as a powerful opponent, and he was a great American. If he was a lesser man than Lincoln it was because, at a moment when national purposes were confused and national identity obscured, patriotism was not enough. Yet I have sought to describe the large measure of consistency—and of dignity—that I believe Douglas's measures genuinely possessed. This, however, required a somewhat different kind of effort than did the interpretation of the fundamentals of Lincoln's thought. Douglas never left any record of reflections upon the issues raised by the whole American experiment in free government (the *Harper's* essay is only an apparent exception), such as Lincoln did in his earlier years, in the Lyceum and Temperance addresses, and in his Gettysburg and Second Inaugural addresses later. To describe convincingly the larger meaning of Douglas's statesmanship in his encounter with Lincoln, it has been necessary to elucidate his policy from a detailed review of his tactical maneuvers in dealing with slavery in the territories, from the Texas annexation resolutions in 1845 until the Senate report accompanying the revised Nebraska bill in January 1854. This I have done in Chapters V through VIII, wherein I also advance and defend the theory that the repeal of the Missouri Compromise was forced upon Douglas against his own intention. It is in the light of this theory that I have passed over, in charitable silence, those utterly meretricious arguments with which Douglas specifically vindicated the repeal.

It has been a problem, for which I crave the reader's indulgence, to know how to draw the line between padding the text with historical information and unwarrantably assuming a knowledge of the facts needed to comprehend the progress of the argument of this book. Because of the demands made by much of the reasoning, I have generally resolved my doubts by omitting anything that would, in my judgment, lengthen the already difficult span between evidence and inference, between premises and conclusions. In Appendix I, I have put in concise form the most important historical facts upon which this study rests and which are not fully explained in the text. I hope it will be adequate for those who have not recently read any general history of the first fourscore years of the Republic.

"Silence," our poet tells us, "is the perfectest herald of joy." And little would I understand of what I owe to others were I to try to say how great my obligations are. Lest silence be misinterpreted—not, however, by those to whom my debts are due—let me mention, first of all, Professor Leo Strauss of the University of Chicago, who directed my graduate studies from 1944 to 1949 at the Graduate Faculty of Political and Social Science of the New School for Social Research. He was and is my teacher, in a sense now archaic but not less vital for being old. The only limits of the scholar's profit have been his own capacity.

Professor Joseph Cropsey, also of the University of Chicago, would have written a better book on these themes had I not pre-empted them. I only add that the offices of friendship have not been merely negative and that he has fulfilled them in overflowing measure.

I owe much to the enthusiastic interest of Professors Allan Bloom of the University of Chicago and Martin Diamond, formerly of Chicago, now of Claremont Men's College. Frequent discussions with these gentlemen during the year I was working on this book in Chicago were invaluable in stimulating and clarifying my thoughts.

My wife typed this, as she has all my manuscripts. Her tactful suggestions, because of their unobtrusiveness, have probably had a more pervasive influence than I am aware of. The foregoing, however, have been the least of her contributions, although they are not little. On the frontiers of scholarship, the work of the pioneer wife continues, abating neither in hardship nor dignity.

Finally, I would speak of those to whom this book is dedicated. It was many years after I first borrowed Lincoln books from the Yale library for my father that I began to read them myself. The exemplary method, if sometimes slow, is the surest. And if, after my father, I became a Lincolnophile, so was I taught to love the things that Lincoln loved by my mother.

Harry V. Jaffa

October 7, 1958
The Ohio State University
Columbus, Ohio

Contents

APPENDICES

O, it is excellent
To have a giant's strength; but it is tyrannous
To use it like a giant.

> *Measure for Measure*, Act II, Sc. ii.

But in these cases
We still have judgment here; that we but teach
Bloody instructions, which, being taught, return
To plague the inventor: this even-handed justice
Commends the ingredients of our poison'd chalice
To our own lips.

> *Macbeth*, Act I, Sc. vii.

Part I

INTRODUCTORY

Chapter I

1958: The Crisis in Historical Judgment

A CENTURY has not diminished the fame of the Lincoln-Douglas debates. They are justly regarded as the greatest in American history, although in a deeper sense they constitute as well a unique episode in the history of free government in the Western world. It is doubtful that any forensic duel, any clash of reasoned argument before a popular audience—or, for that matter, before any legislative body—ever held the power of decision over the future of a great people as these debates did. Whatever their intrinsic merits, the magnitude of their consequences, for good or evil, is as undeniable as it is incalculable. By opposing Douglas for the senatorship in the Illinois campaign of 1858, Lincoln prevented the Little Giant from capturing the leadership of the free-soil movement, possibly even of the Republican party itself, at a moment when Douglas was being looked upon with the greatest favor by eastern leaders of the party. At the same time that he forced Douglas into a warfare with the Republicans that opened an impassable breach between them—and thereby kept open the place for leadership which he himself soon filled—Lincoln also compelled Douglas to take ground that brought about a new and more disastrous split in the Democratic party, a split which contributed mightily to the election of a Republican, and minority President, in 1860. Thus did Lincoln forge a great link in the chain of events that led to secession and civil war.

Popular tradition has surrounded the debates with the aura which, in retrospect at least, always attends a clash of champions. It has ascribed to them a level of dialectic and rhetoric befitting such a match. As to the intensity of the campaign and the emotions it stirred in the principals and followers on both sides, there can be no question. But the real worth of the debates cannot be judged merely by popular tradition, particularly when it is remembered that that tradition is today largely the tradition of the descendants of Lincoln's camp, for the debates proved the springboard whose momentum carried Lincoln to the White House and to the chief responsibility for the nation's safety in its greatest crisis. This tradition, finding a dramatic foil for its hero in Douglas, has pictured Douglas as a brilliant but unscrupulous "dough-face," a "northern man with southern principles," whose high-flying career was finally brought to earth by Lincoln's supreme political logic. According to this view, what Socrates was to the Sophists, what Sherlock Holmes was to Dr. Moriarty, what St. George was to the dragon, so Lincoln was to Douglas. The analogy with Socrates is perhaps the most apt, when it is remembered that Lincoln is thought to have wrought Douglas's downfall with a certain famous question.

But this view of the debates is not regarded highly today by leading authorities of the historical profession. "Solely on their merits," writes Albert J. Beveridge in a classic biography published in 1928, "the debates themselves deserve little notice." This judgment is repeated nearly twenty years later by James G. Randall, widely regarded today as the foremost academic authority on Lincoln, who also quotes with approval the opinion of George Fort Milton, the leading biographer and advocate of the cause of Douglas. "Judged as debates, they do not measure up to their reputation. On neither side did the dialectic compare with that in the debates between Webster, Hayne, and Calhoun."[1]

If this were a mere dash of critical cold water upon a piece of folklore, it would perhaps not much matter. The literary insignificance of campaign speeches is notorious, and the debates were, after all, campaign speeches. Yet this agreement of more recent opinion contrasts remarkably, not only with the folklore, but with the mature and scholarly judgment of the more distant past. James Ford Rhodes, writing in the early 1890's, said that Lincoln, in the campaign of 1858 as well as in his speeches on the repeal of the Missouri Compromise and on the Dred Scott decision, had formulated "a body of Republican doctrine which in consistency, cogency, and fitness can nowhere be equalled." And Rhodes, who was the supreme admirer of the great apostle of the Union, could write that "such clearness of statement and ir-

refragable proofs had not been known since the death of Webster."
As for rhetoric, Lincoln's "bursts of eloquence, under the influence
of noble passion, are still read with delight by the lovers of
humanity and constitutional government." "Listening to the arguments of Lincoln and Douglas," said Rhodes, "the meanest voter
of Illinois must have felt that he was one of the jury in a cause
of transcendent importance, and that . . . the ablest advocates
of the country were appealing to him . . ."[2] Lord Charnwood,
writing his famous memoir a generation after Rhodes, goes even
further, in his opinion that Lincoln, in the debates, had "performed what, apart from results, was a work of intellectual merit
beyond the compass of any American statesman since Hamilton."[3]

The alteration of historical judgments is a phenomenon all too
familiar to every student. It is no accident that the school of which
Randall was the leading member and exponent calls itself, self-
consciously, revisionist. The work of "revision" is characterized by
him in the preface to his masterpiece, the multi-volumed *Lincoln
the President,* as follows: "If sources are diligently re-examined,
then by the same token the product may become 'revisionist.'
Even in a simple matter it is not easy after the passage of years
to recover the true picture. If the past situation was complicated,
if many factors went into its making, if observers at the time
lacked full understanding or differed as to what it meant, and
especially if it has become controversial, then an uncommon effort
is needed to disengage reality from the accumulated deposit
which the years have brought . . . Evidence is . . . unearthed . . .
Discoloring is corrected, partisan misrepresentation . . . is exposed . . . Historical insight cuts through with a new clarity . . .
This is called 'revision,' but that suggests mere change or rewriting; a much better word for it would be historical restoration."
Randall then likens the work of the true historian to that of an
archaeologist: "Where a building belonging to a past age has
disappeared or fallen into ruin, there is the process of studying
available traces and records, examining the period, and gradually
building up a 'restoration' to show the structure as it originally
stood. With a like motive the historian seeks out original records,
excavates, so to speak, clears away unhistorical debris, and
endeavors, if he can, to restore events and essential situations of
the past." Randall does not, therefore, like some contemporary historians,[4] think it sufficient to replace the prejudices of one
generation with those of another in the rewriting of history. While

the revisionist does not expect to achieve perfection in his work, "he does hope by fresh inquiry to come nearer to past reality." "New conclusions come not from preconception, assuredly not from a wish to overthrow or destroy. The historian searches; he presents his findings; if he works validly he destroys nothing except misconception and unfounded tradition." It is in this spirit, we are told, that "the Lincoln-Douglas debates [have been] reanalyzed."

The impression is, I think, inescapable that the severe judgment upon the merits of these debates, coming after generations had looked upon them as an intellectual and moral contest of the highest order of which democratic politics admits, is a consequence of the rise and application of scientific historical method. This impression is greatly strengthened when it is discovered that revisionism differs from both the popular and scholarly tradition concerning the debates, not merely in the judgment of quality to which we have adverted, but on a substantive question of the first magnitude. For the depreciation of the debates is accompanied by—indeed, it may be the consequence of—a debunking of the belief which is at the root of their fame: the belief that Lincoln had opposed Douglas on a great issue and for the sake of a great cause. Randall, in his "reanalysis,"[5] concludes that Lincoln and Douglas only *seemed to differ* (Randall's italics) while actually they were in substantial agreement on all important questions. "For the debate to have had significance," he writes with marked emphasis, "the contestants would . . . have been expected to enter upon the practical and substantial results of their contrary positions." When, however, early in the canvass, "each candidate sought to impale his opponent upon the spikes of formal interrogation," it turned out that only upon the question of the prohibition of slavery in the national territories was there a difference. "Yet even on that point the difference was not vital in its practical effect upon the results. That is to say, in the territories that existed or might later be organized, Lincoln's demand of Congressional prohibition for slavery would produce freedom, but so would Douglas's principle of popular sovereignty honestly applied." The "only point of difference," then, itself turns out, according to Randall, to be "a talking point rather than a matter for governmental action, a campaign appeal rather than a guide for legislation."

It must be apparent that the judgment now confronting us is

as shocking and paradoxical as any rendered upon our national history. How paradoxical this example of revisionism is, how greatly it contradicts the common—or common-sense—conception of this historic episode, may be further gathered from the following contemporary estimate of the Illinois campaign of 1858 by a man who had labored in Douglas's camp: "It was no ordinary contest, in which political opponents skirmished for the amusement of an indifferent audience, but it was a great uprising of the people, in which the masses were politically, and to a considerable extent socially, divided and arrayed against each other. In fact, it was a fierce and angry struggle, approximating the character of a revolution."[6] That it is also shocking is evident the moment one remembers the immense importance of these debates in furthering the breakup of national parties and drawing the nation toward the abyss of civil war. For if the issue between Lincoln and Douglas was a mere talking point, if Douglas had as good a solution to the problem of slavery in the territories as Lincoln had, then what justification did Lincoln have to oppose Douglas and to bring on such an angry and deep-seated struggle? The inference is well-nigh inescapable that Lincoln opposed Douglas only to further his own ambitions, that he deliberately accepted the chance of civil war (which Douglas repeatedly accused him of inviting) by his house divided doctrine and by his "prediction" that the nation was faced with the awful choice of becoming all slave or all free. If Lincoln forced an illusory alternative upon the country, he must be accused of bringing on the very crisis he predicted, with the end in view not the future freedom of the nation's soil (which Randall insists that Douglas had already guaranteed) but the political future of A. Lincoln. We may even better appreciate the devastating character of the moral judgment herein implied if we ask: What would have happened had Lincoln accepted Greeley's advice and the Illinois Republicans had supported, or at least not opposed, Douglas's return to the Senate? The answers to such "iffy" questions are at best problematical, but we may venture the following with as much confidence as Randall advances the hypothesis that popular sovereignty would of itself have kept slavery out of the territories.[7]

Douglas, who had so recently led the Republicans in Congress to victory over the Buchanan forces upon the issue of a fraudulent slave constitution for Kansas, would not have moved away from them had Lincoln not forced him to do so. Thus his position

vis-à-vis the Danites, or administration Democrats, would have
been stronger throughout the North. This strength he might then
have used, either to dictate terms of reconciliation within his own
party, or to move over to the Republicans completely. Or, if
Douglas had headed a new free-soil party (it might have been
called Democratic-Republican, reviving the original simon-pure
Jeffersonian nomenclature), including Douglas Democrats as well
as all the principal ingredients of the combination that supported
Lincoln in 1860 (exclusive of lunatic-fringe abolitionists and
Know-Nothings), he might have led a party with a far broader
base than Lincoln achieved in the next presidential campaign.
It should be remembered that, although Lincoln would have been
elected in 1860 even if all the votes actually cast for other candidates had been combined in favor of any one of them, he received
only a fraction under 40 per cent of the popular vote in that
year. At the same time Douglas received nearly 30 per cent of
the popular vote in the country. Of the combined Lincoln-
Douglas vote in the free states, Lincoln received 60 per cent
and Douglas 40 per cent, and this tells why Lincoln's victory
was so decisive in the electoral college. Yet, although the split
in the Democratic vote did not directly cause Lincoln's election,
indirectly it must have played a tremendous, if immeasurable,
role. For the split made the election of Douglas (whose strength
in 1860 was far more diffused throughout the country than that of
any other candidate) by the electoral college a virtual impossibility. This fact, moreover, was well known throughout the
campaign. Had Americans chosen their President by direct popular vote in 1860, it is far from improbable that, notwithstanding
the damaging campaign of 1858, Douglas might have polled many
more votes than Lincoln.

Because of the peculiarities of the electoral system, the only
real alternative to Lincoln's election by the electoral college was
an election in the House or, still more probably, in the Senate.
Had Douglas carried New York or Pennsylvania, for example, in
both of which there were fusion tickets in the field against Lincoln
in 1860, then the electoral college might very likely have failed
to produce a majority. The South might have prevented the election of any candidate in the House, where voting would have
gone by states, and under the Twelfth Amendment the President
inaugurated in 1861 might have been the man chosen by the
Senate to be Vice-President. The cry of "Lincoln or Lane" un-

doubtedly sent many Douglas men into Lincoln's camp in 1860. This suggests the extreme probability that a coalition of Douglas Democrats and Greeley-Seward Republicans in 1860 might have produced a far greater electoral triumph for the free-soil movement in that year, even if the candidate had been Seward and not Douglas.

Had the free-soil candidate of 1860 enjoyed the vastly greater popular plurality that an addition of the Lincoln and Douglas vote suggests, it would have taken far greater moral courage for the South to have seceded. That a large minority had voted against Lincoln in the free states helped to convince opinion in the South that the North would never coerce them to remain in the Union. The South had long been warned by Calhoun that it ought not remain in a union in which the constitutional minority should be defenseless against the power of a constitutional majority. In the eyes of many, however, that the power of the constitutional majority should be exercised by an actual minority was not merely intolerable but contemptible.

In contemplating a possible alliance of Douglas with the Republicans we must keep in mind that, prior to the Illinois campaign of 1858, this party was by no means fixed in the mold which, however tenuously, Lincoln cast upon it as a result of that campaign. The radicalism of the house divided speech, so much deplored by Randall, was so little ingrained in the rank and file that even in the nominating convention of 1860 an amendment to affirm the principles of the Declaration of Independence as part of the party platform was voted down. A threatened revolt caused it to be included later, but without general enthusiasm and "without any application in terms of racial equality."[8] Any analysis of Lincoln's campaigns (in 1858 or 1860) makes it clear that, by opposing Douglas and thereby losing to the Republicans the free-soil Democrats whom Douglas could have carried into a Republican (or coalition) camp, Lincoln was forced to appeal to abolitionist elements which his party might otherwise have dispensed with. Having staked out a position in the house divided speech to which abolitionists could rally, Lincoln characteristically drew back from it in order to keep as much as possible of the anti-abolitionist free-soil opinion marshaled behind him. It was, however, the careful specification of Republican orthodoxy in the house divided speech, breaking up the anti-Lecompton coalition of the winter and spring of 1857-58, which read Douglas and his dyed-in-the-wool followers out of the free-soil party[9] and thus made it imperative that the Republicans recruit their ranks from abolitionists, however much these remained a minority in the party as a whole. Further, once Lincoln staked out a radical claim, whether he meant to be radical himself or not, it was inevitable that Douglas would pursue the obvious strategy of identifying Lincoln and his party with its most radical element. This was no more than Lincoln himself was doing when he insisted throughout the campaign that Douglas's position of alleged indifference to slavery was the most effective and dangerous proslavery policy possible.

Lincoln was responsible then not only for a definite shift in Republican oratory toward the inclusion of abolitionist slogans (Lincoln's house divided speech was in June 1858; Seward's "irrepressible conflict" came the following October; and Seward was one of those reported to have considered a coalition with Douglas!) but for assuring that his party would be advertised and identified throughout the country, above all in the South, as *the* abolition party. Thus, by furthering the split in the Democratic party, as we have suggested, Lincoln did more than merely promote the election of a minority Republican president in 1860. By creating the chasm between Douglas Democrats and Republicans he caused to be fastened upon the Republicans a character that would, to the existing mind and temper of the South, be indistinguishable from abolitionism, thus increasing beyond measure the likelihood of secession when such a party should carry a national election. If a Democrat had been elected in 1860, whether Douglas or another, it is improbable in the extreme that secession would have followed. But if Douglas had effected a coalition with the Republicans, and if the combination which carried the fight against Buchanan Democracy over the Lecompton fraud in Kansas and kept the soil there free under the banner of popular sovereignty had carried the presidency in 1860, it is equally difficult to imagine secession. For such a coalition would have possessed other advantages than the moral authority of a far greater weight at the polls, as suggested above. If the campaign of 1858 in Illinois had seen a united Douglas Democracy-Republican free-soil movement beating down the miserable fraud of Lecompton-Buchanan Democracy, there would have been no necessity to flaunt before the South either the Freeport Doctrine of Douglas or the abolitionism of the Republicans. It was by making both Douglas Democracy and Republicanism bitterly unacceptable to the South that Lincoln, above all others, made the Civil War the "irrepressible conflict" it became.

It is the great revisionist thesis that the Civil War was a "needless war," that it was a "whipped-up crisis," not the result of "fundamental motives," but of "war-making agitation."[10] If Lincoln was not a fanatic or agitator in the sense in which Randall uses those terms, it is indubitable that he, more than any man, helped produce the situation in which fanaticism and agitation could do their deadly work. To say that Lincoln did so, not for a substantial good that might not otherwise have been attained, but only to keep alive a "talking point," a point that might and did "talk" the country into fratricidal war, is to give him a character that, in the profundity of its immorality, is beyond treason. A Benedict Arnold sells out for gold, but while he may destroy his country he degrades only himself. But a man who makes enemies and aliens of friends and fellow citizens corrupts the soul of the body politic. To create strife where there was none, or where there need have been none, as a means to one's own fame, is to make honor the reward not of virtue or public benefit but of baseness and mischief-making. If the order of talents of the man who does this is high, so much the more reprehensible is his action.

If this conclusion concerning Lincoln appears unbearably harsh, we must protest that we have done no more than draw inferences from premises firmly fixed in the pages of revisionist historiography. We can see no way of questioning the conclusion but by questioning the premises. Was there no substantial difference between Lincoln's policy and Douglas's at the time of the debates? Would Douglas's policy have produced freedom as surely as Lincoln's, without the additional hazard of letting slip the dogs of fanaticism and the dogs of war? In short, how successfully does Randall's "valid" historiography contradict the illusion of a century, that the clash of Lincoln and Douglas was a great contest for the highest stakes and that these stakes were not the personal stakes of the principals but the future of free government not only for the people of the United States but, by reason of their example, for the world?

Chapter II

1858: Lincoln versus Douglas.
The Alternatives

IN A most remarkable obiter dictum, Randall observes that "one of the most colossal misconceptions is the theory that fundamental motives produce war. The glaring and obvious fact is the artificiality of war-making agitation."[1] Unfortunately Randall never explains to us the ground for his distinction between fundamental and non-fundamental (or "artificial") motives. He regards it as "obvious." But every historian knows that what is obvious to one generation may not be at all obvious to the next; that the self-evident truths of Jefferson may become self-evident lies to Calhoun. In like manner, Randall contemplates the two practical questions upon which the North-South controversy focused in the immediate pre-Civil War period: "What should be done about an almost non-existent slave population in the West, or about a small trickle of runaway bondsmen, was magnified into an issue altogether out of scale with its importance."[2] But again, we ask, important to whom? We agree that judgment upon such issues as those that divided Lincoln and Douglas and the North and the South is of the essence of the historian's function. But if we consider revisionism's primary aim, of historical "restoration"—an aim we accept unreservedly—the attempt first to see the past as it appeared in the past and not only in the light of the opinions of a later and different age, it is strange that Randall should so beg the question of why Lincoln, Douglas, and their contemporaries treated as real, fundamental, and important the differences he refers to as illusory, artificial, and slight. For the most superficial reading of the debates shows that the debaters themselves regarded their differences as radical and profound. Randall himself confesses wonderingly that "the intensity of the discussion baffled description."[3]

Among the Lilliputians, the greatest of all human differences was conceived to be the difference between those who opened their eggs at the big end and those who opened their eggs at the little end. Randall would no doubt feel confirmed in his opinion of war by the conflict between Lilliput and Blefuscu. Yet, however justified he might be, even in this case one would, we should think, want to hear how the issues might be stated by, or in behalf of, a Big-Endian and a Little-Endian. Many a throat has been cut for theological differences no more readily intelligible to the bystander than those satirized by Swift in the voyage to Lilliput. But who will boldly say that theological differences may not be fundamental?

Randall, in his zeal to do what he thinks is justice to Douglas, has written that "any attempt to add luster to Lincoln's fame by belittling Douglas or by exaggerating the differences between the two men would be a perversion of history."[4] Now, to exaggerate, except perhaps as a rhetorical device, is always a perversion of history because, by definition, exaggeration is a form of misrepresentation. And there can be no merit, of course, in contributing to the undeserved reputation of any man. Whatever fame may justly belong to Lincoln is cheapened by its admixture with undeserved fame, and the attempt decried by Randall would be foolish as well as dishonest. If exaggerating differences is wrong, so is it wrong to minimize them. And if we are to regard reputations, it may be remarked that Douglas's no less than Lincoln's suffers by trivializing the issues between them, for Douglas did not regard the difference between himself and Lincoln, which Randall treats as a mere matter of method in keeping slavery out of the territories, as a small one. For Douglas, as for Lincoln, it was immensely important that the form of the government of the territories accord with what he believed to be the true spirit of free political institutions. The principle of popular sovereignty, as he interpreted it, was to Douglas the key to political freedom, both in the United States and in the world. The American Revolution, he observed (echoing Webster), had been fought over a preamble—the preamble to the Stamp Act asserting the right of Parliament to bind the colonies in all cases whatsoever. The tax on tea was itself of no consequence, but the concession of principle involved in paying it was of transcendent importance. According to Douglas, it was the violation of the right of self-government which was the cause of the revolt of the thirteen colonies. Lincoln's principle, he maintained, that Congress might intervene to prevent the spread of slavery, meant that it might legislate the domestic institutions of territories and thereby determine the character of future states. The power so to do, Douglas maintained, rightfully belonged only to the inhabitants of those communities, and for anyone else to exercise this power would be of a piece with the attempt of the British King and Parliament to do for the colonists those things, whether good or bad, which the colonists believed might rightfully be done only by their own legislatures.

The principle of popular sovereignty meant the principle whereby each distinct political community, whether state or territory, determined for itself the institutions by which its daily life was lived, subject only to those general rules, embodied in the Constitution, which guaranteed to each its equal right to pursue its own way. Douglas, no less than Lincoln, saw in the American experiment the trial of the cause of political freedom for all humanity. The unity in diversity which the democratic federal Republic embodied was for him, no less than for his opponent, the world's best hope. Yet Lincoln and Douglas understood the nature of that unity, and the nature of that diversity, in radically different terms. On the fact of their antagonism and on its importance they were in agreement with each other and in disagreement with Professor Randall.

Lincoln held that free government was, in principle, incompatible with chattel slavery. The sheet anchor of American republicanism, he held, was that no man was good enough to govern another without that other's consent. There was no principle, Lincoln often argued, that might justify the enslavement of Negroes that might not also, with equal force, be used to enslave white men. Every concession made to Negro slavery weakened by so much the attachment of white men to the charter of their own freedom, and by so much prepared them to be subjects of the first cunning tyrant who should arise among them. Lincoln frequently compared slavery to cancer. It is not possible always to excise the malignancy without causing the patient to bleed to death, but neither is it possible for it to spread without causing death. The primary aim in both cases is to arrest the growth or spread of the element which is alien and hostile to the life principle, whether of the natural body or of the body politic.

Douglas's doctrine of popular sovereignty, with its self-proclaimed neutrality toward whether slavery was voted up or voted down, was a sheer absurdity on its face, according to Lincoln. How could anyone, he asked, at one and the same time advocate self-government and be indifferent to the denial of self-government? Anyone *sincerely* desirous of self-government—which popular sovereignty allegedly meant—*could not*, Lincoln held, be indifferent to slavery. The relation of master and slave was a total violation of self-government; to justify despotism was of necessity to condemn self-government, and to justify self-government was of necessity to condemn despotism. A popular sovereignty which could, even in theory, issue in the despotic rule of one man by another was a living lie, said Lincoln, and to embalm such a lie in the heart of a great act of national legislation—an act which announced to the world the principle by which the American republic incorporated vast acquisitions into its empire—would be a calamity for human freedom. For whatever the immediate practical effects of the Kansas-Nebraska Act, either in introducing or excluding slavery from the remaining Louisiana territory, its ultimate effects would have been no less disastrous to Lincoln than a change in the First Commandment from the singular deity to a plural would have been to a pious Jew or Christian.

As Lincoln held that no man was good enough to govern another without that other's consent, so Douglas held that no community of free men or group of such communities was good enough to dictate the domestic institutions of another community of free men. Lincoln, while holding that slavery in the abstract was unjust, conceded that it might be a necessary evil in some circumstances. But who should determine when such a necessity existed? Those who went out to populate the plains of Kansas, like those who had gone earlier to California, were not to be supposed inferior in wisdom or virtue to their less adventurous and hardy kinsmen whom they had left behind in the older states. Yet these pioneers, like their colonial forebears vis-à-vis the Parliament at Westminster, were not represented in Congress. If Congress could not legislate on slavery in the states, which *were* represented in Congress, why should it legislate on slavery in the territories, which were *not* represented in it? As for any man not being good enough to govern another, Douglas maintained:

> The civilized world have always held, that when any race of men have shown themselves so degraded, by ignorance, superstitution, cruelty, and barbarism, as to be utterly incapable of governing themselves, they must, in the nature of things, be governed by others, by such laws as are deemed applicable to their condition.

That Douglas was not simply hearkening back to the antiquated distinction between "Greeks and barbarians" is shown by the language of that advanced liberal, John Stuart Mill, in his essay *On Liberty*, published first in the year 1859:

> Despotism is a legitimate mode of government in dealing with barbarians . . . Liberty, as a principle, has no application to any state of things anterior to the time when mankind have become capable of being improved by free and equal discussions.

That the Negroes of America, by and large, were not "capable of being improved by free and equal discussion" was common ground to all but an infinitesimal minority in 1858. Lincoln, as we shall see, repeatedly declared himself against doing anything to "bring about the political and social equality of the white and black races." Douglas just as often hurled the allegation of utter inconsistency, of political trimming, against Lincoln on this score. If the Negroes were admittedly not to be our equals, then they must be our inferiors and governed by us, Douglas argued. Humanity and Christianity enjoin that the Negro be accorded every right, privilege, and immunity consistent with the safety and welfare of society. The practical question is: What are those rights? This question, Douglas averred, must be answered by each state and territory for itself.

Illinois had decided that the Negro should be neither a slave nor a citizen; other states had decreed slavery; still others had decided that Negroes might vote. Of the latter, some decreed special qualifications for Negro voters in addition to those required of white men, while others did not draw any such invidious distinction. Douglas's central practical contention came to this: that as Negro rights had, by the nature of the case, to be decided by white men, the white men competent to decide were those closest to the Negroes whose rights were to be decided. Conditions in Maine differed widely from those in Mississippi. Would anyone contend that the laws proper for the few free Negroes of New England were proper for the masses of still primitive Africans of the Deep South? Or vice versa? If Congress might leave it to the territorial legislatures to determine the laws governing the relation of husband and wife, parent and child, to establish entire civil and criminal codes, why might it not also leave it to them to decide concerning master and servant?

For Douglas, the essence of free government lay in the power of decision by free men on issues of vital importance to themselves. To deprive communities of free men of their power of decision over grave questions simply because they were grave was to strike at the main ground of justification of both federalism and democracy. He once said that the principle of the Kansas-Nebraska Act originated when God made man and placed good and evil before him, allowing him to choose for himself. As man's humanity lay in his power so to choose, so also did political freedom. Whether the external force was an absolute monarch, a parliament, or the Congress of the United States did not alter the case. The argument for self-government rested upon the competence of the people to decide all questions, including those of right and wrong, or there was no valid argument for self-government. Like Lord Randolph Churchill, Douglas's motto was "Trust the people." Lincoln and the Black Republican party treated the Declaration of Independence as if it insisted upon a universal leveling of the conditions of men everywhere, instead of raising the heads of free men above the common level, in virtue of their uncommon virtue and sacrifices. Their interpretation was a slander upon the Fathers, who would have been hypocrites had they meant to declare slavery against natural and divine law and then continued one and all to represent slaveholding constituencies and, most of them, to hold slaves themselves. Douglas's interpretation of the famous proposition was, in substance, that it meant "equality for equals only," and he believed that Lincoln's interpretation, by giving equality to unequals, was subversive of all order and justice. If Negroes might not justly be enslaved where their inferior natures or the interests of society required, they might not justly be denied any other equal right. The Black Republican credo, if adopted, would set in motion forces which could not stop short of full political and social equality, of miscegenation and mongrelization, such as had come to pass in Central and South America, where the natives had shown themselves utterly incapable of the self-government that flourished in the former British colonies.

To all this Lincoln replied that Douglas had drawn a false issue. Lincoln conceded that there was a physical difference between the white and black races which would probably forever forbid their living together upon a plane of equality. It was the ancient faith of the Fathers that all men are created equal. Yet that faith did not categorically forbid the denial of any kind of equality to Negroes any more than it immediately placed all white men upon a plane of complete equality. But Negroes were equal to white men in certain inalienable rights, and in virtue of those inalienable rights it was wrong to deny any man the right to put into his mouth the bread that his own hand had earned. Douglas's bogey—the slaveocrats' bogey—that the alternative to slavery was full political and social equality, Lincoln called a horse-chestnut argument, "a specious and fantastic arrangement of words, by which a man can prove a horse-chestnut to be a chestnut horse." Lincoln said it did not follow that if he did not want a Negro woman as a slave he must want her as a wife; he could just leave her alone. If it was true that less had been given to the Negro, the Negro was not for that reason less entitled to keep the portion that was his. Lincoln's ancient faith taught him, he said, that the Negro was a man and entitled to justice, but slavery was a total abrogation of justice. Although it might in some circumstances be a necessary evil, it was an evil all the same. To call it otherwise would be to pervert all truth, to poison the wells of public morality at their source—in that public opinion which is the foundation of all political action in a free society.

But, Lincoln insisted, he did not advocate abolition or any interference with slavery where it already existed. He conceded fully that part of Douglas's argument which placed the primary responsibility for determining the master-servant relation with those who lived with it. Living in a free state, he would not chide his southern brethren for their tardiness in adopting schemes of gradual emancipation, much as he was in favor of such action. But although as a citizen of Illinois he had neither the responsibility nor the right to act with respect to slavery in the slave states, this did not forbid him to express his opinion and advocate legislation with respect to virgin territories, the common possession of the Union, where no master-servant problem yet existed. There the question was not what laws were best suited for dealing with the Negro but should slavery and its concomitant evils be permitted to exist there at all? If the United States had somehow suddenly found itself possessed of a land with a large Negro population, such as Cuba, the question would then have been: What laws are best for these Negroes? But the vast virgin lands of Nebraska, like the lands acquired from Mexico, to which Lincoln had voted "forty times" to apply the Wilmot Proviso, had virtually no Negroes in them. To keep them out, and with them the train of problems their introduction would bring, was something no rational person devoted to civil liberty could, according to Lincoln, fail to desire. If Douglas really feared miscegenation, let him join the Republicans in restricting slavery, for slavery was precisely the cause of at least nine tenths of all miscegenation in this country. Free Negro girls were not likely to become the mothers of mulattoes without their own consent, at least.

When Douglas professed indifference as to whether slavery was voted up or voted down, he meant that not humanity or Christianity, or even the safety of society, but material self-interest was to determine Negro rights. John Stuart Mill, while admitting that despotism was a legitimate mode of government for barbarians, added, "*provided* the end be their improvement, and the means justified by actually effecting that end." Said Douglas, however:

. . . we ought to extend to the negro race, and to all other dependent races, all the rights, all the privileges, and all the immunities which they can exercise consistently with the safety of society. Humanity requires that we should give them all these privileges; Christianity commands that we should extend those privileges to them. The question then arises, What are those privileges, and what is the nature and extent of them? My answer is that that is a question which each State must answer for itself. We in Illinois have decided it for ourselves. We tried slavery, kept it up for twelve years, and finding it was not profitable, we abolished it for that reason, and became a Free State.

Or, on another occasion:

Whenever a territory has a climate, soil, and productions making it the interest of the inhabitants to encourage slave property, they will pass a slave code and give it encouragement. Whenever the climate, soil, and productions preclude the possibility of slavery being profitable, they will not permit it. You come right back to the principle of dollar and cents.

Such statements, according to Lincoln, showed that Douglas "has no very vivid impression that the negro is a human; and consequently has no idea that there can be any moral question in legislating about him. In his view, the question of whether a new country shall be slave or free, is a matter of as utter indifference, as it is whether his neighbor shall plant his farm with tobacco, or stock it with horned cattle." Popular sovereignty, so called, was thus wrong, "wrong in its direct effect, letting slavery into Kansas and Nebraska, and wrong in its prospective principle, allowing it to spread to every other part of the wide world, where men can be found inclined to take it." This policy, Lincoln said, first in 1854 and ever after:

I can not but hate. I hate it because of the monstrous injustice of slavery itself. I hate it because it deprives our republican example of its just influence in the world—enables the enemies of free institutions, with plausibility, to taunt us as hypocrites—causes the real friends of freedom to doubt our sincerity, and especially because it forces so many really good men amongst ourselves into an open war with the very fundamental principles of civil liberty—criticizing the Declaration of Independence, and insisting there is no right principle of action but *self-interest*.

But did not Lincoln see by the summer of 1858 what virtually the whole country saw, that Kansas would never become a slave state and that it was only a matter of time until it became a free state *under popular sovereignty?* And that there was no place in the remaining Louisiana territory so favorable to slavery as Kansas? Was his doctrinal moral opposition to Douglas worth continuing? Had not Washington himself said that slavery could in fact be abolished only by making it unprofitable? Had not Washington sought to link the valleys of the Potomac and the Ohio with roads and canals so that the spread of commerce and industry into Virginia and the upper South would render the slave labor system unprofitable?[5] And was not Douglas as much a practical idealist as Washington by trying to open the West as rapidly as possible and thereby develop a continental railroad system? Was not Douglas's policy far more effective in its anti-slavery bearing than any merely doctrinal moral crusade?

It seems incontestable that, while both men could not have been equally right in the positions they took in 1858, neither held his position out of mere expediency, although we may be sure that each was convinced of the expediency of the position he took. Both men approached the climax of political careers extending over a quarter of a century. Though Douglas's contemporary success and fame greatly exceeded Lincoln's, the latter's political apprenticeship had been thorough; and his 1838 speech "On the Perpetuation of Our Political Institutions" showed a conscious dedication of his life to preparation for just such a moment as this. Nor did the policy of either man reflect light or transient causes; rather it was the result of applying principles of whose validity each was deeply convinced and which alone seemed to illuminate the path of the American people as they struggled to find their way through the darkest enigma ever to perplex a democratic nation.

Although Douglas was the far better known man in 1858—indeed, it is doubtful that any party chieftain and statesman who has not occupied the presidential chair has enjoyed such fame and power in his own lifetime, unless it be Henry Clay or Robert A. Taft—his career prior to the debates is today relatively unknown. We shall try to restore the proportions of 1858 by first presenting an account of the highlights of Douglas's political life and thought, from his entry upon the national scene in 1843 until his great duel with Lincoln. In this account we shall be as sympathetic as possible, seeking the highest ground from which to survey Douglas's embattled career. For we wish, in such an account, to see the best justification of Douglas's course *in 1858* that a devoted follower or, rather, that Douglas himself may have seen as he surveyed his record and came to grips with his supreme antagonist.

Part II

THE CASE FOR DOUGLAS

Chapter III

Slavery

THE charge most damaging to Douglas's reputation through the years, given the widest currency among historians by James Ford Rhodes, was that he thought moral considerations had no place in politics. In recent years this has been repeated and elaborated by Allan Nevins.[1] Yet it is hardly an exaggeration to say that Douglas has suffered more from his defenders than from his detractors. George Fort Milton, his most violent contemporary partisan, calls him a "realist in an emotional age" who "sought to buttress his policies of economic intelligence" with "dialectics" because "he lived in an age when speech in any other vocabulary would not have been comprehended." This suggests that Douglas was a kind of commissar dealing with a backward proletariat. Yet there is no evidence that Douglas himself would have comprehended his own policies in any other idiom than the one he used, or that such a distinction as that between "economic intelligence" and "dialectics" existed in his mind. In his devotion to what he understood to be the mission of free republican institutions Douglas was as emotional as any man who lived in his age.

Douglas entered politics as a follower of Andrew Jackson. The image of Old Hickory was the star to which he hitched his wagon and to which he ever remained loyal. Like his hero, he loved and hated well. He loved the Union and was a fierce and belligerent nationalist. He joined hands with Jackson's old enemy, Henry Clay, to drive through the compromise measures of 1850 (even as Clay had assisted Jackson in the nullification crisis of 1832), because he believed the compromise would preserve and strengthen the Union. But, as he said in 1860, when he went into the heart of the secessionist country, convinced that the election of Lincoln was impending, he would hang higher than Haman (echoing Jackson's words a quarter century before) any man who resisted by force the execution of any provision of the Constitution. In this, his finest hour, Douglas's patriotism burned as intensely as did that of Washington or Lincoln.

Douglas was, moreover, an enemy of prejudice—ethnic, religious, or sectional. The heir of Jackson was devoted to enlarging the basis of participation in American democracy. But how to enlarge the basis of democracy in the 1850's was a difficult question, involving to a considerable degree choosing between the rights of Negroes and the rights of white immigrants. In contrasting his record with Lincoln's concerning the Negro, we must also contrast their records concerning the Know-Nothings, the "Native Americans" who sought to make second-class citizens of the foreign-born, particularly those of non-Anglo-Saxon stock. While Lincoln kept almost silent about them in public, expressing his strong hostility only privately, Douglas attacked the Know-Nothings openly, repeatedly, and vehemently. Moreover, it should be realized that, in speaking ill of Negroes as he did, Douglas only took one horn of a profound dilemma. That dilemma was whether to condemn the moral code of white men in the slave states who were his friends, relatives, and fellow citizens or, by speaking tolerantly of the right of the South to its "peculiar institution," to concede the only premise upon which such a right seemed justified; namely, the inferiority of the black race. The concession to pro-slavery opinion which Douglas made—the minimum concession needed to maintain the Democratic party as a national party and to preserve popular government in a nation increasingly rent by a deep moral cleavage—may thus have appeared to him as the choice of a lesser evil. That Douglas did, in the last analysis, feel more in common with pro-slavery opinion than with abolitionism (which Lincoln also opposed) does not mean that he accepted it. Douglas, like Lincoln, had deep personal as well as party ties with the South. The intolerance of the abolitionists seemed to him the more provocative as well as the more aggressive of the two extremes, and his passionate concern with the constitutional rights of the South led him to pour scorn upon the racial egalitarianism of its detractors.

Allan Nevins calls Douglas a man of "dim moral perceptions" who failed to see that "the irresistible tidal forces of history are moral forces."[2] According to Nevins, the forces of history, the movements of world opinion in the nineteenth century were irresistibly away from irresponsible autocracies and toward responsible democracies; away from slavery, in its many world-wide forms, toward personal freedom. Yet Nevins fails to explain how a statesman standing at the juncture of conflicting currents can infallibly know which way the tide of history is flowing. Lincoln at Gettysburg called the Civil War a *test* and meant thereby a genuine crisis whose event was doubtful. Lincoln certainly saw no predetermined direction of history. Moreover, Nevins does not tell us why swimming with the tide of history—assuming it has one—is morally superior to opposing it. May not a man choose nobly to oppose the "tide" of events? Has not many a good cause been saved by a stand, against all odds, by one who refused to count the odds? In the somewhat overblown peroration of a speech in 1839, Lincoln expressed this old-fashioned thought as follows:

> If I ever feel the soul within me elevate and expand to those dimensions not wholly unworthy of its Almighty Architect, it is when I contemplate the cause of my country, deserted by all the world beside, and I standing boldly and alone and hurling defiance at her victorious oppressors. Here without contemplating consequences, before High Heaven, and in the face of the world, I swear eternal fidelity to the just cause, as I deem it, of the land of my life, my liberty, and my love . . . Let none falter, who thinks he is right, and we may succeed. But if, after all, we shall fail, be it so. We shall still have the proud consolation of saying to our consciences, and to the departed shade of our country's freedom, that the cause approved of our judgment, and adored of our hearts, in disaster, in torture, in death, we never faltered in defending.[3]

When Douglas undertook to repeal the Missouri Compromise in 1854, he is reported to have said that he knew it would raise a "hell of a storm." But he had determined upon a course which he believed to be right and in the long-run interests of all he held dear. He too felt that a crisis had been reached and must be passed, that the rising tide of abolitionism was threatening to wrench American politics from its normal channels, within which national majorities and minorities could peacefully divide, and substitute a sectional issue upon which compromise would not be possible. When that was accomplished, the Union he loved would perish; and no more than Webster or Lincoln did he wish to see that day. If Douglas's doctrine of popular sovereignty, of allowing local majorities everywhere to decide the slavery question, had been accepted by the main body of northern opinion as an acceptable principle for dealing with the "vexed question," Douglas would have proved the master of the irresistible tidal force he roused against himself in 1854. And, in fact, only Lincoln's opposition in 1858 hurled Douglas down as he stood near, very near, the pinnacle of success.

Douglas was not blind to the moral implications of the slavery question. If he was constrained to profess indifference as to whether it was voted up or down, this was a logical implication of his commitment to popular sovereignty, according to which slavery ought to be dealt with at the local level. What his policy of "Don't care" really meant was that he believed he ought not to express an official opinion on a subject which he did not believe ought to come within the scope of his official responsibility. Taking the stand that the Constitution did not give Congress any rightful power over slavery—except the power, coupled with the duty, to provide for the rendition of fugitives—Douglas felt it was the duty of every member of Congress, by a kind of self-denying ordinance, to abstain from expressing views on the substantive issues raised by slavery, issues belonging by right to the state and territorial governments alone. As far as the federal government was concerned, Douglas wished to treat slavery as a jurisdictional question, and he knew that if he permitted himself to express opinions on the merits of slavery he would defeat his own purpose, which was to deny jurisdiction over it to the national legislature. For Douglas was convinced that the Union would not survive differences of opinion on slavery in that forum. To repeat: Douglas did not wish to speak on the merits of the slavery question because he did not wish Congress to become the forum for policies he believed could properly and effectively be framed only at the local level, state or territorial. In 1858, after the Lecompton battle royal, but one public word from Douglas on the immorality of slavery—one word merely to the effect that popular sovereignty, instead of "not caring" whether slavery was

voted up or down, was in fact the best constitutional instrument
for giving effect to the overwhelming northern free-soil condemnation of slavery in the territories—and Douglas could have
destroyed Lincoln's whole claim to leadership and made himself
the unquestioned free-soil leader in the Northwest. Lincoln well
knew this when, in his house divided speech, he said:

> Now, as ever I wish not to misrepresent Judge Douglas's
> *position*, question his *motives*, or do aught that can be per-
> sonally offensive to him.
> Whenever, *if ever*, he and we can come together on *princi-
> ple*, so that our *great cause* may have assistance from his
> *great ability*, I hope to have interposed no adventitious
> obstacle.

Nevins, in his indictment of Douglas, says that Douglas's biographers "have found in all his speeches and letters only one or
two intimating a dislike of slavery. A hundred can be found which
show that, as he once said, he did not care whether it be voted
up or down." In fact, Douglas used the famous "Don't care" phrase
in one or another form a number of times, although not nearly as
often as its incessant repetition by Lincoln and other Republicans
would make one think. And while Nevins gives several examples
of Douglas's alleged moral obliquity in relation to slavery, he gives
none of the "one or two" anti-slavery expressions. In 1860 the
Illinois Republican State Central Committee compiled a pamphlet entitled *The Political Record of Stephen A. Douglas on
the Slavery Question*. In it there are four double-column pages,
of the smallest-size type, which give his supposed anti-slavery
record, and eleven giving his supposed pro-slavery record. Even
this campaign document by the Republicans places Douglas more
on the side of the angels than Professor Nevins does! The charge
of inconsistency, however, leveled against Douglas in 1860 by
the Republican party may reveal the ground of Douglas's best
justification. For consistency, in any narrow sense, is seldom if
ever the path of wise statesmanship. We may anticipate Douglas's
justification in Winston Churchill's remarks about consistency in
politics, remarks specifically applied to Burke, who had once
attacked the British Court and defended the American Revolution, then later had defended the French monarchy and attacked
the French Revolution:

. . . a Statesman in contact with the moving current of events and anxious to keep the ship on an even keel and steer a steady course may lean all his weight now on one side and now on the other. His arguments in each case when contrasted can be shown to be not only very different in character, but contradictory in spirit and opposite in direction: yet his object will throughout have remained the same. His resolves, his wishes, his outlook may have been unchanged; his methods may be verbally irreconcilable. We cannot call this inconsistency. The only way a man can remain consistent amid changing circumstances is to change with them while preserving the same dominating purpose.[4]

Let us try then to grasp the dominating purpose of this brilliant, passionate, tenacious, and flexible man. According to the Illinois Republican State Central Committee, Douglas had worked steadily for the containment of slavery from 1845, when he introduced the amendment incorporating the Missouri Compromise line into the resolutions annexing Texas, until the fourth of January 1854, when he made his report as chairman of the Senate Committee on Territories, which introduced a new Nebraska bill, "neither affirming nor repealing the eighth section of the Missouri Act." However, on January 23, 1854, "nineteen days after he was 'not prepared to recommend a departure' from the Missouri prohibition," says the Republican State Central Committee, "Mr. Douglas brought in a new bill, dividing Nebraska into two Territories—Kansas and Nebraska—and repealing the Missouri Compromise . . ." This, says the committee, "constitutes the turning point in Mr. Douglas's political highway. From this sharp corner, his course is wholly and utterly pro-slavery, down to the introduction of the Lecompton bill in the Senate, where he takes a position of indifference, best expressed in his phrase, 'Don't care whether slavery is voted down or voted up.' The indifferent mood is preserved a little more than two years, when, as will be seen by the record, he becomes more wrathfully pro-slavery than ever before."

We shall then, in the words of another famous American, look at the record. Before doing so, however, we may be permitted to hear Douglas "off the record." It is, we believe, essential that such permission be granted, because Douglas's position as a party leader always depended upon maintaining an alliance of the Northwest with the South, even before the breakup of the Whig party made the survival of the Union depend so heavily upon the preservation of Democratic harmony. For it was this alliance which gave each wing of the party the prospect of membership in a majority coalition, without which either would almost certainly have been condemned to minority status in the nation. And an overt condemnation of slavery or expressed hostility to it would have shattered such an alliance instantly, at any moment of Douglas's career. In like manner, it would be impossible to do full justice to Lincoln's policy in the 1850's without reading his off-the-record denunciations of the Know-Nothings. And so, in 1854, in the first shock of the terrific attack by Chase and the other "Independent Democrats" in Congress upon Douglas's character and motives, amid the pealing of the tocsin that was to arouse the spirit of John Brown, a spirit that did not rest until the institution of slavery was dissolved by the blood of fratricidal war, Douglas spoke as follows to a young man, the son of an old friend and benefactor:

> I am not pro-slavery. I think it is a curse beyond computation to both white and black. But we exist as a nation by virtue only of the Constitution, and under that there is no way to abolish it. I believe that the only power that can destroy slavery is the sword, and if the sword is once drawn, no one can see the end.[5]

This "anti-slavery" sentiment, be it noted, came at the moment of the repeal of the Missouri Compromise, the supreme "pro-slavery" action of his life. But, he then observed in this *private* interview, repeal also meant that "slavery could no longer crouch behind a line which freedom dared not cross." By repealing the implied presumption in favor of slavery south of the line (and that the Missouri Compromise line implied such a presumption Lincoln conceded) Douglas expected that freedom would spread farther and faster. While no such out-and-out anti-slavery sentiments can be found in the public records, we are justified in asking, as we scan those records, whether anything in them is inconsistent with such an anti-slavery bias. By and large we shall find that Douglas's record with respect to slavery rests upon two axioms: first, that the question must be kept out of the halls of Congress, where it could do only mischief by destroying national feeling; and, second, that the boundaries of the United States must be extended and new territory organized as rapidly as possible on the basis of popular sovereignty. The connection between these axioms is this: Douglas believed that the organization of new territory would rapidly result in new free states, would lead to an overwhelming preponderance of freedom over slavery in the Union and an absorption in the constructive task of filling and building up the vast continental domain, a task which would so engage the energies of the nation as to leave the subject of slavery neglected and largely forgotten.

If one expression were needed for Douglas's policy, it would not be "popular sovereignty" but "expansion." Indeed, in Douglas's political lexicon it would be difficult to distinguish accurately between the two. Expansion was the keynote of Douglas's foreign policy, popular sovereignty of his domestic policy, but they were related as the obverse and the reverse of a single coin. Douglas, more than Lincoln, identified the cause of political freedom with the freedom then known in the United States and therefore saw the central domestic task not, as Lincoln saw it, in preserving or perfecting that freedom, but in spreading it. Unlike Lincoln, Douglas had little or no confidence in the power of the American *example* to bring freedom to other lands or peoples. For Douglas the only effective security for American freedom lay in its own physical resources and power, and the only effective agency for increasing freedom lay in the expansion of American boundaries. The freedom-seeking oppressed peoples of the Old World, poured into the indefinitely expansible matrix of the American constitutional system, would in this way have a chance to share in enlightened political institutions. It was not Douglas's custom to indulge in remote speculations, but it is hardly an exaggeration to say that the ultimate logical consequence of his foreign policy would have been a federal republic of the world. Something like the Roman dream of a universal republic was the driving force behind his policies, but it was a universal republic in which local autonomy was genuine, not spurious. The American republic, unlike the Roman, would not be characterized by the ascendancy or hegemony of any one of its parts within the whole. The name "American" would belong originally, and of equal right, to each constituent community. It was the constitutional equality of each distinct political community within the federal system which provided the guarantee that each accession of territory and population to the Union would mean an increase of human freedom and welfare. It was this which made American imperialism, unlike every other imperialism, a blessing to all humanity as well as to itself. It was popular sovereignty which made expansion both feasible (by disarming malice and envy) and desirable (by extending republican freedom).

But we must now show how, from Douglas's viewpoint, the policy of expansion also served, in turn, the cause of popular sovereignty. In the Union as it was when Douglas's political career in Congress began in 1843, free and slave states were evenly balanced (at thirteen each). A rising tide of attack upon slavery in the North was matched by a rising tide of defense of slavery in the South, a defense which increasingly insisted upon slavery as a "positive good." How Douglas saw the political problem presented by the threat to the survival of American freedom from abolitionists on the one hand and Calhoun's "positive good" school on the other may be gathered from these widely circulated remarks in the Senate in 1848. In the midst of angry criminations and recriminations by the abolitionist Senator Hale of New Hampshire, and Calhoun, Foote, and Davis of the southern ultra side, Douglas addressed his fellow Democrats as follows:

I said that the Senator from South Carolina, by the violent course pursued here, has contributed to the result which we deplored, and the abolitionism at the North was built up by Southern denunciation and Southern imprudence. I stated that there were men of the North who are ready to take advantage of that imprudent and denunciatory course and turn it to their own account, so as to make it revert upon the South . . . I have no sympathy for abolitionism on the one side, or that extreme course on the other which is akin to abolitionism. We [Northern Democrats] are not willing to be trodden down, whilst you hazard nothing by your violence, which only builds up your adversary in the North. Nor does he hazard anything; quite the contrary, for he will thus be enabled to keep concentrated upon himself the gaze of the abolitionists, who will regard him as the great champion of freedom . . . so that it comes to this, that between those two ultra parties, we of the North, who belong to neither, are thrust aside. Now, we will stand up for all your constitutional rights, in which we will protect you to the last . . . But we protest against being made instruments—puppets— in this slavery excitement, which can operate only to your interest and the building up of those who wish to put you down.[6]

It is instructive that this essentially moderate and middle ground of Douglas had already been characterized by the grim and uncompromising Calhoun as more offensive than abolitionism itself. The reason is brilliantly exposed by Douglas in the foregoing passage: the extremes have a common interest against the mean. Calhoun's political goal in 1850, the consolidation of southern nationalism, depended upon the enemy in the North, abolitionism. The abolitionists, likewise, could not grow strong without Calhoun's "positive good" school. Southerners like Jefferson or Patrick Henry (or Henry Clay) were not convenient targets for abolitionist propaganda. Although such men did think that abolition was incompatible with the safety of the white South ("Justice is in one scale, and self-preservation in the other," Jefferson had said), they were willing and even anxious to have gradual emancipation if some way could have been found to remove the freed Negroes; but the last thing that abolitionists wanted was a responsible statesmanship that would face the very real question of race adjustment that emancipation would pose.

But Calhoun, before he became an overt disunionist, had been converted from an American to a southern nationalist. His disciple, Hayne, in the celebrated debate with Webster, had already identified as the enemies of American liberty those who would convert this from a federal into a *national* union. American nationalism was thus conceived to be the deadly enemy of southern freedom. But Douglas, like Jackson, was nothing if not a nationalist. Where, however, southern extremists placed an extreme interpretation of the rights of the states under the federal Constitution, abolitionists denounced the Constitution out of hand. The Constitution not only sanctioned slavery but gave slaveholders the right to represent three persons in the House of Representatives for every five slaves. This, said the abolitionists, meant offering a kind of perpetual bonus for enlarging the extent of human bondage. Such "compromises" were bargains with the devil, and the Constitution was a "covenant with hell." "No Union with slaveholders," cried abolitionists.

Between these upper and nether millstones Douglas sought a formula of compromise and conciliation. An emergent American nationality was confronted with this gigantic obstacle of slavery. The sections would not, he saw, and could not agree upon the issue itself. The only way out was an agreement to disagree and a concentration of all loyalties upon that Constitution which safeguarded this very precious right—the right to disagree. Douglas's confidential words to young George McConnel are the tacit premise of his entire policy with respect to slavery: ". . . we exist as a nation by virtue only of the Constitution, and under that there is no way to abolish [slavery]." If we would understand why Douglas in the last analysis seems to sympathize more with the pro-slavery extreme than with the abolition extreme, we must remember that the pro-slavery party always took its stand upon the Constitution, albeit according to its own interpretation. Douglas's rhetoric appealed to a principle that the pro-slavery party at least recognized. The abolitionists, on the contrary, appealed to a "higher law," were willing to damn the Constitution, and admitted no premise to which Douglas might appeal in the interest of any compromise.

Within the framework of the Constitution, thought Douglas, the only way to abolish slavery was to appeal to the people of the states and the territories, who did possess the constitutional power and right to deal as they wished with it. If abolitionists could not persuade the people morally and constitutionally competent to deal with slavery, they had no right to address themselves to those who were incompetent. It meant appealing from persuasion to force, the very antithesis of political freedom. To alter the Constitution, as abolitionists wished, so as to bring slavery in the slave states under the power of the free states, meant removing a vital domestic question from the jurisdiction of a free community because it failed to meet the approval of those outside that community. Such an appeal was subversive of the very idea of free government, was the very formula of arbitrary power. The abolitionists might as well have appealed to foreign powers to enable them to accomplish their dearest wish. The genius of the federal system, its ability to extend itself and freedom simultaneously, lay in the scrupulous observance of this division of federal and local authority and the loyal acceptance of the decisions of constitutional majorities, however unpleasant, under the terms of that division. Despite Douglas's frequent statements to the effect that the slavery question would be decided by the people in each locality on the basis of self-interest, his appeal to the genius of federalism was in fact an appeal to self-restraint, to the denial of self-indulgence, to virtue. Like Lincoln, who once wrote that he bit his lip and kept silent about slavery as long as the South did no more than exercise its constitutional power over the subject, Douglas too believed that freedom—including freedom of speech—sometimes depended upon the ability of men to keep silent.

Since, however, Douglas was indeed the "realist" George Fort Milton calls him, he had another solution of the problem than a dependence upon virtue thus conceived. This was the solution represented by the policy of expansion and was, in essence, an application of the theory of the *Federalist Papers* as expressed in the following passage from #51: "In a free government the security for civil rights must be the same as that for religious rights. It consists in the one case in the multiplicity of interests, and in the other in the multiplicity of sects. The degree of security in both cases will depend on the number of interests and sects; and this may be presumed to depend on the extent of country and number of people comprehended under the same government." And so Douglas felt that the danger of disunion and oppression which loomed large while the contest was between North and South might be dissipated as and when the country comprised still other sections. In short, he wished, through expansion, to submerge factionalism in the melting pot of Union.

The following is from an exchange with Webster in the Senate in 1850:

We have heard so much talk about the North and the South, as if those two sections were the only ones necessary to be taken into consideration, when gentlemen begin to mature their arrangements for a dissolution of the Union . . . that I am gratified to find that there are those who appreciate the important truth, that there is a power in this nation greater than either the North or the South,—a growing, increasing, swelling power, that will be able to speak the law to this nation, and to execute the law as spoken. That power

is the country known as the great West . . . We indulge in
no ultraisms—no sectional strifes . . . Our aim will be to do
justice to all . . .[7]

The West, Douglas felt, while destined to be free soil, would
not have that factious interest in slavery which characterized the
abolition strongholds in the old free states. Douglas was confident
that his own "plague on both your houses" attitude toward the
old sectional dispute would be the attitude of the new states.
For the West, constituting in this respect a kind of third force (or
faction), would hold the balance between the other two. It would
be able to give overwhelming preponderance to the North in
opposing secession, or to the South in opposing abolition. It would
have no vested interest besides the Constitution and the Union.
The decisive constructive task of statesmanship, in Douglas's
view, was to build the West rapidly enough so that it could
play this role before the disruptive forces in the older sections
became uncontrollable.

Although Douglas never unequivocally denounced slavery as
an evil or curse in public, he once came so close to doing so that
his words should be carefully noted. It was in the same debate
in which Calhoun and Hale figured so prominently in 1848.
Douglas then said:

In the North it is not to be expected that we should take
the position that slavery is a positive good—a positive blessing. If we did assume such a position, it would be a very
pertinent inquiry, Why do you not adopt this institution?
We have moulded our institutions at the North as we have
thought proper; and now we say to you of the South, if
slavery be a blessing, it is your blessing; if it be a curse, it
is your curse; enjoy it—on you rest all the responsibility![8]

One feature of this passage is the question it raises concerning
the isothermic theory to which we have adverted above and upon
which Douglas relied increasingly from 1854 onward. According
to that theory, it was both expedient and right for white men
to adopt slavery wherever soil and climate made it profitable.
Here Douglas suggests that the North may have rejected slavery
not because it was unprofitable but because it was a curse. That
slavery, whatever its intrinsic good or evil, was an apple of discord and thereby a fruitful source of evil to the American

republic, Douglas certainly believed. But whereas Lincoln insisted upon the public recognition of the intrinsic evil of slavery
as the only sound basis for any and all practical dealings with
the institution, Douglas came increasingly to the conviction that
practical measures directed toward the containment of slavery
could succeed only if they did *not* involve the abstract question
of the intrinsic good or evil of slavery. This, it would seem, explains why Douglas never again spoke so openly of the vicious
tendency of the Southern "positive good" school or openly defended his own northern constituents' "right to disagree" on the
intrinsic merits of slavery.

The speech from which we have just quoted was delivered
only a decade before the joint debates. In the intervening period
a number of changes occurred which greatly enforced the wisdom
of this change of tactics. The ground for the conviction that
popular sovereignty *meant* freedom became, in Douglas's opinion,
immeasurably firmer; and as it did, the need to emphasize this
agreeable truth to the North became proportionately less urgent,
even as it became urgent to avert the gaze of the South from
this disagreeable prospect. What were some of these changes?
First was the admission of California as a free state in 1850,
destroying forever the balance of free and slave states. No less
important was the fact that California had become free by the
completely unsupervised action of the Californians themselves;
i.e., by popular sovereignty. The inhabitants of the new state
were fairly evenly divided between those of free- and slave-state
nativity, but opinion against slavery there was fairly unanimous.
Yet California's political complexion was strongly Democratic,
with a marked sympathy for the political demands of the slave
states. In 1854 both her senators and representatives voted for the
Kansas-Nebraska bill on a heavily sectional vote. Abolitionist
sentiment there was virtually nonexistent. California was free soil
because Mexican labor was cheaper, more economical than slave
labor. And southern California was the only part of the vast Mexican acquisition believed to be suitable to slave culture. Douglas's
increasing emphasis on the dollars-and-cents argument—which
involved a willingness to concede the desirability of slavery in
such places as Louisiana, a desirability he implicitly repudiated
in the remarks of 1848 already cited—certainly seems to bear the

impress of the success of popular sovereignty, as an instrument of freedom, in California.

Another reason for Douglas's shift in tactics in the decade 1848–58 is the change in his northern constituency, meaning thereby the whole North, not only Illinois. That change was largely due to the amazing immigration of that decade. It has frequently been recorded that in each of the two decades before the Civil War immigration passed the two-million mark. But immigration in the ten years preceding the joint debates actually was well over three million. Of this, 44 per cent was Irish and 33 per cent German. Douglas was the first and perhaps the most popular national leader Irish-born Americans have ever had.[9] The Irish went overwhelmingly into the Democratic camp, although the Whig-Republican Seward in New York sharply challenged Douglas's appeal there by taking a strong anti-Know-Nothing stand. And the Irish, more strongly than any other group in the North, felt what was probably uniformly if less keenly felt by nearly all elements of Lincoln's free-soil coalition except the radical abolitionists. This was a hatred of the Negro exceeding the hatred of slavery. The Irish, who constituted the central reserve of cheap unskilled free labor, a reserve which pushed forward railroad development, always a major plank in Douglas's platform, bitterly detested the thought of competition with Negro labor. The Irish, therefore, like the great majority of laboring whites of the North, were against both the spread of slavery, which might have brought them into contact with Negroes, *and against any tendency toward Negro emancipation,* which would have had the same consequence. Douglas had no stronger rhetorical trump in 1858 than the one he sounded at Ottawa, in the first joint debate, when he said: "Do you desire to turn this beautiful state into a free Negro colony, in order that when Missouri abolishes slavery she can send one hundred thousand emancipated slaves into Illinois . . . ?"

A further consequence of the vast immigration we have noted was to render largely theoretical the abolitionist charge against the Constitution, that in effect it offered, in its three-fifths clause, a reward for enslavement. This clause in the Constitution had weighed heavily in the opposition of men like Daniel Webster to territorial expansion. Lincoln always incorporated Webster's arguments against the three-fifths clause in his indictment of the slave power. Yet the vast augmentation of the population of the free states, over and above natural increase, by reason of foreign immigration (for only a tiny fraction of immigrants went into slave states, where they might have had to compete with black labor), gave the free states an overwhelming preponderance in the House of Representatives and in the electoral college. One Southerner testily remarked that when it was made a capital crime to import a Negro from Africa it should at least have been made a felony to bring in an Irishman.

The potato famine in Ireland, the crop failures in Germany, the abortive European revolutions, particularly in Germany in 1848, all swelled the tide to this country. Until the relatively short-lived panic of 1857 there was general prosperity, both here and abroad, during the decade. Great Britain's repeal of the Corn Laws in 1846, the California gold rush, the Crimean War, all conspired to place American agriculture under forced draft. The same forces that enormously expanded the cotton culture of the South were setting the prairies on fire with the demand for American grain.

The crisis over slavery was largely brought on by the sharpening competition, within the American agricultural system, of the grain and cotton interests for new lands and new laborers. But the agricultural economy which centered upon grain production (but including much more general diversified farming than that centered upon cotton) was a free-labor economy. In such an economy both capital and labor were more mobile. The agricultural entrepreneur of the free state could put his capital entirely into land and equipment. Slavery did not require of him any capital accumulation for labor, nor did his dignity prevent him or his children from laboring in their own fields. If he needed more labor, he could hire it and pay for it out of current production. Indeed, the very prosperity of the southern economy in the fifties made it a poorer competitor in the western territories where popular sovereignty was to rule. For the skyrocketing of slave prices made slaves too valuable to risk in regions not protected by the elaborate system of racial control of the slave states: slave codes, slave patrols, and judges, juries, and police all thoroughly devoted to the institution. Moreover, the high prices of slaves in the fifties also reflected the increasing profitability of the employment of slaves in the older South, which for nearly a generation had been mainly concerned with exporting them to newer regions. In short, never had slaveowners had less incentive to risk slaves in places where their tenure might prove insecure.

Free labor did not need any elaborate system of controls; wages and profits and the hope of bettering one's lot generated the conditions for its success spontaneously. The mobility, flexibility, and spontaneity of the free-labor system meant clearly, as it must have appeared to the keenly observant vision of Douglas, that the odds were overwhelmingly in favor of free-stater and free-soil in any contest for western lands conducted under the rules of popular sovereignty. In Allan Nevins's words, ". . . it was plain that *if* the country held together, every step forward would strengthen the free society as against the slave society." But precisely if this were true, does it not mean that the primary task of statesmanship in this period was to hold the country together rather than to indulge in moral condemnation of slavery? Nay, did it not mean to hold the country together even if it required the condonation of slavery, a propitiation of the slave interest by a kind of pretended agreement with its prejudices, which would thus lull it into a false sense of security and thereby give it a kiss of death? Douglas, during the fifties, had far more extensive contacts and acquaintances throughout the South than did Lincoln, and he was impressed, as Lincoln apparently was not, with the immediate danger from the unreconstructed disciples of Calhoun, who would break up the Union rather than permit the slave states to become a minority.

Douglas had been confronted with this resolve in 1849, when Calhoun had rallied support for a constitutional amendment guaranteeing that the number of free and slave states would always be in balance. It is probable in the extreme that Calhoun was as much interested in promoting secession as in promoting the amendment, by laying down an ultimatum to the North upon which the South would rally. To the idea itself, Douglas then responded as follows:

As I understand [the Senator from South Carolina] he desires such an amendment as shall stipulate that, in all time to come . . . there shall always be as many slaveholding as free states in this Union. In my opinion, the adoption and execution of such a constitutional provision would be a moral and physical impossibility. In the first place, it is not to be presumed that the people of the free states would ever agree to such an amendment . . . and secondly, if they should, it would be impossible to carry it into effect. I have already had occasion to remark, that at the time of the adoption of the Constitution, there were twelve slaveholding states, and only one free state, and of those twelve, six of them have since abolished slavery. This fact shows that the cause of freedom has steadily and firmly advanced, while slavery has receded in the same ratio. We all look forward with confidence to the time when Delaware, Maryland, Virginia, Kentucky, and Missouri, and probably North Carolina and Tennessee, will adopt a gradual system of emancipation, under the operation of which, those states must, in process of time, become free. In the meantime, we have a vast territory, stretching from the Mississippi to the Pacific, which is rapidly filling up with a hardy, enterprising, and industrious population, large enough to form at least seventeen new free states . . . Now let me inquire, where are you to find the slave territory with which to balance these seventeen free territories, or even any one of them? . . . Will you annex all Mexico? If you do, at least twenty out of twenty-two will be free states, if the "law of the formation of the earth, the ordinances of Nature, or the will of God," is to be respected, or if the doctrine shall prevail of allowing the people to do as they please . . . Then, sir, the proposition of the Senator from South Carolina is entirely impracticable. It is also inadmissible, if practicable. It would revolutionize the fundamental principles of the government. It would destroy the great principle of popular equality, which must necessarily form the basis of all free institutions. It would be a retrograde movement in an age of progress that would astonish the world.[10]

That Douglas in 1858 could make Missouri emancipation a bogey after regarding it as a logical step forward in an age of progress in 1849 does not of necessity imply any fundamental change of view or purpose. The rise of a political party in the free states whose central unifying principle was hostility to the institution of slavery was consolidating all political lines in the South upon the single principle of defense of the institution of slavery. Douglas's political life depended upon destroying pro- or anti-slavery tests as the basis of political orthodoxy, North or

South. This meant attacking the attackers of slavery in the North and the defenders of slavery in the South. It meant political trimming, to be sure. But it was trimming of a high, even noble quality. To keep the ship of state on an even keel it was necessary at different times to throw his weight in opposite directions.

Once the Republican party had been formed and had shown its inherent capacity to carry a national election on the central rallying point of hostility to slavery (as it had done in 1856),[11] the problem of political balance was entirely different from what it had been when the Whig party was a vital force in all parts of the country. Douglas could say in 1848, almost in so many words, that slavery was the curse of the South, and then say in 1858 that if he were a citizen of Louisiana he would vote to keep slavery. But 1848 was the year in which a Louisiana slaveholder was elected President of the United States as the nominee of the Whig party. In 1848 there were fifteen free and fifteen slave states. In 1858 there were no new slave states, but California and Minnesota had been added to the ranks of the free states. The entry of Oregon was imminent. By the summer of 1858 the final rejection of the Lecompton Constitution under the terms of the English bill meant the definite victory of the free-soil party in Kansas. There was scarcely a man in the country who soberly and seriously believed that any of the remaining territory, organized or unorganized, north of 36'30" would ever become slave states. While there might be more doubt concerning New Mexico Territory because of its more southerly location and its greater susceptibility to the political pressures of the South, the overwhelming weight of opinion was that the deserts and mountains which made up so much of its area would never render slavery profitable there.

As the conditions making for the certain triumph of the free-soil movement were growing ever stronger as Douglas viewed the scene, so were fear and hatred of the Negro, whose ultimate emancipation was thus apparently becoming assured, growing worse. This painful and melancholy fact must be faced by the historian no less than by his subjects. In 1853 the legislature of Illinois acted to carry out a provision of the state constitution adopted in 1847. This provision had been adopted in a special referendum by a vote of more than two to one. The legislature was authorized to exclude free Negro immigration into the state, which it now proceeded to do, providing heavy fines for any

Negro apprehended entering Illinois. Any Negro caught entering the state who could not pay the fine was to be sold at public auction to whoever would pay his fine in exchange for the shortest term of his service. The treatment of the free Negro throughout the North was steadily worsening. Let it be remembered that in 1820 virtually the entire North had voted against the admission of Missouri into the Union, even after the admission of Maine, and the prohibition of slavery in the remaining Louisiana territory north of 36'30", because of the clause in Missouri's constitution forbidding the entry of free Negroes. For this provision was then held to violate Article IV, Section 2, of the United States Constitution, which guarantees to the citizens of each state all privileges and immunities of citizens of the several states. Thirty-seven years before the Dred Scott decision it was hardly doubted that Negroes might be among the "citizens of each state" to whom the Constitution guaranteed "privileges and immunities"! That Negroes were "so far inferior that they had no rights which the white man was bound to respect" was an opinion Taney in 1857 attributed to the Revolutionary generation, to men of the stamp of Jefferson, Washington, Franklin, and Hamilton, every one of whom denounced slavery as against the unalienable natural right of every man, white or black, to liberty! Lincoln was certainly right when he insisted, against Taney, that opinion in regard to the Negro had become far more unfavorable than it had been when the Constitution was framed, and that public opinion was rapidly becoming what Taney erroneously said it had formerly been.

In the face of this increasingly unfavorable opinion of the Negro, however, even in the free states, was not Douglas, as a popular leader who was necessarily limited to achieving his ends in and through popular opinion, thereby justified in echoing back that opinion? Was he not thus justified, *particularly* when it appeared to him that to oppose such opinion would be destructive of the free-soil cause itself? For it is practically certain that, had the conservative rank and file of the free-soil movement become convinced that the absolute containment of slavery, for which Lincoln and the radicals stood, involved the immediate or near prospect of large-scale emancipation, the whole movement would have suffered a tremendous and possibly fatal shock.

Hatred of the Negro was almost indistinguishable from hatred of slavery as the dynamic of the Northern free-soil movement.

Lincoln's demand for putting slavery where the public mind could rest in the belief that it was "in course of ultimate extinction" was compatible with a gradualness of almost indefinite extent. And Lincoln was frequently careful to co-ordinate any mention of "ultimate extinction" with equally vague suggestions of the gradual removal of emancipated Negroes to Africa or some other congenial clime. It has not been sufficiently noted that Lincoln's advocacy of colonization schemes, apart from its manifest seriousness, also served the practical purpose of gaining acceptance of the idea of the "ultimate extinction" of slavery by his rabidly anti-Negro free-soil followers. It made possible thereby the maintenance in the movement of high moral tone, because it encouraged the feeling of moral indignation at the Negro's enslavement, without interfering with the luxury of prejudice against the Negro himself. But if the free-soil movement had come to fear that large-scale emancipation might have resulted from strict confinement of slavery within its existing boundaries, it would have faced a crisis of its own. A prospect of large-scale migration of freed Negroes to the North might have turned the movement toward support of the southern filibusterers, who wished to carve a slave empire in Mexico or Central America. Douglas desperately attacked this Achilles' heel of Lincoln's argument; on the one hand attacking the alleged humanitarianism of the anti-slavery crusade, by insisting upon the immorality of confining Negroes in the old South, where their rapid natural increase would lead to starvation when they could no longer be profitably employed there, and on the other by stressing the danger of freed Negro immigration into the North. Allowing white men everywhere to use or not to use them, according to their own best judgment, was Douglas's formula. In the circumstances, this meant capitalizing chiefly on the anti-Negro feeling of the North, while Lincoln capitalized chiefly on the anti-slavery feeling there. The practical coincidence of both feelings should not, however, be minimized, nor should the fact that both men made appeals to the other's staple argument. For Douglas did not hesitate to point out how popular sovereignty was achieving freedom in Kansas, as it had in California; nor did Lincoln hesitate to abjure all intention to give political or social equality to the Negro race anywhere in this country. If Lincoln's rhetoric with its frequent appeals to the universalism of the Declaration of Independence seems today to be couched in terms of greater dignity, we must remember that it involved the deliberate risk of civil war, something that Douglas as resolutely undertook to avoid. Had popular sovereignty been advertised as a free-soil device, it would have lost all its efficacy as a dampener of sectional strife. Indeed, the more it *became* such a device, the more necessary it became to avoid the appearance, the more necessary it was for Douglas to insist upon his neutrality on the morality of slavery.

When Calhoun in 1850 spoke of the rights of the South in the common territories of the nation, Douglas resoundingly denied that the South or the North had any such rights. The Constitution, he said, knows only the states and the people. The only ones who had rights in the territories, he maintained, were the people in the territories. If the doctrine of popular sovereignty were only recognized as the true doctrine, slavery agitation could be banished from the halls of Congress and sectionalism effaced. The gallant stand which Douglas took against Calhoun's determined and, alas, successful attempt to replace American with southern nationality in the South must be placed alongside his refusal to condemn the peculiar institution on moral grounds in the fifties. His bold attempt simultaneously to open the floodgates of free-soil expansion and to avert civil war was a dominating purpose to which all other purposes remained subordinate. Whether right or wrong, there is a large consistency in all Douglas's dealings with the "vexed question," a sustained and unchanging conception of what was good for the nation, to which his individual moral judgments remained subordinate. And this purpose and this conception command respect for their moral worth, whether or not we finally accept them as the highest possible moral goals for a statesman of his time.

Chapter IV

Manifest Destiny

THE foregoing is an explanation of the general principles governing Douglas's approach to the "vexed question." We believe that
it exonerates Douglas from any charge of shallow opportunism or
moral obtuseness. Certainly no one has the right to denounce his
"moral perceptions" who has not shown, first, that it was wrong
to subordinate the slavery issue, upon which North and South
could not agree, to an aim and purpose upon which they could
agree; and, second, that the aim upon which sectional agreement
and subordination of slavery was pitched was itself immoral. The
emergence of the Republican party foreshadowed the possibility
that there might be a constitutional majority formed without the
necessity of a single vote from a slave state, a majority which
might thus be able to dispense with those restraints which such
a necessity would have imposed. In the developing crisis of the
fifties, Douglas's was the only powerful voice faithful to the idea
that national political platforms must be framed to satisfy the
moral and constitutional sentiments recognized by majority opinion North *and* South.[1] The least that can be said for the platform
upon which he stood was that it represented the highest common
denominator of sectional agreement. If at last such agreement
proved too slight to preserve the Union without war, it does not
follow that Douglas was at fault for not abandoning it.

The historian has the duty to say those things in behalf of
Douglas's policy which he himself could not say without endangering whatever chances it possessed. When, therefore, the
"Don't care" statements and the "dollars and cents" arguments of
the later fifties are repeated, it is right also to go back to such

earlier speeches as that of 1849, from which we have quoted, speeches uncontradicted if unrepeated in later years, in which Douglas expressed the firm conviction that slavery would be unprofitable everywhere in the West and even in twenty of twenty-two possible states that might be carved out of the remainder of Mexico, should that country be entirely annexed to the United States. It is also right to emphasize that in 1849 he did not say economic conditions *alone* favored freedom. The lands would be free, he said, *either* because of soil, climate, and productions *or* "if the doctrine shall prevail of allowing the people to do as they please."

We can think of nothing more damaging to Douglas's reputation as a statesman than such an explanation of his conduct as the following by his unreserved devotee, George Fort Milton: "Douglas had premonitions of trouble over the repeal of the Missouri Compromise, but he saw so clearly the inevitable effect climate, soil and natural productions would have on human institutions in Kansas and Nebraska that he unduly discounted the effect on the emotions of men, of aroused fears, passions and hates."[2] But how could Douglas, who in 1849 expected slavery to wither away in Delaware, Maryland, Virginia, Kentucky, Missouri, and North Carolina, have been seriously convinced that soil and climate ineluctably determined moral attitudes toward chattel slavery? There had been no noticeable change in the soil, climate, or productions of those states. Either slavery should not have gone there in the first place or Douglas should not have expected it to wither away, if there was any truth to the isothermic theory. Nor could the expansion of cotton culture in the fifties, with the renewed vitality of the peculiar institution accompanying it, have changed any well-founded convictions on this subject. The cultivation of cotton did not require the exclusive use of Negro labor, nor did the utilization of that labor require that Negroes be chattels. Far from discounting the effect of fear and hate, these were the passions that Douglas strove to neutralize. What had happened, in Douglas's view, was that the processes of gradual emancipation, of gradual attenuation of slavery, were first arrested, then reversed, as a result of abolitionist propaganda and the rise of the free-soil movement in the North. Allowing the people to do as they pleased was not understood by Douglas to be a policy of indifference, of voting slavery up *or* down; it meant voting slavery down. Under the pressure of the anti-slavery crusade, however, the South could no longer do as it "pleased." Fear that control over slavery, control over the process of transformation in the relation of the races, which Douglas foresaw in 1849, would be taken out of its hands, had perverted the evolution of moral sentiment in the South. Douglas's policy, founded upon the doctrine of popular sovereignty, by guaranteeing to all localities, North and South, the unquestioned control of their domestic institutions, would then have looked to the reassertion of this "normal" anti-slavery opinion, an opinion in conformity with the "spirit of the age." It is an insult to Douglas's great intelligence to think that he took with full seriousness the "soil and climate" argument, a doctrine which seems to have been designed to win acceptance of popular sovereignty rather than for any independent merit of its own.

In 1849 it was clear to Douglas that Calhoun's amendment, attempting to give slave states a guarantee of political equality with free states, would have been a "retrograde movement in an age of progress which would astonish the world." Douglas, like Professor Nevins, believed that the tendency of the age was toward freedom. But, as the South's reversal of direction showed, the problem of how to assure progress, even in an age of progress, was exceedingly complex. And the future of the Republic involved more than the resolution of the inner cleavage over slavery and sectional antagonism; it also involved the external antagonism between a free republic and the forces of despotism, the forces of predatory imperialism abroad in the world outside the United States. We must observe now how Douglas's tactics with respect to slavery formed part of a broad strategy, of advancing the cause of republican freedom in the mid-nineteenth century.

When Douglas first took his seat in Congress in 1843, the absorbing question was the annexation (or, according to the Democrats, "re-annexation") of Texas. It was linked, in the course of the session, with that of the occupation (or, again, "re-occupation") of Oregon. From the ensuing impulse of expansion, the United States increased its territory upon the continent between the years 1845 and 1848 from about 1.8 million square miles to about three million. For the annexation of Texas was presently followed by the Mexican War and the addition to the Union, by conquest and purchase, of California and the territories of Utah and New Mexico. Meanwhile, a diplomatic settlement with Great Britain confirmed our title to all of Oregon south of the forty-ninth parallel. These lands, together with the Gadsden Purchase of 1853, rounded out our present continental domain and, notwithstanding much mountain and desert, included some of the fairest upon this or any other continent. The collapse of the Spanish Empire in the New World was the primary condition of these acquisitions (as it had been that of Louisiana), but the feebleness and political imbecility of Mexico were the secondary ones.

While in retrospect it may seem inevitable that such a vacuum of power would be filled by the virile force of the nascent American republic, the rapid occupation of these vast spaces must have dazzled the imagination in 1848, as it certainly dazzled that of Stephen A. Douglas. A nation that might expand by nearly a million and a quarter square miles in three years might surely be expected to expand by some millions more in, say, a century! Such at least was the impact of the forties upon the horizon of Douglas, the background of his plans and projects in the fifties. Without appreciating Douglas's vision of future American empire, *and* Lincoln's reaction to it, one cannot grasp the scope or magnitude of the issues between them.

In 1843 we had no recognized titles to any of the aforementioned lands and the question of whether the United States would be of continental extent was as unsettled as most of the disputed territory. West of the Mississippi only Louisiana, Arkansas, and Missouri had become states. While it was reasonably certain that the tier of Louisiana states on the west bank of the Mississippi would be extended to the Canadian border, as it was by the admission of Iowa in 1846 and Minnesota in 1858 (after territorial organization in 1849), there was no clear national intention that the political organization of states would ever proceed further. Most of the remaining Louisiana territory was secured "in perpetuity" to Indian tribes by treaty and lay unorganized and wild. Only by the acquisition of the Pacific coast was the die cast that made it economically and politically necessary for the United States to develop the vast heartland west of the Mississippi to the Rockies, the center of which, Kansas and Nebraska, was to supply the immediate issue over which Lincoln and Douglas were to clash.

Before the annexation of Texas and the consequent embroilment with Mexico, the whole question of westward expansion was unresolved. The decision in favor of expansion is today so much taken for granted that it is difficult for us to realize how deeply it divided the country at the time. Today it is almost inconceivable that we should be involved in a foreign war in which the President would be denounced as the aggressor and the foreign enemy referred to as the victim by leading members of the political opposition. Lincoln's denunciation of Polk, in the House, comes very close to what both a later and an earlier age would call treason, or at least criminal disloyalty. And, it is fair to add, Lincoln as President put men in jail for criticisms of his administration no more severe than his of Polk. The division over the Mexican War was a foreshadowing of the Civil War.

Wholly apart from the question of the profit from, or loss of, the immensely valuable Mexican lands to the west and south were the questions whether the area now embraced by the United States would eventually consist of one ocean-bound republic or several; whether British power in North America would equal or exceed that of the United States; and whether Mexico, with none of the Anglo-Saxon traditions or capacity for self-government or civil liberty, would one day give her law and civilization to the entire American Far West and Southwest. Together, these comprised the question of whether the political future of North America would be divided or subdivided among a number of widely differing regimes and relatively equal powers—or powers sufficiently equal so that, with alliances, they might hope to balance or overcome each other—or whether the continent would be subject to the overmastering hegemony of one giant republic. While the Whigs, whose greatest spokesman was Webster, opposed the annexation even of Texas, the exponents of Manifest Destiny, than whom none was more articulate than Douglas, spoke without hesitation of the acquisition of the whole of Canada, Mexico, Central America, and the islands of the Caribbean.

Douglas's speech on Texas annexation is, for the most part, an elaborate legalistic justification: the original Louisiana Purchase had included Texas and a guarantee of United States citizenship to all inhabitants of the territory ceded by France, but in 1819 we had traded Texas and the Texans to Spain in exchange for Florida, thus violating our plighted national faith. Because of this justification, Douglas would not, he said dwell upon the numerous advantages that would attend the annexation of Texas, in stimulating the industry of the whole country; in opening new markets for the manufactures of the North and East; in the extension of commerce and navigation; in bringing the waters of the Red River, the Arkansas, and other streams flowing into the Mississippi, entirely with [in] our territorial limits; in the augmentation of political power; in securing safer and more natural boundaries, and avoiding the danger of collisions with foreign powers—without dwelling upon these and other considerations, appealing to our interests and pride as a people and a nation, it is sufficient argument with me that our honor and violated faith require the immediate re-annexation of Texas to the Union.

In contradiction to Webster's repeated warnings that "it is of very dangerous tendency and doubtful consequences to enlarge the boundaries of this country" and that there "must be some limit to the extent of our territory, if we would make our institutions permanent," Douglas replied:

. . . in regard to the extension of territory. He regarded all apprehensions unfavorable to the perpetuity of our institutions from this source as ideal. The application of steam power to transportation and travel has brought the remotest limits of the confederacy, now comprising twenty-six states (if we are permitted to count by time instead of distance) much nearer to the center than when there were but thirteen. The revolution is progressing, and the facilities and rapidity of communication are increasing in a much greater ratio than our territory or population.[3]

By a strange paradox, we find the heir of Jefferson, via Jackson, defending the expansion of the Union in terms of the technological revolution, while the heir of Hamilton, Webster, was to ask:

What sympathy can there be between the people of Mexico and California and the inhabitants of the Valley of the Mississippi and the Eastern States in the choice of a President? Do they know the same man? Do they concur in any general constitutional principles? . . . Arbitrary government may have territories and distant possessions, because arbitrary governments may rule them by different laws and different systems. Russia may rule in the Ukraine and the provinces of the Caucasus and Kamtschatka [the Russian name for Alaska] by different codes, ordinances, or ukases. We can do no such thing. They must be of us, *part* of us, or else strangers.[4]

Thus the arch-Whig, the Publius of the *Federalist Papers* redivivus, employing the classic argument of the party that opposed adoption of the Constitution! The idea that liberty was essentially local, dependent upon intimacy, was the argument of Jeffersonian democracy, the argument that justified, if not opposing the Constitution, at least construing the powers of the federal government so narrowly as to leave it little to do beyond providing for the common defense. Jeffersonian democracy involved moreover a preference for agriculture over other occupations, because an agricultural society was precisely the kind in which the tasks of the federal government could be kept minimal.

When in 1837 Webster first spoke against the annexation of Texas, he said he believed the Founders of the republic never intended it to include states from any lands not possessed by the Union in 1787. The Louisiana Purchase he attributed to the necessity to control the mouths of the rivers that rose in the western states, the navigation of which was vital and had already been disputed. The acquisition of Florida was due, he said, to a like, if less urgent, necessity. Webster apparently gave little thought to the possibility that the Founders would have wished to expand the boundaries of the Union to secure advantages for manufacturing, commercial, or shipping interests. Perhaps Jefferson would have advised against such a policy, but we cannot help believing that it would have been warmly endorsed by Hamilton. The strict constructionist principles of Jefferson fit the idea of a relatively loosely knit union, because an agricultural society is relatively independent in its parts, the states or sections. By comparison with an industrial society, its parts exchange little of their agricultural surpluses with each other and much with foreign nations who supply them with manufactured goods. In the Hamiltonian union, there is much greater interdependence, much more internal trade, many more and different interests to regulate and adjust, much more of a *common* good, and hence a great deal more for the federal government to do. The Hamiltonian union must, therefore, be a much stronger union, stronger because of the power the central government must have if its business is so much greater, and stronger because of the loyalties it must command if its decisions are to be accepted. Clay's "American system," to which Webster was vigorously committed, was the lineal descendant of Hamilton's *Report on Manufactures.*

Webster's intense ultramontane unionism was thoroughly consistent with this inheritance, but his view of the territorial confinement of the Union was, in itself, anomalous. Hamilton's protectionist views implied the desirability of a high degree of autarchy; but autarchy meant bringing under one's own domination as much of one's market and sources of supply as possible. Hamilton would never have shrunk from expansionism in pursuit of such goals. In 1798 he had a bold scheme for entering the war then raging in Europe on the side of Britain: ". . . in co-operation with the Venezuelan patriot Francisco de Miranda, the allied American and British fleet would liberate Spanish America and annex Florida and Louisiana as our share of the conquests . . . [and the] wavering West, grateful for the Mississippi River freed at last, would be securely attached, not only to the United States, but to their benefactors, the Federalists."[5] Hamilton's uninhibited imperialism would have been after Douglas's heart. The irony is that the torch for such imperialism should have been carried forward in the name of Manifest Destiny by Jefferson's party. We venture the hypothesis that it was the acquisition of Louisiana under Jeffersonian instead of Hamiltonian auspices, rather than any profound and principled opposition to expansion as such, which turned Federalist-Whig foreign policy into one of traditional hostility to all projects of aggrandizement. The West was indeed grateful to its benefactors, but they were the wrong benefactors, from the Federalist-Whig viewpoint! Moreover, it was Federalism, whose historic mission was to convert a loose confederation into a strong union, that, soured by defeat and frustration, engendered the first potent secession movement. Like the vision of Macbeth beholding the royal line which was to descend from Banquo, Louisiana became a nightmare to unreconstructed Federalists in which a procession of new states entered the Union, firmly wedded to the interests, convictions, and party espoused by the hated Jefferson. Later the embargo and the War of 1812 gave new intensity to New England Federalism's sense of hopeless submersion in the Union, and the Hartford Convention may have proved abortive only because of the sudden ending of the war. There were few arguments in favor of secession, except those relating directly to slavery, that did not have a trial in New England before 1815, prior to their employment in the South in 1861.

The split between Hamilton and Adams, which ended any hope for Hamilton's scheme of entry into the European war in 1798 on the side of Britain, gave a sharper twist to the course of our history than the wrecking of the Federalist party, sharp as that was. It meant that this country's partnership with Great Britain in maintaining a balance of power in the world favorable to the development (or survival) of free political institutions, a ruling fact of the twentieth century, did not strike deep roots until the Civil War. Lincoln's administration was to mark a turning point in Anglo-American relations, as in almost every other aspect of American politics.

The anti-British animus of the Revolution had died in the breasts of men like Washington, Adams, and Hamilton almost as soon as the treaty of peace was signed. In the wars of the French Revolution their sympathies were markedly Anglophile, while those of Jefferson's party were Francophile. While both Washington and Jefferson strove to maintain American neutrality, the electoral revolution of 1800, which enthroned Jefferson's party for a quarter century, meant that American foreign policy was "neutral against" the British. The embargo struck at the British, for example, who controlled the seas, rather than the French. And fighting for the freedom of the seas in 1812 meant, concretely, aiding Napoleon. But it is the legacy of that war for domestic politics that must command our attention here. As in the Revolution, the British in 1812 supplied whisky, money, and leadership "to bring on the inhabitants of our frontiers, the merciless Indian Savages, whose known rule of warfare is an undistinguished destruction of all ages, sexes, and conditions." As a result, hatred of the British and hatred of the Indians became almost indistinguishable passions among frontiersmen in ensuing decades. The West that would have been gained in partnership with Britain, had Hamilton prevailed, looked upon Britain as a deadly enemy. Jackson was raised to power in large measure because of his reputation as a fighter against both British and Indians. The importance of this reputation may be better appreciated by remembering that when in 1840 the Whigs finally did break the Jacksonian hold on the presidency it was by running another supposedly successful Indian fighter, "Old Tippecanoe" Harrison. In that campaign the Whigs did not bother to have a platform, except "log cabins" and "hard cider." To such as these was their imperishable rhetoric largely devoted, as well as to such alleged facts as that the Easterner, Van Buren, wore lace shirts. The Whigs' only other presidential victory was also won with a successful general who was minus a platform. And although Taylor is better remembered for his Mexican War exploits, he too had done many years' service on the Indian frontier. Jacksonian democracy thus had a deeper anti-British motivation than the rather intellectual and pacifistic Anglophobia of Jefferson. And its roots were deeper than the experience even of the frontier.

"The nucleus of Jacksonian democracy," writes Professor Wilfred E. Binkley, "was an ethnic group, the Scotch-Irish stock. These were the descendants of the unfortunates . . . harried from their Ulster homes and finding refuge in the American wilderness, where they nursed an undying hatred of their British persecutors. The rifles that blazed across the cotton-bale breastworks at New Orleans on January 8, 1815 and mowed down the redcoat lines were to them but the avenging instruments of a just God in the hands of the faithful. Jacksonian democracy knew no stronger emotional bond of unity than its universal hatred of the British. It was peculiarly appropriate that the eighth of January became the fixed date of the annual party banquet."[6]

It is more than curious that all the greatest Whig names—e.g., Adams, Webster, Clay, Harrison and Tyler, Taylor and Fillmore, and Lincoln—were of predominantly English ancestry. It is only in the opposite party that we find other ethnic strains conspicuous among the leaders. Jackson and Polk were both of Scotch-Irish descent, Van Buren Dutch, Buchanan Scotch, among the presidents. Even Jefferson traced his ancestors to Wales. Calhoun was of Scotch-Irish stock and, although for a time after his break with Jackson he joined the Whigs, it should be remembered that he was Jackson's first Vice-President. Douglas, of course, bore one of the most famous of all Scottish names. It is amusing that, although Winfield Scott was the last full-fledged Whig candidate for President (1852), he was not of the covenanting breed of Caledonian, whence came the Jacksonians, but was descended from a follower of the Pretender who fled to America after Culloden in 1746. We would not wish to push the ethnic thesis too far. Henry Clay, Lincoln's beau ideal of a statesman, was a leader of the "war hawks" of 1812 along with Calhoun. Manifest sectional interests frequently make the quest for subtler influences superfluous. It is a fact of some impressiveness, however, that from Washington to Lincoln, the Federalist-Whig-Republican presidents are exclusively of English ancestry.

In the light of this fact and that of a contrary quality in the opposite party, it is not surprising to learn that the nativism flourishing in the decades before the Civil War was largely "old English stockism" and made its appeal mainly to groups that were traditionally Whig. When Fillmore, the last Whig President, ran again in 1856, it was not only as candidate of the moribund Whigs but of the "Americans"—i.e., Know-Nothings. One of the great accomplishments of the Republicans in 1860 was in assimilating, for the most part, both the old-line Whigs and the Know-Nothings of the free states. This, even more than the split among the Democrats, was the key to their victory. The foregoing also makes intelligible the fact that it was the Democratic party which in the forties and thereafter welcomed the floods of Irish into its fold. These Irish did not, to say the least, detract from the anti-British feelings of the older Jacksonians in the party. They probably did contribute to minimizing the older anti-episcopal feelings, and made the animus more exclusively ethnic. Or, if religious feelings continued to play a role, they did so by making the Democratic party more hospitable to Catholics, while the nativism which weighed heavily upon the opposition took on an increasingly anti-Catholic bias. Lincoln wrote to his old friend Speed in the summer of 1855:

> I am not a Know-Nothing. That is certain. How could I be? How can any one who abhors the oppression of negroes, be in favor of degrading classes of white people? Our progress in degeneracy appears to me to be pretty rapid. As a nation, we began by declaring that "all men are created equal." We now practically read it "all men are created equal, *except negroes.*" When the Know-Nothings get control, it will read "all men are created equal, except negroes, *and foreigners, and Catholics.*" When it comes to this I should prefer emigrating to some country where they make no pretence of lov-

ing liberty—to Russia, for instance, where despotism can be taken pure, and without the base alloy of hypocrisy.[7]

What has been insufficiently noticed in this widely quoted passage is that Lincoln, in writing to the man who was once his closest personal friend, should find it necessary to make such an elaborate disavowal of anti-foreign and anti-Catholic prejudice. It suggests how common this charge must have been against old-line Whigs. And one must not forget that this, Lincoln's only thoroughgoing written denunciation of Know-Nothingism, was in a personal private letter. On July 21, 1860, Lincoln addressed a letter to Abram Jonas, a prominent Jewish attorney of Quincy, Illinois. In it Lincoln gives a circumstantial denial of ever having stopped at a Know-Nothing lodge in Quincy. But he ends with these words: "And now a word of caution. Our adversaries think they can gain a point, if they could force me to openly deny the charge, by which some degree of offence would be given to the Americans. For this reason it must not publicly appear that I am paying any attention to the charge."[8]

Lincoln wanted and expected the Know-Nothing vote, but it was no indiscriminate desire that motivated him. There was a kinship between the roots of nativism and the roots of the anti-slavery movement, as there was between both of these and the temperance movement. The mid-nineteenth century witnessed a whole host of such "reform" movements, and the movement against slavery was hardly more virulent or fraught with more political consequences until its climactic phase than the movements against liquor and foreigners. In many cases the crusade against liquor and the crusade against Irishmen (and, to a lesser extent, Germans, who also had a reputation for bibulousness) tended to merge into one. The groups that warred against liquor tended also to war against slavery. Lincoln took the stump against liquor before he did so against slavery. As the slavery question became his overriding concern he became silent on the liquor question, particularly as German immigration came to swell the Republican ranks. But he served cold water to the committee that notified him of his nomination for President. It would have been extremely difficult for Lincoln to attack the temperance movement or the nativist movement without dividing the forces of the anti-slavery movement.

The abolitionist movement in America, like the anti-liquor

movement, was in large measure an offshoot of similar movements
in Great Britain. The dynamic force animating both in Britain
was the evangelical movement among the dissenting sects.
Abolitionism in particular spread to America with the spread of
evangelism and was thus strongly identified with radical Protestantism. The Irish reciprocated the scorn of the temperance
reformers and the nativists by hating them for their English
affinities and their Protestantism, as they in turn were hated for
their popery and alleged addiction to drink. Thus the Irish tended
also to hate abolitionism as something English and Protestant and
therefore intolerant of themselves. It is worth mentioning, although it would be difficult to measure its significance, that slavery
was not held to be contrary to natural law, according to the most
famous of Catholic doctors, Thomas Aquinas, while it was categorically denounced as such by the English Protestant John Locke,
whose *Second Treatise of Civil Government* so largely inspired
the famous phrases of the Declaration of Independence.

Douglas, we have said, was a great hero of the Irish and, we
might add, was as well known to be a hard drinker as Lincoln
was notorious for his teetotaling! Moreover, Douglas's second
marriage after the death of his first wife was to the daughter of
a prominent Maryland Catholic family, and the two sons of his
first marriage were educated in a Catholic school and eventually
adopted their stepmother's faith. But Douglas showed his political
colors in nothing more revealingly than when he twisted the
British lion's tail.

We return now to Douglas's Texas annexation speech and find
that the peroration has almost no apparent connection with what
has preceded it, although it should not surprise the reader of the
foregoing paragraphs, as it assuredly did not surprise Douglas's
followers:

> Our federal system is admirably adapted to the whole con-
> tinent; and while I would not violate the laws of nations,
> nor treaty stipulations, nor in any manner tarnish the national
> honor, I would exert all legal and honorable means to drive
> Great Britain and the last vestiges of royal authority from the
> continent of North America, and extend the limits of the re-
> public from ocean to ocean. I would make this an *ocean-
> bound* republic, and have no more disputes about bounda-
> ries or red lines [i.e., British claims] upon the maps.[9]

If we ask what Britain had to do with Texas, we must remind ourselves that in the presidential election of the autumn (1848) preceding this speech Henry Clay and the Whigs had come to grief mainly upon the Texas annexation issue. The Democratic party rallied from the defeat of 1840 above all by espousing this issue *and* by linking it with the occupation of the whole of Oregon, all the way to 54'40", thus balancing southern with northern expansion. Clay's misfortune was due in large measure to his failure to appreciate how popular the annexation of Texas would be, even in the North. Here again the anti-British feeling of Jacksonian Democracy undoubtedly played a leading role, for the rumors of a threatened alliance of the Texans with the British, should annexation fail, seems to have acted as a great lever upon opinion. To the South, it meant the exposure of their "soft underbelly" to abolitionism, and the specter of the Canadian border, the sanctuary of fugitives, suddenly reproduced along the border of their densest slave populations. Slavery was not so firmly planted in Texas that it might not become more advantageous for Texans, if thrown upon the British, to substitute the free labor system. But in the Northwest the old anti-British feelings also stirred, for British power in Canada could have far greater strategic effect if it could be applied simultaneously from Texas. In the Northeast there was fear of a Texan tariff on American goods while British goods entered free. And so support for Texas's annexation was redoubled, both by the prospect of cutting off any flanking movement of British power to the south and by the simultaneous move further to offset British power to the north by the occupation of Oregon.

Although Douglas warmly supported Texas's annexation, as a northwestern Democrat he naturally espoused the cause of Oregon with even greater enthusiasm. Here is an extract from an Oregon speech. The repetitiveness is worthy of inclusion because it indicates how incessantly he hammered at the anti-British theme:

It therefore becomes us to put this nation in a state of defense; and, when we are told that this will lead to war, all I have to say is this, violate no treaty stipulations, nor any principle of the law of nations; preserve the honor and integrity of the country, but, at the same time, assert our right to the last inch [of Oregon, that is], and then, if war comes, let it come. We may regret the necessity which produced it, but when it does come, I would administer to our citizens Hannibal's oath of eternal enmity, and not terminate the war until the question was settled forever. I would blot out the lines on the map which now mark our national boundaries on this continent, and make the area of liberty as broad as the continent itself. I would not suffer petty rival republics to grow up here, engendering jealousy of each other, and interfering with each other's domestic affairs, and continually endangering their peace. I do not wish to go beyond the great ocean—beyond those boundaries which the God of nature has marked out, I would limit myself only by that boundary which is so clearly defined by nature.[10]

To "drive Great Britain and the last vestiges of royal authority from the continent of North America," to "make this an ocean-bound republic," to render "the area of liberty as broad as the continent," and not to suffer "petty rival republics to grow up here" was a policy of a scope and import of the first magnitude and one which Douglas was to pursue with fierce tenacity and energy.

Let us reflect on this broad purpose. Lincoln is justly famous for preserving the Union—to which Douglas was no less dedicated. Lincoln in 1861 refused to allow this Union to be divided into "petty rival republics," but we must credit Douglas, and all those others who espoused the cause of Manifest Destiny, with the vision and determination that created the continental Union that Lincoln finally saved. In giving this credit we must, in fairness, also remember that Lincoln and his party (i.e., the Whigs) did not have such a vision. *They* warned, as with the voice of Webster, that territorial expansion would undermine the principles of a free republican government. The annexation of Texas alone meant the certain addition of one slave state and the possible addition of five slave states, since the annexation resolution permitted Texas's future division. The compromise with the original slave-holding states, which added to the number of free inhabitants three fifths of the slaves in calculating representation in the House of Representatives, would prove a monstrosity if it were not sharply circumscribed, said Webster. "But," he added,

there is another consideration of vastly more general importance . . . because it affects all the States, free and slave-

holding; and it is, that States formed out of territories thus
thinly populated . . . break up . . . the intended relation
between the Senate and the House . . . The Senate, aug-
mented by these new Senators coming from States where
there are few people, becomes an odious oligarchy. It holds
power without any adequate constituency . . . it is but
"borough-mongering" upon a large scale . . . I hold it to be
. . . an outrage upon all the principles of popular republican government . . .[11]

Again we must be struck by the fact that, just as Douglas saw
clearly the implications of the technological revolution for transportation, so he also saw that the new West to be carved out of
Mexico would not long remain the few sparse settlements that
were there then but would rapidly become the home of teeming
millions. By 1850 the miracle of California showed that the Far
West was no more apt to change the representative character of
the Senate than the old Northwest or Southwest. Meanwhile, as
we have already noted, the mighty influx from Europe into the
free states was making the argument against the three-fifths
clause highly abstract.

Douglas's intention to extend the area of liberty was not an
idle one either: the American constitutional system knew no way
to acquire "provinces," in the old Roman sense. Congress had
power to admit new states, and all lands acquired were to be
presumed states, *in statu nascendi*. Moreover, the Constitution
knew no way to admit states except upon the footing of full
equality. Just because of this assurance of equality of old with
new states, American imperialism had a moral quality unlike any
other imperialism the world had ever known. What if California
and the other Mexican cessions were in reality a conqueror's booty
(not that Douglas would have admitted so much)? Was not the
admission of these regions into the Union a guarantee to them
of a republican form of government? The political condition of
Mexico, as Douglas viewed it, was one of virtual and perpetual
anarchy. The United States, in the Monroe Doctrine, had warned
European powers that they might not re-establish dominion on
any soil in the New World from which they had been expelled.
To stand by the doctrine, however, meant to accept responsibility
for the political stability of the regions from which we insisted
others must be excluded. The political credo announced in the

Declaration of Independence, it should be remembered, asserted a right against anarchy no less than against despotism. The accessions of parts of Mexico to the United States did not mean a denial of self-government to the inhabitants of these regions but the first effective assurance of self-government they would have had. Suppose there was some temporary distortion in our federal system resulting from these accessions. Was the risk not worth it? Douglas sensed the drift of world politics toward massive aggregations. He did not, like Tocqueville, foresee a bi-polarity centering in the United States and Russia, but he did see that the old European balance of power would not endure indefinitely. The great competitor was Britain, whose star of empire was rising toward its zenith. Nothing less than complete domination of the Western Hemisphere would assure this country's future. Expansion was necessary, not only as a solution of the leading domestic question but as the policy, both morally right and politically necessary, of giving political freedom the power of survival in a predatory and hostile world.

Of all Webster's arguments against expansion, the most telling has to do with slavery. Webster tacitly rejected Douglas's claim that expansion would make the area of liberty as broad as the continent, because he foresaw the outspreading of the institution of chattel slavery. Not the three-fifths clause nor the perversion of the Senate from its representative basis, but the arming of the interest in chattel slavery was the true danger. In the 1837 speech against annexing Texas the following classic passage occurred, a passage often repeated in later years and to a considerable extent paraphrased by Lincoln in his great Peoria speech of 1854:

> Gentlemen, we all see that, by whomsoever possessed, Texas is likely to be a slave-holding country; and I frankly avow my entire unwillingness to do anything that shall extend the slavery of the African race on this continent, or add other slave-holding States to the Union. When I say that I regard slavery in itself as a great moral, social, and political evil, I only use language which has been adopted by distinguished men, themselves citizens of slave-holding States. I shall do nothing, therefore, to favor or encourage its further extension. We have slavery already amongst us. The Constitution found

it in the Union; it recognized it and gave it solemn guaranties. To the full extent of these guaranties we are all bound, in honor, in justice, and by the Constitution. All the stipulations contained in the Constitution in favor of the slave-holding States which are already in the Union ought to be fulfilled . . . Slavery, as it exists in the States, is beyond the reach of Congress. It is a concern of the States themselves; they have never submitted it to Congress, and Congress has no rightful power over it . . .

But when we come to speak of admitting new States, the subject assumes an entirely different aspect. Our rights and duties are then both different.

The free States, and all the States, are then at liberty to accept or reject. When it is proposed to bring new members into this political partnership, the old members have a right to say on what terms such new partners are to come in, and what they are to bring along with them. In my opinion, the people of the United States will not consent to bring into the Union a new, vastly extensive, and slave-holding country, large enough for a half a dozen or a dozen States. In my opinion they ought not to consent to it . . . On the general question of slavery, a great portion of the community is already strongly excited. The subject has not only attracted attention as a question of politics, but it has struck a far deeper toned chord. It has arrested the religious feelings of the country; it has taken strong hold on the consciences of men. He is a rash man, indeed, and little conversant with human nature, and especially has he a very erroneous estimate of the character of the people of this country, who supposes that a feeling of this kind is to be trifled with or despised. It will assuredly cause itself to be respected. It may be reasoned with, it may be made willing . . . to fulfill all existing engagements and all existing duties . . . But to coerce it into silence, to endeavor to restrain its free expression . . . should this be attempted, I know nothing, even in the Constitution or in the Union itself, which would not be endangered by the explosion which might follow.

I believe it to be for the interest and happiness of the whole Union to remain as it is, without diminution and without addition.[12]

Without at present considering the intrinsic merit of what Webster has said, we call attention to what he has omitted; namely, the alternative danger, the expansion of British influence. The election of 1844, as noted above, was to suggest that anti-British as well as anti-slavery feeling was a deep and durable element in popular opinion. In truth, popular opinion was not altogether consistent with respect to the compatibility of all the objects it wished to achieve, as it seldom is. The task of statesmanship, in part, is to clarify the alternatives that are before the country and to compel the people to a genuine and not a spurious or illusory choice. While Webster gave ear and voice to the deep-toned chord of anti-slavery opinion, Douglas beat the tribal drums of anti-British feeling. While Douglas prodded Southerners to follow his expansionist policies, by reminding them that Britain was the home of abolitionism, Webster "wished that this country should exhibit to the nations of the earth the example of a rich, and powerful republic, which is not possessed by a spirit of aggrandizement." Yet Webster tacitly accepted the proposition that the spread of British influence south of our borders would be wholesome rather than harmful, precisely because the spread of British influence would be likely to arrest the spread of slavery. It is difficult to escape the feeling that, as between Websterian Whiggery—and, later, Lincolnian Republicanism—and Douglas Democracy a profound difference, perhaps the profoundest difference, lay in the differing relative estimate placed upon slavery on the one hand and the British Empire on the other as threats to the future of American freedom. For Douglas, Britain was the great enemy, and differences over slavery had to be subordinated to meet her; for Webster, as for Lincoln, the enemy was the slave power.

There is an astonishing disparity between the seriousness with which Lincoln's contemporaries heard his warning in 1858 of a danger that they might wake up one morning to find slavery lawful in all the states, old as well as new, North as well as South, and the unbelief, not to say contempt, with which that warning has been treated by recent historians. This has been paralleled, if not quite equaled, by the treatment of Douglas's conviction that the future welfare of the country demanded an exclusion of Britain from North America, if not from the Western Hemisphere. Except for noting his advocacy of Manifest Destiny, even Douglas's sympathetic biographers have given short shrift to his long Senate speeches on foreign policy. Yet there is every reason to believe that Douglas himself regarded them as of the utmost importance and that, as senator, his responsibilities in the field of foreign affairs were not surpassed in dignity and gravity by any others. Douglas was, moreover, the recognized chieftain of a movement known as "Young America," a movement largely unofficial and unsanctioned by himself but devoted both to advancing his presidential prospects and to asserting a more vigorous foreign policy than that of the "old fogies" of the party.

That Douglas's warnings against British guile and greed had a deep response can hardly be doubted, and we must try to comprehend why what seems so unsubstantial a fear today did not seem so then. That a war to drive "the last vestiges of royal authority" from North America was a supreme aim of policy for Douglas, we have seen. But it is worth remembering that in 1861 William H. Seward, Lincoln's Secretary of State and the leading Republican in the nation until the nomination of Lincoln, proposed measures aimed at provoking war with several European powers, measures which must in fact have been directed mainly against Britain.[13] Seward's motive, presumably, was to arouse national feelings as a means to ending the secession crisis. Yet he must have seen the same potentialities in an anti-British policy that Douglas did.

To appreciate why Douglas and countless others felt as they did we must recapture something of the international outlook of the mid-nineteenth century. Although it was an "age of progress," actual progress toward political freedom elsewhere in the world, progress toward realizing the rights proclaimed in the Declaration of Independence was extremely doubtful and uncertain. Webster said in 1824:

> It cannot be denied that the great political question of this age is that between absolute and regulated governments . . . The main controversy is between that absolute rule, which, while it promises to govern well, means, nevertheless, to govern without control, and that constitutional system which restrains sovereign discretion, and asserts that society may claim as matter of right some effective power in the establishment of the laws which are to regulate it. The spirit of the times sets with a most powerful current in favor of these last mentioned opinions. It is opposed, however, whenever

and wherever it shows itself, by certain of the great potentates of Europe . . .[14]

Webster spoke these words in support of a resolution of sympathy with the embattled Greek revolutionists fighting for freedom against their Turkish oppressors. In their fight, the Greeks met the active hostility of the Christian crowned heads of the Holy Alliance as well as their infidel imperial masters.

While the "spirit of the times" may have been on the side of freedom, its prospects before the American Civil War could hardly have been called bright. The downfall of the first Napoleon had ushered in a period of intensely reactionary government. Napoleon himself had done much to discredit those principles of the French Revolution which were so nearly identical with the principles of the American Revolution. When the spirit of liberty again took heart, the members of the Holy Alliance, learning nothing and forgetting nothing, undertook to suppress it by every and all means. The revolutions of 1830 and 1848 proved largely abortive. If the Bourbons were finally run out of France, the Second Republic nonetheless proved short-lived; and whatever enlightenment was to be attributed to Napoleon III did not include much political freedom. Meanwhile, British diplomacy and British power were frequently exerted in favor of some of the worst and most oppressive governments in putting down the efforts of their subjects to assert their natural rights. That Britain herself, after the fright of Napoleon subsided, moved slowly but steadily down the path toward constitutional democracy was a fact neither clear nor unequivocal in these years. The full meaning of the Reform Act of 1832 was not visible immediately at so great a distance. The social system of Great Britain was enormously unegalitarian. "In those days," said Disraeli, "England was for the few—and for the very few." It was hardly the home of republican freedom as known to men like Douglas and Lincoln, who, without wealth or birth or influential connections, made their way to the highest positions. Briefly and crudely we may say that, prior to the Third Republic, France's erratic progress toward equality was not accompanied by much liberty; that Britain exhibited a good deal of liberty without much equality; while in the United States alone were liberty and equality substantial realities of social and political existence.

Within this mid-century horizon Lincoln and Douglas would

have agreed that the American republic had a unique responsibility, that it held in trust the cause of republican freedom for all mankind. Americans could not view with indifference the struggle for liberty of men anywhere in the world. Lincoln would surely have agreed fully with the following passage from Douglas's Senate speech (December 11, 1851) on the Kossuth resolutions:

> I do not deem it material whether the reception of Governor Kossuth will give offence to the crowned heads of Europe . . . for I well know that they will not be pleased with any action of this republic which gives encouragement to European movements favorable to liberal institutions . . . Sir, I know of no principle of the law of nations that deprives a republic of the right of expressing its cordial sympathy in all movements tending to the establishment of free principles throughout the world. I hold it is our duty to demonstrate our heartfelt sympathy and profound admiration, by every act which is appropriate to the occasion and the subject-matter. It is due to our own character, in vindication of the history of our revolutionary struggles, which resulted in the establishment of republican principles upon this continent.[15]

For Lincoln had spoken earlier, of the right of revolution, as follows:

> Any people anywhere, being inclined and having the power, have the *right* to rise up and shake off the existing government, and form a new one that suits them better. This is a most valuable, a most sacred right—a right which, we hope and believe, is to liberate the world.[16]

But the classic statement of how the American example was to sow the seeds of revolution throughout the world is Webster's famous Hülsemann letter, vindicating the action of the American government in sending an "observer" to Hungary, an observer whom the Austrians accused of actively abetting the patriot cause. Writing in 1850 as Secretary of State, Webster said he freely admitted that

> in proportion as these extraordinary events appeared to have their origin in those great ideas of responsible and popular

government, on which the American constitutions themselves are wholly founded, they could not but command the warm sympathy of the people of this country . . . They could not, if they desired it, suppress either the thoughts or the hopes which arise in men's minds, in other countries, from contemplating their successful example of free government . . . True, indeed, it is, that the prevalence on the other continent of sentiments favorable to republican liberty is the result of the reaction of America upon Europe; and the source and center of this reaction has doubtless been, and now is, in these United States.[17]

For Webster and Lincoln, however, the central responsibility of America in advancing what Lincoln distinctly referred to as a *world* revolution was to inspire the hearts of men, to hold forth to them the assurance that a republic, a political order devoted to the freedom and happiness of all its members, was not only possible but actual. European liberals might look to America for inspiration and sympathy and, where they succeeded, prompt recognition. But America ought not to jeopardize this precious example of republican freedom by rash adventures. Its primary action upon the international scene was to be moral, not political.

At this point there is a sharply differing emphasis of far-reaching importance in Douglas's speeches. Douglas did not, of course, think we could actually rescue the Hungarian patriots from the clutches of the Russian and Austrian emperors. But he clearly favored a more belligerent tone in all pronouncements upon the conflict abroad between liberal and reactionary forces. For Douglas, the test of republican purity and fidelity was to be found more in the vigor with which we asserted ourselves against anti-republican forces abroad than in any introspective concern. Lincoln, on the contrary, expanding Webster's theme, summoned his countrymen to the great crusade which began in 1854, as follows:

> Our republican robe is soiled, and trailed in the dust. Let us repurify it. Let us turn and wash it white, in the spirit, if not the blood, of the Revolution . . . Let us re-adopt the Declaration of Independence, and with it, the practices, and policy, which harmonize with it . . . If we do this, we shall not only have saved the Union; but we shall have so saved it, as to make, and to keep it, forever worthy of the saving.

We shall have so saved it, that the succeeding millions of free happy people, *the world over* [our italics], shall rise up, and call us blessed, to the latest generations.[18a]

Because the Kansas-Nebraska Act, with its implied rejection of the Declaration of Independence, "deprives our republican example of its just influence in the world—enables the enemies of free institutions, with plausibility, to taunt us as hypocrites," it was a blow at America's foreign policy, no less than against its true domestic policy, according to Lincoln. With Douglas, however, the uncompromising insistence upon purity finds a no less vehement but characteristically different expression. In the same speech on the Kossuth resolutions, from which we have quoted above, Douglas spoke as follows:

Sir, something has been said about an alliance with England, to restrain the march of Russia over the European continent. I am free to say that I desire no alliance with England, or with any other crowned head. I am not willing to acknowledge that America needs England as an ally to maintain the principles of our government. Nor am I willing to go to the rescue of England to save her from the power of the Autocrat, until she assimilates her institutions to ours. Hers is a half-way house between despotism and republicanism. She is responsible, as much as any power in Europe, for the failure of the revolutionary movements which have occurred within the last four years. English diplomacy, English intrigue, and English perfidy, put down the revolution in Sicily and in Italy, and was the greatest barrier to its success even in Hungary . . . I am utterly averse to an alliance with her to sustain her monarch, her nobles, and her privileged classes. She must sustain her constitutional monarchy, even against absolutism without receiving aid from republican America with my consent, and especially so long as she condemns to imprisonment and transportation for life the noble Irish patriots, whose only crime consisted in attempting that for which the great Hungarian is now idolized by the English people. She must do justice to Ireland, and the Irish patriots in exile, and to the masses of her own people, by relieving them from the oppressive taxation imposed to sustain the privileged classes, and by adopting republican institutions, before she can have my sympathy, much less my aid, even against Rus-

sia. I wish no alliance with monarchs. No republican movement will ever succeed so long as the people put their trust
in princes. The fatal error committed in Italy, Germany, in
France, wherever the experiment was tried, consisted in
placing a prince at the head of the popular movement. The
princes all sympathized with the dynasties from which they
were descended, and seized the first opportunity to produce
a reaction, and to betray the people into the hands of their
oppressors. There is reason to believe that much of this was
accomplished through British diplomacy and intrigue. What
more natural? The power of the British Government is in the
hands of the princes and nobility. Their sympathies are all
with the privileged classes of other countries, in every movement which does not affect the immediate interests of their
own kingdom. Republicanism has nothing to hope, therefore,
from England so long as she maintains her existing government, and preserves her present policy. I repeat, I desire
no alliance with England. We require no assistance from her,
and will yield none to her until she does justice to her own
people. The peculiar position of our country requires that we
should have an *American policy* [the italics are Douglas's]
in our foreign relations, based upon the principles of our
own government, and adapted to the spirit of the age. We
should sympathize with every liberal movement—recognize
the independence of all Republics—form commercial treaties,
and open diplomatic relations with them—protest against all
infractions of the laws of nations, and hold ourselves ready
to do whatever our duty may require when a case shall
arise.[18b]

A present-day reader of the foregoing passage must be struck
by the resemblance between what Douglas calls an "American
policy" and the foreign policy advocated by the movement called
"America First" prior to World War II. The persistence of this
theme in American politics is astonishing. In both centuries we
see a refusal to join Britain in opposing a threatened destruction
of the European balance of power by an autocratic continental
power. In both cases there is visible the resentment of non-Anglo-
Saxon nationalities against the idea of war for the sake of British
interests, and the conviction of a radical opposition between
British and American interests. There is, moreover, the peculiar

insistence upon the direct moral claim of American principles of government upon the governments and peoples of Europe, combined with a kind of revulsion from the entire European scene and a withdrawal of American diplomacy, of such power as America could exert through alliances upon that scene in behalf of liberal movements. And in both cases there is the same insistence that America's true reaction to the failure of European liberalism is to be found in establishing an incontestable hegemony in the Western Hemisphere. There is, moreover, a difference between the foregoing policy and the classic "isolationism" of Washington's and Jefferson's neutrality policy and of its quasi-reaffirmation in the Monroe Doctrine. The earlier policies were meant to secure the infant republic from rash adventures, from overcommitments which might needlessly endanger our security. Douglas's policy, on the contrary, looked toward involvement, because it was a summons to a crusade to expel European powers from the New World.

For Douglas, Britain's "half-way house between despotism and republicanism" is the analogue of Lincoln's "house divided." When Webster in 1823 said the greatest question of the age was that between absolute and limited government, he thought "whether the form of government shall be that of limited monarchy, with more or less mixture of hereditary power, or wholly elective or representative, may perhaps be considered as subordinate." For Douglas, however, this "subordinate" question was paramount. Lincoln, in the letter to Speed, spoke of going to Russia, where he could "take his despotism pure, without the base alloy of hypocrisy." Lincoln would not tolerate the impurity represented by successive exceptions to the universal creed of the Declaration of Independence. Douglas's defenders have frequently contrasted his flexibility, as represented by his policy of allowing diversity in the domestic institutions of the states, with Lincoln's doctrinal rigidity. Lincoln did oppose Douglas's popular sovereignty, because it countenanced, in theory at least, the spread of slavery; and Lincoln did demand the ultimate extinction of slavery. But while Lincoln looked to the assimilation of slave to free institutions within the United States, Douglas demanded that Great Britain "assimilate her institutions to ours"! Each man, we might say, called for the elimination of a divided house and denounced what he believed hypocritical betrayal of liberal principles; but whereas

Lincoln saw the fatal division and betrayal at home, Douglas saw them concentrated in "perfidious Albion."

In his Texas and Oregon speeches, one could say that Douglas was simply voicing Jacksonian prejudices, but by 1850 experience had given those prejudices—if they were such—a new dimension and a new plausibility. The revolutions of 1848 had largely failed; bloodshed, persecution, and oppression seemed more than ever the fate of European patriots and liberals. But of all events, none left a deeper mark upon American politics than the Irish famine. Here was a human catastrophe of gigantic proportions. The history of American Negro slavery disclosed no such physical suffering as the starvation and deaths in vast numbers of the Irish peasantry. Nor is it likely that the enforced separation of families, frequently accounted the worst evil of slavery, equaled in a hundred years the separations caused by the enforced emigration from Ireland. That the sufferings of the Irish were attributable to British misrule was widely conceded. And that Douglas, as the spokesman of the Irish in America should, in the scale of human abominations, subordinate the oppression of Negroes to that of the people of his own constituents is hardly a paradox of democratic government.

Certainly it was no mere chauvinism to believe at mid-century that the political structure of the Old World was too rotten to expect any great transplantation to it of the blessings of the New. The continued growth of the New World, the viability of whose free institutions was demonstrated fact, was the true aim of policy.

I insist that there is a difference, a wide difference [said Douglas], between the system of policy which should be pursued in America and that which would be applicable to Europe. Europe is antiquated, decrepit, tottering on the verge of dissolution. When you visit her, the objects which enlist your highest admiration are the relics of past greatness; the broken columns erected to departed power . . . The choicest products of her classic soil . . . bring up memories of the dead, but inspire no hope for the living! Here everything is fresh blooming, expanding, advancing . . . Sir, the statesman who would shape the policy of America by European models, has failed to perceive the antagonism which exists in the relative position, history, institutions—in everything pertaining to the Old and the New World.[19]

The foregoing is from a speech in the special Senate session summoned by the incoming President, Pierce, in March 1853. The debate on foreign policy which had marked the closing months of the Thirty-second Congress, the last under Fillmore and a Whig administration, had been resumed. A controversy had arisen with Britain concerning the interpretation of the Clayton-Bulwer Treaty, which had been signed and ratified in the spring of 1850. This treaty was probably the most unpopular of all our international agreements, at least until Yalta achieved the peak of its ill fame. We shall shortly hear from Douglas precisely why this was so. We should note, however, that it was negotiated and signed amid the gravest internal crisis through which the nation had hitherto passed. It was a Whig treaty, presented to a Democratic Senate, and yet passed by a vote of 42 to 11. This suggests that Whigs and "old fogy" Democrats alike believed in a prudent abatement of national assertiveness while the domestic peril lasted. This was to be Lincoln's view in the next decade, but it was certainly not Douglas's view, then or ever. The deliberations of 1850 were secret, but Douglas tells us in 1853 what he had said before, and these views are expanded on other subsequent occasions of record.

But here is another point of chronology which must command notice. Between Douglas's two major speeches in 1852–53 on foreign affairs there occurred the last unsuccessful attempt to pass a bill to organize Nebraska. It passed the House by an overwhelming margin and failed in the Senate by being laid on the table in the closing hours of the session—in fact, in the early hours of the morning of March 3. This bill, of which we shall take further notice later, was warmly endorsed by Douglas, although it had not a word casting doubt upon, much less repealing, the Missouri Compromise. The Nebraska bill of 1853, however, did not command a fraction of the attention of Douglas (or of anyone else) that its famed successor did; his preoccupation this year was far more with foreign affairs. We shall later expound the view that the repeal provision in 1854 was an aberration from Douglas's true policy; that he never intended it, but that a peculiar set of unhappy circumstances forced him to profess to have intended it, after the fact, and so defend it.

The storm that broke over it was to place Douglas's policy in a false perspective, subordinating a major to a minor theme. He was never again able to push the foreign policy he so dearly believed in, although he never abandoned the attempt.

We would venture as a hypothesis that Douglas, at the end of the Thirty-second Congress, while the lame ducks awaited the return of the Democrats to power in 1853, wished to set the stage for the reassertion of Manifest Destiny. The platforms of both parties in 1852 had asserted that the Compromise of 1850 would be regarded as a definitive settlement of sectional differences. Pierce, in his inaugural address, gave grounds for hoping that Polk's policies would be resumed. But in the following year the Democratic party was rent by internecine feuds and Pierce disclosed his utter incompetence in dealing with them. What the country needed desperately was a policy—and leadership. The Whig party had immolated itself in the fires of sectionalism by taking the lead in, and throwing its weight behind, the Compromise of 1850. The Democratic party appeared to be disintegrating while in power. A vigorous policy with other nations seemed out of the question. Congress could take the lead in forging domestic policy, as it could not in the foreign sphere. Douglas therefore undertook to exert a leadership in 1854 upon an issue he could hope to control through his place in the party and in the Senate. That Douglas was playing the "presidential game" is neither doubtful nor discreditable; what is important is its significance—and success for Douglas, whether as a Democrat or, as was possible in 1858, as Republican, would have meant the reassertion of the primacy of foreign policy. As we shall later show, Lincoln always understood this, and no passages in the joint debates are more meaningful than those in which Lincoln places his own construction upon Douglas's ulterior motives in the external sphere. For this reason it is essential, before turning to the language of the debates, to hear what Douglas said on foreign affairs in 1852–53, in the interval between the domestic crisis of 1850 and its renewal in 1854.

The Clayton-Bulwer Treaty, like that other Whig treaty negotiated in 1842 by Webster and Lord Ashburton, was a settlement of a broad area of irritating and ulcerating differences with Great Britain, differences which could easily have led to war but were as easily removed from that dangerous condition as soon as the principle of compromise was accepted. The 1842 agreement had settled the long-festering dispute over the northeast boundary, between Maine and Canada, a dispute which seemed hopelessly irreconcilable under Democratic administrations but was almost magically dissipated by the diplomacy of Webster and the congenial Ashburton. In 1850 the aftermath of the Mexican War brought not only the domestic sectional controversy but a serious clash of British and American interests in Central America. In the words of Allan Nevins:

> California had no sooner been acquired than a large emigration began to pour across the Panama and Nicaraguan routes. The building of a canal then seemed a much easier enterprise than it actually was, and most Americans inevitably felt that it ought to be under their own control. Great Britain for her part exercised sovereignty over Belize, or British Honduras, asserted a protectorate over the savages who inhabited the so-called Mosquito Coast, and took an interest in the islands of the region. The British had the largest ocean commerce in the world, and no small part of it would pass through any Isthmian canal which was constructed.[20]

The heart of the ensuing treaty was a stipulation that neither Britain nor the United States would "ever obtain for itself any exclusive control over any ship canal," but that both would protect any private company which might undertake to build it. It was also agreed that "the parties owning or constructing the same shall impose no other charges nor conditions of traffic than the aforesaid governments shall approve as equitable," and that "the said canals or railways [shall be] open to the citizens and subjects of Great Britain and the United States on equal terms, [and] shall also be open on like terms to the citizens and subjects of every other state."[21] The "self-denying ordinance" upon which the storm of criticism mainly broke, however, was the following:

> The governments of the United States and Great Britain hereby declare that neither one nor the other will ever . . . occupy, or fortify, or colonize, or assume, or exercise, any dominion over Nicaragua, Costa Rica, the Mosquito Coast, or any part of Central America . . .

The Clayton-Bulwer Treaty, in short, was founded upon the assumption that Anglo-British friendship was the durable basis upon which the international system of the New World might be built. As Clayton wrote to Bulwer at the time, "We have produced a new era in the history of the relations between Great Britain and the United States. We have bound together these two great kindred nations as joint pioneers and partners in spreading the blessings of commerce and civilization."[22] Disillusionment with the treaty set in almost immediately for Clayton, Webster, and the Whigs, as well as for Democrats. The Americans thought that the self-denying ordinance applied to present as well as prospective colonies, etc., while the British interpreted it to mean future ones only; in short, the British meant to retain all the strategic advantages of their existing bases in the vicinity of the Nicaraguan route. But whether the treaty froze existing British advantages in the region or gave us full equality, there can be no question that its Whig authors never looked for more than a full partnership in the area.

The protectorate of the Mosquito Coast included more than half the area of Honduras and Nicaragua, on the Atlantic side. Britain's foothold here (in addition to full possession of Belize, or British Honduras) was, nominally, to prevent the Nicaraguans and others from exterminating the Mosquito Indians. In this situation the Nicaraguans were quite willing to concede to Americans exclusive privileges in the region as an offset to British power. And Douglas wished to pay the British that sincerest form of flattery, imitation, by exploiting native weakness in order to establish an American overlordship that would exclude the British as effectually as the British were in the habit of excluding others. According to Douglas, speaking in the Senate on February 14, 1852, one Hise, Polk's chargé d'affaires (under Buchanan's administration of the State Department) had already negotiated a treaty with Nicaragua, giving this country exclusive and perpetual privileges to build and fortify a canal there, together with land grants for the establishment of free ports and towns at the termini of the interoceanic communications. That such a "treaty" would have been the prelude to another Texas, that the "colonists" would eventually have taken the country from the natives, Douglas was at no pains to deny or conceal. Nor was Douglas unmindful that a treaty with Nicaragua, without a prior understanding with Great Britain, would hardly be worth the paper it was written on. Before the Clayton-Bulwer agreement the British had already obtained from the Nicaraguans navigation rights on the San Juan River entirely inconsistent with the privileges which were now to be bestowed on the Americans.[23] But here, as in the Oregon boundary controversy, Douglas only wanted a scrap of evidence to supply a claim under what he was pleased to call "international law," upon which extravagant demands might be based, demands serving to bring on war. Here are Douglas's main objections to the Clayton-Bulwer Treaty, in his own words:

> In the first place, I was unwilling to enter into treaty stipulations with Great Britain or any other European power in respect to the American continent, by the terms of which we should pledge the faith of this republic not to do in all coming time that which in the progress of events our interests, duty, and even safety may compel us to do. I have already said, and now repeat, that every article, clause, and provision of that treaty is predicated upon a virtual negation and repudiation of the Monroe Doctrine in relation to European colonization on this continent. The article inviting any power on earth with which England and the United States are on terms of friendly intercourse to enter into similar stipulations, and which pledges the good offices of each, when requested by the other, to aid in the new negotiations with the other Central American states, and which pledges the good offices of all the nations entering into the "alliance" to settle disputes between the states and governments of Central America, not only recognizes the right of European powers to interfere with the affairs of the American continent, but invites the exercise of such a right, and makes it obligatory to do so in certain cases. It establishes, in terms, an alliance between the contracting parties, and invites all other nations to become parties to it. I was opposed also to the clause which stipulates that neither Great Britain nor the United States will ever occupy, colonize or exercise dominion over any portion of Nicaragua, Costa Rica, the Mosquito Coast, or any portion of Central America. I did not desire then, nor do I now, to annex any portion of that country to this Union . . . Yet I was unwilling to give the pledge that neither we nor our successors ever would . . . California being a state of the Union, who is authorized to say that the time will not arrive when our interests and safety may

require us to possess some portion of Central America, which
lies half way between our Atlantic and Pacific possessions,
and embraces the great water lines of commerce between
the two oceans?

And further:

But there was another insuperable objection to the Clayton
and Bulwer Treaty . . . I allude to the article in which it
is provided that "The government of the United States and
Great Britain, having not only desired to accomplish a particular object, but also to establish a general principle, they
hereby agree to extend their protection, by treaty stipulations, to any other practicable communications . . . across
the isthmus which connects North and South America . . ."

According to Douglas, this clause extended the treaty to include
not only Central America but Mexico on the north and New
Granada (Colombia and Venezuela) on the south. Since the
treaty recognized a partnership not only with Britain but with
any other foreign powers with whom Britain or the United States
was friendly and who wished to join, then, he said,

the American continent shall have passed under the protectorate of the allied powers, and her future made dependent
upon treaty stipulations for carrying into effect the object
of the alliance, [and so] Europe will no longer have cause
for serious apprehension at the rapid growth, expansion, and
development of our federal Union. She will then console
herself that limits have been set and barriers erected beyond
which the territories of this republic can never extend, nor
its principles prevail.

It would be difficult to imagine words more expressive of the
underlying assumptions of Douglas's entire political career than
the foregoing, in which he co-ordinates the extent of the territory
of our republic with that of its principles. Not only did Douglas
believe that Europe was rotten to the core, but he had no regard
whatever for the political capacity of the Latin Americans, apart
from the fostering hand of the United States.

I do not meditate or look with favor upon any aggression
upon Mexico . . . But who can say that, amid the general
wreck and demoralization in Mexico a state of things may

not arise in which a just regard for our own rights and safety, and for the sake of humanity and civilization, may render it imperative for us to do that which was done in the case of Texas . . .[24]

The principal assumption underlying Whig diplomacy, we have said, was the desirability of permanent friendship with Great Britain. In the continuation of the debate in the March special session Douglas dealt with this as follows:

> . . . I do not sympathize with that feeling which the senator expressed yesterday, that it was a pity to have a difference with a nation so *friendly to us as England* [Douglas's emphasis]. Sir, I do not see the evidence of her friendship. It is not in the nature of things that she can be our friend . . . Sir, we have wounded her vanity and humbled her pride. She can never forgive us. But for us, she would be the first power on the face of the earth . . . She is jealous of us, and jealously forbids the idea of friendship . . . why close our eyes to the fact that friendship is impossible while jealousy exists? Hence England seizes every island in the sea and rock upon our coast where she can plant a gun to intimidate us or annoy our commerce. Her policy has been to seize every military and naval station the world over . . . Does England hold Bermuda because of any profit it is to her? Has she any other motive for retaining it except jealousy which stimulates hostility to us? Is it not the case with all her possessions along our coast?

In the same debate he replied to a remark of Senator Butler, that England was the "mother country," in this vein:

> I can not recognize England as our mother. If so, she is and ever has been a cruel and unnatural mother. I do not find the evidence of her affection in her watchfulness over our infancy, nor in her joy and pride at our everblooming prosperity and swelling power since we assumed an independent position. . . . But, that the Senator from South Carolina, in view of our present position and of his location in this confederacy, should indulge in glowing and eloquent eulogiums of England . . . is to me amazing. He speaks in terms of delight and gratitude of the copious and refreshing streams which English literature and science are pouring into our

country and diffusing throughout the land. Is he not aware that nearly every English book circulated and read in this country contains lurking and insidious slanders and libels upon the character of our people and the institutions and policy of our government? Does he not know that abolitionism, which has so seriously threatened the peace and safety of this republic, had its origin in England, and has been incorporated into the policy of that government for the purpose of operating upon the peculiar institutions of some of the states of this confederacy, and thus render the Union itself insecure? Does she not keep her missionaries perambulating this country, delivering lectures, and scattering broadcast incendiary publications, designed to incite prejudices, hate, and strife between the different sections of this Union? I had supposed that South Carolina and the other slaveholding states of this confederacy had been sufficiently refreshed and enlightened by a certain species of English literature, designed to stir up treason and insurrection around his own fireside, to have excused the senator from offering up praises and hosannas to our English mother![25]

Douglas did not give up this theme until he had wrung it a good deal harder, but we abstain from further quotation. This passage does, however, illustrate how a number of separate strands were woven into the thread of Douglas's policy. We have already seen him contend that England's aristocracy had betrayed the liberal movements in Europe, that their class loyalties, except when in conflict with national advantages, took precedence over any feeling for political freedom. But here we find the most virulent hatred of England as the home of abolitionism, although abolitionism had its home in the middle and lower classes, certainly not in the aristocracy. Slavery was abolished throughout the British colonies (it was mainly concentrated in the West Indies) in 1833, by the first Parliament elected after the great act of reform, an act representing the first major step by Britain toward democracy in the nineteenth century.

The language which Douglas uses to describe English "missionaries" recalls the expressions and tone of the old "tory" Federalists toward the Jacobins, the same Federalists who passed the Alien and Sedition Laws, and is familiar in our day in the attitude and regard toward Communists. In short, Douglas regarded Britain as both reactionary and revolutionary. This may seem inconsistent; but, if so, it is only a superficial inconsistency. Douglas saw British diplomacy conducted by the old ruling classes, who would support liberal causes abroad if they happened to coincide with British interests; e.g., by weakening the hands of rival monarchical powers. But they would with equal or greater alacrity sacrifice those same causes when no selfish advantage promised to accrue from them. These rulers of Britain had no more sympathy for republican freedom in America than for Russian autocracy. British abolitionism was unleashed upon America in precisely the same spirit in which the revolutionaries of eastern Europe were supported against the Czar. The "humanitarian" spirit which abolished slavery in the British West Indies cost nothing to the parliamentarians in Westminster, who did not have to live among the emancipated Negroes. The West Indian slaveholders were not asked to give their consent, which would never have been given, and the power exerted by Parliament to secure abolition was as autocratic, as little based upon the consent of the governed, as the Stamp Act or the tax on tea which precipitated the American Revolution.

Since Douglas identified political freedom with the greatest degree of local autonomy, the coincidence of the emergence of the forms of British democracy with abolition caused him to regard the former in the light of the latter. Douglas no doubt construed the quality of British democracy very much in the light which abolitionism cast upon democracy in this country, for the political aim of abolitionism in America was, quite clearly, to convey to the federal government the power to do to the southern slave states what the Parliament at Westminster had done to the Bahamas. Hardly a man before the Civil War believed the Constitution gave the federal government power over slavery in the states, but if a militant anti-slavery party controlled all branches of the federal government, how long would that belief continue? Or, more concretely, if such a party controlled the formation and growth of new states, how long would it be before three fourths of the states would have the power and the will to change the Constitution so as to give the federal government this power? Does not the Thirteenth Amendment give the answer?

Douglas's remarks last quoted were directed against Butler of South Carolina, who sat in the seat once occupied by Calhoun.

Butler's Anglophilism reflected the community of taste and feeling of the plantation aristocracy with the British gentry that stood the South in good stead during the Civil War. And Butler also reflected the anti-expansionist feeling common among many of the largest slaveholders of the South and slavery's most rigorous defenders. Calhoun himself did not wish any annexation beyond Texas, concerning which he was no more than lukewarm. He knew in 1850 that his proposal for an amendment to keep the slave and free states in balance would never be accepted. And so Calhoun and the conservative wing of the extreme pro-slavery school of the South always saw that their protection within the Union against that three-fourths constitutional majority lay more in limiting the number of future states than in seeking new territory, which might or might not become slave states. As we shall again notice, the strongest slavery men in Congress (and out of it) never wished the repeal of the Missouri Compromise, for its retention enabled them to block the further organization of the West altogether. They were driven to support a measure they hated, because the issue was taken out of their hands when opposition to it became the rallying cry of the abolitionists. We here see Douglas trying to beat down the conservative pro-slavery resistance to expansion in Central America and the Caribbean and trying also to beat down the spirit of conciliation with England, as he later overcame resistance to the organization of the western states, with the Kansas-Nebraska Act.

We conclude our excerpts from Douglas's major foreign-policy pronouncements with some passages from a speech in December 1858, the month following the election in which he defeated Lincoln for the Senate. It was in New Orleans, the city whence the Cuban filibusterers were wont to sail. In this speech his language regarding future annexations was less restrained, if possible, than in the Senate: Cuba, Mexico, Central America (as far as Cape Horn, we should guess!) were all certainly included in Manifest Destiny. In passing he recounted a conversation with Sir Henry Bulwer that occurred in 1850.

He took occasion to remonstrate with me that my position with regard to the treaty was unjust and untenable; that the treaty was fair because it was reciprocal, and it was reciprocal because it pledged that neither Great Britain nor the United

States should ever purchase, colonize, or acquire any territory in Central America. I told him that it would be fair if they would add one word to the treaty, so that it would read that neither Great Britain nor the United States should ever occupy or hold dominion over Central America or Asia. But he said, "You have no interests in Asia." "No," answered I, "and you have none in Central America." "But," said he, "you can never establish any rights in Asia." "No," said I, "and we don't mean that you shall ever establish any in America."[26]

This speech concludes with a peroration in which Douglas says, with one qualification, that he is in favor of an indefinite expansion in which "the more degrees of latitude and longitude embraced beneath our Constitution the better," in which "the principles of free trade [shall] apply to the important staples of the *world* [our italics], making us the greatest planting as well as the greatest manufacturing, the greatest commercial as well as the greatest agricultural power on the globe." There was but one thing that would modify this advocacy: ". . . but I am not in favor of that policy unless the great principle of non-intervention and the right of the people to decide the question of slavery and all other domestic questions for themselves shall be maintained."

We thus see explicitly co-ordinated, just after the end of the great debates, what was implicitly co-ordinated almost from the outset of Douglas's career: popular sovereignty and expansion. But the co-ordination of these two, in the light of a full reading of Douglas's speeches on foreign affairs, casts added light upon the doctrine of popular sovereignty. For Douglas clearly intended a different kind of union from that conceived by Lincoln. Lincoln, like Webster, thought in terms of greater homogeneity, because he thought in terms of sharply circumscribed boundaries; and he accepted these because, in the Whig-Federalist tradition, he tacitly accepted Britain's partnership in deciding vital matters affecting the American future.

Douglas's union would have been a new kind of Rome. Unlike the British Empire, it would have been radically democratic, and yet it could not admit the peoples of all the lands it absorbed into full civic privileges. "If experience shall continue to prove, what the past may be considered to have demonstrated, that those little Central American powers can not maintain self-government, the interests of Christendom require that some power should preserve order for them."[27] Precisely how self-governing Americans would deal with the natives when they took over Central America, Mexico, etc., Douglas does not say. What is clear, however, is that the variety, not only in soil, climate, and productions, but of peoples, that American expansion would involve would require policies of great suppleness and flexibility. The absolutely necessary condition of such flexibility, and the one condition which could be dealt with contemporaneously, was a policy of local self-determination, of popular sovereignty, as Douglas used the term. That the spread of the federal Union to new lands and climes would have involved us in more conspicuous exceptions to general egalitarianism did not disturb Douglas. Why should it? He was satisfied that American principles could and would accompany the flag, and he did not believe they would be extended any other way. The British Empire has in our day been transformed into a commonwealth under far more autocratic auspices than those conceived by Douglas. Mexicans and Orientals in our Far West and Southwest have suffered a good deal of second- and third-class citizenship, giving a good indication of what might have happened on a much larger scale. But have these Mexicans been governed worse than their kinsmen across the border? And where, in the Orient, are Orientals more fortunate? Within the framework of our constitutional system the leaven of free principles has operated steadily in favor of equal treatment of the groups suffering most unequal treatment. Are people better abandoned to systems which deny them even the hope or promise of equality?

In the great Chicago speech[28] in defense of the Compromise of 1850, from which we have quoted above, Douglas spoke, in the vein of John Stuart Mill, of the necessity of barbarians being governed by civilized men. In the same context he observed, "The history of the world furnished few examples where any considerable portion of the human race have shown themselves sufficiently enlightened and civilized to exercise the rights and enjoy the blessings of freedom. In Asia and Africa we find nothing but ignorance, superstition, and despotism. Large portions of Europe and America can scarcely lay claim to civilization and Christianity; and a still smaller portion have demonstrated their capacity for self-government." For Douglas, to strengthen boldly

the political and material foundations of the one indubitably
successful modern republic could not be an anti-republican
policy, simply because all of those comprehended within the republican boundaries would not themselves immediately become
full members of the republican polity. The counsels of perfection
are not for the kingdom of this world. Lincoln, as we shall presently see, approved of the policy of the Founding Fathers which
gave full legal sanction to slavery, where it already existed, as
a "necessity" without which this republic could not have been
founded. Cannot any evil, without which a greater good seems
unattainable, be similarly regarded as a "necessity?"

Douglas was convinced that he lived in an age of progress,
yet he did not regard progress as something to be taken for
granted. The optimism of the age of Tom Paine and Tom Jefferson had received some rude shocks in the catastrophe of the
French Revolution, the subsequent dominance of continental
reaction, and the squalid misgovernment exhibited by the recently emancipated Latin Americans. Something might be done
for world freedom, but it must be done by expanding American
freedom. We should not forget that Douglas was the very prototype of the American politician of the melting pot. As the most
popular leader of America's largest and most downtrodden immigrant group before the Civil War, he demonstrated, no less
than Lincoln, how and why the New World could offer hope
to the people of the Old. But that hope would be stultified if
the United States was not the undisputed mistress of the New
World.

As Douglas viewed the political scene at mid-century, he too
saw the anti-slavery movement and the nativist movement as
obverse and reverse of the same coin. The anti-slavery movement,
with its talk of the "higher law," was distinctly aimed at destroying
the Constitution, was distinctly aimed at a *coup d'état* in which,
when abolitionists held the power of the federal government, the
powers of the states would be stripped from them. As we have
amply shown, Douglas was the enemy of extremists North and
South, yet his enmity was greater for abolitionists, not simply because it was more convenient to attack enemies outside the ranks
of his party, but because he felt they were the aggressors. Secession and abolition were equally unconstitutional, but secession would be morally justified as the exercise of a revolutionary
right—as Lincoln was to concede in his First Inaugural Address—

if it were the only means to security. And if the abolitionists had
their way they could eventually, through control of the federal
machinery, jeopardize the security of Southerners far more than
King George III had ever done. But the anti-slavery movement
was also the profoundest obstacle to expansion. Yet it was only
through expansion that Douglas saw the United States continuing
to assimilate the bruised and crushed sufferers from European
despotism. The opponents of expansion were the same who
would make Britain a "partner" with this country in the New
World, who would thus "contain" and ultimately strangle us in
the toils and tangles of Old World diplomacy. And these same
opponents to expansion, these same devotees of England, were
the ones who wished to preserve the Anglo-Saxon purity of
American society, who wished to exclude foreigners from political rights and to keep the benefits of our free institutions to themselves. In short, the movements against slavery, against expansion,
against foreigners were all movements for British interests and
for those Americans who conceived their own interests in kinship
to England's. The high moral tone which permeated all three
was nothing but snobbishness. The crocodile tears that were shed
for the Negro were only pretexts for destroying the constitutional
equality of the states, that equality which alone guaranteed that
a large republic could remain a free republic; and which, hence,
alone permitted the extension of our boundaries as far as the
fulfillment of our republican mission to the world might require.

Chapter V

The Repeal of the Missouri Compromise I

THE LEGAL POWER AND PRACTICAL IMPOTENCE OF FEDERAL PROHIBITIONS OF SLAVERY IN THE TERRITORIES

IN 1860 the Illinois State Central Committee of the Republican party asserted that Douglas had been anti-slavery until January 4, 1854. On the twenty-third day of that month, to repeat their accusation, "the turning point in Mr. Douglas's political highway" was reached. "From this sharp corner," they say, "his course is wholly and utterly pro-slavery." That Douglas's shift in tactics did not mean a change in his ultimate aims or views with respect to slavery, we have already proposed. We have seen that some such alteration was the natural response of a wise statesman attempting to retain control of events amid the dramatic and rapidly shifting scenes of the fifties. Yet this defense of Douglas is clearly insufficient for at least one simple reason: the country was enjoying a respite from the slavery controversy after the Compromise of 1850 had been confirmed by the election of 1852; and the dramatic scenes of the later fifties, to which we have said Douglas adapted himself, were all directly attributable to his own action in repealing the Missouri Compromise. The bloody struggle in Kansas, the attempted Lecompton fraud, the Dred Scott decision, John Brown, all are virtually inconceivable except as consequences of the Kansas-Nebraska Act. We cannot then credit a man with statesmanship for trying to ride the whirlwind which he himself has sown.

Of the great political facts which we have said dominated

Douglas's judgment in the later fifties, paramount was the Republican party, an anti-slavery party capable of representing a constitutional majority without drawing a single vote from a slave state. Yet Douglas had a primary responsibility for its existence, since the Republican party was originally simply the anti-Nebraska party. Moreover, we must see that the question of the morality of Lincoln's opposition to Douglas in 1858 is identical in principle with the question of the morality of Douglas's action in 1854. This is true, first of all, because either action was an absolute *sine qua non* of the advent of the Civil War. We have spelled out Lincoln's responsibility in Chapter I, but of course the opportunity Lincoln seized would not have existed had not Douglas espoused the repeal of the Missouri slavery restriction. Lincoln's action, which in 1858 denied to Douglas any continuing partnership in the free-soil coalition, forced the slavery controversy back to the pristine issue which had engendered Republicanism in 1854. After the house divided speech, and because of it, the central demand of the Republican party, the centripetal force in the free-soil coalition, again became the restoration of the Missouri Compromise. Thus the debate of 1858 turned more upon the question of the justice and expediency of what had happened in 1854 than upon any other practical question. Only the most complete understanding of the nature of the repealing action will enable us to judge well of the issues between the two men.

We have observed in a previous chapter that, in our judgment, Douglas never desired and never intended to repeal the Missouri Compromise. But we have also maintained that in 1854 Douglas came to the conviction that only the full and consistent application of the doctrine of popular sovereignty—the true principle of republican institutions as he understood them—could resolve the territorial question and provide a firm basis for future national development. These assertions are paradoxical in two respects: First, because Douglas, *after* the repeal, always insisted that he had always intended it. Second, because there is a manifest incongruity between the proposition that Douglas did *not* intend the repeal and that he *did* intend full recognition of popular sovereignty. It must be our task, in this and the succeeding chapters of Part II, to reconcile these assertions. Only by seeing to what extent they can be reconciled can we see how Douglas himself must have viewed the repeal, and only in this light can we see the case for Douglas in its full dimensions.

To comprehend how such a reconciliation is possible, we must grasp in detail the progress and consistency of Douglas's views on the question of federal power and duty in the territories, from his amendment to the Texas annexation resolutions in 1845 until his report and revised Nebraska bill of January 4, 1854. In the present chapter we shall analyze Douglas's proposals in dealing with territorial questions for the period 1845–50 and his various subsequent explanations of them. This we shall do with the accusations made against Douglas by the Republicans in the 1860 campaign, as a foil. Despite the notorious perversity of campaign charges, these accusations constitute a principal source of the understanding of Douglas's motives which has characterized a great body of historical literature. We know no better way to transcend the polemics upon this subject than by a critical confrontation of them at their point of origin. We will then attempt to show how Douglas himself must have viewed his policies, in the periods in question, in their tendency to promote or hinder slavery, to promote or hinder that genuine local control of domestic institutions he called popular sovereignty, to promote or hinder sectional peace.

In Chapter VI we take up the charge of "manifest falsification" hurled first by the Independent Democrats and then by the entire free-soil movement against Douglas's assertion, in his first "quasi" repeal amendment, that the Missouri Compromise restriction of slavery had been "superseded" by the Compromise of 1850. It is our contention that when Douglas made the explicit "supersession" assertion he had already been driven from the ground he intended, on January 4, 1854, to occupy. Yet the conception of the "supersession" of the Missouri Compromise is the central conception of the strategy which constituted Douglas's intention when he first introduced his revised Nebraska bill. The logic of the "supersession" thesis would not, we believe, be intelligible except in the light of his previous record upon the territorial question. We shall demonstrate how, in this light, it is intelligible, and how it partakes of a meaning radically different from that imputed to it by Douglas's detractors.

In Chapter VII we shall first propound the reasons why, in January 1854, Douglas must have felt obliged to abandon the Nebraska bill of 1853, which he had ardently supported and in which no suggestion of repealing the Missouri law occurs. Thence we proceed to an analysis of the great report accompanying

Douglas's revised Nebraska bill. In this report, and in it alone, is to be found the key to Douglas's original intentions in bringing in this revised bill. The many books and articles on this question, from the work of Mrs. Dixon (wife of the Kentucky senator who first moved the repeal on the Senate floor, after Douglas's bill had been reported) to that of P. O. Ray and Frank Hodder (to mention only some leading names), are all beside the point in the decisive respect. Although they all contribute collateral insights by pointing to good reasons why Douglas *might* have accepted the idea of repeal (to get a central or northern railroad route, to help Senator Atchison in his fight with Benton, to gain southern support for the next presidential nomination, etc.), they are needlessly conjectural in saying why he *did* accept it. This, we believe, can be adjudged only in the light of Douglas's intentions *before* the repeal; and the only authentic contemporary record of those intentions is Douglas's report and bill of January 4, 1854. Nowhere, to our knowledge, in the literature on this tremendous historical *crux*, is there a thorough analysis of the report. We have here attempted to supply it, and by it to show how and why (in our judgment) Douglas believed that he could establish popular sovereignty as the ruling principle for territorial government *without repealing the Missouri Compromise*.

Finally, in Chapter VIII, we record the tragic denouement of the strategy *intended* by Douglas but never carried out. From this record we may elucidate a judgment of responsibility for the catastrophe which will do justice to Douglas's intentions, even though it may deplore the action he was driven to endorse. And if we find it impossible to believe what he subsequently said about his own intentions, we must evaluate his disingenuousness in the light of the public good he meant to achieve by it, and in comparison with the alternatives he felt compelled to reject. For if, because of reasons he could not have foreseen, the repeal, as the lesser of evils, appeared necessary, it was surely right for him to represent it in the only light in which he thought he could defend it.

*   *   *   *   *

The "sharp corner" visualized by the Illinois Republican Committee in 1860 is made to appear much more acute by the manner in which they interpret Douglas's pronouncements prior to

January 23, 1854. The plausibility of imputing to Douglas some anti-slavery bias in the earlier period we also have maintained, and evidence for it has been already presented. Yet the impression intended to be conveyed by the Republicans, that he was anti-slavery in the same sense that they were, and that he was an apostate from their principles, is certainly wrong. The extent to which they succeed in producing this impression in their pamphlet is by employing the technique of highly selective quotation. For they would have us believe that Douglas had been, even as they were, a passionate believer in the inviolable sanctity of the Missouri Compromise; that he had believed, no less than they, in the constitutional power of Congress to prohibit slavery in the national territories; and that he had professed to believe, no less than Seward or Lincoln, in a policy which looked toward the ultimate replacement of slavery by free institutions in all the states of the Union.

It is curious that each of these propositions, stated in terms of sufficient generality, is true. Douglas *had* subscribed to them. But he had never done so *in the same sense* as the Republicans. It was only by exploiting equivocations that they made out their case against him as an anti-slavery turncoat. To take the leading example, when Douglas spoke of the Missouri Compromise, *he did not mean by it the same thing the Republicans meant*. To Lincoln the Missouri Compromise meant a system of equivalents —as did the Compromise of 1850. It meant all the parts of the bargain taken together and in their relation to each other. To Douglas it meant the principle of an equitable division of national territory along a geographical line, as represented by the parallel of latitude at 36′30″. In other words, Douglas understood the Missouri Compromise to be the *Missouri Compromise line*. In many of his speeches "the line" and "the compromise" are interchangeable terms. This usage, we add, was not uncommon. Indeed, one of the captions in the Republican tract is: "He thought the Missouri Compromise should have been extended to the Pacific." Whether such usage involved a misunderstanding remains to be seen. In any case, we will show why a strong case can be made for its political legitimacy and why Douglas's espousal of the Missouri Compromise *as he understood it*, before 1850, is not inconsistent with his abandonment of it in 1854.

Before doing so, let us dispose of the charge that Douglas had, in the absurd exaggeration of the Republican pamphlet of 1860, actually advocated Seward's doctrine of an "irrepressible conflict." This charge rested mainly on the passage in the speech directed against Calhoun in 1850, in which Douglas had spoken of an "age of progress" and correlated progress with the gradual abolition of slavery. Yet in this speech Douglas said nothing of conflict, irrepressible or otherwise; he merely contemplated the same peaceful progress of emancipation that had led six of the original thirteen states to emancipate their slaves in the half century that followed independence. Moreover, since the agency of emancipation was local opinion, operating through the machinery of state government, it was an example to him of the true method by which freedom extinguished slavery in an "age of progress," without any reference to the federal government of the republic whatever. Further: when men like Lincoln and Seward spoke of the opposition of freedom and slavery, they thought, as Lincoln said at Peoria, of an "eternal antagonism," of a "collision" so fierce that "shocks, and throes, and convulsions must ceaselessly follow." But Douglas never conceded any such antagonism. Progress was the result of enlightened self-interest: there was no more "eternal antagonism" between freedom and slavery, in his view, than between the horse and the steam engine. As the advantages of the one came to be understood it naturally replaced the other. This, we believe, is another aspect of the "dollars-and-cents" argument to which we have sufficiently adverted above. But further: Douglas's expectation that slavery would be replaced by freedom was not, in and of itself, a policy. Like the opening of Lincoln's house divided speech, Douglas in 1850 was expressing what he believed would happen rather than what ought to happen.

When Lincoln in 1858 expressed the conviction that the Union must become all slave or all free, Douglas accused him of advocating a war between the sections. And Lincoln's persistent retort was that he did not, by these words, advocate anything at all; he only said what he believed would happen. The two men differed in their estimates of the direction events were taking, but the difference in their "predictions" was of course symptomatic of the difference in their policies. From an anti-slavery viewpoint, Douglas was an optimist and Lincoln a pessimist. It was in large measure because Douglas did not believe in the possible victory of slavery over freedom in the nation at large that he chose a policy which would put out of sight, as far as possible, the harsh moral contrast. Lincoln, on the contrary, saw nothing irreversible in "progress," no guarantee that the principles of republican government might not perish. He would never, therefore, acquiesce in a policy that promised sectional peace, on the assumption that a decision by default with regard to slavery must inevitably be a decision against slavery. This Republican charge only conceals the gulf which always existed between Lincoln and Douglas.

Let us now clarify Douglas's general stand with regard to the power of Congress to prohibit slavery in the territories. The Dred Scott decision, of course, forced Douglas to perform remarkable but not invariably successful mental gymnastics in order to harmonize that monstrosity with his previous pronouncements. But before the debacle of this decision—which was a personal catastrophe—Douglas was remarkably consistent in his views. And this consistency is easily appreciated if a simple distinction is kept in mind. It is that, while Douglas always granted the *legal* power of the federal government to prohibit slavery in a territory, he also always insisted upon the superior *moral* right of such action being reserved to the inhabitants of a territory when organized into a political community. Douglas's position on the exercise of federal power over slavery in the territories paralleled Lincoln's position on the legitimacy of slavery in the states. Lincoln believed slavery to be against natural right, to be intrinsically unjust. Yet he conceded there were circumstances in which it might be the lesser evil. Since it is wise to choose the lesser of two evils when no other alternative is possible, the decision in favor of slavery, in a concrete case, might be morally right, even though slavery itself is morally wrong. In essence, although without the same casuistical clarity, this was Douglas's conception of the relation of popular sovereignty to such exercises of federal authority as the Ordinance of 1787 and the Missouri Compromise. Popular sovereignty was the true principle upon which our republican institutions rested; but in certain actual situations federal legislation better served to pacify sectional antagonisms, to preserve the Union. Douglas was inclined to be indifferent about accepting the federal restriction of slavery in these cases—and in the cases where he proposed the extension of the Missouri Compromise line—because he was morally certain that the results of such federal law would only mean the placing of a seal of approval upon the results of popular sovereignty. Douglas was no doctrinaire; he would never insist on what he believed was a purely abstract principle, without regard for consequences. What Douglas was prepared to do if the right of a people to exclude slavery from a territory was seriously interfered with was demonstrated to the world in the battle against Lecompton. To sum up: Douglas never believed that Congress, as distinct from the people of a territory, should decide for or against slavery. But as long as a congressional enactment served to produce general acquiescence in a settlement throughout the nation, and as long as such a settlement was not a substantive denial of popular sovereignty, Douglas was willing to "prefer" such a mode of dealing with slavery in the territories. The legal power of Congress he always conceded—before Dred Scott—but the expediency of its exercise depended upon contingent factors. Among those factors, the chief one was the state of public opinion, North and South, that had made such an enactment as the Missouri Compromise a cause of harmony and not of mutual grievance. Whenever such restriction of slavery became a bone of contention, there was no moral claim which would cause Douglas to cling to it. The Missouri Compromise never had any other merit in Douglas's eyes than its utility as a cause of intersectional harmony.

We shall now take up some points in the documentation of the charge that Douglas had been false to his own principles when he renounced federal restriction of slavery in Nebraska and consented to the repeal of the Missouri Compromise. The first Republican allegation was that in 1845, as a member of the House, he had introduced the amendment to the joint resolution for the annexation of Texas which provided "and in such States as may be formed out of said territory north of the Missouri Compromise line, slavery or involuntary servitude—except for crime—shall be prohibited." "Let it be observed," crowed the Republicans, "that while Thomas Jefferson and the fathers of the Republic proposed to prohibit slavery in the *Territories* only, and while the Republican party of today propose no more and no less, Stephen A. Douglas sought, in 1845, to prohibit it in *States*, even though the people wanted it!"

The foregoing amendment had been offered on January 25, and on February 23 Douglas spoke in the House on the question of the admission of Iowa and Florida, at which time he made the following remarks, which the Republicans quoted against him:

The father may bind his son during his minority, but the moment he attains his majority his fetters are severed, and he is free to regulate his own conduct. SO WITH THE TERRITORIES; THEY ARE SUBJECT TO THE JURIS-DICTION AND CONTROL OF CONGRESS DURING THEIR INFANCY—THEIR MINORITY; but when they attain their majority AND OBTAIN ADMISSION INTO THE UNION, they are free from all restraints and restrictions, except such as the Constitution of the United States has imposed upon each and all of the States. [Capitals supplied by the Republican Committee.]

It is, we think, reasonable to interpret the constitutional thinking of Douglas's amendment in the light of this speech, made less than a month afterward. The Republicans think this passage exhibits Douglas as an exponent of the constitutional power of Congress to place any restriction it might have seen fit to place upon the territories. But the passage also cuts another way: it denies the power of Congress to place any restrictions that are binding *beyond* the territorial period. It says, in effect, that the amendment to the annexation resolutions could not bind states formed from Texas north of the Missouri Compromise line to forbid slavery *after* they had been admitted to the Union as states. We must recall that, although the Missouri Compromise "forever prohibited" slavery in the remaining Louisiana territory north of the line, this was generally understood to apply only to the territorial period. Legal opinion in 1820 was divided, but we are told in John Quincy Adams's diary that President Monroe and all his Cabinet, Adams himself alone excepted, so believed.[1] By 1845 opinion was overwhelming in favor of the doctrine advanced by Douglas, and in 1858 Lincoln himself did not dispute it. In the joint debates he conceded that if Congress kept slavery out of a territory before it became a state, and the people thereafter adopted slavery, there was no power under the Constitution to say them nay. From this, as will presently appear, Douglas's amendment to the Texas annexation resolution had exactly the same force and effect as the Missouri Compromise.

The Republicans also overlooked a distinction between the Missouri legislation and the annexation resolution. The enabling act for the admission of Missouri was, while the latter was not, a statute in the ordinary sense. It was originally sought to annex

Texas by treaty, but the partisans of the measure were unable to secure the support of two thirds of the Senate, whereas they did command majorities in both houses. Whatever the constitutional merits (or demerits) of the method employed to secure Texas, what was admitted to the Union via the joint resolution was not a "territory," in the sense of a community inferior in legal political capacity to a state. Texas, prior to admission, was a republic, as free and independent of the United States as the United States was of Great Britain. The word "territory" in the amendment to the joint resolution refers to the extent of land lying north of the compromise line, not to the political condition of that land. Douglas in 1854 explained his amendment correctly when he said that Congress did not have the power to bind the action of "States" formed out of Texas and applying for admission, but that the joint resolutions formed a compact with the Republic of Texas which, as an independent power, could commit her citizens, while subjects of Texas, to the fulfillment of such obligations. This power of Texas over "applying" states, however, also ended the moment they became actual states, equal in all constitutional respects to their "parent." When the Republic of Texas joined the Union, all of it became the State of Texas. Thus all "States" formed out of Texas and applying for admission to the Union would remain under the jurisdiction of the State of Texas until the moment of admission. We leave aside the question of the true boundaries of Texas, later decided by compromise. Much territory claimed by Texas was later joined to New Mexico Territory, and some to other territories to the north. But whatever Texas's true boundaries, it was provided in the terms of annexation that this same state might in future be subdivided into four additional states with the consent of Texas and Congress. It will be observed that the word "territory" in Douglas's amendment was not capitalized; while the word "States," following the usual but not invariable custom of that day, was capitalized. When the Republicans, in their scathing comment, refer to "Territories" in the sense that includes political capacity and not mere extent of land, they too capitalize. In short, because all of Texas was transformed by annexation from an independent republic to a state in the Union, the law did not contemplate "Territories" there, or to be formed there, to which the slavery prohibition could extend. Douglas's language is strictly correct and means that, when applying for admission *as states*, such "States" as are formed north of 36′30″ shall apply with constitutions prohibiting slavery. It does not, however, prohibit these prospective states, any more than the Ordinance of 1787 prohibited Illinois, Indiana, Ohio, Wisconsin, or Michigan—or the Missouri Compromise prohibited Iowa after 1846—from adopting slavery as a domestic institution at any time after admission to statehood. However unthinkable such a development may in fact have been, the legal situation was generally thus understood at the time of the Lincoln-Douglas debates.

This view of the Constitution is vehemently set forth in another portion of that same speech of February 13, 1845. It is omitted in the Republican tract but immediately precedes, in the original, the passage already given.

> It was clear in his mind [said Douglas] that whenever a new State was admitted into the Union, it came in on an equal footing, in all respects, with the original States; and all attempts to deprive her of that equality, by act of Congress, was in derogation of the Constitution of the United States, and consequently void . . . Many of the northern States have, at different periods, asserted and exercised the right of establishing and abolishing slavery, each for itself, without reference to the wishes of Congress, or of any other States. If the old States had this power, he could not discover how it could be denied to the new ones . . . A man might as well attempt to impose restraints upon the free action of his son after his arrival at full and lawful age, as Congress to fetter the action of the Territories after their admission into the Union as States.[2]

It will be seen that the burden of the two passages, taken together, is not so much that Congress has legal power to bind during the territorial period—although this is, incidentally, affirmed—but that it does *not* have such power when once that period has passed.

In the same speech Douglas already indicates, albeit indirectly, the opinion that his own state had never been affected by the Northwest Ordinance. "Illinois," he says here, "by the free will of her own people, came into the Union without slavery, and with a constitution declaring that slavery shall never exist." This assertion in 1845 is paralleled by another of 1850, which is among those quoted in the Republican tract to show his earlier antislavery feelings:

I undertake to say that there is not one of these States that
would have tolerated the institution of slavery in its limits,
even if it had been peremptorily required to do so by act of
Congress. It is a libel on the character of these people to
say that the HONEST SENTIMENTS OF THEIR HEARTS
were smothered, and their political action upon this question
constrained and directed by act of Congress. Will the Senators from Ohio, Indiana, Michigan, Wisconsin and Iowa make
any such DEGRADING ADMISSION in respect to their
constituencies? I WILL NEVER BLACKEN THE CHAR-
ACTER OF MY OWN STATE BY SUCH AN ADMIS-
SION . . . [Capitals supplied by the Republican Committee.]

Let us note that what is common to these two passages is the
inefficacy of federal legislation concerning slavery in the territories. The Republican Committee comments on the 1850 selection thus: "Let the reader contrast this fine assertion of the
conscientious convictions of the people of Illinois with the horrible libel upon them contained in his speech of February 29th,
1860 . . . and see how he has kept his promise 'never to blacken
the character' of his own State by such an admission." Here are
the remarks of 1860—which, incidentally, are practically identical
with passages in the joint debates of 1858:

We in Illinois tried slavery while we were a Territory, and
found it was not profitable; and *hence* we turned philan-
thropists and abolished it.

And again:

But they (the people of Illinois) said "experience proves that
it is not going to be profitable in this climate." . . . *They
had no scruples about its being right,* but they said, "we cannot make any money by it . . . perhaps we shall gain population faster if we stop slavery and invite in the northern
population"; and as a matter of political policy, State policy,
they prohibited Slavery themselves.

Now an unbiased reading of the 1850 and 1860 statements will
show that there is no contradiction between them. The pledge
"never to blacken the character" of his constituents refers to the
absence of constraint or direction by Congress of their action in

excluding slavery, and has no reference whatever to their motive in so doing. The intended impression, that Douglas had once imputed a moral repudiation of slavery to Illinois, which he later denied, is destroyed the moment one reads further in the 1850 speech. Douglas never believed that qualms as to the morality of slavery had ever had any influence in determining political action with respect to it—certainly not in the old Northwest. Slavery, he maintained, did not prove highly profitable north of the Ohio River. If the economic development of the area could not be carried on in the manner traditional in the South—from which most of the Northwest was originally settled—then free labor must be invited in. Since free labor and slave labor did not mix—this is Douglas's tacit rather than explicit premise, but it was universally understood—then slavery on the soil of the Northwest must be ended. What is impressive, above all, is Douglas's steady insistence that popular sovereignty was not only the right principle but the only practical one. This must be kept in mind when noting his attempts to extend the Missouri Compromise line. In his mind, the extension of the line to new territories, or its retraction from the old, was never more than a token concession to fallacious—albeit politically important—opinions.

We now present evidence substantiating the foregoing interpretation, drawn from the same 1850 speech. The major contention of this 1850 speech is its denial of Calhoun's thesis; viz., that the rights of the South had been persistently violated by the North and that the South was entitled to guarantees of equal rights in the common territories of the nation. The core of Douglas's denial is that the Constitution—the bond of Union—recognizes and represents in the federal legislature the states and the people, but not sections. The following passage is, incidentally, among those used in the Republican campaign tract.

The territories belong to the United States as one people, one nation, and are to be disposed of for the common benefit of all, according to the principles of the Constitution. Each State, as a member of the Confederacy, has a right to a voice in forming the rules and regulations for the government of the Territories; but the different sections—North, South, East, and West—have no such right. It is no violation of southern rights to prohibit slavery [at this point the Republicans leave

off quoting in their pamphlet!], nor of northern rights to
leave the people to decide the question for themselves. In
this sense no geographical section of the Union is entitled
to any share of the territories.[3]

Precisely why there could be no violation of southern rights, by
either the Ordinance of 1787, the Missouri Compromise, or the
provision excluding slavery from the Oregon Territory, is now
set forth. The following is *not* reproduced in the Republican campaign tract.

But I must proceed to the consideration of the particular
acts of aggression of which the Senator complains. And first
of the Ordinance of 1787 . . . This ordinance, the Senator
from South Carolina informs us, had the effect "to exclude
the South entirely from that vast and fertile region which
lies between the Ohio and Mississippi rivers, now embracing
five States and one territory." Is not the Senator mistaken in
his facts? . . . at the time the constitution of the State of
Ohio was formed, at least one half of the people of that
State, and probably more, were natives of, were immigrants
from southern States: that fully two-thirds of the people of
Indiana, at the time she adopted her constitution, were natives of the South; and that a much larger proportion of the
people of Illinois, at the time she was admitted into the
Union, were also from the South. These facts do not indicate
that the Ordinance had the effect to exclude the South entirely from those territories. Let us next inquire what effect
it had upon slavery there. The ordinance . . . was adopted
. . . when the whole country was a vast unpeopled wilderness . . . The object of the ordinance was to prohibit, not
to abolish, slavery in the Northwest territory. And as an
evidence that the ordinance has produced the effect intended
by its framers, we have been repeatedly referred to those
five free States carved out of that territory.

Here we interject the comment that the insistence that the
ordinance had produced its intended effect—*post hoc, propter hoc*
—was a central contention of Lincoln throughout the debates.
Lincoln agreed with Douglas that the South had not been debarred from the old Northwest. Had not the Lincolns migrated
from the slave soil of Kentucky? But he emphatically insisted

that the prohibition of slavery was a necessary cause of the difference between the states south of the Ohio River, in which slavery existed, and the states north of it, not one of which permitted slavery. Lincoln's argument, one must observe, conceded the grounds upon which the southern sense of grievance fed— the grounds of Calhoun's argument. For Lincoln not only conceded, but insisted, that slaveholding had been debarred by federal enactment. This was gall and wormwood to the South. What we should never lose sight of, in reading what follows, is that Douglas employed the identical argument to attack Calhoun in 1850 and to attack Lincoln in 1858 and 1860. The ambidexterity of the argument, as well as its historical merits, must be taken into account in its evaluation.

True, these five States are now free, with provisions in the constitutions of each prohibiting slavery in all time to come; but was it the ordinance that made them free States? The census returns show that there were three hundred and thirty-one slaves in Illinois in 1840, and more than seven hundred in 1830. I do not recollect precisely how many there were in the other States; but I remember there was quite a number in Indiana. How came these slaves in Illinois? They were taken there under the ordinance and in defiance of it. Illinois was a slave territory. The people were mostly emigrants from the slaveholding States, and attached to the institution by association, habit, and interest. Supposing that the soil, climate, and productions of the country were adapted to slave labor, they naturally desired to introduce the institution to which they had been accustomed during their whole lives. Accordingly, the territorial legislature passed laws, the object and effect of which was to introduce slavery under what was called a system of indentures. These laws authorized the owners of slaves to bring them into the territory, and there enter into contracts with them, by which the slaves were to serve the master during the time specified in the contracts or "indentures," which were usually for a period reaching beyond the life of the slaves; and in the event the slaves should refuse to enter into the indenture [a most unlikely contingency!], after being brought into the territory, the master was allowed thirty days to take them back again, so as not to lose the right of property in them. Under the operation of these laws, Illinois became a slaveholding territory under the ordinance, and in utter defiance of its plain and palpable provision. The convention which assembled at Kaskaskia, in 1818, to form the constitution of the State of Illinois, was composed, to a considerable extent, of slaveholders, representing a slaveholding constituency. This body of men had become satisfied, from experience, that the climate and productions of the country were unfavorable to slave labor, and that the institution was prejudicial to their interests and welfare. Accordingly, we find three important principles established in the constitution which they framed, and with which Illinois was admitted into the Union:

1st. The right of property in all slaves, or indentured persons then in the State, was confirmed:

2nd. That no slaves should thereafter be brought into the State;

3rd. Provision for a gradual system of emancipation, by which the State should eventually become entirely free.

. . . These facts furnish a practical illustration of that great truth, which ought to be familiar to all statesmen and politicians, that a law passed by the national legislature to operate locally upon a people not represented, will always remain practically a dead letter upon the statute book, if it be in opposition to the wishes and supposed interests of those who are to be affected by it, and at the same time charged with its execution . . . In free countries, laws and ordinances are mere nullities, unless sustained by the hearts and intellects of the people for whom they are made, and by whom they are to be executed.

This last passage places a finger upon one of the most vital of the nerves of the controversy between Lincoln and Douglas. In a passage in the first joint debate, to which we shall return, Lincoln was to say, "In this and like communities, public sentiment is everything. With public sentiment, nothing can fail; without it, nothing can succeed. Consequently, he who molds public sentiment goes deeper than he who enacts statutes or pronounces decisions. He makes statutes and decisions possible or impossible to be executed." Thus Lincoln, no less than Douglas, believed that the execution of laws, ordinances, and decisions, *in a free society*, depended upon "the hearts and intellects of the people for whom they are made." Now how were the Ordinance of 1787 and the Missouri Compromise restrictions upon slavery to be enforced? The statutes in question contained nothing but simple declarations that slavery "shall be prohibited." Concerning how or by whom the prohibitions were to be enforced, nothing whatever was said. The only compulsion resulting from such enactments would occur if a federal court refused to uphold a territorial slaveholder's claim should it come to be adjudicated.

What good such "enforcement" might be to Negroes held as slaves on "free" soil—assuming the federal courts were to regard the congressional prohibition as valid—is indicated by a passage in Lincoln's Peoria speech:

> But it is said, there is now [October 1854] *no* law in Nebraska on the subject of slavery; and that, in such case, taking a slave there, operates his freedom. That is good book-law; but is not the rule of actual practice. Wherever slavery is, it has been first introduced without law. The oldest laws we find concerning it, are not laws introducing it; but *regulating* it, as an already existing thing. A white man takes his slave to Nebraska now; who will inform the negro that he is free? —Who will take him before court to test the question of his freedom? In ignorance of his legal emancipation, he is kept chopping, splitting and plowing. Others are brought, and move on in the same track. At last, if ever the time for voting comes, on the question of slavery, the institution already in fact exists in the country, and cannot well be removed. The facts of its presence, and the difficulty of its removal, will carry the vote in its favor. Keep it out until a vote is taken, and a vote in favor of it, can not be got in any population of forty thousand, on earth, who have been drawn together by the ordinary motives of emigration and settlement. To get slaves into the country simultaneously with the whites, in the incipient states of settlement, is the precise stake played for, and won in this Nebraska measure.[4]

But how much did the Missouri Compromise and the Northwest Ordinance differ from the "book-law" that no law is free law? Lincoln asserted that it made a great difference: ". . . the positive congressional enactment is known to, and respected by all, or nearly all; whereas the negative principle that *no* law is free law, is not much known except among lawyers." As a practical illustration of the difference, Lincoln pointed to the difference between Illinois and "the adjoining Missouri country, where there was no Ordinance of '87 . . . [and] they [i.e., slaves] were carried ten times, nay a hundred times, as fast, and actually made a slave State." Douglas's historical brief is a powerful denial that "respect" for a positive congressional enactment, an enactment unsupported by any enforcement legislation, could have made any such difference as Lincoln implied it had.

May not a strong prima-facie case in favor of Douglas be found in that the history of the American frontier shows little respect or regard for laws which the settlers did not believe to be in their immediate interest? Moreover, the moral sense of Americans has always been, as Douglas indicates, strongly prejudicial to the enactments of a legislature in which they were not directly represented. Lincoln's argument rests heavily on the physical contiguity of Missouri and Illinois. Yet Lincoln does not consider whether, despite this and apart from federal law, there might not have been sufficient economic differences in the situations of the two states to tip the balance for and against slavery in opposite directions. Missouri was not only farther west than Illinois but in closer contact with the Deep South. Illinois, touching only the border state of Kentucky, was much closer to the Northeast via the Great Lakes. The navigation of the Mississippi, always highly important to both states, nevertheless was relatively more important to Missouri. It was symptomatic of the economic futures of both states, futures which must have been visible relatively early, that their two greatest cities should have faced in different directions. St. Louis had its strongest links with New Orleans, Chicago with the great Atlantic ports. The economic heart of Illinois was the grain- and hog-producing prairies, which were deemed highly unsuited to slave labor. But the richest grain lands extended across only the northern tier of Missouri counties. Missouri, however, had found the use of slave labor profitable in the cultivation of hemp. In the presence of such considerations, it seems highly unlikely that "book-law" and federal law differed as much as Lincoln says they did. Who would have told slaves carried into Nebraska that their legal rights had been violated? As Lincoln liked to point out, no one had bothered to tell Dred Scott that he was a free man during his long residence on free soil. Indeed, after 1857 the federal judiciary would not have enforced such "rights." Lincoln's argument of "respect" for the Northwest Ordinance is hardly supported by the evidence of the system of indentures, which was a practical circumvention of the slavery prohibition. Local law seems to have been the effective law, as Douglas asserted. Only if Congress had enacted a federal *anti-slave code,* to be enforced locally, would the broad declarations have had much practical effect. Yet Lincoln and the Republicans never even dared to ask for this.

Further illustrations of Douglas's attitude toward federal restrictions of slavery—illustrations cited in 1860 as examples of a "Republican" attitude in 1850—are Douglas's amendment to the Oregon bill and his espousal of the cause of the constitutionality of the Mexican law prohibiting slavery in New Mexico. Calhoun had declared that the provision in the law organizing Oregon Territory which forbade slavery was another of the "aggressions" of the North upon the South. To this also Douglas replied by pointing out that it was not the federal law but the settlers themselves who had excluded slavery. During the period of joint occupation with Great Britain, the frontiersmen had formed a government for themselves which came to be known as the provisional government of Oregon.

> By one of the fundamental articles of that government [said Douglas], slavery was forever prohibited in that territory . . . That bill [organizing Oregon as an American territory after the settlement of the northwest boundary with Great Britain], so far as the question of slavery was concerned, did nothing more than re-enact and affirm the law which the people themselves had previously adopted, and rigorously executed, for the period of twelve years. It was a mere dead letter, without the slightest effect upon the admission or exclusion of slavery . . .[5]

Here we find the federal law conceived as a mere endorsement of a decision previously rendered by "popular sovereignty." The only question is why Douglas urged the inclusion of an amendment that had no practical effect if it was so irritating to the South. The answer to this will appear shortly. First we present another passage quoted against him in the Republican campaign tract. It was delivered in the Senate on February 12, 1850:

I am ready . . . to show that by the constituted authority
and constitutional authority of Mexico, slavery was prohibited in Mexico at the time of the acquisition, and that prohibition was acquired by us with the soil, and that when
we acquired the territory, we acquired it with that attached
to it—that covenant running with the soil—and that must
continue, unless removed by competent authority. And because there was a prohibition thus attached to the soil, I
have always thought it was an unwise, unnecessary, and
unjustifiable course on the part of the people of the free
States, to require Congress to put another prohibition on
the top of that one. *It has been the strongest argument
that I have ever urged against the prohibition of slavery in
the Territories, that it was not necessary for the accomplishment of their object.* [Italics in the Republican excerpt
only.]

Before offering comment, we continue the passage as it appears
in the *Congressional Globe:*

It was unwise, it was unnecessary, it was irritating one section
of the Union against another, without doing any good, or
even accomplishing the object in view by the other section.
I have always held that doctrine. I have opposed the Wilmot
Proviso on other grounds; that it was in violation of the great
fundamental principle of self-government; that it was a question which the people should be left to decide for themselves.
I have always held, and hold now, that if the people of California want slavery they have a right to it, and if they do
not, it should not be forced upon them. They have as much
right as the people of Illinois or any other State to settle the
question for themselves. I go further, and I hold that to prohibit slavery in the territories, whilst it is a violation of the
great fundamental principles of self-government, is no violation of the rights of the southern States. I go further, that
to recognize the institution of slavery in the Territories is
no violation of the rights of the northern States. In that sense,
neither have a right there, in my opinion, to do either. Either
to prohibit or establish slavery, by an act of Congress, over
a people not represented here, is a violation of the rights
of the people of California . . . Why, sir, the principle of
self-government is, that each community shall settle this

question for itself; and I hold that the people of California have the right either to prohibit or establish slavery, and we have no right to complain, either in the North or the South, whichever they do. I hold that, till they do establish it, the prohibition of slavery in the territories which we acquired by treaty attached to the soil . . . remains in force. I hold it as a legal proposition.[6]

It will be seen that the main burden of the speech is its attack upon the Wilmot Proviso, and the contention in favor of the Mexican law abolishing slavery is incidental—a fact which considerably mitigates the strength of the anti-slavery sentiment emphasized by the partial selection. The legal proposition concerning the force of the Mexican anti-slavery law, although bitterly contested by Calhoun and Jefferson Davis, was widely accepted. Henry Clay, the chief architect of the 1850 compromise, maintained it vigorously, and Lincoln followed Clay's view, as he generally did. This was one of the chief arguments—besides Webster's espousal of the "soil and climate" thesis in his March 7 speech—which enabled the compromise to be accepted in the free states. Yet there was an apparently slight but potentially vast difference between the Clay-Lincoln conception of the force of Mexican law and Douglas's: according to Douglas, popular sovereignty permitted the people of New Mexico (or California) *to introduce slavery prior to statehood.* That Douglas, accepting Webster's argument of the unsuitability of slavery in these regions, considered this a mere hypothetical alternative ought not to be permitted to obscure it.

Douglas in 1850 was then less anti-slavery, or at least anti-slavery in a different sense, than he is represented to have been by the Republicans. Yet we must always remember the modifications in his anti-slavery views in the perspective of his continuing struggle against the Calhoun-Jefferson Davis wing of the Democratic party. The anti-slavery Whigs of the North believed that slavery was not only forbidden throughout the Mexican acquisition by Mexican law but that it would so remain, even after the 1850 legislation, until the people of the territories applied for admission into the Union as states. What Douglas thought of the precise legal situation created by the New Mexico and Utah territorial legislation is somewhat obscure, but the practical situation was clearly thus, as he viewed it: The people of the territories might introduce slavery whenever they chose and not only when they organized themselves for statehood. In an "age of progress," however, this possibility was merely hypothetical. Jefferson Davis, on the other hand, although denying the validity of the Mexican anti-slavery law upon American soil, wished specifically to deny to the territorial legislatures any power to exclude slavery. Davis clearly believed what Lincoln always maintained: that, unless the slaveholders went into the territories *with* slaves, the territorial legislature would never vote a slave code. Davis, in short, understood popular sovereignty, as propounded by Douglas in 1850, as a guarantee of free soil. Douglas fought Davis bitterly on this issue in 1850 and at length prevailed, at least to the extent that the 1850 territorial bills extended to the territorial legislatures' power over "all rightful subjects of legislation, consistent with the Constitution of the United States," without either the exception or specification of slavery.

However, whether it was consistent with the Constitution for a territorial legislature to introduce or exclude slavery—the former proposition being denied by Wilmot Proviso men and the latter by Calhoun-Davis men—was not decided by Congress. The question was shunted off by provisions of the law which said that "all cases involving title to slaves" and "questions of personal freedom" might be appealed to the Supreme Court. We shall in Chapter VII have further occasion to see how the Compromise of 1850 in fact compromised very little of the outstanding differences on the slavery issue; what it really did was to sweep them under the rug. Or, more accurately, it entrusted them from 1850 on to the Supreme Court. What is surprising is that it took seven years for that tribunal to pronounce upon any of these differences. It is probable that Douglas succeeded in his struggle with Davis only because nothing was really decided against Davis but rather postponed for the decision of the Court. It is passing strange how quiet the pro-slavery extremists became when the fate of their convictions was put into the hands of this Court! However, the concession made by the free to the slave states in 1850, that the people of the Utah and New Mexican territories might choose to have slavery when applying for statehood—which choice they could in any case make the day after being admitted—did not make the law in New Mexico and Utah appreciably different from what it had been in the old Northwest or in the lands covered by the Missouri Compromise prohibition.

Douglas's assertion of the validity of Mexican law meant that—as in the old Northwest—pro-slavery men might go into the territories but would not take slaves with them until they had decided, after arrival, to establish slavery there. Then they might establish slavery if they found it desirable to do so. Douglas, as we have noted, no more expected this to happen than Daniel Webster did. Yet it might be well to note here that it *did* happen in 1859, when the Territory of New Mexico passed a slave code. It is debatable, however, whether the New Mexico slave code of 1859 ever was intended or expected to extend slavery. There never were more than a few slaves there. In the overheated atmosphere just before the Civil War, it may have signified no more than an expression of the solidarity of the New Mexicans with the Deep South. In 1859, as Douglas strove to repair the damage of his Freeport doctrine, he was frantic in his efforts to use the New Mexico slave code as an example of how popular sovereignty had "spread" slavery. But, again, this may have represented far less of a reversal than it appeared. With secession imminent, Douglas was attempting to convince the South that there was little reality in its imagined grievances.

But why, if Douglas regarded the Wilmot Proviso as an unnecessary irritant because of the previous prohibition of slavery attached to the soil by Mexican law, had he moved the amendment prohibiting slavery in Oregon, where it had already been effectively excluded? The answer is twofold. In the first place, the Wilmot Proviso went much farther than any other legal prohibition had ever gone. It would have pledged the faith of the nation to guarantee the freedom of the soil for all future time. This, in Douglas's view, was unconstitutional, because the federal government had no power thus to abridge the freedom of future states. In the second place, Oregon was far north of the Missouri Compromise line, while nearly half of the former Mexican lands were south of that line. The unconditional prohibition—which would, on its face, have been an unrepealable prohibition—was vastly more irritating.

Yet there is a third reason: the Oregon bill passed in 1848. At that time Douglas was striving with might and main to extend the Missouri Compromise line to the Pacific. By 1850 he had abandoned this cause as hopeless. That the legislation of 1850, in Douglas's mind, caused a change in the moral status of the

Missouri Compromise can be shown from his speeches just before and after the mid-century "measures of adjustment." In 1849 Douglas made the Springfield speech quoted at length by Lincoln in his Peoria speech of 1854 and by the Republican Committee in 1860. We give some leading passages:

> The Missouri Compromise had been in practical operation for about a quarter of a century, and had received the sanction and approbation of men of all parties in every section of the Union. It had allayed all sectional jealousies and irritations growing out of this vexed question, and harmonized and tranquilized the whole country . . . it had its origin in the hearts of all patriotic men, who desired to preserve and perpetuate the blessings of our glorious Union—an origin akin that of the Constitution of the United States, conceived in the same spirit of fraternal affection, and calculated to remove forever, the only danger, which seemed to threaten, at some distant day, to sever the social bond of Union. All the evidence of public opinion at that day, seemed to indicate that this Compromise had been canonized in the hearts of the American people, as a sacred thing which no ruthless hand would ever be reckless enough to disturb.

Notice that Douglas says not a word about the function of the Missouri Compromise with respect to the extension of slavery. For him its wisdom consisted only in its soothing effect on sectional passions. When Douglas made this speech he had already been rebuffed in his efforts to extend the Missouri line. The "quarter of a century" referred to would have ended in 1846—at the outbreak of the Mexican war. But it appears that he had not finally abandoned the attempt to utilize the Missouri legislation's prestige and was thus still trumpeting its supposed "sacredness." As we shall presently see, it was the Wilmot Proviso, according to Douglas, which destroyed the halo about the Missouri line. But let us listen to Douglas, in a speech to the Senate in December 1851, reviewing his course in the troubled years ending with the Compromise of 1850:

> . . . I will take a brief review of my course on the whole slavery agitation, and show clearly and distinctly the principles upon which my action upon the subject has always been governed. . . . I have always opposed the introduction of the

subject of slavery into the halls of Congress for any purpose
—either for discussion or action—except in the cases enjoined
by the Constitution of the United States, as in the case of
the reclamation of fugitives from labor . . . When the stormy
agitation arose in connection with the annexation of Texas,
I originated and first brought forward the Missouri Compromise as applicable to that Territory, and had the gratification
to see it incorporated in the bill which annexed Texas to
the United States. I did not deem it a matter of much moment
as applicable to Texas alone, but I did conceive it to be of
vast importance in view of the probable acquisition of New
Mexico and California. My preference for the Missouri Compromise was predicated on the assumption that the whole
people of the United States would be more easily reconciled
to that measure than to any other mode of adjustment; and
this assumption rested upon the fact that the Missouri Compromise had been the means of an amicable settlement of
a fearful controversy in 1821, which had been acquiesced
in cheerfully and cordially by the people for more than a
quarter of a century, and which all parties and sections of
the Union professed to respect and cherish as a fair, just, and
honorable settlement. I could discover no reason for the
application of the Missouri line to all the territory owned
by the United States in 1821 that would not apply with equal
force to its extension to the Rio Grande and also to the
Pacific, so soon as we should acquire the country.

Douglas then detailed his struggle against the Wilmot Proviso,
and his efforts to extend the Missouri line. The Wilmot Proviso
was finally defeated—by circumvention—in the peace treaty. And
the Senate, by a large majority, accepted Douglas's proposal to
extend the Missouri line to the Pacific; but it was heavily defeated in the House, where the Proviso men were largely in
control. After that, Douglas told how he too finally "abandoned"
the Missouri Compromise. This is of great moment, because in
1854 the entire free-soil opinion of the nation reviled Douglas
for asserting that the Compromise of 1850 had in any way touched
the Missouri Compromise, that anyone in voting on New Mexico
or Utah had ever dreamed the Missouri Compromise was involved. A major portion of Lincoln's Peoria speech is devoted
to denouncing this proposition, as the inflammatory *Appeal of*

the Independent Democrats had done almost at the moment the repeal was proposed. Moreover, the flat contradiction of Douglas by the free-soilers, and vice versa, is paralleled by equally flat contradictions, nearly a century later, by professional historians of the highest authority. First let us hear Douglas in 1851:

> At the opening of the next session [the second day of the Thirtieth Congress], upon consultation with the friends of the measure, it was generally conceded—with perhaps, here and there an individual exception—that there was no hope left for the Missouri Compromise, and consequently some other plan of adjustment must be devised. I was reluctant to give up the Missouri Compromise, having been the first to bring it forward, and having struggled for it in both houses of Congress for about five years . . . I gave it up reluctantly, to be sure—and conceived the idea of a bill to admit California as a State, leaving the people to form a constitution and settle the question of slavery afterwards to suit themselves . . . The great argument in favor of this bill was that it recognized the right of the people to determine all questions relating to their domestic concerns in their own way . . . Mr. President, I may be permitted here to pause and remark that, during the period of five years that I was laboring for the adoption of the Missouri Compromise, my votes on the Oregon question, and upon all incidental questions touching slavery, were given with reference to a settlement on that basis, and are consistent with it.[7]

Douglas, in retrospect, "gave up" the Missouri Compromise in 1848. This might seem to contradict his praise of it in 1849. However, his first countermove was to propose the admission of the *entire Mexican acquisition* as the single state of California, only reserving the right to Congress, whenever it might choose to exercise it, to form new states out of any portion of California that lay east of the Sierra Nevada. This was a breath-taking proposal, and we must pause to consider it. We should recall it was made when the gold rush was already on. A "great revolution has taken place in the prospects and condition of that country since the adjournment of the last session of Congress," Douglas said in making his proposal, and this revolution was such as made it all but impossible that any decision in favor of Negro slavery would ever be made by the hordes of settlers and prospectors, should Congress entrust them with that power. Slave property was of all chattels the least movable to new regions. When slavery spread in the United States, it was always from contiguous slave states, by a kind of natural extension of an existing economy. But California was now being reached mainly by the long sea route—only later was it common to go overland. In any case, slaveowners had little or no incentive to risk expensive slaves in a distant region whose soil and climate were relatively untested in regard to slave staples. Moreover, this was a period when the old cotton kingdom was entering its greatest boom, when slaves could be sold or employed very profitably without the trouble or risk of sending them to such distant places as California. And, as noted above, there was cheap Mexican labor almost for the asking in California. Douglas was certain, far more certain than Webster ever had a right to be concerning New Mexico, that slavery would be forbidden in California if the settlers were left to decide the matter for themselves.

But this was only one dimension of his proposal. The other was that, by making the whole Mexican acquisition one state, the decision against slavery taken by the settlers on the Pacific coast would automatically be extended over the whole of the remaining Mexican acquisition, or what became the territories of Utah and New Mexico. In short, Douglas's proposal was an indirect but an almost certainly more effective anti-slavery proposal than the Wilmot Proviso itself! Although it contained no promise such as the Wilmot Proviso attempted, that the states Congress might later choose to carve out of California east of the Sierra Nevada would exclude slavery—a promise he believed could not have been fulfilled if challenged, since Congress had no constitutional right to make it—it would have absolutely precluded such a thing as the New Mexican territorial slave code of 1859. Indeed, Douglas's proposal would have cut almost the whole Gordian knot of constitutional entanglements with the slavery questions. It would have ended all controversy concerning the effect of the Mexican law against slavery; it would have ended the dispute over whether the Constitution automatically carried slavery into the former Mexican provinces or automatically excluded it; it would have ended the question of whether, among the "rightful subjects" to which the territorial legislative powers extended, slavery was included. It would probably also have deprived the Dred Scott decision, in advance, of most of its power for mischief. It is hardly credible that there would have been half the concern that slavery might enter Nebraska, if it had already been excluded from the lands south and west of it. By skipping the territorial period for the whole Mexican acquisition, and not only the area later included in California, it would have made the California interdiction of slavery in the entire Mexican acquisition as undeniably constitutional as that which forbade it in New York or Massachusetts. This was stronger anti-slavery medicine than the Northwest Ordinance or the Missouri prohibition. It is strange that this, Douglas's most extreme anti-slavery proposal, was never cited by the Republicans to illustrate the extent of his later tergiversations. Perhaps the reason is that the Wilmot Proviso men—the predecessors of the anti-Nebraska men—did not rally to Douglas's support; for they were still intent upon the direct interdiction of slavery and not satisfied to accept it as a result of popular sovereignty. That Calhoun was cold is understandable. The measure received little support and was killed by the Senate judiciary committee.

It is desirable now to estimate the merit of Douglas's previous espousal of the extension of the Missouri Compromise line. This too had an anti-slavery aspect denied to it by Lincoln, for example, in his Peoria speech. For the extension of the line would have placed slavery under a categorical ban in all of the Utah Territory and would have pushed the northern boundary of New Mexico Territory down a degree and a half. It would also, in all likelihood, have caused California to be divided into two states. That, however, would have meant *two free* states instead of one, since there was no difference between northern and southern Californians concerning the desirability of slavery. But further: the extension of the Missouri Compromise line to the Pacific would have meant a ban on slavery north of the line, while it would not have done more than make slavery optional south of the line. Now Lincoln said that he, in common with all Wilmot Proviso stalwarts in the House, had steadily refused to support the extension of the Missouri line because, by implication, it gave up the territory south of it to slavery. Yet Lincoln's leader, Clay, was chief architect of the Compromise of 1850, and Lincoln eventually gave that Compromise at least tacit approval. And the Compromise of 1850 opened *all* of Utah Territory and *all* of New Mexico Territory to slavery, to as great an extent as

Douglas had proposed to open to slavery only that part of New Mexico which lay south of 36′30″. In short, the Wilmot Proviso men—Lincoln included, for he was in the House voting against Douglas's proposed extension during his one term in Congress—eventually settled for, or were forced to accept, less than half the loaf that Douglas had originally offered them. This must certainly be kept in mind when evaluating Douglas's assertion, after the repeal, that he had been faithful to the Missouri Compromise when its supposed supporters had deserted it.

Chapter VI

The Repeal of the Missouri Compromise II

DID THE COMPROMISE OF 1850 "SUPERSEDE" THE MISSOURI COMPROMISE?

THE *Appeal of the Independent Democrats in Congress to the People of the United States,* which fired the train attached to the powder keg of anti-slavery passion in the free states, is reprinted in the *Congressional Globe* under the date of January 19, 1854. To it is appended a note, presumably added on or after January 23, since it responds to amendments to Douglas's revised Nebraska bill which were reported only on that date. The note, which follows, sets forth the bitter core of the controversy, thus:

> The *amended* Nebraska bill, introduced by Mr. Douglas [i.e., the bill introduced as a substitute for the Dodge bill on January 4, 1854], was promptly printed at length in the Washington *Sentinel.* As printed, it did not meet the views of certain southern gentlemen, and it was then discovered that an important declaratory section, legislating into the bill the *principles* of the compromise [of 1850] had been omitted by a *clerical error.* Even after this remarkable clerical error had been rectified, the bill was unsatisfactory, and now Mr. Douglas proposes more amendments—to divide the Territory into two: to charge the Treasury with the expense of two Territorial Governments; to strike out the clerical error section, and insert elsewhere in the bill a clause excepting from the laws of the United States, extended over the Terri-

tory, the Missouri prohibition. The proposed amendment will read thus:

"That the Constitution, and all laws of the United States, which are not locally inapplicable, shall have the same force and effect within the said Territory of Nebraska as elsewhere within the United States, *except the eighth section of the act preparatory to the admission of Missouri into the Union, approved March 6, 1820, which was superseded by the principles of the legislation of 1850, commonly called the compromise measures, and is hereby declared inoperative.*"

This amendment is a manifest falsification of the truth of history, as is shown in the body of the foregoing address. Not a man in Congress or out of Congress, in 1850, pretended that the compromise measures would repeal the Missouri prohibition. Mr. Douglas himself never advanced such a pretence until this session. His own Nebraska Bill of last session rejected it. It is a sheer afterthought. To declare the prohibition inoperative, may, indeed, have effect in law as a repeal, but it a most discreditable way of reaching the object. Will the people permit their dearest interests to be thus made the mere hazards of a presidential game, and destroyed by false facts and false inferences?

We observe that the original "repeal" clause only declared the Missouri Compromise "superseded" and hence "inoperative," although in its final form the bill added "and void." Concerning the "truth of history," we now summon two recent witnesses. Allan Nevins writes as follows:[1]

One essential question of fact was raised by Douglas's bill and the accompanying report. Had Congress, applying the popular sovereignty principle to the newly conquered and peculiar region of New Mexico and Utah, really intended universal application of that principle to *all* areas not yet organized? Had it intended a repeal of the long-revered, the supposedly inviolable, Missouri Compromise? If it had, then most members of Congress in 1850 had grossly deceived themselves. Douglas had not once hinted during the debates of 1850 that the new Compromise altered the position of the huge unorganized area of the Missouri Valley.

And again:

> The thinness of Douglas's arguments of precedence, the ob-
> vious shiftiness and subterfuge of his course, inspired instant
> question of his motives.

And finally:[2]

> As for Douglas's statement that the Utah-New Mexico legis-
> lation in the Compromise of 1850 had established a new
> "principle" which must be extended to all other territories,
> this was simply dishonest.

But with regard to the identical "question of fact," we find
Professor Randall taking an exactly contrary position. In his commentary on the debates, Randall writes:[3]

> . . . they [Lincoln and Douglas] were concentrating on the
> question whether Federal prohibition of slavery in western
> territories, having been dropped after full discussion in 1850,
> should be revived as if it were the only means of dealing with
> the highly improbable chance that human bondage would
> ever take root in such places as Kansas, Nebraska, or New
> Mexico.

Randall's language is even stronger than Douglas's in his original
repeal clause, in which, as noted, Douglas only said that the 1850
legislation had "superseded" the Missouri Compromise, rendering
it "inoperative." Randall says flatly that the federal prohibition
of slavery in "western territories," by which he explicitly means
Kansas and Nebraska as well as New Mexico, was "dropped"
in 1850. Now we do not know anyone, least of all Professor Nevins,
who would suggest that Professor Randall ever dishonestly or
manifestly falsified the truth of history. Is not Randall's endorsement of Douglas's interpretation of the 1850 compromise, in the
face of Nevins's equally unqualified acceptance of the Independent Democrats', a manifest sign that the "truth of history"
is open to manifestly opposite interpretations and that the "facts"
speak differently to different men?

As to the charge that "not a man in Congress or out of Congress" pretended that the 1850 measures affected the status of
the 1820 law, the reply depends upon whether one thinks in narrowly legalistic or broadly political terms. We have seen that
Douglas declared in 1851 that the 1850 measures were predi-

cated upon the abandonment of the Missouri Compromise. To be sure, Douglas referred technically to the non-extension of the line to the Pacific. But when he said that he "could discover no reason for the application of the Missouri line to all the territory owned by the United States in 1821 that would not apply with equal force to its extension . . . to the Pacific," the inference is almost inescapable that its non-extension had a broader bearing on the whole sectional controversy than what was involved in determining the fate of Utah or New Mexico. Whether or not Douglas was correct in his judgment of the equal applicability of the Missouri line to the two acquisitions, it is consistent with this belief to regard the refusal to extend the line as tantamount to its "supersession."

The 1820 line, as Douglas saw it, attempted so to divide the national territory that the public mind in the free states would be satisfied that there was in federal law a guarantee that, of the future states applying for admission, no less than half, in all probability, would apply with constitutions prohibiting slavery. It was a guarantee that the free states would not be outnumbered by the slave states. Now by 1850 opinion in these same free states was utterly unwilling to accept this kind of guarantee, although the Senate, in which the slave states were relatively more powerful, was willing to give it. Why had free-state opinion shifted? Had it not done so because the free states, having grown relatively far more powerful in wealth and numbers, felt able to strike a better intersectional bargain? Moreover, were not the anti-slavery forces in the free states better organized and more militant? Did not Douglas express a free-soil attitude when he said privately to young George McConnel that to dispense with a dividing line meant a "step toward freedom," because slavery could "no longer crouch behind a line which Freedom could not cross"? As noted above, the legal situation created by the Missouri line did *not* forbid freedom on its southern side. What the law did was only to forbid slavery to the north, while making it optional to the south. Technically, that is, popular sovereignty ruled south of the line. But the legal situation was not the real one, as is shown by Lincoln's understanding that the line in fact reserved the lands to the south of it for slavery. This was why, as Lincoln said in his Peoria speech, the Wilmot Proviso men in the House would not accept the extension of the Missouri line to the Pacific: they would not, by implication, give up any new lands to slavery; they were bent upon having them *all* free. But was this not an implied endorsement of Douglas's interpretation of 1850? If free-state men preferred having *no* line in *new* territory because a line meant giving some lands up to slavery by implication, why should they not prefer no line in *old* territory, where the "supersession" of the line would mean that freedom could, in all the confidence of its new strength (for this was, remember, an "age of progress"), wrest the unorganized lands *south* of 36'30"? It is true that the Proviso men, as such, never gave the 1850 measures unqualified support, and many fought the fugitive law to the bitter end. Yet moderate anti-slavery men like Lincoln, accepting Clay's and Webster's leadership—and, moreover, seeing California made irretrievably free by local action, as Douglas ceaselessly pointed out —had in fact acquiesced to popular sovereignty in New Mexico and Utah, as they had not done in the extension of the line. As Douglas interpreted 1850, free-soil opinion in the free states had then deemed the chances of freedom better everywhere under popular sovereignty than under a dividing line which, by implication, gave up almost half the territories to slavery.

We thus see how Douglas, long before 1854, expressed his understanding that popular sovereignty had "superseded" the Missouri Compromise in 1850. In a precise sense, the Missouri Compromise line, as a device for settling the slavery question in the Mexican acquisition, was all that had been superseded. But in politics, the narrow sense of an expression of such import can easily glide into a larger sense without contradicting the general understanding of its meaning. Of course "supersession" is not repeal, and the story of how supersession was transformed into repeal remains to be told. For the present, we maintain only that the language Douglas used in 1851 to explain the course he had recently followed sufficiently justifies his statement in 1854 that the abandonment of the Missouri Compromise as a device for dealing with slavery in the former Mexican provinces constituted, in his view, its supersession.

As evidence of the political intelligibility of this terminology, we recall its ready acceptance by Professor Randall. The present writer asked that eminent scholar, in the year before his death, precisely what he had meant when he said that federal prohibition of slavery in western territories had been "dropped" in 1850, since the Missouri Compromise was not repealed until 1854, nor declared unconstitutional until 1857. In a reply dated December 2, 1952, he wrote that what he intended "was merely the obvious fact that the proposal to pass a national law prohibiting slavery in *all* [emphasis by Randall] the territories was not adopted. This proposal," the letter continued, "favored by the Liberty and Free Soil parties, and later by the Republican party, seems reasonable and proper to us now, and is strengthened by admiration for Lincoln, but in 1850 and in the decade of the fifties there was virtually no chance that such a law could be passed by Congress." Now a purist might object that something cannot be "dropped" before it has been raised, and that no federal barrier against slavery had been erected in Utah or New Mexico. The Wilmot Proviso men, morever, had not sought a national law against slavery in *all* the nation's territories, but only in the newly acquired ones. This at least is affirmed by Lincoln in the Peoria speech:

> The most conclusive argument, however, that, while voting for the Wilmot Proviso, and while voting against the extension of the Missouri line, we never thought of disturbing the original Missouri Compromise, is found in the fact that there was then, and still is, an unorganized tract of fine country, nearly as large as the state of Missouri, lying immediately west of Arkansas, and south of the Missouri Compromise line [the present state of Oklahoma]; and that we never attempted to prohibit slavery in it . . . In all our struggles to prohibit slavery within our Mexican acquisitions, we never so much as lifted a finger to prohibit it, as to this tract.[4]

Clearly, Professor Randall saw the matter through Douglas's and not Lincoln's eyes. The legislation of 1850, as Douglas and Randall saw it, was a solution of the question of slavery in "all" the territories, because the struggle of 1850 involved the whole political question of the future status of slavery in the Union. Moreover, Professor Randall's apparent confusion of the struggle over the Mexican territories with "all" the territories reproduces precisely the ambiguity contained in Douglas's "supersession" thesis. And in this ambiguity is contained one of the strongest justifications of Douglas's policy in this period: for by opening Nebraska to slavery, however hypothetically, it also opened to freedom—much less hypothetically—the future Oklahoma, which would have remained written off to slavery by the precisionist Lincoln.

Douglas, as we have seen, constantly identified the Missouri Compromise with the line of 36'30" and treated the line as if it were the "principle" of that compromise. In the same way he found the popular-sovereignty provisions of the Utah and New Mexico territorial bills to contain the "principle" of the Compromise of 1850. Lincoln categorically denied that either the line or the aforesaid provisions constituted any kind of principle whatever. Regarding the first, he said (in the Peoria speech):

> Another fact showing the *specific* character of the Missouri law—showing that it intended no more than it expressed—showing that the line was not intended as a universal dividing line between free and slave territory, present and prospective —north of which slavery could never go—is the fact that by that very law, Missouri came in as a slave state, *north* of the line. If that law contained any prospective *principle,* the whole law must be looked to in order to ascertain what that *principle* was. And by this rule, the South could fairly contend that inasmuch as they got one slave state north of the line at the inception of the law, they have the right to another given them *north* of it occasionally—now and then in the indefinite westward extension of the line. This demonstrates the absurdity of attempting to deduce a prospective *principle* from the Missouri Compromise line.[5]

But does Lincoln succeed in his demonstration? All the parts of the Missouri Compromise may have been specific, yet all the facts together must have been justified by some principle or principles, for the compromise to deserve the respect of principled men. And the justification of the Missouri Compromise was assuredly that it preserved the Union while placing definite limits to the number and extent of future slave states to be formed upon the national domain. In the Missouri Compromise the admission of Missouri was balanced by the admission of Maine. Yet Maine was not a weighty *desideratum,* for the reason that its admission could not have been indefinitely delayed solely because it was a free state. Certainly it was the prohibition of any further slave states north of the line of 36'30" that was the true price exacted by the free states for Missouri's admission. That Missouri itself lay north of the line may be viewed less as a sign of the absence of any principle embodied in the line than as an unprincipled exception to which the free states were compelled because of their relative weakness in 1820–21. For the Missouri Compromise was in fact a very poor bargain from an anti-slavery point of view. Not only was Missouri north of the line but, as we have seen, the adoption of a line contained an implied acquiescence in slavery in all states to be formed south of it. Arkansas, south of the line, had been organized in 1819 and was, in 1820, a much nearer candidate for admission than any territory likely to be organized north of it. Arkansas did come into the Union, in 1836, while Iowa was not admitted until 1846, and Minnesota was not even given territorial organization until 1849. If the bird in hand is twice as valuable, then the slave states certainly received the greater consideration.

But what of the vast unorganized wilderness not yet known in 1820 as Nebraska? We recall our assertion in Chapter IV that no one before the Mexican War, and assuredly no one in 1820, had certain (or even probable) knowledge that the organization of states would proceed beyond a single tier on the west bank of the Mississippi. If this had remained the case there never would have been more than two free states north of Missouri to balance the three slave states on the west bank. In a recent study of the Missouri controversy, Professor Glover Moore[6] surveys opinion in 1820–21 in quest of an answer to whether the South favored and the North opposed the compromise because it was thought the North's share was a worthless desert. The answer to this question is a decided negative. It was generally believed that the soil and climate of the region were healthy and fruitful. Professor Moore does not raise directly the question we would have liked answered; namely, whether the North or South expected free states in anything like the number that eventually resulted north of the line. He adduces a wide scattering of views, but nothing to suggest a widespread public expectation of future free states except directly north of Missouri; i.e., from the lands from which Iowa and Minnesota were to come. In view of the strong conservative opposition to territorial expansion as represented by men like Webster, and the fact that the lands beyond the west bank were secured "in perpetuity" to the Indians, it is unlikely that general opinion could have foreseen more than the two free states as consequences of the Missouri Compromise. It is almost inconceivable that the South would have given it the support it did—for the Missouri Compromise resulted from an overwhelming majority of southern votes combined with a small

minority of northern ones—had a procession of another half dozen
free states been contemplated. What the Republicans were one
day to insist was "nominated in the bond," if it was so nominated,
must have been in exceedingly fine print in 1820. It is one of the
ironies of history that the tremendous expansion of the forties,
which received much of its impulse from the desire for new lands
for slavery, transformed the old Missouri Compromise into a far
more favorable anti-slavery bargain than it could reasonably have
been supposed to be at the time it was made! This suggests an
explanation of the sanctity that it achieved in the eyes of a man
like Lincoln. But it also suggests a moral if not a technical legal
justification for Douglas's attempt to identify the Missouri Compromise with the Missouri line. For, as we have shown, the
employment of the line at the end of the Mexican War was far
more favorable to the free-soil cause than its original employment
had been. The principle that would have justified its original
employment—if any did—would thus certainly seem to have
justified its extension. And if this is true, then was not Douglas
justified, in virtue of the familiar shorthand vocabulary of politics,
in identifying the principle with its application?

Lincoln similarly denied that any new principle had been
established by the 1850 compromises which superseded the
alleged Missouri "principle."

The particular part of those measures [Lincoln said in the
Peoria speech], for [sic] which the virtual repeal of the
Missouri Compromise is sought to be inferred (for it is admitted they contain nothing about it, in express terms) is the
provision in the Utah and New Mexico laws, which permits
them when they seek admission into the Union as States, to
come in with or without slavery as they shall then see fit. Now
I insist this provision was made for Utah and New Mexico,
and for no other place whatever. It had no more direct
reference to Nebraska than it had to the territories of the
moon. But, say they, it had reference to Nebraska, *in principle*. Let us see. The North consented to this provision, not
because they considered it right in itself; but because they
were compensated—paid for it.—They, at the same time got
California into the Union as a free State. This was far the
best part of all they had struggled for by the Wilmot Proviso.

They also got the area of slavery somewhat narrowed in the settlement of the boundary of Texas. Also, they got the slave trade abolished in the District of Columbia. For all these desirable objects the North could afford to yield something; and they did yield to the South the Utah and New Mexico provisions.[7]

But the inference that Lincoln permits in this passage, that the Utah and New Mexico provision was a sheer concession by the free states, is a possible but not a necessary inference. The North made another concession in 1850, which Lincoln duly recorded in an earlier account of the 1850 compromise in this same Peoria speech. It was a concession that achieved a far greater contemporary notoriety; namely, the new Fugitive Slave Law. The abolition of the slave trade in the District of Columbia and the reduction of Texas's boundaries were more than paid for, in most northern eyes, by the infernal statute that paid a federal judge five dollars for setting an alleged fugitive free and ten dollars for declaring him an escaped slave. But what of California? Did the North really have to "pay" an additional price for California in the form of the popular-sovereignty provisions of the Utah and New Mexico laws? Zachary Taylor never thought so, nor did William H. Seward. And Stephen A. Douglas did not think so when he proposed bringing the entire Mexican acquisition into the Union as the state of California. And, as we have already stressed, the extension of the Missouri line to the Pacific would have involved acquiescence in California's (or the Californias') statehood without as much concession to slavery as had been made in 1820–21. In short, it is not necessary to regard the 1850 territorial laws, as Lincoln regarded them, as a concession by the North. Or, if they are to be so regarded, the concession can be attributed to the Wilmot Proviso men (of whom Lincoln was a stalwart), who had raised the South's price for the admission of California by refusing to accept it without imposing terms humilating to the slave states.

We have argued that, by a legitimate construction of Douglas's pre-1854 statements, he was justified in his subsequent assertion that the measures of adjustment of 1850 had "superseded" the Missouri Compromise. Yet it would be unnecessary and unwise to claim that what existed as a possible and legitimate construction existed contemporaneously as a clear-cut public understanding. Douglas gave what might be called a creative interpretation of 1850 (including his own role therein), an interpretation supported by the facts, which nonetheless brought the facts of 1850 into a focus different from that of 1850, a focus designed for 1854. As we shall see, this was just what Lincoln did with the anti-slavery policy of the Founding Fathers. Lincoln assumed that a subordinate aspect of their thoughts and measures would have retained the same value had it become paramount. But Lincoln did not know what sacrifices Jefferson or Washington would have made for their anti-slavery convictions if the price of maintaining them had been enormously increased. Jefferson, in particular, wavered woefully in his last years. At the time of the Missouri crisis in 1820, he took a distinctly southern position, looking upon the anti-slavery agitation in the North as a Federalist plot to break up the political dynasty he had founded in 1800[8] and which had ruled unchallenged thereafter. In particular, he accepted the "diffusionist" thesis, that allowing slavery to spread into new country such as Missouri did not tend to its perpetuation but only spread it "thinner." Lincoln was to blast and wither this argument and to heap upon it his bitterest contempt. But its connection with Jefferson is carefully concealed; only sentiments worthy of the hero of the Declaration and the patron of the Northwest Ordinance are presented to our view. Lincoln does much the same with Henry Clay, who had no real connection with the slavery restriction in the Missouri Compromise. All that Clay actually did was to get the slave state of Missouri into the Union in 1821—while free-soil opinion in the North was still resisting its admission because of the discrimination against free Negroes in Missouri's constitution. Others had got the slavery restriction written into the enabling act of 1820. A few of Clay's eloquent moral condemnations of slavery are quoted by Lincoln over and over again. But the policy that Lincoln framed, and adorned with famous names, was his own. Both Lincoln and Douglas sought precedents for what they wanted, and the precedents were worth little more than what they wanted them for. Each had independent arguments sufficient to convince himself, but in politics it is a good rule not to appear to do anything for the first time. History as precedent is an essential ingredient of political life; it is often a necessary condition of such stability and intelligibility as politics can aspire to. Yet the discovery by the true statesman of the right precedents is as much an act of imaginative perception as that whereby any great teller of old tales renews the life of a people for the present and the future by a vision of the past.

Supersession, we have observed, is not synonymous with repeal. Douglas, we say, intended to "supersede" the Missouri Compromise in 1854 but not to repeal it. That distinction now requires elaboration and explanation. What we believe is that Douglas intended in 1854 that repeal of the Missouri Compromise remain a possible inference, in the same way that supersession of the Missouri Compromise was, in 1850, a possible inference from the Compromise of 1850. What would remain as a possible inference in 1854 might then be presented as a necessary inference on some future occasion, when the practical question would not involve lands north of 36'30".

What Douglas sought above all else in January 1854 was to make the doctrine of popular sovereignty, which had been an article of languid party faith since Cass's Nicholson letter in the '48 campaign, into a passionate creed. Hitherto it had been strongly held only by the northwestern Democracy; Cass was senator from Michigan. As a party doctrine for resolving the slavery controversy, and for laying the foundation for an American empire, popular sovereignty was something of a novelty.

Its aptness for American party politics lay in its shrewd turning to political advantage of some of the deepest-rooted American traditions. Tocqueville's *Democracy in America* was written on the basis of observations made during the formative years of Lincoln's and Douglas's adolescence and early manhood. And Tocqueville began his study, not with the federal government, but with the states. And the key to understanding the states he found in the township.

> The form of the Federal government of the United States was the last to be adopted; and it is in fact nothing more than a summary of those republican principles which were current in the whole community before it existed, and independently of its existence . . . The great political principles which now govern American society undoubtedly took their origin and their growth in the state . . . It is not without intention that I begin this subject with the township . . . municipal institutions constitute the strength of free nations.

Town meetings are to liberty what primary schools are to
science; they bring it within the people's reach, they teach
men how to use and how to enjoy it. A nation may establish
a free government, but without municipal institutions it cannot have the spirit of liberty.[9]

What Douglas meant to do was to appeal to the spirit of, and
attachment to, the principles of town-meeting democracy as a way
of removing the slavery incubus from American politics. In Illinois
itself, this spirit had been appealed to successfully as settlers from
the Northeast and the South had clashed on the subject of township versus county government. The Illinois constitution of 1847,
allowing local options, had reconciled these conflicting demands.
As already noted, the moral condemnation of slavery emanated
largely from the evangelical movement in radical Protestantism,
itself in large measure a re-creation of the Puritan spirit. But the
town meeting was a secular by-product of the congregational
form of church government which characterized the Puritan
bodies in old New England. The profound attractiveness of the
popular-sovereignty idea lay in its seizing upon the old and deep
connection of the idea of morality with the idea of local self-
government. This connection might thus be used to neutralize, if
not to defeat, the moral fervor of the anti-slavery crusade emanating from other roots in that same tradition. The spirit of local
independence had, of course, received new vitality from the
conditions of western community life. It was not the aristocratic
families of the old South who tended to migrate—the ones who
ruled their counties like English squires and, we might add, were
probably more accustomed to episcopal than congregational
church government. To them popular sovereignty was anathema,
as it was to the abolitionists, who meant to impose their moral
ideas in the spirit of Cromwell's saints. But Douglas believed
it in accordance with that spirit of moderation and mutual trust
which alone made democratic government possible.

One further point, by way of prologue to the analysis of Douglas's Senate report: that is to remark upon the congeniality in
public opinion of the doctrine of popular sovereignty, as a loosely
held general idea, and the Missouri Compromise. We have seen
that Douglas advocated and believed in the effective adoption
of popular sovereignty in the territorial legislation of 1850, yet also
believed in the continued legal effect of the Mexican anti-slavery

law. In Missouri, in November 1853, where excitement over Nebraska was then keenest and where Thomas Hart Benton, anti-slavery leader of the state's Democracy, was locked in political death battle with the pro-slavery Democratic leader David Atchison, we find resolutions passed at meetings of Benton's partisans that ". . . we are in favor of the people who go there [Nebraska] and settle to determine the question as to whether it shall be a slave or free state"; and, almost in the same breath, that ". . . we are opposed to the agitation of the slavery question in the organization of this Territory by any attempt to repeal the Missouri Compromise."[10] Of course popular opinion before the repeal was hardly conscious that the 1850 laws were silent as to whether the people who went to the Southwest to settle and decide in favor of free or slave states might go *with* or *without* slaves. The public, not yet instructed by Douglas in the nature of the differences undecided in 1850, permitted itself to desire and believe in things that were presently to appear incompatible. Yet we must emphasize the extent to which general opinion, and in particular free-soil opinion, on the eve of Douglas's Nebraska bill of 1854, was prepared to respond to the popular-sovereignty appeal, without any sense of jar to its attachment to the Missouri Compromise.

Chapter VII

The Repeal of the Missouri
Compromise III

WHAT DOUGLAS INTENDED ON
JANUARY 4, 1854

OF ALL criticisms of Douglas's course in 1854, none appears on its face to be more devastating than that drawn from the evidence of the 1853 Nebraska bill. "In 1853," said Lincoln at Peoria, "a bill to give [Nebraska] a territorial government passed the House of Representatives [by a vote of 98 to 43, with 20 affirmative votes from slave states], and, in the hands of Judge Douglas, failed of passing the Senate only for want of time. This bill contained no repeal of the Missouri Compromise. Indeed, when it was assailed because it did not contain such repeal, Judge Douglas defended it in its existing form."[1] In the principal Senate speech for the 1853 bill Senator Atchison of Missouri had spoken thus:

> Now, sir, I am free to admit at this moment, at this hour, and for all time to come, I should oppose the organization or the settlement of that Territory unless my constituents and the constituents of the whole South, of the slave States of the Union, could go into it upon the same footing, with equal rights and equal privileges, carrying that species of property with them . . . Yes, sir, I acknowledge that that would have governed me, but I have no hope that the restriction will ever be repealed.[2]

Because, Atchison continued, the tide of population would roll over the Nebraska frontier in defiance of law, unless law was provided, it was as well to organize the territory now as later. As to its chances, Atchison spoke thus:

> I trust now that the bill will be taken up, and that we will act upon it and pass it . . . The President will sign it, as a matter of course, if he signs any of the appropriation bills. There is no question about that. We have votes enough, and I have no doubt but there is a majority of the Senate in favor of the organization of the Territory of Nebraska, if you will only give us an opportunity to vote.[3]

And Douglas, concluding the discussion in the early hours of the morning of March 4, 1853 (Franklin Pierce was to be inaugurated at noon), remarked:

> I have merely said as much as was necessary to vindicate the action of the Committee; and now I should be delighted if the Senate, by common consent, would unite and pass the bill; for if it be taken up, I am sure it will be passed. My fears are that it will not be taken up.[4]

Douglas's fears were justified. The bill was never voted upon. On a motion to lay it on the table, the vote was yeas 23, nays 17. A shift of four votes and the tempest of the year following, in which the Republican party was born, might have been averted! According to George Fort Milton, "Once more Southern opposition kept a Territory from being organized," for the bill, he says, was set aside by "an almost exclusively sectional vote."[5] However, this is misleading, for among those voting to shelve the bill were senators from Pennsylvania, Massachusetts, New York, Vermont, and Connecticut. And a third of the Senate was absent, including some of the strongest free-soilers. Even more difficult to understand, in the light of the Atchison speech, is Professor Randall's statement[6] that "the Missouri Compromise . . . was in 1854 beyond the sphere of practical politics," or that "anti-slavery people . . . had no better chance in 1854 than that offered by the Douglas bill . . ."[7] Professor Randall seems, again, to be confusing the political effort needed to re-enact the Missouri Compromise restriction with what was needed merely to leave it alone. As to the "chance" offered by the Kansas-Nebraska bill, the question is why Douglas did not simply report the Dodge bill, introduced in December 1853, which was the same bill he had supported the previous March. In this connection we reproduce the following interesting colloquy that took place during those after-midnight hours of March 4, 1853, when that early Nebraska bill was so unfortunately set aside. Almost the whole discussion, we should mention, had concerned the rights of Indians in Nebraska, an issue which could be, and was, discussed by northern and southern men as if no sectional question were involved.

MR. ADAMS. I know that my friend from Illinois is a good compromise man, and I wish to propose to him a compromise on this subject, and that is, that by common consent it be postponed until the Friday after the first Monday of December next, when we shall have ample time and opportunity to discuss and investigate it; and if we think it right we can then pass the bill.

MR. DOUGLAS. I must remind my friend from Mississippi that eight years ago, when he and I were members of the House of Representatives, I was then pressing the Nebraska bill, and I have ever since been pressing it. I have tried to get it through for eight long years. I would take it as much more kind if my friend should propose that by common consent we take up and pass the bill. The members of the body are in very good humor, all having got what they have wanted except the Territories. I hope we shall do something for them.[8]

This passage is extremely revealing of the vastly different atmosphere surrounding the 1853 bill. Douglas even had hopes of slipping it through by common consent, without a roll-call vote, in the rush of adjournment business! His reference to "eight long years" is factually correct, although it must have been said without any great sense of urgency. Douglas had not said a word about Nebraska in Congress for the last several of those eight years. But most significant of all is the expectation, voiced by Adams of Mississippi, that the bill might be taken up the following December and passed without much difficulty after the matters under debate—mostly concerning the Indians—could be ironed out.

Now there may, of course, have been more opposition to the 1853 bill than Douglas and Atchison in 1853 or Lincoln in 1854 admitted. It was natural for Douglas and Atchison to exaggerate the support the bill had, as an argument for bringing it to a vote. They had a common interest in such a bill, since a chain of territorial governments in mid-continent would make possible central and/or northern railroad routes to the Pacific. While Nebraska was closed, the only organized territories across which such roads could be built lay between Texas and southern California. And Atchison and Douglas represented the interests of St. Louis and Chicago. Conservative pro-slavery men—the great Whig slaveowners who had opposed the Mexican War—never desired the repeal of the Missouri Compromise. They much preferred to keep Nebraska closed, both as a means of keeping out new free states and because the southern railroad route meant an economic advantage to the South. Moreover, they still maintained their alliance with the millowners, the "cotton Whigs" of the North. Crocodile tears could always be shed for the Indians as a way of opposing the organization of new territories. And here we note a constitutional eccentricity whose influence is imponderable but may have been great. To admit settlers lawfully into Nebraska, it was necessary to extinguish Indian claims, which encompassed virtually the entire region. We need not enter the maze of complicated interactions of municipal and international law, but only note that new treaties *might* have been necessary to extinguish the claims, and new treaties could be defeated in the Senate by one third plus one of the votes.

Sometime in the intervening ten months Douglas certainly decided that a completely new approach to the Nebraska question was in order. He may have felt that only a new approach, which would create a positive nationwide interest in the measure, could overwhelm the "old fogies" North and South. In our judgment, that interest was to be created, not so much by specific expectations with regard to Nebraska—the demands of prospective homesteaders and the railroad interests, for example, were not enough—but by the erection of popular sovereignty, as we have said, into a national dogma. And popular sovereignty, thus canonized, would be the basis in national opinion upon which a policy for action in a much broader field than Nebraska might be erected. As we have argued in the chapter on Manifest Destiny, Douglas had during these months become disappointed with Pierce's leadership, and the party was tearing itself to pieces. The Whig party had supplied the chief leadership, in Clay and Webster, for the 1850 compromise. But the Whig party had been dealt a death blow by outraged free-soil opinion as a consequence. The tensions which destroyed the Whigs were now racking the Democrats, particularly in the North. Something dramatic had to be done. Douglas, we have said, determined upon the greatest assertion of political leadership possible to a Senate chairman of the Committee on Territories. This could not have been accomplished by the mere endorsement of the old Nebraska bill. Moreover, the opening of the Thirty-third Congress was the first under a Democratic administration since the retirement of Polk, and the first since the 1850 "measures of adjustment." It was not possible for Douglas, the previous year, to make a statement, such as he was now to make, the basis of party orthodoxy, if the bill had had to be signed by a Whig president. And it was essential to Douglas's 1854 plans and projects that he become the high priest of the party's faith.

* * * * *

Douglas's intentions, in sidetracking Senator Dodge's old Nebraska bill and bringing in an entirely new one, accompanied by an elaborate report, must now be gleaned from that report. This document, a masterpiece of political rhetoric, deserves the closest scrutiny by every student of the legislative process. Of it we may say what Macaulay said of the Toleration Act, that "it will not bear to be tried by sound general principles. Nay it will not bear to be tried by any principle, sound or unsound." And yet not quite so. Unlike the English with their "national distaste for whatever is abstract in political science," the sensitive and inflammatory public for whom Douglas wrought conceived of their demands in terms of general principles. Douglas's report also abounds in contradictions, but whereas the great English law achieved its purpose by an innocent disregard of its own inconsistencies, Douglas's report is highly and articulately self-conscious on this subject. Since his public demanded principles, and since principled differences are peculiarly difficult to compromise, Douglas attempted to make the ignoring of principled differences itself a principle. Yet, again, this is not entirely correct. It fits one of Douglas's arguments, wherein he says, in substance: In 1850 we struck a good bargain, a bargain in which each party got something and gave something, and which all greatly preferred to the alternative, which would have been no bargain, but disunion. But this bargain, Douglas shows, was accepted by the different parties for different reasons and understood in different terms. If any attempt had been made to reach agreement on the *reasons* for the compromise, there could have been no compromise. The moral, however, should have been: Let us now follow the precedent of 1850 and ask what it is each party hopes to accomplish by a Nebraska bill and see if there is not an attainable common denominator of these demands. It is not the moral Douglas draws, however. He has another argument, which introduces a new level of contradiction. And while Douglas points clearly to the one kind of contradiction, he shrewdly averts attention from the other. Instead of the superficial inconsistency of an "agreement to disagree," Douglas moves on to associate a simple dictate of prudence with a new higher principle. This new higher principle, of course, is popular sovereignty. However, on the evidence Douglas himself offers in the report, no one in 1850 subordinated any differences of principle to the supervening principle of popular sovereignty. The warring factions of 1850 no more agreed on popular sovereignty, on committing "all questions pertaining to slavery in the territories . . . to the decision of the people residing therein," than the warring sects in 1689 had agreed that "mere theological error ought not to be punished by the civil magistrate." According to Macaulay, "This principle the Toleration Act not only does not recognize, but positively disclaims . . . Persecution continues to be the general rule. Toleration is the exception." But in 1689 the exceptions were sufficient to accomplish most of what would have been accomplished had the principle of toleration been recognized. The right end was achieved, but for the wrong reasons.

So in 1850, California could have been admitted and New Mexico and Utah organized on the popular-sovereignty principle, but they were not. The conflicting claims of the Wilmot Proviso men on the one hand and the Calhoun-Davis men on the other tended to cancel each other out as the bargain was struck, but the negative act of abstaining from any decision whatever on the merits of these positions (as Douglas points out was done) was not a positive affirmation of any third position. Treating the negative as if it were a positive affirmation, while yet declaring that there was no positive affirmation, is what transforms Douglas's report from the level of superficial to that of profound inner contradiction. It is as if someone had told the English people four

years after the Toleration Act that they had repudiated the
principle of persecution and adopted the principle of religious
liberty. The principle of religious liberty was not recognized in
English law for nearly another century and a half. In like manner,
Wilmot Proviso men did not abandon the principle of congressional exclusion of slavery in the territories; but while still asserting the principle, as Webster did in his March 7 (1850) speech,
they relaxed their demand as unnecessary in the circumstances.
In like manner, Calhoun-Davis men, while continuing to believe
in the right to protection of slave property in the territories, abated
that demand in the face of the uncertainty that slaveowners would
go into New Mexico—or, perhaps, believing that if they did they
would be able to protect this property themselves (even as the
neighboring Texans had done) so long as no positive ban existed
in federal law. The only question concerning slavery distinctly
left to the decision of the people of the territories by the 1850
legislation had to do with the constitutions with which they might
one day apply for admission to the Union. It had nothing to do
with the status of slavery during the territorial period. The 1850
laws, as we shall see Douglas aver in his report, were silent on
this question. Perhaps this *may* have meant allowing the people
residing therein to decide. But a decision by default is hardly a
higher principle, and Douglas's sleight-of-hand consists precisely
in his attempt to produce the appearance of such a principle, not
only despite this evidence, but from this evidence. That he does
in large measure succeed is evidence of a supreme piece of political legerdemain—a virtuoso sleight-of-hand trick, in which a
principle, like a rabbit, is pulled from a principle-proof hat!

"The principal amendments which your committee deem it
their duty to recommend to the favorable action of the Senate,"
Douglas began in his famous special Senate report of January 4,
1854,

are those in which the principles established by the compromise measures of 1850, so far as they are applicable to territorial organizations, are proposed to be affirmed and carried
into practical operation within the limits of the new Territory.
The wisdom of those measures is attested, not less by their
salutary and beneficial effects, in allaying sectional agitation
and restoring peace and harmony to an irritated and dis-

tracted people, than by the cordial and almost universal approbation with which they have been received and sanctioned by the whole country.

The report thus begins with a hypothesis which is something of a paradox: that *compromise* measures established principles. That this is even more than a paradox will appear when Douglas says in the report that there was in 1850 no agreement beyond the specific terms of the Utah and New Mexico 1850 territorial laws. And there is this further implicit contradiction: Douglas alludes to the existence of parts of the Compromise of 1850 other than the territorial laws. What right does he have to assume that what is part of a larger whole can stand on its feet as a precedent apart from that whole? We have already shown that an argument can be made to the effect that other parts of the Compromise, as parts of a bargain, balanced and canceled each other and that this part might stand alone. But this required such a demonstration as we have suggested; it is hardly warranted as an assumption. One cannot assume without proof that one particular part of a compromise embodies the "principle" of the compromise more than any other parts of the compromise. Further: the idea of "cordial and almost universal approbation" is, to put it mildly, a somewhat overoptimistic viewing of the scene in the free states that greeted, for example, the Fugitive Slave Law. It is true that the country, weary with strife, had quieted down in the realization that disunion or war would probably result from any attempt to reopen the controversy. But the immolation of the Whig party upon the altar of the compromise was hardly evidence of its vast popularity. It is true that both the "major" parties had in 1852 endorsed, with uncertain enthusiasm, the settlement of 1850. But one of them was already well on the way to becoming a minor party, and the other was being threatened with a similar fate. What Douglas was in fact attempting in these sonorous opening paragraphs was not history but a new propaganda in favor of the 1850 measures, a propaganda designed to endow them with a sanctity such as the Missouri Compromise had come to have and which Douglas well knew the Missouri Compromise had not had until long after 1821.

In the judgment of your committee [the report continues], those measures were intended to have a far more comprehensive and enduring effect than the mere adjustment of the difficulties arising out of the recent acquisition of Mexican territory. They were designed to establish certain great principles, which would not only furnish adequate remedies for existing evils, but, in all time to come, avoid the perils of a similar agitation, by withdrawing the question of slavery from the halls of Congress and the political arena, and committing it to the arbitrament of those who were immediately interested in it, and alone responsible for its consequences. With the view of conforming their action to what they regard the settled policy of the government, sanctioned by the approving voice of the American people, your committee have deemed it their duty to incorporate and perpetuate, in their territorial bill, the principles and spirit of those measures. If any other considerations were necessary, to render this course imperative upon the committee, they may be found in the fact, that the Nebraska country occupies the same relative position to the slavery question, as did New Mexico and Utah, when those territories were organized.

Here we find the report's first version of the popular-sovereignty idea as the supervening principle of the 1850 compromise. But committing slavery to the arbitrament of those immediately interested and alone responsible is loose enough for many meanings. It certainly does not require us to believe more than that the people of the territories would not be confronted with any federal mandate to prohibit slavery when they came to draft constitutions preparatory to seeking statehood.

We turn now to another massive difficulty: Daniel Webster had by common consent gone to the very farthest verge that free-soil opinion could go in conciliating pro-slavery opinion in 1850. Indeed, it is probable that no other northern leader had the prestige to go so far, and Webster himself had spent that prestige prodigally. But Webster had said in 1850, in one passage of the March 7 speech, that "there is not at this moment within the United States, or any territory of the United States, a single foot of land, the character of which, in regard to its being free territory, or slave territory, is not fixed by some law, and some irrepealable law, beyond the power of the action of the government."[9] If this was so, or if the belief that it was so had been part of the purchase price of support by the North for the 1850 legislation, for what territory could that legislation serve as precedent? Indeed, was it not the conviction, in 1850, that the compromise measures were a final settlement of the question of slavery in the territories, that induced men on all sides to make concessions? For the belief that the relaxation of a principle will never serve as a precedent, that therefore such evil as flows from the case will be limited to the case, is the very thing that will induce men to relax their principles.

But what did Webster mean by "irrepealable law"? *After* Douglas had been driven to the repeal of the Missouri slavery restriction, when he was locked in combat with the free-soil senators over his *amended* Kansas-Nebraska bill, Douglas asserted that Webster (now dead) did *not* include the Missouri Compromise in that category, and cited as evidence another passage from Webster's March 7 speech:

> Now, Mr. President, I have established . . . the proposition with which I set out . . . and that is, that the whole territory within the former United States, or in the newly acquired Mexican provinces, has a fixed and settled character, now fixed and settled by law which cannot be repealed; in the case of Texas without a violation of public faith, and by no human power in regard to California or New Mexico; that, therefore, under one or other of these laws, every foot of land in the States or in the Territories has already received a fixed and decided character.

"One or other of these laws," Douglas was to insist, distinctly referred only to laws affecting Texas and the Mexican provinces, and these and these alone were "irrepealable." But what Douglas did not mention was that Webster had also said, in the very paragraph preceding the foregoing, that "wherever there is a foot of land to be prevented from becoming slave territory, I am ready to assert the principle of the exclusion of slavery."[10] And when Webster on June 3, 1850, voted for the provisions of the 1850 bills permitting the people of the new territories to adopt state constitutions with or without slavery, he said: "And let it be remembered that I am now speaking of New Mexico and Utah, and other territories acquired from Mexico, and of nothing else . . . *as to them* [our italics] I say that I see no occasion to make a provision against slavery . . ."[11] Nothing can be more certain than that Webster never understood the Missouri restriction to have been disturbed by 1850; and Douglas was certainly guilty of disingenuousness in twisting the one sentence to his purpose. Our defense of Douglas on this point is the one already suggested: he no more intended repeal than Webster did, and was driven to such tortuous explanations by the same unforeseen contingency that drove him to repeal.

To the objection, however, that the very idea of the Compromise of 1850 was founded upon the belief that it could *not* serve as a precedent, we offer a twofold reply. In the first place, one virtue of the 1850 compromise, as Douglas expounded it, was that it permitted the different parties to accept it for different, even contradictory, reasons. Thus Webster might reconcile important elements of free-soil opinion on the assumption that there would be no further territorial acquisitions; that was his privilege as a northeastern Whig. But by the same token Douglas, as a northwestern Democrat, had a right to different expectations.

Yet this explanation is not sufficient. However notoriously alive Manifest Destiny may have yet been in the Democratic party in 1850, the idea that the compromisers were establishing a precedent for "all time to come" was certainly remote from public consciousness. Indeed, it is virtually certain that, if there had been any serious attempt to introduce such a consideration into the compromising, compromise would have been at an end. Yet how "unhistorical" is this use of history? Lincoln was one day to write: "All honor to Jefferson—to the man who, in the concrete pressure of a struggle for national independence by a single people, had the coolness, forecast, and capacity to introduce into a merely revolutionary document, an abstract truth, applicable to all men and all times, and so to embalm it there, that today, and in all coming days, it shall be a rebuke and a stumbling block to the very harbingers of re-appearing tyranny and oppression."[12] Yet Lincoln knew that the anti-slavery implications that he, in 1858, perceived in the Declaration were far from fully grasped by the public for whom Jefferson wrote. It was notorious that the Declaration itself had been emended more than once out of tenderness for the sensibilities of those who profited—North and South—by the slave trade, whether as buyers or sellers. If the Declaration of Independence meant no more than what it was generally understood to mean in 1776, Lincoln's statement is profoundly unhistorical. Yet had not Jefferson himself said of the Declaration that it was only meant ". . . to be an expression of the American mind . . . [and that] All its authority rests on the harmonizing sentiments of the day"?[13] Jefferson, in writing the Declaration, may have expressed no more than what he thought all believed. But it is also true that men in 1776 subscribed to propositions which had consequences of which they were not fully aware and which they may not have accepted if they had been aware of them. That Jefferson intended the Declaration, or the philosophy it expressed, to have far more drastic consequences than were possible in 1776 is hardly open to question. And if the intention of the legislator is the law, then did not the historical meaning of the Declaration comprehend also its historic mission, and was not that mission the attainment as well as the promise of equality?

Applying the same construction to Douglas's interpretation of the Compromise of 1850, may we not say that he, as one of the chief architects of that legislation, had a right to find in it more than was unequivocally expressed, more even than was generally understood as a condition of its acceptance at the time it was accepted? In our judgment, such a "constructive interpretation" of the past would have been unjustifiable if Douglas's present intention was not justifiable. In so far as that intention was repeal of the Missouri Compromise, which we deny that it was, he should be condemned. But in so far as his aim was propaganda in behalf of 1850, which we affirm, with a view to lend dignity to those measures so that support of them would not be a kiss of death to national political parties, his aim is eminently justifiable. And essential to that propaganda was the discovery that 1850 was not merely the rubbish heap for the principles of frightened men but the rallying ground for a better principle.

Let us now hear how Nebraska country in 1854 occupied the "same relative position" as Utah and New Mexico in 1850.

It was a disputed point, whether slavery was prohibited by law in the country acquired from Mexico. On the one hand it was contended, as a legal proposition, that slavery having been prohibited by the enactments of Mexico, according to the laws of nations, we received the country with all its local laws and domestic institutions attached to the soil, so far as they did not conflict with the Constitution of the United States; and that a law, either protecting or prohibiting slavery, was not repugnant to that instrument, as was evidenced by the fact, that one-half of the States of the Union tolerated, while the other half prohibited, the institution of Slavery. On the other hand it was insisted that, by virtue of the Constitution of the United States, every citizen had a right to remove to any Territory of the Union, and carry his property with him under the protection of law, whether that property consisted in persons or things. The difficulties arising from this diversity of opinion were greatly aggravated by the fact, that there were many persons on both sides of the legal controversy who were unwilling to abide the decision of the courts on the legal matters in dispute; thus, among those who claimed that the Mexican laws were still in force, and consequently that slavery was already prohibited in those territories by valid enactment, there were many who insisted upon Congress making the matter certain, by enacting another prohibition. In like manner, some of those who argued that the Mexican laws had ceased to have any binding force, and that the Constitution tolerated and protected slave property in those territories, were unwilling to trust the decision of the courts upon that point, and insisted that Congress should, by direct enactment remove all legal obstacles to the introduction of slaves into those territories. [Jefferson Davis in 1850 only wished to prevent a territorial legislature from prohibiting the introduction of slavery. He had not yet moved to the demand for full congressional protection.]

Such being the character of the controversy, in respect to the territory acquired from Mexico, a similar question has arisen in regard to the right to hold slaves in the proposed territory of Nebraska when the Indian laws shall be withdrawn . . . Under this section [of the 1820 enabling act for Missouri], as in the case of Mexican law in New Mexico and Utah, it is a disputed point whether slavery is prohibited in Nebraska country by *valid* enactment. The decision of this question involves the constitutional power of Congress to pass laws prescribing and regulating the domestic institutions of the various territories of the Union. In the opinion of those eminent statesmen, who hold that Congress is invested with no rightful authority to legislate upon the subject of slavery in the territories, the eighth section of the act preparatory to the admission of Missouri is null and void;

while the prevailing sentiment in large portions of the Union sustains the doctrine that the Constitution of the United States secures to every citizen an inalienable right to move into any of the territories with his property, of whatever kind and description, and to hold and enjoy the same under the sanction of law.

Let us watch the political legerdemain whereby Douglas extracts a new principle from an old event. Notice the last sentence quoted, in which Douglas describes one doctrine (and only one) as being held by *eminent* statesmen. According to this doctrine, the Missouri Compromise was null and void because Congress had no rightful power whatever to legislate upon the question of slavery in the territories. The opinion of the "eminent statesmen" is presented as an objection to the Missouri law, but there is nothing analogous to it in the preceding paragraph, wherein objections to the Mexican anti-slavery law were presented. Certainly it could not refer to Douglas's 1850 opinions, for we have heard Douglas's well-known 1850 advocacy of the legal effectiveness of the Mexican prohibition as the strongest reason why he had opposed the Wilmot Proviso. And no Mexican law could have been legally effective which the Constitution had denied Congress the power to enact. Now, in the first of the two paragraphs just quoted, Douglas gave as the basis of the argument of those who had opposed the legal proposition in favor of Mexican law that "by virtue of the Constitution of the United States, every citizen had a right to remove to any Territory of the Union, and carry his property with him under the protection of law, whether that property consisted in persons or things." In the latter paragraph he repeats this doctrine, in the second half of the last sentence quoted, after the semicolon. But the manner in which it is repeated, within the same sentence as the one quoting the opinion of "eminent statesmen," obscures the fact that the doctrine that Congress has no power to legislate on slavery in the territories is completely different from the doctrine that every citizen has an inalienable right to move into any territory with any description of property. For the latter doctrine, by necessary inference, conveys to Congress the right to pass laws *protecting* the slave property to which the citizen is said to have an inalienable right. Both doctrines support the view that the Missouri Compromise was invalid, but one is the old Calhoun-Davis doctrine, whose culmination was the demand for a congressional slave code for the territories; and the other was Douglas's *subsequent* doctrine of complete non-interference, a doctrine maintained in the debates with Lincoln and given full form only in the *Harper's Magazine* article, "Popular Sovereignty in the Territories," published in 1859.

But if this is "pure" popular sovereignty, and if this is expressly stated to imply the invalidity of the Missouri restriction, do we not here have an unmistakable sign that repeal was Douglas's aim from the outset in 1854? The answer is no. For Douglas had not yet identified *himself* with "pure" popular sovereignty. That Douglas was preparing the ground for such a declaration of invalidity, we have no doubt. But preparing is not occupying. Everything hinges on timing. To declare the invalidity of the Missouri law after all the territory north of the Missouri line had been organized and settled would be very different from doing so earlier.

But who were the "eminent statesmen"? There is something "funny" in this expression, in both senses of the colloquialism. While we would not positively assert that there were no such persons, it would be difficult to say who they were. Certainly neither Douglas nor any of the other compromisers held such views in 1850—a fact attested by the omission of any such objection to the Mexican law in this very report. Popular sovereignty had been common political coin at least since 1848, and yet no one had said that Congress had *no* power over slavery in the territories. As a *political* doctrine, it was widely believed that the people of the territories ought to be accorded the fullest measure of self-government; but the general *legal* doctrine still held that it was the right and duty of Congress to accord this measure, and not that the Constitution did it of its own force. The 1850 territorial law not only provided for a governor and judges appointed by the President of the United States and a veto power (which required a two-thirds vote of the territorial legislature to override) by this same governor (who was not responsible to the territories but to the President), but every territorial statute was subject to an absolute veto by Congress. Even in the final version of the Kansas-Nebraska Act, which supposedly embodied more of this new "pure" popular sovereignty, the non-responsible executive and his veto remained.

Even if we confound the political desirability, with the legal requirement, of a hands-off policy by Congress concerning slavery in the territories, no one had yet (January 4, 1854) maintained even the desirability that congressional hands should be off to the extent now indicated. At the most, popular sovereignty had meant that Congress should not decide, even in the territorial period, whether slavery might be established in a territory. But that Congress had no power over the conditions under which the people who went into the territories might decide—e.g., whether they went *with* or *without* slaves—had not been a recognized feature of popular sovereignty. Those who held that Congress had no such power—the Calhoun-Davis school—also held the whole idea of popular sovereignty in contempt. Douglas thus transforms the contemporaneous 1854 "dispute" (a dispute that was sleeping, if not moribund, until his report gave it vitality) concerning the validity of the Missouri law by introducing a doctrine which has no equivalent in the supposed analogy. And the boldness of Douglas's originality is concealed when he endows this new doctrine with the prestige of "eminent" statesmen who, so far as we know, existed only in his imagination.

Final judgment on this comparison of Nebraska and the Mexican acquisition can be arrived at only after evaluating Douglas's intention; but the manner in which Douglas makes the comparison reveals a further downgrading of the Missouri Compromise. That there were objections by the Calhoun-Davis school to both the Mexican and Missouri slavery restrictions is certainly correct, and it is also true that at bottom they were founded upon a single constitutional doctrine. This was given its final and precise formulation in 1857 in Taney's opinion in the Dred Scott case: that the right to property in a slave was affirmed in the Constitution, and that the Constitution (by the Fifth Amendment) forbade Congress (and, *a fortiori*, Mexican law) to deprive any person of property without due process of law. Yet there was a great practical and political difference between Mexican law, transferred by international law to American soil, and the at least once-sacred Missouri Compromise. The Texans had been heroes in the North as well as in the South for revolutionizing against Mexican law. But even those Southerners who believed the Missouri law unconstitutional would have recognized in Congress an authoritative arbiter of the meaning of the Constitution.[14] It was a striking departure for Douglas to put the scruple against Mexican law, which had not been the subject of any solemn affirmation by any branch of the American government, upon the same level as a scruple against the Missouri Compromise, even if the scruple in both cases had the same technical foundation. Moreover, it was well known that the constitutional objection to the Missouri Compromise had its head and inspiration in the teachings of John Caldwell Calhoun. It was also known that this worthy had discovered his objection only in later years, after he had discovered the "positive good" of slavery. When Calhoun sat in Monroe's Cabinet and was among those consulted on the constitutionality of the famous eighth section of the enabling act for Missouri he found no flaw in it. Indeed, he then "heartily endorsed" the Compromise of 1820, according to an authoritative recent study.[15] The Missouri Compromise had been passed by both houses of Congress and signed by a president. And this President, who was subsequently re-elected, had received the approval by his Cabinet of the eighth section, a Cabinet including both Calhoun and John Quincy Adams. Disrespect to Mexican law could hardly outrage the North. Disrespect to the Missouri Compromise assuredly would. Douglas, of course, had said in 1850 that American settlers cared nothing for congressional legislation of their domestic affairs unless it suited them. However, in the old Northwest and in Iowa and Minnesota, it was indisputable that the settlers *had* decided in accordance with the federal declaration. Whether federal law there was powerless or not, it derived dignity from the fact that it had never been seriously challenged.

But the downgrading of the Missouri Compromise goes still farther. In discussing the Mexican prohibition of slavery Douglas cites the opinion—which he himself once expressed with utmost emphasis—holding that it was valid on American soil until repealed by American authority. But when he comes to the "disputed point" concerning the Missouri Compromise restriction of slavery, he gives two opinions holding this law invalid—the new "pure" popular-sovereignty opinion, and the Calhoun-Davis opinion, repeated from the preceding paragraph—but no opinion supporting the Missouri law's validity. It is of particular importance in this context to realize that among extreme anti-slavery men it was firmly believed that the provision in the Fifth Amendment forbidding any person to be deprived of life, liberty, or property, without due process of law, forbade that any man be *enslaved* in consequence of federal law. By omitting this challenging antithesis to "the doctrine that the Constitution of the United States secures to every citizen an inalienable right to move into any of the territories with his property, of whatever kind and description," he clothes that doctrine with excessive dignity. Certainly he treats this view with a consideration that is a surprise to anyone who has witnessed the savage attacks he made upon it in 1850. And the omitted doctrine was the one held most vehemently by Chase and Sumner, the men who were presently to issue a flaming challenge to the Nebraska bill. Whether or not this was a tactical error, Douglas was to pay heavily for it. Did Douglas think that, by not presenting any other doctrine antithetical to the extreme pro-slavery position, this new "pure" popular sovereignty might be construed to be such an antithesis? Did he, in 1854, visualize "pure" popular sovereignty as the fighting free-soil doctrine it became—for a short time—in the fight against Lecompton?

We now come to the first specific statement of what Douglas's committee proposed that Congress actually do. Until now we were told only that it meant to follow the precedent of 1850 and then were presented with a complicated statement concerning the nature of the precedent, in the form of an analogy between the dispute in 1850 over Utah and New Mexico and the "dispute" in 1854 over Nebraska, and its relation to current questions. The analogy suggested a heavy weighting of the scales against the Missouri Compromise. But the weight is more than redressed by a downright denial of the force of the deleterious inferences. Douglas wrote:

> Your committee do not feel themselves called upon to enter into the discussion of these controverted questions. They involve the same grave issues which produced the agitation, the sectional strife, and the fearful struggle of 1850. As Congress deemed it wise and prudent to refrain from deciding the matters in controversy *then*, either by affirming or repealing the Mexican laws, or by any act declaratory of the true intent of the Constitution and the extent of the protection afforded by it to slave property in the territories, so your committee are not prepared *now* to recommend a departure from the course proposed on that memorable occasion, either

by affirming or repealing the eighth section of the Missouri act, or by any act declaratory of the Constitution in respect to the legal points in dispute. [Italics not in the original.]

The adverb "now" in the last sentence was soon to take on ominous meaning. But in the context it stands in opposition to "then," and it would have taken an unusually wary mind to suspect that "now" meant only "for the time being." The crucial proposition contained in the last sentence is that the committee *did not recommend the repeal of the eighth section of the Missouri act.* That it did not affirm it is of minor significance, since it was not the custom of Congress to reaffirm the constitutionality of its own actions, and there was no demand for such an affirmation. The refusal to reaffirm is, in itself, merely perfunctory. But the refusal to repeal stands as massive evidence that Douglas, on January 4, 1854, had no intention that the barrier to slavery in the Nebraska country would be thrown down as a condition of its territorial organization.

The report then continues:

Your committee deem it fortunate for the peace of the country, and the security of the Union, that the controversy then resulted in the adoption of the Compromise measures, which the two great political parties, with singular unanimity, have affirmed as a cardinal article of their faith, and proclaimed to the world, as a final settlement of the controversy and an end of the agitation. A due respect, therefore, for the avowed opinions of Senators, as well as a proper sense of patriotic duty, enjoins upon your committee the propriety and necessity of a strict adherence to the principles, and even a literal adoption of the enactments of that adjustment in all their territorial bills, so far as the same are not locally inapplicable.

Having climbed to the clarity of an unequivocal refusal to repeal, Douglas again descends to the murky ambiguities of his 1850 precedent. If he had limited himself to the "literal adoption . . . so far as the same are not locally inapplicable" of the language of the 1850 territorial acts, then the only important question could have been whether the right granted in the 1850 laws to apply for admission with slavery was or was not "locally inapplicable" in the face of the eighth section of the Missouri act. But this would have been hardly worth quarreling about. In the joint debates, Lincoln conceded this right to the people of any territory, *provided* slavery had been excluded during the territorial period. For, as we have often noted, all it meant was conceding to them the right to do, the day before statehood, what they could in any event do the day after. But now—after maintaining that in 1850 Congress had refused to decide all such questions of principle as whether the Constitution of the United States made freedom national and slavery an exception, or slavery national and freedom an exception, or that the Constitution reserved the question of freedom versus slavery to localities because Congress had no power over it whatever—now Douglas insists upon following the example of 1850, not only in the letter of the law, but in its "principles" as well. And the denouement of that fateful January of 1854—which we shall describe in the next chapter—began, not with the report we are now reading, but with the subsequent inclusion into the Nebraska bill of an alleged "principle" of 1850, *as if it had been* "a literal adoption" from the 1850 territorial laws.

Let us now hear Douglas report the "letter" of the earlier laws:

Those enactments embrace, among other things less material to the matters under consideration, the following provisions:

"When admitted as a State, the said Territory or any portion of the same, shall be received into the Union, with or without slavery, as their constitution may prescribe at the time of their admission."

"That the legislative power and authority of said Territory shall be vested in the governor and a legislative assembly."

"That the legislative power of said Territory shall extend to all rightful subjects of legislation, consistent with the Constitution of the United States and the provisions of this act . . . [We omit repeating a clause dealing with disposition of the soil and discriminatory taxes.]

"Writs of error and appeal from the final decisions of said [territorial] supreme court shall be allowed, and may be taken to the Supreme Court of the United States in the same manner and under the same regulations as from the circuit courts of the United States . . . except only that, in all cases involving title to slaves, the said writs of error or appeals shall be allowed and decided by the said supreme court without regard to the value of the matter, property, or title in controversy; and except, also, that a writ of error or appeal shall also be allowed to the Supreme Court of the United States . . . upon any writ of habeas corpus involving the question of personal freedom. . ."

Then, after a short paragraph citing the extension of the 1850 Fugitive Slave Law to the new territories in 1850, Douglas goes on to enunciate the "principles" (otherwise called "propositions") of the 1850 territorial laws.

From these provisions it is apparent that the compromise measures of 1850 affirm and rest upon the following propositions.

First: That all questions pertaining to slavery in the territories, and in the new States to be formed therefrom, are to be left to the decision of the people residing therein, by their appropriate representatives, to be chosen by them for that purpose.

Second: That "all cases involving title to slaves," and "questions of personal freedom" are referred to the adjudication of the local tribunals, with the right of appeal to the Supreme Court of the United States.

Third: That the provisions of the Constitution of the United States, in respect to fugitives from service, are to be carried into faithful execution in all "organized territories" the same as in the States.

This famous document then ends as follows:

The substitute for the bill which your committee have prepared, and which is commended to the favorable action of the Senate, proposes to carry these propositions and principles into practical operation, in the precise language of the compromise measures of 1850.

Let us observe the same kind of transformation flowing from the juxtaposition of the *provisions* of the 1850 territorial acts with *propositions* (or "principles") upon which they are said to rest, as we previously noted in the juxtaposition (and presumed analogy) of the dispute concerning the validity of the Mexican anti-slavery law and the dispute concerning the validity of the

Missouri restriction. Now the first provision cited by Douglas actually says nothing whatever concerning the power of the people of the territories over slavery in the territories; it says only that *when admitted as a state* said territory (or any portion of the same) shall be received into the Union with or without slavery. This provision neither precludes nor assumes the existence of slavery as a subject of territorial legislation, for the simple reason that it does not hold the question of slavery during the territorial period in contemplation at all. The first *proposition* then makes a giant and wholly unwarranted leap (from the point of view of logical inference) when it says that *all* questions *in* the territories are to be decided by representatives of the people of the territories. This proposition, incidentally, even if the compromise measures of 1850 had in some unseen way "rested upon" it, certainly is nowhere "affirmed" in them. However, as an alleged inference from the first provision cited, we must say that the first proposition states the exact reverse of the truth: i.e., by itself the first provision refers *no* question pertaining to slavery *in* a territory to the decision of the people therein.

But could the first proposition be inferred from the third provision (of the 1850 territorial laws) cited in Douglas's report or from some combination of the first and third provisions? The answer is that it could not be, by any process of construction we know. On Douglas's own showing, in this very report, Congress did not decide or declare what degree or kind of power over questions pertaining to slavery "in the territories" was "consistent with the Constitution of the United States." And Congress had not, in 1850, left it to the territorial governments or to the people of the territories acting in a constituent capacity to judge the extent of their own powers under the Constitution. This is shown by the fact that "all cases involving title to slaves" and "questions of personal freedom" were left to decisions of the courts and ultimately to the Supreme Court of the United States. And these courts, whether territorial or federal, were neither chosen by nor responsible in any way to the people of the territories. It is clear that the aforesaid "cases" and "questions" would surely have involved some or all of the points of controversy which Douglas praised Congress for *not* deciding in 1850. If, for example, the Dred Scott decision had issued before January 1854, it would have been plain, in accordance with that decision, that all questions pertaining to slavery *had not* been left to the people of Utah

and New Mexico or to their representatives—and *could not* be left
to them or to the people of Nebraska—because according to the
Dred Scott decision neither Congress nor a territorial legislature
had any power consistent with the Constitution to forbid the
introduction of slaves into any United States territory. In citing
the Calhoun-Davis opinion that every citizen of the United States
had an inalienable right to go into any federal territory with his
slave property, Douglas had by clear implication raised the
hypothetical possibility of such a Supreme Court decision as that
in the case of Dred Scott. Hence he must have known on January
4, 1854, that the first of his "propositions," according to which
"all questions pertaining to slavery in the territories . . . [were]
to be left to the people residing therein," might not have involved
any legislative power to forbid the bringing of slaves into these
selfsame territories. In short, as long as there was no understanding of what powers over slavery in the territories were "consistent
with the Constitution of the United States," it was impossible to
deduce from the 1850 grant to the people of Utah and New
Mexico of legislative power in "all rightful subjects of legislation"
any power to decide "all questions pertaining to slavery in the
territories."

What Douglas has done, and in our opinion done quite
deliberately, is to create, by his first proposition, a vastly greater
presumption in favor of a much "purer" popular sovereignty than
had ever been made before. Because Congress left vital constitutional points undecided, Douglas in his first proposition presumes
that it left them, not to the Supreme Court, but to the people of
the territories to decide. Because Congress left it to the people
to decide the status of slavery after the territorial period ended,
Douglas presumes that it had also left it to them to decide it
before it ended. Yet there is a tactical and rhetorical, if not logical,
consistency in all this: Douglas steadily pushes forward the whole
popular-sovereignty idea as a kind of residual legatee of all
the mutually incompatible contending doctrines. Popular sovereignty emerges as a kind of dark horse as the popular favorites
kill each other off.

But further: Douglas had found, and found truly, that the
genius of the 1850 compromise lay in a practical agreement which
admitted of divergent and even contradictory interpretations; but
the January 4, 1854, Nebraska bill, as authoritatively expounded
by its author, does not rest simply on the first or "pure" popular-

sovereignty "proposition"; it rests also on the second, which, if it does not flatly contradict the first, renders it altogether obscure. By this peculiar rhetoric—which permits the same kind of divergent interpretations as persisted after 1850—Douglas is true to the "principle" of 1850.

Two things, and only two things, emerge clearly as immediate political conclusions of the report: It is the hope and intention of its author that all questions pertaining to slavery will be left— or will be believed to be left—to the decision of the people residing in the territories; and second, that the Missouri Compromise is not repealed.

Chapter VIII

The Repeal of the Missouri
Compromise IV

TRAGEDY. THE EXTREMES CRUSH THE MEAN

Now intervened a strange episode. Douglas's special report, accompanied by the bill, was issued on January 4 and printed in the Washington *Sentinel* on the seventh. This bill, despite the elaborate prologue of the report, actually contained no statement regarding slavery, except the language of the 1850 territorial acts which we have seen as the first of the provisions cited in the report. But on January 10, after the bill had been twice read in the Senate and ordered to be printed, it was reprinted by the *Sentinel* with an additional twenty-first section which, Douglas explained, had been omitted in the first published version because of a "clerical error." This famed "clerical error" section read as follows:

Section 21. *And be it further enacted,* That, in order to avoid all misconstruction, it is hereby declared to be the true intent and meaning of this act, so far as the question of slavery is concerned, to carry into practical operation the following propositions and principles established by the compromise measures of 1850, to wit:

First. That all questions pertaining to slavery in the Territories, and in the new States to be formed therefrom, are to be left to the decision of the people residing therein, through their appropriate representatives.

Second. That "all cases involving title to slaves" and "questions of personal freedom," are referred to the adjudication of the local tribunals, with the right of appeal to the Supreme Court of the United States.

Third. That the provisions of the Constitution and laws of the United States, in respect to fugitives from service, are to be carried into faithful execution in all "the organized Territories" the same as in the States.

It will be seen immediately that these three "propositions and principles" correspond to the ones with which the report had concluded. But whereas the second and third propositions of the report and of the twenty-first section are virtually identical, there is a slight change in the initial proposition as it occurs in the bill. The report spoke of the "decision of the people . . . by their appropriate representatives, *to be chosen by them for that purpose.*" The final portion of this sentence is now dropped. Why? The idea of representatives chosen for a special purpose suggests a constitutional convention, an exertion of constituent or original power, and not power delegated by Congress. This clause is the nexus in the report between the first provision and the first proposition. Both suggest (without specifying) the exercise of an extraordinary power, and not the legislative power vested in a territorial governor and legislative assembly. However, the first proposition of the twenty-first section does retain a vestige of its predecessor in the word "appropriate." All this makes it difficult to believe that Douglas did not have the twenty-first section as part of his grand design on January 4, and still more difficult to believe that a clerk was responsible for its omission on that date. Certainly the metamorphosis of the first provision into the first proposition in the report, and the latter into the first proposition of the twenty-first section, shows a steady progress of the idea of popular sovereignty, as applied to questions pertaining to slavery, from an extraordinary power exerted on the threshold of statehood, to an extraordinary power exerted during the territorial period, to an *almost* ordinary exertion of territorial legislative power. Yet the "almost" is an important reservation. For the word "appropriate" is an anomaly. And the second proposition raises as massive a question mark as to the meaning of the first proposition, when it occurs in the twenty-first section of the bill, as it raised in the report.

A succession of historical authorities, following the main theme of *The Appeal of the Independent Democrats*, has accepted the

view that the twenty-first section of Douglas's Nebraska bill, as
reprinted on January 10, 1854, represented a complete and
radical departure. In the words of Allan Nevins, "it enacted the
popular sovereignty principle. The plain implication was that the
Missouri Compromise was dead."[1] But in the face of the question
mark with which we have just seen Douglas himself punctuate
"the popular sovereignty principle," is it not impossible thus to
assert what effect its enactment, if it was enacted, would have
had on existing law? So far as anyone could tell, on the basis of
Douglas's report or bill, including the twenty-first section, popular
sovereignty was protean and might assume almost any shape or
form. Indeed, there was no plain implication in the entire bill and
report. It was a mass of contrary and contradictory statements,
inferences, and implications. In the face of the many eminent
scholars who speak with the voice of Professor Nevins, we
summon as a single witness Abraham Lincoln. The following
passages are from the Peoria speech (October 16, 1854):

> On January 4, 1854, Judge Douglas introduces a new bill to
> give Nebraska territorial government. He accompanies this
> bill with a report, in which last, he expressly recommends
> that the Missouri Compromise shall neither be affirmed nor
> repealed.
>
> Before long the bill is so modified as to make two territories
> instead of one; calling the southern one Kansas.
>
> Also, about a month after the introduction of the bill, on
> the Judge's own motion, it is so amended as to declare the
> Missouri Compromise inoperative and void . . .[2]

It will be noted that Lincoln's expression "about a month" implies
that he drew no distinction between the January 4 and January 10
versions of the first Douglas bill. The decisive fact concerning the
first bill, with or without the twenty-first section, was that it
expressly did not affirm or repeal the eighth section of the Missouri
law. If there was any doubt that Lincoln had brushed aside the
twenty-first section of the first bill, it should be removed by this:

> I am aware Judge Douglas now argues that the subsequent
> *express* repeal [italics ours, not Lincoln's] is no substantial
> alteration of the bill. This argument seems wonderful to me.
> It is as if one should argue that white and black are not
> different.[3]

The difference between white and black, to Lincoln, was the difference between the bill before and after express repeal. As far as Lincoln was concerned, to pretend, as Douglas did, that the bill, even with the twenty-first section, was not essentially and fundamentally different from the bill with express repeal was as "wonderful . . . as if one should argue that white and black are not different." But this judgment of Lincoln, sufficient, as we think, to refute the idea of any "plain implication" that the Missouri Compromise was to be killed by the twenty-first section, has other far-reaching implications. For Lincoln's statement, crucial as it is to his case against Douglas, raises the question of the validity of the whole outcry raised against Douglas's report and bill *before* the express repeal. And with it is involved the question of whether Douglas really bore the responsibility of the repeal when it finally came. We must now observe the sequence of events in which that express repeal was involved.

Despite the fact that the bill Douglas reported on January 4 contained nothing more revolutionary than the provision for admitting future states from Nebraska with or without slavery, it was immediately attacked by Greeley in the New York *Tribune,* and the hue and cry in the North began. Nothing better illustrates the volatility of the political left wing of the anti-slavery movement than the hare-and-tortoise relationship of Greeley and Lincoln. Greeley exploded at the first appearance of a suggestion of a challenge to the Missouri Compromise, despite the disclaimer in the report. Lincoln would not be moved to action by an insult not at the same time certain to be an injury. The gauntlet had to be thrown down in terms altogether unmistakable before he would assume the vast responsibility of joining such an issue. But once the issue was joined, Lincoln never rested in carrying on the fight. It was Greeley who flinched in 1858 and sought accommodation with Douglas, even as he was later to flinch when the election of Lincoln was seen to involve war or disunion. But the brilliant and unstable editor, as the war progressed, was to harry Lincoln again, demanding a radical abolition policy which would have been a fundamental departure from the platform upon which Lincoln had been elected and which he had re-affirmed in his first inaugural address. Now in 1854 Greeley set the deep-toned chords vibrating in the North, and there was an answering cacophony from the opposite direction. "Clay's Whig successor in the Senate, Archibald Dixon, a . . . lawyer-planter of precise mind," writes Professor Nevins, "pointed out the flaw" in the twenty-first section. "Unless the Missouri Compromise restriction were explicitly repealed, it would remain in force until the people had acted to end it. No slaveholder could emigrate to the Territory with slaves until after the people living therein had met, and through their representatives passed affirmatively on the question whether slavery could exist or not. This being so, argued Dixon, the decision would certainly go against slavery; for the laws up to that point would exclude all slaveholders while admitting free-soilers, abolitionists, Britons, Germans, and others opposed to the peculiar institution."[4] According to Mrs. Dixon, in her *True History of the Missouri Compromise and Its Repeal,* her husband

> saw that Judge Douglas's bill, though seemingly framed on the plan of non-intervention, would not in reality carry out that principle at all; that as far as practical participation of the Southern people in those territories was concerned, the Wilmot Proviso . . . could not more effectually exclude them than they were already excluded by the Act of 1820 . . . and, until it should be directly repealed, it would effectually and practically preclude the Southern people from settling in Kansas and Nebraska . . . If they were *effectually,* even though indirectly, excluded from entering these Territories, what good would it do them that there was in the twenty-first section a provision that "all questions pertaining to slavery in the Territories and New States to be formed therefrom are to be left to the decision of the people residing therein, through their appropriate representatives?" *Cui bono?* When they were to be no part of the people.

We can think of no more accurate statement of the force of Douglas's first Nebraska bill, even with the twenty-first section, nor more eloquent testimony in support of our thesis that Douglas never intended that the Missouri slavery restriction would, "practically and effectually," be repealed. Nor, in our view, was it repealed by unequivocal indirection. This Douglas might have done by presenting the twenty-first section as an amendment to the January 4 bill. Then it might have "superseded" any contrary implications in the original version. But by presenting the twenty-first section as a part of the original version, he presented it as part of a bill of which the special report stood as an authoritative explanation. And this report, to repeat, expressly denied an intention to repeal. Lincoln, as we have seen, wisely disregarded the whole business of "clerical error," as *The Appeal of the Independent Democrats* unwisely did not do. As long as Douglas's denial of an intention to repeal was uncontradicted by Douglas himself, it rendered nugatory any repeal implication of the twenty-first section. At this juncture the anti-slavery leaders should have been content to take their stand on this denial and keep their powder dry.

Alas, extremists on both sides were unwilling to await the unraveling of the mysteries Douglas had propounded. Douglas hoped that while each extreme would find something doctrinal with which to be appeased, if not satisfied, the loaves and fishes of new territorial governments might "supersede" such doctrinal appetites as were disappointed. The probability that Nebraska would quickly yield several new free states should have satisfied the free-soilers. Meanwhile, the doctrine of the special report, steadily and progressively interpreted in favor of an ever "purer" popular sovereignty, would render it morally certain that in any future territorial acquisitions there would be no federal prohibition of slavery. And it was toward such acquisitions that Douglas would have turned the nation's energies.

On January 16, Dixon informed the Senate of his intention to offer an amendment to the Nebraska bill that would in express terms have removed the slavery restriction of the eighth section of the Missouri act and have affirmed

> that the citizens of the several States or Territories shall be at liberty to take and hold their slaves within any of the Territories of the United States, or of the States to be formed therefrom, as if the said act . . . had never been passed.

This amendment, according to all accounts, amazed and agitated Douglas. And well it might. Far from being a mere repeal, it was virtually a statement of the extreme Calhoun-Davis position. For the expression "take *and hold*" their slaves implied that territorial enactments might not forbid slaveholding. And the reference to future states as well as territories made the amendment a kind of reverse Wilmot Proviso. Of course there was an equivocation in "as if the said act . . . had never been passed"; yet "shall be at liberty" was strong medicine. No doubt Dixon expressed a more extreme position here than he meant to insist upon. Later he expressed himself satisfied with Douglas's much-watered-down repeal provision. Yet it is instructive to see how radical the demands of border-state senators had become; and Dixon was sitting in the seat of Henry Clay!

Dixon's proposed amendment instantly rallied the pro-slavery forces. If a Whig would do so much for the South, could Democrats do less? The next few days were thick with secret conferences, from which fateful decisions were to emerge. That a crisis no less than that of 1850 impended was foreshadowed when on the next day, January 17, Senator Sumner arose and gave notice of his intention to offer an amendment to the Nebraska bill expressly reaffirming the slavery prohibition of the Missouri act of March 6, 1820. The fat was in the fire.

Sumner's initial move was more restrained than Dixon's. Whether for bargaining purposes or not, Dixon had announced an intention of positively establishing the legality of slavery in *any* territory of the United States. Sumner might have responded by proposing that slavery was unlawful in any territory of the United States, but he merely stood firm on the Missouri Compromise. Now did the goddess of moderation prove fickle. While Dixon and Douglas worked together to find an acceptable compromise, the anti-slavery leaders in the Senate, Chase and Sumner, took steps which made all compromise or even polite intercourse between themselves and Douglas a virtual impossibility. They issued *The Appeal of the Independent Democrats in Congress to the People of the United States,* one of the most successful pieces of political propaganda the world has seen. Among its resounding paragraphs were such expressions as the following:

> We arraign this bill as a gross violation of a sacred pledge; as a criminal betrayal of precious rights; as part and parcel of an atrocious plot to exclude from a vast unoccupied region immigrants from the Old World, and free laborers from our own States, and convert it into a dreary region of despotism, inhabited by masters and slaves.

And:

> These pretences . . . that the territory, covered by the

positive prohibition of 1820, sustains a similar relation to slavery with that acquired from Mexico . . . are mere inventions, designed to cover up from public reprehension meditated bad faith.

It concluded by imploring "Christians and Christian ministers to interpose. Their divine religion requires them to behold in every man a brother, and to labor for the advancement and regeneration of the human race." It exhorted all men to "protest, earnestly and emphatically . . . against this enormous crime."

The *Appeal* was printed, as we have noted above, in the *Congressional Globe* of January 30; and the dateline then given it by its authors was January 19. Yet the note appended to the body of the *Appeal*, which we have already reproduced, inveighs against the January 10 "clerical error" and all subsequent changes down to the amended version of January 23, which incorporated Douglas's own repeal. But it is inconceivable that the original draft of the body of the *Appeal* was not composed before January 10. For it is inconceivable that the twenty-first section would not have been flayed in the body of the *Appeal* if its existence was known when the first draft of the *Appeal* was prepared. Precisely when the *Appeal* was written we do not know. But it reached the nation through the press on January 24. On January 23 the bill, as finally amended in Douglas's committee, was reported to the Senate, but consideration was postponed until the thirtieth. According to Douglas, this was an act of courtesy to Chase, who requested the additional week's time to study the bill as now further amended. Clearly, however, the week's delay was to enable the *Appeal* to sow the wind. This it certainly did and, when Douglas rose to open the debate on the thirtieth, the whirlwind raged about him.

Douglas claimed to know nothing about the *Appeal* until after it had been published. Exactly when he found out about it, when therefore he knew that Chase and Sumner were not interested in any form or shape of compromise with him, is less important than the brute fact that they applied the torch to anti-slavery passions at the precise moment when bargaining among the senators was going on as to the form that a Nebraska bill might take. Chase, who was the principal author of the *Appeal*, had come to the Senate in 1849, after the 1848 elections had left the Ohio legislature deadlocked between Whigs and Democrats and a handful of free-soilers were able to prevent the election of either

a Whig or regular Democrat. Chase, who was above all a free-
soiler, finally went to the Senate as an "Independent Democrat."
Such a man, of course, was nothing in the national councils of
either major party. Until the principle of the Wilmot Proviso
agitation was revived and made the basis of national party
organization, he would remain a cipher. Much the same was true
of Sumner. But both men had seen, from their experience of the
Proviso, that such a party might yet take hold. Douglas's report
and bill of January 4 gave them their opportunity, and they took
it.

If Chase and Sumner had come to Douglas privately, if the
Appeal had been used as a bargaining counter with which he
might have offset the pro-slavery demands upon him, how different might the results have been? We can never know; but we
are convinced that Douglas would have understood as well as
Chase and Sumner the value of the weapon they held in their
hand. His remark to Dixon that he knew the repeal would raise
a "hell of a storm" suggests that he never underestimated free-soil
passions. But within the Senate at the moment, in January 1854,
the free-soil strength was negligible; and its potential influence,
instead of being mobilized to strengthen Douglas against pro-
slavery demands, was used entirely to destroy him. If Douglas
was wrong in saying later that the express repeal had not changed
the bill in any important respect, what are we to say of Chase
and Sumner, who went to the country on the basis of that earlier
—nay, earliest—bill? Does not Lincoln's condemnation turn back
upon his future associates as much as upon Douglas?

Certainly the *Appeal* burned all bridges in one direction.
Douglas was thus thrown entirely upon his southern associates if
he wanted a Nebraska bill. Should he have abandoned the effort
altogether then? Douglas was now the prisoner of his own report.
With such a weighty invocation he could hardly have turned back.
The repealers could give him the votes, the votes a bill, and the
bill two new territories. Douglas had fought the same fight against
the Wilmot Proviso men in '48, and by '49 California had come
knocking at the door for admission as a free state. Douglas had
flung this in the face of the doctrinaire exclusionists throughout
the debate in '50. He was certain he could do it again.

Did he not in fact do it again? By the spring of 1858 Kansas
seemed as surely on the way to becoming a free state as Iowa

or Minnesota had been. Douglas himself had led the fight to assure that Kansas be free—under the banner of popular sovereignty. Were not the house divided speech and the campaign that followed it as wanton a destruction of the spirit of compromise and of the chances of sectional peace as Chase's and Sumner's *Appeal* had been four years earlier?

Part III

THE POLITICAL
PHILOSOPHY OF
A YOUNG WHIG

Analytical Outline of Lincoln's Address before the Young Men's Lyceum of Springfield, Illinois, January 27, 1838*

A. Introduction
  I. Our Subject (1)
  II. Our Problem: The Achievement of the Fathers; Our Duty to Preserve and Transmit (2)
B. Dangers to Be Forestalled
  I. Introduction: That They Are Internal, Not External (3, 4)
  II. The Dangers and Their Remedies (5–22)
    a. Present Danger: Mob Rule; and Its Remedy
      1. Mob Rule (5–11)
        a′. Its Direct Evils (5–8)
        b′. Its Indirect Evils (9–11)
          1′. From Bad Examples
          2′. From Alienation of Feelings of Best Citizens
      2. Remedy (12–15)
        a′. Political Religion (12, 13)
        b′. Redress of Grievance by Better Laws (14, 15)
    b. Future Dangers to Be Anticipated
      1. Introduction: Why Suppose Future Dangers? (16)
      2. How Future Must Differ from the Past
        a′. With Respect to Leaders of Genius and Ambition (17–19)
        b′. With Respect to the Passions of the People (20–22)
C. Exhortation to Rebuild the Temple of Liberty
  I. The Materials Must Be Hewn from Reason; Passion Now Our Enemy (23)
  II. That the New Temple May Last as Long as "the Only Greater Institution." (24)

*Note: Numbers in parenthesis correspond to the paragraphs of the text as printed in the *Sangamo Journal*, February 3, 1838, and reprinted in *Collected Works*, I, pp. 108–15. The paragraphs are not numbered in the printed text.

Chapter IX

The Teaching Concerning Political
Salvation

WE have said that Lincoln's 1838 speech "On the Perpetuation of Our Political Institutions" showed conscious dedication to preparation for the crisis with which he one day grappled on so vast a scale. This may disturb the image of the folklore Lincoln, the hero who resembles Everyman, fashioned from the clay of the common people, sharing their joys and sorrows, yet able to turn from the concerns of everyday life to discharge, with deeper wisdom, duties heretofore regarded as the province of kings and potentates. This is the Lincoln who is supposed to have written the Gettysburg Address on the back of an envelope as he rode from Washington. Yet a careful reading of the earlier deliverance will show that the ideas crystallized in 1863, in prose not unworthy of the greatest master of our language, had been pondered and matured full twenty-five years before.

Of the myriad writers on Lincoln, Edmund Wilson alone, so far as we are aware, has grasped something of the hidden reservoirs of that "startlingly prophetic" utterance delivered to the Young Men's Lyceum of Springfield. Its most electrifying passage, as Wilson notes, contains a warning against a "towering genius," thirsting and burning for distinction, who would disdain to perpetuate a government which would only be a monument to the fame of others, and might destroy the existing fabric either by "emancipating slaves or enslaving freemen." As Wilson observes, the warning is ambiguous, and this *Ubermensch* is described "with a fire that seemed to derive as much from admiration as from apprehension." The ambiguity, Wilson perceives, stems not only from the mingling of attraction and dread with which Lincoln seems to regard the figure he has conjured, but from his apparent neutrality with respect to the moral quality of acts of emancipation and of enslavement. "It was as if," writes Wilson, "he had not only foreseen the drama but had even seen all around it, with a kind of poetic objectivity, aware of the various points of view that the world must take toward its protagonist."[1] Thus the indictment we have drawn in the first chapter of this work, the indictment of Lincoln as master villain of American history, was conceived long before revisionist historiography; indeed, it was conceived as an abstract possibility long before the events the historians recorded. For when Lincoln in 1838 saw that the emancipation of the slaves might be possible, or might be believed to be possible, only by the overthrow of the government established by the Fathers, he anticipated in principle every profound objection to the role he one day unhesitatingly played. "He had in some sense imagined [the] drama himself—had even prefigured Booth and the aspect he would wear for Booth when the latter would leap down from the Presidential box crying 'Sic semper tyrannis!' "[2] For in the Lyceum speech Lincoln had compared the possible future American Emancipator—who might be the destroyer of the American republic—to Caesar. And thus had he, as Wilson indicates, cast the role of the American Brutus twenty-seven years before it was played by Booth.

The task of interpreting the thought of Lincoln is very different from interpreting that of Douglas. In part this stems from the difference in the situations of the two men: Douglas early became and remained a national figure and was almost continuously occupied with politics on the highest level. From the fact that he was a leading contender for his party's presidential nomination from 1852 on, he was a prisoner of that peculiar difficulty of American politics, "availability." That there was a large consistency to everything he did, we believe and have maintained; but to educe it from the heat of the political battles, in which everything he did and said was struck off, has been like resolving many contrary component forces into a single vector. Lincoln's career, on the contrary, until 1854, was as undistinguished as Douglas's had been brilliant. He became a skilled practitioner of the arts of party politics; he was a ranking Whig in his home state; but his record was that of a party faithful, a wheel horse of the machine, adept in caucuses, "smoke-filled rooms," and on the stump. His most notable achievement was in securing the removal of the state capital from Vandalia to Springfield. His speeches in the state legislature, and in Congress during his one term, contain rhetorical flights—and some robust humor—suggestive of powers capable of greater objects than the advocacy of Whig orthodoxy. Yet it is difficult to imagine this oratory commanding much attention today had the career of its author not taken such a dramatic and unexpected turn.

Or was it unexpected? Here we touch a tantalizing question, one assuredly close to the heart of Lincoln's amazing fascination. Did Lincoln, all the years he was, to put it bluntly, a hack politician, secretly fancy himself in the stupendous drama he had contemplated in the Lyceum speech? Was he serving his apprenticeship in politics with the conscious expectation of one day playing the master craftsman? We cannot answer these questions except by showing, as we propose to do, that all the while Lincoln was engaged in the more or less petty bread-and-butter party questions, during his early years, he also produced occasional pieces, of permanent value, upon "the great and durable question of the age." There are, in particular, two public addresses by Lincoln—the Lyceum speech already mentioned and the Temperance Address delivered on Washington's Birthday, 1842, to the Springfield Washington Temperance Society—in which Lincoln forecasts and diagnoses a political and moral crisis of popular government. In neither of these speeches does he openly present the problem of slavery in the leading position it occupies in the Second Inaugural. Rather does he see the difficulty of free government in the broader context of the eternal problem created by the power of evil passions—of which slavery is but a particular manifestation—over mankind. Because the young Lincoln observed the forms of the occasions upon which he spoke, the highly unconventional content of his thought has been overlooked for its conventional expression. Yet both these pieces are intellectual *tours de force*, and at least one of them, the Temperance Address, is a literary masterpiece and a masterpiece of political satire. The two speeches complement each other. The central topic of both is the same, but the first emphasizes the political side, the second the moral. For Lincoln, the question of the "capability of a people to govern themselves" was always twofold: it referred both to the viability of popular political institutions and to their moral basis in the individual men who must make those institutions work. If the men who exercised the decisive influence in a popular government were not themselves "self-governed"—i.e., self-controlled—then it was vain to expect the institutions to be so. The two speeches describe the leading dangers, as Lincoln saw them, that evil passions might insinuate themselves into the operation of a free government and thereby destroy it.

*   *   *   *   *

To say that Lincoln, as he was mastering the politician's craft and outwardly leading a life hardly distinguishable from countless others, had all the while contemplated and exerted himself to prepare for the greatest role in the greatest crisis he could imagine coming in his lifetime is, as we have said, to disturb somewhat the popular image of Lincoln as the prototype of the common man. And it is no light matter, for anyone deeply affected by Lincoln's Civil War oratory, to trouble this much-loved image. For no one did more than Lincoln himself to promote belief in the uncommon resources of the common man. In so far as Lincoln as President permitted himself to be celebrated, he was ever careful that his own achievement, no less than his office, be considered representative. That Lincoln's "uncommon commonness" was a studied effect—a work of art so successful that all traces of art have vanished from it—may therefore prove somewhat unsettling. In a sense, it throws doubt upon the truth of the assumption upon which Lincoln's advocacy of the people's cause rested: that the "people," without leaders uniquely endowed or specially trained, could furnish out of their midst men for any office or contingency. Lincoln sounded this theme in his very first message to Congress, July 4, 1861, upon the outbreak of hostilities:

This is essentially a people's contest . . . a struggle for maintaining in the world that form and substance of government whose leading object is to elevate the condition of men . . .

And from the outset this meant a government that was not only *for* the people but *by* and *of* them:

It may be affirmed, without extravagance, that the free institutions we enjoy have developed the powers and improved the condition of our whole people, beyond any example in the world . . . there are many single regiments whose members, one and another, possess full practical knowledge of all the arts, sciences, and professions . . . and there is scarcely one from which there could not be selected a President, a Cabinet, a Congress, and perhaps a court, abundantly competent to administer the Government itself!

And again:

Great honor is due to those officers who remained true, despite the example of their treacherous associates; but the greatest honor, and most important fact of all, is the unanimous firmness of the common soldiers and common sailors. To the last man, so far as known, they have successfully resisted the traitorous efforts of those whose commands, but an hour before, they obeyed as absolute law. This is the patriotic instinct of plain people. They understand, without an argument, that the destroying the Government which was made by Washington means no good to them.[8]

Toward the end of the war he addressed an Ohio regiment, saying:

I happen temporarily to occupy this big White House. I am a living witness that any one of your children may look to come here as my father's child has.

But Lincoln's praise of the ability, fidelity, and wisdom of plain people, of common soldiers and sailors, is raised to a higher and different level at Gettysburg. Upon this level it is transformed into a capacity for glory:

The world will little note, nor long remember, what we say here, but it can never forget what they did here.

The acid title of Richard Hofstadter's widely read essay in *The American Political Tradition*, "Abraham Lincoln and the Self-Made Myth," ungraciously expresses an important truth. Simple souls have indeed been harmlessly imposed upon to think that Lincoln really did not expect his words to be recalled. Yet Lincoln knew, as well as Pericles or Churchill, how utterly the immortality of the deed depends upon the immortality of the word. "In the beginning was the Word." Lincoln knew that only as the incantation upon the silent field renewed the sacred fire which had passed from those who had given their last full measure would freedom be born again. It is entirely improbable that Lincoln performed his task with such skill and did not know what he was doing. It is impossible he should have understood the function of his own oratory—whose premise is that, unless its exhortation is obeyed, these dead shall have died in vain— without understanding the even greater renown success would confer upon him. But again this brings us to the question with which we began this work. Was the cause of popular government but the matter from which Lincoln's own fame was to be wrought? Glory was traditionally the prerogative of kings and noblemen, and in war the path of glory was supposedly found. The common people, in their wretched anonymous millions, had perished through the ages for the triumphal processions of these usually unscarred heroes. Did Lincoln, like the "towering genius" of the Lyceum speech, deliberately lead the American people down the path to war because in no other way could he escape the common fate and lot for which his otherwise commonplace career seemed destined?

More, probably, has been written of Lincoln in less than a single century than of any political figure of whom the records survive. Yet in some respects the vast accretion of Lincolniana has shrouded rather than disclosed the figure of the man within. One reason, we suggest, is that few of those who have literally left no stone (or log or rail) unturned in the quest for every day in his life have asked what that life consisted in, from the point of view of their subject. Lincoln himself was singularly uninterested in the facts that have so fascinated posterity. Lord Charnwood recounts that "when he had been nominated for the Presidency he was asked for material for an account of his early life. 'Why,' he said, 'it is great folly to attempt to make anything out of me or my early life. It can all be condensed into a single sentence; and that sentence you will find in Gray's *Elegy*: 'The short and simple annals of the poor.' That's my life, and that's all you or anyone else can make out of it.'" Of course when he said this he was running for office, and Lincoln's identification with the "poor," the "plain people," and the "common" folk was as much a part of his platform as opposition to the spread of slavery. Lincoln was a great actor, and he did not step out of character. Yet the lack of interest he displayed in the story of his own life was not affected. Great acting is also born of conviction, and Lincoln believed in the role he played. The difficulty lies in identifying that role. Lincoln was not uninterested in himself, as is shown by the extreme self-consciousness he sometimes displayed, nor assuredly did he undervalue himself. But Lincoln did not see in commonplace occurrences the record of the life of which he was so conscious.

I was born and have ever remained in the most humble walks of life. I have no wealthy or popular relations to recommend me. My case is thrown exclusively upon the independent voters of this county, and if elected they will have conferred a favor upon me, for which I shall be unremitting in my labors to compensate. But if the good people in their wisdom shall see fit to keep me in the background, I have been too familiar with disappointments to be very much chagrined.[4]

With such statements in mind Professor Hofstadter has well said that "the first author of the Lincoln legend and the greatest of the Lincoln dramatists was Lincoln himself." It is not surprising, then, that so much effort has been made to find in the humble walks of his life and in his acquaintance with grief and disappointment the secrets of Lincoln's strength.

Yet in this same address to the people of Sangamon County, when he first ran for elective office (for the state assembly, for which he was defeated), Lincoln also used these highly revealing words: "Every man is said to have his peculiar ambition. Whether it be true or not, I can say for one that I have no other so great as that of being truly esteemed of my fellow men, by rendering myself worthy of their esteem." Since this statement was made in an election handbill, there can be no question that "being truly esteemed" included receiving their suffrages. And we know that in a democracy a man does not render himself worthy—i.e., does not cause himself to be thus "esteemed"—merely by cultivating virtue, as virtue was traditionally understood.

"That man," wrote Herndon, his law partner for seventeen years in Springfield, "who thinks Lincoln calmly gathered his robes about him, waiting for the people to call him, has a very erroneous knowledge of Lincoln. He was always calculating and planning ahead. His ambition was a little engine that knew no rest." Lincoln was ambitious, and ambition, as he one day wrote to General Hooker, "within reasonable bounds does good rather than harm." But what bounds does reason prescribe? To put the problem in its classic form: Are the things that make a man worthy of the esteem of his fellow men the same as the things that cause him to be esteemed? In a sense the whole case for popular government rests upon the affirmation of the ultimate identity of the two; even as the case against popular government, from Plato's *Apology of Socrates* on down, has rested upon the denial of their compatibility, much less identity. If the things a man must do to achieve office in a democracy, particularly high office, are degrading to him—as is so frequently believed—then it is impossible to believe seriously that the government of such men is elevating. If the "best men" hold in contempt the esteem Lincoln so avidly sought, then government of and by the people cannot long endure. How to reconcile the demands of virtue, of a self-respect conscious of no stooping in its conquest of honor, with the achievement of the honor which flows from popular recognition, *hoc opus, hic labor est.* Woodrow Wilson once remarked that the phenomenon of Lincoln had made it possible to believe in democracy. Wilson was acutely sensitive to the tension between love of fame and love of excellence; he knew that their reconciliation was problematical and that democracy, not as something to be suffered, but as something to be loved, as an embodiment of man's aspiration, required a conviction that a man of the people, chosen by the people, could exemplify moral and intellectual greatness.

Lincoln has been understood—and correctly understood—as the supreme advocate of the cause of popular government. But it is not because he saw no problem, no difficulty, in adopting that advocacy. Noble things are difficult, said Aristotle, and the nobler more difficult. Lincoln saw popular government as most noble and most difficult. His First Inaugural address exhorts "a patient confidence in the ultimate justice of the people." Yet the Second Inaugural tells us that this same people had offended divine justice; and a terrible punishment, willed not by man, was necessary to expiate the offense. The "ultimate justice" of the people depends, therefore, upon a purification which it is not in their own unaided power to accomplish. A case against the people, as well as for them, was present in Lincoln's thought from beginning to end. Because he grappled with this antagonism, Lincoln's thought, for all the pristine clarity with which he expressed himself, is extraordinarily complex. Whether Lincoln grappled successfully in the first great phase of his career, the long duel with

Douglas, it will be our duty to inquire. The answer to the question will, in considerable measure, tell us whether, in Wilson's sense, we are entitled to believe in democracy. Of one thing, however, we may be certain. Lincoln would never have accepted as his own justification the fact that, in the end, he was chosen by the people and Douglas rejected. For the whole struggle with Douglas revolved precisely around the question of the moral demands which must be obeyed by a people if the people themselves are to possess the title deeds to respect and obedience. How conscious Lincoln was of this difficulty, we may now observe by turning to his Lyceum speech of 1838.

*   *   *   *   *

This speech, being a set piece, has its exordium and peroration. It begins by stating its subject, "the perpetuation of our political institutions," and continues celebrating the happy circumstances of the American people, in peaceful possession of the fairest portion of the earth and with a political system "conducing more essentially to the ends of civil and religious liberty, than any of which the history of former times tells us." But, says Lincoln, "We toiled not in the acquirement or establishment of them— they are a legacy bequeathed us, by a *once* hardy, brave, and patriotic, but *now* lamented and departed race of ancestors. Theirs was the task (and nobly they performed it) to possess themselves, and through themselves, us, of this goodly land; and to uprear upon its hills and valleys, a political edifice of liberty and equal rights; 'tis ours only, to transmit these . . . to the latest generation . . ." We are immediately struck by the resemblance to the great speech of a quarter century after, whose opening sentence is an exquisite condensation of the foregoing. Yet the differences are not merely literary. This is not an immature version; its more elaborate presentation will help considerably to throw into relief the majestic austerities of the Gettysburg Address. Let us note for the present this further resemblance: both speeches begin with a pious invocation of the Fathers; they are the Founders who, like Abraham, Isaac, and Jacob, by their merit brought blessings to us, their descendants; and, like Moses, gave the laws which we have the lesser task of maintaining. Yet both speeches, of 1838 and 1863, as they proceed—the one prophesying, the other proclaiming—tell of a crisis and test greater than that of the Fathers, which must be passed if the good allegedly possessed, or brought into the world by them, is truly to be achieved. But still more: the greatness of the test is also a measure of the greatness of the good and of the men who achieved it. The "new birth of freedom" is not a mere renewal of the old; it is also a transcendence of it. We shall see this theme expressed with great subtlety in the 1838 speech, although without the Shakespearean pathos of the words spoken upon the battlefield.

Now Lincoln asks how shall we perform this duty—the duty to transmit the land "unprofaned by the foot of the invader," the institutions "undecayed by the lapse of time and untorn by usurpation"? In good Whig fashion he dismisses all foreign danger. "As a nation of freemen we must live through all time, or die by suicide." Then comes the body of the address, in which are spelled out the principal dangers threatening our polity from within.

This has three main parts. The first deals with the present evils of mob rule, which has been sweeping the country. The second, the future danger of the "towering genius" who will seize the opportunity created by the confusion raised by the mob to erect one-man rule. Third is also a future danger, resulting from the fading public spirit of the Revolution, the release of base passions originally held in check by or turned against a common enemy and for some time subdued by the memory of the Revolution.

The section dealing with mob rule is the lengthiest, although that dealing with the dangerous leader is, conspicuously, the central one. The evils of mob rule, in Lincoln's account, are threefold: the direct evils of unlawful violence; the indirect evil, by which unpunished crimes encourage the "lawless in spirit . . . to become lawless in practice"; and last and worst, the alienation of the feelings of "good men" and the "best citizens" from the government. It is this alienation which sets the stage for the unprincipled leader.

Let us examine Lincoln's account of the "mobocratic spirit, which all must admit, is now abroad in the land." Although he says its depredations are confined to no single part of the country, but "Alike . . . spring up among the pleasure hunting masters of Southern slaves, and the order loving citizens of the land of steady habits," his preface can hardly be said to show sectional impartiality. And all his actual episodes are lynchings in slave states. However, there is more impartiality than strikes the eye. Events in Illinois, we shall see, are in the foreground of Lincoln's attention, and his choosing to discuss home problems by referring to happenings elsewhere is characteristic of his rhetorical technique. "Those happening in the State of Mississippi, and at St. Louis, are, perhaps, the most dangerous in example and revolting to humanity."

> In the Mississippi case, they first commenced by hanging the regular gamblers; a set of men, certainly not following for a livelihood, a very useful, or very honest occupation; but one which, so far from being forbidden by the laws, was actually licensed by an act of the Legislature, passed but a single year before. Next, negroes, suspected of conspiring to raise an insurrection, were caught up and hanged in all parts of the State: then, white men, supposed to be leagued with negroes; and finally, strangers, from neighboring States, going thither on business, were in many instances subjected to the same fate.

Thus, Lincoln exclaims, the process went on, from gamblers to Negroes, to white citizens, to strangers, "till dead men were seen literally dangling from the boughs of trees upon every road side; and in numbers almost sufficient, to rival the native Spanish moss of the country, as a drapery of the forest."

The second "horror-striking scene" concerns a mulatto man in St. Louis whose "story is short; and is perhaps, the most highly tragic, of anything of its length . . ." This man was "seized in the street, dragged to the suburbs . . . chained to a tree, and actually burned to death . . . within a single hour from the time he had been a freeman, attending to his own business, and at peace with the world."

Next Lincoln turns to explain how the indirect consequences are worse than the direct. In so doing he employs one of his curious rhetorical *démarches*, which interrupts the edifying but nonetheless platitudinous moralizing. We would expect him to say, "Bad as these things are, their potential for evil is still greater." Instead, he goes to considerable—nay, almost shocking—length to show that at least in the case of the gamblers and the St. Louis mulatto no great harm had been done at all.

Abstractly considered, the hanging of the gamblers . . . was of but little consequence. They constitute a portion of population, that is worse than useless in any community; and their death, if no pernicious example be set by it, is never matter of reasonable regret with any one. If they were annually swept, from the stage of existence, by the plague or smallpox, honest men would, perhaps, be much profited, by the operation.

And:

Similar too, is the correct reasoning, in regard to the burning of the negro at St. Louis. He had forfeited his life, by the perpetration of an outrageous murder, upon one of the most worthy and respectable citizens of the city; and had he not died as he did, he must have died by sentence of the law, in a very short time. As to him alone, it was as well the way it was, as it could otherwise have been.

We must remark the way in which Lincoln deliberately paints a contrast between a "mulatto" dragged to a flaming death within an hour of the time he had been free, minding his own business and at peace with the world, and a "negro" who had murdered a leading citizen. Surely the portrayal of the former hardly suggests the latter! But is it ever "as well . . . as it could otherwise have been" to burn a man who has not even been convicted of a crime? As to the gamblers, when is it "never matter of reasonable regret" for men to be lynched, particularly, as Lincoln has been at pains to point out (thus also heightening the contrast, as with the peaceful mulatto turned negro-murderer), when they have pursued a vocation sanctioned by law? These strange passages, however, are not nearly so conspicuous in context. For there they are prefaced with the observation that the direct consequences of mob rule "are, comparatively speaking, but a small evil; and much of its dangers consists, in the proneness of our minds, to regard its direct, as its only consequences." Hence the "abstract consideration" concerning the gamblers and the "correct reasoning" concerning the St. Louis lynching are presented as examples of erroneous judgments toward which our minds are said to be prone. Such reasoning, according to Lincoln, may extenuate or even justify mob violence; and he tells us that it is important both to distinguish this reasoning from the blind prejudice of the mob and to realize that it may also mislead us.

Yet Lincoln did not go to the lengths he did to present these cases in such different lights, in successive paragraphs, only to make the simple point above. The entire speech is a defense of the rule of law from all forms of arbitrary rule. The mob is one extreme of arbitrariness, the Caesar-dictator another; and the extreme of one kind of arbitrariness tends to engender the other, as the sequel will tell us. The idea of the rule of law rejects the notion that any individual or any group has sufficient wisdom and virtue to be trusted with the decision of individual cases on their own merits, without regard to general rules established by and through the authority of the whole community. Yet the fact remains, as Lincoln insinuates, that, abstractly considered, the rule of law *is* inferior to discretionary rule, just because each case would be better decided if it could be decided on its own merits. And it is as important to recognize the abstract superiority of discretionary rule as it is to recognize its practical inferiority.

Why so? Because all law aims at abstract justice, with respect to which it is a means. This end, which is translegal, is a perception of the discretionary judgment of wise men; and the law must be informed by such judgment—or be believed to be so informed—if it is to command respect. Men will submit to abuses tolerated by the law if they feel these abuses are tolerated rather than enjoined or abetted by the law. In the fifties Lincoln was again and again to refer to the proposition, "all men are created equal," as an "abstract truth," a truth which was the life principle of American law. The implications of this truth were only partially realized, even for white men, and largely denied as far as black men were concerned. Yet it supplied the direction, the meaning, of all good laws in this country, although the attempt at that time to achieve all that might and ought ultimately to be demanded in its name would have been disastrous. A law is foolish which does not aim at abstract or intrinsic justice; and so is it foolish to attempt to achieve abstract justice as the sole good by succumbing to the fallacy to which the mind is prone, which regards direct consequences as if they were the only consequences. Those who believe anything sanctioned by law is right commit one great error; those who believe the law should sanction only what is right commit another. Either error might result in foolish laws; and, although a foolish law may be preferable to a wise dictator, a wise law is preferable to both.

Lincoln minimized the intrinsic evil of hanging gamblers and burning murderers without due process of law. But there is, by contrast, no attempt, as there was no possibility, of minimizing the evil of the many lynchings caused by the frenzied fear of servile insurrection. The case of the gamblers, it is clear in retrospect, was mentioned chiefly because of its involvement in this more serious episode. The St. Louis affair, moreover, whose intrinsic importance Lincoln downgrades sharply, also was involved in a chain of events. Lincoln does not choose to identify these explicitly, for reasons we must attempt to fathom. Toward the end of paragraph nine, however, he enumerates as follows some of the kinds of mob violence which, if they are not stopped, will certainly lead to the overthrow of our political system:

> . . . whenever the vicious portion of the population shall be permitted to gather in bands of hundreds and thousands, and burn churches, ravage and rob provision-stores, throw printing presses into rivers, shoot editors, and hang and burn obnoxious persons at pleasure, and with impunity; depend upon it, this Government cannot last.

At this point there is, in the new (1954) collected edition of Lincoln's works, the following annotation:

> Dwelling as he does on the horrors of lynch law in Mississippi and Missouri, Lincoln may seem remiss in ignoring, save for this phrase, the lynching at Alton, Illinois, on November 7, 1837, of the abolitionist editor Elijah Parish Lovejoy. It is somewhat too obvious and naïve to assume that Lincoln was being politic in avoiding reference to an episode so recent and so vivid in the recollection of his audience. Rather it seems possible that he chose a subtler way of pricking the conscience of his audience than by direct denunciation. Members of the Lyceum who listened to Lincoln without sensing the specter of Lovejoy in their midst must have been obtuse indeed.[5]

It is somewhat incongruous that Mr. Basler, Lincoln's editor, thinks it naïve to assume a politician is being politic. In fact, however, the subtlety which he correctly imputes to Lincoln exemplifies that very quality. It should be known that the Lovejoy killing, some eleven weeks before the Lyceum speech, was the most famous abolitionist martyrdom until John Brown. And

Alton (to be the scene of the last joint debate) was a town in southern Illinois, some fifty or sixty miles from Springfield, on the east bank of the Mississippi, near St. Louis. It was a wealthy and growing community, the commercial rival of St. Louis for the trade of the Deep South. Alton's traders were mostly New Englanders, and their attitudes were much like those of the cotton Whigs of Boston: they had no use for either slavery or abolition. Lovejoy, a Presbyterian minister turned anti-slavery (and also anti-Catholic) crusader, had been operating in St. Louis for some time. In his paper he had castigated both the crowd which had lynched McIntosh and the judge who had charged the grand jury not to return indictments for the lynching if, as he pointed out for their convenience, they found that "the deed was done by 'congregated thousands' whose names could not be ascertained."[6] It was Lovejoy's activity in the McIntosh business which led the mob to throw his press into the river for the first time (there were three more times to come) and caused him to move across the Mississippi to Alton. There his activities led to renewed mob violence, and he was finally shot down as, gun in hand, he and a band of armed supporters sought to defend his newly arrived fourth press in the warehouse in which it had just been stored.

It should be realized that the economic well-being of Alton, in competition with St. Louis, depended upon the favor of New Orleans customers. And Illinois, during the previous year, had been bombarded (in common with other northern states) with petitions and memorials from slave-state legislatures to take action against abolitionism. The legislature had responded, in January 1837—a year before the Lyceum speech—with resolutions denouncing abolitionism, although not recommending any further action against it. Six weeks after these resolutions, a protest against them was spread upon the journal of the House, signed by Dan Stone and A. Lincoln, representatives of Sangamon County, which declared that "the institution of slavery is founded on both injustice and bad policy, but that the promulgation of abolition doctrines tends rather to increase than abate its evils . . ." The protest is mild enough. Where the resolutions had said that Congress "cannot abolish slavery in the District of Columbia, against the consent of the citizens of said District without a manifest breach of good faith," Lincoln and Stone insisted that Congress had the power but ought not to exercise it "unless at the request of the people of said District." The crucial difference, without question, was the insistence that slavery itself was unjust. Even here there is more of a shift of emphasis than a break with the majority. For the joint select committee which had reported the resolutions, even while denouncing abolitionism in unmeasured terms, had deeply deplored "the unfortunate condition of our fellow-men, whose lots are cast in thraldom in a land of liberty and peace."[7]

But why the delay of six weeks? Beveridge at least does not hesitate to suggest that Lincoln was being "politic." "If Lincoln and Stone held the opinions expressed in their protest . . . they were not without reasons of practical politics for their delay. They were intent upon securing the permanent location of the state capital at Springfield. Nothing must interfere with that supreme purpose, no member be offended unnecessarily, no risk hazarded of losing a single vote without urgent cause. Not until that matter had been settled did they submit their views on the slavery question."[8] It is not necessary to add, as Beveridge does, that "Lincoln subordinated everything to Springfield's interest," to see that he was not a man to squander political credit. The problem of political rhetoric is treated more explicitly in the Temperance Address; yet Lincoln's protest with Stone against the anti-abolition resolutions of the Illinois legislature and his handling of the same question in the Lyceum Address already exemplify his lifelong conception of political leadership. That conception calls for mollifying, never antagonizing, the feelings of those whom he would lead. So to do was for Lincoln more than an act of prudence, it partook of a moral imperative: for if the cause of free government was noble, then a necessary condition of leadership in such a government could not be ignoble. But this, in turn, would have been absurd if deference to popular feelings were indiscriminate: Lincoln's attack upon the mob, and the passions the mob represented, shows that this is not his drift. But Lincoln believed, and always found, in popular demands an aspiration for justice, an aspiration for what was noble. Even the mob that killed Lovejoy might have felt it was defending the Constitution—or the rights of Catholics, whom Lovejoy vilely slandered. The task of a leader is to find the point of coincidence between the moral demands which are dear to the men he would lead and their self-interests, and to turn this, not only against the unjust self-interests of others, but against the unjust self-interests of his own followers. The popular leader must be prepared to gratify the less-than-noble but not immoral demands of his would-be supporters if he is to have their support for the higher purposes of statesmanship. To hold these meaner services in contempt is to abandon popular government to those who have only mean ends, and to make of popular government a mean thing. Men may be led toward higher purposes of which they are scarcely conscious, if those who hold these purposes first show concern for and an ability to gratify their less noble demands.

There can be no doubt that the mob violence Lincoln had in mind when he composed the Lyceum speech, the violence which supplies the subject matter for nearly two thirds of that speech, was exclusively violence arising from abolitionism and the reaction to it. Or, to be more just, we should say that it was violence arising from the renewed life and vigor of the institution of chattel slavery, which was caused by the cotton gin. This economic renewal of slavery falsified all the Fathers' expectations concerning the institution. Without this renewal there would have been neither northern abolitionism nor the southern reaction to abolitionism. Yet Lincoln keeps this crucial cause of mob violence out of sight, choosing not to make pro- and anti-slavery passions his theme. The prudential reasons for this are easy to see: abolitionism was probably not appreciably more popular in Springfield than in Alton; if he had attacked the Alton mobs for their attack on Lovejoy, he would have accomplished nothing but his own political ruin. But if Lincoln could not afford to be identified with Lovejoy's cause, neither did he have any wish to advance it, since Lovejoy's cause was in certain respects the same as the mob's. For abolitionism was precisely one of those things that, with an eye fixed on "abstract" justice alone, and careless of consequences, would also have overthrown the Constitution.

The theme of abolitionism is dealt with explicitly only once in the address. It occurs at the end of the section on mob rule, as the second part of the discussion of the remedy for mob rule. The principal remedy is "political religion," which shall be treated at length later; but redress of grievances through change of laws is a supplement to the aforesaid religion. Lincoln's sole example of grievances is "the promulgation of abolitionism." In any such case, he says:

one of two positions is necessarily true; that is, the thing is right within itself, and therefore deserves the protection of all law and all good citizens; or, it is wrong, and therefore proper to be prohibited by legal enactments; and in neither case, is the interposition of mob law, either necessary, justifiable, or excusable.

It is remarkable that Lincoln apparently considers positive action based upon the intrinsic rightness or wrongness of the doctrine as exhaustive alternatives, saying nothing of the right of speech to be protected irrespective of its quality. This could hardly have been an oversight, since freedom of speech was ground on which the abolitionists stridently took their stand. One reason, we suggest, is that Lincoln had publicly gone on record that slavery was unjust; and it followed that abolition of slavery was, "within itself," therefore just. That Lincoln believed the abolitionists deserved the protection of law is, in one sense, the burden of the entire speech; but it is a message which Lincoln believes can better be conveyed if mob law is attacked as wrong rather than abolition defended. For abolitionism, although right "within itself," is not unqualifiedly right. Abolitionism, as we have suggested, wished to overthrow slavery, not by means sanctioned by the Constitution, but by means outside the Constitution. Abolitionists did not claim freedom of speech in order to persuade men lawfully to rid themselves of slavery. The lawful undermining of slavery, which had seen six of the original thirteen states abolish it in the fifty years after independence, and active agitation against slavery continue to win public favor in many southern states, had been arrested and reversed. The abolitionism of the Garrison and Lovejoy variety which did much to reverse this trend was directed exclusively toward opinion in the free states, toward convincing those who had no constitutional power over slavery where it existed. Although abolitionists sometimes denied the illegality of their aims, they were as unconvincing as the Communists in our day who have said they intend nothing but victory at the polls. As we have already observed, many denounced the Constitution and Union openly. For the rest it made absolutely no sense to seek converts to their cause in New York, Massachusetts, or Illinois, unless the power of the free states was to be eventually exerted against slavery in the slave states. Abolition aimed to create an opinion which would sanction the use of federal power by national majorities to interfere with slavery; and the fear that the government itself would become an agency of unlawful violence was at the root of much of the passion directed against abolitionists. Lincoln's position was that slavery, like gambling, might be wrong in itself and yet be sanctioned by law. But to take the short, illegal way with slavery or gambling is also wrong, just as it was wrong to take the short, illegal way with abolitionists. The abolitionists, taking their unpopular stand under the claim of a right to freedom of speech, had constitutional sanction (generally speaking, for the Fourteenth Amendment had not yet brought the First Amendment to bear upon the states) for their means, although none for their ends. The anti-abolitionist mobs, on the other hand, had good constitutional ground for their opposition to abolitionism but none for their violent methods. Both abolitionism and anti-abolitionism undermined respect for the law, and Lincoln attacked both at the point common to both, in their tendency to lawlessness.

But what of Lincoln's silence on the right of free speech? That abolition was abstractly right, and therefore deserved legal protection, does not explain Lincoln's apparent readiness to place under legislative ban any doctrine wrong "within itself." Here, however, there is no equivocation or reserve: Lincoln never apparently gave the slightest credence to the doctrine widespread in our time, that there is any indefeasible right to promulgate freely doctrines "wrong within themselves." Lincoln thought, as he said during the Civil War, that a government "thoroughly imbued with a reverence for the guaranteed rights of individuals" is slow to move against abuses of personal liberty. But there are circumstances in which such a government may be endangered by such abuses and the attempt at indiscriminate protection of all so-called personal liberties would be a vain folly. For not only may the government whose existence alone protects all rights be endangered by some of them, but the abuse of some rights by some people may lead to the invasion of other rights of other people. It is not always possible simultaneously to protect all rights, and then a choice must be made between those of greater and those of lesser importance. "Must I shoot a simple-minded soldier boy who deserts," asked Lincoln, in that memorable wartime pronouncement, "while I must not touch a hair of a wily agitator who induces him to desert? This is nonetheless injurious when effected by getting a father, or brother, or friend into a public meeting, and there working upon his feelings till he is persuaded to write the soldier boy that he is fighting in a bad cause, for a wicked administration of a contemptible government, too weak to arrest and punish him if he shall desert. I think that, in such a case, to silence the agitator and save the boy is not only constitutional but withal a great mercy."[9] Freedom of speech is very precious, but so are justice and mercy, and there are times when the latter take precedence of the former. Can it be doubted that if the spread of the doctrine of the "positive good" of chattel slavery could have been arrested by legal enactment (we do not say that it could have), its suppression would have been just and merciful? It was Lincoln's belief that the spread of the opinion that slavery was morally right—as distinct from expedient—was the sufficient cause of all the differences which, in 1860, were beyond compromise. Without it there would have been no war. As a rule, Lincoln was inclined to regard the indirect evils of suppressing speech as outweighing any direct good. But what he said in 1838 about the propriety of suppressing doctrines wrong in themselves is fully consistent with what he said at Cooper Union in 1860. When he then pointed out to the South that the Republican party had no abolitionist aims, never had had them, and had always disavowed them, he asked:

> These natural, and apparently adequate means all failing, what will convince them? This, and this only: cease to call slavery wrong, and join them in calling it *right* . . . Senator Douglas's new sedition law must be enacted and enforced, suppressing all declarations that slavery is wrong . . .
> Nor can we justifiably withhold this, on any ground save our conviction that slavery is wrong. If slavery is right, all words, acts, laws, and constitutions against it, are themselves wrong, and should be silenced, and swept away.[10]

If slavery is right, all words against it are wrong *and should be silenced*. But if slavery is not right, all words advocating it are wrong. In a free society, in which the opinions formed by speech are the basis of all government, it is idle to forbid changes in the government while permitting changes in the opinion upon which the government rests. The Constitution guarantees to each state a republican form of government. Such guarantee—like the guarantee that the representation of each state in the Senate shall not be reduced without its own consent—implies a perpetuity in certain fundamentals of the Constitution, beyond the reach of all majorities, even in three fourths of the states. For Lincoln the primary task of political leadership was to maintain and strengthen the opinion upon which these fundamentals rested. There was no question that the advocacy of the opinions favorable to freedom was the only durably effective means of combating opinions hostile to freedom. This is what Lincoln believed he was doing throughout his long struggle with Douglas. And Lincoln himself never advocated sedition laws—even in the Cooper Union speech. All he did was to concede the justice of Douglas's demand for such a law, *if slavery was right*. Freedom of speech, to Lincoln, was logically a subordinate right, subordinate to the right of personal freedom, of which it was an implication. A man cannot be a slave and have freedom of speech; and if the right to personal freedom is in question, there is no point in defending freedom of speech. Since Lincoln denied there was any difference in principle between the enslavement of white men and Negroes, and since the challenge of slavery extension involved the whole question of the right to personal freedom, he thought the issue must be joined on the paramount ground of the rightness or wrongness of slavery. Thus it was that he regarded Douglas's demand for a cessation of the discussion of the slavery question as wholly absurd. It was the only thing worth discussing. And upon the decision of this question hinged the fate of all liberties that men can enjoy only if they are legally free. However inexpedient it may be to suppress the speech of those who advocate slavery, it would have been absurd to Lincoln to speak of an indefeasible right to advocate slavery. Certainly men threatened with enslavement by the spread of pro-slavery opinion—and Lincoln believed the long-range threat to free white labor was nothing less than their reduction to the condition of Negro slaves —have a moral right to any means that will destroy this threat.

We have seen why, from the viewpoint both of prudence and abstract principle, it would have defeated Lincoln's purpose either to attack or defend abolitionism. But Lincoln had still another and more profound reason in the Lyceum speech to keep the slavery controversy for the most part out of sight. For Lincoln meant to present an analysis of the problem of popular government in the light of the eternal antagonism within the human soul of reason and passion. For this purpose it was necessary not to permit the supposition that any immediate cause of conflict, however grave, was the sole or sufficient cause of a threat to the perpetuation of our political institutions.

Of the indirect consequences of mob rule the worst, according to Lincoln, is that which breaks down the attachment of the people to their government. Of particular danger is the alienation of "the feelings of the best citizens," leaving it "without friends, or with too few, and those few too weak." "At such a time and under such circumstances, men of sufficient talent and ambition will not be found wanting to seize the opportunity, strike the blow, and overturn that fair fabric, which for the last half century, has been the fondest hope, of the lovers of freedom, throughout the world." The *coup d'état* Lincoln appears to visualize is suggestive of what our century knows as Fascism; i.e., a political movement combining the bread and circuses of Caesarism with the demand for security by the middle classes, the "good men" described by Lincoln who "love tranquillity" and cannot abide the turmoil and constant danger to the security of their persons, families, and property that an undisciplined populace, intoxicated by power, may threaten. A Whiggish protest against Jacksonian democracy may be sensed in this part of Lincoln's speech, as well as the spirit of the *Federalist*, the spirit of protest against the turbulence of Shays's rebellion, and the excesses of "democracy" that culminated in the Constitutional Convention of 1787. Yet Lincoln's analysis of the Caesarian danger, although it does not contradict the thesis of the *Federalist*, goes beyond it. Lincoln sees a danger which Hamilton and Madison did not take into account and for which constitution building, however excellent, is insufficient. The following from #51 would seem representative of the doctrine of the celebrated papers: "Ambition must be made to counteract ambition. The interest of the man must be connected with the constitutional rights of the place . . . the private interest of every individual [must] be a sentinel over the public rights." It is Lincoln's teaching, however, that there are certain ambitions which cannot be counteracted by ambition, that there are circumstances, far from remote in their probability, in which there would be such a division of private interests as practically to nullify these interests as sentinels over public rights. Such dangers, according to Lincoln, can only be confronted by a mighty resolve which has no private motive. There must be a people capable, in the last resort, of sacrificing every conscious private interest and leaders capable of sacrificing every conscious ambition.

Lincoln would grant that it is foolish to rely upon men's virtue
when it is possible to prompt them by self-interest. But he would
say that it is worse than foolish to think that self-interest can be
the ultimate reliance of republican freedom. For men claiming
republican freedom—the right to self-government, a right whose
very name is a synonym for virtue—cannot doubt that they must
vindicate their claim by their virtue, when the supreme test
comes.

Lincoln's prophetic account of the coming crisis begins with a
question. Why should we, after fifty years, suppose any danger
different from those already faced and overcome? The answer is
that "There are now, and will hereafter be, many causes, dangerous in their tendency, which have not existed heretofore . . ."

> That our government should have been maintained in its
> original form from its establishment until now, is not much
> to be wondered at. It had many props to support it through
> that period, which now are decayed, and crumbled away.
> Through that period, it was felt by all, to be an undecided
> experiment; now, it is understood to be a successful one.—
> Then, all that sought celebrity and fame, and distinction,
> expected to find them in the success of that experiment.
> Their *all* was staked upon it:—their destiny was *inseparably*
> linked with it. Their ambition aspired to display before an
> admiring world, a practical demonstration of the truth of a
> proposition, which had hitherto been considered, at best no
> better, than problematical; namely, *the capability of a people
> to govern themselves.* If they succeeded, they were to be
> immortalized; their names were to be transferred to counties
> and cities, and rivers and mountains; and to be revered and
> sung, and toasted through all time. If they failed, they were
> to be called knaves and fools, and fanatics for a fleeting
> hour; then to be sunk and forgotten. They succeeded. The
> experiment is successful; and thousands have won their
> deathless names in making it so.

It may be observed that the argument concerning the *maintenance* of the government applies with equal force to its *establishment,* although this is not said explicitly at this point. What
ambition is here said to aspire to applies to the entire work of
the generation of the Founding Fathers and most especially to
the Fathers themselves. And now we are confronted with another

of those rhetorical reversals which, like the earlier justification of lynchings by "abstract" and "correct" reasoning, although it barely ripples the flow of conventional sentiments upon the surface, shows a startling detachment not far below. And in this case our shock may prove a good deal more severe. For there appears to be a systematic process of detraction of the Fathers that borders upon the savage. Their heroic deeds, deeds whose heroism no one celebrated more resoundingly than Lincoln himself, we are here told, are "not much to be wondered at." Their work was not nearly so difficult as it has been supposed, because it had "many props to support it" then. A little later on Lincoln elaborates this theme as follows:

By this ("the powerful influence which the interesting scenes of the revolution had upon the *passions* of the people as distinguished from their judgment") the jealousy, envy, and avarice, incident to our nature . . . were, for the time, in a great measure smothered and rendered inactive; while the deep-rooted principles of *hate*, and the powerful motive of *revenge*, instead of being turned against each other, were directed exclusively against the British nation. And thus, from the force of circumstances, the basest principles of our nature were either made to lie dormant, or to become the active agents in the advancement of the noblest cause—that of establishing and maintaining civil and religious liberty.

That the Fathers were in a position to employ and did employ "the basest principles of our nature" for the "noblest cause," while it may detract somewhat from the magnitude of their accomplishment and is a reflection upon the people they led, is no moral reflection upon them. But such reflections are not long to be suppressed. Lincoln echoes Hamilton, in the seventy-second *Federalist*, who spoke of "love of fame, the ruling passion [the precise expression used later by Lincoln] of the noblest minds." However, Lincoln questions the nobility of those who have fame as a ruling passion, because the beneficence of passion, as such, cannot be taken for granted. We shall see Lincoln develop the thesis that love of fame is, in itself, morally neutral, that it was once the friend of the "noblest cause" purely because of circumstances, and that, equally because of circumstances, it is now the enemy of that same cause. The fame of individuals (as distinct from that of nations), which is here considered, is essentially a private good,

conceived as being enjoyed by those whose names are immortal-
ized. This private good was, as noted, not only compatible with
the public good in the lifetime of the Fathers but absolutely
required it *then*. But whether the Fathers sought the good for
the sake of fame, or fame for the sake of the good, we cannot
say. Hence we cannot say that they were virtuous men. Yet this
is not all. Lincoln said at the beginning of the speech that the
Fathers were "hardy, brave, and patriotic," that they performed
their task "nobly." But one does not think of noble deeds as being
undertaken solely or mainly for the doers' own benefit. Yet here
he attributes to them no motive other than "celebrity, fame, and
distinction." This was to be gained by "success," upon which their
"*all*" was staked and with which their destiny was "*inseparably*"
linked (Lincoln's italics). According to this eschatology, success
gains the heaven of praise and immortality and failure the hell
of execration and oblivion. Let us compare this notion of reward
and punishment with the ending of the Sub-Treasury speech,
December 26, 1839: Thinking of what might give his soul a
dignity "not wholly unworthy of its Almighty Architect," Lincoln
pictures himself defending his country's cause alone. He there-
upon swears, "Without contemplating consequences . . . eternal
fidelity to the just cause. Let none falter," he continues in accents
that were to resound in 1858 and 1860, "who thinks he is right,
and we may succeed. But," he concludes, "if after all, we shall
fail, be it so.—We still shall have the proud consolation of saying
to our consciences, and to the departed shade of our country's
freedom, that the cause approved of our judgment, and adored
of our hearts . . . we never faltered in defending." In the 1839
speech Lincoln says that the choice of a cause—of ends as distinct
from means—is made by a soul worthy of its eternal artificer,
without regard to consequences; i.e., without regard to the
chances of success or failure. In the eternity from which the soul
emanates, success or failure has nothing to do with reputation
in this world. For such a soul there is a different seat of judgment
than that of the highly unstable source of reputations which allots
political fame. In the 1838 speech he contrasts the passions of
the people with their judgment; he shows that the passions of
people and leaders supported the popular cause, but he does
not say that the judgment of the leaders, any more than that of
the people, supported that cause. This contrast does not suggest
any intimation in the 1838 speech that the leaders of the Revolu-

tion had that dignity which in 1839 he claims for himself, of having first submitted his cause to the judgment seat of conscience, of an unseen but all-seeing judge, without whose approval all other approval is valueless and in the light of whose approval all condemnation is but vindication. Finally, in the 1839 speech Lincoln says that the just cause must be adored in the heart. Here alone is a passion which is good in itself because it is, by definition, a passion caused by what is good in itself; it is a passion which expresses itself not in self-reflecting contemplation but in the self-abnegation of adoration. It is the soul's link, as the invocation of the 1839 peroration shows, not with the spurious immortality of human opinions, but with eternity. Such a passion, while it compels men to hold political fame in contempt, alone makes them worthy of the greatest fame. Of such judgment, passion, and dignity in the Fathers, Lincoln gives no hint in the Lyceum speech. While he positively asserts nothing incompatible with such higher dignity, he more than suggests that we ought not to give them the benefit of doubt. For does he not say, almost in the same breath, that while they aspired to be admired by the world—i.e., *wondered at*—their success *is not much to be wondered at?*

There is still further irony in the fact that Lincoln attributes the demonstration of the proposition that the people are capable of governing themselves not to the people but to those relatively small numbers who aspire to fame. It is true that Lincoln here speaks of "thousands" winning "deathless names," which would probably include all the local heroes in the far-flung regions in which the Revolutionary struggles took place. Yet as the passage continues Lincoln reveals that his true subject is not the glory shared by thousands—for, as Hobbes says, "glory is like honor, if all men have it, no man hath it"—but the distinction which brooks no equality, no rivalry. As we shall see, Lincoln was quite convinced that the decisive factor in the great political equations is "towering genius" of the caliber of Washington and Jefferson or of Caesar and Napoleon. It is they, above all, who demonstrate the capacity—or incapacity—of "the people" to govern themselves. Yet Lincoln here tells us that the people led by Washington co-operated with him in very large measure because of "the basest principles of our nature," while Washington himself may have been animated primarily by the hope of a personal gain, a gain which he neither shared with anyone else nor which could be regarded as a result of the processes of popular government. Thus he may have had little love for or interest in popular government, except as it was incidentally necessary to his own fame. In short, Lincoln tells us there is no real reason to suppose that "our fathers," whether as leaders or followers, were sincerely devoted to the cause they have bequeathed to us! If the true test of self-government is a test of the ability of reason to control passion, a test of the fidelity of a people and their chosen leaders to the rights entrusted to them by the nature of popular government, then there is no reason to believe that such a test has yet occurred. The capability of a people to govern itself has not yet been demonstrated!

How are we to interpret these amazing and dramatic reversals of what have always seemed to be Lincoln's deepest convictions, as well as the explicit theses of this very speech? Provisionally we would make these suggestions. First, the reversals occur only upon analysis, and the surface of the speech does not disturb the conventional picture of the heroic character of the Revolution. Second, throughout these central passages, which we have not yet followed to their end, Lincoln warns against the danger *now* of overweening ambition, of the ambition of the man who cannot bear to share a place in glory's sun, who would build if he can but tear down if he must. But before Lincoln's warning is made fully explicit, he gives a demonstration more convincing than any mere exhortation to beware of the ambitious man. He enacts the role of such a man before our eyes, showing how the board of honor might be swept clean by one whose talent and audacity might crop the honors on the crest even of a Washington to make a garland for his own head. Yet does Lincoln not, at the same time, indicate still more how vain is mere political reputation? Does he not show (*Honi soit qui mal y pense*) that malicious speculation upon the motives of men can sully the fame of the clearest judgments and the most disinterested hearts, that the extrinsic good of fame is only the lure or bait that wise men use to lead great souls in their formative years to taste the good that is intrinsically rewarding and which supersedes and displaces the appetite for fame? In the long run, we may even conclude, those who have chosen the intrinsically just cause, the cause approved of their judgment and adored in their hearts, will be recognized and hailed by those other men, of whatever time or place, who succeed them in the pilgrimage to the temple of liberty. It is the contemplation of such approbation which alone can truly gratify the highest human type.

The passage of the Lyceum speech describing the "success" of the experiment of self-government continues thus:

But the game is caught; and I believe it is true, that with the catching, end the pleasures of the chase. This field of glory is harvested, and the crop is already appropriated. But new reapers will arise, and *they*, too, will seek a field. It is to deny, what the history of the world tells us is true, to suppose that men of ambition and talents will not continue to spring up amongst us. And, when they do, they will as naturally seek the gratification of their ruling passion, as others have so done before them. The question then is, can that gratification be found in supporting and maintaining an edifice that has been erected by others? Most certainly it cannot. Many great and good men sufficiently qualified for any task they undertake, may ever be found, whose ambition would aspire to nothing beyond a seat in Congress, a gubernatorial or a presidential chair; *but such belong not to the family of the lion, or the tribe of the eagle*. What! think you these places would satisfy an Alexander, a Caesar, or a Napoleon?—Never! Towering genius disdains a beaten path. It seeks regions hitherto unexplored.—It sees *no distinction* in adding story to story, upon the monuments of fame, erected to the memory of others. It *denies* that it is glory enough to serve under any chief. It scorns to tread in the footsteps of *any* predecessor, however illustrious. It thirsts and burns for distinction; and, if possible, it will have it, whether at the expense of emancipating slaves, or enslaving freemen. Is it unreasonable then to expect, that some man possessed of the loftiest genius, coupled with ambition sufficient to push it to its utmost stretch, will at some time, spring up among us? And when such a one does, it will require the people to be united with each other, attached to the government and laws, and generally intelligent, to successfully frustrate his designs.

Distinction will be his paramount object, and although he would as willingly, perhaps more so, acquire it by doing good as harm; yet, that opportunity being past, and nothing left

to be done in the way of building up, he would set boldly
to the task of pulling down.

Here then, is a probable case, highly dangerous, and such
a one as could not have well existed heretofore.

At the point at which Lincoln prepares his question, as to whether
the men of heroic mold can find gratification within the framework
of institutions erected by others, Edmund Wilson, in the essay
referred to above, interjects the following comment: "You may
think that the young Lincoln is about to exhort his auditors to
follow the example of their fathers, not to rest on the performance
of the past but to go on to new labors of patriotism, but the
speech takes an unexpected turn . . . He has been, it seems,
preparing to deliver a warning."[11] The speech does take an
unexpected turn, but the warning is its least unexpected and
certainly its least unorthodox aspect. For in these sentences we
find the future author of the Gettysburg Address denying, in a
wholly relevant sense, that all men are created equal!

Let us first be clear as to the meaning of the famous proposition.
Although it has given rise to countless differing interpretations,
yet does it not indisputably mean that the government of man
by man, unlike the government of beasts by man, is not founded
in any natural difference between rulers and ruled? Any man
is by nature the ruler (actual or potential) of any dog, for example.
As Jefferson was fond of saying, and Lincoln sometimes echoed,
some men are not born with saddles on their backs to be ridden
and others with spurs to ride them. The government of man over
other species is rooted in a natural difference, but political
government cannot be traced to any such difference. The government of men may be based upon force or fraud, in which case it
is illegitimate, or it may be based upon consent. Such is assuredly
the irreducible meaning of the Declaration of Independence, and
no one has ever been more sensitive to it or to all the changes
that could be rung upon it than Lincoln. Yet Lincoln here tells
us that there are men whose genius for and will to domination
virtually makes them a species apart. They belong to "the family
of the lion and the tribe of the eagle." Even as it is natural and
rational for men who are equal to seek in consent the basis of
political rule, so is it natural (and rational) for men who are
surpassingly superior to seek in the unfettered acknowledgment
of their superiority the basis of such rule. Such men, therefore,

are the born enemies of any political institutions which they are not by law destined to rule, but most especially are they the enemies of republics, as is implied in the examples Lincoln gives of the world's most famous destroyers of republics. Lincoln does not even entertain the possibility of taming or accommodating such natures, or "rehabilitating" them, in the modern parlance. What he says is far more suggestive of ancient than modern thinking. For example, there is the following passage from Plato's dialogue *Gorgias*, spoken by a character named Callicles, who is a follower of the teacher of oratory for whom the dialogue is named and who holds the view Lincoln appears to attribute to the Caesar-type:

> . . . the makers of laws are the majority, who are weak; and they make laws and distribute praises and censures with a view to themselves and to their own interests; and they terrify the stronger sort of men, and those who are able to get the better of them, in order that they may not get the better of them; and they say, that dishonesty is shameful and unjust; meaning, by the word injustice, the desire of a man to have more than his neighbors; for knowing their own inferiority, I suspect they are too glad of equality . . . whereas nature herself intimates that it is just for the better to have more than the worse, the more powerful than the weaker . . . Nay but these are the men [i.e., tyrants and conquerors] who act according to nature; yes, by Zeus, and according to the law of nature: not, perhaps, according to that artificial law, which we invent and impose upon our fellows, of whom we take the best and strongest from their youth upwards, and tame them like young lions,—charming them with the sound of the voice, and saying to them, that with equality they must be content, and that the equal is honorable and just. But if there were a man with sufficient force, he would shake and break through, and escape from all this; he would trample under foot all our formulas and spells and charms, and all our laws which are against nature: the slave would rise in rebellion and be lord over us, and the light of natural justice would shine forth.[12]

According to Callicles, a government founded upon a doctrine of equal human rights is a lie, a myth imposed upon the stronger by the weaker, in order to deprive them of the just share to which they would be entitled by their strength. Callicles also, like Lincoln, distinguishes between the stronger natures who may be satisfied by the conventional honors bestowed by the weaker, on the basis of their morality of weakness, who might be "charmed" with a presidential chair, and those true "lions," the *Ubermenschen,* whose strength includes the intellectual penetration of the spurious quality of such pleasures and the consequent refusal to accept them. Such men will not accept the highest honor in the gift of a society of equals because they cannot—indeed honestly cannot—acknowledge a right in their inferiors to grant as a gift what they have a leonine right to claim as their own. To speak of these men as immoral is a mistake, for they do not recognize any obligation to what is commonly called morality. All such obligations are predicated upon an equality whose truth they deny. If their superiority is real, as Lincoln no less than Callicles appears to affirm, then morality must in fact consist in whatever vindicates their superiority. The Declaration of Independence affirms the natural equality of men and conceives political obligation in the light of that equality. But by equal reason obligation must correspond to inequality if men are as naturally unequal as they are here asserted to be. Now we are confronted with the most acute problem of the Lyceum Address: Did Lincoln seriously believe in the existence of men so superior that their submission to "equal" men was a violation of natural right? Is there not a strong presumption in favor of an affirmative answer to this question in the fact that Lincoln does not, in his warning against this alleged type, propose any alternative gratification for that ruling passion which he foresees engendered by Caesarian natures? He says that the true Caesarian, who will assuredly arise, "would as willingly, perhaps more so," do good as evil. But Lincoln does not, as we might expect, propose any good for him to do. If, in fact, no good exists which is both adequate to the fulfillment of his nature and consistent with republican freedom, then it would follow that republican freedom cannot long endure. It cannot because it is in a decisive sense against nature, because it is in a decisive sense unjust. We must then inquire, above all, whether Lincoln does not show us, in the perpetuation of a republic based upon equal rights, a task equal to or surpassing in glory what future Caesars might find in the ruins of a republic.

We have previously noted Edmund Wilson's observation that

Lincoln described his heroic destroyer "with a fire that seemed to derive as much from admiration as apprehension." May this not be due in part to the fact that the vision of a man who, by force of his own qualities, seizes what is rightfully his own is always admirable? Is this additional evidence that Lincoln really accepted the truth of the proposition that some men are by nature the rulers of others? Before attempting an answer we would produce another ancient parallel to this passage in the Lyceum speech from Aristotle's *Politics*:

> If . . . there be some one person, or more than one, although not enough to make up the full complement of a state, whose virtue is so pre-eminent that the virtues or political capacity of all the rest admit of no comparison with his or theirs, he or they can be no longer regarded as part of a state; for justice will not be done to the superior, if he is reckoned only as the equal of those who are so far inferior to him in virtue and in political capacity. Such a one may truly be deemed a god among men. Hence we see that legislation is necessarily concerned only with those who are equal in birth and capacity; and that for men of pre-eminent virtue there is no law—they are themselves a law. Anyone would be ridiculous who attempted to make laws for them: they would probably retort what, in the fable of Antisthenes, the lions said to the hares, when in the council of the beasts the latter began haranguing and claiming equality for all ('Where are your claws and teeth?!'). And for this reason democratic states have instituted ostracism; equality is above all things their aim, and therefore they ostracised and banished from the city for a time those who seemed to predominate too much . . .[13]

In his comment on Lincoln's ambiguous attitude toward his dangerous hero Wilson also says "it is evident that Lincoln has projected himself into the role against which he is warning . . ." We believe this is true, in the sense that Lincoln envisioned himself playing the highest political role. But we do not believe he envisioned himself as the destroyer, except in so far as every true strategist imagines himself in the position of his enemy. The warning against Caesar is sincere, and its sincerity is rooted in Lincoln's conception, in the same sense as Aristotle's, of a political role transcending that of Caesar and opposed to Caesar. The guarantee of his sincerity is his conviction that the man who can play such a role possesses a ruling passion of greater magnitude and may achieve greater glory than Caesar. There is evidence of such a role in Lincoln's simple exhortation to the people to remain united, faithful to the government and laws, and watchful against the destroyer. Yet this advice in itself is purely perfunctory. It is not for the people, but for their leaders, to penetrate the disguises in which their enemies come. Lincoln knew that both Caesar and Napoleon had overthrown republics by posing as their defenders, preserving republican forms until there was no power in the republics to resist them.

> You all did see, that on the Lupercall,
> I thrice presented him a kingly crown,
> Which he did thrice refuse. Was this ambition?

Anthony's rhetorical question may be answered as the crowd answered it, but we know that Anthony himself answered it differently. But the antithesis to Caesar is not, as Mr. Wilson appears to suppose, Brutus. For Brutus—at least Shakespeare's Brutus— although a man of purest intentions, was a guileless bungler. It was Cassius who possessed the wisdom of the serpent, who would have murdered Anthony instead of allowing him to speak at Caesar's funeral. The man who would be a match for Caesar must somehow combine the virtues *and* political capacity of which Aristotle speaks; he must somehow unite, in his single person, the goodness of Brutus and the wiliness of Cassius.[14] Because these qualities were divided in Caesar's enemies they were impotent against Caesar, who was mightier in death, as Brutus found at Philippi, than in life. The conspiracy ended in civil war and the destruction of the conspirators, but the regime founded by Caesar was re-established more firmly than ever.

It is the Calliclean thesis that the passion for domination of the natural ruler cannot brook submission to a regime of equal rights. But the Calliclean thesis is not pushed far enough by its advocates. For the passion it celebrates cannot be gratified by victory over the weaker, for whom the strong man has such contempt. Callicles demonstrates the contempt that the strong man has for the opinions of the weak, as represented by their opinions of justice. But what of the Caesarian reputation, which is founded in the adulation of these selfsame weaklings?

And then he offered it the third time; he put it the third time by, and still he refus'd it, the rabblement shouted, and clapp'd their chopp'd hands, and threw up their sweaty night caps, and uttered such a deal of stinking breath, because Caesar refus'd the crown, that it had almost chok'd Caesar . . .

Does not a really strong man despise glory founded in such praise or in any praise founded in the mental, moral, or physical infirmity of those who give it? A Harry Monmouth seeks out a Harry Percy upon the field of Shrewsbury. The measure of a lion or eagle can be taken only against other lions or eagles; the victor in such a contest compels admiration whether he seeks it or not.

Callicles and Aristotle agree in the doctrine that the man of superlative virtue is not subject to the laws of "equals"—i.e., of inferiors—but that he is a law unto himself. But Callicles again fails to take the measure of his own thesis by assuming a qualitative similarity in the superior and inferior men, believing that the superior have the same pleasures as the inferior and differ only in their ability to gratify themselves. This is the same fallacy which Lincoln imputes both to the Fathers and to the Caesar type; it may also have been the fallacy of Hamilton when he said that love of fame was the ruling passion of the noblest minds. Lincoln, like Aristotle (and Plato), holds that the fame achievable by political success is the greatest good from the popular point of view, but it is not absolutely the greatest good. The folly of placing the highest human aspiration in political immortality Lincoln has subtly demonstrated by showing how the most apparently secure of all fame, that of the Fathers, might be annihilated. As the peroration of the Sub-Treasury speech indicated, there must then be a good beyond political fame, which replaces the appetite for fame, in the highest human type. But the appetite for this higher good makes the highest type man self-controlled with respect to all those appetites which the law forbids us to indulge, except in a moderate or "equal" fashion. Just as the athlete who has a consuming passion for victory in an Olympic game forgoes of his own will many of the pleasures of other men, so this highest type man is controlled by his passion for a greater good. He is, as Aristotle says, above the law, because there is that in him which more than fulfills the law's requirements without either fear of the law's punishments or desire of the law's rewards. Such a man, Aristotle says, is like a god as compared to other men. This assertion has a very precise meaning. When we see the would-be Olympic victor abjuring the pleasures of other men, we do not, in any profound sense, wonder at his self-denial. Neither do we wonder at the honesty of the banker, the piety of the preacher, or the affability of the politician. Wonder is the offspring of mystery, and these instances present no mystery. The Roman mob was struck with amazement when Caesar thrice put by the kingly crown, because it could not comprehend how a man who might have had a crown should deny it to himself. Yet it was not in the least wonderful to Casca, who knew perfectly well why Caesar had refused it. Within the political horizon, political success, above all that "immortality" conferred by the highest political success, which preserves a man's memory in honor "to the latest generation," appears as the ruling passion of the noblest minds. But for a man to have such glory within his grasp and yet not to seize it must appear supremely wonderful to those whose vision is bounded by the political horizon. What greater good can there be to which this might be subordinated? To those who regard the political good as the highest good, anyone who can act as if there is a greater good must be more than a man. In this sense he must be a god. Lincoln's conception of the highest political role fits the Aristotelian conception of the man of godlike virtue. For the antithesis to the Caesarian destroyer of republics is, as we have maintained, one who is greater than Caesar, who is, therefore, the savior of republics. Political salvation, it would appear, like the salvation of the individual soul, cannot be achieved without superhuman or divine virtue.

The man of godlike virtue, said Aristotle, is no proper part of a political community. This is true because, as we have just observed, the law which is rooted in the requirement to check the grasping passions of men, to enable them to live peaceably together, has nothing to control in him. But further: such a man is said also to possess Caesarian power, to be able to overthrow the law; and even though he does not do so, the fact of his ability means that there is no element of submission in his attitude toward the law. The laws are not for him, yet there is no tension between the requirements of his well-being and the continued existence of the law for the simple reason that he has no desire for those things with respect to which the law lays constraints.

But why should his attitude not be that of indifference instead of that of the protector? In one of Lincoln's great wartime utterances the true statesman is likened to a shepherd protecting his flock. He differs from the wolf, not because he is inferior in power to injure the sheep, but because he chooses to protect them. But why does the shepherd abstain from inflicting injury? Is he not merely a disguised wolf, who will eventually sacrifice the sheep to his own gain even more thoroughly than the wolf? Lincoln's answer to this, it is plain, is that the figure of the shepherd is only a similitude under which the human mind conceives of the divine nature. Lincoln's shepherd is like the shepherd of David's psalms and Isaiah's prophecies.[15] When the sheep see the shepherd slay the wolf, their adulation is not founded only in self-interest; it is genuine admiration of the shepherd's strength. But the cause of this admiration, the sense of wonder at the shepherd's might, comes not only from the sense of his strength. The strength of the wolf inspires terror, yet there is nothing wonderful about it because it is joined to the wolf's predatory nature. Indeed, if the sheep are, as Callicles suggests, themselves entirely selfish, the gentleness of the shepherd would be all the more incomprehensible. It is the contrast between the shepherd's gentleness and his strength, and the mystery of why he denies himself "human"— i.e., selfish—gratification, that arouses wonder. It is this *imitatio Dei* which creates a glory exceeding anything awarded for political success. Such a glory may, in fact, exceed any merely political glory, even on the political level. Yet it is understood that the actual achievement of such glory is incidental or accidental; the political savior is capable of being the savior only because he has no wish to see the thing he can save endangered. The Lord had no wish to see man sin; the divine nature offered man salvation nonetheless; yet it is inconceivable, or at least inconsistent with the idea of the divine nature, that God needed glorification as man needed salvation. Lincoln had a corresponding conception of the nature of the true statesman in the highest sense. He alone can save his country who can forgo the honors of his countrymen. Like Aristotle's great-souled man, described in the *Nicomachean Ethics,* he alone is worthy of the highest honor who holds honor itself in contempt, who prefers even to the voice of his countrymen the approving voice heard only by himself, "Well done, thou good and faithful servant." That the question of the measure of the man who might live up to this standard was involved in Lincoln's mind from the beginning to the end of his contest with Douglas is shown by Lincoln's last speech in the 1858 campaign:

> Ambition has been ascribed to me. God knows how sincerely I prayed from the first that this field of ambition might not be opened. I claim no insensibility to political honors; but today could the Missouri restriction be restored, and the whole slavery question replaced on the old ground of "toleration" by *necessity* where it exists, with unyielding hostility to the spread of it, on principle, I would, in consideration, gladly agree, that Judge Douglas should never be *out*, and I never *in*, an office, so long as we both or either, live.[16]

There is in this passage something of a suggestion that there is no place in democratic politics for the man who would act only on the grand scale, in the great crises. Such a suggestion is, of course, belied by Lincoln's life and by his obvious relish for the ways, low as well as high, of the politician. Yet there is a sense in which Lincoln's career bears out this aristocratic interpretation. For Lincoln, like Aristotle's great-souled man, who is a man of few but great actions, seems to have concentrated his whole inner life upon preparing for the crisis foretold in the Lyceum speech. Lincoln, unlike Douglas, found himself unable to play anything but a minor political role throughout the agitation caused by the Wilmot Proviso. And he accepted the leadership of Clay—and of Douglas himself—as Whigs and Democrats joined hands in the Compromise of 1850.[17] The arts that he learned in his political apprenticeship were not learned for the sake of moving the state capital from Vandalia to Springfield, Senator Beveridge to the contrary notwithstanding. When Woodrow Wilson said that the phenomenon of Lincoln had made it possible to believe in democracy, he implied that great moral restraint was traditionally associated with aristocratic virtue and had always seemed particularly incompatible with deference to popular opinion. It was Lincoln's task to demonstrate how magnanimity might find its lodgment with the cause of the people.

There is yet another sense in which the man of surpassing merit is not part of a political community, in which sense also Lincoln is in agreement with Aristotle. Let us think first of the role of the founder as distinct from that of the savior. It is the task of a Moses, a Lycurgus, a Romulus, or a Washington to give an impress to the political order he founds, even as the sculptor gives form to the statue. To do so implies, as in the case of the artisan, a separation and detachment of the worker from his work. The founder, *qua* founder, is then never a part of the order he founds. In a somewhat different sense this is true of the entire founding (or Revolutionary) generation. They are not bred under the law of the republic they help to found; they are never so thoroughly molded by it in their inner beings as those who come after them. This relationship, we should observe, is also indicated in the story of Exodus by the fact that those whom Moses led out of Egypt, like Moses himself, were not permitted to enter the Promised Land. Only their children, bred under Mosaic law, entered it. Lincoln's argument in the Lyceum speech parallels the Bible, in that he imputes to the Revolutionary generation, in particular the leaders, passionate personal motives for attachment to the new order, motives which betoken inferiority to the attachment which is habitual and which flows from a character disposed from within to choose rightly, without any supervening direction by the passions. Hatred of the Egyptians led to independence, but not hatred of Egypt, but love of Israel, must perpetuate Israel. Love of Israel must come from reverence of the Law, from those bred by the Law, in whom the Law has been implanted from birth and grown with their growth.

And yet there is another viewpoint, from which posterity is inferior to the founding generation. When Lincoln states the case against the Fathers, by maintaining that the passion for "fame, celebrity, and distinction" gave adventitious support to their cause, he was deliberately shaping the argument to focus attention upon the Caesarian destroyer. But the "detachment" of the Founders may certainly be viewed in a more inspiring light. They were compelled to take great risks for their cause, as Lincoln indicates. But while it is true that, as he says, their destinies were inseparably linked with the *maintenance* of republican institutions, they were not linked with their *establishment* except by their own deliberate choice. They incurred the risks by choosing their cause. Washington and Jefferson might have stood high in the service of King George III, as Moses might have continued to do in the service of Pharaoh. The detachment of the Founders enables them to see the republic in a light in which it does not appear to posterity. Those bred by the law are bred to affirm republican principles, not as a matter of deliberative choice, but spontaneously, as an immediate consequence of their republican natures. But the founder must reject much of what he has been bred to believe. He sees the republic as an alternative, and his affirmation is a triumph of the republican cause over all the alternatives he rejects. Moreover, the glory of Washington, for example, like that of Moses, is that of a founder of an order which holds out a unique promise of good to the entire family of man, a good which mankind has always desired but has never known to be possible. All the weary experience of the past is against such men; the boundlessness of the infamy which surrounds the prospect of failure on their lonely pinnacles of largely unshared responsibility is unimaginably terrible. They do not have the comforting assurances of communal conviction because the community which would shelter their assurance exists only in their own vision of the future. Meanwhile they must bear the reproaches of those who yearn for the fleshpots of Egypt or watch the summer soldiers depart as winter closes over Valley Forge. Such a founder comprehends the affirmation of his decision in all its terror, majesty, and solitude. He thus estimates the value of the thing to which he would give life as perhaps no one again will estimate it. For such a man alone knows what it is to affirm its value while all the alternatives he has rejected crowd around him, beckoning him from the uncharted voyage to the easier, safer, and conventional paths.

Let us consider the consequences of the foregoing reflections as they bear upon the nature and role of the would-be preserver. The principal danger to the republic comes, according to Lincoln, from the Caesarian type. Men of this type are of the same order of genius as the Founders, in that they too do not savor what they deem to be conventional pleasures. Although bred by the law, they do not see it as other citizens do; they shake off their loyalty as if it were a dream or mirage and see it as the Founders did, as an alternative—and an opportunity. Yet in the last analysis Caesar is a victim of the delusion he thinks he has thrown off. For the ambition which he chooses to gratify, the ambition for fame, we have seen to be but a conventional pleasure transfigured. But the antagonist of Caesar, no less than Caesar, must comprehend the republic as an alternative: an alternative to be chosen or—to become the mere instrument of his own ambition. The sense in which the founder stands outside the order he founds is fairly obvious, but it is no less true that its preserver must stand outside it. He too must know, nay, he must feel, all the reasons which might wrench him from his republican loyalty. The qualifications of a savior, whether of the individual soul or of the political soul of a free nation, require a temptation in the wilderness. The savior must know all the attractions of becoming the destroyer before he can become the savior. It is no accident that the Lyceum speech, whose highest theme is political salvation, ends by saying that the "proud fabric of freedom" may yet rest upon a "rock," and that if it does, "as truly as has been said of the only greater institution, 'the gates of hell shall not prevail against it.'"

Lincoln's deliberate invocation of the analogies with the New and Old Testaments indicates that the trials of the faith of the forefathers must be reduplicated by their subseqeunt political savior. And Lincoln has methodically indicated the nature of the trials by indicating the gravest grounds for the gravest doubts of the most sacred tenets of the citizens' creed: the moral and intellectual eminence of the Founding Fathers, the heroic character of the Revolution, and, above all, the proposition that all men are created equal. Lincoln has shown that these things were not matters of unquestioning faith for him but subjects of extreme and anxious doubt. Yet Lincoln has not only indicated his doubts but his triumph over them. All men *are* created equal, because those who are really superior are in the decisive sense above humanity. For them to claim superior rights would be absurd, because such a claim would imply an appetite for those political goods for which they have no desire. "All men are created equal" remains the decisive *political* truth, because those who might with justice deny it have no motive to deny it, while those who do deny it can only do so because of an unjust motive.

That the Founding Fathers were truly a heroic breed we have also suggested must have been Lincoln's serious final conviction. This may be stated decisively when we point out that Lincoln has really shown that the situation of the Founder is reproduced, in all its essentials, in the situation of the preserver. The passage on the Caesarian menace concluded by saying that this danger is one which could not have existed before. If this is true, then it follows that a unique task exists now, even as one existed in the revolutionary era. And since Lincoln correlates the opportunity for glory with uniqueness, the opportunity for glory still exists. But now we see that the passion which merits true glory is not a passion *for* glory. We understand that both founder and preserver must transcend mere ambition. The heroic character of the Fathers is re-established by the same considerations that point to the savior, as distinguished from the destroyer.

Yet the task of the savior differs from, and is in crucial respects more noble because it is more difficult than, the task of the original Founders. It was no expression of a transient mood that led Lincoln to say, as he left Springfield to take the nation's helm on February 11, 1861, that he went "with a task before me greater than that which rested upon Washington." The original founder leads a fight against avowed enemies of republican freedom—in Washington's time against a largely alien foe. The Caesarian danger is an inner danger, arising mainly from the coincidence of vaulting ambition and mob violence.[18] But mob violence is peculiarly dangerous to popular government when it is—as Lincoln clearly believed it was—an expression of the impatience of the people, intoxicated with the idea that they are the source of all legitimate power. For intoxication with their own supremacy may lead to the conviction that the constitutional forms erected to secure their rights are barriers to their rights. The people, in short, tend to identify their rights with their passions and to oppose obstacles to their passions as if they were obstacles to their rights. The Caesarian danger comes when demagogues indulge the people in this very delusion. When those who thus flatter the people become masters of the government, then the forms of law may themselves become prostituted. Caesar may come into possession of the government by carefully observing legal requirements which he means to do away with when his control is secure. Thus may the substance of popular government, the security of individual rights, be completely abolished in the name of the people and the rights of individuals. In his diagnosis of the Caesarian menace Lincoln is, among other things, expressing a Whig view of Jacksonian democracy. In our opinion Lincoln did not feel the repulsion toward Jackson that was official Whig dogma. We cannot, for example, believe that Lincoln ever shared the Whig view that Jackson had overextended the powers of the presidency. Douglas, far more than Jackson, embodied the menace implied in Jacksonianism. The celebration of "military glory—that attractive rainbow that rises in showers of blood—that serpent's eye that charms to destroy," as he said during the Mexican War, Lincoln did indeed fear greatly. Such glory, upon which Jackson certainly capitalized, intoxicated Jackson's followers far more than it did their chief and, among these, none more than Douglas. As we have amply seen, all Douglas's policies culminated in a Catonian cry for the destruction of British power in the New World. All the disruptive forces in American life would have been "pacified" by a gigantic crusade against Britain. Yet the message of the Lyceum speech is that such a policy as Douglas's would be in effect a confession of defeat for free popular government. In the passage in the Lyceum speech in which Lincoln says that the future destroyer will seek distinction "whether at the expense of emancipating slaves, or enslaving freemen," he is not thinking primarily, as Edmund Wilson supposes, of his own future role and the objections that might be made to it. He is thinking of the passions of the rival factions at Alton, Illinois, and of the politicians who would seek votes without regard to the intrinsic rightness or wrongness of the methods or the goals of the men in the mobs. He is thinking, above all, of such a monstrosity as Douglas's popular sovereignty—which was itself but a particular formulation of Jacksonian democracy and which "didn't care" whether slavery was voted up or voted down. The doctrine of popular sovereignty as preached by Douglas was of the essence of the Caesarian danger; it was a base parody of the principle of popular rights. It implied that whatever the people wanted they had a right to, instead of warning the people that the rights which they might assert against all the kings and princes of the old world were rights which they must first respect themselves.

Thus we see that, for the republic to live, the act of creation or founding must be repeated. Indeed, we may go further and say that Lincoln's argument carried to its logical conclusion requires that the re-creation of the republic is something that may have to be accomplished at any time and that only as there are men of transcendent ability and virtue who, in the sense indicated, stand guard outside the community can those within it remain in possession of their republican rights. The demonstration of the "people's" capacity to govern themselves is possible because of the Washingtons and Jeffersons of the first generation and because of such men as Lincoln fourscore and seven years after. The Caesarian danger may arise at any time; it is rooted in the strength of the passions of the people and in the evil genius of some men to offer the people the gratification of these passions in forms which are spuriously represented as legitimate exercises of the people's rights. But Caesar must be encountered by one who has all Caesar's talent for domination, one who could, if he would, govern the people without their consent, but who prefers the people's freedom to their domination. Such statesmanship is predicated upon the truth that Caesar is, in the last analysis, not the people's master but their fool. For his own ambition is but vulgar ambition transfigured; he is capable of enslaving the people only by first becoming enslaved to their desires. He overthrows republican self-government by leading the people to foreign conquest, bread, and circuses. Those who would teach the people that they may not eat the bread others have earned, whether abroad or at home, have a much harder task. Yet they alone are true masters, they alone have enslaved the people—to a noble enslavement—the restraint of their own passions. The true ruler of men, with the highest of all ambitions, sees in the idea of equality the principle which requires, both logically and politically, the highest degree of moral self-government. His own sense of superiority can be vindicated only by the knowledge that he has been responsible—whether by the shepherd's silent watchfulness or his stern and unrelenting encounter with the wolf—for the restraints which keep his flock in the paths of righteous endeavor.

* * * * *

The work of the Founding Fathers was excellent and noble, but it was incomplete. Its incompleteness is no necessary reflection upon the Fathers themselves. In asserting their independence of the British they could not help appealing to passions of revenge and hatred; nor could they, in appealing to the principle of equal rights, avoid setting in train passions which would resist both just and unjust restraints. The people must be taught, as Jefferson taught them, to assert their rights. But they had not yet learned to respect what they had asserted. The people had not yet learned to be submissive in the presence of their own dignity. That this is peculiarly difficult to learn is easy to see. Whoever sees the law as the product of his will—whether it be a Louis XIV or the American people—is prone to think that all things are lawful. Yet however easy or inevitable the error, it is still an error. Whoever fulfills the law does not destroy the law. But that the people can destroy themselves, that they can be led by the Pied Piper of

Caesarism to their own destruction, was Lincoln's profound conviction. For the people to have the respect to which their rights entitle them they must be made subject to a discipline in virtue of which they will demand only those things in the name of their own supreme authority that are reasonable; i.e., consistent with the implications of their own equal rights. There is only one way in which this self-respect on the part of the people can, according to Lincoln, be achieved. The Lyceum speech is designed, as the whole idea of political salvation implies, to give force to the one practical proposal of the Lyceum speech; namely, the proposal for a "political religion." We have noted that the speech ends with a comparison of the American republic to the "only greater institution," as we have earlier noted parallels of the Revolutionary generation to the Israelites led out of Egypt by Moses. We would now observe that Lincoln's political thought is cast almost wholly in the metaphor of a double perspective, in which the function of his statesmanship is seen either on the analogy of the salvation of Israel from Egypt or the salvation of the world by the Messiah. Lincoln's moral imagination worked in and through a kind of conflation of the symbols of Old and New Testaments. It is, for example, impossible to grasp fully what Lincoln believed he was doing in his debates with Douglas throughout the period of 1854–60 without seeing it as a performance of a prophetic role in the Old Testament sense. Neither is it possible to understand his conception of his Civil War role without seeing the Messianic idea at work. In discussing "political religion" as presented in the Lyceum speech, we will go beyond the framework of the speech itself to show how it involved Lincoln's whole conception of political salvation and of the role of statesmanship as necessarily agreeing in its higher reaches with the purposes and methods of the divine teacher. Because of the importance of its anticipations, we reproduce the following with all its rhetorical flourishes:

> Let every American, every lover of liberty, every well wisher to his posterity, swear by the blood of the Revolution, never to violate in the least particular, the laws of the country; and never to tolerate their violation by others. As the patriots of seventy-six did to the support of the Declaration of Independence, so to the support of the Constitution and Laws, let every American pledge his life, his property, and his sacred honor;—let every man remember that to vio-

late the law, is to trample on the blood of his father, and
to tear the charter of his own, and his children's liberty.
Let reverence for the laws, be breathed by every American
mother, to the lisping babe, that prattles on her lap—let it
be taught in schools, in seminaries, and in colleges; let it be
written in Primers, spelling books, and in Almanacs;—let it
be preached from the pulpit, proclaimed in legislative halls,
and enforced in courts of justice. And, in short, let it become
the *political religion* of the nation; and let the old and the
young, the rich and the poor, the grave and the gay, of all
sexes and tongues, and colors and conditions, sacrifice unceas-
ingly upon its altars.

We cannot help noticing that here, unlike the Gettysburg
Address, Lincoln calls only for dedication to the legal order, not,
as we might have expected, to the Declaration *and* the Constitution and laws. Yet in this difference we are reminded of the
problem from which the Lyceum speech starts: the problem of
disorder arising from base passions, passions set in motion *by the
Revolution* and hence by the summons to independence. In fact,
the difference between the Lyceum speech and the Gettysburg
Address is more apparent than real. For the latter effects a subtle
but profound change in the doctrine which it adapts (rather than
adopts) from the Declaration of Independence. Throughout the
period of the debates with Douglas, the "prophetic period" of his
career, whose keynote was a return to ancestral ways, Lincoln
constantly referred to the great central tenet as an "ancient faith."
And so, in the Gettysburg Address, what was called a self-evident
truth by Jefferson becomes in Lincoln's rhetoric an inheritance
from "our fathers." This is not to suggest that Lincoln doubted
the evidence for the proposition—although we have seen that his
assent was far more complicated than that of "the people" could
well be—but that he found its political efficacy, "four score and
seven years" after, to reside more in the fact of its inheritance
than in its accessibility to unassisted human reason. Lincoln transforms a truth open to each man as man into something he shares
in virtue of his partnership in the nation. The truth which, in the
Declaration, gave each man, as an individual, the right to judge
the extent of his obligations to any community in the Gettysburg
Address also imposes an overriding obligation to maintain the integrity, moral and physical, of that community which is the bearer

of the truth. The sacrifices both engendered and required by that truth—for the lapses from the faith are, in a sense, due to the moral strain imposed by its loftiness—transforms that nation dedicated to it from a merely rational and secular one, calculated to "secure these rights"—i.e., the rights of individuals—into something whose value is beyond all calculation. The "people" is no longer conceived in the Gettysburg Address, as it is in the Declaration of Independence, as a contractual union of individuals existing in a present; it is as well a union with ancestors and with posterity; it is organic and sacramental. For the central metaphor of the Gettysburg Address is that of birth and rebirth. And to be born again, to Lincoln and his audience—as to any audience reared in the tradition of a civilization shaped by the Bible and by Plato's *Republic*—connoted the birth of the spirit as distinct from the flesh; it meant the birth resulting from the baptism or conversion of the soul. This new birth is not, as we have said, mere renewal of life but the origin of a higher life. Thus Lincoln, in the Civil War, above all in the Gettysburg Address and Second Inaugural, interpreted the war as a kind of blood price for the baptism of the soul of a people.

When the opportunity came, Lincoln was prepared by long forethought to shape from the materials of the American tradition that political religion which in 1838 he had seen to be necessary for the perpetuation of our political institutions. He found in the experience of that people two pre-eminent obstacles, or antagonisms, whose reconciliation it would be the essential task of that religion to effect. One was the antagonism between the American secular and religious traditions and the other the inner conflict, to which we have adverted, engendered in part by the Declaration of Independence itself, between the principles of popular government and the passions of the people.

We may observe that American civilization was, in a high degree, formed by the conjunction of two main currents of thought and conviction. One was the Puritan religious tradition, the other the secular tradition known in the eighteenth century, and since, as the Enlightenment. Although accommodations on the popular and political level were increasingly made as the eighteenth century progressed (as in that laughable compromise between fidelity and infidelity known as Deism), these elements of American life were largely hostile to each other. The impact of the French Revolution on America tore away most of the veils of compromise and exacerbated enmities that had been superficially smoothed over. Although Jefferson could on occasion use religious language, he was the lifelong enemy of clerical influences, especially those emanating from New England. While he repeatedly exhorted men to the ethic of Christianity—as he understood it—he never concealed his detestation of the theology of its churches. Such doctrines as those of the Trinity, original sin, predestination, redemption through faith (not works), etc., he considered relics of man's barbaric past or sophistries spun by priests to bemuse men's minds and aid in their own seizure of power. Although Jefferson is the arch-apostle of religious freedom, there is no question but that he hoped and believed the effect of religious freedom would be a withering away of credence in all, or nearly all, revealed theology. It is hardly an exaggeration to say that, for Jefferson, such an attrition of what he was pleased to call superstition was essential if men were to claim their natural rights and republican freedom was to endure. The preamble to the Declaration of Independence invokes not the God of Israel or the persons of the Trinity but the God of Nature and is wholly a document of the rationalistic tradition. This God reveals himself, not in thunder from Sinai, nor through any gift of faith, inspiration, or private judgment upon sacred scriptures. He reveals himself through "self-evident" truths; i.e., through the unassisted natural processes of ratiocination. Lincoln, however, achieved, on the level of the moral imagination, a synthesis of the elements which in Jefferson remained antagonistic. He incorporated the truths of the Declaration of Independence into a sacred and ritual canon, making them objects of faith as well as of cognition. Through his interpretation of the Civil War as both a Hebraic and Christian ritual atonement, this canon was made sacred to the American people as the Declaration of Independence, of itself, could not be made. This interpretation did not depend for its conviction upon the intellectual acknowledgment of the truth alone—an acknowledgment which, of itself, Lincoln in 1838 showed was a feeble barrier to the passions—but upon a passionate and passion-conquering conviction born of the sense of the awful price exacted by that truth of its votaries. For the experience of the price paid for infidelity, but which measured the value of fidelity, might create a presumption in favor of the truths of the Declaration, which the evidence supplied by reason, apart from such experience, could never create.

Lincoln's conception of a political religion which would create "reverence for the laws" is first expressed in the Lyceum speech and is given fulfillment in the unsurpassed beauties of the Gettysburg Address. The 1863 speech tacitly obscures the rational foundations of the proposition to which it says the nation was dedicated. It associates the new birth of freedom with the idea of the release of the spirit from the bondage of sin, the idea with which the people were familiar from their ancient revealed religion. By this very association Lincoln gave the idea of political freedom, which was so new to the Western world, a sense of the dignity which is naturally associated only with things that are old. The connection between venerability and stability is nowhere expressed more brilliantly than in the forty-ninth number of the *Federalist*, which we may with profit reproduce in this context:

If it be true that all governments rest upon opinion, it is no less true that the strength of opinion, in each individual, and its practical influence on his conduct, depend much on the number which he supposes to have entertained the same opinion. The reason of man, like man himself, is timid and cautious when left alone, and acquires firmness and confidence in proportion to the number with which it is associated. When the examples which fortify opinion are *ancient* as well as *numerous*, they are known to have a double effect. In a nation of philosophers, this consideration ought to be disregarded. A reverence for the laws would be sufficiently inculcated by the voice of enlightened reason. But a nation of philosophers is as little to be expected as the philosophical race of kings wished for by Plato. And in every other nation, the most rational government will not find it a superfluous advantage to have the prejudices of the community on its side.

The lapse of the American people from the faith of their fathers, like that of the people led by Moses, was a lapse from a truth immediately accessible. Neither the pillar of fire by night, and the cloud by day, nor the rational self-evidence of human equality, had the "practical influence" upon the conduct of one or the other which their missions required of them. The Jews were led out of Egypt in fulfillment of a promise gained not by their merits but by those of Abraham, Isaac, and Jacob. So, we have seen, were the American people foreordained to the blessings of a government of equal rights by the merits of the Founding Fathers. Yet, like the Jews who were still corrupt from their sojourn in Egypt, the American people were not worthy of their mission. By their infidelity they were destined to sufferings, sufferings from which they would gain that purity of heart and tenacity of conviction which neither miracle nor reason, of itself, seems able to implant.

The necessity of a political religion has, as we have seen, particular meaning within the framework of Lincoln's analysis of the problem of free popular government. Over and again, in the debates with Douglas, Lincoln said that in a government like ours public sentiment is everything, determining what laws and decisions can or cannot be enforced. For here there is no monarch or ruling class with a will apart from that of the people. Thus self-control by the people is a particular necessity, and there is, accordingly, an especial need for that "double effect" spoken of in the forty-ninth *Federalist*, that "prejudice" in favor of moral restraint which comes from reverence for the laws. But reverence is a species of veneration, and veneration is for things venerable; i.e., old. A regard for ancient opinions is a peculiar necessity and a peculiar difficulty for free popular government. For such government is, as no one believed more passionately than Lincoln, founded in the proposition that all men are created equal, but that proposition implies an equality not only between individuals but between generations; it is, therefore, peculiarly subversive of reverence. The Declaration of Independence thus not only expresses the central truth upon which free government is based but undermines the possibility of reverence which alone can stabilize government founded upon that truth. As the forty-ninth *Federalist* says, such reverence would not be necessary were men able to be governed by the voice of enlightened reason alone. But the *Federalist* warns, as Lincoln warned, that it would be singularly unenlightened to depend upon that voice as the sole restraint upon popular passions.

The tension between the truth and the reverence which that truth undermines is but another expression of the irreconcilability of passion and reason. We said before that Lincoln sought, in a political religion, the reconciliation of the hostile elements in the American secular and religious traditions. We might conveniently oversimplify that antagonism by saying that one element called for reverence without reason and the other reason without reverence. Yet neither was politically true or viable without the other.

In Lincoln's republican theology this tension may be compared to original sin in the Christian tradition. The idea of political salvation, as expressed in the Lyceum speech in 1838, points, as we have observed, to the political savior. Clinton Rossiter, in his *The American Presidency*, well says that "Lincoln is the supreme myth, the richest symbol in the American experience. He is, as someone has remarked neither irreverently nor sacrilegiously, the martyred Christ of democracy's passion play." Many things in Lincoln's life, like the accident of his death, may have been fortuitous —or providential—but the myth that came to life with his passing was neither. It was the finely wrought consummation, of philosophic insight and a poetic gift, of a life devoted to the problem of "the capability of a people to govern themselves."

Analysis of Lincoln's Temperance Address*

A. Present Success of the Temperance Cause (1–18)
  I. Celebration of Present Success (1–2)
  II. Causes of Present Success: Contrast Between the Old and New Temperance Champions (3–18)
    a. Want of Approachability of Old-School Champions: Wrong Men (3–4)
      1. Their Want of Approachability
        a'. Because of Supposed Want of Sympathy
        b'. Because of Supposed Want of Disinterestedness
      2. The Washingtonians Contrasting:
        a'. Sympathy
        b'. Disinterestedness
    b. Unwisdom of Old-School Champions' Tactics: Wrong Measures (5–18)
      1. Unwisdom of Denunciation (5–16)
        a'. Its Impolicy (5–8)
          1'. Its Ineffectiveness
            a". Because Unsympathetic
            b". Because Necessarily Productive of Antagonism
          2'. The Washingtonians Effectiveness
        b'. Its Injustice (9–16)
          1'. Drinking Sanctioned by Universal Public Opinion: Hence Not Unjust
            a". Evidence of This Opinion
            b". Interpretation of This Opinion
            c". Evaluation of This Opinion
          2'. Its Denunciation Inhumane: Hence Unjust
            a". Against the Grain of the Altruistic Passions: Hence Base
            b". Against the Grain of the Egotistic Passions: Hence Foolish
      2. Contrasting Wisdom of the Washingtonians (16–18)
B. Causes of Future Success (19–24)
  I. The Missionary Work of Reformed Drunkards (19)
  II. The Co-operation of Non-Drinkers (20–24)
    a. Doubts of the Non-Drinkers As to Benefits of Their Co-operation (20–22)
      1. Doubt of the Benefit of Banishing Drink

a'. The Doubt

b'. Removal of Doubt: Testimony of "Universal" Opinion

2. Doubts of Benefit from Non-Drinkers' Taking the Pledge

a'. First Doubt

1'. Emptiness of the Gesture

2'. Doubt Removed: Moral Example Not an Empty Gesture

b'. Second Doubt

1'. Moral Example Ineffective

2'. Doubt Removed: Moral Example Extremely Powerful When Fashionable

b. Fear of the Non-Drinkers of Injury from Their Co-operation (23–24)

1. Fear: That They Will Identify Themselves With Drunkards

2. Removal of Fear:

a'. Argument from Christianity: In Taking Pledge, They Imitate Christ, Who Is Above Them, Not Drunks, Who Are Below Them

b'. Argument from Reason and Experience: Drunkards As A Class Not Inferior, Hence No Danger of Demeaning Themselves

C. Relation of Temperance Revolution to '76 (25–30)

I. Comparison of the Two Revolutions As To Misery Inflicted and Relieved

a. The Political Revolution

1. Its Benefits (25)

a'. Past and Present

1'. Political Freedom Beyond Anything Achieved Elsewhere

2'. Solved the Problem of Man's Capability to Govern Himself

b'. Future: The Germ of the Universal Liberty of Mankind.

2. Its Cost: Famine, Death, and Desolation (26)

b. The Moral Revolution (27)

1. Its Benefit: Superiority of Moral to Political Freedom

2. Its Cost: "Widow's Wail" Compared with "Universal

Song of Gladness"
II. Consequences of the Two Revolutions: Universal Reign
of Reason (28)
III. Glory of the Two Revolutions (29–30)
a. For the Land That Will Be the Birthplace and Cradle
of Both (29)
b. For the Name of Washington (30)

*Note: Numbers in parenthesis correspond to the paragraphs of the
text as printed in the *Sangamo Journal,* March 25, 1842, and reprinted
in *Collected Works,* I, pp. 271–79. The paragraphs are not numbered
in the printed text.

Chapter X

The Teaching Concerning Political
Moderation

THE Lyceum speech contains a prognosis, twenty years before
the house divided speech, of a crisis which must be reached and
passed before the capability of a people to govern themselves
might be said to be demonstrated. Lincoln saw the gathering
storm clouds of that crisis in the wave of mob violence sweeping
the country in 1838. His diagnosis of the causes of that violence
showed he did not believe it to be any transient wave of popular
feeling, but a disease endemic to the government inherited from
the Revolution. Certainly his own exhortation to self-restraint
could not have been expected to be even a palliative of such
evils. Such exhortation serves only to indicate the nature of the
role required by him who would administer the true remedy, but
it is clear that the opportunity to apply that remedy lay only in
part in the power of its possessor. The political savior, like that
other Messiah, must await the fulfillment of prophecies implicit
in the very conception of his own function before he could step
forth.

The Lyceum speech ends by saying that the old "pillars of
the temple of liberty . . . have crumbled away" and the "temple
must fall, unless we . . . supply their places with other pillars,
hewn from the solid quarry of sober reason." The pillars of the
first temple, the work of the Revolutionary Fathers, were, alas,
not quarried from a solid substance, and because they were not
the temple did not endure. A second temple must be built, of
rock, which shall last as long as the "only greater institution."
Like that other institution, this one also finds its consummation

in an apocalyptic vision, when "the last trump shall awaken our
WASHINGTON," to find the republic still free, its soil undese-
crated by a hostile foot, and his name still revered. It is typical
of the many paradoxes of the Lyceum speech that this passionate
summons to passionate rededication is characterized as a plea
for "cold, calculating, unimpassioned reason!"

We have seen that the work of the Fathers was, in a sense,
predestined to at least temporary failure because of the inner
tension, engendered by the idea of equality, between the people's
rights and the people's duties. Life, liberty, and the pursuit of
happiness required institutions of government "to secure these
rights." The people had a sacred duty to maintain a constitution
and laws designed to secure them; but the strength of anarchic
passions in the people was such that it would have been utopian
to expect mere intellectual recognition of this fact to be sufficient
to produce obedience. Since the first and most successful enterprise of the Fathers was to produce *disobedience* to an ancient
established order, it would have been peculiarly difficult for *them*
to inculcate reverence. We have already seen that the need for
reverence was well understood by the authors of the *Federalist*.[1]
In the same forty-ninth number, from which we have already
quoted, occurs this further statement of the theme of the Lyceum
speech:

> We are to recollect that all the existing constitutions were
> formed in the midst of a danger which repressed the passions
> most unfriendly to order and concord; of an enthusiastic
> confidence of the people in their patriotic leaders, which
> stifled the ordinary diversity of opinions on great national
> questions; of a universal ardor for new and opposite forms
> produced by a universal resentment and indignation against
> the ancient government . . . The future situations in which
> we must expect to be usually placed, do not present any
> equivalent security against the danger which is apprehended.

Although the *Federalist* presents Lincoln's problem with great
clarity, its fundamental approach to the solution is predicated
on the idea that it is possible to build a political system on the
"policy of supplying, by opposite and rival interests, the defect
of better motives."[2] Hamilton and Madison thought that somehow
passions might be controlled by the government, while reason
would control the government.[3] "Ambition must be made to

counteract ambition. The interest of the man must be connected with the constitutional rights of the place."[4] Lincoln, we have seen, denies the ultimate adequacy of this approach—affirming its insufficiency, not its incorrectness—because he denies that there is a constitutional place for the highest ambitions. It is true that there is a sense in which ambition in Lincoln's scheme still must counteract ambition. The Messianic ambition must counteract the Caesarian. But the loyalty which the Constitution must command must be generated by a nobler vision of excellence than that of a well-contrived machine. Lincoln's verdict upon a document such as the *Federalist* may be inferred from his association, at the end of the Lyceum speech, of "cold, calculating" reason with the Last Judgment.

Lincoln's solution involved, as we have seen, an engrafting of the passion of revealed religion upon the body of secular political rationalism. How this differed from what the founding generation attempted may be seen by comparing the cadences of the Gettysburg Address not only with the Declaration but with the following passage of Washington's Farewell Address (upon which both Hamilton and Madison had collaborated with the author):

> Of all the dispositions and habits which lead to political prosperity, Religion and Morality are indispensable supports. In vain would that man claim the tribute of Patriotism who should labor to subvert these great pillars of human happiness, these firmest props of the duties of Men and Citizens. The mere Politician, equally with the pious man ought to respect and to cherish them . . . Where is the security for property, for reputation, for life, if the sense of religious obligation desert the oaths, which are the instruments of investigation in Courts of Justice? And let us with caution indulge the supposition that morality can be maintained without religion. Whatever may be conceded to the influence of refined education on minds of peculiar structure, reason and experience forbid us to expect that national morality can prevail in exclusion of religious principle.

It would be difficult to find a more condensed expression of Lincolnian doctrine which was at the same time more alien in tone and feeling to the sense of what Lincoln believed. Washington's discussion of the utilitarian function of religion and morality is of a piece with the *Federalist's* discussion of the mechanical distribution of the powers of government under the Constitution. Whereas Lincoln spoke of "the only *greater* institution," the politician is here said to have an "equal" motive with the pious man, as if "human happiness" and immortal felicity were on the same level! Washington bids us indulge with caution the supposition that "morality" can be maintained without religion. But in the very next sentence he says, with contrasting emphasis, that reason and experience forbid us to expect "*national* morality" thus to prevail. And he conspicuously sets aside the question of a religious requirement for superior minds with a superior education. We here see the mingling, like oil and water, of the rationalism and religion of the eighteenth century. Compare Washington's "equalizing" of piety and policy with the following statement of Lincoln from a handbill to the voters of the Seventh Congressional District in Illinois in 1846, when he was running for the House and his opponent, the evangelical minister Peter Cartwright had circulated a charge of infidelity against him:

> I do not think I could myself, be brought to support a man for office, whom I knew to be an open enemy of, and scoffer at, religion.—Leaving the *higher* [our italics] matter of eternal consequences, between him and his Maker, I still do not think any man has the right thus to insult the feelings, and injure the morals, of the community in which he may live.[5]

Washington propounds the need for reverence and concedes (more then he insists) that reverence (or obligation) is born of the sense of the sacred that religion bestows. But there is no trace of reverence in Washington's discussion of the need for reverence; the sacred is treated as a necessity of the profane. In Lincoln the profane is transformed into the sacred, but in Washington the profane order merely profits from the existence in it of men who fear God.

It is worth our while also to consider some parallel reflections from Jefferson's *Notes on Virginia,* produced in the years 1781 and 1782, and a commentary of unsurpassed authority on the spirit of '76. The following is from Query XVII, concerning the different religions of Virginia. Jefferson has just enumerated some surviving relics of the old common-law penalties for heresy.

This is a summary view of that religious slavery under which

a people have been willing to remain, who have lavished
their lives and fortunes for the establishment of their civil
freedom. The error seems not sufficiently eradicated, that the
operations of the mind, as well as the acts of the body, are
subject to the coercion of the laws. But our rulers can have
no authority over such natural rights, only as we have submitted to them. The rights of conscience we never submitted,
we could not submit. We are answerable for them to our
God. The legitimate powers of government extend to such
acts only as are injurious to others. But it does me no injury
for my neighbor to say there are twenty gods, or no God.
It neither picks my pocket nor breaks my leg.[6]

The view of the nature and value of religious and civil liberty
here expressed by Jefferson was unquestionably Lincoln's own.
Or, we should say, it was as much Lincoln's view as it was Jefferson's; for we can discover expressions by both men which imply
similar qualifications to the foregoing doctrine. Jefferson could
hardly have meant with full seriousness that the object of government was solely to prevent damage to the body—or the pocket.
On the other hand, when Lincoln says no man has a right to
insult the feelings or injure the morals of his fellow citizens, he
does not mean that the citizen has a political right to legal protection against such injury. He means that the offender suffers
just punishment when he loses the esteem and good will of his
fellow citizens. Jefferson accepts this, too, when he says, "If it
be said, his [i.e., the scoffer's] testimony in a court of justice
cannot be relied on, reject it then, and be the stigma on him."
Both men accept the idea of social stigma as the natural and
appropriate reward for contemptuous heterodoxy. Lincoln, however, would never have expressed as openly, or rather as irascibly,
as Jefferson does his contempt for the older religious tradition,
which sees eternal salvation as something to which the powers
of government might contribute positively. Why he would not
has never been better expressed than by Jefferson himself in the
very next query in the famous *Notes*. The following embraces
a passage which was, to Lincoln, a jewel whose price was surpassed only by the Declaration of Independence itself:

And can the liberties of a nation be thought secure when
we have removed their only firm basis, a conviction in the
minds of the people that these liberties are the gift of God?

That they are not to be violated but with his wrath? Indeed I tremble for my country when I reflect that God is just; that his justice cannot sleep forever . . .[7]

How did Jefferson suppose that one man could not injure another by spreading atheism and skepticism if the only firm basis of our liberties was a conviction of particular providence, of dependence upon a personal God for the receiving of our rights, and of his rewards and punishments for honoring or dishonoring them? The answer is, presumably, that "Reason and free inquiry are the only effectual agents against error. Give a loose to them, they will support the true religion by bringing every false one to their tribunal, to the test of their investigation."[8] There is a suggestion of naïve optimism, however, in this celebrated aphorism. How do we know that the tribunal of reason and free inquiry will have the power of subpoena? That Jefferson was not naïve, however, the following passage from the same paragraph (from Query XVII) assuredly indicates. Its summons to shore up the people's respect for the principles of the people's government indicates an impressive agreement concerning the fundamental problem of American government by Washington, Hamilton, Madison, Jefferson, and Lincoln.

Let us . . . get rid, while we may, of those tyrannical laws [of heresy, perpetuated by the old common law]. It is true, we are yet secured against them by the spirit of the times . . . But is the spirit of the people an infallible, a permanent reliance? . . . the spirit of the times may alter, will alter. Our rulers will become corrupt, our people careless . . . It can never be too often repeated, that the time for fixing every essential right on a legal basis is while our rulers are honest, and ourselves united. From the conclusion of this war we shall be going downhill. It will not then be necessary to resort every moment to the people for support . . . They will forget themselves, but in the sole faculty of making money, and will never think of uniting to effect a due respect for their rights.[9]

Jefferson saw in the revolutionary fervor a rare opportunity for fixing the principles of civil and religious liberty in public law. The backsliding that Lincoln was to lament in 1838 and thereafter, Jefferson amply anticipated. But Jefferson did not seem to antici-

pate what a broken reed the law itself would be once the spirit of
the people departed from it. And there was a fundamental inconsistency in Jefferson's faith in "reason and free inquiry" and his
belief that the people would normally be preoccupied, not with
their rights, but with the avid pursuit of gain. For the people to remain united in effecting due respect from their "rulers" for their
rights, they must themselves first have such respect. And this respect, according to Jefferson no less than Lincoln, depends upon a
firm conviction that they are the gift of a just God. No responsible
statesman can then be indifferent to anything that weakens such a
conviction. He must, on the contrary, hold that the strengthening
of that conviction is the first and highest task of statesmanship, because it is the condition of every other political good. This task,
however, Lincoln, no less than Jefferson, held to be outside the
framework of politics in the ordinary sense. It is not for the law
to command assent to religious doctrines; on the contrary, it is
the function of religious doctrines to command assent to the rule
of law. Reason and free inquiry will support the true religion,
in Jefferson's sense, if the people support the rule of law erected
on the foundation of their own rights. But reason and free inquiry
cannot pursue their vocation in an atmosphere of mob violence;
reason and free inquiry presuppose, for their efficacy, Lincoln's
"political religion," Jefferson's "firm basis" in the conviction of
divine justice.

It is of some importance that the central thought not only of
the Gettysburg Address but of Lincoln's second inaugural has its
literary foundation—apart from the Old and New Testaments—
in the writings of Thomas Jefferson, whom Lincoln called "the
most distinguished politician of our history." The passage in the
eighteenth query of the *Notes*, from which we have quoted in
part,[10] contains a prophecy by Jefferson of a tremendous "revolution of the wheel of fortune," in which he foresaw the possibility
that the position of the white and black races on this continent
might one day be reversed. Nay, more, such "an exchange of
situation . . . may become probable by supernatural interference.
The Almighty has no attribute which can take side with us in such
a contest," he says, in anticipation of, "It may seem strange that
any men should dare ask a just God's assistance in wringing their
bread from the sweat of other men's faces." But Jefferson ended
this discussion in the *Notes* by flying completely in the face of his

previous prediction that "From the conclusion of this war we shall be going downhill" and optimistically envisaged "the spirit of the master abating, that of the slave rising from the dust, his condition mollifying, the way I hope preparing, under the auspices of heaven, for a total emancipation . . . with the consent of the masters, rather than by their extirpation."

Yet Jefferson was far more correct when he saw that the people's preoccupation with money-making would undermine their respect for human rights, particularly when money could be made by trafficking in bodies and souls possessed of those rights. It is impressive and significant beyond words that Jefferson, who was such a confirmed detractor of revealed theology, and whose works are filled with contempt for it, of the quality of the pocket-picking, leg-breaking order, could not but express himself in the most solemn language of that theology when he contemplated the institution of Negro slavery. On Jefferson's own premises it would seem that nothing would have been efficacious in abating the avarice in the master's spirit but a conviction that a living God would one day cause all the wealth piled up by the bondman's unrequited toil to be sunk and a conviction that the master's own life and liberty might perish in the convulsion. Jefferson's warfare against clerical influences was a noble warfare in so far as it meant establishing religious liberty. But Jefferson carried that warfare too far, if we are to take seriously what he himself says about the basis of civil and religious liberty. And Jefferson's notoriety as a free thinker made it difficult, if not impossible, for him to be taken seriously when he did warn his countrymen of divine vengeance for their sinful adherence to slavery.

It must not be thought, however, that because Lincoln wished to enlist the religious feelings of the American people in full support of their form of government that he saw no dangers to civil liberty from religious passions. The truth is the exact opposite. The struggle for separation of church and state, for disestablishment, for most of the legal forms of religious freedom, had been largely won; Jefferson's victory had been virtually complete. But theological intolerance in American political life now took a subtler and more dangerous form. Mid-nineteenth-century America was swept by a whole series of alleged reform movements—temperance, abolitionism (and its southern counterpart, the positive-good advocacy of slavery), nativism, Young Americanism, feminism (in its early manifestations)—and many of these received their dynamic impulse by the encouragement they received from, and their association with, the churches. A single word sums up the common core of many of these mid-century movements, and that is *millennialism*. The vision animating reformers was not that of a better world but of a well-nigh perfect world, of a New Jerusalem. Theirs was secularized Puritanism, combining the spirit of religious messianism with the substance of a naïve rationalism and this-worldly utopianism. In the peroration of Lincoln's Temperance Address, to which we shall shortly turn, he characterizes the aim of this movement as the final subjection of *all* passions to reason, of all matter to mind. It is not the amelioration of the human condition but the transformation of human nature which is here meant by "reform."

The temperance movement and the abolitionist movement were both nurtured by the evangelical spirit, and what Lincoln has to say about temperance will give us a remarkable insight into his whole view of reform, as that was understood in both these movements. "Temperance" is, in a sense, the more fundamental of the two, since it meant not the Aristotelian golden mean of the passions but the entire elimination of the influence of passion over human conduct, chattel slavery being only one consequence of such influence. That the root of slavery was indeed in bad human passions Lincoln certainly believed. Jefferson had said that, particularly in a warm climate, no man will earn his own bread if he can compel another to earn it for him, and Lincoln had repeated this thought in many variants.[11] But Lincoln was sensitive to the danger that extreme expectations of worldly perfection would engender extreme political solutions, requiring extreme measures and extreme power in those who would carry them through. The expectations that were proper and fitting for the kingdom of heaven might be fatal to the freedom of a republic. The spirit of theological intolerance, denied by Jefferson the instrument of power for theological ends, might be vindictively triumphant if it seized the goals of secular rationalism as its own.

We saw in Lincoln's Lyceum speech not only a far-sighted anticipation of dangers threatening the perpetuation of our political institutions but a serious critique of the principles upon which they were originally based. This critique had the purpose not of weakening the faith of its would-be preserver but of making it more enlightened. We saw how and why a critical detachment

from the object of their highest devotion was a necessary attribute of founders and of saviors. But Lincoln saw himself not only
as the savior of the political institutions, but by that fact the
founder of a political religion. And that implied and required
another, similar kind of critical detachment. Lincoln's temperance
speech contains a theological critique which parallels his critique
of the dogmas of the Revolution.

*   *   *   *   *

Like the Lyceum speech, the Temperance Address had its
occasion in contemporary political developments. When Lincoln
delivered it, it would have been difficult to say whether temperance or slavery would be the dominating vote-producing question
of the years just ahead. The famous Maine liquor law was passed
in that state shortly after the Compromise of 1850, and laws
modeled on it were passed in Massachusetts, Vermont, Rhode
Island, and Connecticut. The prohibition ferment reached a peak
in Illinois in 1855, and a version of the Maine law passed there
two weeks after Lincoln had failed in his first bid for the Senate.
By that time, however, he had hitched his wagon to the anti-
slavery star and found it prudent to keep silent on the liquor
question. In 1842, however, he was espousing the temperance
cause energetically. That Lincoln did not believe in temperance,
as the reformers believed in it, we believe it is easy to demonstrate. In the address we shall see Lincoln disavow the spirit of
intolerance which characterized the "old school champions" of
temperance, as he was later to disavow John Brown and abolition.
Yet even as he one day became the Great Emancipator, after a
lifelong disapproval of abolition, so we find him here, in a kind
of anticipatory gesture, accomplishing a similar feat by placing
himself, rhetorically, at the head of a movement in which he
found more to disapprove than to approve.

Although Lincoln had little sympathy with abolitionist or temperance reformers, it was because he disapproved of their temper
and their methods. His sympathy with the ultimate aims of
abolition cannot be doubted, nor his sympathy with temperance,
if the term is understood rightly and not as the alleged reformers
understood it. For the nativists, the anti-immigrants, the Know-
Nothings, self-styled "Americans," Lincoln felt only loathing and
contempt. How could he, he once said, who abhorred the op-

pression of Negroes, approve the degrading of classes of white men? Yet it was Lincoln's political fate one day to need the Know-Nothing vote in much the same way that Douglas needed the pro-slavery vote. And the temperance movement, as we have noted, being an offshoot of radical Protestantism, had anti-Catholic, anti-foreign overtones. Particularly were there anti-Irish overtones, for the Irish were hated both for their Popery and their alleged addiction to drink. In the Temperance Address there is, incidentally, a good-natured Irish joke. The joke is harmless enough, yet plays on both the risibilities and prejudices of the audience, neatly drawing attention from what might otherwise have been a dangerous doctrine: the absurdity of other-worldly in contrast to this-worldly sanctions for morality. The Whig Lincoln might thus tell Irish jokes; it is doubtful that the Democrat Douglas would have done so. In short, Lincoln's Temperance Address, on the surface a merely conventional oration, strongly praising virtue and condemning vice, is a well-appointed ship for navigating some of the strongest voting tides of mid-century America: temperance, abolition, nativism.

Yet the theme of the speech is one of the four cardinal virtues, not a concrete political proposal. How did Lincoln on this one occasion discuss moral virtue? Consider the nature of the occasion on which he spoke. The following is from the first volume of Beveridge's *Lincoln:*[12]

The Temperance movement . . . which had been in progress all over the country, was now in full swing throughout Illinois; and . . . an extraordinary temperance agitation was in progress. The feeling against excessive drinking, which had shown itself by petitions to the legislature had come to a head, and fervent temperance meetings were being held in every township. Lincoln joined this crusade and made temperance speeches in many villages and hamlets. The Washingtonian Society, largely made up of reformed drunkards, had swept over the nation . . . When a unit of this society was formed in Springfield, he delivered a temperance address before it on Washington's birthday 1842.

It was a great occasion. From eleven o'clock until noon a procession paraded the streets. At the head marched "the beautiful company of Sangamo guards under the command of Captain E. D. Baker."[13] An "immense crowd" gathered at the Second Presbyterian Church where the exercises were held. Brightly shone the sun on that joyous day and loud rang the songs of temperance. So "delighted" was the audience with the singing, that "several pieces were a second time called for and repeated." Finally, soon after twelve o'clock Lincoln rose and addressed the audience that packed the church.

In this atmosphere, a quaint indigenous mixture of revival meeting, political jamboree, and football rally, Lincoln discoursed on a theme that had taxed the wisest heads of Athens and Jerusalem and of the great universities. One can hardly imagine an occasion better calculated to bring forth all the clichés of a man's soul, yet Lincoln's performance on this occasion was not unworthy of a pupil of the greatest of the masters who had preceded him.

Lincoln did in a way produce all the clichés that the occasion called for. But they were not the clichés of *his* soul. Clichés, in one sense or another, are indispensable to public speaking. The problem, we believe, is whether a speaker, in identifying himself with his audience, thereby surrenders any independent identity of his own or achieves, at least in speech (the indispensable basis for achieving it in deed), a new identity for the audience. This rhetorical question is discussed explicitly within the Temperance Address:

> When the conduct of men is designed to be influenced, *persuasion*, kind, unassuming persuasion, should ever be adopted. It is an old and true maxim "that a drop of honey catches more flies than a gallon of gall."—So with men. If you would win a man to your cause, *first* convince him that you are his sincere friend. Therein is a drop of honey that catches his heart, which, say what you will, is the great high road to his reason . . .

We may assume then that Lincoln will give us an example of that maxim applied. While the formal or apparent subject of the speech is the praise of a movement devoted to banishing intoxicating liquor, its real subject is the difference between the wrong and the right way of effecting *any* moral reform in society. More specifically, it is the difference between a temperate and an intemperate approach to moral reform. Since Lincoln in the speech presents himself as a moral reformer, Lincoln's speech, which is also Lincoln's deed upon the occasion, should be an example of temperate action. But "actions speak louder than words," and men's actions sometimes bely their words. "Don't do as I do; do as I say," may sometimes be good advice, but no one ever takes it. Every moralist knows that precept without example is vain, and the political moralist knows that the pattern of behavior he sets before his audience will influence them more deeply than the arguments he employs while setting that pattern. Now no man has ever been more credited with self-control than Lincoln; and if it is true, as Aristotle says, that we must look to the men we credit with the virtues to understand what virtue is, then we must not only listen to what Lincoln says but observe how he himself exercised self-control on this occasion. To comprehend his behavior, we must attend not only to the explicit argument of the speech but to the argument implicit in the consequences which we discern are intended by the speech. How the implicit and explicit arguments may differ may be indicated by some brief anticipations of the analysis to follow. When Lincoln criticizes the means employed by others to effect moral reform we must ask precisely how the means he is at that moment employing differ from those he rejects. And if we sometimes find, as we shall, that Lincoln pays his antagonists the sincerest kind of flattery, that of imitation, we may suspect that the explicit argument is, in part at least, specious and that the real controversy is not limited to means but concerns ends. Reflecting further, we may conclude that the reason for the partial substitution of a specious issue for a real one is that Lincoln differs not only with his alleged antagonists but with his alleged friends. In this way we may also find that real temperance is far more a virtue of the appetites of the mind than of those of the body, that it has more to do with the control of one's thoughts, or the expression of those thoughts, than with the control of one's thirst.

In the passage we have quoted Lincoln says that you must convince a man that you are his sincere friend if you would win him to *your* cause. The impression throughout the speech is that the temperance cause *is* Lincoln's cause. Yet, whether this were true or not, Lincoln would be required by his own rhetorical principle to give such an impression; otherwise, how could he convince the temperance people (including, of course, those who would vote temperance "as long as they could stagger to the

polls") that he was their friend? As a politician Lincoln always
was compelled to adopt, to "befriend," professed causes and beliefs of his fellow citizens and hoped-for constituents. Yet to adopt
the opinions of others, for public purposes, does not mean to
believe in them. The Temperance Address shows, as do few
documents of modern politics, a method whereby a public man
can both accept and reject the prejudices of his contemporaries;
how he can, at one and the same time, flatter their vanity and
chasten their egotism; how he can, appearing to agree with their
opinions, modify them, however little, or failing that, so to promote his own leadership that, when these opinions come to be
applied, they will be applied by a man whose judgment is not
chained to them and who can thus utilize them for wiser purposes.

A broad survey of Lincoln's Temperance Address discloses a
plan with a chronological pattern.[14] It begins with a celebration
of the *present* success of the movement, reviews its *past* history,
and ends with an apocalyptic vision of its *future* complete triumph. Now it is a principle of rhetoric, of public speaking, that
the beginning and the end are the parts which particularly arrest
attention, just as the contrasting dialectic principle focuses attention on the center. The beginning and the end are the "ex-
ternals," the parts best calculated to strike the notice of the
unobservant many, who are the typical addressees of rhetoric.
It is in these parts of his speech that we would especially look
for the clichés or conventional opinions called for by the occasion.
And Lincoln does not disappoint us—on the contrary, he exceeds
every legitimate expectation! Let us hear him celebrate the
present success of the cause with almost every excess of allitera-
tion, assonance, repetition, and metaphor:

> The list of its friends is daily swelled by the additions of
> fifties, of hundreds, and of thousands. The cause itself seems
> suddenly transformed from a cold, abstract theory, to a
> living, breathing, active, and powerful chieftain, going forth
> "conquering and to conquer." The citadels of his great ad-
> versary are daily being stormed and dismantled; his temples
> and his altars, where the rites of his idolatrous worship have
> long been performed, and where daily sacrifices have long
> been wont to be made, are daily desecrated and deserted.
> The trump of the conqueror's fame is sounding from hill to

hill, from sea to sea, and from land to land, and calling millions to his standard at a blast.

If the foregoing sample of buncombe seems overdone, listen to the following, from the peroration, to which we adverted above, in which the millennial vision of the final triumph of the temperance cause is hailed in frenzied accents suggestive of passages in the Book of Revelation:

> . . . its march cannot fail to be on and on, till every son of earth shall drink in rich fruition the sorrow quenching draughts of perfect liberty. Happy day, when all appetites controlled, all passions subdued, all matters subjected, *mind*, all conquering *mind*, shall live and move the monarch of the world. Glorious consummation! Hail, fall of fury! Reign of Reason, all hail!

That contemplation of the final victory of temperance should induce such verbal intoxication is an incongruity which, we think, did not escape the author of the passage, especially in consideration of the malicious play on the sense of the word "drink."[15] With this we state plainly our opinion that Lincoln, in the beginning and end of his Temperance Address, was caricaturing the style of the enthusiasts of the movement. The caricature is close enough to reality to please the enthusiasts, while exaggerated enough to indicate to any shrewd non-enthusiast that Lincoln was not such an enthusiast himself. In short, Lincoln's exaggerated style, in the most rhetorical parts of his speech, is a rhetorical device to show how purely rhetorical are the sentiments therein expressed! However, it is not so much the stylistic metaphor in the extremities of the speech as the argument at its center that contains Lincoln's considered views. Before turning to that argument we observe that, throughout the speech, Lincoln employs this same device whenever he presents, even in indirect discourse, the rhetoric of the devotees, old or new, of the movement. When he presents his own commentary or criticism, it is in a style as simple and free from affectation as the Gettysburg Address. Humorless critics, who have failed to perceive the difference between the sober accents that are Lincoln's own and the high style of his mimicry, have called the speech an immature work. We can not readily recall a more precocious example of literary skill.

The central section of the address is introduced by the following sentence:

> For this new and splendid success, we heartily rejoice. That that success is so much greater *now* than *heretofore*, is doubtless owing to rational causes; and if we would have it to continue, we shall do well to inquire what those causes are.

This plain prose follows immediately after the passage from the exordium concerning the conqueror's blast. Lincoln turns from the celebration of the success of the temperance movement to an inquiry into the causes of that success. The alleged purpose of such an inquiry is to enable the success to continue. On the assumption that no one has previously supplied this knowledge, Lincoln implies that true understanding has not hitherto guided the movement; its present success is then due to providence—or chance. We must remember this in observing the praise of the Washingtonians, wherein their wisdom is contrasted with the folly of the old reformers. The wisdom of the Washingtonians is not true wisdom; it is at most what Aristotle would call successful experience, and without a correct knowledge of the cause of that experience it will never be true wisdom. Only as Lincoln supplies that knowledge of causes will it be a true reform movement.

But Lincoln's turn to the quest for "rational causes" leads in a somewhat unexpected way to deeper questions. The rational causes are said to consist, for the most part, in the human passions, which Lincoln here treats, almost like Spinoza, as if they were governed by a necessity as much a part of the order of nature as that whereby a stone falls. The old temperance reformers were the fire-and-brimstone type who used denunciation instead of the persuasion we have already seen Lincoln recommend. What was the result of their tactics?

> To have expected them [i.e., the dram sellers and the dram drinkers] to do otherwise than as they did—to have expected them not to meet denunciation with denunciation, crimination with crimination, and anathema with anathema, was to expect a reversal of human nature, which is God's decree, and can never be reversed.

The quest for "rational causes" is thus a quest for causes rooted in human nature. That men should be governed in their behavior by such causes is here attributed by Lincoln to God: natural law and divine law appear to coincide. However, Lincoln's manner of reference to the divine decree is somewhat heterodox: he says that it "can" never be reversed, not that it "will" never be reversed. Traditionally the God of Israel was thought to be bound by his own promises but not by necessity. It is rather the God of Aristotle and Spinoza who is so bound.[16] Now we believe it was, at least in Lincoln's day, ground common to all Christian sects that the strength of some passions, at least, was not to be attributed to God's decree but to man's sinfulness. While different sects estimated differently the extent of the weakening of man's nature as a result of the Fall, all agreed that in man's fallen condition a knowledge of human nature alone does not suffice. Lincoln's attack on the intemperance of the old temperance movement involved, necessarily, an attack on the premise upon which that movement rested, namely, its theology. That theology taught that the prime conditions of moral reformation were faith and grace and that natural knowledge of natural causes would be worthless without these; Lincoln, to say the least, reverses this priority and seems to argue that rational knowledge of human nature is sufficient and that the intrusion of the doctrine of man's sinfulness into the work of moral reform has been an obstacle to the beneficent operation of these natural causes. It is true that Lincoln also implies in the course of the speech that the Washingtonians not only work in harmony with human nature but that they are *ipso facto* the bearers of a true Christianity, as distinct from the Pharisaical Christianity of the old-school champions. But whether, according to Lincoln, the provenience of the "true" Christianity is the Christian revelation or natural knowledge of human nature is not easy to say. The relation of moral virtue to revelation on the one hand and to unassisted reason on the other is the deepest problem of Lincoln's Temperance Address.

The topical arrangement of the body of the speech is detailed and complex. It has two clearly distinguishable parts, but the relation of these is problematic. Of the thirty paragraphs of Lincoln's text, we refer to numbers three to twenty-four as the body.[17] Of these, numbers three to eighteen may be classified under the heading "causes of present success" and numbers nineteen to twenty-four under the heading "causes of future success." The ratio is thus roughly three to one (roughly, because the paragraphs are not of equal length). However, the part dealing with present success is, in fact, chiefly an account of the causes of past failure. Although the new movement is praised by way of contrast with the old, twice as much space is devoted to condemning the old as to praising the new. When we come to the much shorter section called "causes of future success," we find that Lincoln devoted less than a third of it to what he says will be the main cause of that success—namely, the missionary work of the reformed drunkards—and more than two thirds to discussing the objections of the non-drunkards whose assistance is supposed to be vital but who want no part in a drunkards' movement, reformed or otherwise. If we add up the space Lincoln devotes to objections to both temperance movements, old and new, we find that more than two thirds of the body of the speech consists of criticisms and attacks on temperance movements.

I have said that the relation of these two central parts is problematic. It is not clear whether the second of the two is thought to succeed the first or is conceived as a subdivision of the first. This uncertainty, in a work so carefully articulated, may not be inadvertent. The section accounting for present success is, as we have noted, mainly preoccupied with past failure. This failure Lincoln in large measure attributes, as we have said, to Christian theology, or one interpretation of that theology. The contrasting success of the Washingtonians is attributed in this section not to a contrasting interpretation of Christianity but to a wise (or, rather, fortunate) co-operation with the beneficial passions of human nature. But then in the succeeding section (if it is in fact the succeeding one), purportedly devoted to the grounds for future success, Lincoln concentrates upon the principal anticipated obstacle to that success. This obstacle is the contempt that virtuous men feel for the vicious and their sense of superiority even to those who have reformed. This attitude of proud contempt toward moral weaklings is, incidentally, fully consistent with the idea of a virtuous man as that idea is expressed in the *Nicomachean Ethics*. Aristotle says that the virtuous man does not possess the sense of shame, for he would be incapable of anything shameful. And a man who regards himself as incapable of shameful deeds cannot possibly possess the sympathy toward those who are capable of them, whether reformed or not, that one may possess who is conscious of weakness within himself. In this context Lincoln appeals to the Christian idea of the original and common sinfulness of humanity, to the idea that there are none who are not moral weaklings, apart from divine grace, to overcome the argument of the contemptuous non-joiners. Thus Lincoln in the first of these two sections accounted for the failure of the old temperance movement largely because of the manner in which theological considerations, specifically a doctrinaire application of the theory of original sin, impeded the beneficent operation of human nature; in the latter section he seems to appeal to another aspect of the identical theological dogma to aid in the final victory of the new temperance movement. The fundamental difficulty, as it seems to us, in interpreting Lincoln's Temperance Address is whether the theology to which he appeals to remove the obstacles to final success is the same or different from that which was the root of the past failure of the movement. If this theology is ultimately one and the same, then the alleged condition of the final victory of the movement would be of a piece with the alleged cause of its past failure. There would then be no final victory over intemperance, and the account of the future would in reality be a part of the account of the past.

Let us now turn to the first of the two foregoing parts of the body of the Temperance Address. This also is divided into two main parts: the first devoted to the proposition that the old movement was championed by the wrong men, the second, that it employed the wrong measures.

The warfare heretofore waged against the demon of intemperance has, somehow or other, been erroneous. Either the champions engaged, or the tactics they adopted, have not been the most proper. These champions for the most part, have been Preachers, Lawyers, and hired agents.—Between these and the mass of mankind, there is a want of *approachability*, if the term be admissible, partially at least, fatal to success.

". . . it is so easy," Lincoln proceeds:

and so common to ascribe motives to men of these classes, other than those they profess to act upon. The *preacher*, it is said, advocates temperance because he is a fanatic, and desires a union of Church and State; the *lawyer*, from his pride and vanity of hearing himself speak; and the *hired agent*, for his salary.

Now, of these three, the central class mentioned is that of lawyers, and Lincoln, we all know, was a lawyer. Lincoln warns his audience against the class to which he himself belonged. Or should we say that he warns them, and us, against the class that he would belong to *if* he had been a temperance reformer? This passage should be remembered when, in the sequel, we come to Lincoln's alleged refutations of the objections of non-drunkards to joining the Washingtonians. For who is there, apart from the reformed drunks, whose motives the dram drinkers and dram sellers might not equally suspect? Do not the butcher and baker each have something to sell, and cannot they too be suspected of joining a public hue and cry for interested reasons? If the motives of all such men are suspect, then it would injure the movement rather than benefit it, on the grounds Lincoln shows, if they were to join it. And if Lincoln does urge such men to join the movement, as he later does, does he not show himself a questionable friend? Does he not thereby raise in our minds a doubt as to his motives, of the kind he assigns here to lawyers as a class?

However, in listing preachers, lawyers, and hired agents as the wrong kind of champions for a temperance movement, Lincoln omits to mention politicians. And it was in his capacity of politician, rather than that of lawyer, that Lincoln appeared on the platform. If infatuation with the sound of their own voices is a vice of lawyers, it is even more the vice of professional vote getters. Certainly the power of vanity over the demagogue, who thinks his voice is the voice of the people and the people's that of God, is infinitely greater. It is difficult to avoid the impression that when Lincoln says "lawyers" he means "politicians." The very reason for Lincoln's swimming in the temperance tide was that it was becoming not merely a movement for moral reform but a movement for legislation, a plank in party platforms. In our opinion Lincoln's concentration upon the peculiar virtues of the Washingtonians points away from such legislation and leads much more logically to such an organization as Alcoholics Anonymous, with emphasis on both A's.

But when one, who has long been known as a victim of intemperance, bursts the fetters that have bound him, and appears before his neighbors "clothed, and in his right mind," a redeemed specimen of lost humanity, and stands up with tears of joy trembling in eyes, to tell of the miseries *once* endured, *now* to be endured no more forever . . . however simple his language, there is a logic, and an eloquence in it, that few, with human feelings, can resist. They cannot say that *he* desires a union of church and state, for he is not a church member; they can not say that he is vain of hearing himself speak, for his whole demeanor shows, he would gladly avoid speaking at all . . . Nor can his sincerity in any way be doubted; or his sympathy for those he would persuade to imitate his example, be denied.

Lincoln, the lawyer-politician, could not help joining a movement which, on its face, was concerned with the relief of real human misery. Yet he saw in the currents of passion that swirled about such a movement many that would exploit that misery rather than relieve it. It was impossible to avoid participation in the movement without abandoning the lambs to the wolves. If Lincoln was compelled by his own rhetoric to class himself among the wolves, yet he nonetheless effectively warns those who will listen of the danger of wolves. In so doing he plays the role not of the wolf but of the shepherd.

We come now to the argument that the old-school champions employed the wrong measures. Such measures are said to be wrong for two reasons. The first of these flows directly from the character of the "wrong men." "Unapproachable" men employ the tactics of "unapproachability." Yet the concept of unapproachability is subtly narrowed. It was said before that it was possible to ascribe narrow and selfish motives to preachers, lawyers, and hired agents. But now Lincoln singles out the tactics of denunciation, the tactics of fanaticism, the special province of the preachers. Why such tactics are imprudent we have already seen. But he says here they are wrong for another reason: because they are unjust. Now Lincoln's announced intention of inquiring into the "rational causes" of the present success of the temperance movement would, we think, have been sufficiently realized if he had limited himself to the instrumental question of how to enlist the passions of drinkers in the cause of reform. To say that the old temperance movement was unjust is to say not only that it employed the wrong means but that it was devoted to the wrong end. For justice is not merely the means but the end of civil society.

Lincoln's attack on the injustice of the old temperance movement is elaborated with great care. It is divided into two main subsections: the first of these maintains that drinking was sanctioned by universal public opinion, that such opinion is, in effect, the social basis of conscience, and that nothing sanctioned by it can justly be condemned; the second subsection, which we shall discuss first, is a renewed attack on the tactics of denunciation, an attack no longer limited to its ineffectiveness but emphasizing its inhumanity and moral baseness. Here is the first part of this second subsection:

> Another error . . . into which the old reformers fell, was, the position that all habitual drunkards were utterly incorrigible, and therefore must be turned adrift, and damned without remedy, in order that the grace of temperance might abound to the temperate *then*, and to all mankind some hundred years *thereafter*. There is in this something so repugnant to humanity, so uncharitable, so coldblooded and feelingless, that it never did, nor ever can enlist the enthusiasm of a popular cause. We could not love the man who taught it—we could not hear him with patience. The heart could not throw open its portals to it. The generous man could not adopt it. It could not mix with his blood. It looked so fiendishly selfish, so like throwing fathers and brothers overboard, to lighten the boat for our security—that the noble-minded shrank from the manifest meanness of the thing.

Comparisons are proverbially invidious. But since we know that *Pilgrim's Progress* was one of the books that the young Lincoln read assiduously, we cannot help asking how the purportedly secular doctrine here attacked differs from the spiritual doctrine incorporated in Bunyan's tale of Christian, leaving behind his own blood and kind that he might alone attain the Heavenly City? Turning from such a speculative question, we observe that, whereas Lincoln had employed merciless ridicule to point out the ineffectiveness of the tactics of denunciation,[18] when he contemplates their moral baseness he himself echoes the language of the old-school champions. Lincoln had begun, you will recall, by lamenting the absence of *"persuasion,* kind, unassuming persuasion," from the old temperance movement. But he "forgets" the sympathetic approach which he recommends toward the drunks when he turns to those who saw in drunkenness an absence of "grace," which is to say the tokens of unredeemed original sin. Lincoln had said, "If you would win a man to your cause, *first* convince him that you are his sincere friend." But he speaks of the old reformers as "fiendishly selfish" and says that the "noble-minded" shrink from their "manifest meanness." Clearly, no friendly intercourse is possible between men who regard each other as Lincoln regarded these men. In other words, by his example, though not by his precept, Lincoln *agrees* with the old reformers that some form of ostracism or excommunication is the just, if not the necessary, response to what appears to us as morally abominable. But, while Lincoln does not regard the drunks as abominable, his language characterizing the old reformers certainly implies that they are.

This in turn throws a different light upon the tactics of reform. These tactics consist for the most part of "persuasion," as we have seen. Persuasion means turning potential friends into actual friends. In identifying yourself with the man you would persuade, you lead him to identify himself with your cause. But the very condition that leads to friendship, love of what is common to the friends, involves hate: hate of what is alien to them. For we cannot love something without hating what would destroy it. If I love someone, I will hate his enemies. Love can be seen in part by affirmation but in part also by negation. It was necessary even for Jesus to demonstrate his identification with humanity, his love of humanity, not only by consorting with sinners and Samaritans but by attacking the money-changers in the temple.

With this our argument appears, not for the first time, to have come full circle. As Lincoln began by ridiculing the tactics of denunciation, only to employ them, so now we find him attacking the doctrine of incorrigibility, of irremediable damnation, yet adopting some such doctrine as the tacit premise of the attack. For it is the argument of the whole Temperance Address that it is our duty, so far as in us lies, to make actual friends of potential friends, never to make potential friends into actual enemies. Yet Lincoln, according to the natural law of the passions he invoked above ("which is God's decree, and can never be reversed"), must here be making enemies of the old reformers.[19] Yet so to do could not be justified, on his principles, unless some men were *only* potential enemies and not potential friends. And this could not be true unless in some sense the doctrine of incorrigibility were true.

We must then inquire whether Lincoln's argument is simply self-contradictory or whether there is a valid difference between the sense in which Lincoln must have accepted the doctrine of incorrigibility and the sense in which he rejected it. To see what this difference might be, let us review some passages in which comparisons are drawn between the two classes of "incorrigibles." The first of these is made by implication in the second paragraph of the address, where Lincoln said that the "cause itself seems suddenly transformed from a cold abstract theory, to a living, breathing, active, and powerful chieftain." What is there implicit becomes explicit when Lincoln says:

> They [the Washingtonians] know they [the drunkards] are not demons, not even the worst of men. *They* know that generally, they are kind, generous, and charitable, even beyond the example of their more staid and sober neighbors. *They* are practical philanthropists; and *they* glow with a generous and brotherly zeal, that mere theorists are incapable of feeling.

We may descry a current of argument here suggestive of Edmund Burke's attack on the French Revolutionists. Lincoln, like Burke, opposes "theory" in the name of "practice." But the differences are profounder than the similarities. Burke's attack on "theory" was so wide-ranging and vituperative as to suggest that every attempt, not only that of the disciples of Rousseau, to find a metaphysical foundation for the principles of morals and politics was either base or foolish. But it would indeed be strange to find any real kinship between such anti-theoretical dogmatism and the convictions of the man who was to build his political career on "an abstract truth, applicable to all men and at all times."[20] Lincoln, far from attacking rationalism, is in fact basing his whole case upon it. For, as we saw, Lincoln attributed the failure of the methods of the old school to its ignorance of human nature. Moreover, as we also saw, the hypothesis upon which the body of the address is based is that the present success of the movement must be attributable to "rational causes" and that the central function of the address is to supply such knowledge of causality. Now knowledge of causality is knowledge of nature, human or non-human; it is theoretical knowledge par excellence. However practical his object, Lincoln also presents himself in the address as a theoretician. The old-school champions are then "mere theorists" because they are bad theorists. It is significant and, we think, characteristic that in the passage in which Lincoln denounces the baseness of the old reformers he speaks of this baseness as flowing from a "position" which is an "error." Earlier he had spoken of drunkards as men whose "failing was [traditionally] treated as a *misfortune*, and not as a *crime*, or even a *disgrace*." True vice is then linked with error, even as drunkenness is treated by Lincoln, rather as Aristotle treats incontinence, which is not properly called vice. Lincoln's association of vice, as distinct from incontinence, with error naturally suggests the converse: the association of virtue with knowledge. The Socratic thesis lurking within the Temperance Address may provide the key to much that is enigmatic in it.

The old reformers' conception of incorrigibility was founded upon an interpretation and application of the doctrine of original sin. And Lincoln seems to be saying something similar to what Rousseau said in the *Social Contract*: Whoever says, "Outside the Church there is no salvation," is a bad citizen and must be cut off from the body politic. Lincoln's practical aim, throughout the address, is friendship and harmony in civil society. True temperance is productive of harmony or concord in the soul of society, as in that of the individual. Bad passions constantly threaten this harmony, yet the attempt to extirpate bad passions, as the old reformers did, is self-defeating or worse. For the passion to extirpate, as distinct from the passion to control bad passion, is the worst of all possible passions and produces discord and enmity more than any other. Love, we said before, involves hate in that we cannot love something without hating whatever would destroy it. But the principle thus stated carries an implied qualification: only the love of destructible things involves us in hatred. The ungenerated, the imperishable, the eternal, can be loved without ever requiring us to hate. We noted above that, according to Aristotle, the man of perfect virtue has contempt for moral weaklings. But the contempt of the great-souled man of antiquity for his moral inferiors is a sign of a greater passion. The passion for wisdom or the reflection in the great-souled man of the passion for wisdom is the cause of his superiority, as it is the cause of his contempt for his inferiors. For it is the philosopher's passionate preoccupation with the eternal, with the divine, as distinct from the ephemeral and the merely human, which makes it possible for him to love without hating. How far Lincoln carried the implications of his own position in his own mind we need not here decide; but it is clear that the dogmas of the theological reformers made it impossible for them, even in the name of a God who was ἀγάπη, to love without hating. That the theological reformers were not genuinely preoccupied with the divine is shown by their morbid attitude toward those who, as they thought, did not stand in the same relation to the divine as they thought they stood. They did not derive pleasure so much from the sense of their own salvation as from that of the damnation of others. The old reformers were the prototype of true intemperance. They did not indulge the pleasures of the body; on the contrary, they denied themselves these. But they subordinated the pleasures of the body not to the true but to the spurious pleasures of the soul. The analysis of Lincoln's argument suggests a portrait, as subtle as it is profound, of the most dangerous of all political types: the ascetic reformer whose underlying motivation is perverted sensuality. It is the Angelo of Shakespeare's *Measure for Measure,* and the asceticism of such men, from Cromwell to Lenin and Hitler, insists upon creating a New Jerusalem upon earth, if necessary by removing from the world all who cannot live by their criterion of saintliness. And this morbid irreconcilability to the earthy quality of an earthly existence is inseparably connected, in Lincoln's analysis, to the spurious character of their conception of the divine and eternal. It is an illicit passion, masked by an intellectual error as a passion for justice. The pleasure that such men derive from the odor of their own sanctity, while it may make them proof against ordinary vices, also makes them capable of extraordinary crimes. For their supposed self-mastery is an absurdly intensified egotism, a cosmic vanity. At the same time that it denies them the common objects of passion it denies them common sympathies. But while it excludes sympathy, it does not exclude hatred. Whereas the great-souled man of antiquity was conscious of his superiority, and his superiority begot contempt, his contempt of moral weaklings was like that of an adult toward children and was entirely consistent with personal kindness and indulgence, even while exercising firmness in checking their faults.

The argument just sketched suggests that not sympathy but contempt is the true attitude toward moral weakness. In contradiction to this is the manifest argument employed by Lincoln in favor of joining the Washingtonians, a reformed drunkards' society, and against the position of the contemptuous non-joiners.

> "But," say some, "we are no drunkards; and we shall not acknowledge ourselves such by joining a reformed drunkards' society, whatever our influence might be." Surely no Christian will adhere to this objection.—If they believe, as they profess, that Omnipotence condescended to take on himself the form of sinful man, and as such, to die an ignominious death for their sakes, surely they will not refuse submission to the infinitely lesser condescension, for the temporal, and perhaps eternal salvation, of a large, erring, and unfortunate class of their own fellow creatures. Nor is the condescension very great.

It would probably be unfair to lay too great stress on the fact that Lincoln says "they" and "their" five times in one sentence when referring to Christians. Perhaps Lincoln meant no more by this than he meant in 1846 when, a candidate for Congress, he was charged by his opponent, a minister, with being an "open scoffer at Christianity." This charge Lincoln indignantly denied, although acknowledging that he was "not a member of any Christian Church." However, whether or not Lincoln included himself among those to whom the foregoing argument might be addressed, he supplements it with another and different argument, which is introduced by the last sentence above.

> In my judgement, such of us as have never fallen victims, have been spared more from the absence of appetite, than from any mental or moral superiority over those who have. Indeed, I believe, if we take habitual drunkards as a class, their heads and their hearts will bear an advantageous comparison with those of any other class. There seems ever to have been a proneness in the brilliant and the warm-blooded, to fall into this vice—the demon of intemperance ever seems to have delighted in sucking the blood of genius and generosity.

We here see Lincoln employing two lines of argument, which we might characterize as arguments from revelation and reason respectively. By the first Lincoln addresses Christians through an appeal to the Incarnation, showing that if they join the Washingtonians they can regard themselves as imitating not the inebriate but Christ. The ambiguity of this argument makes it, however, of doubtful value.[21] In the first place, it depends upon the doctrine of man's sinfulness—for the Incarnation was necessitated by the Fall—a doctrine which, as we have seen, Lincoln treats elsewhere as an obstacle to that knowledge of human nature which would be sufficient of itself to effect the work of moral reform. But we may also be permitted to doubt its edifying character even within the context of the theology it invokes. Would those who joined for the motive here suggested imitate Jesus in any spiritual sense? It is to be presumed that Jesus identified himself with sinful humanity from compassion, from love. But would Lincoln's addressees do as much? In taking Jesus as their model, would they not in fact overcome their repugnance to what was below them by identifying themselves with what was above? Would not pride, rather than compassion, be their motive? And would not the act of condescension intensify, rather than attenuate, their sense of superiority? It seems to us that the condescension of "Christians" who thus joined the Washingtonians, not out of spontaneous good will, but from a deliberate decision to mortify their feelings, would have been "positively insufferable."[22] Indeed, such condescension would seem to be the breeding ground of precisely that spiritual arrogance which Lincoln so much deplored in the old reformers. The attempt to overcome that natural contempt which flowed from the natural sense of superiority of the morally strong for the morally weak would then lead only to an unnatural contempt. In short, the appeal here to revelation, apart from the fact that it hardly fits into the category of "rational causality" into which the body of the speech is designed to fall, would overcome the attitude of the contemptuous non-joiners by making of them even more contemptuous joiners. It could hardly contribute to the success of the temperance movement.[23]

Turning to the argument from "reason," we find that it, too, is of doubtful value and full of ambiguity. In the first place, does it strengthen the argument from Christianity to say that, after all, no condescension is involved? If there is no condescension, why mention the Incarnation? If the Incarnation is mentioned, why doubt the necessity of condescension? Whatever independent merits these two arguments have are not enhanced by their proximity.

There is, of course, a large and important truth in Lincoln's assertion that there is a proneness to intemperance in the blood of "genius and generosity," but the inferences which he appears to draw do not seem to be correct. As to the fact, the passions of some men *do* seem to run far stronger than others. Moreover, "nothing great is achieved without passion," and the measure of a man's greatness is the greatness of the passion which his virtue directs toward its proper objects. Yet the powerful appetites which "great natures" have are in themselves morally neutral. Those who succeed in mastering their appetites, subordinating them to the work of virtue, are rightly honored and praised. But, by the same token, those who fail are doubly blamed: blamed for the evil they do, and blamed for the good which they fail to do and of which they more than others were capable.[24] To exempt men of superior talents from blame because their temptation to self-indulgence is greater would be to destroy the ground for the praise of those who overcome temptation. One exception, or rather qualification, to the foregoing criticism may be made. There are situations or circumstances which test a man's virtue beyond anything that virtue itself could anticipate or withstand. From this it is that tragedy results. The catastrophe of a Macbeth, a Lear, or an Othello is beyond mere moral condemnation. Because not even a man of the highest virtue can feel assurance that he would be proof against the slips that led to their falls; he can feel pity, terror, and horror at their fate but not contempt or the indignation that betokens a sense of superiority. This suggests the wisdom of the author of the *Nicomachean Ethics*, in replacing (in Book VII) the simple antithesis of virtue-vice with the wider horizon which includes heroic virtue and bestiality. Within the sphere of virtue-vice, praise and blame imply superiority and inferiority. But there is a region, beyond that embraced by virtue, in which failure does not necessarily involve blame or inferiority.[25] However, to treat the Washingtonians as tragic heroes could only be an act of cosmic condescension or Olympian humor.

Lincoln's argument in the passage under consideration partakes, albeit on a different level, of the same tacit irony which we saw in the Gettysburg Address, when he said that the world would "little note nor long remember." When Lincoln says here that "such

of us as have never fallen victims, have been spared more from
absence of appetite," he says what was literally true of himself
in respect to whisky, but not to a far more dangerous intoxicant.
We have heard Lincoln, in the Lyceum speech, warn of a passion,
as naturally powerful in his own blood as in that of any man,
which "thirsts and burns for distinction." The passion for political
fame might be gratified as Caesar, Alexander, or Napoleon gratified it, by destroying republics; or it might be gratified as our
Founding Fathers did, by constructive works, such as finding a "solution of the long-mooted problem, as to the capability
of man to govern himself." In the earlier speech Lincoln had
indicated that he regarded himself as the heir of the work of
the Founding Fathers but that the discharge of his trust might
require virtue transcending even that of the Founding Fathers.
For they were lured by the pleasing hope, the fond desire, of
that immortality of fame which their work in fact achieved for
them. But Lincoln showed the possibility that their work could
be preserved only if there were those who, though worthy of
equal fame, might have to prove this worth by the silent sacrifice
of fame. But the man who can thus hold even fame in contempt
must be able to hold the value of human opinion in contempt. He
must, in a sense, be above mankind. So here, it would seem, Lincoln's indulgent attitude toward moral weakness is not the condescension of compassion but the condescension of a godlike sense
of superiority which does not hold other men to a standard which
it imposes on itself. For Lincoln has already maintained that it
is rational knowledge which alone can guide a movement which,
however much of "genius and generosity" there has been in it,
has nonetheless been largely a child of fortune. But Lincoln has
also shown us his deliberate refusal to exploit that movement for
narrow political advantage and his dissociation from those who
would. The words by which Lincoln classifies himself among those
whose "virtue" is due to lack of temptation are but symptomatic
of that larger act of self-denial, to which the whole address is
witness and which belies those words.

There is, moreover, little doubt that universal public opinion,
Lincoln's chief witness against the old reformers in his denunciation of their injustice, does not favor his own explicit argument
in favor of joining a reformed drunkards' society. For the same
universal opinion which sanctioned the use of intoxicants and regarded its abuse more as a misfortune than a crime also sanctioned

the exclusion of habitual drunkards from polite society. The common-sense view of the matter was neither that of the old reformers with their theological thunder nor the social and moral egalitarianism Lincoln seems to recommend here. One can treat drunks, reformed and unreformed, with tolerance and humanity and still draw the conventional moral and social distinctions concerning them. How valid these distinctions are may perhaps be better appreciated if we restate Lincoln's argument in more radical form. For although the Washingtonians were themselves concerned only with one kind of incontinence, their principle would apply equally to all.

> By the Washingtonians, this system of consigning the habitual drunkard to hopeless ruin, is repudiated. *They* adopt a more enlarged philanthropy . . . *They* teach hope to all—*despair* to none. As applying to *their* cause, *they* deny the doctrine of unpardonable sin. As in Christianity it is taught, so in this *they* teach, that
> > "While the lamp holds out to burn,
> > The vilest sinner may return."

Since the Gospel also offers thieves and fornicators hope of salvation, we should, if Lincoln's argument were valid, be as ready to join societies of the supposedly reformed among these as of reformed drunkards.[26] But I think it is clear, from all that we know of the human nature to which Lincoln has recourse for his key argument, that this is absurd. That the kingdom of heaven will draw no distinction between the salvation achieved by lifelong sinners and lifelong saints (unless it rejoices more for the former than for the latter) is no sufficient ground for rejecting the moral and social distinction drawn by natural reason between these classes.[27] Universal public opinion sees no contradiction between praying in the same church with publicans and sinners while abstaining from their company outside of it. There will be time enough for that in the life to come.

We have already given our considered judgment that Lincoln did not seriously believe that non-drinkers should join a reformed drunkards' society. The movement properly belonged to the alcoholics alone, and the intrusion of outsiders, far from bringing new success, was bound to make it the game of other ambitions. Lincoln was, however, speaking to a reformed drunkards' society. When considering all the kindly things he says *about* the Washingtonians, one must not forget that he is speaking directly *to* them. He could hardly have taken the position that it was a dishonor to be one of them. The egalitarianism of the kingdom of heaven already existed to a limited extent in the principle of American democracy, in which one man had one vote, irrespective of virtue. Of this fact Lincoln the politician was prudently aware. Yet Lincoln could have pointed out many other ways in which non-drinkers might, by sympathy, generosity, and kindly acts, aid the cause of reform. Instead he chose to raise, in an acute form, the issue of the necessary proportion between virtue and full membership in a good society. By his bad arguments he shows how utopian it is that "good" men should be asked to join a society of "inferior" men. By this he shows still more the truth of the converse: if "good" men are "disqualified" by their goodness from a society of their inferiors, how much more true is it that the "inferior" are disqualified by their inferiority from a society of the "good"? How bad Lincoln must have thought his overt arguments in this section we may glean from the testimony of a silent witness: Lincoln himself never joined the Washingtonians.[28] In concluding this discussion we may then say that the sense of superiority which the virtuous man feels toward those of lesser virtue, and which we have called, perhaps somewhat harshly, contempt, is not repudiated by Lincoln. For the hierarchic moral and social distinctions to which this sense of superiority gives rise are implicit in the consciousness of virtue, a consciousness indispensable to virtue, and hence indispensable to the constitution of a good society.[29]

We now return to Lincoln's thematic discussion of the relation of justice to universal public opinion. You will recall that Lincoln had said that the old-school reformers were unjust in their condemnation of drinking because it had been sanctioned by general opinion. The argument consisted of three parts. In the first Lincoln set forth the evidences of this opinion in the universal practice of using intoxicants ("From the sideboard of the parson, down to the ragged pocket of the houseless loafer, it was constantly found"). In the second he interpreted this opinion from the manner in which people referred to both the good and the ill which came from drinking (". . . none seemed to think the injury arose from the use of a *bad thing*, but from the abuse of a *very good thing*"). In the third he evaluated such opinion. It is to this third part of Lincoln's discussion of the justice of universal opinion that we now turn.

> The universal *sense* of mankind, on any subject, is an argument, or at least an influence, not easily overcome. The success of the argument in favor of the existence of an overruling Providence, mainly depends upon that sense; and men ought not, in justice, to be denounced for yielding to it in any case, or for giving it up slowly, especially, where they are backed by interest, fixed habits, or burning appetites.

It will be observed that Lincoln does not say that whatever universal public opinion pronounces right *is* right but rather that no one can be justly denounced for following it. Clearly Lincoln believed that universal public opinion can change (". . . is it wonderful that *some* should think and act *now*, as *all* thought and acted *twenty years ago?*") and hence that it can contradict itself. But to be capable of transcending such opinion means, in effect, to be capable of living without self-contradiction, something certainly beyond the power of most men. And no one can be held responsible for what is not in his power.

To understand Lincoln's attachment to public opinion it is necessary only to remind ourselves again of the larger meaning of his career. This is shadowed forth as well in the Temperance Address as in any speech of Lincoln's prior to Gettysburg.

> If the relative grandeur of revolutions shall be estimated by the great amount of human misery they alleviate, and the small amount they inflict, then indeed, will this be the grandest the world shall ever have seen.—Of our political revolution of '76 we all are justly proud. It has given us a degree of political freedom, far exceeding that of any other of the nations of the earth. In it the world has found a solution of the long-mooted problem, as to the capability of man to govern himself. In it was the germ which has vegetated, and still is to grow and expand into the universal liberty of mankind.

The revolution of '76 meant, as we all know, the revolution dedicated to the proposition that all men are created equal. But it also meant the revolution which insisted that governments derive their just powers from the consent of the governed alone. And, as the Gettysburg Address was to show, the consent of the governed and the opinion of the governed were understood by Lincoln to mean the same thing. Yet there is a tension between the doctrine of human equality and the requirement that the opinion of the governed shall rule. In a later chapter we shall propound at greater length the significance of this tension in Lincoln's thought. For the present we note that equality and consent coincide in the agreement that, because men are by nature politically equal, majority rule is the right way of deciding political questions. But the right way of deciding does not necessarily produce right decisions. For the majority may even act to destroy the basis of its own legitimacy by repudiating the proposition that all men are created equal. This, of course, is what Lincoln one day believed threatened when, with the repeal of the Missouri Compromise and the Dred Scott decision, the nation appeared on the verge of turning its back on the Declaration of Independence. Without enlightened leadership, capable of enlisting people in the service of a principle higher than their own selfish interests, a leadership which would prevent them from incorporating injustice into those opinions which, by their universality, became the foundation of most men's sense of justice, popular government would not be worth saving. Yet the attempt to enlist men in the service of a higher principle is itself fraught with the gravest danger. The old reformers would plant a theocratic seed in the heart of reform opinion, a seed which could, in Lincoln's judgment, choke liberty. But the Washingtonian movement, and all movements akin to it, could also lead to the same result. For the attempt in a modern democracy to make moral reform a subject of partisan politics could be fatal, both to political life and to morality. Let us try to understand why this is so.

First let us observe that Lincoln says that the revolution of '76 "has found" a solution to the problem of man's capability to govern himself. Now the term "self-government" has from antiquity been understood in the double sense of referring both to political self-government and moral self-government. In the political sense it seems rather to be metaphorical, meaning governing and, in turn, being governed by others.[30] However, self-rule may be spoken of in a sense which is at least partially non-metaphorical when applied to morality. For when a man rules his own passions it is one part of himself which rules another. When Lincoln speaks of the "Happy day, when, all appetites controlled, all passions subdued . . . *mind*, all conquering *mind*, shall live and move the monarch of the world," he is speaking, hyperbole apart, of moral virtue. It is not by accident, moreover, that Lincoln refers to the rule of the intellect over the passions as a monarchic rule. Man's moral freedom is gained by the destruction of equality within the soul of the individual, by the total subjection of many passions and appetites to one mind. Political freedom, on the contrary, is achieved by the overthrow of the subjection of the many to the one. Egalitarianism, which is destructive of moral freedom, is indispensable to political freedom, and vice versa. If, therefore, moral reform becomes the object of politics, if politics is "moralized," so that the emancipation of man, the goal of the political revolution, is reinterpreted to mean the regeneration of man, it will mean the re-establishment in authority of the monarchic principle. Moreover, this authority will be far greater than before, because the reintroduction of the monarchic principle, under democratic auspices, will introduce a far different despotism than that which the revolutions of '76 and '89 overthrew. When the people insist that the people become regenerate, when what is required is not good behavior but purity, then the requirement for participation in political life will have drastically changed. For in the work of regeneration only the pure can take part. Once a democratic government convinces itself, or permits itself to be convinced, that the work of regeneration has been committed to it, then it must cut itself off from the contamination of the unregenerate. How inescapable is the compulsion to escape the contamination of the unregenerate Lincoln's inner argument has amply demonstrated. The moralizing of politics in this sense can only lead to a secular version of the theocratic despotism which Lincoln warned against in the case of the old reformers. Only, in the latter case we could discern in the background the despotism of Cromwell or Massachusetts Bay. In the foreground we can discern Lenin and Stalin.

That Lincoln did not believe in the "moral revolution" which he celebrates in such extravagant language at the end of the Temperance Address is indicated not only by the excesses of the rhetoric. He says, as noted, that the world has already found a solution of the problem of self-government in the principles of '76. From *this* germ, he says, "the universal liberty of mankind" is "still to grow and expand." Now it was axiomatic to the Founding Fathers, as it had been to Plato in antiquity, that political government was necessary only because and in so far as the passions, the requirements of the body, played a role in human motivation. ". . . what is government," wrote Hamilton and Madison, "but the greatest of all reflections on human nature? If men were angels, no government would be necessary." And what was an angel but a being ruled by mind, because his substance was purely intellectual? If the day which Lincoln hails ever came, when "all matters subjected," mind alone ruled, then men would indeed be angelic, political government would be at an end, and the state would wither away. If political government were thus essentially supererogatory, Lincoln could never have regarded the revolution of '76 as decisive for the problem of self-government. He would, like Marx, have regarded it only as a preparation for the true revolution.

It will be recalled that Lincoln spoke, a bare twenty years earlier, of a universal public opinion as favorable to the practice of using intoxicating drink. This, it should be noted, leaves a generation to spare, between 1776 and 1842. The pristine age of political freedom was wholly unconcerned with what is now called by Lincoln the moral revolution. Lincoln ends the Temperance Address with a dazzling invocation of the name of Washington, "the mightiest name of earth—*long since* mightiest in the cause of civil liberty; *still* mightiest in moral reformation." If we had any doubt that the revolution of '76, which occurred by Lincoln's chronology forty-six years before the temperance revolution began, had solved the moral problem of self-government, so far as that problem can be solved by political action, this should put it to rest. For if Washington's name is "*still* mightiest in moral reformation," then it was mightiest before the temperance revolution began. If the Washingtonians, appropriating the name of the Father of their country, had added to his fame, it would have been "*now* mightiest in moral reformation." But the work of moral reform undertaken since the revolutionary era, of which the temperance movement was symptomatic, was not viewed by Lincoln as representing any advance upon the work of the Founders.

The age which gave birth to both the temperance and abolition movements was an age of optimism, of utopianism, of impatience with the imperfections of man's state. The era ushered in by the Declaration of Independence was looked upon by many not as the consummation of the long struggle for political freedom, and against feudalism and superstition, but as an invitation to wage total war against the imperfections of the human condition. For Lincoln too the Declaration was a promise as well as an achievement. The doctrine of human equality, the idea that all should have an equal chance in the pursuit of happiness, expressed an aspiration toward which human life must ever struggle. But Lincoln also saw in the requirement of consent a requirement that that struggle must ever come to terms with the actual conditions of human imperfection, ignorance, and fallibility. To think that we can not only safeguard ourselves from tyranny but rid ourselves of folly would have been regarded by him as the greatest folly.

The mid-nineteenth century was gripped by the idea of progress and the assurance that the later age would be the best. The dangerous delusion was taking hold of men's minds that, since the upward direction of social change was assured, success would ever trammel up the consequences of evil means. It was no longer necessary to restrain one's impatience in dealing with evil. If the cause was right, everything could be permitted. Lincoln, to the extent that he was utopian, was utopian rather in the manner of the ancients, placing the golden age not in the future but in the past. He constantly found that "we are not what our fathers were." His later struggle to restore our "ancient faith" that "all men are created equal" is sufficiently well known. In the Temperance Address we see a paradigm of that coming struggle. We see, moreover, a diagnosis of the totalitarian impulse within the heart of modern egalitarianism of surpassing brilliance.

Part IV

THE CASE FOR LINCOLN

Chapter XI

The Legal Tendency toward Slavery
Expansion

THERE is no better illustration of the moral confusion in contemporary historical literature on the Lincoln-Douglas debates than Allan Nevins's conflicting judgments concerning the repeal of the Missouri Compromise. In his chapter on the Kansas-Nebraska Act he bitterly condemns Douglas, as we have seen, as a man of dim moral perceptions who, feeling no repugnance for slavery himself, could not fathom the depths of anti-slavery feeling in the free states. However, in the final chapter of his four massive volumes, in a review of the causes of the Civil War which gives full prominence to the repeal as the first of a series of ill-fated steps, Nevins has this to say: "Had an overwhelming majority of Americans been ready to accept the squatter sovereignty principle, this law might have proved a statesmanlike stroke; but it was so certain that powerful elements North and South would resist it to the last that it accentuated strife and confusion."[1] One would have thought, from the earlier condemnation of Douglas in effecting the repeal, that northern anti-slavery opinion was *right* in rejecting a doctrine professing indifference to the morality of slavery and that, had an overwhelming majority of Americans accepted such a position, it would have been not a statesmanlike stroke but a calamity. Nevins appears very close to endorsing the view that what is acceptable to the overwhelming majority is right, that slavery is right where an overwhelming majority desire it and wrong where they reject it; in short, that Douglas's popular sovereignty was the true doctrine.

In still another place Nevins observes that "by the late spring of 1858, [Douglas] could feel that as a champion of honesty and democratic principle he had won a memorable triumph . . . The Lecompton constitution was as dead as the Yazoo Fraud. His victory was a moral triumph . . ."[2] But the fight against Lecompton, as far as Douglas was concerned, was a fight entirely on a popular-sovereignty basis. From the beginning to the end of that fight he had asserted that his only aim was to see that the constitution of Kansas should be the act and deed of the people of Kansas, not the work of outsiders, whether emigrant-aid societies, border ruffians, or the President and Congress of the United States, nor, of course, a fraudulent minority masquerading as a majority. If Douglas's victory was truly a moral triumph, if, that is, it did not produce morally desirable results incidentally or accidentally, then it was as much a victory over the free-soil opinion which had condemned him in 1854 as it was a victory over Buchanan's vicious Directory. In truth, Douglas had brought the majority of the free-soil North to the point of accepting popular sovereignty, and it was precisely this imminent possibility that Abraham Lincoln in the spring of 1858 regarded as the greatest disaster that could befall the American people.

Now let us again examine the question raised in the first chapter of this work. Was there no substantial difference between Lincoln's policy and Douglas's at the time of the great debates? Would Douglas's policy have produced freedom as surely as Lincoln's? Would the country have been as well advised to adopt the popular-sovereignty formula for dealing with the slavery issue? What confronts us first of all is Lincoln's massive insistence that the spread of slavery be halted by a principle that treated slavery as wrong *everywhere*. Was this insistence doctrinaire or opportunistic? No one was, in general, more prone than Lincoln to follow that dictate of prudence by which one attempts always to remove evils without shocking the prejudices that support them—allowing time and circumstances to wear down the prejudice. We shall see that this was implicit in the gradualism with which Lincoln approached all concrete questions of reform. Although Lincoln thought all sound policy was based on an "abstract truth" of universal applicability, he also denounced "pernicious abstractions" that set people by the ears for no practically good ends. But Douglas's doctrine of allowing the people of a territory to decide whether or not they wanted slavery was not, in Lincoln's eyes, a formula for avoiding a dispute that had no practical consequences. It was a formula for depriving the North of its moral armor against slavery extension, extension which was threatening to engulf "*all* the States, *old* as well as *new—North* as well as *South*." Professor Nevins has denounced Lincoln's warning, in the house divided speech, that "we shall lie down pleasantly dreaming that the people of Missouri are on the verge of making their State free, and we shall awake to the reality instead that the Supreme Court has made Illinois a slave State" as an "absurd bogey."[3] Professor Randall, in gentler but firmer language, dismisses Lincoln's fears as "imaginary," "extremely unlikely," and based upon "something of a non-sequitur."[4] If these learned gentlemen are correct, if Lincoln's prediction of the real danger of the spread of slavery was simply nonsense, *then* Lincoln was, as we have said, either knave or fool: fool for not seeing what is so obvious to the professors, or a monster of wickedness for deliberately risking the peace of the nation. No defense of Lincoln is possible that agrees with this judgment.

The rhetorical heart of the speech[5] with which Lincoln began the memorable campaign of 1858 and which gave an intensely personal tone to the joint debates is the charge of a conspiracy to nationalize slavery between Douglas, Taney, Pierce, and Buchanan (the four "workmen," "Stephen, Roger, Franklin, and James"). The idea of such a plot is treated by Professor Randall as "quite fanciful and non-existent,"[6] and he apparently regards it a charity to Lincoln to pass over his evidence without examination. Professor Nevins does take some slight cognizance of the evidence supporting Lincoln's charge but regards it as a "partisan conclusion," which, "in the eyes of posterity, was pitched on a disappointingly low plane."[7] He seems to think Lincoln was foolish to give Douglas the opportunity to fling at him the words "infamously false" and to declare "that he [Douglas] had never exchanged one word with Taney or Pierce on the Dred Scott decision and had not spoken of it to Buchanan until long after it was made." Nevins seems to have taken Douglas's word and unhesitatingly pronounces the accusation "unfounded."[8] Yet in his own chapter on the Dred Scott decision, Nevins cites an extensive correspondence between Judge Catron and President-elect Buchanan, a correspondence in which Judge Grier joined and which the Chief Justice is said in the correspondence to have seen.

Whether or not this amounted to collusion is a very fine point of casuistry. But if Buchanan and Taney were in communication, then it is altogether probable that Pierce was privy to what Buchanan knew, since, as Lincoln noted, the outgoing President's endorsement of the anticipated decision matched the incoming President's advance exhortation in favor of it. That there was pre-concert on the part of three of the four "conspirators" is heavily implied in evidence Professor Nevins himself churns up.[9] In the course of the debates Lincoln modified his original charge to the extent that he admitted the possibility that Roger, Franklin, and James might have *used* Stephen and that Douglas might have been innocent of the intention imputed to the other three, but not of the folly of contributing to their ends.

At the end of the famous exordium, with which the house divided speech begins, wherein Lincoln warns of a crisis in which it shall be decided whether the nation shall follow a path leading to the ultimate extinction of slavery or to its legalization throughout the nation, he concludes by asking, "Have we no *tendency* to the latter condition?" This sentence is frequently overlooked. But it is important to keep in mind that the evidence Lincoln assembles in the speech is not so much evidence of a plot as it is evidence of a *tendency* toward a condition in which slavery shall be lawful everywhere in the United States. Lincoln was careful then and thereafter to point out that he did not *know* a conspiracy existed, only that he *believed* it. All his evidence, so far as a plot is concerned, is circumstantial. Yet the vital question which we must ask is *not* whether the circumstances overwhelmingly suggest pre-concert among the principals concerned in them but whether they overwhelmingly indicate a *tendency* toward spreading slavery. Let us ask then first of all whether Lincoln was reasonable in alleging such a tendency. If the answer is affirmative, we may further inquire whether it was also reasonable to assign as a cause of the tendency some kind of plot or conspiracy.

We shall focus attention upon the two massive pillars of evidence upon which Lincoln built his case. The first is the Kansas-Nebraska Act; the second is the Dred Scott decision. The Nebraska bill threw down the congressional prohibition of slavery in the remaining Louisiana territory but asserted that it was its "true intent and meaning . . . not to legislate slavery into any

Territory or States, nor to exclude it therefrom; but to leave the people thereof perfectly free to form and regulate their domestic institutions in their own way, subject only to the Constitution of the United States." The ambiguity in the meaning of "subject only to the Constitution" left doubtful the meaning of "perfectly free to form and regulate." Lincoln pointed out that opponents of the bill (principally Chase) tried to have it amended "so as to expressly declare that the people of the Territory *may* exclude slavery" but that its friends refused. We remark that in the joint debates, when Lincoln reiterated this charge, Douglas replied that Chase had only done this to obstruct the progress of the bill, that Chase's amendment was unfair because he refused to have it said that the people may exclude *or* introduce slavery. To this Lincoln retorted that Douglas knew perfectly well that Chase's principles forbade any countenancing of the right of slavery but that Douglas or one of his friends could have moved the addition of the words that Chase refused.

Here we would remind the reader that in his January 4, 1854, committee report, analyzed at length above, Douglas had enumerated the conflicting conceptions of the relation of the Constitution to slavery in the territories, both in 1850 and 1854. He there noted the school which held that the Constitution protected every citizen in his right to move into any territory, with any kind of property whatever, "and to hold and enjoy the same under the sanction of the law." And the Nebraska bill, in its earliest version, incorporated the provisions of the 1850 laws which left the decision of all constitutional questions to the Supreme Court. Thus Douglas knew, or at least believed it possible, that the Supreme Court might decide that "perfectly free" would not include the power to exclude slavery. We cannot say, of course, and Lincoln could not justly say, that Douglas knew in 1854 what the Court would decide. But the possibility which became a reality in the Dred Scott decision was distinctly contemplated in Douglas's committee report. For in that 1854 report the view adopted by Taney in 1857 is set forth as one of the interpretations of the Constitution the Court might, under the terms of the act, be called upon to adopt or reject. And Douglas must have known, as it was generally known, that in any intersectional issue the Court's membership would be markedly weighted toward the South. This is an obstacle to the belief that, if Douglas was "used," he was used unwittingly.

The Kansas-Nebraska Act threw down the Missouri Compromise barrier to slavery extension. It encouraged the inference—which, however, its author refused to permit to be made explicit in the bill—that slavery might be either introduced or excluded by the people who would go to live in the newly organized territories. Its author alleged that the purpose of removing the congressional restriction was solely to enable these people to be "perfectly free." When, however, the great decision in the case of Dred Scott came, it turned out that "subject to the Constitution" would permit "neither *Congress* nor a *Territorial Legislature* . . . [to] exclude slavery!"

According to Lincoln, the most objectionable and dangerous feature of the Dred Scott decision was not that under it "'squatter sovereignty' [was] squatted out of existence," because the "perfect freedom" of the settlers to form their domestic institutions proved to be exactly no freedom at all. The core of the Dred Scott decision is found, above all, in the proposition that "no negro slave, imported as such from Africa, and no descendant of such slave can ever be a *citizen* of any State, in the sense of that term as used in the Constitution of the United States." "This point," said Lincoln, "is made in order to deprive the negro, in every possible event, of the benefit of that provision of the United States Constitution, which declares that 'the citizens of each State shall be entitled to all the privileges and immunities of citizens in the several States.'" Yet the immediate legal use made by the Court of the foregoing dictum was of less ultimate significance than was the evidence adduced by Taney to support it, evidence culminating in the infamous phrase (which Lincoln did not quote) that Negroes were "beings of [such] an inferior order . . . that they had no rights which the white man was bound to respect." Taney, it is true, did not say that this was what he believed to be true; he only insisted it was what the Fathers of the Constitution believed and held himself bound to give the Constitution such practical meaning as would be justified by the intention of the Fathers. The consequence, however, was that under the Constitution expounded by Taney the Negro had no rights which federal courts would respect. Thus the central tenet of the Dred Scott decision agreed perfectly with the central tenet of the Kansas-Nebraska Act, according to which it was a matter of indifference whether slavery was "voted up or voted down." For "voting up" slavery could not be indifferent to anyone who believed the Negro was included in the Declaration of Independence and was possessed of the same inalienable right to liberty as the white man. What Douglas called the " 'sacred right of self-government' . . . though expressive of the only rightful basis of any government, was so perverted in [Douglas's] attempted use of it as to amount to just this: That if any *one* man, choose to enslave *another*, no *third* man shall be allowed to object." Certainly there was no power under the Constitution, as interpreted by Taney and his coadjutors upon the Court, which would enable any man to protect another man from enslavement if that man was a Negro. Under the doctrine of the Court, Lincoln pointed out, "whether the holding a negro in actual slavery in a free State, makes him free, as against the holder, the United States courts will not decide, but will leave to be decided by the courts of any slave State the negro may be forced into by the master." However, when Lincoln said that, according to popular sovereignty, if one *man* chooses to enslave another, no third man may object, he picked his words with utmost precision. For the Negro was a man, and Lincoln was entirely satisfied that the logic of Douglas's popular sovereignty did not stop with the Negro. If the white man did not respect the rights appertaining to the Negro's humanity, he equally struck at his own. There was no principle, we shall presently hear Lincoln argue, which justified enslaving Negroes which did not at the same time justify enslaving whites.

In what way, however, did Lincoln think that the Dred Scott decision might lead to the legalization of slavery in the free *states?* We have already noted Lincoln's opinion that it denied Negroes any real protection by federal courts. Thus it deprived them of protection from kidnaping into slavery, unless they might find that protection in the courts of slave states. But in judging the possible future by the known past Lincoln was struck by the strange wording in the declaratory section of the Kansas-Nebraska Act, wherein was contained the assertion of the intention not "to legislate slavery into any Territory or State." What business, Lincoln asked, had a mere territorial bill to speak of the power of the people of a "*State*" to introduce or exclude slavery? Indeed, in view of Douglas's long insistence that the Congress of the United States had no power to regulate the domestic institutions of a state, he should have been the last man to have permitted, much less to have introduced, the implication that it had such power. Yet the inference that Congress had such a power can hardly be avoided when Congress declares that it is its intention *not* to exercise such a power.

In the territorial legislation of 1850 Congress had said that states formed from Utah and New Mexico might enter the Union with or without slavery, as their constitutions might prescribe. This, however, was no more than a declaration of how Congress would receive applications for statehood from these quarters. In like manner, the old Ordinance of '87 and the eighth section of the Missouri Act of 1820 were declarations, in effect, first, that the territories in question should be free *as territories*, and, secondly, that applications for statehood from the respective areas would not be entertained unless slavery was forbidden in the constitutions accompanying the requests for admission. Congress might use its undoubted power to admit—or refuse to admit—new states, to lay down conditions of admission. But the principle of the equality of the states meant that Congress had no power over states already admitted that it did not have over the original states. In the Kansas-Nebraska Act, however, it was affirmed that the people of any territory *or state* should be "perfectly free to form and regulate their domestic institutions in their own way, subject only to the Constitution of the United States." The author of the bill refused to have language incorporated in it spelling out the meaning of "perfectly free," and he confessed that there were opposing interpretations of the Constitution, among which he would not decide, some of which would have reduced that perfect freedom to a nullity. And now, as noted above, the Supreme Court, to which the selfsame measure remanded all such questions for decision, had declared such freedom to be a nullity by denying that the Constitution to which territories and states alike were subject permitted either Congress or territorial legislatures to exclude slavery. But the Court, although it had every opportunity to do so—in an opinion which has been widely regarded as three-quarters obiter dictum—did *not* affirm the power of states to exclude slavery.

Although Professor Nevins utterly disbelieves that slavery might have spread to the free states, he concedes that "Judge Nelson had hinted at constitutional restraints upon State power over slavery."[10] Nelson had indeed insisted that the decision by the highest court of Missouri, that Dred Scott's residence in

Illinois did not make him free, was binding in federal court and that the federal court might not question the competence of the state court in such a matter. Then he spoke as follows: "In other words, *except in cases where the power is restrained by the Constitution of the United States,* the law of the State is supreme over the subject of slavery within its jurisdiction. As a practical illustration of the principle, we may refer to the legislation of the free States in abolishing slavery, and prohibiting its introduction into their territories. Confessedly, *except as restrained by the Federal Constitution,* they exercised, and rightfully, complete and absolute power over the subject."[11] But what did the exception mean? Nelson had just asserted that the laws prohibiting slavery in Illinois did not make Dred Scott free if he could be forced to return to a slave state. Now, clearly, Dred Scott had been held in Illinois as a slave. Could the state of Illinois have prevented his owner from bringing him into the state? Could anyone have gone into an Illinois court and secured a writ of habeas corpus for Dred Scott? And, if the Illinois court had declared him free, would an appeal carried to the Supreme Court have upheld the Illinois court, or would the Taney court have again declared that Dred Scott was a slave under Missouri law and that either the full faith and credit clause or the privileges and immunities clause of Article IV of the Constitution "restrained" the free state from thus depriving a citizen of Missouri of his property? We do not know the answers to these questions, but, in the light of the fate of the "perfect freedom" *subject to the Constitution* granted to the people of Kansas and Nebraska by the territorial act of 1854, can it be wondered that Lincoln was suspicious of Nelson's "except as restrained by the Federal Constitution"? Indeed, did not Nelson's exception, in the light of this history, raise precisely the same degree and kind of doubt concerning the constitutional powers of the states that Douglas's original report raised concerning the powers of Congress in the territories?

The Dred Scott decision had pronounced the eighth section of the Missouri Act of 1820 unconstitutional by denying that Congress had power to forbid slavery in any territory acquired as the common property of the nation. We have already observed that in 1820 "Monroe and all the cabinet [including John Quincy Adams and John Calhoun] agreed that Congress could prohibit slavery in a territory."[12] It is safe to say that, prior to the sharp turn by the South toward the defense of slavery as a "positive good" in the 1830's, it would have been difficult to have found anyone, even among the strict constructionists, who doubted the power of Congress over slavery in the territories. The Taney decision denied the validity of a law which had stood upon the statutes of the country for thirty-four years, a law which Douglas himself in 1849 had described as having an origin akin to that of the Constitution, canonized in the hearts of the American people, and as a sacred thing which no ruthless hand would ever be reckless enough to disturb. But it did more. It denied that the first Congress which sat under the Constitution and which had re-enacted the Ordinance of '87—the ordinance which had originally been drafted by Jefferson and which had forbidden slavery in the old Northwest Territory—had acted within the limits of its constitutional competence! In this Congress, as Lincoln was to point out in the Cooper Union speech, there were sixteen of the thirty-nine signers of the Constitution, including James Madison, and the measure "passed both branches without yeas and nays, which is equivalent to unanimous passage."[13] It was signed by President Washington, who did not, so far as we know, have any doubt as to its constitutionality. Taney's argument explaining away the congressional prohibition of slavery in the old Northwest is so tortured that it would require at least a chapter to trace its many involutions. We will quote a single sentence, however, which should suffice for present purposes: "It appears, therefore, that this Congress regarded the purposes to which the land in this territory was to be applied, and the form of government and principles of jurisprudence which were to prevail there, while it remained in the territorial state, as already determined on by the States *when they had full power and right to make the decision;* and that the new government, having received it in this condition, ought to carry substantially into effect the plans and principles which had been previously adopted by the States, and which no doubt the States anticipated when they surrendered their power to the new government."[14] When Taney speaks of the previous action of the states, he refers to their joint action under the Articles of Confederation. In short, Taney attempts to justify the action of the first Congress, in adopting a law enforcing the slavery restriction in the Northwest Territory, on the assumption that the Congress under the Articles of Confederation had greater power to govern territory than had the Congress under the Constitution. We will not attempt to demonstrate, as Lincoln hardly thought it worth demonstrating, that the Fathers of the Constitution did not believe they were establishing a government in any point less competent than that which subsisted under the Articles. And if the action of the first Congress, which re-enacted the Northwest Ordinance, was such a refined point of construction as Taney makes it seem, it could hardly have passed, as Lincoln notes, without yeas and nays.[15]

To the foregoing we would also add that the case of *Dred Scott v. Sandford* was the second in which the Supreme Court had held invalid an act of Congress, the only other being that of *Marbury v. Madison*, decided in 1803. But the case of *Marbury v. Madison* was a far less unequivocal exercise of what is now called judicial review. For Marshall had denied that Congress had the right to add to the original jurisdiction of the Supreme Court; he was insisting on the right of the Court to decide the meaning of the grant of power to it in the Constitution. It was not clear beyond a doubt that he asserted an equal power to determine the powers granted to the other branches of the government by the Constitution. In the course of the joint debates, Lincoln cited both Jefferson and Jackson to the effect that the policy of the United States government, on political questions, might not be established by the judges. Jackson had repeatedly refused to accept the opinion of the high court on the constitutionality of the Bank of the United States as binding on himself. Each officer of the Constitution is sworn to uphold it *as he understands* it, Jackson had said. Although Marshall had in the *Marbury* case used broad language to defend the invalidation of a very narrow area of legislation, the question involved in the case was, from a political standpoint, moot. Taney's decision had a vastly different bearing. The demand for the restoration of the Missouri Compromise slavery restriction was at that time the only real unifying force in the Republican party, the absolute *sine qua non* of its continued political existence. The election of 1856 had revealed that the Democratic party was now a minority party in the nation as far as the presidential vote was concerned. The Whig and Know-Nothing parties were breaking up rapidly, and it was highly probable that the Republican party would become the majority party in the not very distant future. The Republican party appeared to be on the threshold of overthrowing the hegemony of the Democratic party, as neither the Federalists nor Whigs had ever threatened to do. The elections of 1856 carried the clear portent of an impending realignment of political strength in the nation, such as had not happened since 1800. And the decision in the case of Dred Scott, coming hard on the heels of those portents, was a declaration that the election of a Republican administration would be the election of a party dedicated to the overthrow of the Constitution —i.e., the Constitution as seen by Taney. Such a decision went far beyond anything implied in Marshall's opinion in the *Marbury v. Madison* case. It would have been a more just analogy if Marshall had declared that the repeal of the Judiciary Act of 1801 by Jefferson's party had been unconstitutional. Marshall never had a fair opportunity to express himself officially on this matter, and we cannot know whether he would have dared such an opinion. Yet even such a decision would not have been a summons to Jefferson to disband his party and hand the reins of government back to the Federalists. The Dred Scott decision was nothing less than a summons to the Republicans to disband. In the light of this history it can hardly be doubted that the Dred Scott decision was the revolution in constitutional law Lincoln asserted it to be and that the acceptance of that decision as politically binding would have been as much an abnegation of the principles of popular government as were the doctrines of nullification and secession.

Lincoln's ever-repeated theme throughout the debates was that in a popular government statutes and decisions are rendered possible or impossible of execution by public sentiment. It is in reference to such sentiment that legislatures and courts determine what they may and may not attempt. Lincoln did not believe that Taney's court would have had either the incentive or the temerity to pronounce the decision of 1857 in 1854. First the Missouri Compromise had to be repealed; second, the doctrine of popular sovereignty, so called, erected into a campaign plank and an election carried under that obscure banner. Next the people had to be taught that, in re-electing the Democrats to office, they had endorsed the constitutional opinion which had repealed the Missouri Compromise and which had looked upon the congressional power to restrict slavery in the territories as somehow improper, if not positively unlawful. Only when the old idea of the moral objectionableness of slavery, an idea enshrined in the Missouri Compromise, as it had been earlier enshrined in the Northwest Ordinance, had been replaced by the idea of the moral indifference of slavery could the Court have attempted what it did attempt. Only as the Kansas-Nebraska Act, and the party strategy which utilized it to change public sentiment, had in a measure succeeded was the Dred Scott decision deemed possible of execution and hence worth attempting. It was Lincoln's contention, therefore, that if the Dred Scott decision could receive the endorsement at the polls which the Kansas-Nebraska Act had received—or, it should be said, of such an appearance of endorsement as Douglas and Buchanan claimed for it from the results of the '56 elections—then still further revolutions might well be in store. Lincoln did not say that another Dred Scott decision impended, but he said that the acquiescence of public sentiment in the principles of the Dred Scott decision, which struck down the power either of Congress or the people of a territory to exclude slavery, would lay a firm foundation for another such decision. Once the idea of the sacrosanct character of property in slaves was firmly established, then indeed there might be another decision, which would declare that no *state* had the power to prohibit slavery. Such a decision might appear intolerable and unenforcible *now*, Lincoln conceded. But did it appear more intolerable and unenforcible than the decision denying Congress the right to prohibit slavery in the territories would have appeared to Jefferson, Washington, Madison, either of the Adamses, or Monroe? If one such change could be effected, why could not another? That such a change was in fact definitely prepared by the Dred Scott decision Lincoln demonstrated, not in the house divided speech, but in the course of the joint debates.

At Galesburg, on October 7, 1858, Lincoln reinforced his charge as to the danger in the Dred Scott decision in the following words:

> In the second clause of the sixth article . . . of the Constitution of the United States, we find the following language: "This Constitution and the laws of the United States which shall be made in pursuance thereof; and all treaties made, or which shall be made, under the authority of the United States, shall be the supreme law of the land; and the judges in every State shall be bound thereby, anything in the Con-

stitution or laws of any State to the contrary notwithstanding."

The essence of the Dred Scott decision is compressed into the sentence which I will now read: "Now, as we have already said in an earlier part of this opinion, upon a different point, the right of property in a slave is distinctly and expressly affirmed in the Constitution." I repeat it, *"The right of property in a slave is distinctly and expressly affirmed in the Constitution!"* What is it to be *"affirmed"* in the Constitution? Made firm in the Constitution—so made that it cannot be separated from the Constitution without breaking the Constitution; durable as the Constitution, and part of the Constitution. Now, remembering the provision of the Constitution which I have read; affirming that that instrument is the supreme law of the land; that the Judges of every State shall be bound by it, any law or constitution of any State to the contrary notwithstanding; that the right of property in a slave is affirmed in that Constitution, is made, formed into, and cannot be separated from it without breaking it; durable as the instrument; part of the instrument;—what follows as a short and even syllogistic argument from it? I think it follows, and I submit to the consideration of men capable of arguing, whether as I state it, in syllogistic form, the argument has any fault in it?

Nothing in the Constitution or laws of any State can destroy a right distinctly and expressly affirmed in the Constitution of the United States.

The right of property in a slave is distinctly and expressly affirmed in the Constitution of the United States.

Therefore, nothing in the Constitution or laws of any State can destroy the right of property in a slave.[16]

Douglas never met the argument that Lincoln thus presented in syllogistic form, and to our knowledge it has not been met by anyone who has denied the force of its conclusion. Lincoln said he could see no flaw in the reasoning, that the conclusion was inescapable, assuming the truth of the premises. The flaw was in the premises. "I believe that the right of property in a slave *is not* distinctly and expressly affirmed in the Constitution,"[17] he said. His third question to Douglas at Freeport had been, "If the Supreme Court of the United States shall decide that States cannot exclude slavery from their limits, are you in favor of acquiescing in, adopting, and following such decision as a rule of political action?"[18] And Douglas had replied "that such a thing is not possible. It would be an act of moral treason that no man on the bench could ever descend to."[19] Professor Nevins uses almost the same language when he calls Lincoln's prediction that the Supreme Court might make Illinois a slave state an "absurd bogey." For "no court would have dared such folly."[20] But, we may ask Professor Nevins, even as Lincoln asked Douglas, how do we know that the judges who were capable of the Dred Scott decision would not have been capable of this additional folly? If Taney had dared the major and the minor, why would he not have dared the conclusion? It was Lincoln's thesis that the change in constitutional law already effected by the Dred Scott decision was not notoriously greater than the one which he anticipated as a further consequence of the premises it established. Lincoln granted that no Court would have *yet* dared such a folly; what he contended was that the premises justifying such a conclusion were contained in Taney's Dred Scott decision and, if they remained fixed in the law *as premises*, then it was only a matter of time until public sentiment, having accustomed itself to the premises, would acquiesce in the conclusion. When public sentiment permitted such a decision to be executed, he did not doubt that it would be forthcoming.

Professor Randall, without addressing himself very directly to Lincoln's precise syllogism, has also denounced its conclusion. "When Lincoln spoke in 1858, his declaration that the Taney property doctrine of 1857 *might* some day lead to a Federal imposition of slavery upon all the states, was something of a non-sequitur," he writes. "Few constitutional lawyers would contend that the domain of the fifth amendment included the vastly broader field of the fourteenth. That a future Supreme Court would ever rule that the Federal government could impose slavery upon unwilling states was extremely unlikely. Such a doctrine would have been opposed where Northern states prohibited slavery and in the South because of state-rights principles."[21] But Professor Randall's allegation of a *non sequitur,* so far as it is meant to apply to Lincoln's syllogism, is open to the following objection. The minor premise, which Lincoln drew from Taney's opinion, *does not rest upon the Fifth Amendment.* After the sentence Lincoln quoted from the opinion, Taney continued, "The right to traffic in it [i.e., slave property], like an ordinary article

of merchandise and property, was guaranteed to the citizens of
the United States, in every State that might desire it, for twenty
years. And the government in express terms is pledged to protect
it in all future time, if the slave escapes from his owner." Thus
it is the first clause of Section 9 of Article I of the Constitution,
which says that "The migration or importation of such persons
as any of the States now existing shall think proper to admit,
shall not be prohibited by the Congress prior to the year one
thousand eight hundred and eight . . ." and the third clause of
Section 2 of Article IV, which says, "No person held to service
or labor in one State, under the laws thereof, escaping into
another, shall, in consequence of any law or regulation therein,
be discharged from such service or labor, but shall be delivered
up on claim of the party to whom such service or labor may
be due," which forms the alleged basis of Taney's assertion that
the right to property in slaves is expressly affirmed in the Constitution. The portion of Taney's opinion just quoted above
continues: "This is done in plain words—too plain to be misunderstood. And no word can be found in the Constitution which
gives Congress greater power over slave property, or which
entitles property of that kind to less protection than property of
any other description. The only power conferred is the power
coupled with the duty of guarding and protecting the owner in
his rights." Now it is clear that Taney did not mean to infer
from the purely negative expressions of the Fifth Amendment,
which prohibit depriving a person of his life, liberty, or property
without due process of law, the positive duty to guard and protect
the slaveowners in their rights. Taney had previously given the
Fifth Amendment as a reason why Congress might not deprive
men of slave property who had migrated with that property to
federal territories. But although he says that slave property is
entitled to no *less* protection than any other, he does not say
that it is not entitled to *greater* protection. We see here the same
kind of ambiguity as in "subject to the Constitution" or "except
as restrained by the Federal Constitution." The niche is open,
as Lincoln said it was, for a still more privileged position for
slavery. There is no doubt that Taney's expression about "guarding and protecting" slave property gave great impetus to the
southern demand for a congressional slave code in the territories,
a demand which was to split the Democratic party in 1860. For
the moment we emphasize that Taney's assertion that the Consti-

tution expressly affirms the right to slave property, and by this reason enjoins a duty to protect slave property, rests mainly upon a construction of Section 2, Article IV, and does not depend upon the Fifth Amendment at all. And this assertion, combined with the supremacy clause, certainly does yield, as a logical necessity, the conclusion that no state may destroy the right of property in a slave.

However, if the Fifth Amendment were involved in Lincoln's syllogism, as it is not, we may still wonder at Randall's assertion that "few constitutional lawyers" would include the domain of the Fourteenth Amendment in that of the Fifth. Clearly he is thinking of lawyers in the mid-twentieth century, but our question concerns the state of constitutional law in 1858, when the Fourteenth Amendment had not yet been conceived. The reigning constitutional opinion, without question, was *Barron v. Baltimore*, delivered by Chief Justice Marshall in 1833. Marshall had stated that the Fifth Amendment was intended solely as a limitation on the federal government and not upon the states. However, this fact by itself cannot tell us what decision would have been rendered if a legal test had come twenty-five years later. In this connection we cite the opinion of Professor Crosskey, in a recent essay on "Constitutional Limitations on State Authority."[22] According to his investigations, many lawyers and judges, partly from ignorance and partly from a disagreement with Marshall's opinion, did not accept it as a binding precedent. There arose a long series of cases, of which Crosskey gives a partial list,[23] "in which lawyers continued to invoke various provisions of Amendments II–VIII against the states." "In 1840," he writes, "in *Holmes v. Jennison*, the Barron decision was most elaborately challenged in the Supreme Court itself, as erroneous. In 1845, the Supreme Court of Illinois, apparently in ignorance of the Barron case, observed . . . that the Due Process Clause of the Fifth Amendment was 'obligatory upon all the States.' And in 1852, the Supreme Court of Georgia denounced the Barron decision in no uncertain terms and refused to be bound by it . . . And though nineteen years had passed since the decision of *Barron v. Baltimore*, the Georgia Court said it was 'aware' the question the case had involved was 'still regarded as an unsettled one.' "[24] It is not necessary for the purpose of the present argument to enter into the merits of Professor Crosskey's broader contentions, such as his view that the Fourteenth Amendment was intended by its Republican authors to confirm the applicability of amendments II to VIII to the states, an applicability they always had believed (according to Crosskey) to exist. Certainly, however, *Barron v. Baltimore* did not occupy the sacrosanct position in public opinion that Douglas in 1849 ascribed to the Missouri Compromise. If the pro-slavery impulse could in such a short time have accomplished the overthrow of that mighty barrier, with the treading under foot of the constitutional opinions of the Fathers which had lain at its foundation, why might not *Barron v. Baltimore* have also been overthrown? The record of the Supreme Court in the decades *after* the Civil War in striking down state interference with corporate property is notorious. The Fourteenth Amendment was, of course, the text upon which the Court then delivered its sermons. In the reconstruction era it was more convenient for the Republicans to enact new amendments than to trust to reinterpretations of old ones. But, had the struggle of the fifties gone in favor of the party of Pierce and Buchanan, whose administrations were dominated by such men as Jefferson Davis and Jacob Thompson, why should it be supposed that courts dominated by their appointees would have done less for their favorite form of property than Republican courts did for theirs?

Randall says that the South would have opposed Lincoln's imaginary new Dred Scott decision because of state-right principles. Nothing was more improbable. In the decade before the Civil War the South never turned to state-right principles except to defend the institution of slavery. If state-right principles were sacred to the South, it would not have demanded the rigorous fugitive slave law it did. The Constitution says that fugitives "shall be delivered up," but it does not say by whom. The clause in question is not among the enumerated powers of Congress. There is no *a priori* reason for thinking the delivering up of fugitives was a federal and not a state function. And if "state-right principles" were principles, in any proper sense, then it was because of some conception of the superior virtue of local autonomy. Yet the South rejected Douglas as a party leader in 1860 precisely because he insisted there ought not to be a federal slave code for the territories.

But Randall also thinks that such a decision would have been "opposed where Northern states prohibited slavery." If this assertion means that a decision legalizing slavery would have been opposed where slavery was opposed, it is, of course, true, because it is (practically) tautologous. But would there have been continued opposition to slavery in the North if the Dred Scott decision and the repeal of the Missouri Compromise were allowed to stand? Here was the heart of the danger as Lincoln saw it. Professors Randall and Nevins, like Douglas himself, believe it "worse than folly" to think that slavery could have been extended to any of the hitherto free states and territories by any combination of legal or political maneuvers. They believe Lincoln was contending with a shadow, not substance; that the spread of slavery by political means was out of the question, because slavery could spread only where it was economically profitable and that it had already reached its limits of profitability. We shall examine this thesis shortly. For the present we assert that if it were accepted as settled legal doctrine that the right to property in slaves was "expressly affirmed" in the Constitution, there could be no *legal* barrier to a future decision pronouncing slavery lawful in all the states, old as well as new, North as well as South.

Taney's dictum was a literal untruth: slave property was not "expressly" affirmed in the Constitution because the words "slave" or "slavery" do not even occur in that document (prior to the Thirteenth Amendment). A "person held to service or labor" might be an indentured servant as well as a slave. Further, such persons are referred to in the Constitution as held not by virtue of a right affirmed in the federal Constitution but under the laws of a "State." Lincoln repeated over and over (citing Preston Brooks of South Carolina as a witness) that, when the Constitution was framed, the Fathers believed that slavery would some day become extinct, and, according to Lincoln (following Clay), they deliberately refrained from using language which would record the former existence of slavery under it when it had vanished. Certainly the Fathers believed that the states had it in their power to abolish slavery, yet when Taney spoke of the fugitive slave clause as pledging the federal government to protect the slaveowner "in all future time," he used language which strongly suggests a legal foundation of slavery in the Constitution as distinct from the states. In short, a Constitution interpreted by judges of Taney's persuasion might mean anything the interests of the slave power required it to mean. The only security against such interpretations lay in the election of a president who would appoint judges of a different persuasion.

Chapter XII

The Political Tendency toward Slavery Expansion

THAT there was *legal* "tendency" toward the spread of slavery to all the states we may take as demonstrated. Let us ask further in what sense this legal tendency constituted a practical or political tendency? Let us observe that in the house divided speech Lincoln spoke only of slavery becoming "lawful" in all the states. His careful phraseology indicates, first of all, his rejection of Douglas's thesis that the extension or non-extension of slavery in America had never been materially affected by general prohibitions or permissions of slavery. According to Lincoln, the legalization of slavery was decisively important for its extension. He repeatedly cited Henry Clay to the effect that "one of the great and just causes of complaint against Great Britain by the Colonies, and the best apology we can now make for having the institution amongst us,"[1] was that the mother country had refused to prohibit it and had withheld from the people of the colonies the authority to prohibit it for themselves. In addition, Lincoln pointed to the circumstantial evidence connected with the old Northwest Ordinance. Douglas, we have seen, ridiculed the notion that this ordinance had decided the freedom of the states of Ohio, Indiana, Illinois, Wisconsin, and Michigan. The settlers who had gone there had decided against slavery because they had decided it was not in their interest to have it. But why had they so decided? Douglas was driven back on his isothermic theory—soil and climate made it unprofitable. But, Lincoln pointed out, a large part of Kentucky, Virginia, Maryland, and Delaware are as far north as parts of Ohio, Indiana, and Illinois. There was no great difference in soil or climate between the

left bank and the right bank of the Ohio River, such as to decide
that slavery would come right up to the river's edge on the one
side and yet be nowhere seen on the other. There was then no
east-west boundary in nature, between free soil and slave soil,
of which the Northwest Ordinance was only a confirmation. Nor
was there a north-south line. For the state of Missouri stood
directly to the west of Illinois and shared in two thirds of the
latitude of that state. Moreover, as an added point we may note
that the heaviest concentration of slaves in Missouri—areas having
more than 15 per cent slave population—was in a line of counties
extending across the state from a point *north* of St. Louis.[2] In
point of latitude most of Missouri's slaves might have been included in Illinois, Indiana, or Ohio. In his Ohio speeches after the
1858 campaign Lincoln added that Indiana and Ohio had both
(but particularly Indiana) petitioned Congress to remove or
suspend the anti-slavery provision of the ordinance, but the Congress, acting on a report of John Randolph of Virginia, himself a
slaveholder, had refused. Hence it was not true that the men
of the territories under the Northwest Ordinance had paid no
attention to the slavery prohibition. In fact, they had sometimes
chafed under it. What Douglas's whole argument disregarded was
the influence the known existence of such a law might have had
in inducing men hostile to slavery to come to the Northwest and
in persuading men friendly to it to keep out.

It is true that in most of the early settlements north of the
Ohio River there was a preponderance of slave-state immigrants.
It is also true that the early history of Illinois, Ohio, and Indiana
is full of struggles between pro- and anti-slavery parties. This
proves no more than that the simple existence of the Northwest
Ordinance was not sufficient in itself to decide whether slavery
would ever be planted in these regions. But can it be doubted
that the existence of the slavery prohibition weighed in favor of
eventual freedom? Lincoln knew from personal experience that
many migrants across the Ohio from the South, like his own family,
preferred free soil as much as any migrants from New England,
that they had fled the degrading effects of competition with slave
labor and came to the Northwest expecting the promise of free
soil in the Northwest Ordinance to be respected. Further, there
can be no doubt that many slaveholders must have refrained
from bringing slaves into the territory because of the fear of losing
them. And, finally, there is the simple fact that, however tenuous

it might sometimes be, respect for law as such is a factor in determining obedience to it.

During the formative period of the old Northwest public sentiment had, broadly speaking, endorsed the moral as well as legal competence which had enshrined the slavery prohibition in the Northwest Ordinance. It was widely known that Jefferson, himself a slaveholding Southerner, had initiated the move for the slavery prohibition in the Northwest. The pro-slavery settlers had then to conduct their political warfare with a heavy presumption, compounded of morality and legality, against them. Lincoln's argument in favor of the federal restriction of slavery in the territories never relied on the effectiveness of law as such. It was always an argument in favor of a law *as* an expression of the moral sense of the people. The moral sense which condemned slavery naturally demanded a law preventing its extension, and the demand for the law was simultaneously a demand for the preservation of that moral sense. Lincoln was certain, not that the Northwest Ordinance as such had excluded slavery from the territory north of the Ohio, but that the moral condemnation of slavery which demanded and was embodied in the ordinance had kept it out. In the same way Lincoln believed that the Missouri Compromise slavery prohibition was at once both a moral and legal condemnation of slavery. The repeal of the Missouri Compromise, in Lincoln's eyes, did indeed throw down an important legal barrier to slavery. But far more important was the implicit repeal of the moral condemnation. It was this repeal which might in time spread slavery to the free states as well as to the hitherto free territories.

Professor Randall says that Douglas's program "would *inevitably* have made Kansas free both as a territory by popular sovereignty and as a state by constitutional processes."[3] But Randall's monstrous assumption is that popular sovereignty in Kansas would have yielded the same result even if the mighty political upheaval which found expression in the Republican party had never occurred or at least had never achieved the political effect it did achieve. It was opposition to the repeal of the Missouri Compromise which gave birth to the party and which placed ninety-odd Republicans in the House of Representatives in the Thirty-fifth Congress. In the House, where the Lecompton fraud was beaten—Douglas could muster just three Democratic votes (including his own) against the Buchanan forces in the Senate—the Republicans supplied nearly five votes for every one supplied by Douglas Democrats.[4] In other words, Douglas's "success" in making popular sovereignty work in Kansas in 1858 and 1861 depended upon the existence of a party committed to the restoration of the Missouri Compromise slavery restriction, a party utterly repudiating his version of popular sovereignty!

Lincoln's insistence, in the house divided speech, that Douglas was no fit leader of a party believing in the superiority of free soil to slave soil was directed in large measure to those eastern Republicans who rated Douglas's achievement high for having led them to victory in the Lecompton fight. But Randall and Nevins commit the same error Lincoln imputed to men like Greeley. They fail to see that the nerve of the opposition to Lecompton was *not* popular sovereignty but anti-slavery passion. And this passion could not be sustained by a policy which didn't care whether slavery was "voted up or voted down." It was the determination that Kansas ought to be free, not that she ought to have a constitution embodying the will of Kansans, that ultimately assured freedom to Kansas. It is trivial that those who believed Kansas ought to be free of necessity believed that the constitution of Kansas should be the act and deed of Kansans, but it is important to realize that the converse is not true. Douglas claimed great credit for having fought the Buchaneers on the Lecompton fraud, a credit which Professors Randall and Nevins give him in unstinted measure. But, said Lincoln, the Lecompton dispute was not one of *principle* but one of *fact:* one side asserted, and the other denied, that the Lecompton Constitution was the actual expression of the will of bona fide settlers. Buchanan men, Douglas men, Republicans admitted that it *should* be such an expression. "This being so . . . is Judge Douglas . . . going to spend his life maintaining a principle that nobody on earth opposes? Does he expect to stand up in majestic dignity, and go through his apotheosis and become a god, in the maintaining of a principle which neither a man nor a mouse in all God's creation is opposing?"[5] Yet Lincoln held that the attempted betrayal of Kansas by the Lecompton fraud was an outcome of the betrayal of principle embodied in the Kansas-Nebraska Act. The repeal of the Missouri Compromise was predicated upon the moral indifference of slavery and freedom and hence upon the moral indifference of a constitution which expressed the will of Kansans *because* it embodied the equal natural rights of man and one which denied these rights by sanctioning slavery. Douglas, like Buchanan's pro-slavery advisers (Buchanan himself was but a tool), only paid lip service to the principle that Kansas should have a constitution of her own free choice. By the time that Lecompton became a critical issue, opinion in the free states had been so enraged by the aggression originally perpetrated by Douglas's own Nebraska bill that it would have been political suicide for Douglas to have done aught but resist Lecompton, in company with the Republicans. But to have accepted Douglas as a leader, because political expediency demanded that he throw himself into the work of averting some of the consequences of his own mischief, would have been arrant folly. The men who opposed slavery in Kansas would have been helpless if there had not been men in Congress, Republicans from the free states, with the power of their votes to back up the free-soil Kansans. The idea that the slavery issue could be left to be decided in the territories themselves was demonstrated to be pure illusion by the history of Lecompton. If there had been no anti-Nebraska party in Congress—no Republican party—a slave constitution would have been fastened upon Kansas, and Douglas could not have done a thing about it—even if he had wished to.

Lincoln's contention throughout the debates was, in brief, that so long as Congress had the power to admit new states Congress would have the decisive voice—whether exercised affirmatively or negatively—as to whether a territory would be free or slave and whether it entered the Union free or slave. Douglas's Kansas-Nebraska Act left the number of inhabitants required for statehood entirely open, and Congress's discretion in deciding when there were enough Kansans to form a state was in itself a lever of great power in helping or hindering the contending parties in Kansas. It could always decide that the time for statehood was ripe whenever the party it wished to help happened to be in the ascendant.[6] In short, Douglas himself would have been helpless against Buchanan in the Thirty-fifth Congress if a party had not existed in the Congress, a party with the potentiality of controlling the national government, which differed with Douglas *on principle*. But to have accepted Douglas as a leader, or to have weakened in any way the purpose to restore the Missouri Compromise, would have completely disorganized the political opposition to the extension of slavery, for it would have stricken down the only distinct ground for the independent existence of the Republicans.

For Randall to think it "inevitable" that slavery would not have gone into Kansas is to suppose that the same historical effect would have followed if the historical cause had been different. The existence of the Republican party was a *sufficient* cause for the defeat of Lecompton and the turning back of the pro-slavery tide in Kansas.[7] Whether there was present at the same time any other cause sufficient to arrest the spread of slavery into Kansas remains to be seen. The only other possibility alleged then or since concerns the effect of soil, climate, and productions. But even granting—for the moment—the tenability of the economic thesis, according to which slavery would not have proved profitable in Kansas, one can only conclude that the Southerners who indubitably wished to *try* slavery in Kansas would in time have abandoned it. There is no historical ground whatever for asserting the inevitable freedom of Kansas in the immediate future—certainly none for asserting the freedom of Kansas as a territory—except on the assumption of the continuing existence of such a party as the Republican, committed to the congressional prohibition of slavery in the territory. And, again, even granting credence to the economic argument, there is no reason to think that the process of rooting slavery out of Kansas, if it had ever got in, would not have been very long and difficult. Keeping slavery out, as Lincoln said repeatedly, was a thousand times easier than getting it out.

It is as certain as anything that can be asserted about the Kansas struggle that, without the active vehicle of the Republican party to support them, Beecher's bibles would have been an arsenal of little worth in the contest with the Blue Lodges and their border ruffians. Slaveowners did not, and would not, risk their extremely valuable property in Kansas in the turbulent conditions of that struggle. Randall notes with emphasis the absence of slaves from Kansas in 1858 and 1861 and concludes that, because there were none there (to speak of), there would not have been any. All his evidence proves, however, is that under existing conditions owners did not take them. Owners were awaiting the outcome of the struggle. It is simply naïve to suppose that the vast political effort the South made to establish the right to hold slaves in the prairies was one that they never expected to exercise. It made all the difference in the world whether the anti-slavery migrants to Kansas were men who merely thought slavery unprofitable or men who thought slavery a profound moral and political evil. Men of the former description might, in a friendly way, urge slaveowners to return home and dispose of their slaves and invest their money in something more profitable. Or they might find that they were wrong and take a try at slaveowning themselves. Men of the latter description might steal their neighbors' slaves or otherwise attempt their expropriation. It was the hostility to slavery which alone assured such a hostile reception to slaveowners in Kansas, a reception that decided most of them to remain in the shelter of ancestral slave codes until the issue was decided for them in the halls of Congress. Without the Republican party Kansas would not have been populated with men so determinedly opposed to slavery, and there is no way of knowing how many more slaveowners would *then* have ventured into Kansas. But without the sustained determination to restore the Missouri Compromise there would have been no Republican party (i.e., no party of that description). Popular sovereignty "worked" in Kansas in 1858 not because of Douglas but because of the Republicans.

Professor Randall has written, "By 1858 it was evident that slavery in Kansas had no chance. Indeed, the decisive step on this matter was taken in the free-state sense on August 2, 1858, before the joint debates began."[8] This assertion, however, is pure conjecture. Only in retrospect can one say that the rejection of Lecompton by the people of Kansas on that date was "decisive." No one knew *then* that the whole weary business might not have to be done over again. Thirteen thousand Kansans balloted on that August day, rejecting Lecompton by a margin of six to one. But in a country as large as Kansas how durable would a margin of nine thousand votes prove, particularly if Congress should withhold statehood for three, four, or five years? And what would prevent another fraudulent minority from attempting the same hoax over again, this time with success, if a President pliant to the wishes of slaveholders should again use the patronage of his administration to bend Congress to his will? There was, in fact, no assurance known to any contemporary other than that supplied by experience, which was, to repeat, the experience of a vital Republican party. And to have gone to sleep on the conviction that freedom in Kansas, or anywhere in the world, was "inevitable" would have been to take the linchpin from the

Republican party. The "decisive step" of August 2, 1858, meant a crisis for the Republican party, for it meant the replacement of a stern and immediate danger with a subtler and longer-term danger. Nothing but the sustained sense of danger which Lincoln succeeded in driving home to his own cohorts on the hot and dusty prairies of that fateful summer preserved the party and ultimately assured that the "decisive step" of August 2 would be succeeded by other steps in the same direction. When Kansas became a free state in 1861, under the operation of Douglas's still unaltered Kansas-Nebraska Act of 1854, it was not because of Douglas that it did so—or the foolish Greeley, who had wanted Lincoln to withdraw from the Senate race in favor of Douglas— but because of Lincoln.

Chapter XIII

The Intrinsic Evil of the Repeal of the
Missouri Compromise

LINCOLN, we have said, believed in the restoration of the Missouri Compromise restriction on slavery as a supreme necessity of national policy. This necessity did not lie, however, solely or even mainly in the efficacy of the restriction as a barrier to slavery in such places as Kansas. That Lincoln, in flat contradiction to Douglas—and to some present-day historians—believed such a barrier was needed is certain. It was needed because the moral and legal opposition to slavery in free territory, and free states as well, were inseparable. Professor Randall thinks that the free states would not have tolerated a Supreme Court decision legalizing slavery within their borders because they were hostile to slavery. Lincoln, of course, would have granted as much, but Lincoln did not believe the free states could abandon their insistence upon the freedom of the territories without losing the root of the conviction which was the foundation of their own freedom. For the free states to abandon the Missouri Compromise restriction could only signal a drastic change in the moral attitude toward slavery in the free states. Such a change, if it were allowed to proceed unchecked, might very well lead in the not-too-distant future to the peaceful acceptance of slavery there. We have yet to examine the thesis that there was no danger of slavery spreading to free territories or states because it would not have been profitable. For the moment we summarize Lincoln's argument by saying that Republican insistence on the maintenance of the legal barrier in Kansas and Nebraska was indispensable for maintaining the moral fiber of the political resistance to the spread of slavery, whether in the territories or the free states.

We have thus far emphasized the practical importance to Lincoln of keeping alive the question of federal restriction of slavery in Kansas and Nebraska. But we would fail completely to grasp the dimensions of Lincoln's argument if we limited ourselves to these considerations. "If Kansas should sink today, and leave a great vacant space in the earth's surface," he said in the course of the debates, "this vexed question would still be among us."[1] We shall presently see that Lincoln regarded Kansas as no more than representative of other territories which might fall prey to slavery on the basis of the precedent of Douglas's Nebraska bill, if the latter were allowed to stand as a model of territorial law. But above and beyond territories, or states, there was a question of intrinsic right and wrong which was at the heart of the controversy. There was the question of whether, as a matter of principle, slavery should be tolerated only by necessity where it already existed and where the public mind might rest in the belief that it was in course of ultimate extinction or whether it might grow, spread, and become perpetual. This issue was raised by the repeal. It was an issue which, once raised, naturally took precedence over all others. It so took precedence because it involved radically different, alternative ways of conceiving the nature and function of the whole American polity. It was impossible to raise the question which was raised, concerning the status of the humanity of the Negro, without at the same time raising an equally vital question concerning the status of the humanity of white men. It was impossible to deny the Negro the natural rights demanded for all men by the Declaration of Independence without denying the natural foundation of the rights of white men. And it was impossible to change radically the way of conceiving of the white man's rights without changing radically the white man's life. Even if the legal foundation of American rights had remained the same —which Lincoln believed impossible—the changed conception of their extra-legal foundation in "the laws of Nature and of Nature's God" would have been catastrophic to him. It would have been a change in the inner consciousness of the American citizen which would have sapped his moral dignity and have deprived him of inner worth, whether any external consequences were to ensue or not.

According to Professor Randall, the debates were without "significance" because the debaters did not "enter upon the practical and substantial results of their contrary opinions." Randall implies that opinions are not politically significant except as they determine "practical and substantial results." Professor Randall may be correct, but his opinion is not Lincoln's. Or perhaps we should say that everything turns upon what is taken to be "practical and substantial." For Lincoln there was nothing more substantially important than whether Americans lived their lives believing that all men are created equal or whether they did not. For Lincoln the material prosperity of America was chiefly valuable as the external sign of inner spiritual health. And that health—the qualitative superiority of American life—was inextricably and inexorably linked to the tenets of the Declaration of Independence.

There is a view widespread today that the principle of a free society is, in itself, neutral with respect to the differences of opinion which may divide the citizens. According to this view, the processes of constitutional democracy exist for the purpose of allowing differing opinions to compete with each other, and public policy may stand upon the ground of any opinions, so long as these command the support of a constitutional majority. One cannot understand Lincoln's policy in the long course of his debates with Douglas from 1854 until 1860 without realizing that it constitutes a categorical denial of this view. Douglas's doctrine of popular sovereignty, unclear as it was on many points, was nonetheless clear in this: that it conceived of a virtually unrestrained right of local majorities to determine the rights of minorities and to determine these minority rights according to the interests of the majority. It involved a flat repudiation of the principle laid down in Jefferson's first inaugural address, "that though the will of the majority is in all cases to prevail, that will, to be rightful, must be reasonable; that the minority possess their equal rights, which equal laws must protect, and to violate which would be oppression." This Douglas's doctrine did directly, in making the rights of Negroes solely a matter for determination by positive law, but indirectly it had the same effect upon the rights of white men. It was Lincoln's insistence that this was the character of Douglas's doctrine, and that such a doctrine was both untrue and immoral, which constituted his central contention, both theoretical and practical, in his long exchanges with Douglas.

In Lincoln's Peoria speech of 1854 he had declared that he hated the principle of Douglas's Nebraska bill, a principle which acknowledged a right to have slavery wherever men find it in their interest to have it. He hated it because of the injustice of slavery, because it enabled "the enemies of free institutions, with plausibility, to taunt us as hypocrites . . . and especially because it forced so many really good men amongst ourselves into an open war with the very fundamental principles of civil-liberty— criticizing the Declaration of Independence, and insisting that there is no right principle of action but *self-interest*." It is not, of course, for a free government to legislate true opinion with regard to the fundamental principles of civil liberty. But it is certainly the task of statesmanship to create conviction in the minds and hearts of the citizens with respect to these principles. And that man is no friend of free government who flatters the people into believing that whatever they wish to have is right and that he will abide by their demands, whatever they are.

At the end of this same Peoria speech Lincoln rebuts a series of arguments that Douglas had advanced against him after he had given the same speech somewhat earlier at Springfield. Among his remarks are the following:

> In the course of my main argument, Judge Douglas interrupted me to say, that the principle of the Nebraska bill was very old; that it originated when God made man and placed good and evil before him, allowing him to choose for himself, being responsible for the choice he should make. At the time I thought this was merely playful; and I answered it accordingly. But in his reply to me he renewed it, as a serious argument. In seriousness then, the facts of this proposition are not true as stated. God did not place good and evil before man, telling him to make his choice. On the contrary, he did tell him there was one tree, of the fruit of which, he should not eat, upon pain of certain death. I should scarcely wish so strong a prohibition against slavery in Nebraska.[2]

The condition of man under a free government, according to Lincoln, resembled that of man in the Garden of Eden. His freedom was conditional—conditional upon denying to himself a forbidden fruit. That fruit was the alluring pleasure of despotism. "As I would not be a *slave*, so I would not be a *master*. This expresses my idea of democracy. Whatever differs from this, to the extent of the difference, is not democracy,"[3] Lincoln wrote on the eve of the joint debates. A democratic people must abide by certain restraints in order to be a democratic people. The moment they cast these off they cease to be democratic, whether a change takes place in the outward forms of their political life or not. Lincoln said he *would* not be either slave or master. But what was true of Lincoln's *will* was a reflection of the conviction in Lincoln's *mind* that "all men are created equal." People could not be expected long to abstain from the forbidden fruit who did not believe that this abstention was in accordance with a higher principle than their own pleasure. If the pleasures of freedom come into competition with the pleasures of despotism, they cannot survive on the basis of their pleasantness alone. That, we have seen, was Jefferson's and Lincoln's explicit judgment—and it would be a rash man who would deny that they were correct. Lincoln's analysis of the problem of popular government in the Lyceum speech had long convinced him that if the choice of free government rested only on the appeal of such government to the passions—i.e., to the pleasure of the people—it would not long endure. The Lyceum speech demonstrated how the highest ambition of the loftiest souls, hitherto believed capable of gratification only in a monarchic order, might be achieved in the perpetuation of a democratic one. It recorded the discovery in the soul of "towering genius" that the highest ambition can be conceived as consummated only in the highest service, that egotism and altruism ultimately coincide in that consciousness of superiority which is superiority in the ability to benefit others. But what is true of the superior individual is also true of the superior nation; and Lincoln argues in the course of his debates with Douglas that the freedom of a free people resides above all in that consciousness of freedom which is also a consciousness of self-imposed restraints. The heart of Lincoln's case for popular government is the vindication of the people's cause on the highest grounds which had hitherto been claimed for aristocratic forms. In the consciousness of a strength which is not abused is a consciousness of a greater strength, and therewith a greater pride and a greater pleasure, than can be known by those who do not know how to deny themselves.

A free popular government, founded upon the doctrine of universal human rights, would not guarantee that for every individual the rewards of life would always be proportionate to his efforts. But it would be the first in which there would be no guarantee that for all but a privileged minority the rewards could in no event be proportionate to their efforts. It would be the first in which there would be no pre-ordained barriers to distributive justice. To those who argued that the Negro was an inferior being, endowed by nature with lesser gifts of intellect and moral capacity, Lincoln replied that, if the Negro had been given less, that was no reason to take from him the little he had. If he has been given little, that little let him enjoy. Lincoln's understanding of "equality" is then nothing but distributive justice or proportional equality. Every man has the right to labor productively, and he has the right to the fruit of his labor. That one man can labor more productively than another no more entitles him to the lesser man's little than the lesser man is entitled to the greater one's much. Every attempt to deny the Negro equality of right, as distinct from equality of reward, Lincoln called that "old serpent," the root of all despotism, "You work; I'll eat."

The price of American freedom, of all civil liberty, was fidelity to the faith that "all men are created equal." Constancy to this was as necessary to the preservation of the paradise of American freedom as the obedience of Adam and Eve to God's single prohibition had been necessary to that other Eden. Both gardens, alas, had their temptations. The existence of Negro slavery and the discovery of vast profits to be made from it led Americans to believe that all men are not created equal, after all, but that some are born to serve and some to be served. But let this conclusion enter, and force and fraud will, in fact, determine who shall serve and who shall be served. The mere existence of slavery, according to Lincoln, was not a fatal transgression, for the American people were not responsible for its introduction. The spirit of the Revolution had placed the institution far along the road toward ultimate extinction; but the spirit of the Revolution had passed, and a new "light" had dawned. In consenting to the extension of slavery the American people had succumbed to serpentine temptation. And now Lincoln, no less than Moses or the prophets, insisted that a time had come when the question had to be answered by every man, "Who is on the Lord's side?"

Chapter XIV

The Universal Meaning of the Declaration of Independence

THE long political duel between Stephen A. Douglas and Abraham Lincoln was above all a struggle to determine the nature of the opinion which should form the doctrinal foundation of American government. No political contest in history was more exclusively or passionately concerned with the character of the beliefs in which the souls of men were to abide. Neither the differences which divided Moslem and Christian at the time of the Crusades, nor the differences which divided Protestant and Catholic in sixteenth-century Europe, nor those which arrayed the crowned heads of Europe against the regicides of revolutionary France were believed by the warring advocates to be more important to their salvation, individually and collectively. Vast practical consequences flowed from the differences in all cases, but we could not understand the meaning of the differences if we did not first see them as the men who fought for them saw them, as having absolute intrinsic importance, apart from all external consequences.

"Swinging up and down and back and forth across Illinois, making the welkin ring and setting the prairies on fire, Lincoln and Douglas debated—what? That is the surprising thing," says Professor Randall.

With all the problems that might have been put before the people as proper matter for their consideration in choosing a senator—choice of government servants, immigration, the tariff, international policy, promotion of education, westward extension of railroads, the opening of new lands for homesteads, protection against greedy exploitation of those lands . . . encouragement to settlers . . . improving the condition of factory workers, and alleviating those agrarian grievances that were to plague the coming decades—with such issues facing the country, those two candidates for the Senate talked as if there were only one issue.[1]

According to Randall, Lincoln and Douglas ignored any such "representative coverage of the problems of mid-century America" while confining themselves almost exclusively to the question of slavery in the territories. But while slavery in the territories was the single practical issue, it was in large measure subordinated in the course of the debates. For Lincoln there was, indeed, "only one issue," but that issue was whether or not the American people should believe that "all men are created equal" in the full extent and true significance of that proposition. Lincoln did not believe that in concentrating upon this sole and single question he was in any sense narrowing and limiting the range of the discussion. "Our government," Lincoln said before the Dred Scott decision, "rests in public opinion. Whoever can change public opinion, can change the government, practically just so much." But public opinion, according to Lincoln, was not essentially or primarily opinion on a long list of individual topics, such as Professor Randall has enumerated, nor was it the kind of thing that the Gallup poll attempts to measure. "Public opinion, on any subject," said Lincoln, "always has a 'central idea' from which all its minor thoughts radiate." And the "'central idea' in our political public opinion, at the beginning was, and until recently has continued to be 'the equality of men.'"[2] For Lincoln, then, to debate public-lands policy, or the condition of factory workers, when the question of the equality of rights of all the people was in dispute would have been utterly inconsequential. Whether the land would be tilled by freeholders or slaves, and whether factory workers might be permitted to strike, would be vitally affected by a decision concerning that "central idea." Until the matter of that central idea was settled, all peripheral questions were required, by the logic of the situation, to be held in abeyance.

In the first joint debate, at Ottawa, Lincoln affirmed in the strongest language the importance of the contest between himself and Douglas, for capturing the public mind. "In this and like communities," said Lincoln, "public sentiment is everything. With public sentiment, nothing can fail; without it, nothing can succeed. Consequently, he who molds public sentiment, goes deeper than he who enacts statutes or pronounces decisions. He makes statutes and decisions possible or impossible to be executed. This must be borne in mind, as also the additional fact that Judge Douglas is a man of vast influence, so great that it is enough for many men to profess to believe anything, when they once find out Judge Douglas professes to believe it."[3] These expressions, with minor variations, were repeated over and over. The decision in the Dred Scott case, as we have already noted, Lincoln did not believe would have been "possible . . . to be executed," had it not been for the fact that since 1854 Douglas had been inculcating in the public mind new "general maxims about liberty," as Lincoln put it at Galesburg, maxims such as Douglas's "assertions that he 'don't care whether slavery is voted up or voted down;' and that 'whoever wants slavery has a right to have it;' that 'upon principles of equality it should be allowed to go everywhere;' that 'there is no inconsistency between free and slave institutions.'"[4]

The Kansas-Nebraska Act had said that men might have slavery in the territories if they wished to have it, and the Dred Scott decision had decided that they might not forbid it if they wished to do so, because the Constitution of the United States affirmed the right of property in slaves and forbade either Congress or a territorial legislature to interfere with that right. The common premise of both the act and the decision was, in the words of the Chief Justice, that the Negro was an "ordinary article of merchandise and traffic," that he "might justly and lawfully be reduced to slavery," and that he was a being "so far inferior that [he] had no rights which the white man was bound to respect." This meant that the proposition that "all men are created equal," upon which the government of the United States was admittedly founded, either could not be understood in its universalistic implications or that the Negro could not be admitted to be a man. Lincoln controverted the Taney-Douglas premise upon the grounds that it was false historically, absurd logically, and immoral politically.

That the Negro was not a man was something that neither Douglas nor Taney would say in so many words; nor was it something that either affirmed to be the opinion of the Fathers. Yet Lincoln insisted that it was an inescapable implication of their denial of the Negro's natural right to freedom. This he demonstrated in the Peoria speech of 1854 when he said, "The law which forbids the bringing of slaves *from* Africa; and that which has so long forbid taking them *to* Nebraska, can hardly be distinguished on any moral principle."

Equal justice to the South, it is said, requires us to consent to the extending of slavery to new countries. That is to say, inasmuch as you do not object to my taking my hog to Nebraska, therefore I must not object to you taking your slave. Now, I admit this is perfectly logical, if there is no difference between hogs and negroes. But while you thus require me to deny the humanity of the negro, I wish to ask whether you of the south yourselves, have ever been willing to do as much? It is kindly provided that of all those who come into the world, only a small percentage are natural tyrants. That percentage is no larger in the slave states than in the free. The great majority, south as well as north, have human sympathies, of which they can no more divest themselves than they can of their sensibility to physical pain. These sympathies in the bosoms of the southern people, manifest in many ways, their sense of the wrong of slavery, and their consciousness that, after all, there is humanity in the negro. If they deny this, let me address them a few plain questions. In 1820 you joined the north, almost unanimously, in declaring the African slave trade piracy, and in annexing to it the punishment of death. Why did you do this? If you did not feel that it was wrong, why did you join in providing that men should be hung for it? The practice was no more than bringing wild negroes from Africa, to sell to such as would buy them. But you never thought of hanging men for catching and selling wild horses, wild buffaloes or wild bears.[5]

Lincoln ever maintained that, as there was nothing in logic or morals, neither would there long be anything in politics to forbid the reopening of the slave trade if the legitimacy of the extension of slavery were once accepted by public opinion. If Negroes were nothing but an article of commerce, as Taney contended, then it was certainly an arbitrary infringement on the right of property to compel men to pay upward of fifteen hundred dollars for field hands, when they might be bought upon the coast of Africa for the price of a red pocket handkerchief. But, in fact, it had never been generally believed by Americans that it was just and lawful to reduce Negroes to servitude, as the capital punishment for the slave trade indicated. Moreover, Lincoln continued, the man who engaged in the domestic slave trade, the slave dealer, was generally despised and held in contempt even in the South.

> If you are obliged to deal with him, you try to get through the job without so much as touching him. It is common with you to join hands with the men you meet; but with the slave dealer you avoid the ceremony—instinctively shrinking from the snaky contact . . . Now why is this? You do not so treat the man who deals in corn, cattle or tobacco.

Again, continued Lincoln, there are nearly a half million free blacks, worth over two hundred millions of dollars, at the average price (in 1854) of five hundred dollars.

> How comes this vast amount of property to be running about without owners? We do not see free horses or free cattle running at large. How is this? All these free blacks are the descendants of slaves, or have been slaves themselves, and they would be slaves now, but for *something* which has operated on their white owners, inducing them, at vast pecuniary sacrifices, to liberate them. What is this *something*? Is there any mistaking it? In all these cases it is your sense of justice, and human sympathy, continually telling you, that the poor negro has some natural right to himself—that those who deny it, and make mere merchandise of him, deserve kicking, contempt and death.

Douglas's Nebraska bill, later joined by the Dred Scott decision, instituted a "tendency to dehumanize" the Negro, although the moral sense of the American people, South as well as North, testified to the Negro's humanity, to the moral baseness of treating him as "mere merchandise." Before the contest between Lincoln and Douglas was finally over, Douglas said in a speech at Memphis, as reported by Lincoln in his 1859 Cincinnati speech:

> . . . that while in all contests between the negro and white man he was for the white man . . . that in all questions between the negro and the crocodile he was for the negro.[6]

This declaration was not made accidentally, said Lincoln; Douglas had said the same thing many times during the 1858 campaign, although it had not been reported in his speeches then. It indicated an equation, according to Lincoln: as the crocodile is to the Negro, so is the Negro to the white man. Thus it was a calculated attempt to reduce the Negro, from the white man's standpoint, to the level of the brute. "As the negro ought to treat the crocodile as a beast, so the white man ought to treat the negro as a beast."

The attempt to legitimize the extension of slavery was impossible without denying the Negro's humanity or without denying the moral right of humanity or both. Taney, in the Dred Scott decision, had attempted to escape the moral responsibility for such implications by ascribing to the Founding Fathers opinions which he (unlike Douglas) could not bring even himself to espouse. Then he found in the principle of constitutional responsibility a justification for enforcing these opinions.

No one, we presume, supposes that any change in public opinion, or feeling in relation to this unfortunate race . . . should induce the Court to give to the words of the Constitution a more liberal construction in their favor than they were intended to bear when the instrument was framed and adopted . . . Any other rule of construction would abrogate the judicial character of this court, and make it the mere reflex of the popular opinion or passion of the day.

Lincoln agreed wholeheartedly with the foregoing conception of the function of the Supreme Court. But he maintained that Taney was doing exactly what he denied doing; namely, adopting an opinion which had never even been dreamed of until the necessities of the Democratic party, as indicated by the results of the November 1856 elections, had engendered it. In the course of the joint debates Lincoln finally gave it as his belief that Taney was the first man, and Douglas the second, who had ever denied that the Negro was included in the Declaration. The "fixed and universal" opinion from 1776 until 1857 was, in short, almost the exact opposite of what the Democratic party, echoing Douglas and Taney, now professed and now said that the Fathers had professed.

At Galesburg, the other day [Lincoln said at Alton], I said, in answer to Judge Douglas, that three years ago there never had been a man, so far as I knew or believed, in the whole world, who had said that the Declaration of Independence did not include negroes in the term "all men". I reassert it today. I assert that Judge Douglas and all his friends may search the whole records of the country, and it will be a great matter of astonishment to me if they shall be able to find that one human being three years ago had ever uttered the astounding sentiment that the term "all men" in the Declaration did not include the negro. Do not let me be misunderstood. I know that more than three years ago there were men who, finding this assertion constantly in the way of their schemes to bring about the ascendancy and perpetuation of slavery, *denied the truth of it*. I know that Mr. Calhoun and all the politicians of his school denied the truth of the Declaration. I know that it ran along in the mouth of some Southern men for a period of years, ending at last in that shameful, though rather forcible, declaration of Petit of Indiana, upon the floor of the United States Senate, that the Declaration of Independence was in that respect a "self-evident lie," rather than a self-evident truth. But I say . . . that three years ago there never had lived a man who had ventured to assail it in the sneaking way of pretending to believe it, and then asserting it did not include the negro. I believe the first man who ever said it was Chief Justice Taney in the Dred Scott case, and the next to him was our friend Stephen A. Douglas. And now it has become the catchword of the entire party.[7]

While we would not attest, as a matter of historical record, that no man had ever said what Douglas and Taney were saying, prior to 1857, Lincoln's statement cannot be much of an exaggeration, if it is an exaggeration at all. That Washington, Jefferson, Adams, Madison, Hamilton, Franklin, Patrick Henry, and all others of their general philosophic persuasion understood the Declaration in its universalistic sense, and as including the Negro, is beyond doubt or cavil. All of them read the Declaration as an expression of the sentiments of Locke's *Second Treatise of Civil Government*, wherein many of them had read, almost from childhood, that all men are naturally in "a state of perfect freedom to order their actions . . . without asking leave, or depending upon the will of any other man. A state also of equality, wherein all power and jurisdiction is reciprocal, no one having more than another; there being nothing more evident than that creatures of the same species and rank . . . should also be equal one amongst another without subordination or subjection . . ." The Declaration of Independence had said that governments are instituted "to secure these rights," which plainly implied that the security, or enjoyment, of the rights which are all men's by nature does not follow from the fact of their unalienability. The Revolution was a great stroke to better secure the unalienable rights of *some* men, but, still more, it was a promise that all men everywhere might *some* day not merely possess but enjoy their natural rights. This promise was to be fulfilled in and through the successful example of a government dedicated to the security of the natural rights of the men who organized that government, the first government in the history of the world so dedicated. If that government had attempted to secure in their fullness the natural rights of all Americans, not to mention all men everywhere, the experiment of such a government would have met disaster before it had been fairly attempted. But the inability of the Founders then and there to secure the rights of all the men whom they believed possessed unalienable rights did not in the least mean that they believed that the only people possessed of such rights were those whose rights were to be immediately secured.

"Chief Justice Taney," said Lincoln in his Springfield speech on the Dred Scott decision (June 26, 1857), "admits that the language of the Declaration is broad enough to include the whole human family,

but he and Judge Douglas argue that the authors of that instrument did not intend to include negroes, by the fact that they did not at once, actually place them on the equality with the whites. Now this grave argument comes to just nothing at all, by the other fact, that they did not at once, *or ever afterwards,* actually place all white people on an equality with one another. And this is the staple argument of both the Chief Justice and the Senator, for doing this obvious violence to the plain, unmistakable language of the Declaration. I think the authors of that notable instrument intended to include *all* men, but they did not intend to declare all men equal *in all respects.* They did not mean to say all were equal in color, size, intellect, moral developments, or social capacity. They defined with tolerable distinctness, in what respects they did consider all men created equal—equal in "certain inalienable rights, among which are life, liberty, and the pursuit of happiness." This they said, and this they meant. They did not mean to assert the obvious untruth, that all men were enjoying that equality, nor yet, that they were about to confer it immediately upon them. In fact, they had no power to confer such a boon. They meant simply to declare the *right*, so that the *enforcement* of it might follow as fast as circumstances should permit. They meant to set up a standard maxim for a free society, which should be familiar to all, and revered by all; constantly looked to, constantly labored for, and even though never perfectly attained, constantly approximated, and therefore constantly spreading and deepening its influence, and augmenting the happiness and value of life to all people of all colors everywhere.[8]

We are familiar with Lincoln's conviction of the necessity of a "political religion" for the perpetuation of our political institutions and his tendency, fully matured in the Lyceum speech, but finally consummated in the Second Inaugural, to transform the American story into the moral elements of the Biblical story. We cannot help then perceiving the resemblance, in such expressions as "a standard maxim," "familiar to all," "revered by all," and "constantly looked to," to the words of the greatest of all lawgivers:

And these words, which I command thee this day, shall be in thine heart: And thou shalt teach them diligently unto thy children, and shalt talk of them when thou sittest in thine house, and when thou walkest by the way, and when thou liest down, and when thou risest up.

Nor did Lincoln forget the concept of political salvation when, in the course of the campaign of 1858, he said (July 10, 1858):

It is said in one of the admonitions of the Lord, "As your Father in Heaven is perfect, be ye also perfect." The Savior, I suppose, did not expect that any human creature could be as perfect as the Father in Heaven; but he said, "As your Father in Heaven is perfect, be ye also perfect." He set that up as a standard, and he who did most towards reaching that standard, attained the highest degree of moral perfection. So I say in relation to the principle that all men are created equal, let it be as nearly reached as we can. If we cannot give freedom to every creature, let us do nothing that will impose slavery upon any other creature.[9]

At this point we must obtrude some critical reflections concerning the adequacy of Lincoln's assertions with regard to the meaning of the signers of the Declaration. If we ask, first of all, if Lincoln's vindication of the consistency of the Fathers was altogether accurate from an historical standpoint, the answer, we believe, cannot be an unequivocal affirmative. It is true that Lincoln's hypothesis as to the meaning of the Declaration is consistent with the language of that document and is at least superficially consistent with its known philosophic antecedent, whereas the interpretation of Douglas and Taney certainly does the "obvious violence" that Lincoln asserts that it does. We may even supplement Lincoln's indictment by pointing out that Douglas's interpretation transforms the Declaration from a document of natural law to one of positive law. Douglas, in his speech on the Dred Scott decision, had said, as Lincoln quoted him, that when the signers

declared all men to have been created equal . . . they were speaking of British subjects on this continent being equal to British subjects born and residing in Great Britain—that they were entitled to the same inalienable rights . . . The Declaration was adopted for the purpose of justifying the colonists in the eyes of the civilized world in withdrawing their allegiance from the British crown, and dissolving their connection with the mother country.[10]

The last sentence is correct enough as stating *one* purpose of the Declaration. But precisely because the revolutionists appealed to the whole civilized world, to men who were under no obligation to the laws of Great Britain, they did not affirm their rights as Britons but their rights as men, and they appealed not to the laws of Britain for justification but to laws common to themselves and all those to whom they addressed themselves, to the "laws of Nature and of Nature's God." The only logical reconciliation of Douglas's statement with the language of the Declaration would be by means of the proposition that all true men are by nature British! Such a proposition might find its place in some undiscovered operetta by Gilbert and Sullivan, but we cannot imagine the Founding Fathers in the chorus! Still further, the very concept of the unalienability of certain rights is inconsistent with the idea of their being rights of British subjects. The rights of Britons *as* Britons were rights conferred by British law and hence alienable by the same process which conferred them. The King in Parliament might add to them or subtract from them; but the rights referred to by the Declaration are conceived as properties of man in virtue of his nature and hence unalterable by any mortal power. Douglas and Taney were indeed shamefully ignorant of the distinction between natural law and positive human law, and the obviousness of the violence they did to Jefferson's language cannot be affirmed too strongly.

Yet despite the consistency of Lincoln's alternative rendering of the signers' and Founders' meaning, it cannot be endorsed on historical grounds without some qualification. For in the passages just quoted Lincoln treats the proposition that "all men are created equal" as a transcendental goal and not as the immanent and effective basis of actual political right. And, in so doing, he transforms and transcends the original meaning of that proposition, although he does not destroy it. His, we might say, is a creative interpretation, a subtle preparation for the "new birth of freedom." Let us try to understand it more precisely.

The idea of the equality of all men, within the eighteenth-century horizon, was connected with the idea of the state of nature, a pre-political state in which there was no government, no lawful subordination of one man to another man. It was a state which was tolerable but only barely so. Because it was but barely tolerable, "mankind are more disposed to suffer, while evils are sufferable, than to right themselves by abolishing the forms to which they are accustomed." But because it *was* tolerable, it was preferable to "absolute Despotism," which was intolerable. The concept of the state of nature, as a pre-political state, highly undesirable, yet tolerable, is among the axiomatic premises of the doctrine of the Declaration of Independence. To indicate the departure that Lincoln's interpretation represents we observe that the idea of such a pre-political state plays no significant role in his thinking. The only use Lincoln ever made of the expression "state of nature" is when he quoted or paraphrased a passage from Clay's famous Mendenhall speech. The following is the passage, used by Lincoln in his reply to Douglas at Alton:

I desire no concealment of my opinions in regard to the institution of slavery. I look upon it as a great evil and deeply lament that we have derived it from the parental government, and from our ancestors. I wish every slave in the United States was in the country of his ancestors. But here they are; the question is how they can best be dealt with? If a state of nature existed and we were about to lay the foundation of society, no man would be more strongly opposed than I should be to incorporate the institution of slavery among its elements.[11]

Lincoln likened Kansas and Nebraska to the state of nature, where the political foundations of society were about to be laid. This usage, however, is widely different from the idea of the state of nature presupposed in the Declaration. Lincoln and Clay presuppose a more or less virgin country and conditions which are more or less optimum. They envisage the kind of act of foundation portrayed in the dramatic dialogue of Plato's *Republic*, in which reason chooses the "elements" it would incorporate in a "good" society. The Lockean state of nature, on the other hand, although a normative concept, is normative primarily in a negative way: it specifies the conditions under which the right of revolution ought to be exercised, and it specifies the purposes for which it ought to be exercised. But because the conditions under which the right ought to be exercised are very bad conditions (although not the worst possible), the purposes for which the right of revolution ought to be exercised are minimal rather than maximal conditions of human welfare. It is true that these minimal conditions, when stated in terms of the political circumstances of the thirteen colonies in 1776, do not appear to us today as so dreadfully undesirable. What the signers termed absolute despotism—forgetting, for the moment, the powerful but overdrawn portrait of the Declaration—would have appeared as a paradise of freedom to the oppressed humanity of the ages. Yet the fact remains that within the range of their experience, and from the point of view of their concept of the state of nature, they were asserting minimal rights, and they claimed they were absolved of their allegiance in the eyes of civilized mankind because of the insecurity which they had come to feel at the hands of the government of Great Britain. On the other hand, Lincoln's interpretation of "all men are created equal" is *not* that it specifies the condition of man in a pre-political state, a highly undesirable state which marks the point at which men ought to revolt, but that it specifies the optimum condition which the human mind can envisage. It is a condition *toward* which men have a *duty* ever to strive, not a condition *from* which they have a *right* to escape. It is conceived as a political, not a pre-political, condition, a condition in which—to the extent that it is realized—equality of right is secured to every man not by the natural law (which governs Locke's state of nature, in which all men are equal) but by positive human law. Lincoln's interpretation of human equality, as we have already indicated, is that every man had an equal right to be treated justly, that just treatment is a matter of intrinsic worth, that a man's rewards from society ought to be proportioned to the value of his work and not to any subjective liking or disliking.

In his Springfield speech of July 17, 1858, Lincoln said:

> Certainly the negro is not our equal in color—perhaps not in many other respects; still, in the right to put into his mouth the bread that his own hands have earned, he is the equal of every other man, white or black. In pointing out that more has been given you, you can not be justified in taking away the little which has been given him. All I ask for the negro is that if you do not like him, let him alone. If God gave him but little, that little let him enjoy.[12]

Or, as he wrote in a fragment which has survived:

> Suppose it is true, that the negro is inferior to the white, in the gifts of nature; is it not the exact reverse justice that the white should, for that reason, take from the negro, any part of the little that has been given him? "*Give* to him that is needy" is the christian rule of charity; but "Take from him that is needy" is the rule of slavery.[13]

According to Lincoln, as we have said, a man's rewards should be proportioned to his labor, and this is (or should be) a function of his moral and intellectual capacity. Lincoln did not, of course, involve himself in any foolish controversy as to whether the Negro did or did not have the same capacity as the white man; he confined himself to asserting that his claims, *whatever they were*, ought to be determined on the same principle as the white man's.

This followed from the proposition that all men have an equal claim to just treatment—and that the Negro was a man.

To sum up: in the old, predominantly Lockean interpretation of the Declaration civil society is constituted by a movement away from the state of nature, away from the condition in which the equality of all men is actual. But in Lincoln's subtle reinterpretation civil society (i.e., just civil society) is constituted by the movement *toward* a condition in which the equality of men is actual. In the older view, which Lincoln shared as far as it went, the actual recognition of the equality of all men is really a necessary condition of the legitimacy of the claims of the government upon the governed. But it is also a sufficient condition. For the language of the Declaration at least permits the view that, if the government of King George III had not been as thoroughly despotic as it is pretended it actually was, the Revolution might not have been justified. In short, the Declaration conceives of just government mainly in terms of the relief from oppression. Lincoln conceives of just government far more in terms of the requirement to achieve justice in the positive sense; indeed, according to Lincoln, the proposition "all men are created equal" is so lofty a demand that the striving for justice must be an ever-present requirement of the human and political condition. While Lincoln most assuredly accepted the Declaration in its minimal, revolutionary meaning, he gave it a new dimension when he insisted that it provided a test not merely of legitimate government—i.e., of government that *may* command our allegiance because it is not despotic—but of *good and just* government—i.e., of a government which may be loved and revered because it augments "the happiness and value of life to all people of all colors everywhere."

Lincoln's interpretation of "all men are created equal" transforms that proposition from a pre-political, negative, minimal, and merely revolutionary norm, a norm which prescribes what civil society ought *not* to be, into a transcendental affirmation of what it *ought* to be. Lincoln does not, of course, abandon the lower-level Lockean-Jeffersonian demands, yet there is visible a tension between them and the higher ones upon which he insists.

The assertion that "all men are created equal" [he says in the Dred Scott speech] was of no practical use in effecting our separation from Great Britain; and it was placed in the

Declaration, not for that, but for future use. Its authors meant it to be, thank God, it is now proving itself, a stumbling block to those who in after times might seek to turn a free people back into the hateful paths of despotism. They knew the proneness of prosperity to breed tyrants, and they meant when such should re-appear in this fair land and commence their vocation they should find left for them at least one hard nut to crack.[14]

Lincoln was trying to perpetuate a government, Jefferson in 1776 to overthrow one, and Lincoln clearly has exaggerated Jefferson's non-revolutionary purpose. In fact, the equality proposition was indispensable to Jefferson in building his case for the right of revolution upon Lockean ground, but the state-of-nature idea with which it was bound up was alien to Lincoln's whole way of thinking. However, Lincoln was probably right when he said that Jefferson did intend to make a statement which would have future as well as present usefulness, although he may have overstated the degree to which such a thought predominated in Jefferson's consciousness. Yet there is a difference between the use which Jefferson might have intended and the one Lincoln ascribes to him. Jefferson was always more concerned to remind the people of their rights than of their duties. He emphasized what they should demand of their government rather than what they must demand of themselves. Jefferson feared above all the usurpations which governments might commit if the people became drowsy and did not exercise that eternal vigilance which is the price of freedom. He thought in terms of a perpetual struggle between the governors and the governed, as epitomized in his famous epigrammatic assertions, as, "the tree of liberty must be refreshed from time to time with the blood of patriots and tyrants," and "that a little rebellion, now and then, is a good thing, and as necessary in the political world as storms in the physical." The moral horizon of such expressions is markedly different from that of Lincoln's Lyceum speech, with its round condemnation of lawlessness and its conviction that any lawlessness, in such a government as Jefferson himself had helped to found, was an invitation to mob rule and mob rule the prelude to the failure of the entire experiment in popular government. While Lincoln never denied the danger of usurpations by the government, he placed far more emphasis on the danger of usurpations of a lawless people, which might become the usurpations of the government in response to popular pressure. Once the government was established upon a popular basis, the great danger, as Lincoln saw it, was the corruption of the people. Jefferson tended to see the people as sometimes careless of their own rights but as primarily motivated only by the desire not to be oppressed. Lincoln saw in the people, too, the desire to oppress. The Caesarian danger arose because of the coincidence of Caesar's ambitions with the people's desire to oppress; one without the other was powerless.

Jefferson, however, was not wholly unconcerned with the possibilities of popular corruption, as shown by his fear of a propertyless, urban proletariat and his advocacy of agrarianism as a preservative of virtue. Yet Jefferson's position was in this respect in hopeless contradiction with itself, in his simultaneous advocacy of science and an education which was predominantly scientific. For the consequence of science, particularly the emphatically practical science of Jefferson (like that of Franklin), was inevitably such an increase in the productive powers of labor as would necessitate an ever-growing division of labor, ever more commerce, ever improved communications, and the ever-growing urbanization and industrialization of America. Jefferson's agrarianism was a sheer anachronism from its beginning, a vestigial attachment to a world he did as much to destroy as any man. It was a reliance upon external conditions which could not possibly long endure to produce a virtue which he was at least occasionally aware was indispensable to preserve the institutions he so valued. Jefferson's agrarianism, however, was an *ad hoc* remedy for a defect in his theory, a defect of which he was in a confused way conscious, but which he could never overcome. For Jefferson's attempt to conceive of a remedy for the people's corruption was vitiated by his Lockean horizon.[15] All obligation within this horizon is conceived in terms of deductions from the state of nature, the state in which all men are actually equal. In this state, however, in which men have equal and unalienable rights, they have no real duties. The embryonic duties which exist in Locke's state of nature are not genuine duties but only rules which tell us to avoid doing those things which might impel others to injure us. Duties in any meaningful sense arise only in civil society and are conceived as logically required if civil society is to perform well its function of securing our rights. But whether in the state of nature or the state of civil society, men are not instructed, on Lockean grounds, to abstain from injuring others because it is objectively wrong, but because it is foolish: it undermines the security for their own rights. In short, there is little beyond an appeal to enlightened self-interest in the doctrine of universal equality when conceived in its pristine, Lockean form. Whereas for Lincoln, egotism and altruism ultimately coincide, inasmuch the greatest self-satisfaction is conceived as service to others; in the ethics just sketched such altruism as there is is ultimately reduced to egotism. That the patriotism engendered by the struggle for independence gave such an ethics a greater dignity than this suggests cannot be gainsaid, any more than the dignity of the character of Washington or the idealism of Jefferson can be vindicated on such low grounds. Yet it is also true that the widespread lack of concern over the moral challenge of Negro slavery to the doctrine of universal rights in the Declaration in the Revolutionary generation can be traced to the egotistic quality of these rights in their Lockean formulation. For this reason we must concede that Lincoln exaggerated the degree in which the men of the Revolution were concerned with the freedom of all men. And thus there is some color, although it is only the faintest, for Douglas's assertion that the signers would have been inconsistent if they had meant to include the Negroes in "all men" and then had continued to hold slaves themselves. In truth, their principle included the Negroes in "all men," but the Negroes' rights did *not* impose corresponding duties upon the white masters. Lincoln, we believe, gave a greater consistency and dignity to the position of the signers than was theirs originally. Let us try to understand precisely how he did so.

All men admittedly have a *right* to liberty by the doctrine of the Declaration. But so does every man have a right to life. Now, if we conceive these rights as operative within the Lockean state of nature, we will immediately see that no man is under any necessary obligation to respect any other man's rights. For example: because I have a right to life, I have a right to kill any man whom I have reason to believe might kill me. That is, I have no obligation to respect the other man's right to life until he has given me adequate pledges that he will not try to kill me. After I have received such a pledge I have an obligation to him. But

I have this obligation then because, and only because, I have a prior concern to preserve myself. By respecting his pledge I increase my own safety. The same holds true of liberty: I have a right to liberty, which right *permits* me to enslave anyone who, I fear, might otherwise enslave me.

Jefferson once remarked, about the Negro's enslavement in America, that justice was in one scale and self-preservation in the other. Or, as he rhetorically asked on another occasion, shall we present our slaves with freedom and a dagger? Jefferson never hesitated in his answer: the Negro must continue to be enslaved so long as, and to the degree that, his freedom might injure (or, what came to the same thing, might be believed to injure) the white man. Lincoln, of course, was never an abolitionist and always granted the right of the slave states to continue the institution of slavery as long as they felt the kind of dangers that Jefferson (in common with most Southerners) avowedly felt. Yet, when Lincoln said that the policy of the Founding Fathers was to place the institution of slavery where the public mind might rest in the belief that it was in course of ultimate extinction, he was also stretching their attitude to fit *his* theory rather than theirs. It would have been truer to say that they *hoped* it was in course of ultimate extinction than that they believed it was actually in course of extinction. Allan Nevins' observation that "their *expectations* regarding its termination had been much more equivocal than their hopes" is entirely justified.[16] We have quoted Jefferson's views in an earlier chapter which show how badly he wobbled on the prospect of future conditions favorable to Negro liberty.

To resume the theoretical analysis, we may say that no man, from the strictly Lockean standpoint, is under an obligation to respect any other man's unalienable rights until that other man is necessary to the security of his own rights. Only men bound to each other by the social contract are, in a strict sense, bound to respect each other's unalienable rights. And so far are they from being under the obligation to respect other men's rights that they may kill or enslave other men whenever in their judgment this *adds* to their own security. It would also be true, however, that the enslaved Negroes always had the right to revolt and to kill their masters. But the masters would have had no *obligation* to free them until and unless the Negroes had the physical power to make good their freedom. No one has ever expressed more clearly or candidly this view of the right of revolution than Lincoln, in his speech on the Mexican War, when he said that "any people anywhere, being inclined and having the power, have the *right* to rise up and shake off the existing government, and form a new one that suits them better."[17] A people who are so servile as to lack the desire for freedom, *or* who lack the power, do not in any practical sense have the right. The "appeal to Heaven," the *ultima ratio juris,* in which Locke's right of revolution culminates, and through which the rights to life and liberty alone receive their sanction, is the appeal to *force.* And those who do not have force at their disposal have no effective Lockean argument for denying the assertion of despotic power over them.

But if the foregoing is true, what interest did Jefferson and those minded like him have in ultimate Negro emancipation or, for that matter, in the emancipation of any one whom they could profitably enslave? The answer, we believe, may be found (apart from the matter of mere moral taste) in the concept of long-run as opposed to short-run egotism. The freedom of a free, popular republic depends upon the indoctrination of people *everywhere* in their natural, unalienable rights. Security is a matter of freedom from oppression at home *and* freedom from foreign domination. The great Enlightenment of the eighteenth century, of which Jefferson was such an ornament, was famous for nothing more than for its cosmopolitanism. And the essence of this cosmopolitanism lay in the conviction that only when the rights of man are secured everywhere will they attain their maximum security anywhere. It was expressed typically in the belief that republican governments are unwarlike, because when the government is of the people, when those whose blood and treasure pay for wars must decide between war and peace, there will be no more aggressive wars, no more wars for conquest or dynastic glory.[18] In this vein Jefferson, in the passage from the *Notes on Virginia* quoted above,[19] feared that some day the Negro would rise up to enslave the white man. In short, Jefferson really did believe, as did Lincoln, that he who would not be a slave ought not to be a master. But the Lockean root of Jefferson's conviction—the deepest root for Jefferson's generation—regarded this precept as pre-eminently a requirement of enlightened self-interest, as a long-run requirement of the security of the rights of the self-regarding, egotistical individual. But in the short run, in the foreseeable future, there could, from this viewpoint, be no pressing conscientious objection to the continued enslavement of those whose slavery was not, but whose emancipation would be, a threat to the masters. Jefferson, it is true, did, in his eighteenth query, state one further objection to slavery. It was that slavery engendered despotic manners, and he implies (although he does not state) that such manners are inimical to the spirit of free republican institutions. But this argument by itself is also a prudential one and is a condemnation of slavery more for its effects upon the whites than for its wrong to the Negroes. How inadequate it is may be seen by recollecting that Burke, in his speech on conciliation with America, observes the same effects that Jefferson does and draws the opposite conclusion.[20]

Lincoln's morality then extends the full length of Jefferson's, but it also goes further. Jefferson's horizon, with its grounding in Locke, saw all commands to respect the rights of others as fundamentally hypothetical imperatives: *if* you do not wish to be a slave, then refrain from being a master. Lincoln agreed, but he also said in substance: he who wills freedom for himself must simultaneously will freedom for others. Lincoln's imperative was not only hypothetical; it was categorical as well. Because all men by nature have an equal right to justice, all men have an equal duty to do justice, wholly irrespective of calculations as to self-interest. Or, to put it a little differently, our own happiness, our own welfare, cannot be conceived apart from our well-doing, or just action, and this well-doing is not merely the adding to our own security but the benefiting of others. Civil society, for Lincoln as for Aristotle and Burke, is a partnership "in every virtue and in all perfection." And, while our duties to friends and fellow citizens take precedence over duties to those who are not friends or fellow citizens, the possibility of justice, and of injustice, exists in every relationship with every other human being. Indeed, if it was not possible to do justice to non-fellow citizens, the possibility of justice and friendship with fellow citizens would not exist. For civil society is the realization of a potentiality which must exist whenever man encounters his fellow, or it is not a potentiality anywhere. And that potentiality, for Lincoln, found its supreme expression in the proposition that "all men are created equal."

According to Lincoln, the Douglas-Taney thesis with regard to the Negro was historically false. We cannot but pronounce

Lincoln right and his opponents wrong; yet it should be understood that Lincoln's affirmation of the Founders' and signers'
meaning, as distinct from his contradiction of Douglas and Taney,
is not itself impeccable on purely historical grounds. But if it is
not impeccable historically, it is superior on logical and moral
grounds to the doctrine it purports to interpret. To what extent
Lincoln was conscious that his interpretation was "creative" we
cannot absolutely say. Yet we cannot forget that in the Lyceum
speech Lincoln warned that the Revolution was supported not
only by the sense of right but by the passions of the revolutionists,
both by the base passions of the people of hatred and revenge
and by the noble but dangerous passion of the leaders for fame
and distinction. And we cannot help noticing that the Lockean
interpretation of unalienable rights, which we have sketched,
ultimately views such rights as reducible to *passions*.[21] For the
right to life and liberty is held to be indefeasible in Locke just
because the passion for life, and for the necessary means thereto,
is held to be indefeasible. But when Lincoln said, as he repeatedly
did say in the debates, that Douglas's "Don't care" policy with
respect to slavery was an absurdity, because it tolerated the notion
that there was such a thing as a right to do wrong, he super-
imposed upon the Lockean doctrine of the unalienable right to
liberty a very different conception of right. The Lockean idea
of a right to liberty meant that no one can consistently appeal
to *my* sense of right to give up *my* liberty, but it does not mean
that a man who enslaves another violates the enslaver's sense
of *what is right*. Lincoln confounds the meaning of *a right*, meaning an indefeasible desire or passion, with *what is right*, meaning
an objective state or condition in which justice is done. Lincoln
does not, however, deny that there are natural rights in the
Lockean sense; i.e., that there are indefeasible passions which
entitle all men to reject allegedly moral claims upon them which
are inconsistent with the gratification of these passions.[22] But
while the Lyceum speech conceded the adequacy of the notion
of natural right as the right of the passions, for the purposes of
the Revolutionary generation, it also denied its future utility.
"Passion has helped us; but can do so no more . . . Reason . . .
must furnish all the materials for our future support . . ." From
Lincoln's 1838 criticism of the Revolution we suspect that he was
not innocent of the nature of his subsequent "reconstruction" of
the meaning of the Fathers. For as passion is subjective so is rea-

son objective. The concept of *what is right* is the concept of an objective condition, a condition discernible by reason. "All I ask for the negro is that if you do not like him, let him alone," said Lincoln with a pathos which anticipates the war years. But his meaning is that the test of right is not how something agrees with our passions but how it agrees with a discernment of what is due to a man. Right conceived as subjective passion does *not* forbid us to do what is objectively wrong; it only directs us to do whatever we deem necessary for *our* lives and *our* liberty. Right conceived as a state or condition in which every man is rendered his due forbids us to dissociate the value to ourselves of our own lives and liberties and the value to themselves of the lives and liberties of any men who may be affected by our actions.

Chapter XV

The Form and Substance of Political
Freedom in the Modern World

DOUGLAS's policy with respect to slavery, we have said in an earlier chapter, constituted a kind of agreement to disagree. The desirability of such an agreement was predicated, in turn, upon his belief that "we exist as a nation only by virtue of the Constitution" and that therefore a scrupulous observance of all constitutional duties was all that was really necessary for the states and sections to live amicably together. Citizens of the several states might continue to hold differing opinions on slavery because they would abstain from any attempt to frame a joint policy on slavery, an attempt which would inevitably produce collision. Lincoln, however, categorically denied the whole foundation of this policy, because Lincoln denied that we existed as a nation solely, or even mainly, by virtue of the Constitution. This denial he was to make the affirmative faith of the nation at Gettysburg, when "fourscore and seven years ago" carefully placed the birth of the nation in the year 1776, not the year 1787. And the life principle of the nation was then said to be not the compromises of the Constitution—which Lincoln, as an honest man, always admitted and freely accepted—but in the dedication and rededication to the equality of all men. The Constitution and the Union might be regarded as *formal* causes of nationhood; although qua forms they were certainly destined to metamorphosis: the Union by the addition of new states, and the Constitution by amendments. But the central proposition of the Declaration was its *final* cause. It was common dedication to this which was the primary constituent element in our nationhood, and no change in the final cause was possible which would not destroy the nation so constituted. Lincoln's attitude toward the "central idea" of American political public opinion, which was also the central constitutive element of American nationality, is again suggestive of a central theme of Aristotle's *Politics*. In the third book of that work Aristotle asks, by virtue of what is it that the identity of a *polis* is established? It is not because men inhabit a certain place, Aristotle says, because a wall could be built around the Peloponnesus—but that would not make those so embraced fellow citizens. Similarly it is not any particular group of citizens, for the citizens who comprise a city (we might say nationals who comprise a nation) are always changing, like the water in a river. A *polis*, Aristotle says, is a partnership or association, a partnership in a *politeia*. And the *politeia* is the form of the *polis*, as the soul is the form of the body.[1] Therefore the *polis* is no longer the same when the *politeia* changes, any more than a chorus is the same when the persons who have comprised a tragic chorus now constitute a comic chorus. The Greek word *politeia* has been employed because it is usually translated *constitution*, as in the expression *American Constitution*. But the Constitution is a set of laws, albeit fundamental laws. However, the *politeia* is not the laws but rather the animating principle of the laws, by virtue of which the laws are laws of a certain kind. Consequently Aristotle says, "The laws should be laid down, and all people do lay them down, to suit the *politeiai* and not the *politeiai* to suit the laws." This relationship is excellently expressed in a fragmentary writing of Lincoln's which has no date and is ascribed to the period after the 1858 campaign but before his inauguration.[2] The language expresses more concisely and more beautifully the essential argument maintained by Lincoln throughout the debates on the relationship of the Declaration of Independence to the Constitution and Union than anything in his actual speeches. It is a meditation upon *Proverbs* 25:11:

> All this is not the result of accident. It has a philosophical cause. Without the *Constitution* and the *Union*, we could not have attained the result; but even these, are not the primary cause of our great prosperity. There is something back of these, entwining itself more closely about the human heart. That something, is the principle of "Liberty to all"—

the principle that clears the *path* for all—gives hope to all—and, by consequence, *enterprize*, and *industry* to all.

The *expression* of that principle, in our Declaration of Independence, was most happy, and fortunate. *Without* this, as well as *with* it, we could have declared our independence of Great Britain; but *without* it, we could not, I think, have secured our free government, and consequent prosperity. No oppressed people will *fight*, and endure, as our fathers did, without the promise of something better, than a mere change of masters.

The assertion of that *principle*, at *that time*, was the word, *"fitly spoken"* which has proved an "apple of gold" to us. The *Union*, and the *Constitution*, are the *picture* of *silver*, subsequently framed around it. The picture was made, not to *conceal*, or destroy the apple; but to *adorn*, and *preserve* it. The picture was made *for* the apple—*not* the apple for the picture.

So let us act, that neither *picture*, or *apple* shall ever be blurred, or bruised or broken.

That we may so act, we must study, and understand the points of danger.

It would thus be no exaggeration to say that, according to Lincoln, the relation of the famous proposition to the Constitution and Union corresponded to the relation of soul to body. The breakup of the Union would have been fatal from one point of view, but what would it have availed for the body to have survived the death of the soul? Douglas wished to preserve the Union of states by a concession to that opinion which looked upon slavery as a positive good. Douglas may not have agreed with that opinion—although his disagreement is highly equivocal, in that he always endorsed the theory of racial inequality which justified Negro slavery—but his doctrine of popular sovereignty gave a stamp of moral approval to the decision of any white majority to have slavery. Douglas thought that only by recognizing the equality of majorities of white Americans could the constitutional equality of the states be maintained and therewith loyalty to the principle of federal union. But, said Lincoln, the "central idea" of the Republic is *not* "that 'all States as States, are equal' nor yet that 'all citizens as citizens are equal,' but . . . the broader, better declaration, including both these and much more, that 'all *men* are created equal.'"[3] The idea of preserving constitutional equality by repudiating human equality was a moral and logical monstrosity.

According to Lincoln, the extension or non-extension of slavery in 1858 would be possible only in so far as the people of the United States adopted, or repudiated, the view that slavery was morally right and socially desirable. This, in turn, hinged upon their denial of the universal meaning of the Declaration of Independence or their return to its "ancient" meaning. The issue that Douglas tried throughout the debates to make between himself and his opponent was that

> Mr. Lincoln asserts as a fundamental principle of this government, that there must be uniformity in the local laws and domestic institutions of each and all the states of the Union . . . In other words, Mr. Lincoln advocates boldly and clearly a war of sections, a war of the North against the South, of the free states against the slave states—a war of extermination—to be continued—until the one or the other shall be subdued and all the states shall either become free or become slave.
>
> Now, my friends . . . I assert that it is neither desirable nor possible that there should be uniformity in the local institutions . . . of the different states of this Union. . . . I therefore conceive that my friend, Mr. Lincoln, has totally misapprehended the great principles upon which our government rests . . . Uniformity is the parent of despotism the world over, not only in politics but in religion. Wherever the doctrine of uniformity is proclaimed, that all the states must be free or slave, that all labor must be white or black, that all the citizens of the different states must have the same privileges or be governed by the same regulations, you have destroyed the greatest safeguard which our institutions have thrown around the rights of the citizen.[4]

Douglas has gained great credit among historians for his accurate prognostication that the end result of Lincoln's policy would be a war between the states culminating in the final overthrow of freedom or slavery. Lincoln never denied that such a war was possible, but he insisted that it was no part of his intention to bring it about. And he would not be frightened from his policy by threats of war against it. Douglas's assertion that Lincoln insisted upon uniformity is, however, true in a certain sense. But in the sense in which it is true Douglas himself also demanded uniformity. For if such an aphorism as Douglas's "uniformity is the parent of despotism" is true, then Douglas must have believed it was as desirable that there be uniformity of conviction on *this* as Lincoln believed it was desirable to have uniformity of conviction on the moral wrong of slavery. The only true issue was *what* are the convictions—and hence what are the institutions—with respect to which it is desirable to have uniformity and what are the ones with respect to which diversity is either permissible or desirable, or both. Lincoln insisted that the diversity which sprang from soil and climate—or the diversity which sprang from religious freedom—was both permissible and desirable. *But slavery was not such a thing.* A free people cannot disagree, or agree to disagree, on the relative merits of freedom and despotism. If the majority favors despotism, it is no longer a free people, whether the form of the government has already changed or not. Jefferson had said: "If there be any among us who would wish to dissolve this Union or to change its republican form, let them stand undisturbed as monuments of the safety with which error of opinion may be tolerated where reason is left free to combat it." Yet the change of opinion in the South, from the age of Washington and Jefferson, who treated slavery as a necessary evil to be gradually done away with, to the present positive good school, culminating in the open denial of equal human rights, had also led to the virtually complete suppression of divergent opinion there. When Senator Foote of Mississippi had in 1848 invited Senator Hale of New Hampshire to visit Mississippi and grace the highest tree in the forest there (which earned him the sobriquet of Hangman Foote), Hale responded by inviting Foote to New Hampshire, where he assured him a respectful hearing in every town and hamlet. Wherever the view that slavery was a positive good gained the ascendancy, a political demand arose for the purge of all dissenting opinion. The culmination of this trend, which came after the joint debates, was Douglas's Senate speech, following John Brown's raid, in which he called for a criminal sedition law which would have banned the Republican party as effectively as any law proposed by the late Senator McCarthy would have banned the Communist party. With the repudiation of human equality vanished the genius of republican freedom. The idea that any society can subsist without an agreement upon fundamentals is, of course, a delusion. But it is peculiarly true of a republican society, where the opinion of all the people enters into the government. Every "agreement to disagree" presupposes a prior agreement with respect to which disagreement can *not* be tolerated. According to Lincoln, it was intolerable that the American people disagree upon the principle of the abstract equality of all men. In so far as they did so they were no longer one nation.

The doctrine of popular sovereignty, as interpreted by Douglas, was the miner and sapper, which was preparing just such a change of opinion in the North as had already come over the South. It was impossible in 1858 to say to the great majority of the North that slavery was *right*. But by treating it as if it was *not wrong* Douglas went as far as it was possible to go in that direction. While the great majority still believed in the principle of freedom, Lincoln held, it was the course of wisdom to have an authoritative showdown at the polls, a showdown that would place despotism beyond the pale of hope of its advocates. That those who would not be able to resist the decision of the ballots might have recourse to bullets never frightened Lincoln, nor must it frighten any man who believes in free government. That is the true answer to those who hold Douglas wise in seeing the possibility of war in Republican victory. In the end it was the answer Douglas himself gave to the South.

Douglas, Lincoln said, professed not to care whether slavery was voted up or down, but this was the very thing about which nearly every man in the country, North or South, cared and cared deeply. As Lincoln said repeatedly, he believed he had no right, and he professed no inclination, to use the power of the federal government to interfere with slavery in the states. But he was convinced that the decision as to whether slavery was to be permitted in the territories would determine, indirectly, whether slavery would eventually become lawful in all the states. And this decision was not, could not be considered, a local one. It was not a question for Kansas alone. It concerned *all* the people, and it was a decision for all to make.[5] A free people cannot allow the most vital question concerning its future to go by default. Hamilton had written in the first *Federalist*, "It has been frequently remarked that it seems to have been reserved to the people of this country, by their conduct and example, to decide the important question, whether societies of men are really capable or not of establishing good government from reflection and choice, or whether they are forever destined to depend for their political constitutions on accident and force." Lincoln did not believe it was possible to perpetuate a government dedicated to a self-evident truth, a government intended to incorporate the principle of rational choice, by a pretense of indifference to the most fundamental of all political choices, the choice between freedom and despotism.

According to Lincoln, a free people cannot disagree on the relative merits of freedom and despotism without ceasing, to the extent of the difference, to be a free people. In choosing to enslave other men it is impossible not to concede the justice of one's own enslavement. The commitment to freedom must simultaneously be a commitment to justice, and the idea of a freedom to be unjust would imply, by equal reason, a freedom to be unfree. Freedom and justice are, in Lincoln's vocabulary, distinguishable, but they are as inseparable as the concavity and the convexity of a curved line. The most concise expression of Lincoln's reasoning on the foregoing theme may be found in another of his great "fragments," in which he distilled the essence of arguments which recur discursively throughout the debates. It too is undated.[6]

If A. can prove, however conclusively, that he may, of right, enslave B.—why may not B. snatch the same argument, and prove equally, that he may enslave A?—

You say A. is white, and B. is black. It is *color*, then; the lighter having the right to enslave the darker? Take care. By this rule, you are to be slave to the first man you meet, with a fairer skin than your own.

You do not mean *color* exactly?—You mean the whites are *intellectually* the superiors of the blacks, and, therefore have the right to enslave them? Take care again. By this rule, you are to be slave to the first man you meet, with an intellect superior to your own.

But, say you, it is a question of interest; and, if you can make it your *interest*, you have the right to enslave another. Very well. And if he can make it his interest, he has the right to enslave you.

The argument against the claim of intellectual superiority, the only serious argument in favor of slavery, was one which Lincoln had apparently inherited from Clay. In a speech at Edwardsville, Illinois, September 11, 1858, when the campaign was far advanced, Lincoln read to his audience the following passages from a letter written by Clay in 1849:

> I know there are those who draw an argument in favor of slavery from the alleged intellectual inferiority of the black race. Whether this argument is founded in fact or not, I will not now stop to inquire, but merely say that if it proves anything at all, it proves too much. It proves that among the white races of the world any one might properly be enslaved by any other which had made greater advances in civilization. And, if this rule applies to nations there is no reason why it should not apply to individuals; and it might easily be proved that the wisest man in the world could rightfully reduce all other men and women to bondage.[7]

It should be noted from the foregoing passages that neither Lincoln nor Clay attempts to *disprove* the claims of intellectual superiority; what they maintain is that the consequences of admitting such claims are such as none of those who raise them are prepared to accept. To raise such claims is then an act of folly, and an act of folly cannot vindicate an assertion of intellectual superiority or wisdom! As Lincoln remarked in another of his fragments, "Although volume upon volume is written to prove slavery a very good thing, we never hear of the man who wishes to take the good of it *by being a slave himself.*" It is implicit in such remarks that a wise man would never proclaim his superiority in wisdom. Other wise men, we may presume, would recognize his wisdom by reason of their own, and the folly of the fool is the very thing that prevents him from recognizing it. There is no surer sign that a man is a knave or a fool than his claim to rule other men because he is wiser than they. The state of the case of all who claim sanction, human or divine, for their enslavement of other men is characterized by Lincoln thus:

> For instance, we will suppose the Rev. Dr. Ross has a slave named Sambo, and the question is, "Is it the Will of God that Sambo shall remain a slave, or be set free?" The Almighty gives no audible answer to the question, and his

revelation—the Bible—gives none—or, at most, *none* but such
as admits of a squabble, as to its meaning. No one thinks of
asking Sambo's opinion on it. So, at last, it comes to this, that
Dr. Ross is to decide the question. And while he considers it,
he sits in the shade, with gloves on his hands, and subsists
on the bread that Sambo is earning in the burning sun. If he
decides that God Wills Sambo to continue a slave, he thereby
retains his own comfortable position; but if he decides that
God wills Sambo to be free, he thereby has to walk out of
the shade, throw off his gloves, and delve for his own bread.
Will Dr. Ross be actuated by that perfect impartiality, which
has ever been considered most favorable to correct decisions?[8]

"Slavery," Lincoln had said in his Peoria speech, the first in which
he came to grips publicly with the peculiar institution, "is founded
in the selfishness of man's nature—opposition to it, in his love of
justice. These principles are an eternal antagonism; and when
brought into collision so fiercely, as slavery extension brings them,
shocks, and throes, and convulsions must ceaselessly follow."[9]

For Lincoln was convinced that slavery was rooted in human
selfishness, and the arguments advanced to justify it were per-
versions of reason, designed to quiet the sense of justice which
must ever denounce the act of enslavement whenever it presents
itself to a man in its true character. It was impossible to vindicate
a claim to self-government, which was at the same time the assertion of a right to be unjust. Political freedom could only be
vindicated, Lincoln believed, on the grounds that it led to greater
justice between man and man than a system in which there was
no political freedom.

But we are then confronted with this paradox: if just government is based upon the consent of the governed, what right to
govern inheres in those who claim political rights not on the basis
of equality but on the basis of their superiority? What right to
govern is there in a community which does not believe in
government by the consent of the governed? Curiously enough,
the case of the white South before the Civil War resembled in
one striking particular the case of the Negroes which it asserted
a right to enslave. That is to say, the whites said the Negroes
were deficient in civilized qualities, but, by Lincoln's definition,
the whites who denied the Declaration were in a crucial respect

also uncivilized. Douglas, expressing the view of the South, said at Ottawa:

> Now, I do not believe that the Almighty ever intended the negro to be the equal of the white man. If he did, he has been a long time demonstrating that fact. For thousands of years the negro has been a race upon the earth, and during all that time, in all latitudes and climates, wherever he has wandered or been taken, he has been inferior to the race which he has there met. He belongs to an inferior race, and must always occupy an inferior position.[10]

In order to understand Lincoln's reaction to Douglas's tiresome reiteration of this theme, one must first do credit to the element of truth which it contains. One need not even inquire into its historical accuracy, as far as "thousands of years" is concerned, in order to see that, within the framework of nineteenth-century civilization, the ascendancy of the civilization of western Europe over that of the peoples of Africa and Asia was unchallenged and appeared unchallengeable. But, to put the case in its hardest form, the promulgation of the doctrines of the Enlightenment, of the principles of political freedom as proclaimed in the English Revolution of 1688, the American Revolution of 1776, and the French Revolution of 1789, was all the work of Western men and of white men. The great tragedy of the Negro in America, as of other non-Western peoples since, lay in the fact that he was compelled to appeal for the recognition of his natural rights to white men and that he could not point to their recognition by black men elsewhere; for it was undeniably true that no government of black men anywhere had yet secured the equal rights of black men in the sense that this government of white men secured the equal rights of its citizens. From this point of view it must be conceded that Negroes did come from an "inferior civilization," that is, from a civilization in which there was no recognition of the universal equal rights of man. However, this argument, as Henry Clay would say, also proves too much. For it is also true that in western Europe, whence the doctrine of universal equal rights emanated, there had been no general recognition of these equal rights until the eighteenth century. The monarchies of the Western world, with few exceptions, and those very recent, did not recognize such rights. And it was not until 1776 that *any* nation had been founded upon the explicit recognition of such rights. In short, if Douglas's argument were to be taken seriously, it would prove that the Almighty had waited many thousands of years to demonstrate the capacity of the white man, no less than that of the Negro, for self-government.

We have already quoted from John Stuart Mill's essay, "On Liberty," published in 1859, to the effect that "despotism is a legitimate mode of government in dealing with barbarians, provided the end be their improvement, and the means justified by actually effecting that end." It must, we believe, be conceded that the justice of despotism is not absolutely and unequivocally refuted by Lincoln's argument. For it follows as a necessary implication of the Declaration itself that, in Mill's words, "Liberty, as a principle, has no application to any state of things anterior to the time when mankind have become capable of being improved by free and equal discussion." In other words, in a world that is duped and befuddled by the obscurantism practiced upon their peoples and upon themselves by, e.g., feudal kings and nobles, or in a world in which the souls of savage peoples are locked within the dark night of primeval barbarism, self-government of the people is inconceivable. But the right of revolution announced in the Declaration, the right to use force against those who would deny us the security of our natural rights to life and liberty, is obviously applicable against corrupt or degraded peoples as well as against rulers of this description. The right to revolution is a right to use violence against *anyone* who would deny us the enjoyment of our rights. From this viewpoint an enlightened minority has the same right to use force against a brutal majority as an enlightened majority has against a brutal king. And, if the minority or majority which is brutalized cannot be exiled, it must be ruled despotically until such time as it can justly be admitted to a share in government. And this argument, be it noted, although it lends color to the enslavement of the Negroes in the South, equally justified the destruction of the Confederacy by war and the institution of reconstruction governments which certainly ruled arbitrarily. The South, in denying the equal natural rights of the Negro, not only denied the foundation of its own rights; it denied as well its own *competence to exercise these rights.*

Was there an element of self-contradiction in Lincoln's position in that it denounces any recognition of a right to despotic rule and yet contemplates violence against those who assert a right to despotic rule? We maintain that there is not. Lincoln had grappled with this problem, and solved it, in the Lyceum speech. It is true that some men are so superior to other men that they might, in theory, justly rule them without the other men's consent. But such a right does not require *recognition* in the sense that universal equal rights must be recognized. It is the nature of superior men, the very essence of their superiority, that it cannot be gratified by exploiting other men. It is the renunciation of the power of exploitation which alone can gratify their sense of superiority. Hence those who use the argument of superiority to enslave—as the Rev. Dr. Ross—are not superior men. Where men are enlightened—meaning thereby where they recognize the moral necessity of the doctrine of equal natural rights—they are capable of being improved by rational discussion, to use Mill's phrase. It is the function of the great man, the sign of his mastery, that he employs his powers by confirming and enhancing his fellow citizens' capacity for self-improvement and chastens any backsliding from the convictions that entitle them to be considered rational men. The great man, be he a Washington or another, will not force the wills of those who will not themselves coerce the wills of others, except to secure their own rights. But neither will rational men hesitate to use force *to* secure their rights. And it does not matter, in principle, whether the threat to that security comes from the one or the many, the majority or the minority.

*   *   *   *   *

The foregoing reflections obtrude upon us another difficulty which must lead us for the moment beyond the horizon of the debates proper. It will be seen from what we have just said what the underlying "necessity" was that, in Lincoln's words, justified the Founding Fathers in tolerating slavery. That necessity was, on the one hand, the avarice of slaveowners, which was too strong to be overcome, and, on the other, the actual condition of degradation of their slaves, partly an inheritance from Africa and partly the consequence of the brutalization of slavery. It was axiomatic for Lincoln that the slavery of the Negroes could be extenuated only on the supposition that the institution was "in course of ultimate extinction," and this in turn could only be contemplated if the Negroes were, in some sense, being prepared for freedom. In his eulogy of Henry Clay, Lincoln quoted the following from Clay's speech to the American Colonization Society in 1827:

> There is a moral fitness in the idea of returning to Africa her children, whose ancestors have been torn from her by the ruthless hand of fraud and violence. Transplanted in a foreign land, they will carry back to their native soil the rich fruits of religion, civilization, law and liberty. May it not be one of the great designs of the Ruler of the universe, (whose ways are often inscrutable by short-sighted mortals,) thus to transform an original crime, into a signal blessing to that most unfortunate portion of the globe?[11]

That the enslavement of Negroes was "just" in a qualified sense, so long as they were being prepared for freedom, must, we believe, be conceded. But what of the "crime" of their enslavement? Lincoln once complained of the Liberty party men, who would not vote for Henry Clay because he owned slaves, that they had helped elect Polk in his stead and thus helped to bring on the Mexican War and with it the extension of slavery. The Liberty men said, "We are not to do *evil* that *good* may come," to which Lincoln replied, "By the *fruit* the tree is to be known. An *evil* tree can not bring forth *good* fruit. If the fruit of electing Mr. Clay would have been to prevent the extension of slavery, could the act of electing have been evil?"[12] But the same argument may be turned to the question of the American Negro's original enslavement. If we are to know the tree by its fruit, and if the final fruit of the African slave trade was to be the possession by Africans of the infinitely precious doctrine of equal human rights and the possibility of erecting an edifice of human freedom, which could only be built upon such a teaching, how can we regard the means to such an end as a crime? To say that God alone may do evil that good may come cannot, we should think, be regarded as more than an evasion.

We have in a number of places suggested analogies between Lincoln's moral teaching, as a foundation for his political teaching, and Aristotle's. Such an analogy must seem paradoxical in the light of the reputation of the one as the great defender of slavery and the other as its supreme antagonist. Yet the paradox, we maintain, lies more in their reputations than in the truth. Aristotle's vindication of *natural* slavery, in the first book of his *Politics,* is a defense of the slavery of the man who lacks sufficient reason to guide himself and can only live a useful life when some-one else directs him. This has reference primarily to the mentally feeble, and no society gives such men their freedom, whether it allows them to be made chattels or puts them in institutions. It would also refer to those who, for whatever reason, are in-corrigible—the Calibans of this world—and all such men are also put under restraint in one way or another.

But Aristotle clearly envisaged the continued existence of a slavery which is *not* natural in any of the foregoing senses, which is, therefore, merely conventional and which is, therefore, by his own terms, unjust. In book seven of the *Politics* Aristotle repeat-edly speaks of the employment of slaves in his best polity, a polity which is either the most just possible or which embodies the greatest degree of justice generally attainable by the *poleis* of his time. Superficially this would stand in marked contrast to Lin-coln's summons to recognize the natural equality of rights of all mankind. But only superficially. For in the ninth chapter of the seventh book Aristotle remarks, "Why it is better for all slaves to have freedom set before them as a prize (or reward), we will say later." This promise is not kept in any surviving portions of the *Politics*, which appears to be fragmentary. The passage indicates, however, two things: first, that the slaves Aristotle has in mind are slaves not by nature but by convention only; and, secondly, that slaves who are slaves by convention only should have their slavery "in course of ultimate extinction." For Aristotle, no less than Lincoln, the hope and, by consequence, the virtuous activity which liberty engenders must not be shut out of the heart of the slave.

But Aristotle, unlike Lincoln, definitely sanctions "slave catch-ing" and envisages a more or less steady supply of slaves, probably always as great as the number set free. Why? The answer, we believe, is somewhat as follows. Aristotle regarded civilization as limited primarily, though not exclusively, to Greeks. This certainly was not because he thought Greeks alone capable of becoming civilized, since he thought that non-Greeks captured and en-slaved by Greeks could be made fit for freedom by the training provided by Greek life. It was because civilization in the world he knew was a rare and difficult plant and, in fact, existed only in extremely fortunate circumstances. Its existence elsewhere was always possible but extremely improbable. The enslavement of barbarians by Greeks was then justified by the fact that it was probably the only way in which barbarians could be civilized. That slave labor contributed to the material elevation of Greek life certainly did not detract from the element of justice in slavery from Aristotle's point of view. The economic scarcity of the ancient world—in contrast to the rapidly increasing abundance of the world Lincoln knew—must also be taken into consideration in accounting for the degree of toleration each has for a phenomenon which was intrinsically unjust from either's point of view.

But there is this further difference. The revolution which began in 1776 was, according to Lincoln, only the beginning of a *world* revolution. In his Mexican War speech of January 12, 1848, Lincoln referred to the right of revolution proclaimed in the Declaration as "a most valuable, a most sacred right—a right which, we hope and believe, is to liberate the world." Lincoln had seen in his own lifetime virtually the whole of Central and South America "revolutionize." And he had seen Texas successfully revolt from Mexico after Mexico had revolted from Spain. Within two lifetimes two whole continents had undergone revolutions in the name of the doctrines of the Declaration; and, although Europe's experience had been less happy, the foundations of absolutism had repeatedly been shaken by unsuccessful revolutions, and the confidence of European liberals in ultimate success was high. In these circumstances Lincoln felt, with Webster, that our prime duty as a nation was to set an example of a free republic dedicated to elevating the conditions of life of its own people without any spirit of aggrandizement toward men elsewhere. In the contest of Lincoln and Douglas we may see the issue of the last great Whig-Democratic contest redefined, the issue in the campaign of Clay and Polk. This issue we may call the issue of internal improvement versus external conquest and aggression. Lincoln's summons to fidelity to the Declaration is the phoenix risen from the ashes of the old Whig call for internal improvement, but the concept of internal improvement has been purified and transformed to mean the improvement of the nation's soul. Internal improvement versus foreign aggression is interpreted by Lincoln, in his contest with Douglas, in precisely the sense in which Socrates interprets those concepts in Plato's *Republic*. When Glaucon rejects the city of primitive moral health, the "city of pigs," it is because he demands luxuries, luxuries which he thinks it is more troublesome to do without than to purchase by aggressive war. All of Douglas's policies pointed to aggressive war as the solution of internal difficulties, difficulties which Lincoln, like Plato, believed could be avoided only through moral restraint. Lincoln saw the road of aggression, whether of the individual or of the nation, as a road of endless involvement, aggression begetting aggression, with the end never nearer. In a world of growing interdependence, particularly the moral interdependence created by the principles of the Declaration itself, this course had become peculiarly impossible. For the Declaration of Independence was the first case in history in which a single people made a national revolution on the assumption that its particular principles were, simultaneously, the universal principles which civilized men everywhere would recognize. The Declaration assumed that its potential, if not its actual addressees, embraced the entire family of man. And it did not think of these addressees as some few "wise men" who, like the ancient Stoics, might live in the interstices of society in widely scattered lands. The Declaration assumed a mass audience throughout the world, capable, sooner or later, of acting upon the principles it announced. There never was a time in the ancient world when a statement of universal principles of right could have been made with the assumption of such an audience. And once the cause of political freedom had been indissolubly associated with such a statement of principles, it could only be maintained by associating with such principles an example of moral restraint, an example of respect for the rights of men everywhere.

For Aristotle, as for Lincoln, the slavery of men who were morally and intellectually capable of managing their own lives without injury to others was intrinsically unjust. For Lincoln, as for Aristotle, there were "necessities" which justified the toleration of slavery, which made it a lesser evil. "Cast into life where slavery was already widely spread and deeply seated," Lincoln said of Henry Clay in his eulogy of his great and revered leader, "he did not perceive, as I think no wise man has perceived, how it could *at once* be eradicated, without producing a greater evil, even to the cause of human liberty itself."[13] That there was a difference in *worlds* between Aristotle and Lincoln may be conceded, but that there was a difference in *principle*, as to the intrinsic justice of slavery, must be doubted. This, we believe, is true even if it is also true that in Aristotle's world the institution of slavery—as distinct from the slavery of individual

men—would always be among the lesser evils and thus could
never be wisely placed "in course of ultimate extinction." In Lincoln's world the chronic economic scarcity which was among the
justifications of ancient slavery did not exist. If in Aristotle's world
the possibility of leisure, and hence the cultivation of the liberal
arts, depended in some ways on slavery, the reverse was true in
Lincoln's world. In the nineteenth century freedom, not slavery,
was productive of economic abundance. The machine was the
slave of the modern world, and property in man by man could not
be defended on moral grounds except as a temporary expedient.
Whether Lincoln's world or Aristotle's world was the better world,
whether the hope engendered by the machine, of the final
abolition of human exploitation, outweighs the fears engendered
by this same machine, is a question upon which we need not
enter here. It was not a question for Lincoln, since he was called
upon to act in a world already governed by the potentialities
of the machine, for good and for evil.

In concluding this analysis we would observe that, although
the relationship of a master to one who is a slave, not by nature,
but by convention only, is always intrinsically unjust, there is no
way of knowing, *a priori*, whether it is just or unjust, whether
it is a greater or a lesser evil, to sanction such a relationship
in particular cases. For it is the essence of practical wisdom to
adapt its judgments to differences in circumstances. The purpose
of practical wisdom is always the same, and the wise statesman
will act to achieve the greatest measure of justice that the world
in which he is acting admits.

Chapter XVI

Popular Sovereignty: True and False

LINCOLN constantly warned those who would either approve or withhold their disapproval of slavery that this was a matter upon which, in principle, there could be no compromise or equivocation. To those Southerners who appealed to the Bible to justify slavery he said that Douglas was wiser than they, for Biblical slavery was the slavery of white men. We have given it as our opinion, in Chapter II, that for Douglas the essence of free government lay in the power of decision of a free people of the most vital, no less than of the most trivial, questions. Lincoln agreed, but he believed that shifting responsibility for the future of the nation upon the first few stragglers into Kansas or Nebraska was a miserable evasion of responsibility. And Douglas's assumption, in his "Don't care" policy, that the doctrine of popular sovereignty was such that the duty of statesmanship was exhausted when the people's power of decision was secured to them was absolutely false. Lincoln's classic refutation of this thesis may be found in the Peoria speech:

The doctrine of self-government is right—absolutely and eternally right, but it has no just application, as here attempted. Or perhaps I should say that whether it has such application depends upon whether the negro is *not* or *is* a man. If he is *not* a man, why in that case, he who *is* a man may, as a matter of self-government, do just as he pleases with him. But if the negro *is* a man, is it not to that extent a total destruction of self-government, to say that he too shall not govern *himself?* When the white man governs himself that is self-government; but when he governs himself, and also governs *another* man, that is more than self-govern-ment—that is despotism. If the negro is a *man*, why then my ancient faith teaches me that "all men are created equal;" and that there can be no moral right in connection with one man's making a slave of another.

Judge Douglas frequently, with bitter irony and sarcasm, paraphrases our argument by saying: "The white people of Nebraska are good enough to govern themselves, *but they are not good enough to govern a few miserable* negroes!!"

Well I doubt not that the people of Nebraska are, and will continue to be as good as the average of people else-where. I do not say the contrary. What I do say is, that no man is good enough to govern another man, *without that other's consent.* I say this is the leading principle—the sheet anchor of American republicanism.[1]

Free government, according to Lincoln, was not the mere *process* of arriving at decisions without coercion by any formula embody-ing the principle of majority rule. It was not even government of, by, and for the people. It was government of, by, and for a people *dedicated* to a certain proposition. Many of those present-day admirers of Douglas who remember the end of the Gettysburg Address forget its beginning. Lincoln's position always embraced both concepts, while Douglas never comprehended the meaning of the principle of equality, nor its relation to popular sovereignty, properly so called.

If self-government was a *right,* and not a mere *fact* character-izing the American scene (more or less), then it must be derived from some primary source of obligation. There must be something, Lincoln insisted, inhering in each man, *as a man,* which created an obligation in every other man. And if any majority anywhere, however constituted, might rightfully enslave any man or men, it could only be because there was nothing in any man which, simply because he was a man, other men were bound to respect. If the latter were true, as Douglas implied, then the mere exist-ence anywhere of the phenomenon of self-government said noth-ing as to its rightness or desirability. It might exist because of merely fortuitous circumstances or of beliefs which had no support beyond the fact of their being believed. It would then be mean-ingless to say that anyone had a duty to perpetuate a self-governing polity or to bring one into existence where there was none. Since Douglas did not indicate any *other* ground than Lincoln's as the foundation of his doctrine of popular sovereignty, he was utterly illogical in claiming for it the status of an eternal principle of political right.

Douglas's popular sovereignty, sanctioning as it did the enslavement of one description of men by another, of necessity sanctioned the enslavement of any other description of men. Douglas affirmed the right to enslave only as a right of the white race in dealing with all other races (which were "inferior" and had no right to self-government, according to Douglas). But Douglas simply had not thought through the implications of such a position. Why, if a white majority, whether in a state or in the nation, decided to enslave a white minority (or to deprive it of political rights or otherwise act in a manner that the Declaration of Independence would classify as "despotic"), might it not rightfully do so? If one answers that such actions would be contrary to the Constitution, the reply follows that any constitution is merely a document of positive law and that the same "sovereign people" which establishes it may alter or abolish, by constitutional or revolutionary measures, any inhibitions to its own authority. Moreover, as Lincoln saw by 1857, a constitutional majority, in the sense of the amending clause of the Constitution, is not necessary to amend that document in any real sense. The majorities which elect President and Congress can, on any point upon which they are really agreed, do anything they wish. For President and Congress together can always reconstitute, overrule, or disregard the Supreme Court. If, then, one majority might, without violating any fundamental moral principle, enslave one minority, whatever its color or composition, there is no principle, certainly none involved in the mere idea of majority rule, which would inhibit it from enslaving another. And if one minority after another is enslaved, the majority itself becomes a minority. In short, the idea of a popular sovereignty divorced from a universal conception of human right is a complete absurdity.

Lincoln's second question to Douglas at Freeport is rightly famous, for it was the immediate cause of the most significant political effects. Yet it is the third question, to which we have already adverted, which leads most directly to the heart of the issues between the two men. "If the Supreme Court of the United States shall decide that states can not exclude slavery from their limits, are you in favor of acquiescing in, adopting and following such decision as a rule of political action?" ran this interrogatory. In contrast to Douglas's downright, although indefensible, answer to the second question, his reply to the foregoing is completely evasive. At Freeport in his initial reply he spoke thus: "I am amazed that Lincoln should ask such a question. ('A school boy knows better.') Yes, a school boy knows better. Mr. Lincoln's object is to cast an imputation upon the Supreme Court . . . He casts an imputation upon the Supreme Court of the United States by supposing that they would violate the Constitution of the United States. I tell him such a thing is not possible. It would be an act of moral treason that no man on the bench could ever descend to." Thus, instead of giving an answer, Douglas says the question is improper because it assumes an impossibility. Yet whether or not the Court *would* decide that states might not prohibit slavery, nothing is more evident than that it was possible, just as it was possible for the justices to go insane. If mental or moral incompetence on the part of Supreme Court justices were impossible, why should the Constitution permit their impeachment? Lincoln hammered away at this vital flaw in Douglas's armor and at Quincy received the following response, which was the last he was to receive, to the third Freeport question:

> But, Mr. Lincoln says that I will not answer his question as to what I would do in the event of the court making so ridiculous a decision as he imagines they would by deciding that the free state of Illinois could not prohibit slavery within her own limits. *I told him at Freeport why I would not answer such a question.* I told him that there was not a man possessing any brains in America, lawyer or not, who ever dreamed that such a thing could be done. I told him then, as I say now, that by all the principles set forth in the Dred Scott decision, it is impossible. I told him then, as I do now, that it is an insult to men's understanding, and a gross calumny on the court, to presume in advance that it was going to degrade itself so low as to make a decision known to be in direct violation of the Constitution.[2]

At this point in the speech a voice from the audience was heard to say, "The same thing was said about the Dred Scott decision before it passed." That voice, with all that it implied, may well pass as the true voice of the muse of History. We have italicized the sentence in which Douglas admits that he has not and will not answer Lincoln's question. And the expressed reasons for the refusal are, of course, inadmissible. Douglas had referred to Lincoln at Chicago at the beginning of the campaign (July 9, 1858) as a "kind, amiable, and intelligent gentleman, a good citizen and an honorable opponent." Perhaps Douglas hoped to tame Lincoln and bring him over to the Greeley view with this "nice doggy" approach. If so, he must have been soon disenchanted. At any rate, this "intelligent" man, who happened also to be a lawyer of some distinction, certainly did believe the decision in question was possible, and he had convinced many thousands that it was possible. This Douglas knew, and in saying that no one believed it he was saying what he must have known to be false. Lincoln had, moreover, at Galesburg, demonstrated by irrefragable logic, as we have shown, that such a decision did *not* contradict the principles of the Dred Scott decision, at least as set forth in the Chief Justice's opinion, which was the opinion of the Court. And Douglas never undertook to grapple with Lincoln's syllogism. He did not because he could not.

To that unnamed voice Douglas replied by repeating what he had said in substance just before the passage we have quoted: ". . . I will not be drawn off into an argument upon the merits of the Dred Scott decision. It is enough for me to know that the Constitution of the United States created the Supreme Court for the purpose of deciding all disputed questions touching the true construction of that instrument . . ." Of course, that the Supreme Court was entrusted with deciding "*all* disputed questions" was itself a disputed point in the debates. Everyone knew that the Constitution itself says nothing of the kind. Lincoln, as we have observed, cited Jefferson and Jackson to the effect that each officer of the government must uphold the Constitution as *he* understands it. Douglas was transfixed on a sharply thrown spear, and no wriggling could do more than fix the spear more firmly.

Douglas's crucial statement in his reply to Lincoln was his assertion that Lincoln's question implied that the judges were capable of "moral treason." This, of course, is precisely what Lincoln believed. Not only did he believe the judges capable of moral treason, but he believed they had actually committed it. For Lincoln believed that moral treason consisted, above all, in denying the proposition that "all men are created equal" or in denying that this was in fact the foundation of the American constitutional system. Douglas was not logically required to accept Lincoln's definition of moral treason, but it was no less fatal to the logic of his position to invoke the concept of such treason. For the very idea of moral treason means that there is a higher, substantive principle to which the idea of "legal treason" must be subordinate. To have invoked such a concept and then to have affirmed a readiness to accept the political consequences of the decisions of the Supreme Court, whatever they might be, made no sense. If moral treason is more heinous than legal treason, then one who unquestioningly obeys a bad law (or legal enactment, such as a court decision) must in principle be inferior to one who is prepared to disobey it. And, by equal reason, to change the law from what is morally right to what is morally wrong—e.g., to change free law into slave law—must in principle be as great a wrong as disobedience to morally good law. Lincoln, in the Lyceum speech, in his most extreme plea for obedience to law—a plea which was, of course, not for obedience to *any* laws, but to those of a free republic—had said that laws, "if not too intolerable," should always be borne with. And he could not have said more, unless he, too, had forgotten the right of revolution proclaimed in the Declaration. To repeat: for Douglas to say it was enough for him to know that the Court had decided something, without inquiring into the merits of the decision, was to imply that there was no higher standard than positive law; but, if there was no such standard, then the idea of moral treason was meaningless. In fact, however, Douglas attempted, as we have seen, to make "popular sovereignty" play a role equivalent to "all men are created equal" in supplying the substance of an idea of intrinsic moral-political worth. But "popular sovereignty," we have also seen, is reducible to the proposition that all political right is positive right. Douglas would no more inquire into the merits of a decision of "the people" than he would inquire into the merits of the decision of the Court. In this, at least, he was consistent.

While the third question is the fundamental question put to Douglas at Freeport, the "Freeport question" itself must not go without comment. No more need be said about its effect in splitting Douglas from the South, as the "conspiracy" charge in the house divided speech was to drive him from his Republican admirers. Let us note principally that it attempted to convict Douglas of "moral treason" by his own definition, in so far as he acknowledged an obligation to abide by the Dred Scott decision when that decision had denied to the territorial legislature, as to Congress, the power to exclude slavery from a territory. Douglas, we assume our readers to know, said that it mattered not how the Court decided the "abstract" question of territorial legislative power, since slavery could not be established anywhere without affirmative legislation, which the territorial legislature was under no obligation to pass. Whether Douglas was factually correct—i.e., whether it was true that positive protection was a necessary precondition for the existence of slavery—we will not now inquire. For the moment we state Lincoln's *moral* objection to such a policy. Lincoln believed such a policy was morally intolerable for a free people just because he believed that in a free society law must express the moral conviction of the people. Douglas's policy amounted to a nullification of the Constitution by destroying the value of a right that the Chief Justice said was "expressly affirmed" in the Constitution. On this point Lincoln was in agreement with the radical Southerners. As he said at Cooper Union in the passage we have quoted in Chapter IX, "If slavery is right, all words, acts, laws and constitutions against it, are themselves wrong, and should be silenced, and swept away."[3] Lincoln believed that slavery was wrong and that its wrong must be acknowledged if the nation's free institutions were to be preserved and perpetuated. But Douglas's conception of popular sovereignty not only denied that slavery was wrong, but it struck at the root of all morality by denying that men had an obligation to act upon *what they themselves believed to be right*. In his answer, or refusal to answer the third question, Douglas conceded that the Dred Scott decision was binding by conceding that it did not constitute "moral treason" and did not violate the "known" meaning of the Constitution. He would not deny that the Constitution "expressly affirmed" the right of property in slaves in the territories. Now was it not "moral treason" to "accept" the proposition that the Constitution affirmed such a right and yet to say that members of a territorial legislature had no duty to secure a right so affirmed? For what purpose did the Constitution exist but to secure the rights it affirmed? Lincoln pounded and pounded at this anomaly and insisted, what we believe every candid person must admit, that there was no qualitative difference between the right to hold and enjoy property in slaves in the territories in the Constitution *as expounded by Taney and accepted by Douglas* and the right to the rendition of fugitive slaves in the states. If there was no obligation either in Congress or in the territorial legislature to secure one "expressly affirmed" right, then where was the duty to secure another? The abolitionists were the only ones in the country who had seriously denied Congress's duty to pass a fugitive slave law, and Douglas's Freeport Doctrine placed him, *a fortiori,* on the same ground. Lincoln's last words in the joint debates are, "Why there is not such an Abolitionist in the nation as Douglas, after all."[4]

In the *Nicomachean Ethics* Aristotle draws a distinction between the antithesis of virtue to vice and that of continence to incontinence. These antitheses are similar yet differ significantly. A virtuous man acts rightly because he knows what is right and has conquered the passions which would prevent him from acting rightly. Indeed, the sign of a virtuous character, according to Aristotle, is not that its possessor does what is right but that he *enjoys* doing it. A continent man resembles a virtuous man, but his passions still resist the good or right action, and hence he cannot act with pleasure. The difference between virtue and continence may not always be perceptible to an observer, but its inner significance is crucial. For the pleasure which accompanies virtuous action inevitably enhances the quality of the action. Incontinence differs from vice in that the latter leads a man to do the wrong thing deliberately. The vicious man enjoys vice as the virtuous man enjoys virtue. The incontinent man, however, does not act wrongly from intention but from weakness. He knows what is right and wishes to do it, but his errant passions are too strong for him. The words of Paul in the Letter to the Romans, 7:15 and 19, describe his plight to perfection.

> For that which I do I allow not: for what I would, that I do not; but what I hate, that I do.

And:

> For the good that I would I do not: but the evil which I would not, that I do.

Superficially it would seem that, even as continence is a lesser excellence than virtue, so incontinence is a lesser evil than vice. The vicious man is malevolent on principle, the incontinent man because he cannot help himself. And presumably, like Paul, the incontinent man can be praised for his intention, if not his action, while the vicious man can be blamed for both.

As a general statement the foregoing conclusion is substantially correct. Moral education is a process wherein refractory passions are subjected to a discipline which must come, for the most part, initially from the outside. Incontinence normally precedes continence in the chronology of such education. And so does continence normally precede virtue. For the yoke of the moral demands rests heavily for a long time for most of us before it is carried lightly, if ever it is. The process of internalizing the moral demands is threefold: first they must be accepted, then obeyed, and only finally rejoiced in. Yet there are those whose development, in whole or in part, is arrested. And of those who remain incontinent it may be said that they are, in a fundamental sense, worse than the vicious. For a person who does what is wrong *on principle*—i.e., believing that it is right—might conceivably reform if he were persuaded that what he is doing is not right but wrong. "But to the incontinent man," says Aristotle, "may be applied the proverb 'when water chokes, what is one to wash it down with?' If he had been persuaded of the rightness of what he does, he would have desisted when he was persuaded to change his mind: but now he acts one way, in spite of having been persuaded of the contrary."

Douglas's Freeport Doctrine was nothing less than a calculated indoctrination in incontinence. In so far as it was not sheer hypocrisy, it sanctioned the refusal to perform the most solemn of recognized constitutional obligations. As such, it was subversive of the entire process of moral education in the principles of free republican government. Douglas's own Kansas-Nebraska Act had said that the people of the territories were subject to the Constitution in the exercise of their legislative powers. And fidelity to the Constitution is the key to the only rational defense of his entire career that is possible: that Constitution by virtue of which, alone, he held, we existed as a nation. And yet, while acknowledging the binding force of Taney's declaration that the right of property in slaves had been expressly affirmed in the Constitution, he advised the people of Kansas to ignore such a right if they did not wish to admit slaveholders into their midst. We have quoted earlier from Douglas's 1850 speech, in which he said that in free countries laws and ordinances are mere nullities unless sustained by hearts and intellects of the people. But this was as true of the Constitution of the United States as of any of the local laws made by, or in consequence of, its authority. It was a mere quibble that he proposed nullifying a constitutional right by non-action. For if one such right might be nullified by local non-action, with no remedy from federal courts or Congress, why might not another right be nullified by positive action? The Freeport Doctrine had all the potentialities for nullification and disunion that the teachings of Calhoun expressed without their intellectual and moral integrity. Lincoln agreed, and rightly agreed, in this with the Jefferson Davis school of thinking: the Union might, as a political entity, survive by recognizing the nationality of slavery and the locality of freedom, or by recognizing the locality of slavery and the nationality of freedom. But it was impossible that it should recognize the nationality of slavery and yet deny the legal consequences of that recognition, or that it should recognize the nationality of freedom and deny the consequences following from that. To say that the Constitution carried slavery into the national domain, where it might be destroyed by men whose political rights were derived solely from that selfsame Constitution, was an anomaly in law and morals too gross to be tolerated. Lincoln's final summary of the meaning of the Freeport Doctrine came after the debates, in his speech in Columbus, Ohio, September 16, 1859. Its aphoristic perfection cannot be improved. When you clear away all "the trash, the words, the collateral matter," said Lincoln, Douglas's Freeport Doctrine was reduced to this "bare absurdity":

> . . . a thing may be lawfully driven away from where it has a lawful right to be.[5]

Douglas was too intelligent a man and too sensitive to his own loyalty to the Constitution to allow Lincoln an unchallenged advantage from this anomaly. His only real attempt at a reply came after the joint debates in his Harper's essay of 1859 on "Popular Sovereignty in the Territories." As has been indicated in the Preface, a full analysis of his argument therein would go beyond the limits of this study. We only notice here that Douglas attempted to maintain the position that the legislative power of the territories was not derived from Congress but that, while Congress had the power to establish a government for the territories, the government *in* the territories derived its authority from the *people* in the territories. He likened the action of Congress in establishing a legislature in the territories to its action in establishing United States courts. Congress might establish courts, but it might not itself act as a court, nor might it overrule decisions of the courts (a proposition in itself highly questionable). The courts, according to this thesis, derived their judicial power from the inherent nature of judicial power, not from the Congress which conferred the judicial power on them. And so Congress had the right to confer legislative power on the territories but not to exercise it. And the power of the territorial legislature, although *conferred* on the territory by Congress, derived from the inherent right of self-government of the people there, which right Congress presumably only recognized when it acted to "confer."

For our present purposes we will merely note that this doctrine vindicates Lincoln's attack in that it recognizes the moral impossibility of the position Douglas took during the debates. It attempts to bottom the Freeport Doctrine on his conception of popular sovereignty as a moral principle—although we have already seen that this conception cannot bear inspection *as* a moral principle. But, as constitutional doctrine, the Harper's essay will not stand up any better. Lincoln had pointed out during the debates that the Kansas-Nebraska Act, like other territorial bills, provided for a governor and courts appointed by the President and that these shared the legislative authority of the territories as much as the President and Supreme Court shared the legislative authority of the United States. Prior to the Kansas-Nebraska Act territorial laws had been subject to nullification by Congress as well as veto by the governor. Douglas's bill had been more "democratic" than its predecessors; but not even Douglas had breathed a suggestion in 1854 that the earlier territorial laws, in subjecting the territories to such supervision by Congress, had been unconstitutional or contrary to the principles of political right. No one had ever doubted before Douglas's Harper's essay— and probably no one but Douglas then—that Congress had a lawful power to nullify or override territorial legislation, *if it chose to do so*, whether or not the exercise of such power was expedient.

The right that Congress has, under the Constitution, to admit new states has been conceded, then and since, to sanction the exercise of all powers necessary and proper to prepare territories to become new states. And "necessary and proper" has never been interpreted other than liberally in this respect. Strict construction of the Constitution, whatever may be said for it in other respects, would be completely absurd here, for the simple reason that, by a strict construction of the Constitution, the nation could never have acquired the lands from which the new territories and states were formed.[6] For two years Jefferson ruled the newly (and, by his own view, unconstitutionally) acquired Louisiana Territory despotically, although it had a Creole population approximating that of some of the states and the treaty with France had guaranteed them United States citizenship. And when Jefferson grudgingly admitted local *participation* in the territorial government, it was on a far more limited basis than the Kansas-Nebraska Act (or, indeed, any intervening territorial acts) provided. But perhaps more to the point is Douglas's own proposal in regard to Utah in 1857. When the Mormon difficulties were at their height, Douglas proposed as a possible solution that the territorial law be revoked and the inhabitants of Utah be brought under complete, direct federal control! In short, Douglas himself was prepared to recall the grant of legislative power to the people of a territory when they did not exercise it in a sufficiently responsible manner. As everyone knows, polygamy was at the bottom of the Mormon troubles, and Douglas would have taken any and all steps that might have been required to see that no state of the Union would ever sanction that indubitably "domestic" institution. The Republican party, we should add, was dedicated from its inception to the extinction of those "twin relics of barbarism," polygamy and slavery. And Douglas never defended the right of the people *anywhere* to choose, if they would, the former of the two.

The Constitution cannot then entrust to Congress such a task as that of ensuring that new states be "republican" in form—meaning practically thereby that they have institutions compatible with harmonious membership in a union with the other states—while denying to Congress legislative power when and where the institutions of future states are being formed. It may be doubted—as Jefferson doubted—that the Constitution grants Congress power to acquire new territory. Yet Douglas was the most violently expansionist national leader the country has ever seen, the last man in the world to have suggested constitutional doubts of such a kind. And Congress could not possibly fulfill its undoubted duty to prepare acquired lands for statehood if it did not have legislative power in the territories. And this again could not be true if the territorial legislature had other than a derivative, conditional, legislative right. The Harper's essay only adds to the confusion inherent in the Freeport Doctrine.

In presenting the case for Douglas we have represented him as the enemy of Know-Nothingism and of all the snobbery and class consciousness engendered by the hostility of the older Anglo-Saxon stock for the new floods of immigrants. Yet Douglas, in opposing Anglo-Saxon prejudices, did so by cultivating the prejudices of the Irish, both for the British and for the Negro. Lincoln, however, opposed all prejudices, so far as they undermined the "ancient faith" which he believed to be the necessary condition of all political and moral well-being in a free popular republic. In his Dred Scott speech, wherein Lincoln gave his classic exposition of the meaning of the Declaration as the standard maxim of a free society, he drew an inference from this thesis which not only illustrated his point but also constituted a challenge to the mistaken devotion of the Irish for Douglas:

> I had thought the Declaration promised something better than the condition of British subjects; but no, it meant only that we should be *equal* to them in their own oppressed and *unequal* condition. According to that, it gave no promise that having kicked off the King and Lords of Great Britain, we should not at once be saddled with a King and Lords of our own.[7]

Lincoln too could twist the lion's tail, but he did so only to assert an obligation on Americans to achieve greater justice among themselves, in consequence of their free principles, than was to be found in any polity of the old world. Lincoln was absolutely convinced, old-line Whig though he had been, that the only hope of the new immigrants of being assimilated into American life on terms of general equality was in and through the religious cultivation of the universal creed of the Declaration. In his Chicago speech of July 10, 1858, Lincoln sounded a theme which echoed through the debates. He spoke of the annual celebration of independence, as he always loved to do, in terms which suggest nothing so much as the Feast of the Passover, celebrating the deliverance of the Hebrew people from Pharaoh's Egypt, or of Easter, celebrating the deliverance of the world from original sin.

We hold this annual celebration to remind ourselves of all the good done in this process of time, of how it was done and who did it, and how we are historically connected with it, and we go from these meetings in better humor with ourselves—we feel more attached the one to the other, and more firmly bound to the country we inhabit. In every way we are better men in the age, and race, and country in which we live for these celebrations. But . . . there is something else connected with it. We have besides these men—descended by blood from our ancestors—among us perhaps half our people who are not descendants at all of these men, they are men who have come from Europe—German, Irish, French and Scandinavian—men that have come from Europe themselves, or whose ancestors have come hither and have settled here, finding themselves our equals in all things. If they look back through this history to trace their connection with those days by blood, they find they have none, they cannot carry themselves back into that glorious epoch and make themselves feel that they are part of us, but when they look through that old Declaration of Independence they find that those old men say that "We hold these truths to be self-evident, that all men are created equal," and then they feel that that moral sentiment taught in that day evidences their relation to those men, that it is the father of all moral principle in them, and that they have a right to claim it as though they were blood of the blood, and flesh of the flesh of the men who wrote that Declaration, and so they are. This is the electric cord in that Declaration that links the hearts of patriotic and liberty-loving men together, that will link those patriotic hearts as long as the love of freedom exists in the minds of men throughout the world.[8]

We may compare the foregoing with the following typical expression by Douglas in his opening speech at Ottawa:

I do not question Mr. Lincoln's conscientious belief that the negro was made his equal, and hence is his brother, but for my own part, I do not regard the negro as my equal, and positively deny that he is my brother or any kin to me whatever.[9]

Such sallies, as may be gathered, caused much hilarity. But the serious contrast is as weighty as anything in the joint debates. Lincoln insisted, what every political philosopher has always recognized, that there must be some conviction, usually embodied in the form of a story that can be told, comprehended, and taken to heart by all, which produces a sense of community and unites the hearts of those who call themselves fellow citizens. Without that fellow feeling there is no basis for mutual trust, and where there is no trust there can be no freedom. For political self-government involves governing and being governed, and where there is insufficient trust, the idea of making others the trustees, for however limited a time, of our dearest interests does not make sense. And the only possible basis for the unity of a people as heterogeneous in origin as the American people was one which transcended their different origins. Such unity could not be found in any revealed religious teaching, because they were as divided in this respect as in any other. Lincoln did, however, in retelling our history, cast it in a form which reflected the *common* elements within the sectarian diversity, as we have seen in the Lyceum speech. But the doctrinal basis of this patriotic history was the universal statement in the Declaration, a statement which must be understood as comprehending the Negro if it were to be understood in a way which would unite white men.

No one who knows anything of the explosive hatreds involved in the clash of Americans of different origins, in consequence of the great tides of immigration before and after the Civil War, can doubt that they contained vast possibilities for caste and class oppressions, oppressions which might have rivaled if they did not exceed those of the enslaved Negro. Indeed, the oppressions that did exist in the later nineteenth century, in the slums of the great cities, in the factories and in the mines, were bad enough. Yet they have proved in large measure transient, and it would be difficult to find any considerable group, unless it be the American Indian, whose position, having once been depressed in relation to other groups, has not been ameliorated. And no group since the Civil War has been so hopelessly degraded as was the Negro, slave and free, in the decades before the Civil War. If this is true, it is so because, and only because, although class and caste oppressions may have existed in *fact*, they have never since been defended, or defensible, as a matter of *right*, before the American people as a whole. That the nation as a whole has never been able to defend inequality as the South defended slavery may be traced, so far as any great political effects can be traced, to Lincoln's success in opposing Douglas as a leader of "American political public opinion."

Chapter XVII

The Meaning of Equality: Abstract and Practical

To THE foregoing argument there is, however, one massive objection. In brief, this objection amounts to the charge that Lincoln never really believed in the principles of the Declaration of Independence and that he never espoused them further than suited his own personal and party purposes. The evidence for this charge is that, although Lincoln insisted in the "abstract," that the Negro undoubtedly had the same right as the white man to life, liberty, and the pursuit of happiness, he was no more willing than Douglas to secure those rights; i.e., to accord to the Negro the concrete means to their enjoyment. For it is indubitably true that, from the first raising of the slavery-extension issue in 1854 by the repeal of the Missouri Compromise, but never more emphatically than in the joint debates, Lincoln pronounced himself against any measure to bring about the political or social equality of the white and black races. Because of this Lincoln's consistency, if not his sincerity, has been widely questioned. And the view has been spread that Lincoln adhered to the universalism of the Declaration so long as, but only so long as, it kept pace with the interests of the Republican party and with his interests as a Republican leader. In this vein, and in line with revisionism's depreciation of the debates, Professor Randall insists that in 1858 "big and fundamental things about slavery and the Negro were not on the agenda of national parties."[1]

The case against Lincoln, on the ground that he limited himself to an "abstract" condemnation of slavery, a condemnation which issued only in the condemnation of the extension of slavery, upon which alone northern abolitionists and Negrophobes agreed, has been stated with great sharpness in a brilliant essay on Lincoln by Professor Richard Hofstadter in his *The American Political Tradition*.[2] Hofstadter, it should be remarked, does not share the political orientation of revisionism, which makes Douglas the hero of the effort to avoid the "needless war." Yet his historiography, apart from some highly personal interpretations, seems to be based largely upon revisionism. We shall present some marked instances of this. On the whole, Hofstadter's political sympathies appear to lean toward abolitionism. Randall, Milton, Craven, and others of their school blame Lincoln, with varying degrees of acerbity, for insisting at all upon the universal meaning of the Declaration and making the moral condemnation of slavery a political question. Hofstadter, however, approves of this but believes that the same argument which condemned slavery should have compelled Lincoln to condemn the political inequality which he tolerated. His conclusion with respect to Lincoln, however, is identical with that of revisionism: the pre-presidential Lincoln was above all a demagogue who thought much of what was necessary to get himself elected and little of the consequences to the country of his being elected.

Professor Hofstadter describes with admirable clarity the practical political problem Lincoln faced and the formula with which he solved it. Lincoln's campaigns reconciled the demands both of abolitionists, for whom opposition to slavery was paramount, and the demands of those who cared nothing that the Negro was enslaved, so long as he was kept out of the territories, whether as a freeman or a slave, where they and their children might wish to go. Lincoln's trick, according to Hofstadter, was to invoke the full moral weight of the Declaration of Independence for the extremely limited demand of keeping slavery out of Kansas and Nebraska (where Hofstadter, in common with the revisionists, does not believe it would have gone anyway). According to Hofstadter, Lincoln's success in enforcing this demand while reconciling (practically, not logically) the divergent and conflicting viewpoints of his followers "entitles him to a place among the world's great political propagandists." Clearly, however, Hofstadter does not believe that Lincoln's success entitles him to any place at all among the world's great moralists.

Hofstadter's charge against the integrity of Lincoln's position may best be gathered from the following passage of his essay: ". . . [Lincoln's] strategy of appealing to abolitionists and Negrophobes at once, involved him in embarrassing contradictions. In Northern Illinois he spoke in one vein before abolition-minded audiences, but farther south, where settlers of Southern extraction were dominant, he spoke in another. It is instructive to compare what he said about the Negro in Chicago with what he said in Charleston.

Chicago, July 10, 1858:

Let us discard all this quibbling about this man and the other man, this race and that race and the other race being inferior, and therefore must be placed in an inferior position. Let us discard all these things, and unite as one people throughout this land, until we shall once more stand up declaring that all men are created equal.

Charleston, September 18, 1858:

I will say, then, that I am not, nor ever have been, in favor of bringing about in any way the social and political equality of the white and black races: that I am not, nor ever have been, in favor of making voters or jurors of negroes, nor of qualifying them to hold office, nor to intermarry with white people . . .

And inasmuch as they cannot so live, while they do remain together there must be the position of superior and inferior, and I as much as any other man am in favor of having the superior position assigned to the white race.

It is not easy to decide whether the true Lincoln is the one who spoke in Chicago or the one who spoke in Charleston. Possibly the man devoutly believed each of the utterances at the time he delivered it; possibly his mind too was a house divided against itself. In any case it is easy to see in all this the behavior of a professional politician looking for votes."

That Lincoln was a professional politician and vote getter may be freely granted, but the case for democracy, we believe, rests upon the possibility that this occupation may be an honorable one. Nay, more, we believe, with Woodrow Wilson, that the example of Lincoln is of crucial significance in the evidence it supplies concerning this possibility. Hofstadter would have us believe that the evidence of the pre-presidential Lincoln, at least, is not evidence to suggest the possibility of reconciling the demands of the vocation of democratic politics with the demands of honor. The passages presented above suggest, moreover, not only a fundamental inconsistency of view but a base adaptation of Lincoln's professions to suit the prejudices of the immediate audience. Let us turn first to this lesser charge, the charge of trimming.

Hofstadter has taken over the trimming charge (as he indicates), as well as the inconsistency charge, from Douglas, who made them in the Galesburg debate. Lincoln, in his reply to the trimming charge—which reply, however, Hofstadter omits to mention—observed first of all:

> When the Judge says . . . that I make speeches of one sort for the people of the northern end of the state, and of a different sort for the southern people, he assumes that I do not understand that my speeches will be put in print and read North and South. I knew all the while that the speech that I made at Chicago and the one I made at Jonesboro and the one at Charleston, would all be put in print and all the reading and intelligent men in the community would see them and know all about my opinions.[3]

The foregoing is part of Lincoln's immediate response at Galesburg, but he added to it at Quincy after Douglas had again pressed the attack:

> Now I wish to show you, that . . . before I made the speech at Charleston, which the Judge [and Professor Hofstadter] quotes from, he had himself heard me say substantially the same thing. It was in our first meeting, at Ottawa . . . [where] I read an extract from an old speech of mine, made nearly four years ago, not merely to show my sentiments, but to show that my sentiments were long entertained and openly expressed; in which extract I expressly declared that my own feelings would not admit a social and political equality between the white and black races, and that even if my own feelings would admit of it, I still knew that the public sentiment of the country would not, and that such a thing was an utter impossibility, or substantially that . . . At the

end of the quotation . . . I made the comments . . . which
I will now read, and ask you to notice how very nearly they
are the same as Judge Douglas says were delivered by me
down in Egypt.[4]

We will not reproduce the entire extract here, since it will be
required a little later. But in the course of it Lincoln did say,
besides much more to the same effect, "I have no purpose to
introduce political and social equality between the white and
black races." After reading he continued:

I now make this comment: That speech from which I have
now read . . . was made way up north in the Abolition
district of this state *par excellence*—in the Lovejoy district—
in the personal presence of Lovejoy—It had been made and
put in print in that region only three days less than a month
before the speech at Charleston, the like of which Judge
Douglas thinks I would not make where there was any
Abolition element.[5]

It seems to us that this is a full and complete refutation of at
least one half of the trimming charge, viz., that Lincoln trimmed
his "inegalitarianism" in the North. As to his trimming his egalitarianism to the southward, it is true that we do not find the
flaming invocations of the Declaration at Jonesboro, Alton, or
Charleston. But the campaign was spread over four months, during which the candidates were continuously speaking, and it
would be difficult to pin down the trimming charge on the ground
that Lincoln did not say at these three places what he had said
dozens of times elsewhere and what the people in these southern
parts of the state must have known Lincoln had often said if they
knew anything about him at all. Paul Angle, in his introduction
to the new edition of the Lincoln-Douglas debates, says of the
campaign, "In two ways, it makes journalistic history. For the first
time correspondents traveled with the candidates, and for the first
time a series of political speeches was reported stenographically."
This would tend to substantiate Lincoln's assertion that he knew
his speeches would be read in all parts of the state. More pertinent,
however, is the fact that Lincoln's two great speeches preceding
the campaign, the Peoria speech of 1854 and the speech on the
Dred Scott decision in 1857, were both delivered in Springfield,
which belonged both geographically and politically to the southern part of the state. Indeed, the Republicans never carried Lin-

coln's home county, either in 1858 or 1860. And both of these speeches contain, in the most emphatic way, Lincoln's assertion of the universalism of the Declaration, its inclusion of the Negro, and its moral condemnation of slavery. And both also contain denials on Lincoln's part, as he said in the Dred Scott speech, of "that counterfeit logic which concludes that, because I do not want a black woman for a *slave* I must necessarily want her for a wife."

Let us say in concluding our discussion on this picayune but troublesome point that we would be surprised if anyone could find any political speeches in which the speaker did not make some adaptations to the known prejudices of his audience. And we are certain that this was true of both Lincoln and Douglas. Lincoln's rhetorical maxim was ever "that a drop of honey catches more flies than a gallon of gall." But it is one thing to approach an audience by emphasizing the points the speaker has in common with it and another to misrepresent his position to it. There is no evidence that Lincoln deliberately suppressed anything in the South that he had said in the North and positive evidence that he did not suppress in the North what he had said in the South. The imputation of baseness in Douglas's charge may be put down as campaign oratory. One cannot say as much of Professor Hofstadter's repetition of the charge and his failure to report Lincoln's answer to it.

The one time in the joint debates when Lincoln may have lost his temper was at Jonesboro. The Douglas newspapers, quoting the senator, had circulated the charge that Lincoln had been so overcome at Ottawa that he had had to be carried from the platform. Lincoln *had* been carried on the shoulders of some of his enthusiastic admirers, but Douglas insisted that he *had to be* carried. After some pretty strong and highly personal language Lincoln remarked, "But really I have talked about this matter perhaps longer that I ought, for it is no great thing, and yet the smallest things are often the most difficult to deal with." And so it is with this foolish trimming charge which has stuck through a century, although Lincoln gave the lie to the most important part of it at Quincy, if not at Galesburg. But although the trimming charge cannot stand on its own feet, it has in all likelihood been believed by many because they have accepted the truth of the inconsistency charge, and this is a most serious matter. In what,

precisely, Lincoln's inconsistency is alleged to have lain is concisely summarized in a note appended by Hofstadter to the passage from his essay reproduced above. It runs as follows:

> Lincoln was fond of asserting that the Declaration of
> Independence, when it said that all men are created equal,
> included the Negro. He believed the Negro was probably
> inferior to the white man, he kept repeating, but in his right
> to eat, without anyone's leave, the bread he earned by his
> own labor, the Negro was the equal of any white man. Still
> he was opposed to citizenship for the Negro. How any man
> could be expected to defend his right to enjoy the fruits of
> his labor without having the power to defend it through his
> vote, Lincoln did not say. In his Peoria speech he had himself
> said: "No man is good enough to govern another man, without
> that man's consent." In one of his magnificent private memo-
> randa on slavery Lincoln argued that anyone who defends
> the moral right of slavery creates an ethic by which his own
> enslavement may be justified. But the same reasoning applies
> to anyone who would deny the Negro citizenship. It is im-
> possible to avoid the conclusion that so far as the Negro was
> concerned, Lincoln could not escape the moral insensitivity
> that is characteristic of the average white American.

In entering this particular inquiry it would be well to remind
ourselves of Sir Winston Churchill's definition of political consistency, which was given in an earlier chapter.[6] Mere verbal
consistency is no criterion of genuine consistency in politics. In
fact, genuine verbal *inconsistency* may be a requirement of true
political consistency. We have applied tests based upon such premises to Douglas's policies and have seen a very large measure of
political consistency in all he said and did. If Douglas's policies
were wrong, it was certainly not because they were inconsistent;
it was because they were based upon a consistent refusal to accept the consequences of the true meaning of "all men are created
equal." Fidelity to a cause, rather than to a stock formula of
words, is what we have a right to demand of a statesman. Different words may advance the same cause in different circumstances, and sometimes words of contrary bearing must be used
at the same time to advance that cause in given circumstances.
A statesman has only a limited control of the conditions within
which he must act. If, within the limits of his control, he acts

inconsistently with the ends of true policy, he is justly to be
blamed. If, however, he professes no intention to alter those conditions which are beyond his control, even though the goal with
which we identify him would make it appear desirable to alter
them, then no sane man will denounce him. The problem of applying the moral judgment of history to a statesman requires,
therefore, a fourfold criterion: first, is the goal a worthy one;
second, does the statesman judge wisely as to what is and what
is not within his power; third, are the means selected apt to produce the intended results; and fourth, in "inconsistently" denying
any intention to do those things which he could not in any case
do, does he say or do anything to hinder future statesmen from
more perfectly attaining his goal when altered conditions bring
more of that goal within the range of possibility? On all these
counts we believe it can be demonstrated that Lincoln spoke and
acted with perfect consistency.

How conscious Lincoln was of this problem we have already
seen when Lincoln answered the argument of Douglas and
Taney that the Fathers and Signers could not have included the
Negro in "all men are created equal" and then have continued
to hold slaves themselves or represent slaveholding communities.
The men who secured our independence and founded the government, said Lincoln, certainly believed all men had certain unalienable rights. But if they had attempted to secure *all* the rights
of *all* men they would have ended in *no* rights secured for *any*
men. The truth of the proposition, or the sincerity of their intention, was in no wise impugned by the moderation of their actions.
In the same Chicago speech of July 10, 1858, from which Hofstadter (following Douglas) has quoted, Lincoln also spoke as
follows:

> . . . there are certain conditions that make necessities and
> impose them upon us, and to the extent that a necessity is
> imposed upon a man he must submit to it. I think that was
> the condition in which we found ourselves when we estab-
> lished this government. We had slavery among us, we could
> not get our constitution unless we permitted them to remain
> in slavery, we could not secure the good we did secure if
> we grasped for more, and having by necessity submitted to
> that much, it does not destroy the principle that is the charter
> of our liberties.[7]

Thus Lincoln understood the task of statesmanship as we have described it: to know what is good or right, to know how much of that good is attainable, and to act to secure that much good but not to abandon the attainable good by grasping for more. Now Lincoln's task from 1854 on, as he saw it, was to place slavery where it would be in course of ultimate extinction. This, he was convinced, could be done by arresting the spread of slavery, by confining slavery within its existing limits. A necessary condition of such an achievement was to restore the Missouri Compromise slavery restriction. Lincoln undoubtedly would have done more; e.g., he would have revived the Wilmot Proviso limitation if that were feasible. Evidence of this may be found in the law the Republicans passed outlawing slavery in *all* the territories in 1862. To this law we will return later. But Lincoln's policy was not only to concentrate upon the possible but to proceed a step at a time. Indeed, only by such caution could he discover how much weight the ground he was on would bear. For one must not forget the reverse of the policy just stated: Lincoln believed, revisionists to the contrary notwithstanding, not only that slavery might be placed in course of ultimate extinction but that if it was not so placed it might become national, lawful in all the states, North as well as South, old as well as new. In other words, the issue, as Lincoln saw it, was not merely whether slavery would be perpetuated within its existing boundaries but whether slavery *or* freedom would be placed in course of ultimate extinction. That is the meaning of the house divided speech. The fate of the antislavery coalition, a coalition made up, as he also said in the house divided speech, "of strange, discordant, and even, hostile elements," depended, in his judgment, on the success of his personal leadership. For he believed that the eastern leaders who thought they could coalesce with Douglas after Lecompton were profoundly mistaken. Thus Lincoln was convinced in 1858, as in 1863, that upon the success of the policy for which he stood, and with which he was identified, the question would be decided of whether free, popular government was to survive. With such a sense of almost more-than-human responsibility Lincoln would not risk the good he believed he could secure by grasping at more.

Hofstadter does not deny that Lincoln's policy in 1858 was well designed to accomplish what it was avowedly designed to accomplish; namely, the exclusion of slavery from the territories by the creating of a major party possessing the political means to enforce such a policy. Nor does he question the proposition that the state of opinion in the country was such that, had Lincoln announced any intention to do more to secure the rights of the Negro than to place the Negro's captivity "in course of ultimate extinction," in the foregoing sense, Lincoln would have ruined his cause along with himself. Lincoln said over and again that he believed opinion was well-nigh universal in the country against any more equality for the Negro than that implied in a policy of turning slavery back on its existing legal rights in the slave states. How true Lincoln believed this to be we may further gather from two letters he wrote to Chase in June 1859. Chase was more of a radical than Lincoln and was particularly conspicuous for his opposition to the fugitive slave law of 1850. Lincoln had read that the Republican State Convention of Ohio had adopted as a plank in its platform the proposal to "repeal . . . the atrocious Fugitive Slave Law." And Lincoln concluded his first letter as follows:

> I enter upon no argument one way or another; but I assure you the cause of Republicanism is hopeless in Illinois, if it can be in any way made responsible for that plank.

And again, at the conclusion of the second letter, he wrote:

> My only object was to impress you with what I believe is true, that the introduction of a proposition for the repeal of the Fugitive Slave law, into the next Republican National Convention, will explode the Convention and the party.[8]

Professor Hofstadter has given Lincoln full credit for political astuteness, and we do not think he disputes the accuracy of the judgment expressed above. But how much more true would it have been of any wildly visionary scheme (as it would then have appeared) for full Negro citizenship? The only hypothesis upon which such a proposal would not have "exploded" the party would be that the proposer would have been quietly confined as a lunatic. But he assuredly could not have led the Republican party in Illinois in the year 1858. To conclude this portion of the argument we would address a question to anyone who, like Professor Hofstadter, believes that Lincoln should have demanded the vote for Negroes in 1858, at the same time that he demanded the enforcement of a policy looking to the end of their enslavement. Was it more important to lead to victory the anti-slavery party which then existed, and existed on a very tenuous foundation, or

to proclaim a policy of full interracial equality, a proclamation
that would have wrecked that party, leaving a pro-slavery party
in control of the national government? We concede that such a
counsel of "perfection" may be demanded in the name of morality.
And it may be that obedience to such counsels gain a man the
kingdom of heaven. But we believe it is as demonstrable as anything in politics can be that, had Lincoln acted upon it, he would
have acted to perpetuate the hell of slavery on earth.

Hofstadter has said, "It is impossible to avoid the conclusion
that so far as the Negro was concerned, Lincoln could not escape
the moral insensitivity that is characteristic of the average white
American." We may doubt that that man was insensitive to the
claims of the Negro's humanity who could write to his most intimate friend that the sight of slaves "was a continued torment to
me," and, "It is hardly fair for you to assume, that I have no
interest in a thing which has, and continually exercises, the power
of making me miserable. You ought rather to appreciate how much
the great body of the Northern people do crucify their feelings,
in order to maintain their loyalty to the Constitution and the
Union."[9] We do not believe anyone with moral sensitivity can
read through the body of Lincoln's speeches on the slavery question without becoming aware of the intensity of the passions he
suppressed, as well as those to which he gave vent. We do not
believe anyone who is conscious of the larger meaning of statesmanship to Lincoln can fail to be aware how real was the
crucifixion which he believed had to be suffered for the sake of
political salvation. We do not believe anyone with moral sensitivity could say of this man that he was "never much troubled
about the Negro . . ."

Hofstadter's accusation that Lincoln showed the "moral insensitivity . . . of the average white American" is suggestive of Gunnar
Myrdal's massive work, *An American Dilemma*, the subtitle of
which is *The Negro Problem and Modern Democracy*.[10] In his
preface Myrdal writes as follows:

> The "American Dilemma," referred to in the title of this
> book, is the ever-raging conflict between, on the one hand,
> the valuations preserved on the general plane which we shall
> call the "American Creed," where the American thinks, talks,
> and acts under the influence of high national and Christian

precepts, and, on the other hand, the valuations on the specific plane of individual and group living, where personal and local interests . . . jealousies; considerations of prestige and conformity; group prejudice . . . dominate his outlook.

But the American dilemma, that "ever-raging conflict," is, in Myrdal's formulation, a moral dilemma, a dilemma arising from the sensitivity of the average American to the demands of the American creed, a sensitivity which rebels against the demands of his prejudices, even as his prejudices rebel against the demands of his creed. That such a conflict has characterized the moral life of the American people we fully concede. But we insist, with Myrdal, against Hofstadter, that such a struggle is as much indicative of sensitivity as of insensitivity. And we deny that the peculiarly American tension, arising from recognition of the demands of equality on the one hand and the practical denial of some of those demands on the other, is in any just sense a morbid condition. It is, on the contrary, the typical condition in which political justice must be sought.

It is generally conceded that the Declaration of Independence is an authoritative expression of the American creed. But it has escaped the attention of Myrdal and of many others that the dilemma which he has celebrated is *not*, as he has thought, between general and specific valuations, between precept and practice, between ideal and reality. *The American dilemma is embodied in the Declaration of Independence itself.* If the dilemma exists at all, it is in the structure of the ideal, which issues in a dual imperative. For the Declaration of Independence does indeed say that all men are created equal. But by reason of this very equality governments are said to derive their just powers from the consent of the governed. Now the meaning of the expression "consent of the governed" is open to much interpretation. However, if the consent of the governed may rightfully be withdrawn from any government which the people do not believe secures their unalienable rights in a satisfactory manner, we believe that the consent of the governed cannot be interpreted in a merely hypothetical sense; it cannot be merely passive; it must embody the *opinion* of the governed. There is no question, at any rate, that for Lincoln, no less than for Professor Hofstadter, a government which did not, in the manner of a representative democracy, embody popular opinion was not a legitimate govern-

ment. Indeed, in Lincoln's Peoria speech of 1854 (first delivered
in Springfield in "southern" Illinois) he made his most radically
democratic statement of his pre-presidential career. After saying,
as we have seen above, that the principle that no man is good
enough to govern another without that other's consent is the sheet
anchor of American republicanism, he went on to declare, "Allow
ALL the governed an equal voice in the government, and that,
and that only, is self-government."[11] From this it is clear that
Lincoln at least held no medieval notions of "passive" consent.
Consent meant for him, as for any Jeffersonian Democrat, active
participation, an "equal voice in the government." For our purposes, then, consent of the governed must mean the opinion of
those who have an equal voice in the government, a voice to
which *all* the governed are entitled.

Now the opinion of the governed, unfortunately for the utopians
of this world, does not always favor the full and unequivocal recognition of that very equality which, alas, constitutes the title
deeds of its own authority. Nay, more, the opinion of the
governed may deny that all men are created equal. The crisis of
the house divided had arisen because a very considerable portion
of the American people had turned its back on the truth upon
which its own rights depended. Lincoln exhorted them again
and again to turn back into the right and true path. He firmly
believed that the explicit renunciation of the central tenet of human equality created a revolutionary situation: without such recognition, without this "sheet anchor," the ship of state was adrift,
and there was no security for any of the rights for which governments are instituted. For Lincoln the recognition of the "abstract"
truth was not barren of practical consequences just because it
was abstract. On the contrary, it was a necessary condition of
every political good. Professor Randall says that Lincoln "cited
Clay as showing that equality was abstract; you could not apply
it."[12] This is erroneous. Lincoln said that, according to Clay, the
equality proposition in the Declaration "is true as an abstract
principle . . . but . . . we cannot practically apply it in all
cases."[13] For Lincoln the equality principle meant that slavery
should if possible be excluded from the foundations of any society; but it also meant that it should guide legislators in any
existing society, teaching them to produce equal security for the
rights of all the governed to as great a degree as conditions would
permit. This was Lincoln's doctrine of the "standard maxim," to

which we have sufficiently adverted. But supreme among the conditions which must limit the wise legislator's actions *in a free society* is the opinion of the governed, to which he is duty bound *by the principle of equality itself*.

If the only thing that counted, the only thing that created obligation for the statesman, was the goal of equality of condition —i.e., equality of security for the unalienable rights of man—then the idea of popular government would be an absurdity. To see that each man received his "equal" measure we would have to have philosopher-kings, endowed with absolute power, to decree and enforce what metaphysicians alone would know how to expound. But if, for good and sufficient reasons, we will not risk the only condition upon which absolute justice seems attainable, then we must be prepared to accept that lesser form of justice which tempers the demand for equality with the demand for consent. Political justice, as a compound of equality *and* consent, requires deference to opinions which deny *many* of the implications of "abstract" equality, just as it required the repudiation of opinions which deny *any* of the implications of such equality.

In the Peoria speech, in a passage he was to read to his audience in the first debate at Ottawa four years later, Lincoln said:

> What next? Free them, and make them politically and socially, our equals? My own feelings will not admit of this; and if mine would, we well know that those of the great mass of white people will not. Whether this feeling accords with justice and sound judgment, is not the sole question, if indeed, it is any part of it. A universal feeling, whether well or ill founded, can not be safely disregarded.

And later in the same speech he also said:

> . . . the Judge has no very vivid impression that the Negro is a human; and consequently has no idea that there can be any moral question in legislating about him. In his view, the question of whether a new country shall be slave or free, is a matter of as utter indifference, as it is whether his neighbor shall plant his farm with tobacco, or stock it with horned cattle. Now whether this view is right or wrong, it is very certain that the great mass of mankind take a totally different view.—They consider slavery a great moral wrong; and their feeling against it, is not evanescent, but eternal. It lies at the

very foundation of their sense of justice; and it cannot be trifled with.—It is a great and durable element of popular action, and I think, no statesman can safely disregard it.[14]

In these two passages we can see the twin poles which constituted the axis upon which Lincoln's conception of political justice rotated. Lincoln was equally dedicated to the principle of equality and the principle of consent. Statesmanship, for him, consisted in finding that common denominator in existing circumstances which was the highest degree of equality for which general consent could be obtained. To insist upon more equality than men would consent to have would require turning to force or to the arbitrary rule of the few. But to turn to oligarchy, as a means of enforcing equality, would itself involve a repudiation of equality in the sense of the Declaration. Precisely because all men are created equal, we have an equal duty to work for equality and to seek consent. Lincoln did not believe he had a moral right to deprecate the opinion of his countrymen which denied political equality to Negroes. To have done so would have meant denying the right of white men to judge the conditions under which their government could best secure their rights. But the Declaration of Independence asserts that the people have an indefeasible right to judge of the security of their rights, and Lincoln could not deny the legitimacy of their judgment concerning the status to be accorded the Negro without denying that right. Lincoln's middle ground, between equality and consent, which is actually the middle ground between the two aspects of equality, is the only thoroughly consistent ground which the principles of the Declaration sanction. Lincoln never ceased to summon the people to fidelity to the principle of equality, considered as the principle of abstract justice. He would not abandon equality, as Douglas had done, when equality proved unpopular or inconvenient. But neither would he abandon equality's other face, reflected in the opinion of the governed who made up the political community of the United States. Because of the requirement of consent, Lincoln felt a duty to adjust public policy to the moral sense of the community. In the tension between equality and consent, in the necessity to cling to both and abandon neither, but to find the zone between which advances the public good, is the creative task of the statesman. For this task there is no formula; for the wise statesman there is no substitute.

The meaning of the Declaration, and the rights which Negroes might justly claim in consequence of its principles, has been greatly misunderstood. Hofstadter approves highly of Lincoln's anti-slavery argument, by which, in his words, "anyone who defends the moral right of slavery creates an ethic by which his own enslavement may be justified." "But," Hofstadter continues, "the same reasoning applies to anyone who would deny the Negro citizenship." This, however, is not correct. Slavery involves the denial of an "unalienable right," the right to liberty, which all men have, according to the Declaration, by the laws of nature and of nature's God. But the privileges of citizenship are not unalienable natural rights but civil rights, to be determined by a civil process. In that civil process the opinions of the members who constitute each civil society may rightfully legislate the terms and conditions by which those who are not members may be permitted to enjoy the advantages of this society.

Let us remind ourselves of the conception of the origin of civil society implicit in the Declaration. Men who are originally equal —no one having more authority over another than the other has over him—join together in order better to secure the rights that each has in virtue of his humanity but which he cannot enjoy except in and through association with his fellows. The authority which arises from their so combining rests upon unanimity, in that no man who does not consent to join is a member, nor is any man who is not accepted a member. Those who form a civil society do so for their *better* security, and no man is obliged to join who does not feel that his joining makes him more secure, and no man need be accepted whose joining does not make the others feel more secure. Whoever does not join a civil society, at its founding, has no claim to the advantages of a citizen, nor does the civil society founded have a right to impose upon him the obligations of a citizen. This does not mean that citizens and non-citizens may treat each other unjustly. A non-citizen who benefits a country that is not his own—e.g., a Lafayette—deserves that country's gratitude. And a non-citizen who enjoys the protection of the laws of a country not his own incurs obligations in proportion to the benefits he enjoys. Still the duty not to injure others and to repay benefits, etc., are duties which men have toward each other irrespective of the bond of civil society. They exist in the state of nature, and the obligations of non-members of a given civil society to members is the same as it was before the formation of the civil society in question. Now, however, although unanimity establishes civil society, it cannot continue to be the basis of decision. Legislation must be by majority rule, because it is the nearest practicable approximation to unanimity and derogates least from the natural equality from which the civil society took its origin. The majority then proceeds to establish such rules and regulations for the conduct of society as in its judgment shall add most to the security (and hence enjoyment) of those rights, for the sake of which the society was formed. In making such rules the opinion of the majority counts as the opinion of the whole. This, of course, is a fiction; but it is a believable fiction so long as, but only so long as, the minority feels that, whether mistakenly or not, the majority is legislating with a view to securing the minority's rights as well as its own. If the minority feels that its rights are more endangered than secured by the legislation of the majority, then it may, if it can, withdraw its allegiance. This consciousness of the right of revolution, a right by which the minority can endanger the majority, if the majority endangers it, is one of the forces which tends to keep the majority "honest"; i.e., to assure that it will make a reasonable effort to think of the minority's interests along with its own.

Now among the rules which each society may justly make for its better preservation are rules dealing with non-members and rules for admitting non-members to membership. And it is clear that Negro slaves were not members of the civil society established in 1776 or of the one perfected in 1787. Some few free Negroes were members, and the opinion of Taney in the Dred Scott case was utterly wrong, in assuming that Negroes could not become citizens. They certainly could become citizens if and when any state within which they were residing chose to make them such. But while their enslavement may have been intrinsically unjust, there was nothing intrinsically unjust in denying them the status of citizens after their emancipation. Admission to the status of citizen is always something for the legislative power in civil society to determine, from the point of view of the advantages of that civil society. There is a certain anomaly in the position of the freed Negro before the Civil War in that he was neither a citizen (in most states) nor an alien. But from the point of view of the principles of the Declaration his status more nearly resembled that of an alien than a citizen. In any case, he was certainly a non-member. The principles of the

Declaration do *not* require that any one who chooses to reside in a land where he is not a member of the polity has a right to a share in the government of that polity merely because he is subject to its laws. The proposition that all the governed have a right to an equal voice in the government applies only to those who are members of the civil society. Any other assumption would make nonsense of the conception of civil society as an association for *better* securing unalienable rights. If foreigners could vote in our elections, without any previous inquiry on our part as to their character and opinions, our enemies could overcome us by sending over an army not to fight but to vote! Whether rightly or wrongly, the overwhelming opinion of white Americans before the Civil War was that Negroes were not fit to exercise the privileges of citizenship and that to admit them would have been subversive of the purpose for which the government was instituted. It was Lincoln's opinion, as it was Jefferson's, that the only natural right which the Negro possessed which required civil recognition, beyond emancipation, was the right to emigrate. The right to emigrate was a corollary of the right to liberty. If a man is not admitted to the full privileges of a society of which he is not a constituent member, or a successor of a constituent member, he is denied no natural right. But he must be permitted to form a society of his own if he so chooses or go where he thinks he can better secure his own rights. He may not justly be deprived *both* of membership in the polity, to the laws of which he is subject, *and* of the possibility of forming a polity in which he will have full membership.

Professor Hofstadter's comparison of the right to citizenship with the right to liberty fails completely as a criticism of Lincoln, who understood the logical and moral implications of the Declaration of Independence as well as, if not better than, any man who has attempted to live by that noble testament. However, Hofstadter's argument would be true today in a sense in which it was not true in 1858. That is, anyone who now attempted to justify depriving Negroes of the privileges of citizenship would set a precedent which might be used against himself. The reason for this is that the Fourteenth Amendment to the Constitution declares that "All persons born or naturalized in the United States, and subject to the jurisdiction thereof, are citizens of the United States and of the state wherein they reside." Since 1868 the Negro populations of the United States as a whole have enjoyed the status of citizens of the United States and of the state wherein they reside. The same amendment, as is, we trust, sufficiently well known, also affirms that "No State shall make or enforce any law which shall abridge the privileges and immunities of citizens of the United States . . . nor deny to any person within its jurisdiction the equal protection of the laws." The recognition of the Negro's claim to the privileges of citizenship, by the most solemn legislative process known to the Constitution, the amending process, has created a moral claim to political equality which the Negro could not claim by the principles of the Declaration of Independence alone. That Abraham Lincoln contributed mightily to this enhancement of the worldly fortunes of the Negro in America, and to that transformation of public opinion which made it possible, we will not attempt to demonstrate. But we do believe it is demonstrable. And we also believe that the still unfulfilled achievement of equal political rights for Negroes would not even be imaginable if there had not first been that recognition of the Negro's humanity that the Declaration of Independence demands. But Lincoln could not have been successful in securing the recognition of the rights which the Declaration *does* demand if he had pretended to assert in their behalf rights which it does *not* demand.

A wisely consistent statesman, we have maintained, will not do or say anything to hinder future statesmen from more perfectly attaining the ends which he recognizes as desirable but not presently possible. Let us now inquire whether Lincoln, in denying any intention in 1858 to make citizens of Negroes, did or said anything that might have served as a precedent for denying them this consummation in the future. What Lincoln believed, or did not believe, concerning racial equality and inequality has been the subject of more loose and uncritical scholarship than almost anything concerning his career before 1860. For example, T. Harry Williams, in his introduction to the recent Rinehart edition of Lincoln's selected writings, says, "Like perhaps ninety-nine per cent of the American people in the nineteenth century, when little attention was given to cultural anthropology or the study of race, he was firmly convinced that the colored race was inferior to the white. He did not think that whites and Negroes could live together without one race, the superior whites, seeking to oppress the other." But Professor Williams does not say *in what*

Lincoln held the Negro to be inferior, nor whether Lincoln held that the respects in which the Negro was inferior constituted reasons for keeping him permanently in the position of a political inferior. And in saying that Lincoln held that the whites would always oppress the Negroes, does he understand this to be a prediction of continued intolerance or an inference from the Negro's inferiority? Let us turn to Lincoln's key statements on this delicate subject.

In so doing, we must first remind ourselves what an extremely delicate subject it was. We must remember that it was Douglas's strategy, in all his long struggle with Lincoln, to fasten the charge of racial egalitarianism upon Lincoln. As Lincoln tried to convict Douglas of being really pro-slavery, so Douglas tried to convict Lincoln of being really an abolitionist and a complete racial integrationist. Lincoln could not have survived politically had there been any widespread suspicion of truth in Douglas's charge. In evaluating the meaning of Lincoln's denials of racial egalitarianism, we must keep in mind the tremendous pressure he was under to deny it and the fact that, as Professor Williams indicates, perhaps 99 per cent of his followers were firmly convinced that the Negroes were so far inferior as to be incapable of exercising the privileges of citizenship in a manner compatible with the public safety and welfare. We would say that opinion in Illinois in 1858 was probably about as favorable to Negro citizenship as opinion in Arkansas today is favorable to public school integration. And we would ask the reader of the following selections to ponder whether any politician of that state or sister states would today be capable of such a restrained indulgence of the opinions of those whose suffrages he was seeking.

We have already produced the classic passage from the Peoria speech in which Lincoln said that his own feelings would not admit of making the Negroes social and political equals or, "if mine would, we well know that the great mass of white people would not." After repeating this passage at Ottawa he went on to say, among other things:

> I have no purpose to introduce political and social equality between the white and black races. There is a physical difference between the two, which in my judgment will probably forever forbid their living together upon the footing of perfect equality, and inasmuch as it becomes a necessity

that there must be a difference, I, as well as Judge Douglas, am in favor of the race to which I belong, having the superior position. I have never said anything to the contrary, but I hold that notwithstanding all this, there is no reason in the world why the negro is not entitled to all the natural rights enumerated in the Declaration of Independence, the right to life, liberty, and the pursuit of happiness. I hold that he is as much entitled to these as the white man. I agree with Judge Douglas he is not my equal in many respects—certainly not in color, perhaps not in moral and intellectual endowment. But in the right to eat the bread, without leave of anybody else, which his own hand earns, he is my equal and the equal of Judge Douglas, and the equal of every living man.[15]

This passage is repeated, with minor differences in wording, at Charleston, where Lincoln had also said, as we have seen above, "I am not, nor ever have been," in favor of making voters or jurors of Negroes or otherwise permitting them social and political equality.

What are we to infer from the foregoing concerning Lincoln's views? In the first place, we must note that Lincoln, in saying, "I am not, nor ever have been," says nothing about the future. Lincoln never said, so far as we know, that he never *would* be in favor of such equality. In the Peoria speech he said his own feelings were against it, but he immediately introduced, as a hypothetical possibility, that his own feelings might not be against it. Why? The sentence, taken as a whole, is an equivocation. Concerning the equality or inequality of the qualities of the Negro, we note that Lincoln says "certainly" only that the Negro is not his equal in color. Lincoln knew, of course, that his audience would assign great value to this inequality. But what value did he assign to it? We do not know.[16] As to moral and intellectual endowment, he says "perhaps" the Negro is unequal in these respects. If we credit Lincoln with the opinion which is implicit in his whole life's work, then he believed that moral and intellectual differences were the only qualitative differences between men of intrinsic importance. On this premise Lincoln never, to our knowledge, said that the Negro was certainly inferior in capacity to the white man. In saying "perhaps," Lincoln was merely echoing the opinion of Jefferson, and of all enlightened Americans, who recognized that, in the barbaric condition of native Africans and in the oppressed condition of American Negroes, there had not been sufficient opportunity to form a conclusive judgment as to their potentialities.[17] We give it as our opinion that, in the actual circumstances, cultural anthropology could not have given a more intelligent answer.

Lincoln was a pessimist on the subject of the possibility of an interracial, egalitarian society. The physical difference of color, he thought, preserved prejudices which would make political equality impossible. But he did not say that the inequality traceable to color was rooted in an inequality of intrinsic worth. Nor did he ever say, as Professor Williams believes, that the "superior whites" would always oppress the inferior Negroes. Lincoln gave it as his opinion *that one or the other* would do the oppressing. And, he said, if there must be a superior and an inferior, an oppressed and an oppressor, he would naturally prefer the advantage being on the side of "the race to which I belong." This reasoning has nothing whatever to do with justice. It contemplates the situation in the ancient conundrum in which there are two men on a raft capable of supporting only one. It is equally just, or unjust, for either to push the other off. What this proves is that there are certain situations in which justice is impossible. Where justice is impossible, the decision between two equally unjust alternatives may justly be decided on the basis of pure self-interest. But because there are some situations in which justice is impossible does not mean that it is never possible or that there is any less obligation to be just when justice is possible.

In the background of Lincoln's pessimism on the race question, as in the foreground of every appeal to natural right, are the classic reflections of Jefferson. In the *Notes on Virginia* Jefferson had written, "Among the Romans emancipation required but one effort. The slave, when made free, might mix with, without staining the blood of his master. But with us a second is necessary, unknown to history. When freed, he is to be removed beyond the reach of mixture."[18] When Jefferson asked himself, "Why not retain and incorporate the blacks into the State," his answer was: "Deep-rooted prejudices entertained by the whites; ten thousand recollections, by the blacks, of the injuries they have sustained; new provocations; the real distinction which nature has made; and many other circumstances, will divide us into parties, and produce convulsions, which will never end but in the extermina-

tion of the one or the other race."[19] The premise of this assertion,
be it noted, is not a doctrine of white supremacy. On the contrary,
Jefferson must have entertained the possibility that the blacks
had very considerable political capacity if he believed it possible
that they might become oppressors in their turn. He supposes
that Negroes and whites alike are given to prejudice—because
such is the nature of their common humanity—and when the roots
of the prejudice go as deep as in this instance, the obstacles to
complete equality of condition in the same society are insuperable. Both Lincoln and Jefferson, we are certain, would have conceded that such prejudices are theoretically capable of being
transcended. Nay, more, we are certain that neither of them held
an opinion on the race question which might justly be called a
prejudice. "But a nation of philosophers is as little to be expected
as the philosophical race of kings wished for by Plato."[20] Both
Lincoln and Jefferson, being committed to government by the
consent of the governed, were committed to the proposition that
unphilosophic opinion must always enter into the actual basis
of political justice. In the Temperance Address Lincoln had
foreseen, with a clarity given to few men, the possibility of
tyranny implicit in the demand that men be governed by reason
alone. No man who was himself governed by reason would attempt to enforce such demands.

Neither Lincoln nor Jefferson believed that genuine friendship
between the races—that is, apart from exceptional individuals—
was possible. And neither believed that, where friendship is
impossible, it is possible for men to be fellow citizens in any but a
partial or incomplete sense of the term. The acceptance of
imperfection was of the essence of the acceptance of popular
government and yet in no wise indicated the inferiority of popular
government to other possible forms of government. For Lincoln,
as for Jefferson, Clay, and others, the only perfect solution of
the American race question was complete separation by the
emigration of the Negroes. For Lincoln the possibility of this solution was demonstrated in the history of the ancient Hebrews,
who had gone out of Egypt, and the colonists who had departed
from the Old World monarchies, to gain their freedom in the New
World and to establish, eventually, the United States. It has been
demonstrated in our own day by the state of Israel. In advocating
emigration and colonization for the Negroes Lincoln was not
depreciating the Negroes; on the contrary, he paid them a high

tribute in supposing they had the same capacity for founding a free society that white men had. Lincoln was impressed, as few of his critics today are, by the vast cost in human genius and sacrifice that must go into the erection of free political institutions. He did not believe that the Negro race would ever fully enjoy the freedom and equality which had been established by the efforts of white men until they had established freedom and equality in a country of their own. Lincoln knew that the opinion of the average white man was unfavorable to the Negro just because there was no example of a free indigenous Negro polity to which Negroes might point as an example of their political capacity. As long as opinions depended on such evidence, and as long as such evidence was lacking, so long would "perfect equality" between the races be utopian.

In the Ottawa debate Lincoln said he did not believe the two races could live together upon a footing of "perfect equality," but he did not say they could not live together upon a footing of much greater equality. His pessimism was, in fact, much more moderate than Jefferson's. In the Civil War, Lincoln went far to impress the white public with the claims to civil rights which Negroes had justly acquired by their sacrifices in saving the Union, a Union which had in some measure become theirs by virtue of these sacrifices. And when Lincoln began to prepare his plan for reconstruction, toward the end of the Civil War, political rights for *qualified* Negroes was included as a matter of course. This policy was perfectly consistent with what he had said in 1858 and earlier. Lincoln never attempted to propose what was more than one step ahead of the great body of political public opinion. But he always led the way.

Chapter XVIII

The "Natural Limits" of Slavery Expansion

WE have already cited the extraordinary statement by Professor Randall that Douglas's program "would inevitably have made Kansas free . . ." We have argued that, in so far as Randall relies for his judgment on the political effects of the doctrine of "popular sovereignty," taken by itself, he is utterly mistaken. For Douglas would have been powerless to resist Buchanan in 1857–58 without the Republicans in Congress, and there would have been no Republicans there if Douglas's policy had been accepted in 1854; and there is no reason to believe that without the continued opposition to Douglas by Lincoln in 1858 "popular sovereignty" would have resulted in freedom in Kansas thereafter. But Randall's thesis, and the whole revisionist case, hinges upon still another hypothesis. It is that causes other than purely political ones would in any case have kept slavery out of Kansas and out of any other parts of the Union where it was not already established. "By 1858 it was evident that slavery in Kansas had no chance," Randall writes. "After that, as Professor W. O. Lynch has shown, 'there was no remaining Federal territory where the conditions were so favorable to slavery.' The fight against the Lecompton proslavery constitution was won not by reason of any debate between Lincoln and Douglas, but by the logical workings of natural causes and by a specific contest in which, with 'the aid of Republicans, he [Douglas] won the Lecompton fight.'"[1]

Anyone reading Randall's text would, we think, suppose that the article of Professor Lynch from which Randall has quoted,

and which is to be found in the *Dictionary of American History,*
Volume IV, page 309, contains some evidence to support the contention that "there was no remaining Federal territory where the
conditions were so favorable to slavery." In fact, however, Lynch's
article contains nothing whatever to that effect, except the bare
assertion Randall has quoted. In Lynch's bibliography, however,
one finds listed the classic essay by Charles W. Ramsdell, "The
Natural Limits of Slavery Expansion," published in *The Mississippi Valley Historical Review,* October 1929. So far as the present
writer has been able to discover, this essay is the headwater from
which has flowed the "natural causes" thesis upon which Randall,
Lynch, and other revisionists have based their conviction that
freedom in the territories was inevitable. This essay must be one
of the most influential works in American historical writing since
the Civil War. What is remarkable is its acceptance by northern
historians, because the author is one of the most redoubtable and
uncompromising apologists of the southern cause. Like most
southern apologists *since* the Civil War, he does not think slavery
was the real issue. The "positive good" theory was only the
reaction to abolitionism—on which Southerners blame everything
for which no apology can be found—but, according to Ramsdell,
abolitionists or not, "There can be little doubt that the institution
of chattel slavery had reached its peak by 1860 and that within
a comparatively short time it would have begun to decline and
eventually have been abolished by the Southerners themselves."
Why the South fought so desperately to preserve an institution it
was about to abolish may be hard to understand. Ramsdell, of
course, would say they were fighting for the rights of the states
which, unlike the Union, were worth fighting for.[2]

A man may always be pardoned, and even admired, for making
a spirited defense of the cause of his forefathers. But to see the
"natural causes" thesis pass from an old Confederate like Ramsdell
to a "Constitutional Unionist" like Randall and then to an
"Abolitionist" like Hofstadter is as bewildering as it is stimulating.
The following occurs in a note to Hofstadter's essay on Lincoln.
"Historians are in general agreement with such contemporaries
of Lincoln as Clay, Webster, Douglas and Hammond, that *the
natural limits of slavery expansion* in the continental United States
had already been reached." We have italicized the phrase which
shows the title of Ramsdell's essay passing into Hofstadter's

language almost as a truism. Strangely neither Hofstadter, in his three-page, fine-print bibliography, nor Randall, in his bibliography of over fifty pages appended to the second volume of *Lincoln the President*, lists the Ramsdell "Natural Limits" essay. This is the more surprising because both list Ramsdell's far less consequential essay blaming Lincoln for the firing on Fort Sumter. Yet Randall *disagrees* with the Sumter piece, which he lists, and *agrees* with the "natural limits" piece, which he does not list. And the firing on Sumter, important as it is as an episode, can hardly be compared in importance with the question of the reality of the slavery-extension issue, which was the avowed political cause of secession. Can it be that Randall and Hofstadter do not wish to acknowledge their debt to the Southerner, even when he helps them damn Lincoln, who was neither secessionist, constitutional unionist, nor abolitionist?

So far as we know, it is Ramsdell, and not Clay, Webster, Douglas, or Hammond, whom recent historians have followed. As for Clay and Webster, we do not know what evidence Hofstadter has—since he gives none—that they believed slavery to have reached its "natural limits" in the continental United States. During the Senate debates on the Kansas-Nebraska bill in the spring of 1854, Chase, Sumner, Seward, and other of its opponents proved beyond a peradventure—as Lincoln was to do in his Peoria speech the following fall—that the compromisers of 1850—certainly the Whig compromisers—had no territories in mind but those acquired from Mexico. Webster's celebrated seventh of March speech, as we have shown in an earlier chapter,[3] only referred to former Mexican soil, from which all antislavery men, *and Douglas*, believed it was banned by Mexican law, until such time as there was a positive enactment sanctioning slavery by American authority. So far as we know, neither Clay nor Webster ever said, or implied, that slavery would not expand *anywhere* in the continental United States if all legal prohibitions were withdrawn. Clay and Webster did, however, speak of natural causes keeping slavery out of the Mexican Southwest. In this sense they did propound a "natural limits" theory of a sort. However, there was a vast difference for statesmen to propound such a belief to gain acceptance of a specific legislative measure and for scholars to employ it as a general theory for the interpretation of history. As we shall shortly show, the concept of a natural limit to slavery is, as a scientific theory, false and should never have commanded the assent of any reflecting person. Certainly no one who has read Lincoln's speeches, where it is thoroughly refuted, should have entertained it for a moment. As propounded by Webster, Clay, and Douglas in 1850, it meant only that it was improbable that slavery would go into such a place as New Mexico Territory *in the foreseeable future.* The justification for Webster is that he used a plausible but specious argument to persuade the North to forgo the Wilmot Proviso, because he believed that the Compromise of 1850, *taken as a whole,* was a Union-saving measure, in the interest of the entire country. And the compromise would have been impossible if the Proviso demand had been insisted upon by the North. The idea that God and nature would keep slavery out of the newly acquired Southwest was an argument addressed to the North and designed to make palatable a concession which, in any case, was being paid for by such southern concessions as the admission of California as a free state. It is almost inconceivable that Webster or Clay would have accepted the "natural limits" theory to defend the repeal of the Missouri Compromise, which was a wholly gratuitous, uncompensated concession to pro-slavery opinion. But even if Webster's argument was more plausible than we believe it ever was, there is no excuse for historians repeating it, nearly a century afterward, when experience has revealed its utter hollowness. For in 1859, as we have already noted, the territorial government of New Mexico actually passed a slave code for that vast region. The revisionists, we are aware, would reply that, even with the slave code, slavery did not go into New Mexico. To this we would rejoin that the sectional crisis came to a head barely a year after the code was passed and that the election of Lincoln persuaded most slaveowners not to venture forth in any direction with their property until the secession issue was settled. The following is from a letter written by the Secretary of the New Mexico Territory to an acquaintance in Washington on August 16, 1858, during the thick of the Lincoln-Douglas campaign:

It is generally believed here that the territorial legislature will pass some kind of a slave code for the territory at the next session. It is true that we have few slaves here, but Otero [New Mexico's delegate to Congress] has let it be known that if N. M. expects any favors from Wash. [i.e., from the Buchanan administration], a slave code would be a wise move. The governor and most of the other officials are favorable to it . . . We have assured the Mexicans that it will protect their own system of peonage . . .[4]

So much for the way in which political causes supplemented "natural causes" in helping "popular sovereignty" along. But less than ten years after Webster had declaimed so about God and nature forbidding slavery in New Mexico, we find such sentiments as the following, expressed in a letter by an Associate Justice of the territory, a native New Englander, to the Attorney General of the United States, February 14, 1859:

This body has passed a law for the protection of slave property in the territory. This was necessary, for the truth is I do not see how Americans are going to get on here without slavery. It can't be done. The Peons are not worth their salt and all other labor is unattainable. Slave labor can be made very profitable by cultivating the soil, and I will venture to say that a man with a half dozen negroes would make a fortune at the present prices of produce . . . and grains. The soil in the bottoms is very rich and productive. You must not place any credence in the story that slave property could not be made available here.[5]

It is our impression that the word "available" in the last sentence is employed in the somewhat archaic sense of "useful," or "capable of succeeding," as an "available" candidate for office. However, to anyone who, like Professor Hofstadter, still takes the Webster argument of 1850 seriously, we offer the foregoing as expert testimony from someone on the spot to the effect that the soil and climate argument, as applied to New Mexico, was nothing but what Lincoln called a "lullaby." Another reason why there were few slaves in New Mexico is that just before the war slave prices were skyrocketing. They were in such demand in the older slave lands that it was almost impossible to buy them for the newer lands. We should note, moreover, that while the New Mexican legislature was passing a slave code it also passed a series of measures to strengthen the system of peonage. Ramsdell and others have maintained that the cheapness of Mexican labor made Negro slavery unlikely in the Southwest. In fact, however, the two systems helped each other. Negro slavery helped to reinforce peonage—or would have if it had remained available as an alternative source of labor. The worst effects of peonage, which was scarcely better than slavery, would have been impossible to ameliorate if slavery had continued to exist nearby. And Lincoln's whole point was that, where men were free to introduce slavery, *any* alternative labor system was bound to be depressed to a condition approximating that of the slaves. To sum up: the "natural limits" and "popular sovereignty" theories had their prime test in New Mexico, and what was happening there even as the Lincoln-Douglas debates were in progress vindicated Lincoln's contentions during the debates.

Ramsdell's essay is very persuasive in establishing a very limited proposition; viz., that by 1860 the traditional southern plantation system of cotton culture had extended about as far as it was likely to extend *within the existing boundaries of the United States.* He does except some large areas of Texas, which the railroads had not yet made accessible to markets and which were also unusable until the invention of the barbed-wire fence made the fields immune to the depredations of cattle, because the lands in question were far from fencing timber. But Ramsdell's essay proves nothing whatever as to the possibility of slavery being extended by the employment of slaves in *other* occupations. Nor does it prove that any existing limitations were *permanent* limitations. It is precisely this last point at which Lincoln took aim when he employed one of his most oft-repeated and prescient arguments in the joint debates. We take the text from the last joint debate at Alton, although he said substantially the same thing at Springfield, July 17, 1858, and at Jonesboro and Quincy in the joint meetings, as well as in innumerable speeches on the stump.

Brooks of South Carolina once declared that when this Constitution was framed, its framers did not look to the institution existing until this day. When he said this, I think he stated a fact that is fully borne out by the history of the times. But he also said they were better and wiser men than the men of these days; yet the men of these days had experience which they had not, and by the invention of the

cotton gin it became a necessity in this country that slavery
should be perpetual. I now say that . . . Judge Douglas has
been the most prominent instrument in changing the position
of slavery . . . and *putting it upon Brook's cotton-gin basis* . . .[6]

"Brooks's cotton-gin basis" means a basis in which any possibility
to make profit from the Negro is not to be prevented by any
considerations of the Negro's rights. But it means still more. It
means that the expectation of the Fathers, an expectation based
on the economic prospects of slavery *before* the invention of the
cotton gin, was utterly confounded *by* the invention of the cotton
gin. If Professor Ramsdell had written an essay on the "natural"
limits of slavery in 1790, he would have seen those limits utterly
destroyed before the end of 1791. If, then, a human invention
can completely overturn limits set by "nature," nature is a most
fickle thing to rely upon. In short, the idea of a "natural" limit
to a human institution is, as we have maintained, an absurdity.
One invention had completely altered the prospects of freedom
of millions of human beings. The mid-nineteenth century was very
self-conscious of the rapid technological changes that were revolutionizing the conditions of human life. Lincoln himself lectured
on science and inventions after the campaign against Douglas
and had patented an invention of his own. "Brooks's cotton-gin
basis" therefore implied the following further questions: shall we
permit the institution of human slavery to be revolutionized by
any future technological development? Shall human rights be the
slave of technology, or shall technology be the slave of human
rights? Without a moral decision against slavery no guarantee for
the future was possible. Certainly there is no scrap of evidence
in Ramsdell's essay that there was in 1860 any more of a guarantee
against the expansion of slavery than that which existed in 1790.

That slavery was wedded, by and large, to cotton in the
antebellum South may be true. But this is to be explained by
the extraordinary profitability of cotton culture and proves nothing
as to the possibility of the exploitation of slave labor in other
fields of human production. That Negro slavery could be maintained only in connection with the simpler forms of unskilled
field labor is a myth contradicted even by those who spread it.
Ramsdell himself refers to "negro mechanics . . . hired at high

wages." He does not say these were slaves, but it is notorious that many were—as well as that their owners kept most of their wages. Kenneth Stampp, in his admirable recent survey *The Peculiar Institution*,[7] says that although, for obvious reasons, the bulk of the slaves were employed in cotton and similar agricultural pursuits, "In 1860, probably a half million bondsmen lived in southern cities and towns, or were engaged in work not directly or indirectly connected with agriculture," and that "in spite of the protests of free laborers," they "worked in virtually every skilled and unskilled occupation."[8] And as revealing as words can be of the truth of Lincoln's position is the following: "Some Southerners were enthusiastic crusaders for the development of factories which would employ slaves. They were convinced that bondsmen could be trained in all necessary skills [for which conviction there was abundant empirical evidence] and would provide a cheaper and more manageable form of labor than free whites."[9] Professor Stampp also gives an example of a famous iron company in Richmond, Virginia, which introduced slaves into its labor force in the 1840's, with the result that the free laborers eventually struck in protest. Then the manager, like countless managers since, "vowed he would show his workers that they could not dictate his labor policies: he refused to re-employ any of the strikers."[10] Thereafter the company employed only slaves. When Lincoln made his New England tour in March 1860, after the Cooper Union speech, he came to New Haven, Connecticut, in the midst of a shoe strike. The strike was, in part, occasioned by the loss of southern business by reason of an attempt to apply pressure, via the boycott, upon Republican businesses and businessmen. Yet Lincoln grasped this nettle firmly when he said:

> I am glad to see that system of labor prevails in New England under which laborers *can* strike when they want to, where they are not obliged to work under all circumstances, and are not tied down and obliged to labor whether you pay them or not! I *like* the system which lets a man quit when he wants to, and wish it might prevail everywhere. One of the reasons I am opposed to Slavery is just here.[11]

Southern apologists who speak of a "natural limit" to slavery are really thinking not of economic "nature" but of the nature of the Negro. What they seem to assume, perhaps half consciously, is that the Negro is a kind of domestic animal, limited in usefulness like a horse or a mule. Lincoln's fundamental objection to the whole "soil and climate" thesis stemmed from his simple assumption that the Negro was a man and that as such he was capable of being exploited in *any* way that human labor might be exploited. Any break in the legal barriers confining slavery was a threat to free labor, because slave labor could be used to degrade free labor wherever there was a legal possibility of their being used side by side. Slavery, moreover, was a protean institution, as Professor Stampp's recent book convincingly shows. There were many forms that the relationship of master and servant could and did take, and there is no reason to suppose that, should slavery in the mines, foundries, factories, and fields of the free states have proved advantageous to powerful groups therein, new systems of discipline might not have been invented to make the exploitation of slave labor highly profitable. The totalitarian regimes of the twentieth century provide us with ample evidence of the variety of ways that this might have been done. Even if it were true that the productivity of a system based on free labor is greater than one based on slave labor, it does not follow that it is more *profitable to the men who run it*. A large portion of a smaller sum may still be more than a small portion of a larger one. All we know of the fierce struggles, the long uphill climb, of free labor in the grip of the industrial revolution that followed the Civil War suggests that it never could have succeeded, as it has, if in addition to all other handicaps the incubus of slavery could have been placed in the scales against it. If the great corporations, the "robber barons" who came to dominate the state legislatures in the postbellum period, had wanted to import slaves as strikebreakers, *then* it would not have required even another Dred Scott decision to spread slavery to the free states. It is simply unhistorical to say that such a thing *couldn't* have happened because it *didn't* happen. It didn't happen because Lincoln was resolved that it *shouldn't* happen. And nothing but his implacable resolve made it impossible.

The thesis that slavery would not have gone into the territories, whether it was prohibited by law or not, is the fundamental thesis of revisionism in dealing with the political causes of the Civil War. But this thesis is itself a subordinate manifestation of an apology for the South which has received a classic formulation in the work of Ramsdell. The main thesis of this apology, which we have already given in Ramsdell's words, is that slavery as an economic institution had reached its peak in 1860 and was about to decline. Gradual emancipation was "just around the corner," if only the Republicans had not placed the South on the defensive. This contention has recently received its most detailed and circumstantial refutation in a monograph written under the auspices of the National Bureau of Economic Research by two Harvard economists, Professors Alfred H. Conrad and John Meyer. "The Economics of Slavery in the Ante-Bellum South," published in *The Journal of Political Economy*, April 1958, is the most enlightening piece of original research we have encountered on the slavery question.

According to the authors, this study is the first attempt to measure the profitability of slavery according to the economic, as opposed to the accounting, concept of profitability. The debate over the profitability of slavery, they note, has been conducted in terms of a variety of accounting methods, usually shaped to prove the debaters' contentions and seldom comparable one with another. Conrad and Meyer have attempted to measure the profitability of southern slave operations in terms of modern capital theory. And what they have concluded is that the rate of return on male slave capital employed in the field ranged between 5 and 7 per cent in the majority of antebellum cotton plantation operations, while the rate on female slave capital, from both field work and procreation, averaged 8 per cent. These returns, they say, compare favorably with contemporary returns of 6 to 7 per cent on genuinely alternative investment opportunities.

Slavery, they maintain, was profitable to the whole South, the continuing demand for labor in the cotton belt ensuring returns to the breeding operations on the less productive land in the seaboard and border states. The breeding returns were necessary, however, to make the plantation operations on the poorer lands as profitable as alternative contemporary economic activities. The failure of southern agriculture on these poorer lands in the postbellum period is probably attributable, they say, mainly to the loss of capital gains from slave breeding and not to the relative inefficiency of the tenant system that replaced plantations or the soil damage resulting from the war. This last point, we observe, is of great importance. It is a reply to those who charge the freed Negroes with incapacity as agriculturists when separated from their old overseers. What the freed Negroes were unable to do to compete with the old plantation system was to sell themselves to balance their budget! Shades of Swift's "Modest Proposal!"

The Conrad and Meyer work is striking for its data on the importance of slave breeding to the entire slave economy. As they mention, this was something that Southerners, then and since, have gone to great lengths to deny and to conceal. We may recall[12] that Douglas in 1849 had expected all the border states, from Missouri to Delaware, to adopt schemes for gradual emancipation. If soil and climate *in these states* had been the sole determining factor, his expectation might have been correct. But the Conrad and Meyer work shows that the employment of slaves in these states, *plus* the sale of the surplus Negroes raised there, maintained the profitability of slavery there. The South, they note, had developed a price structure for slaves and efficient market mechanisms for transferring slaves. Because of this no argument based on the soil and climate in a region which did not take into account the profits from breeding can be accounted adequate. Thus, they further conclude that *continued expansion of slave territory was both possible and, to some extent, necessary.* The maintenance of profits depended, they say, upon *either* intensive or extensive expansion. Intensive expansion, we would add, could only mean greater use of more skilled slaves, and this in itself would have suggested the feasibility of, and have encouraged the use of slaves in, the kinds of farming supposedly reserved for the yeoman farmers of the West. As to the alleged inefficiency of slave labor in all but certain kinds of farming, Conrad and Meyer are, like Stampp, entirely unimpressed. They note that slaves were employed in cotton factories throughout the South, in coal mines, in lumbering, and in iron works (as already noted), and they say that southern railroads were largely built by slaves. In short, there is almost nothing to suggest that slaves, like free Negroes since the Civil War, might not have gone almost anywhere the law and the whites allowed, doing any work white men did, if given the chance.

In concluding this portion of our argument, we would merely note that the Conrad and Meyer paper is not only a refutation of the Ramsdell "natural limits" theory, but it is a vindication of another argument that Lincoln used, with ever greater emphasis, as the Civil War approached. In commenting on the difficulties of finding support for a plan of gradual emancipation and colonization, he had observed at the end of his Dred Scott speech, "The plainest print cannot be read through a gold eagle; and it will be ever hard to find many men who will send a slave to Liberia, and pay his passage, while they can send him to a new country, Kansas for instance, and sell him for fifteen hundred dollars, and the rise."[13] And in the New Haven speech, from which we have quoted above, Lincoln also spoke as follows:

> The owners of these slaves consider them property. The effect upon the minds of the owners is that of property, and nothing else—it induces them to insist upon all that will favorably affect its value as property, to demand laws and institutions and a public policy that shall increase and secure its value, and make it durable, lasting and universal . . . The slaveholder does not like to be considered a mean fellow . . . and hence he has to struggle within himself and sets about arguing himself into the belief that Slavery is right. The property influences his mind. The dissenting minister, who argued some theological point with one of the established church, was always met with the reply, "I can't see it so." He opened the Bible, and pointed him to a passage, but the orthodox minister replied, "I can't see it so." Then he showed him a single word—"Can you see that?" "Yes, I see it," was the reply. The dissenter laid a guinea over the word and asked, "Do you see it now?" So here, whether the owners of this species of property do really see it as it is, it is not for me to say, but if they do, they see it as it is through 2,000,000,000 of dollars, and that is a pretty thick coating.[14]

The necessity for the expansion of slavery, and the reality of the need for new lands, if the value of that multi-billion dollar investment was to be safeguarded, was implicitly confessed by Douglas himself in his last rejoinder in the joint debates at Alton. Lincoln's idea, said Douglas,

> is that he will prohibit slavery in all the territories, and thus force them all to become free states, surrounding the slave states with a cordon of free states, and hemming them in, keeping the slaves confined to their present limits whilst they go on multiplying until the soil on which they live will no longer feed them, and he will thus be able to put slavery in a course of ultimate extinction by starvation.[15]

Of course, Douglas did not entertain the thought that the schemes of emancipation proposed by Jefferson might be revived again, even by Southerners, once the confinement of slavery lowered the rate of return upon slaves. Certainly schemes of compensated emancipation would stand a chance if the compensation was for an investment of dwindling value. In this sense Douglas has accurately stated Lincoln's purpose. But it is difficult to comprehend how any one could have said, as Professor Randall has, that in 1858 "big and fundamental things about slavery and the Negro were not on the agenda . . ."

Chapter XIX

Did the Republicans Abandon Lincoln's Principles after the Election of 1860?

Of all the distortions concerning the significance of the Lincoln-Douglas debates circulated by revisionists, none is more damning to the reputation of the Republican party led by Lincoln than the charge that the main plank in the campaigns of 1858 and 1860 was abandoned after Lincoln's election. A concise statement of this charge may be found in Hofstadter's essay on Lincoln: "But the supreme irony [of the Lincoln-Douglas debates] can be found in the fact that early in 1861 the Republicans in Congress gave their votes to measures organizing the territories of Colorado, Nevada, and Dakota *without prohibiting slavery*. After beating Douglas in 1860, they organized the territories along the pattern of his policy, not Lincoln's."[1] Hofstadter has clearly taken this theme from Randall, but it is so important for an appreciation both of history and of historians that we trouble the reader with the parallel passage in Randall's work:

> . . . any serious student of the subject should turn to the proceedings in Congress early in 1861. If Lincoln had been elected senator, and if in that period he had voted as did the great majority of Republicans in Congress on bills organizing the territories of Colorado, Nevada, and Dakota, he would actually have been taking the Douglas position, for these territories were organized by Republican votes without prohibition of slavery . . . This seems to suggest that . . . in a broader analysis, the "issue" of abolition in the territories

was a talking point . . . a campaign appeal rather than a guide for legislation.[2]

We pause only to note that there was no issue of "abolition" in the territories. Randall has again fallen into Douglas's vernacular. Lincoln always pointed out that there was no need to *abolish* slavery in the territories; his aim was to keep it *out*. The foregoing passage is from Randall's chapter on the debates, but in his chapter on the secession crisis of the winter of 1860–61 he returns to the charge thus:

> It has been noted above how Douglas was able in 1861 to taunt the Republicans with abandonment of those princi- ples on which the Lincoln-Douglas debates had been waged in 1858. That point deserves further notice here. When the aforementioned acts organizing Colorado, Nevada, and Da- kota were passed (February–March 1861), the prohibition or permission of slavery was not mentioned in these statutes, which left the question of slavery in the territories exactly where it was in Douglas's Kansas-Nebraska act of 1854, so far as congressional legislation was concerned . . . After the proceedings had been completed regarding the three ter- ritorial bills . . . Douglas could not refrain from making his comment. "This very session," he said, "the Republican party, in both Houses of Congress . . . have backed down from their platform and abandoned the doctrine of congressional prohibition . . . They have abandoned the doctrine of the President elect . . ."[3]

The foregoing passages, from both Hofstadter and Randall, are as remarkable for what they omit as for what they say. Let us consider the situation during this last, lame-duck session of the Thirty-sixth Congress, and then we will also take note of certain subsequent events.

In the first place, the election of Lincoln in the fall of 1860 had been followed by the secession of South Carolina on Decem- ber 20, 1861, and South Carolina was soon followed by Georgia, Florida, Alabama, Mississippi, Louisiana, and Texas, all of which "left" the Union before the inauguration of Lincoln. It was in the midst of the desperate efforts to preserve the Union that the three territorial bills mentioned were passed. The most notable of these efforts was the Crittenden Compromise. The provisions of this last-ditch attempt to stem the tide of secession, and apparently the only one that southern leaders would support, may be summarized in the words of Professor Randall in his *The Civil War and Reconstruction.*

> Let slavery be prohibited in national territory north of the line 36 degrees 30 minutes, but let it be established and maintained by Federal protection south of that line; let future states, north or south of the line, come into the Union with or without slavery as they wish; restrain Congress from abolishing slavery in places within national jurisdiction which may be surrounded by slave states . . .[4]

We forbear at this point because the main points have been given. The key to the Crittenden Compromise, of course, is the division of the nation's territory along the parallel of the Missouri Compromise line. And it was at this point at which most Republicans in Congress stuck. The purpose of the Republican party was, as we have seen, to restore the Missouri Compromise prohibition. But it meant to do this because it meant, as a matter of principle, to forbid slavery *anywhere* that the authority of Congress extended. Lincoln never would have tampered with the Compromise of 1850 if the slave power had not tampered with the Compromise of 1820. But now that *all* the territories had been opened to slavery, by the Kansas-Nebraska Act and the Dred Scott decision, he meant to close them all to slavery the moment the political means for doing so were available. While the measures in the Crittenden Compromise were being discussed, Lincoln passed the word of the incoming administration to its congressional followers. We quote from a letter addressed to William Kellogg from Springfield, December 11, 1860:

> Entertain no proposition for a compromise in regard to the *extension* of slavery. The instant you do, they have us under again; all our labor is lost, and sooner or later must be done over. Douglas is sure to be again trying to bring in his "Pop. Sov." Have none of it. The tug has to come & better now than later.[5]

And again, to another Republican, December 18, 1860:

> I am sorry any republican inclines to dally with Pop. Sov. of any sort. It acknowledges that slavery has equal rights with

liberty, and surrenders all we have contended for. Once fastened on us as a settled policy, filibustering for all South of us, and making slave states of it, follows in spite of us, with an early Supreme Court decision, holding our free-state constitutions to be unconstitutional.[6]

With secession in full cry, and with the imbecile Buchanan wringing his hands and saying secession was unconstitutional but the Constitution forbade him to do anything about it, the Republicans in Congress were under enormous pressure to make some concessions to keep the country together, at least until a President of their choice took office. It is indicative of that pressure that Kellogg, to whom the first letter above was addressed, in spite of Lincoln's advice, introduced a bill to amend the Constitution so that slaves could be taken into any territory south of the Missouri line latitude. But the whole weight of the President-elect was thrown against any compromise that would admit the right of slavery to go into a single foot of the national domain. Upon the rock of Lincoln's fidelity to the principle of his campaign against Douglas every compromise foundered in that fateful winter. Whether Lincoln was doctrinaire in this insistence may be debated, but that he stuck to his principle can in no wise be doubted.

When the bills organizing Colorado, Nevada, and Dakota were passed, Buchanan was still in the White House. And since he was thoroughly committed to the Dred Scott decision, any bill containing a prohibition of slavery in the territories would certainly have been vetoed. But the Republicans did not, in any case, have a majority in both houses of the second session of the Thirty-sixth Congress. They had a slight majority in the House, but in the Senate there were twenty-six Republicans, thirty-six Democrats, two Americans, and two vacancies.[7] It is true that after the congressional delegations from the seceding states had withdrawn the Republicans *might* have pressed for the slavery prohibitions in the territorial bills. But the secession issue was not finally settled, and the attitude of the border states still hung in the balance. It would have been madness to have pressed a temporary voting advantage when the attitude of the border states, upon which all might yet depend, still was unsettled. The fact that they stood firm against any *commitment* to abandon their intention to ban slavery in the territories is surely as much an exhibition of principle as practical wisdom could have required.

The denouement of this story, which is omitted altogether by Hofstadter, and which is not omitted by Randall, but told without any suggestion of its relevance to the Lincoln-Douglas debates, came the following year. We give it in Randall's words from the second volume of *Lincoln the President*:[8]

> Two months after having provided emancipation in the District, Congress abolished slavery in the territories of the United States then existing or thereafter to be formed or acquired [Act of June 12, 1862]. In this instance, as in the District case, Congress passed and Lincoln signed a bill which, by ruling law according to Supreme Court interpretation, was unconstitutional. This fact, as well as the legal extinction of that explosive territorial situation which had produced such prodigious prewar agitation, was allowed to pass over with little comment.

This grudging record of the "legal extinction" of any possibility of slavery in United States territories may also, with charity, be allowed to pass with little comment. What should not be passed over, however, is the fact that in June 1862, six months after the meeting of the *first* regular session of the *first* Congress sitting during the presidency of Abraham Lincoln, slavery in the territories of the United States "then existing or thereafter to be formed or acquired" was prohibited. If this constituted an abandonment of the principles of the campaign of 1858, if this was not a consummation of everything Lincoln had fought for that fateful summer, then words have no meaning.

Chapter XX

The End of Manifest Destiny

HAVING just noted Lincoln's iron refusal, in the midst of the secession crisis of the winter of 1860–61, to concede any right to slavery *south* of 36'30" latitude, we can understand why he would never have viewed with approval any of the devices by which Douglas attempted in the years 1848, 1849, or 1850 to secure any division of the nation's territory by extending the Missouri line. For Lincoln was perfectly convinced that any such division, however superficially unfavorable it might appear to be to the interests of slavery, involved a wrongful concession of principle. It would have been wrongful in itself, and it would have been utterly unreliable. Lincoln knew that the vast acquisitions of the Mexican War were only a foretaste of what Douglas himself believed to be in store if he ever gained control of the nation's foreign policy. Only a national commitment to confine slavery, Lincoln believed, would put an end to the drive for foreign conquest and domination. Many historians have doubted that there was any considerable support in the South for filibustering. And, of course, there is widespread disbelief that Douglas was interested in extending slavery. What they have failed to take into account, however, was the dynamism in the *coincidence* of the ambitions of Douglas and the slave power. It was this coincidence that repealed the Missouri Compromise. For, say what one will as to the precipitating force of the *Appeal of the Independent Democrats*, Douglas *did* strike a bargain with the Southerners, and there was nothing in his policy or principles which inhibited him from indulging any requirement of slavery. That Douglas would have consented to the expansion of slavery as a means to other ends we can hardly doubt. No end was more potently desired by Douglas than the destruction of British power in the Western Hemisphere. To accomplish this Douglas would always have permitted the Devil to name his price. And the Devil was Slavery.

The fourth question Lincoln put to Douglas at Freeport has also been overshadowed by the famous second question. It, too, has a significance that can hardly be exaggerated. Lincoln asked: "Are you in favor of acquiring additional territory, in disregard of how such acquisition may affect the nation on the slavery question?" Here is an extract from Douglas's reply:

. . . this is a young and growing nation. It swarms as often as a hive of bees, and . . . there must be hives in which they can gather and make their honey. In less than fifteen years, if the same progress that has distinguished this country for the last fifteen years continues, every foot of vacant land between this and the Pacific Ocean, owned by the United States, will be occupied. Will you not continue to increase at the end of fifteen years as well as now? I tell you, increase, and multiply, and expand, is the law of this nation's existence. You cannot limit this great republic by mere boundary lines, saying, "thus far shalt thou go, and no further." Any one of you gentlemen might as well say to a son twelve years old that he is big enough, and must not grow any larger, and in order to prevent his growth put a hoop around him to keep him to his present size. What would be the result? Either the hoop must burst . . . or the child must die. So it would be with this great nation. With our natural increase . . . with the tide of emigration that is fleeing despotism in the old world to seek a refuge in our own, there is a constant torrent pouring into this country that requires more land, more territory upon which to settle, and just as fast as our interests and our destiny require additional territory in the north, in the south, or in the islands of the ocean, I am for it, and when we acquire it will leave the people, according to the Nebraska Bill, free to do as they please on the subject of slavery and every other question.[1]

Let us note that, according to this doctrine, the land area of the Western Hemisphere became usable only by being incorporated into the United States! Neither Mexico nor Canada, by Douglas's calculations, could provide population outlets except by being first sacrificed to the Moloch of Manifest Destiny. But as Douglas could not bear to contemplate any partnership of British and American power, so Lincoln always tacitly assumed it to be a sound basis for American freedom. In 1845 Lincoln had written that he could never see much good to come of Texas annexation "inasmuch as they were already a free republican people on our own model." This was Clay's attitude, and it cost Clay the presidency, because he underestimated the popular fear that Texas might form an alliance with Britain. Still, Lincoln could see no reason in 1858 why every expansion of freedom would have to take place by an expansion of the boundaries of the United States. How Lincoln scorned Douglas's expansionism we may gather from the following rebuttal to Douglas's answer to his fourth Freeport question. It was delivered at Galesburg:

> If Judge Douglas's policy upon this question succeeds, and gets fairly settled down, until all opposition is crushed out, the next thing will be a grab for the territory of poor Mexico, and invasion of the rich lands of South America, then the adjoining islands will follow, each one of which promises additional slave fields. And this question is to be left to the people of those countries for settlement. When we shall get Mexico, I don't know whether the Judge will be in favor of the Mexican people that we get with it settling this question for themselves and all others; because we know the Judge has a great horror for mongrels, and I understand that the people of Mexico are most decidedly a race of mongrels. I understand that there is not more than one person there out of eight who is pure white, and I suppose from the Judge's previous declaration that when we get Mexico or any considerable portion of it, that he will be in favor of these mongrels settling this question, which would bring him somewhat into collision with his horror of an inferior race.[2]

The ugly potentialities of a policy of *lebensraum* combined with *racial supremacy* should hardly need explanatory comment today. The accents of sarcasm in the foregoing extract can scarcely escape notice. Of the "mongrels" to the south Douglas had spoken thus at Springfield, July 17, 1858:

We are witnessing the result of giving civil and political rights to inferior races in Mexico, Central America, in South America, and in the West India Islands. Those young men who went from here to Mexico to fight the battles of their country in the Mexican war, can tell you the fruits of negro equality with the white man. They will tell you that the result of that equality is social amalgamation, demoralization and degradation, below the capacity for self-government.[3]

Douglas's white supremacy, American empire, would have been a very different polity from anything envisaged in the pristine purity of the republican ideal of the Founding Fathers. There would have been precious little "popular sovereignty" for the natives for whom Douglas had such contempt. And there might be many American states today in which, as in the case of the French in Algeria, a privileged minority would be engulfed in the swirling tides of hatred of an unprivileged majority of a different complexion. The problem of racial adjustment in America today is of an order of magnitude that we could hardly exaggerate. And this problem, as every informed person knows, although dramatized by the struggle of the Negro, is not limited to the Negro. Indians, Mexicans, Orientals have all had a desperate struggle, varying in times, places, and intensity, to achieve the dignity which our fundamental law and principles hold out to all. Aspiration must, as Lincoln implied in his "standard maxim" doctrine, always transcend fulfillment. Yet it is essential that the possibility of fulfillment does not fall so far short of the aspiration as to make it not a source of hope but a mockery. Douglas's formula for solving the slavery question, in which the nation was already hopelessly entangled, would have made that question infinitely more complicated. It is almost inconceivable that democratic processes could have survived such complications. And we can only shudder to think what the twentieth century would be like if the United States had entered it as first and foremost of totalitarian powers.

❊   ❊   ❊   ❊   ❊

The only moral justification of Douglas's policy—as of revisionist historiography—is a tacit belief in the idea of progress, an idea that economic forces were "inevitably" working for freedom, both on the plains of Kansas and elsewhere. Only such a belief could justify the principle that all harsh moral alternatives were to be avoided, that one could safely "agree to disagree." The silent forces of history were working for freedom, if only the politicians would give them time. Lincoln's whole policy, on the contrary, was a denial that things would take care of themselves, that progress would result from anything but man's foresight, judgment, and courage. The impulse of the Revolution had been a mighty one, Lincoln believed, and great things had been achieved because of it. But the spirit of '76 and the spirit of Nebraska were utter incompatibilities. The Nebraska bill could never even have been considered if there had not been an enormous change in public opinion, a change for the worse that augured still further changes for the worse, changes which portended the utter extinction of a weary mankind's hope that there might at last be a demonstration of man's capability to govern himself. To avert these changes no reliance could be placed on anything so absurd as "soil and climate." The only reliance, the only rock upon which man's political salvation might be built, was man's moral sense, the determination of some men to be free, and the awareness that no man can rightfully achieve freedom for himself or, in the presence of a just God, long retain his freedom if he would deny to any other man, of whatever race or nation, the right to equal freedom.

Notes

Chapter I

1. *Lincoln the President* (New York: Dodd, Mead & Company, 1945), I, p. 127.
2. *History of the United States from the Compromise of 1850*, II, pp. 330, 332, 338.
3. *Abraham Lincoln*, Pocket Book Edition, p. 161.
4. See the introductory essay on Carl Becker by George H. Sabine, prefaced to Becker's *Freedom and Responsibility in the American Way of Life* (New York: Vintage Books, 1955). Sabine explains that Becker was a "relativist" according to whom history must be "continually rewritten," not because of the discovery of new facts, but because the historian is necessarily dominated by the "preconceptions" and "value judgments" of the age in which he lives, and it is these preconceptions which determine the meaning he finds in the facts. Becker would have derided Randall's idea of restoring "reality," as a masquerade of the historian's prejudices in the guise of "detachment." Randall, we presume, might have questioned Becker's cogency when the latter affirmed, "Everything is unstable . . . except the idea of instability."
5. Op. cit., Chapter V, "Lincoln and Douglas."
6. Quoted by Rhodes, op. cit., II, p. 329.
7. Randall maintains (op. cit., pp. 126, 129–31) that popular sovereignty actually did keep slavery out of Kansas and that, since the Republicans in 1861 actually organized the territories of Dakota, Nevada, and Colorado without congressional prohibitions of slavery, the Douglas of the debates was thoroughly vindicated. But, as we shall argue at length later, this assertion involves a number of hypotheses and is no mere statement of fact; e.g., did the "principle of popular sovereignty" keep slavery from these places, or did free-soil opinion and determination, which rejected that principle when it rejected Douglas's leadership, keep it out?
8. Randall, op. cit., p. 158.
9. On the conflict between the Illinois and eastern Republicans, see Don E. Fehrenbacher, "The Nomination of Abraham Lincoln in 1858," in the *Abraham Lincoln Quarterly*, March 1950.
10. The expression "needless war" is taken from George Fort Milton's

Eve of Conflict: Stephen A. Douglas and the Needless War. (New York: Houghton Mifflin, 1934.) That it expresses the key theme of revisionist historiography is ably set forth by Thomas J. Pressly, *Americans Interpret Their Civil War* (Princeton University, 1954), Chapter Seven, "Repressible Conflict," pp. 257 ff. The other expressions I have chosen (they could be endlessly multiplied) are Randall's. The beginnings of a reaction to revisionism, particularly in the reviews, are also documented in Pressly's book. Of particular distinction is Arthur M. Schlesinger, Jr.'s "The Causes of the Civil War: A Note on Historical Sentimentalism," *Partisan Review*, October 1949. This short but remarkable essay certainly anticipates in principle some of the major elements in the critique of revisionism in the present study.

Chapter II

1. Randall, op. cit., I, p. 76. We omit annotating citations from speeches of Lincoln and Douglas in this chapter, which presents a concise synoptic impression of the two positions confronting each other.
2. Ibid., p. 86.
3. Ibid., p. 122.
4. Ibid., p. 127.
5. Cf. Brooks Adams's introduction to Henry Adams, *The Degradation of the Democratic Dogma*, (New York: Peter Smith, 1949), pp. 17–20.

Chapter III

1. Nevin's denunciation of Douglas is chiefly in the second volume of *Ordeal of the Union*, published in 1947 by Scribner. The sequel, the third and fourth volumes of *Ordeal of the Union*, published in 1950 under the subtitle *Emergence of Lincoln*, praises Douglas as highly as he had earlier been denounced. We shall have occasion below to comment on Nevin's differing criteria of statesmanship.
2. Op. cit., II, p. 108.
3. *The Collected Works of Abraham Lincoln*, (hereafter cited as *Collected Works*) Roy P. Basler, editor (Rutgers University, 1953), I, pp. 178, 179. Unless otherwise noted, all italics in quotations from Lincoln are Lincoln's own.
4. Winston S. Churchill, *Thoughts and Adventures* (London, 1932), p. 39.

5. Milton, op. cit., p. 150.
6. *Congressional Globe,* 30th Congress, 1st Session, Appendix, 506–7.
7. Ibid., 31st Cong., 1st Session, Appendix, p. 365.
8. Cf. note 6 above.
9. The importance of the Irish to Douglas is indicated in Lincoln's passing reference in 1852 to "those adopted citizens, whose votes have given Judge Douglas all his consequence . . ." *Collected Works,* II, p. 143. Cf. also Mr. Dooley on "The Negro Problem," in *Mr. Dooley's Philosophy* (New York: R. H. Russell, 1900), p. 218. "I was fr strikin' off the shackles iv th' slaves, me la-ad. 'Twas thrue I didn't vote fr it, bein' that I heerd Stephen A. Douglas say 'twas onconstitootional . . ."
10. *Congressional Globe,* 31st Congress, 1st Session, Appendix, p. 371.
11. It was only the division of free soil votes between Fremont and Fillmore that saved the Democrats from defeat in 1856.

Chapter IV

1. Douglas, we might observe, attempted, through the wise conduct of party politics, to achieve what Calhoun wanted when he called for the "concurrent majority." How much better was Douglas's policy, which would have attempted to secure the substance without the offensive form!
2. Milton, op. cit., p. 155.
3. January 6, 1845: *Congressional Globe,* 28th Congress, 2nd Session, Appendix, p. 95.
4. In the Senate, March 23, 1848. *The Works of Daniel Webster* (Boston, 1860), V, p. 300.
5. W. E. Binkley, *American Political Parties* (New York: Alfred A. Knopf, 1947), p. 82.
6. Ibid., p. 121.
7. *Collected Works,* II, p. 323.
8. Ibid., IV, p. 86.
9. Cf. note 3 above.
10. Cf. *Life of Stephen A. Douglas,* by James W. Sheahan (New York, 1860), p. 92.
11. Webster, *Works,* V, p. 289.
12. Ibid., I, pp. 355–57. Webster incorporated much of this passage into his March 7, 1850, speech.
13. Randall, op. cit., II, pp. 29–31.
14. Webster, *Works,* III, p. 65.
15. *Congressional Globe,* 32nd Congress, 1st Session, p. 70.

16. *Collected Works*, I, p. 438.

17. Webster, *Works*, VI, pp. 494, 495.

18ª. *Collected Works*, II, p. 276.

18ᵇ. But see also the "Resolutions in Behalf of Hungarian Freedom," reported by Lincoln to an Illinois meeting, January 9, 1852. *Collected Works*, II, p. 115. They include a denunciation of British oppression of Irish patriots, a denunciation which is reserved by comparison with Douglas's.

19. Sheahan, op. cit., p. 114.

20. Nevins, op. cit., I, p. 550.

21. Cf. *A History of the Foreign Policy of the United States*, by R. G. Adams (New York: Macmillan, 1924), p. 233.

22. Nevins, op. cit., p. 551, n. 14.

23. Adams, op. cit., p. 231.

24. Sheahan, op. cit., pp. 105–8.

25. Ibid., pp. 113, 115.

26. Ibid., pp. 122, 123.

27. Ibid., p. 123.

28. Ibid., pp. 168–86. It is interesting and significant that Professor Nevins, after quoting from this speech the passage we have cited on p. 31, beginning "The civilized world have always held," goes on to condemn Douglas in these words: "It was impossible for such a man to comprehend the fervent emotion with which millions of freedom loving Northerners regarded the possibility that half the great West might become a land of slaves . . ." (*Ordeal of the Union*, II, p. 108.) The significance lies in the fact that Nevins should so single out this 1850 speech, which is the one speech of Douglas that Lincoln praised highly. Cf. Lincoln, *Collected Works*, II, p. 138: ". . . a very able production . . . comparing favorably with anything from any source, which I had seen on that general subject. The reading of it afforded me a good deal of pleasure . . ." We would further note that, in this same speech, in which he praises Douglas, Lincoln speaks of the error of those who had attempted to stir up insurrection in Cuba against Spanish rule. The heart of the error, Lincoln said, lay in the fact that the Cubans were unfit for civil liberty, a statement which would suggest a measure of agreement with the proposition of Douglas which Nevins finds so unfeeling.

Chapter V

1. *The Missouri Controversy*, by Glover Moore (University of Kentucky, 1953), p. 124.

2. *Congressional Globe*, 28th Congress, 2nd Session, p. 284.
3. Ibid., 31st Congress, 1st Session, Appendix, p. 369.
4. *Collected Works*, II, pp. 262–63.
5. Cf. note 3 above.
6. *Congressional Globe*, 31st Congress, 1st Session, Appendix, p. 343.
7. Sheahan, op. cit., pp. 163–66.

Chapter VI

1. *Ordeal of the Union*, II, p. 100.
2. Ibid., p. 115.
3. *Lincoln the President*, I, p. 122.
4. *Collected Works*, II, p. 258.
5. Ibid., II, p. 257.
6. Op. cit., pp. 115–18.
7. *Collected Works*, II, p. 259.
8. Moore, op. cit., p. 251.
9. *Democracy in America*, Reeve-Bradley trans. (New York: Vintage, 1954 Books), Vol. I, pp. 61–63.
10. P. Orman Ray, *The Repeal of the Missouri Compromise*, 1909, pp. 163 ff.

Chapter VII

1. *Collected Works*, II, p. 254.
2. *Congressional Globe*, 32nd Congress, 2nd Session, p. 1113.
3. Ibid.
4. Ibid., p. 1117.
5. Op. cit., p. 104.
6. Op. cit., p. 82.
7. Ibid., p. 81.
8. *Congressional Globe*, 32nd Congress, 2nd Session, p. 1117.
9. Webster *Works*, V, p. 340.
10. Ibid., p. 383.
11. Ibid.
12. *Collected Works*, III, p. 376.
13. Quoted by Carl Becker, *The Declaration of Independence* (New York: Knopf, 1942), p. 25.
14. The Supreme Court, before the Civil War, was very far from having achieved the unique position it occupies today, as the judge of the legality of the actions of the other two branches. Today it is even held by some scholars that the Dred Scott decision was the

first in which the Court ruled distinctly that a provision of a federal statute violated the Constitution. But whether *Dred Scott vs. Sandford,* or *Marbury vs. Madison* a half century before, was the first, we should note that even in the case of Dred Scott the Court did not declare the act of Congress unconstitutional until three years after it had been declared "void" by Congress itself.

15. Moore, op. cit., pp. 124, 247.

Chapter VIII

1. Op. cit., II, p. 95.
2. *Collected Works,* II, p. 254.
3. Ibid., p. 261.
4. Op. cit., II, p. 95.

Chapter IX

1. Edmund Wilson, "Abraham Lincoln: The Union as Religious Mysticism," in *Eight Essays* (New York: Doubleday Anchor Books, 1954), p. 202.
2. Ibid., p. 202.
3. *Collected Works,* IV, pp. 437, 438–39.
4. Ibid., I, p. 8.
5. *Collected Works,* I, p. 111.
6. Cf. Albert J. Beveridge, *Abraham Lincoln,* I, p. 220; and for the entire episode, pp. 219–24.
7. Cf. *Collected Works,* I, p. 75.
8. Beveridge, op. cit., I, p. 195.
9. Letter to Erastus Corning and Others, June 12, 1863. *Collected Works,* VI, p. 266.
10. *Collected Works,* III, pp. 547, 548, 549.
11. Op. cit., p. 190.
12. Jowett translation, pp. 483, 484.
13. *Politics,* 1284 a 3–20. Jowett translation.
14. This interpretation of *Julius Caesar* was suggested to me by Prof. Leo Strauss.
15. See Lincoln's address at a Sanitary Fair in Baltimore, April 18, 1864. For an extremely interesting discussion of this address see "The Dilemmas of Freedom," by Hans J. Morgenthau, and the "Comment on Morgenthau's Dilemmas of Freedom," by Howard B. White, in *The American Political Science Review,* September 1957. Our interpretation of the metaphor of the shepherd follows

that of Professor White (p. 733), who locates its source not only in the Bible but in Plato's *Republic*, 343 A ff., and *Statesman*, 271 E 6–8, and 275 B 1 ff. There is no evidence that Lincoln read Plato, but that he knew that Plato was the source of some central conceptions of Western thought is suggested by the following: "As Plato had for the immortality of the soul, so Young America has a 'pleasing hope—a fond desire—a longing after' territory," *Works*, III, 357. The line occurs in Addison's *Cato* (Act V, Sc. i), but Lincoln appears to have moved at his ease among ideas of the Platonic tradition, particularly those infused into the Christian tradition.

16. *Collected Works*, III, p. 334.
17. See Lincoln's praise of Douglas's 1850 Chicago speech defending the Compromise of 1850, *Works* II, 138. Excerpt quoted above, Ch. IV, n. 28 (p. 442).
18. It will be observed that Lincoln has fully anticipated and in a sense agrees with the revisionist thesis that the Civil War was a "whipped-up crisis," the product of irresponsible leadership playing upon irrational hopes and fears. But how far removed is Lincoln's diagnosis of this danger, almost a generation before the crisis broke in all its fury, from the revisionist view of the war as something eccentric, improbable, and unnecessary! Compare the Lyceum speech's expectation of the moral-political crisis of Caesarism, as something inherent in the attempt to demonstrate man's capacity to govern himself, and the following: "That America, devoted to peace and busy with the affairs of a growing nation, should have become a snarling area of internal conflict, however voluminously explained, is a matter whose 'causes' seem unconvincing. It happened; otherwise it would seem incredible." Randall, op. cit., I, p. 75.

Chapter X

1. For present purposes we limit ourselves to this broad comparison of the general approach to reverence by the Founding Fathers in such a book as the *Federalist*—which was praised as an authoritative exposition of the principles of the Constitution by both Washington and Jefferson—with that of Lincoln. Two supplementary comments would, however, appear in order. First, the awesome figure of Washington served, in the first eight years, to produce the restraints which must flow, in the long run, from reverence for the laws. Washington thus played a quasi-monarchial role in the early days of the Republic, using a personal authority

which was really greater than that of the law—which he certainly could have overthrown had he so chosen—to establish the law. Second, we would take cognizance of the notorious preference of Hamilton for some of the aristocratic institutions of English Whiggery to stabilize the democratic passions. The difference between Lincoln and Hamilton—his greatest intellectual predecessor in the Federalist-Whig-Republican tradition—was that Lincoln grasped the necessity of evolving aristocratic restraints upon democracy, not by borrowing contra-democratic devices from a non-democratic past, but by evolving them from within the democratic ethos as perfections of that ethos.

2. *Federalist*, #51, Modern Library edition, p. 337.
3. Ibid., #49, p. 331.
4. Cf. note 2 above.
5. *Collected Works*, I, p. 382.
6. *The Complete Jefferson*, assembled and arranged by Saul K. Padover (New York: Duell Sloan & Pearce, 1943), p. 675.
7. Ibid., p. 677.
8. Ibid., p. 675.
9. Ibid., p. 676.
10. Cf. note 7 above.
11. Compare Jefferson's remark to this effect in Query XVIII (Padover ed., p. 677).
12. P. 324.
13. A fellow Whig, but rival for political preferment, although a personal friend. Lincoln named his second child after him.
14. It is worth noticing how "time" was a motif in Lincoln's rhetoric from early years. It is, of course, the key to many of the profoundest effects of both the Gettysburg Address and the Second Inaugural.
15. Compare the following *double-entendre:* "Whether or not the world would be vastly benefitted by a total and final banishment from it of all intoxicating drinks, seems to me not *now* to be an open question. Three-fourths of mankind confess the affirmative with their *tongues,* and, I believe, all the rest acknowledge it in their *hearts.*" Apart from the possibility that the "now" may be meant in the most literal sense—viz., in the presence of the Washingtonians—there is the horrible suspicion that three fourths do not acknowledge it in their hearts. Here, as elsewhere throughout this chapter, all italics in quotations from Lincoln are Lincoln's own.
16. The difference between a God who cannot and one who will not reverse himself has, of course, well-nigh unlimited ramifications. How far Lincoln was aware of these, we do not venture to say. However, Lincoln does say, in a later passage which must be discussed in its proper place, that the argument for Providence, like

that for whisky, rests upon universal public opinion. Now it is precisely because the philosophic God is subject to ontological necessity that he cannot be conceived as changing and hence cannot be conceived as "Providence"—i.e., concerned with particular beings or particular events. For this reason *He* could not change his "decree," while the biblical God could (and frequently did). Moreover, the argument for a God whose "decree" is subject to necessity would be an ontological argument, not an argument from universal public opinion.

It may be objected that we are laying too great stress upon the distinction between "can" and "will" and that, in any case, there is no necessity for conceiving the two conceptions of deity in the form of a radical opposition. In Thomistic theology, for example, the antinomy is overcome by the proposition that all apparent "reversals" of the divine fiat are themselves predetermined by an aboriginal necessity. Without inquiring whether the Thomistic synthesis is philosophically successful, I think it clear that Lincoln's language is inconsistent with such a synthesis. For the Thomistic doctrine, while holding that the divine reversals are apparent rather than real, denies to human wisdom the possibility of penetrating to its core the necessity of the divine nature, anticipating thereby all future reversals. Revelation remains a necessity of human life precisely because central facts concerning human life—e.g., man's sinfulness and the remedy therefore—are beyond unassisted human reason. From the Thomistic view, therefore, Lincoln would have had no basis to assert as a matter of natural knowledge that the strength of the passions would always remain the same. Since Lincoln does assert this as a matter of natural knowledge, he must have here presupposed only a natural theology. And from the point of view of a natural theology, the force of the opposition of the two conceptions of deity recurs in full.

17. It is advisable that the reader consult the analytical outline of the Temperance Address which we have prepared for a precise understanding of our references to sections and subsections. We have, where convenient, given in parentheses the numbers of the paragraphs comprehended in a given section.

18. See fifth paragraph of the address, which has not been quoted.

19. "I was at the door of the church as the people passed out," records the faithful Herndon, "and heard them discussing the speech . . . 'It's a shame,' I heard one man say, 'that he should be permitted to abuse us so in the house of the Lord.' The truth was the [Washingtonian] society was composed mainly of the roughs and drunkards of the town, who had evinced a desire to reform. Many

of them were too fresh from the gutter to be taken at once into the society of such people as worshipped at the church where the speech was delivered . . . The whole thing, I repeat, was damaging to Lincoln, and gave rise to the opposition on the part of the churches which confronted him several years afterwards when he became a candidate against the noted Peter Cartwright for Congress." Beveridge, op. cit., I, p. 329, n. 2.

20. *Collected Works*, III, p. 376.

21. It might be argued that, in presenting objections to Lincoln's argument, we are producing a hybrid mixture of interpretation and critique. Whether this is so or not depends upon whether or not certain criticisms of his overt argument were intended by Lincoln to be made by the intelligent addressee of his speech. When the criticism required by the manifest deficiencies of Lincoln's argument correspond heavily with the defects which he has openly imputed to the position of others, we may be permitted to suspect that Lincoln was as conscious as we are of such weaknesses in his reasonings. If this is so, we are entitled to think that Lincoln also had a covert argument which transcends these difficulties and that it is this argument which is the true aim of interpretation. To discover this argument requires that we supply, by means of such criticism as the foregoing, the intermediate premises lacking in Lincoln's explicit exposition.

22. Lincoln's expression in a somewhat different context. See paragraph ten of the address.

23. We might notice Lincoln's equally spurious argument that nondrinkers should take the pledge so as to make the refusal to take the pledge as unfashionable as wearing one's wife's bonnet in church. The idea of thus turning "temperance" into a fashion would mean, of course, to deprive it of any inner moral significance. The morally indifferent example chosen by Lincoln indicates this. How this would contribute to real temperance may be gathered from the experience of another President. Harry S. Truman, in his memoirs, tells of working in a drugstore as a boy. The local temperance leaders regularly trooped into the store for their matutinal medicine on the way to work. Truman said he learned then and there to prefer the barroom drinkers to the prescription-counter drinkers. I doubt that Lincoln, whose proposal here amounts to turning thousands into prescription-counter drinkers, would have disagreed.

24. The foregoing reflection requires this further comment. Men of "genius and generosity" may have a proneness to intemperance—i.e., to self-indulgence in the broader sense (not only with respect to drink)—but they also have a "temptation" to virtue that lesser men

do not have. Let us consider female virtue, by way of analogy. A beautiful woman is subject, no doubt, to temptations that an ugly one does not have. But it is also true that the pleasure she gives by her beauty gains advantages for her that an ugly woman may not have at all or may have only at a sacrifice that the beauty need not make. Similarly, men of genius and generosity, having access to noble pleasures, have less need of ignoble ones. It would be truer to say that they have less temptation to ignoble pleasures but that, if they do turn to them, they will do so with far more force and vehemence. But this, it seems, leads to an opposite conclusion from Lincoln's: society should be harsher to the man of talents who forgoes noble for ignoble pleasures; increasing the penalty of moral failure will strengthen the resolve for success. With the same inner (and valid) logic, it also appears, society has always penalized more harshly the unchastity of beautiful women.

25. See the discussion of heroic virtue in my *Thomism and Aristotelianism* (University of Chicago, 1952), pp. 98 ff.

26. This reflection suggests that the Washingtonians might have been a convenient symbol of early Christianity, which must also have been assembled largely from the outcasts of the society of its period. Such at least is suggested by the idea that in the kingdom of heaven the last shall be first, etc., not to mention the social and moral standing of most of those to whom Jesus addressed his Gospel. Lincoln's attack on the old-school reformers in like manner calls to mind the attack of the early Protestants upon the pomp and intolerance of Rome. That the old-school reformers were the lineal descendants of the early Protestants may perhaps give us a supplementary insight into the probable fate of the Washingtonian movement, from Lincoln's point of view, should it continue on the path Lincoln discerned, as an organized political force.

27. We might observe this difference, which undoubtedly underlies the common-sense distinction between the pledge taken by the Washingtonians and the "pledge" which gains entrance into the kingdom of heaven. It is presumed, we take it, that the blessed have such enjoyment from their blessedness there that temptation to sin is inconceivable in the celestial abode (bypassing the question of whether the passions of the body are even possible in heaven). Unfortunately this is not the case of the Washingtonians, so that a sober community dignitary who joined could not be absolutely sure that it was a "reformed" drunkards' society he was joining.

28. The evidence for this statement is not indubitable, as the proof of a negative never is. Roy P. Basler, in his one-volume edition of Lincoln's *Writing and Speeches*, p. 129, says, "It is not certain that Lincoln was ever a member of the organization." To which we would add the observation that Lincoln, in the Temperance

Address, says that the whole purpose of teetotalers like himself
joining is the value of their public example. From the point of
view of this argument, not to be notoriously a member would be
tantamount to not being a member at all. However, there is in
addition a direct statement (in Beveridge, op. cit., II., pp. 241,
242) reported of Lincoln himself, although many years after the
speech.

> A decanter of "red liquor," . . . stood on the sideboard, and,
> as the usual act of politeness of former days, Douglas invited
> callers to have a drink if they wished. "Mr. Lincoln, won't
> you take something," Douglas is reported to have said when
> Lincoln rose to go. "No, I think not," said Lincoln. "Why!
> are you a member of the Temperance Society?" asked Doug-
> las. "No! I am not a member of any Temperance Society,"
> Lincoln answered, "but I am temperate *in this,* that I don't
> drink anything."

29. The moral "leveling" which is the object of Lincoln's satire in these
passages is characteristic of the utopianism so strong in the
nineteenth century. The abolition of "artificial" distinctions by the
French Revolution, so that "citizen" became a greater title of
honor than king or lord, lay behind this utopianism. But the term
"citizen" was still parochial by comparison with the term "com-
rade," whose history in 1842 was still largely before it. That
communism sprang from the same soil as the temperance movement should be obvious from much of this chapter.

30. Whether by rotation in office, as in classical times, or as the voter
in a modern democracy "rules" on election day and is ruled
thereafter.

Chapter XI

1. *Emergence of Lincoln,* II, p. 463.
2. Ibid., I, pp. 347, 348.
3. *Emergence of Lincoln,* I, p. 362.
4. Randall, op. cit., p. 116.
5. The house divided speech, June 16, 1858, is to be found in
Collected Works, II, pp. 461–69. No further footnote references to
it will be given.
6. Randall, op. cit., I, p. 108.
7. Nevins, op. cit., I, p. 362.
8. Ibid.
9. Compare also the following from Nevins's appendix on the respon-

sibility of Curtis and McLean for the Dred Scott decision: "It remains to say a few words about President-elect Buchanan's intervention. While no 'conspiracy' was concocted between him and Taney, he did let key members of the Court know just what kind of decision he wanted, and just why he wanted it . . . He moved the hesitant Grier to act . . . He had always taken a realistic view of the bench. He had long thought that politics should govern it." *Emergence of Lincoln,* II, p. 477. Among the definitions given by Webster of "conspiracy" is the following: "Combination of men for a single end; a concurrence or general tendency, as of circumstances, to one event; harmonious action." We believe the candid reader will find sufficient evidence to support Lincoln's conspiracy charge in this sense of "conspiracy." Nevins and Randall have rejected Lincoln's charge in its *legal* sense, in which sense it was never meant. Lincoln's rhetoric is deliberative, not forensic. Its forensic quality is metaphorical; he was, after all, a lawyer. But he is not trying to convict of crime; he is attempting to convince the people that they cannot entrust their liberties to the Democratic Party of Taney, Pierce, Buchanan, and Douglas. For such men had collaborated in the "harmonious action" implied by the agreement of the purposes of the Kansas-Nebraska Act, the Dred Scott decision, and the other circumstances he elaborates. His charge was never intended to impute guilty purposes in the legal sense. He could not have intended this, since legal conspiracy means an intention to violate the law, and these men were law *makers.*

10. Op. cit., I, p. 362.
11. Italics not in the original.
12. Moore, op. cit., p. 124.
13. *Collected Works,* III, p. 527.
14. Italics not in the original.
15. That the re-enactment of the Northwest Ordinance, including the slavery prohibition, must have been regarded contemporaneously as an exertion of ordinary legislative power by Madison, Washington, et al., is sufficiently demonstrated in Curtis's disserting opinion.
16. *Collected Works,* III, pp. 230–31.
17. Ibid., p. 231.
18. *Collected Works,* III, p. 43.
19. Ibid., p. 54.
20. *Emergence of Lincoln,* I, p. 362.
21. *Lincoln the President,* I, p. 116.
22. *University of Chicago Law Review,* Autumn 1954.
23. Ibid., p. 142, n. 266.
24. Ibid., p. 142.

Chapter XII

1. *Collected Works*, II, p. 518.
2. Nevins, *Emergence of Lincoln*, I, p. 165.
3. Randall, op. cit., I, p. 124. Our italics.
4. Lincoln developed this argument most fully in his July 17, 1858, speech. *Collected Works*, II, pp. 504 ff.
5. Ibid., p. 509.
6. The English bill which submitted the Lecompton Constitution to Kansas on August 2, 1858, itself contained an enormous bribe of public lands if the slave constitution were adopted. Men who did not care deeply about slavery and freedom were not apt to have voted as those Kansans did. And it is idle to think that their support by a national party committed to the federal prohibition of slavery in the territories did not affect their caring.
7. The sufficiency of the Republican party as a cause assumes that the Republicans' growing strength made Douglas's break with Buchanan both possible and necessary. Although the Republicans outnumbered Douglas men five to one in the showdown on Lecompton in the House, they did not have enough votes in the 35th Congress to defeat it by themselves alone.
8. Op. cit., I, p. 127.

Chapter XIII

1. *Collected Works*, II, p. 180.
2. Ibid., II, p. 278.
3. Ibid., p. 532.

Chapter XIV

1. *Lincoln the President*, I, pp. 121, 122.
2. *Collected Works*, II, p. 385.
3. Ibid., III, p. 27.
4. Ibid., pp. 225, 226.
5. Ibid., II, p. 264.
6. Ibid., III, p. 445.
7. Ibid., pp. 301, 302.
8. Ibid., II, pp. 405, 406. Most of this passage was quoted by Lincoln in the Alton debate, ibid., III, p. 301.
9. Ibid., II, p. 501.
10. Ibid., p. 407.

11. Ibid., III, pp. 303, 304.
12. Ibid., II, p. 520.
13. Ibid., III, p. 204.
14. Ibid., II, p. 406.
15. Jefferson never remained wholly Lockean. There are passages—e.g., in his letter to John Adams, October 28, 1823—in which he speaks of a natural aristocracy and that man is "formed for the social state," which would seem to premise a rejection of the whole egalitarian-state-of-nature theory. It is hard to tell whether such departures are purely *ad hominem* or whether Jefferson simply was unable to make up his mind.
16. *Emergence of Lincoln*, I, p. 392.
17. *Collected Works*, I, p. 438.
18. Compare Lincoln's letter to Herndon, February 15, 1848, especially the following: "The provision of the Constitution giving the war-making power to Congress, was dictated as I understand it, by the following reasons. Kings had always been involving and impoverishing their people in wars, pretending generally, if not always, that the good of the people was the object. This, our convention understood to be the most oppressive of kingly oppressions . . ." Tom Paine's *Rights of Man* is the most famous popular statement of this view of the relation of monarchies and republics.
19. Cf. above, p. 257.
20. Thus Jefferson, in the aforesaid query XVIII, *Notes on Virginia*: "The whole commerce between master and slave is a perpetual exercise of the most boisterous passions . . . This quality is the germ of all education in him . . . The man must be a prodigy who can retain his manners and morals undepraved by such circumstances. And with what execration should the statesman be loaded, who, permitting one half the citizens thus to trample on the rights of the other, transforms those into despots, and these into enemies, destroys the morals of the one part, and the *amor patriae* of the other . . ." This is an amazing statement for many reasons, perhaps most for the reference to slaves as citizens. Yet Jefferson never wavered in his insistence that these "citizens" should be deported as a price of their freedom. Consider, however, the classic counterpart to the foregoing, from Burke's speech on conciliation with American, paragraph 42: ". . . in Virginia and the Carolinas they have a vast multitude of slaves. Where this is the case in any part of the world, those who are free are by far the most proud and jealous of their freedom. Freedom is to them not only an enjoyment, but a kind of rank and privilege . . . I do not mean, Sir, to commend the superior morality of this sentiment, which has at least as much pride as virtue in it; but . . . The

fact is so: and these people of the southern colonies are much more strongly, and with a higher and more stubborn spirit, attached to liberty, than those to the northward." Although Burke and Jefferson do not flatly contradict each other—for Burke reserves the difference between pride and virtue—yet the tendency of their evaluations is clearly opposite. Needless to say, the evaluation of the British statesman is the one that became the dominant conviction in the South. Lincoln, of course, accepted fully Jefferson's views in the eighteenth query—except for its optimistic conclusion about the spirit of the master abating, which we have noted above to be a *non sequitur.*

21. For an authoritative exposition of Hobbesian and Lockean natural-right doctrine, with particular reference to the respective roles of reason and passion, see Leo Strauss, *Natural Right and History* (Chicago, 1953), especially Chapter V, "Modern Natural Right."

22. For Lincoln's reasoning, implicit and explicit, concerning the "rights" in the passions, see the discussion of political and social equality below, Chapter XVII.

Chapter XV

1. The soul is the form of the body, hence its *formal* cause. The *function* of the soul—i.e., rational activity—is the *final* cause. Strictly speaking, not the principle "all men are created equal," but the activity which it engenders, the activity arising from the hope it plants in the hearts of all, is the final cause of the American polity. We have not attempted a more precise explication of Aristotle's doctrine of causality or of its application to Lincoln's language than seemed necessary for the use herein made of it.

2. *Collected Works,* IV, p. 168.

3. Ibid., II, p. 385.

4. Douglas at Chicago, July 9, 1858. In *Created Equal? The Complete Lincoln-Douglas Debates of 1858,* edited by Paul M. Angle (University of Chicago, 1958), p. 18.

5. From the Peoria speech: "Finally, I insist that if there is ANYTHING which it is the duty of the WHOLE PEOPLE to never entrust to any hands but their own, that thing is the preservation and perpetuity, of their own liberties, and institutions. And if they shall think, as I do, that the extension of slavery endangers them, more than any, or all other causes, how recreant to themselves, if they submit the question, and with it, the fate of their country, to a mere handful of men [i.e., the early settlers in the territories who, according to Douglas's doctrine, would decide the issue for

all who would come after], bent only on temporary self-interest."

6. *Collected Works,* II, p. 222.
7. Ibid., III, p. 93.
8. Ibid., p. 204.
9. Ibid., II, p. 271.
10. Ibid., III, p. 10.
11. Ibid., II, p. 132.
12. Ibid., I, p. 347.
13. Ibid., II, p. 130.

Chapter XVI

1. *Collected Works,* II, pp. 265, 266.
2. Ibid., III, p. 267.
3. Cf. p. 202.
4. *Collected Works,* III, p. 318. Douglas had maintained in 1850 that slave property was like any other property with which a citizen of the United States migrated to a territory; viz., it was subject to local law. Banks, whisky, and slaves were three different things which had been prohibited by local territorial laws somewhere and at sometime, and there was no more reason for slaveholders to complain of the exclusion of slaves than for liquor owners to complain of the exclusion of liquor. In 1858 he modified this to the extent that he said that slaves might be "regulated" like any other property by local law. Lincoln made merry with this equivocation: what kind of "regulating" is it that totally destroys the enjoyment and thereby the value of the property? Douglas's position was sound in 1850 when he insisted that slaves were incident to the same liabilities as other property, but the Dred Scott decision, by asserting that the right to property in slaves was affirmed in the Constitution, placed it on a totally *different* footing from other property. "All property is based upon local law," says Professor Hodder (op. cit., p. 19) in rejecting Taney's assertion of a property right asserted within the federal Constitution. Douglas could then not assimilate the obligation to protect slave property to that of other property without rejecting Taney's opinion. As long as he refused to do this, Lincoln's analogy of Taney's supposed right with that of the fugitive-slave clause held.
5. Ibid., III, p. 417.
6. We omit, as immaterial to the point under discussion, the distinction between territories owned originally and territories acquired after 1787.

7. Ibid., II, p. 407.
8. Ibid., p. 499.
9. Ibid., III, p. 10. We may wonder at some other implications of Douglas's denial of the brotherhood of man.

Chapter XVII

1. *Lincoln the President*, I, p. 122.
2. New York: Knopf, pp. 93–136. First published as a trade edition and reprinted three times. Reprinted as a Vintage paperback edition in 1954, and reprinted in this edition six times by March 1957. From the present writer's experience, it is the main source from which college students today are imbibing their opinions concerning Lincoln.
3. *Collected Works*, III, p. 221.
4. Ibid., p. 248.
5. Ibid., pp. 249, 250.
6. Cf. p. 46.
7. *Collected Works*, II, p. 501.
8. Ibid., III, pp. 384, 386.
9. Ibid., II, p. 320.
10. New York: Harper, 1944.
11. *Collected Works*, II, p. 266.
12. Randall, op. cit., I, p. 123.
13. *Collected Works*, III, p. 303.
14. Ibid., II, pp. 255, 256, 281, 282.
15. Ibid., III, p. 16.
16. There is no evidence that Lincoln assigned intrinsic importance to the color difference. But Jefferson did, as the following remarks indicate: "And is this difference [viz., of color] of no importance? Is it not the foundation of a greater or less share of beauty in the two races? Are not the fine mixtures of red and white, the expressions of every passion by greater or less suffusions of color in the one, preferable to that eternal monotony, which reigns in the countenances, that immovable veil of black which covers the emotions of the other race? Add to these . . . their own judgment in favor of the whites, declared by their preference of them . . ." Padover ed., p. 622. The last-mentioned point—namely, that the blacks as well as the whites preferred the color white—suggests that if color as a basis for evaluating human worth is a prejudice, it is so universal a prejudice that it must be counted politically, so long as the opinions of non-philosophers are to have political weight; i.e., always.

17. Again let us hear Jefferson: "The improvement of the blacks in body and mind, in the first instance of their mixture with the whites, has been observed by everyone, and proves that their inferiority is not the effect of their condition of life." And further: "I advance it, therefore, as a suspicion only, that the blacks, whether originally a distinct race, or made distinct by time and circumstances, are inferior to the whites in the endowments both of body and mind. It is not against experience to suppose that different species of the same genus, or varieties of the same species, may possess different qualifications." Padover, pp. 663, 664, 665.
18. Padover, p. 665.
19. Ibid., p. 661.
20. Cf. p. 245.

Chapter XVIII

1. Randall, op. cit., I, p. 127.
2. Cf. *Americans Interpret Their Civil War*, by Thomas J. Pressly (Princeton University, 1954), pp. 244–46. The quotation from Ramsdell in this paragraph is taken from Pressly, p. 245.
3. Cf. p. 165.
4. *New Mexico and the Sectional Controversy*, 1846–1861, by L. M. Ganaway (University of New Mexico, 1944), p. 66.
5. Ibid., p. 72.
6. *Collected Works*, III, p. 316.
7. New York: Knopf, 1956.
8. Op. cit., pp. 60, 62.
9. Ibid., pp. 63, 64.
10. Ibid., p. 65.
11. *Collected Works*, IV, p. 24.
12. Cf. p. 59.
13. *Collected Works*, II, pp. 409, 410.
14. Ibid., IV, p. 16.
15. Ibid., III, p. 323.

Chapter XIX

1. The italics are Hofstadter's.
2. *Lincoln the President*, I, p. 126.
3. Ibid., pp. 229, 230.
4. Boston: D. C. Heath & Company, 1937, pp. 202, 203.

5. *Collected Works,* IV, p. 150.
6. Ibid., p. 155.
7. Randall, *Civil War and Reconstruction,* p. 232.
8. P. 136.

Chapter XX

1. *Collected Works,* III, pp. 54, 55.
2. Ibid., p. 235.
3. Angle, op. cit., pp. 64, 65.

Appendices

Appendix I

Some of the Historical Background to the Lincoln–Douglas Debates

THE Lincoln-Douglas debates are quite naturally identified, above all, with the seven joint debates of the summer and fall of 1858, which were the most sensational feature of the great senatorial campaign. And yet if we attend to the actual dialectical exchanges, the joint debates will be seen to be only a part of a much longer series of argumentative encounters. For the beginning of this larger debate we must go back to the Illinois state fair in Springfield in the first week of October 1854. Douglas spoke there on the third of the month, reviewing his arguments, now familiar to the whole country, defending the Kansas-Nebraska Act, which had become law the previous spring and which had, by the repeal of the Missouri Compromise, renewed the pro- and anti-slavery convulsions of the year 1850. Lincoln replied to this speech on the following day, October 4, 1854. The same speech was repeated by Lincoln on the evening of the sixteenth of the month at Peoria, Illinois, where Douglas had spoken in the afternoon. It is from the text delivered at Peoria that the printed version was taken, and for this reason it has passed into history as the Peoria speech. It is the longest of all Lincoln's pre-presidential speeches and a more complete statement of his position in the controversy with Douglas than is to be found in any other single deliverance. It is noteworthy that he frequently quoted from it, and more frequently paraphrased it, in the joint debates, and it is the primary source for an understanding of Lincoln's position throughout the period 1854–61. Of the great Lincoln speeches which precede the campaign of 1858, the next in importance to the Peoria speech is the one on the Dred Scott decision. It, too, was delivered in Springfield, June 26, 1857. But it, too, is a direct reply to a speech Douglas had made in the same place two weeks earlier, when Lincoln had—as was his custom—sat in Douglas's audience.

The house divided speech, which formally began the senatorial contest on June 16, 1858, was delivered to the convention which had just resolved that "Abraham Lincoln is the first and only choice of the Republicans of Illinois for the United States Senate, as the successor of Stephen A. Douglas." Both resolution and speech were unprecedented in a number of ways, not least because senators were then elected by joint sessions of the state legislature, and such electioneering as went on usually took place in the halls of the legislature *after* the election of its members. By making the choice of United States senator an issue in the general election, the Illinois Republicans initiated the first long step toward the Seventeenth Amendment. On July 9, 1858, Douglas returned to Chicago from Washington, where he had been delayed several weeks after the Congress had adjourned. With Lincoln seated beside him on the balcony of the Tremont House he delivered a fiery reply to the house divided speech. From the same balcony, on the very next evening—Douglas having already left Chicago—Lincoln retorted in a speech whose peroration was, and is, among the most moving of his many invocations of the Declaration of Independence. From Chicago both orators moved again toward Springfield. On July 16 Douglas spoke at Bloomington. Again Lincoln was present. On the seventeenth Douglas delivered substantially the same speech in Springfield. Lincoln was not in the audience this time; but the reason, it may be supposed, is that he was busy at the time preparing his third major speech of the campaign, which rebutted Douglas's Bloomington speech and which he delivered in the evening of the same July 17 in the State House in Springfield.

Less than a week later, on July 24, 1858, began the correspondence, which shortly concluded in the arrangements for the seven joint debates. Lincoln issued the challenge, and Douglas named the times and places as follows:

1. Ottawa, La Salle County .... August 21st
2. Freeport, Stephenson County .... August 27th
3. Jonesboro, Union County .... September 15th
4. Charleston, Coles County .... September 18th
5. Galesburg, Knox County................ October 7th
6. Quincy, Adams County .... October 13th
7. Alton, Madison County .... October 15th

The idea was, as Douglas put it, to choose "one prominent point in each Congressional District in the State, except the Second and Sixth districts, where we have both spoken." There is a curious footnote to history in a postscript to Lincoln's letter to Douglas of July 29, 1858, the letter in which he acknowledges Douglas's formal agreement to the proposal to have joint meetings. "As matters now stand, I shall be at no more of your exclusive meetings." Douglas and his managers were extremely annoyed at Lincoln's habit of turning up at Douglas's rallies—and then inviting the same crowd to return later to hear him!

The procedure at the joint debates was for one man to open, speaking for exactly one hour—a timekeeper being present, just as at a boxing match. His opponent would then reply for an hour and a half. Finally the man who opened would have the rebuttal for half an hour. Douglas opened and closed at Ottawa, Jonesboro, Galesburg, and Alton; Lincoln at Freeport, Charleston, and Quincy. Since there were seven debates, one man had to have the advantage on rebuttals, but it is doubtful that, in such a long series of exchanges, there was any unfairness to Lincoln in this. He, being the lesser known man, certainly gained more from the mere fact of the joint meetings.

The colorful descriptions of the debates in Carl Sandburg's *Prairie Years* and in other volumes too numerous to mention need not be added to here. Suffice it to say that the atmosphere for each debate resembled that of the day of the Big Game in any American college town of today. To quote from the Chicago *Press and Tribune* coverage of the first debate: "Ottawa was deluged in dust . . . At eight o'clock [the speaking began at 2:30 P.M.] the avenues leading from the country were so enveloped with dust that the town resembled a vast smoke house. Teams, trains, and processions poured in from every direction like an army with banners. National flags, mottoes and devices fluttered and stared from every street corner. Military companies and bands of music monopolized the thoroughfares around the court house and the public square. Two brass twelve pounders banged away in the centre of the city and drowned the hubbub of the multitude with their own higher capacities for hubbub. Vanity Fair never boiled with madder enthusiasm." At Ottawa the crowd was estimated at about 12,000, at Freeport still more. The smallest crowd, about 1500, was at Jonesboro, a little town 350 miles south of Chicago. Galesburg is estimated to have furnished a crowd larger than any that preceded it. At Alton, the last debate, 4000 to 5000 were said to be present. It must be remembered that these were open-air affairs, with no accommodations during the three hours of speaking other than the ground upon which the audience stood. And there was just about every kind of weather —the blazing sun at Ottawa, rain at Freeport, and some chill days for the October debates. It was both spectacle and event that fastened the eyes of the farmers of Illinois upon these protagonists, a spectacle and event that must continue to fascinate every reflective observer of the drama of popular government.

*   *   *   *   *

Behind the Lincoln-Douglas debates are a series of famous compromises, once familiar to every schoolboy. First, of course, there are the compromises concerning slavery in the United States Constitution. Of these, the third clause of Article I, Section 2, says that "Representatives and direct taxes shall be apportioned among the several States . . . according to their respective Number, which shall be determined by adding to the whole Number of free persons . . . three-fifths of all other persons." This "three-fifths" clause, which caused the representation of the slave states in the lower house of Congress to be increased in the ratio of three "persons" for every five slaves, came to be a particular sore point, not only because of its obvious unfairness from the point of view of representative democracy, but because subsequent developments destroyed its character as a compromise. Originally the clause intended to increase *both* representation *and* liability to direct taxes by the three-fifths ratio. Because of the aversion of Jeffersonians and Jacksonians to direct taxes, however, the liability aspect dropped almost completely from view. When the northern states abolished slavery and the South sought to extend it to new territories, this clause became a thorn in the side of the free states that the Founders could hardly have anticipated.

In addition, the Constitution of 1787 provided that the importation of slaves from abroad might *not* be prohibited before 1808. This clause (the first of Article I, Section 9) was a compromise between the demand for outright prohibition and the demand for an outright denial of a power to prohibit the foreign

slave trade. It represents a much more positive anti-slavery bias
in the men who wrote the Constitution than might appear today
on its face. For if Negro slaves, as Taney was to assert in 1857,
were considered in 1787 as mere articles of commerce, to be
bought and sold as ordinary merchandise, it is hardly conceivable
that the trade in them should be so distinguished and set apart
from the "Commerce with foreign Nations" which, in the third
clause of Section 8 (of Article I), it is said that Congress shall
have power to "regulate."

The so-called "fugitive slave" clause of the Constitution (the
third of Article IV, Section 2) does not, as often noted, mention
slaves at all. (See page 290.) We can hardly regard it as a compromise of the Constitution, since there seems to have been no
significant opposition in 1787 to the inclusion of such a provision.
All responsible men were then agreed that, however contrary to
abstract justice slavery might be, to the extent that it constituted
property according to positive law, it must be protected. No
matter how favorable men like Washington or Jefferson might
be to gradual emancipation, to encourage slaves to escape was
not thought by them to be a defensible method to accomplish it.

Of the political measures dealing with slavery, the Missouri
Compromise is, of course, one which students of the debates must
keep constantly in mind. In actual fact, however, there were *two*
compromises in the course of the settlement of the Missouri
question. When the territory of Missouri applied for permission
to frame a state constitution early in 1819 there were eleven free
and eleven slave states. To a bill enabling Missouri to become
a state a New York congressman proposed an amendment that, in
effect, would have provided for the gradual abolition of slavery
in Missouri. The amendment passed the House but was defeated
in the Senate, and all action on Missouri's application was stale-
mated for the session amid violent controversy. When Congress
again met, in December 1819, Maine was requesting admission
as a free state, and a way out of the impasse appeared. In its
final form the *first* Missouri Compromise saw Maine admitted
to the Union and an enabling act for the admission of Missouri
as a slave state, with a provision in the act that, in the remainder
of the Louisiana Purchase north of 36'30", slavery should be
"forever" prohibited.

On the basis of the March 1820 enabling act Missouri held a

convention which drafted a constitution, with which it then applied for admission. But this constitution empowered the legislature to exclude free Negroes and mulattoes from the state. When it was presented to Congress another storm broke, for sentiment in the free states was strongly convinced that such a provision contravened Article IV, Section 2, of the Constitution, which says, "The Citizens of each State shall be entitled to all Privileges and Immunities of Citizens in the several States." And free Negroes and mulattoes indubitably possessed privileges of citizenship under the constitutions of free states. It was the stumbling block of this free Negro provision of Missouri's constitution which required the *second* Missouri Compromise. And it was this compromise of which Henry Clay was the moving spirit and which his conciliatory skill in Congress produced. By it Clay secured support for Missouri's admission whenever Missouri would give a satisfactory pledge that nothing in her constitution should be interpreted to abridge the privileges and immunities of citizens of the United States. This pledge Missouri soon gave, *without* repealing the offensive clause in her constitution, and was admitted to the Union. In short, the second Missouri Compromise was a face-saving form of words which enabled the original compromise to take effect. It was of no consequence with respect to the power of Missouri (or any other state) to discriminate against free Negroes as much as it pleased.

In 1836 the creation of the Republic of Texas, by a successful revolution against Mexico, initiated the long struggle for Texas's annexation to the United States, a struggle consummated by Texas's entry into the Union in the summer of 1845. Although the phrase "manifest destiny" made its appearance only in 1845, throughout the nine years that the annexation of Texas was debated it became increasingly well understood that the extension of both slavery and the Union, over the vast and (by white men) largely unoccupied lands of North America owned by Mexico, was indirectly at stake. The Mexican War, which followed the annexation of Texas and which was the expected and virtually certain consequence of it, then added the great regions to the Union which were to precipitate the territorial issues thenceforward to dominate American politics until the Civil War.

The genesis of the Civil War was seen, above all, in the controversy concerning the Wilmot Proviso. This famed measure came soon after hostilities with Mexico began. President Polk requested $2,000,000 from Congress to be used in peace negotiations—negotiations in which "purchase" would underwrite conquest in wresting California and the other Mexican provinces manifestly destined for the Stars and Stripes. To a bill to appropriate this sum, moved in the House August 8, 1846, David Wilmot, a Pennsylvania Democrat, offered an amendment which "provided, that, as an express and fundamental condition to the acquisition of any territory from the Republic of Mexico by the United States, by virtue of any treaty which may be negotiated between them, and to the use of the moneys herein appropriated, neither slavery nor involuntary servitude shall ever exist in any part of said territory . . ." The bill with Wilmot's amendment passed the House by a vote of 87 to 64 after a bitter debate in which all efforts to water it down—e.g., by limiting its prohibitions to lands north of 36'30"—were beaten. It died, however, in the Senate. But the next Congress, the one in which Abraham Lincoln was a little known member, revived the Proviso in a multitude of guises, and it was repeatedly supported by large majorities in the House and as repeatedly rejected in the Senate. The point contended for by the Wilmot Proviso, and endorsed again and again by the representatives of a large majority of the American people, was, however, defeated by the Treaty of Guadalupe Hidalgo, which ended the Mexican War, February 2, 1848. This treaty was approved by the Senate, where the Proviso was always unpopular, and it secured the Mexican provinces without any restriction as to slavery. The collaboration of the Senate, in which the interests of slavery were vastly overrepresented, and the President in defeating the will of the "direct representatives of the people" was a lesson deeply impressed upon the free-soil North. And the breaking up of old party lines, in the support of the Proviso, foreshadowed the Republican party of the next decade.

At the end of the Mexican War, as before the Missouri controversy, the number of free and slave states—there were now fifteen of each—was equal. Thus the application of California in 1849 for admission, with a constitution forbidding slavery, again fanned into violent conflagration the passions aroused by the Wilmot Proviso. The Nashville Convention, summoned at the behest of John C. Calhoun, attempted to lay down as a southern ultimatum the doctrine that Congress had no power to exclude slaveowners from going into any of the national territories with their peculiar property, but that, on the contrary, Congress had a duty to protect the rights of the owners of slaves. Although the Convention expressed a willingness to compromise by extending the Missouri line to the Pacific, it also threatened secession as the alternative to a satisfactory settlement. Against this background the Compromise of 1850 was thrashed out in the spring and summer of that year. Because of it, but perhaps only because of it, the threat of secession proved abortive. The program of the Nashville Convention was, however, revived a decade later and its threats turned into deeds.

In actuality the 1850 compromise was a series of five separate statutes. These reflected the recommendations of Henry Clay who, as chairman of a select committee, had embodied them in an omnibus bill. The omnibus, however, instead of uniting the friends of the separate provisions, united its enemies and accordingly failed to pass. It was when Douglas took command of the legislation, seeing that it might be enacted if, for example, some northern Senators were not required to vote for a fugitive slave bill and some Southerners were not required to vote for the admission of California, that the whole was put through. The "measures of adjustment" were, then, as follows: the admission of California as a free state; acts for the establishment of territorial governments for Utah and New Mexico, which provided that the states to be formed therefrom might enter the Union with or without slavery, as their constitutions should prescribe; an act compensating Texas for the abandonment of large territorial claims in New Mexico and definitely fixing the boundaries between the two; an act abolishing the slave trade (but not slavery) in the District of Columbia; and finally an act designed greatly to improve upon the efficiency of the old fugitive slave law, now deemed by the South to be wholly inadequate.

The Kansas-Nebraska Act of 1854, providing two new territorial governments, repealed the eighth section of the 1820 enabling act for Missouri, which had prohibited slavery "forever" in the area for which the new governments were established. This repeal rested upon the hypothesis that the Compromise of 1850 had "superseded" that of 1820. Against this hypothesis is the fact that the bill Douglas introduced in January 1854 was itself a

substitute for the one introduced some weeks earlier by Senator
Dodge of Iowa, who had merely revived the Nebraska bill of
the previous session which had passed the House and failed in
the Senate, apparently only by being lost in the rush of adjournment business. And this bill had not even alluded to the Missouri
Compromise. Yet in successive amendments to Douglas's bill the
Missouri restriction was declared "inoperative" and then "void."
In a famous clause called by Thomas Hart Benton a "stump
speech in the belly of the bill," it was declared to be the true intent
and meaning of Congress neither to legislate slavery into the territories, nor to exclude it therefrom, but to leave the people there
"perfectly free" to form and regulate their own domestic institutions. One obvious difficulty with respect to such a declaration
was that when it was made the "people" to which it referred
did not yet exist—except for some few trespassers upon the public
domain—since Kansas and Nebraska were not lawfully open to
settlement until after the bill became law. The "people" of Kansas,
where the issue was joined, had yet to come from either free
or slave states and were certain to be either pro-slavery or anti-
slavery. The Kansas-Nebraska Act legislated civil war on the
plains of Kansas.

The story of "bleeding Kansas" need not be retold here. The
contest between the anti-slavery emigrant-aid societies, equipped
with "Beecher's bibles"—i.e., rifles—and the "border ruffians" and
Blue Lodges of Missouri was the practical result of introducing
"squatter sovereignty." Both sides employed fraud and violence
freely, but the proximity of Missouri gave the first advantage
to the pro-slavery settlers. Consequently the territorial legislature
elected in March 1855 was pro-slavery and was prepared to use its
obviously temporary advantage to force the issue and make Kansas a slave state before the anti-slavery people could do anything
about it. And the anti-slavery settlers, who must have been in
a majority almost immediately after the first elections (if they
were not already so at the time), reacted by boycotting the
"legal" government and setting up one of their own, to be known
in history as the Topeka Movement. The contest between the
two "governments" was prosecuted both in Kansas and Washington—but it was in Washington that the decisive field of action
lay.

Much has been said of the "fraudulent" Lecompton Constitution in the foregoing pages of this book. We have not hesitated

to use such a pejorative expression, since it represents ground common to Lincoln and Douglas. Yet the reader should know somewhat more precisely the nature of this attempted fraud. It was the direct consequences of that early advantage of the pro-slavery settlers. Determined, as we have said, to make Kansas a slave state, the Kansas legislature passed a law over the governor's veto which provided for a constitutional convention, which in due course met at Lecompton, Kansas, September 7, 1857. The vote for the delegates to this convention had taken place the preceding June 15, but the free-state men had refused to participate in it for the very good reason that the entire electoral machinery was in the hands of the slave-state men and an honest vote was impossible. The convention completed its work early in November, submitting to the voters of the territory the alternative of adopting their constitution with or without an article securing the institution of Negro slavery. The fraud, however, consisted in this: the voters did *not* have the option of rejecting the constitution as a whole, and the constitution "without" slavery did *not* provide for the emancipation of slaves *already in Kansas*. On the contrary, it expressly *forbade* the future state legislature to emancipate slaves already in Kansas without their owners' consent and without full compensation. Further, no amendment of the state's constitution was to be permitted before 1864—obviously to prevent changes in the status of slavery. There were only about two hundred slaves in Kansas at the time, but so long as their slave status, and that of their progeny, was guaranteed to remain, Kansas must in principle be a slave state, no matter which way the voters voted. This was the heart of the fraud. Of course, with the security of even a small number of slaves assured in law, it might not be possible to distinguish them from slaves subsequently smuggled in from Missouri. To help assure that no such distinction would in fact be made, the Lecompton delegates also provided in their constitution that the provisional electoral machinery, to go into effect as soon as the state was admitted into the Union, would be in the hands of the Lecompton men themselves. They would "supervise" the first elections to the state legislature.

The Lecompton Constitution was "approved" almost unanimously by a vote taken on December 21, 1858. This "approval" represents both the abstention from the election by the free-staters and the sifting of the ballot boxes by the pro-slavery election judges. The constitution was, however, transmitted to Washington, where the full power of the slave states was lined up behind the pliant Buchanan, who now showed more determination in a bad cause than he was ever to show in a good one. Lecompton was approved in the Senate but was defeated in the House by a vote of 120 to 112, the victors including 92 Republicans, 22 Douglas Democrats, and 6 Know-Nothings. Lecompton, by this fact, became moribund but not yet quite dead. A compromise was adopted, bearing the name of Representative English of Indiana, which provided for it to be again submitted to the voters of Kansas. Only now it was a vote on outright acceptance, without evasiveness on the slavery article, or outright rejection. If they accepted it, Kansas would become a state immediately, receiving a huge grant of government lands, and with the receipts from the sale of other government lands promised. If they rejected Lecompton, the territory must attain a population of 90,000 (the ratio for a member of the House) before again applying for statehood. Clearly the English bill bribed Kansans to accept Lecompton and enter the Union as a slave state (the population was then no more than 25,000). Yet a clear chance to vote on the whole Lecompton iniquity was all the free-staters wanted. With the entire country watching, and fraud at the ballot boxes now minimized, Lecompton was duly buried on August 2, 1858 by a vote of 11,812 to 1,926. Kansas was now firmly in free-state hands, notwithstanding the fact that, by the Dred Scott decision of 1857, slaveowners might, if they chose, still take slaves there. With the virtual monopoly of the instruments of violence, lawful and unlawful, now possessed by their enemies, it was unlikely that any slaveowners would do so.

Appendix II

Some Notes on the Dred Scott Decision

AMONG the attempts to shift all blame for the coming of the Civil War on the Republicans, especial notice is due to the brilliant and highly influential essay by Frank Hodder, "Some Phases of the Dred Scott Case," published in *The Mississippi Valley Historical Review*, Volume XVI, pp. 3–22, June 1929. According to Hodder, the Supreme Court had originally decided only that the decision of the highest court of Missouri was final as to the status of persons within the boundaries of that state. It was not necessary, says Hodder, for the Court to have entered the question of the constitutionality of the Missouri Compromise, and it would not have entered upon it if Justices McLean and Curtis had not announced *their* intention to go over this ground in dissenting opinions. McLean was an active candidate for the Republican presidential nomination, and so he is the chief villain of Hodder's scenario, although he blames Curtis even more for supporting McLean, since Curtis was (according to Hodder) mending fences in anti-slavery New England, whither he intended soon to retire to enter upon a money-making legal practice. McLean was then the ambitious fanatic but Curtis the baser of the two, since he acted rather from avarice. All such speculations concerning motives are pure conjecture and tell us more about Hodder than about the judges. Let us, however, assume that Hodder is correct and that Justice Nelson's opinion would have been the opinion of the Court but for McLean and Curtis. Then let us ask whether a reasonable man who was genuinely concerned, as was Lincoln, about the nationalization of slavery would have nonetheless objected (as did McLean and Curtis).

"The opinion of Nelson, which but for the dissent of McLean and Curtis would have been the opinion of the Court," writes Hodder, "held that when a slave returns to a slave state his status is determinable by the courts of that state. That question had been decided by unanimous opinion of the Court, in 1850, in the case of *Strader v. Graham*. The Ordinance of 1787 and the

Compromise of 1820, whatever their validity, had no extra-territorial force. Scott was a slave because the Supreme Court of Missouri had decided that he was a slave. The judgment of the lower court should therefore be affirmed. This was the only respectable opinion delivered by the Court. It was not only correct in law, but it was best for the free states. It relieved them from any obligation to give effect to the laws of slave states except as they were bound by the fugitive slave clause of the Constitution."

Now Hodder's assertion that Nelson's opinion was "correct in law" rests on the hypothesis of both the soundness of the decision in *Strader v. Graham* and the identity of the legal questions involved. How sound the precedent was we may briefly indicate as follows. Hodder shows that in Nelson's opinion the analogy worked thus: "As Nelson pointed out, if a proper respect for the laws of Illinois required Missouri to give effect to them, then a proper respect for Missouri required that Illinois give effect to her laws and Scott would not have been free in Illinois." But this reasoning is patently based upon the assumption of the equality of free law and slave law—an assumption which Missouri herself had never made in the eight precedents which the Missouri Supreme Court overruled in 1852! But, more important for present purposes, *Strader v. Graham* was not identical with *Dred Scott v. Sandford.* In the earlier case slaves had passed from Kentucky to Ohio, which was a state and not a territory free under a federal prohibition. The plaintiffs in *Strader* had claimed that the Northwest Ordinance had made the land north of the Ohio River forever free, but the Court rejected this and decided that the old ordinance had been supplanted by a statute after the adoption of the Constitution and that the principle of state equality supplanted the statute after Ohio had become a state. All that the Court had really decided in the 1850 case was that the extraterritorial force of Ohio law, after the slaves returned to Kentucky, was a matter of interstate comity and not a matter of federal adjudication. But this differs vitally from Dred Scott, since Scott had been held not only in Illinois, a free state (and, like Ohio, originally under the Northwest Ordinance), but for about two years in Wisconsin Territory, in a place where slavery was prohibited by the Missouri Act of 1820. This involved a distinct issue as between federal law and state law and differed from the issue of state law versus state law in the 1850 case.

Hodder's precedent utterly fails him. If Dred Scott had been as-similated to the Strader case, this would have been to put very new wine into an older bottle. It might have averted the storm Taney's decision created in the North, as Hodder in company with all revisionists dearly wishes. But it might for that reason have been even more perilous to the anti-slavery cause. Let us see.

As we have already observed, Hodder admits that when, in 1852, the Supreme Court of Missouri decided against Dred Scott by a decision of two to one, they "repudiated eight Missouri precedents in Scott's favor upon the ground that 'times had changed' and that the free states, by obstructing the return of fugitive slaves, refused to recognize the law of slave states." Times had indeed changed, for in times past courts of slave states had repeatedly honored both the Ordinance of 1787 and the Missouri Compromise. Behind the Missouri Supreme Court's decision, how-ever, was the whole bitter controversy of 1850. We have demon-strated above at some length that the Compromise of 1850 was, in vital respects, no compromise at all, since Congress declared nothing on the most bitterly controverted of all points (the power of Congress over slavery in the territories) but had rather passed the buck on that question to the Supreme Court of the United States. The Kansas-Nebraska Act, we have also seen, although re-pealing the eighth section of the Missouri Act of 1820, still left open the same question by appearing to give all power over slav-ery to the territorial legislature but actually giving it all power "subject . . . to the Constitution" and leaving it to the Supreme Court to decide how much power the Constitution permitted the territorial legislature to have. Since the territorial legislature de-rived its powers from Congress, it obviously could have no powers that Congress lacked, and so the issue of the powers of Congress and of the territorial legislature was really one and the same.

Now Nelson's opinion was really nothing but a cautious and surreptitious attempt to accomplish the results of Taney's opinion, and it is easy to see why McLean and Curtis might have determined to force the whole thing out into the open. Hodder's assertion that Nelson was "correct in law" is absurd, unless he is prepared to maintain, as he does not, that the Missouri Compro-mise was in fact unconstitutional. Nelson's opinion, no less than Taney's, had the effect, in Lincoln's words, of deciding that "whether the holding of a negro in actual slavery in a free State [or free territory] makes him free, as against the holder, the United States Courts will not decide, but will leave to be decided by the courts of any slave State the negro may be forced into by the master." It is true that Nelson's opinion does not constitute an open repudiation of the Missouri law. But if we remember the supremacy clause of the Constitution—according to which valid federal law takes *precedence* over conflicting state law—we cannot doubt that this was an implied repudiation. Nor could McLean, who certainly had a more intimate knowledge of his colleagues' minds than Professor Hodder could possibly have had, doubt it. If McLean did force the issue, it was because he knew that the majority on the Court was prepared to strike down any attempt by either Congress or a territorial legislature to prohibit slavery in the territories, and he was rightly convinced that the time had come when the country should know the meaning of the Democratic slave power's strategy in entrusting to the Supreme Court the mystery of the legal status of slavery in the territories.

Hodder laments the political character of the opinions of Taney and McLean and Curtis. But this was inevitable, once Congress had handed over the greatest political question of American history to the Court. Ever since the Wilmot Proviso agitation the slave power had been weakest in the House of Representatives, strongest in the Senate. As long as weak presidents and strong southern senators could keep the Supreme Court favorable to the South, the cards were stacked in favor of the South on the territorial issue. The only recourse of free-soilers was in a party which would elect a free-soil President, who would appoint free-soil judges. That Nelson was, in fact, prepared to denounce the Missouri Act of 1820 is shown by his subsequent endorsement of Taney's opinion. McLean must have seen that Nelson and Taney were playing a party game and playing it to the hilt, as indeed they were. Anyone who cannot see that today must be blind indeed. Professor Hodder finds McLean an ambitious politician, but Taney acted only from "a mistaken sense of duty" and not from "any partiality for slavery." Perhaps so; perhaps Taney never intended that the President, who was of his party, should soon crow in a message to Congress, "It has been solemnly adjudged by the highest judicial tribunal known to our laws that slavery exists in Kansas by virtue of the Constitution of the United States. Kansas is therefore as much a slave state as Georgia or South Carolina."

Index

INDEX

P9-CNE-565

~

Marriage in the Early Republic

Gender Relations in the American Experience

Joan E. Cashin and Ronald G. Walters,
SERIES EDITORS

Angel Kwolek-Folland,
Engendering Business: Men and Women in the Corporate Office, 1870–1930

Margaret Creighton and Lisa Norling, eds.,
Iron Men, Wooden Women: Gender and Seafaring in the Atlantic World, 1700–1920

Stephen M. Frank,
Life with Father: Parenthood and Masculinity in the Nineteenth-Century American North

Anya Jabour,
Marriage in the Early Republic: Elizabeth and William Wirt and the Companionate Ideal

ANYA JABOUR

Marriage in the Early Republic

Elizabeth and William Wirt and the Companionate Ideal

The Johns Hopkins University Press
BALTIMORE AND LONDON

The Johns Hopkins University Press
2715 North Charles Street
Baltimore, Maryland 21218-4319
The Johns Hopkins Press Ltd., London

Library of Congress Cataloging-in-Publication Data will be found
at the end of this book. A catalog record for this book is
available from the British Library.

ISBN 0-8018-5877-1

FRONTISPIECE: William Wirt and Elizabeth Wirt. Photos
courtesy of the Virginia Historical Society.

Portions of chapters 1, 2, and 3 first appeared in Anya Jabour,
" 'No Fetters But Such as Love Shall Forge': Elizabeth and William Wirt and Marriage in the Early Republic," *Virginia Magazine of History and Biography* 104 (Spring 1996), 211–50. Portions
of chapter 4 first appeared in Anya Jabour, " 'It Will Never Do
For Me To Be Married': The Life of Laura Wirt Randall, 1803–
1833," *Journal of the Early Republic* 17 (Summer 1997), 193–236,
and in Anya Jabour, " 'Grown Girls, Highly Cultivated': Female
Education in an Antebellum Southern Family," *Journal of Southern History* 64 (February 1998), 23–64.

For my mother,
Jane Elizabeth Cress Jabour

Contents

~

Acknowledgments

Researching the Wirts' marriage has been facilitated by the support of numerous individuals and institutions. John B. Boles, who edited the microfilm edition of the William Wirt Papers at the Maryland Historical Society, introduced me to the Wirts in the first place. By bringing the twenty-four-reel collection to Rice University, he gave me the opportunity to do a great deal of my research without leaving home. The Department of History at Rice University generously funded research trips to the Southern Historical Collection, the Virginia Historical Society, the Library of Virginia, and Duke University's Special Collections Library. The Boone Endowment from the Department of History at the University of Montana enabled me to chase down elusive documents at the Maryland Historical Society, the Maryland State Archives, and the Maryland Hall of Records. The College of Arts and Sciences supplied important financial assistance in the final stages of preparing the book for publication. A grant from the Colonial Dames of America also helped to finance my work on the Wirts. Mary Elizabeth Glade took time out from her own research to make a trip to the Richmond Circuit Court to photocopy the Wirts' wills for me, and Aubrey Russell Bowles III, the current owner of the Wirts' last Richmond residence, gave me a personal tour and shared his architectural plans of the house with me.

Many valued colleagues have contributed their insights to this book. Sally G. McMillen, Steven Mintz, Carol Quillen, and the members of the Houston Area Southern Historians read an exploratory essay on the Wirts in 1992; their comments and criticisms have informed my work on the Wirts from the very beginning. Fellow scholars at conferences of the Society for Historians of the Early American Republic, the Omohundro Institute of Early American History and Culture, the Carleton Conference on the History of the Family, and the Southern Association for Women Historians also have given me valuable feedback. I am especially indebted to Laura McCall, Mary Elizabeth Glade,

Stephanie Cole, Gail S. Terry, Susan E. Klepp, Jesse Battan, Debra M. O'Neal, and Konstantin Dierks for their interest in my work and for sharing their own research with me. My fellow members of the women's studies research group at the University of Montana have generously given me more than my share of time and have asked probing questions that forced me to clarify my thinking about the Wirts. Series editors Joan E. Cashin and Ronald G. Walters have read and reread the manuscript and have offered me their comments and suggestions.

The advice and support of many people have been indispensable along the path from dissertation to book. I owe Tammy C. Whitlock for many long-distance phone calls that helped me through my first two years as a junior faculty member and aspiring author. Sara Hayden served as a sounding board while we hiked the switchbacks up Mount Sentinel to the concrete "M" that overlooks our offices in the Liberal Arts building. Through the miracle of e-mail, Cynthia Lynn Lyerly shared the trials and triumphs of producing a first book cross-country. Dee Garceau, my neighbor on the hallway during a long summer of revisions, took breaks from her own revisions to talk with me about the process. Robert J. Brugger, history editor for the Johns Hopkins University Press, guided me from submission to contract, and Sarah B. Cline, of acquisitions, patiently answered my questions about preparing the manuscript for copyediting. My colleagues in the history department have been encouraging and supportive throughout the process.

Finally, I must thank my husband, Bill Zollinger, who gave up summer vacations to accompany me on research trips, cooked gourmet meals while I agonized over revisions, and finally helped trouble-shoot when my computer failed me two weeks before deadline.

The Beau Ideal

In 1828, Margaret Bayard Smith, a Washington, D.C., resident and a popular domestic author, described a most congenial "evening social visit" in a letter to her son. The hosts, Elizabeth and William Wirt, had impressed Smith with the "splendor" of their accommodations and their "intellectual" conversation. Margaret Smith, whose novels and essays celebrated love, marriage, and family life, found many reasons to praise the Wirts, who had moved from Virginia to the nation's capital in late 1817 when William was appointed U.S. attorney general. Her most extravagant compliments, however, were reserved for the qualities of the "heart." Smith spent many social evenings with the Wirts, and she was repeatedly moved by the "caressing manner" and "ardent affections" they demonstrated in their "domestic circle." Smith gave the Wirts the highest possible accolade. "The domestic habits, style of living, and character of this family," she pronounced, "come nearer to my beau-ideal, than that of any other I know." So impressed was the popular writer that she modeled the characters in one of her domestic novels, *A Winter in Washington*, on "this charming family."[1]

The blissful unity that this sentimental author observed in Elizabeth and William Wirt's domestic circle was not borne out in the Wirts' own writings. Although they never attained true gentry status as great planters, the Wirts were prominent, respected southerners with close ties to many of Virginia's leading families. White, well-to-do, and literate, they left an extraordinarily rich record of their lives. William, a successful lawyer and occasional politician, wrote essays and other works that contributed to the legend of the Old South, particularly of his adopted state, the Old Dominion. Elizabeth, the second daughter of one of Richmond's most prominent merchants, was the first

American to write a book on the language of flowers. The Wirts' most prolific writings, however, were personal and family correspondence. Rather than presenting an idyllic romance of uninterrupted happiness, the Wirts' letters to each other reveal a relationship that often was marred by serious differences of expectation and experience.

The Wirts longed for an emotionally fulfilling, egalitarian, and loving relationship. Despite their shared commitment to a blissful togetherness, Elizabeth and William Wirt spent much of their life apart, were often divided on important issues, and never achieved their goal of mutual happiness in marriage. Instead, the Wirts experienced marriage in different, even divergent, ways, which mirrored the very real differences between men and women in the early Republic—differences that were at odds with the ideal of companionate marriage.

This study joins a fascinating scholarly dialogue on family history, women's history and male studies, and southern history. Historical inquiry into Americans' most intimate relationships in the past has led many students of the past to conclude that, by the early nineteenth century, many women and men had placed a new value on affectionate ties between family members, particularly within the immediate family, whose nucleus was a married couple joined by romantic love. This new desire for intimacy and companionship displaced a domestic patriarchy in which men wielded authority over the other members of the immediate and extended family and in which an emphasis on harmony and order limited the open expression of affection. By the early nineteenth century, growing numbers of Americans shared Margaret Smith's enthusiasm for the ardent affections of the heart, making the early American Republic a period of particular promise for egalitarian, loving relations between men and women within marriage.[2]

As scholars of women's experiences remind us, however, women and men continued to occupy very different positions in the nineteenth-century United States. Women could not vote or hold office, could not hold property in their own name if married, had few economic resources and very restricted employment options, and had limited opportunities for education, travel, or independence. Focusing on the urban Northeast, women's historians have revealed an emerging set of interlocking ideologies by which "true women," by advancing a new code of "domesticity," established a unique female influence over their home and family and elevated the importance of "woman's sphere." By promoting the ideology of "separate spheres," American women called attention to the central importance of their tasks in the domestic arena and criticized the values of the male-dominated marketplace. Over the course of the nineteenth century, the "bonds of womanhood" provided a basis for women's organization and spawned a movement for women's equal rights. In the opening decades of the century, however, female influence within the home remained central to women's quest for higher status. As the new field of male studies has made clear, by acceding to their wives' dominance at home, men in the antebellum United States were able to devote themselves with increasing vigor to the cult of the "self-made man." Working ceaselessly for self-advancement in the public realm of business, they only sporadically (and sometimes reluctantly) entered woman's sphere and succumbed to female influence. Despite the new ideals of romantic love, therefore, women and men filled different roles and looked for happiness in different ways. Men devoted their lives to self-advancement; women looked for fulfillment in self-sacrifice.[3]

Studies of the American South further complicate our understanding of relations between men and women in the past. Some research on southern women and families has suggested that patriarchy persisted much longer in the South. Buttressed by the political economy of slavery, patriarchal norms, several scholars contend, created strained relationships between men and women in the Old South. At the same time, however, many studies indicate that southerners enthusiastically embraced the new ideals of affectionate, egalitarian personal relationships. Scholars of other sections of the United States have noted a tension between the new ideals of affection, equality, and mutuality in marriage and the enduring distinctions between men's and women's access to political, economic, and social power. The South, however, offers an example of a peculiarly acute conflict between competing ideals of the relations between women and men.[4]

Elizabeth and William Wirt's marriage demonstrates the difficulties that confronted men and women in the early Republic—especially in the South—in their attempt to achieve what historians have labeled companionate marriage. The Wirts were lifelong border residents. Living in the upper South's cities—Williamsburg, Norfolk, and Richmond, Virginia; Washington, D.C.; and Baltimore, Maryland—they resided on the outskirts of a region that is often described as a hybrid of traditional and modern culture. The Wirts were intimately acquainted both with the plantation lifestyle of the Old South and with the urban, professional milieu more commonly associated with the Northeast. At the crossroads of North and South, the Wirts experienced the pressures of different gender roles and unequal power relations in a peculiarly charged atmosphere. The Wirts felt both the tension between mutual love and increasingly demarcated gender roles commonly associated with the urban Northeast and the contest between new ideals of companionate marriage and the patriarchal ideals that many scholars argue still flourished in the South. A fundamental inequity between men and women—a difference felt throughout the nineteenth-century United States, but with particular force in the Old South—undermined the Wirts' attempts to achieve a truly companionate marriage. As southerners and as Americans, the Wirts experienced the contradictions of companionate marriage in all their force.

The principal source for this study is the Wirts' own correspondence. Like many other wealthy white southerners, Elizabeth and William Wirt were separated frequently, and like other married people of their class, they took full advantage of the mails to send each other weekly, daily, and even twice-daily missives, ranging from brief, scrawled notes to lengthy, introspective letters. The Wirts' letters, carefully preserved, offer the researcher "an animated & interesting history" of "the lives & loves" of this nineteenth-century southern couple.[5]

The Wirts' letters are a testament to the power of the emerging ideal of companionate marriage. Like other couples in early-nineteenth-century Virginia who embraced the new standards for romantic love, the Wirts commented on the marriages of their acquaintances, measuring their success by the degree to which they achieved the ideal relationship of "affection & respect." Above all, in a truly companionate marriage, each partner would value the love of the other above all else. Elizabeth and William often assured each other of their total devotion with phrases that suggested that the loss of the other's love would threaten their very existence. In their correspondence, Elizabeth and William Wirt enthusiastically promoted the idea that women and men could and should find absolute personal fulfillment within the bounds of marriage.[6]

Elizabeth Wirt did not strike her contemporaries as a romantic. Margaret Smith described her as "a woman of sound common sense, a great manager and economist." Elizabeth's correspondence generally supports Smith's impression of her. Like many women in the early Republic, Elizabeth tended to write short, unreflective letters that were, as she often described them, mere bulletins of business. However, the steady pattern of daily updates on housework, child care, and the family's health was punctuated by brief, but intense, outbursts of emotion. Elizabeth often lamented that she lacked William's facility with the language of love, but her expressions of affection for her husband had an unmistakably heartfelt quality. In 1810, she told William, "If increasing admiration and ever glowing love, would be a suitable return [for his love letters], I can faithfully declare myself not insolvent, but ready boldly to meet you with my heart in my hand, and demand an acknowledgement of value received." Smith admitted that despite Elizabeth Wirt's lack of apparent "genius, with all its ardent affections, [and] enthusiasm," she was "wholly devoted to her husband."[7]

William Wirt, by contrast, was profoundly sentimental. "His manners in the domestic circle," Margaret Smith confided to a friend, "have a charm peculiar to himself." Like other gentlemen in the early Republic, William made letter writing an art. His copious correspondence was addressed not only to Elizabeth but also to a wide circle of friends and acquaintances. Men in early America originally honed their letter-writing skills to advance their careers, but by the start of the nineteenth century they had adapted correspondence to serve a new purpose: forwarding intimacy. Style and substance merged in William's correspondence with his wife. Where Elizabeth's writing was direct and unembellished, William's prose was stylized and polished. Unlike his wife, William often quoted from literature, frequently using stock phrases to describe his own feelings. Finally, while Elizabeth sandwiched relatively brief expressions of love between recommendations on her husband's diet and medication, news of the children's progress, and reports on household affairs, William frequently devoted entire letters to rhapsodies on what he liked to call conjugal bliss. Despite William's use of highly conventional language to convey his feelings, his sentiments generally ring true. In 1811, after reading through the Wirts' correspondence to date, William wrote a typically effusive eighteen-page epistle to his wife. "Beloved of my soul," he declared, "that I have ever loved you most tenderly and respected you most deeply, no one who reads these letters can ever doubt; for they bear a stamp of love that no human power can counterfeit."[8]

The extensive correspondence of this southern couple, spanning the formative opening decades of the nineteenth century, suggests the difficulties that confronted husbands and wives in the early Republic. Marriage in the nineteenth-century United States ideally united couples in a loving partnership, but men's and women's different gender roles and unequal power relations were problems that struck at the heart of companionship.

The Wirts' marriage reveals how the promise of a companionate marriage defined by symmetry, reciprocity, and mutuality was shaped by the realities of women's and men's different lives. Elizabeth and William Wirt's gender roles were played out in the context of three issues that surface repeatedly in their correspondence: domestic economy, home and family, and love and marriage. It was in these crucial areas that Elizabeth and William attempted to put their ideals into practice as partners in finances, parenthood, and romance. Throughout their marriage, the Wirts repeatedly redefined their roles in marriage as master and mistress, father and mother, and husband and wife. As they did so, the challenges posed to companionship by men's and women's different roles became apparent. Margaret Smith once remarked that Elizabeth was "a domestic woman." While Elizabeth Wirt devoted herself entirely to household economy, home and child care, and marriage, her husband's commitment to these tasks always competed with his other responsibilities beyond the domestic arena. As a result, William Wirt's contributions to domestic life, while significant, were always shaped by his participation in men's party politics and in the male-dominated workplace. The Wirts fulfilled their domestic duties in different contexts and in different ways.[9]

The ideal of companionship in marriage, which promised a loving partnership of equals, both concealed and exacerbated men's and women's inequality in the new American nation. Elizabeth Wirt never demanded full equality between men and women. In the era in which the Wirts met, fell in love, and married, only a few very exceptional women openly denounced inequality between men and women. Elizabeth was no Mary Wollstonecraft or Judith Sargent Murray, but she did expect her husband to shoulder an equal burden in maintaining the Wirts' relationship. William Wirt, while sharing his wife's enthusiasm for a relationship predicated on affection, rather than authority, did not fully comprehend the importance that Elizabeth placed on reciprocity and symmetry within such a relationship. Although Elizabeth Wirt would never have demanded political or economic equality with her husband, inequality was an important obstacle to her vision of companionship, for inequality resulted in William's lengthy absences from home and reinforced his difficulties in understanding the sources of his wife's unhappiness. William's letters to Elizabeth repeatedly affirmed his belief in the doctrine of love, but at the same time, they attested to the lure of fame and fortune away from her. With few resources outside marriage, Elizabeth depended on her husband for her happiness. "She is wholly devoted to her husband," Margaret Smith remarked, "and does not disguise her indifference to all other things and persons." Love was important to both Elizabeth and William Wirt, but the degree to which they depended on marital bliss for personal happiness was not the same.[10]

Elizabeth and William Wirt's marriage reveals the persistent differences in men's and women's lives in the nineteenth-century United States—differences that were felt all the more acutely because of their dissonance with the beau ideal. The Wirts both had high expectations of marriage, but those expectations—and the extent to which they were met—were very different for Elizabeth and William. From the very start of their marriage, the Wirts spent a great deal of their time apart. The Wirts' separations escalated in length and frequency throughout their marriage, until by the mid-1820s they spent only two months of the year together. William, who felt loneliness and anxiety— but also personal satisfaction and contentment—during his work-related ab- sences, experienced the Wirts' attenuated relationship positively. Like northern men who lauded woman's sphere from afar and like southern men determined to make their reputation in politics, William viewed the time he spent at home as a refreshing, but temporary, retreat from his work beyond its walls. He might long for more time together, but he viewed separation as an integral part of marriage. To his friend and fellow lawyer, Dabney Carr, William mused: "I imagine there is no man, however happy in the circle of his family, who does not find himself made more conscious of that happiness, and his feelings of enjoyment quickened by these occasional separations." Elizabeth, however, like many southern women, did not fully comprehend her husband's obsession with public life. In her opinion, the time that she and William were apart endangered their relationship. Far from heightening Elizabeth's enjoyment of their time together, the Wirts' separations caused her anxiety and depression. Without William's constant company, Elizabeth could not be happy. Like many southern plantation mistresses, she suffered from intense feelings of isolation, which appear not to have been relieved by her urban lifestyle. For William, mutual love, respect, and trust—by mail—were what was necessary to com- panionate marriage; for Elizabeth, companionship demanded her husband's presence. "These separations, so long protracted, are vexatious drawbacks to happiness," she chided in 1821, "and if I knew how to better my self, I would not submit to them, so I wouldent." Elizabeth and William Wirt shared a commitment to companionate marriage, but they defined companionship in very different—even divergent—ways.[11] Thus, their marriage can be seen as a lengthy attempt to negotiate a workable compromise on the meaning of mar- riage in the American Republic.

CHAPTER ONE

Forming a Life Partnership

Courtship in Richmond,
1799–1802

"O! my Betsey, my soul assures me that we were indeed made for each other," rejoiced William Wirt in a letter to his bride, Elizabeth Gamble Wirt, in December 1803. "Not merely to bear the name of husband & wife, but reciprocally to render to each other this system of being as happy as its nature will permit. How delightful it is thus to love you!"[1] William's letter to his wife of three months indicated that by the time Elizabeth and William Wirt agreed to "bear the name of husband & wife," they had formed clear ideas of what being "husband & wife" in the early-nineteenth-century United States meant: marriage partners should strive "reciprocally" to further each other's happiness. However, the Wirts' three years of courtship and three months of engagement were more complicated than William's high praise for their union might suggest. The Wirts' lengthy and sometimes stormy courtship revealed the fault lines between their new ideals of companionship, reciprocity, and mutuality in an egalitarian, romantic relationship and older and enduring notions of marriage as a hierarchical bond between a superior patriarch and a submissive wife. New ideals of romantic love softened, but did not eliminate, the patriarchal structure of marriage in nineteenth-century America, and a celebration of equality and mutuality in marriage blurred, but did not erase, the divisions between male and female gender roles.

Courtship is always a crucial period for a couple. Elizabeth and William Wirt's courtship also had a specific importance rooted in historical time and place. When William and Elizabeth met, courted, and wed, the meaning of marriage and family and the assumptions about gender roles within marriage were in flux. A patriarchal, autocratic ideal of male leadership and female obedience was gradually being replaced by an ideal of companionate marriage, emphasizing mutual respect and romantic love between the marriage partners. This idea of marriage as an affectionate partnership affected middle- and upper-class men and women on both sides of the Atlantic, beginning in the seventeenth century. Ideally, companionate marriage permitted individual choice in marriage based on personal affection and sexual attraction and encouraged loving, rather than authoritarian, relationships between husbands, wives, and their children.[2]

Companionate marriage and the more egalitarian relationships between men and women which it recommended were especially in vogue in the early national period when Elizabeth Gamble and William Wirt courted and wed. As the United States experimented with nationhood, so men and women experimented with their lives in marriage. A whole genre of the new nation's literature was devoted to prescriptions for marriage. Literature in the new nation recommended that men and women should cherish equality, not hierarchy, in their relationships, and they should strive for reciprocity and mutuality, not sharply differentiated gender roles. Magazines in early America presented marriage as a meeting of equals and glorified the marriage relationship as freed from patriarchy, egalitarian, and symmetrical in its expectations of men and women.[3]

Marriage and family were invested with special importance in the South following the Great Awakening of the 1740s and the South's Great Revival (or Second Great Awakening) in the Wirts' own time. Beginning in the mid-eighteenth century, southerners channeled the emotion unleashed by evangelical religion into interpersonal relationships, investing the family with new emotional intensity. By the early nineteenth century, the new understanding of marriage and family as loving and companionable relationships affected many well-to-do plantation families in the upper South as well as urban people in the Northeast.[4]

New ideals of marriage were especially important for women, who had occupied a clearly subordinate status in the domestic patriarchy of the colonial American family. Although some scholars have argued that domestic patriarchalism strengthened its hold in Tidewater Maryland and Virginia at the turn of the century, the revolutionary and postrevolutionary eras fomented new ideals of womanhood, marriage, and family which undermined patriarchy as an ideal. The Revolutionary War itself has been interpreted as a revolution against patriarchal authority. A broader range of ideas about women's abilities and duties accompanied this revolution. One historian has suggested that the postrevolutionary years offered at least four competing ideals of womanhood: a conservative ideal of piety, purity, domesticity, and self-sacrifice; a liberal ideal that condemned female weakness and supported equality between the sexes within the bounds of marriage; a radical ideal that held the individual's rights to be supreme, even if this meant a disruption of the family unit; and a final ideal that taught women to follow where their hearts or natural understandings led. Of all these ideals, the liberal ideal—which defined a role for women as the equal companions of men in a relationship of reciprocal love and respect—was most consonant with the emerging ideal of companionate marriage.[5]

Ideals of manhood also changed in the new republic. In evangelical churches in the South, men were warned to restrain their use of authority in the marital relationship. In place of patriarchal authority and displays of manly honor in combat, evangelical men were advised to embrace self-control, love, and the open expression of emotions. Similarly, popular novels of the time advocated an ideal of sensibility, in which men were urged to share a sentimental attachment to home life with women.[6]

New ideals of marriage, a fundamental reassessment of womanhood, and changing ideals of manhood all combined to lead couples to expect marriage to be a loving partnership of equals. In their courtship, Elizabeth and William expressed high expectations of marriage consonant with the new ideal of companionate marriage: they looked forward to a marriage partnership in which they would strive for mutuality, equality, and reciprocity. In companionate marriage, women expected more control over at least some aspects of their lives, while men anticipated yielding patriarchal privilege in favor of a close emotional attachment to their wives. The Wirts' expectations would be contradicted and limited by other factors, however. Although marriage in the early-nineteenth-century South could be a partnership, it was always an unequal one. Both Elizabeth's and William's high hopes and potential disappointments were foreshadowed during their courtship and engagement.

Elizabeth Washington Gamble and William Wirt probably met at church in Richmond in 1799. After their marriage, William recalled how Elizabeth would cast her "dark, brilliant eyes" and "sweet smiles" on him from the "ladies' side" of the building. Elizabeth came from one of Richmond's most prominent and prosperous families. Born on January 30, 1784, Elizabeth Washington Gamble was the second daughter of Robert and Catharine Gamble. The Gambles built their wealth and reputation on trade, an occupation that Tidewater Virginia shared with northeastern port cities yet made distinctive with a focus on items produced and used primarily in a region set apart by the presence of slavery. Robert Gamble, whose father, uncle, and grandparents had joined the Scotch-Irish migration to backcountry Virginia by way of Pennsylvania in 1735, was born in Augusta County, Virginia, in 1754. Shortly before the outbreak of hostilities with Britain, he married another member of Augusta County's Scotch-Irish community, Catharine Grattan, who had migrated, while still a girl, to Virginia with her Irish-born father and Scottish-born mother. After serving in the Revolution and gaining the rank of colonel, Gamble inherited a portion of his father's "good landed estate" but chose to take advantage of the nearby Great Wagon Road to become a successful merchant in Staunton, where he stayed until 1792. He then sold his land in Augusta County to his only brother, John, and moved to Richmond, where he was soon a well-to-do merchant and a respectable member of Richmond society. In 1799 he celebrated his success with the purchase of an imposing new residence atop what came to be known as Gamble's Hill. Elizabeth grew up in Richmond surrounded by eminent men such as Chief Justice Marshall and "friends of [her father's] early days and native country," in a setting of "elegant hospitality."[7]

Elizabeth Gamble and her older sister, Agnes Sarah Bell, known as Nancy, attracted many suitors to what William called the "*blanche maison*" on Gamble's Hill. A crayon portrait made several years later exhibited Elizabeth as slender and poised, her regular classic features brought to life by her large, dark eyes. Her stern expression as she posed for the French artist Charles Balthazar Julien Fevret de Saint-Memin contrasted with the riotous curls that escaped the ribbon Elizabeth used to keep her hair loosely coiled at the back of her head.[8]

As Elizabeth sat to have her likeness done, her composure and slight smile hinted at her intelligence and wit. Elizabeth was the beneficiary of a national drive for improved women's education. In the attempt to realize the promises of a more egalitarian society implicit in revolutionary rhetoric (if often overlooked for groups other than property-holding white men), some women in the postrevolutionary era created a rationale for wider access to education and interest in the political process as republican wives and mothers who would influence their husbands for good and train their sons to virtuous, self-sacrificing citizenship. Many men, including William Wirt, enthusiastically endorsed this idea, which allowed women to aspire to new goals while still tying them to their domestic duties.[9]

Elizabeth's education reflected the dual thrust of female educational reform: to introduce women to a classical curriculum and to remind them that their calling was marriage and family. Richmond did not open its female academy until 1807. Instead, Elizabeth and her older sister, Nancy, attended a private female seminary under the direction of a family friend, pastor, and local schoolmaster, John D. Blair. Parson Blair demanded high achievement in everything necessary to "high mental culture." Blair schooled his students in French and arithmetic, and he may have anticipated the curriculum of the Richmond Female Academy, which included Latin, Greek, mathematics, history, geography, and natural philosophy. If so, he did not neglect more traditional ornamental accomplishments; William admired Elizabeth's skill at the piano. Like other advocates of improved female education, Elizabeth's teacher probably believed that women could attain a complete classical education and still excel in the feminine graces. This was particularly true in the South, where even the women's colleges trained their students in the wiles of the southern belle well into the nineteenth century. True to the pattern of female educational reform, Blair's seminary prepared graduates for specifically female "duties of life. They could give an appearance of neatness and comfort to everything around them," one conservative Richmonder recalled many years later, "and make their homes pleasant retreats for their families and friends." Perhaps, like the model curriculum proposed by educational reformers, Elizabeth and her schoolmates' schedules combined math and history with needlework, music, and dancing. But while certificates were presented to Blair's students for both "moral deportment" and academic achievement, only the heads of academic classes were awarded with silver medals, which served "to gratify their ambition and stimulate those who were to succeed them." Certainly Elizabeth seems to have been fired with ambition. Although she did not distinguish herself at Blair's seminary, she exhibited a keen interest in intellectual development throughout her life. Elizabeth may have learned bookkeeping skills from her father, and the botanical details she included in the book on flowers she published in 1829 suggest that Elizabeth did not hesitate to augment her formal training with skills she could pick up during her life.[10]

By the time Elizabeth Washington Gamble began to exchange glances with William Wirt, at the age of fifteen, she had developed into an intelligent, widely read, and opinionated young woman. Elizabeth was the younger daughter, and the Gambles probably expected her older sister, Nancy, to marry first. However, men who came to the Gamble home to court Nancy soon were joined by Elizabeth's suitors. In her interaction with these men, Elizabeth displayed a maturity beyond her years. Perhaps, as some scholars have suggested, she found that being a belle gave her a source of power that most southern women enjoyed only during the courtship ritual. In addition, Elizabeth's sound education must have given her additional confidence to express her views to the men who came to vie for her attentions. William later described Elizabeth as possessed of "vigorous intelligence and solid judgment."[11]

Courtship was an important time for women to use their best judgment. Elizabeth's response to one of her suitors, Thomas Bayly, indicated that she was prepared to meet men with graciousness but with a firm commitment to retaining her own personality. She had no intention of flattering men by seconding their every thought. Elizabeth told Bayly that her 1801 letter was the first she had written to a man other than a relative, but she did not hesitate to express her political views, which were in opposition to his. (She was an ardent Federalist; he was a Republican.) Elizabeth also informed Bayly that she and her sister had spent the evening "very agreeably" with "two very smart Beaux . . . One a Fedt. the other a Demot." Perhaps the Democrat was William Wirt, a widowed lawyer who had recently moved to Richmond. By the time Elizabeth wrote to Thomas Bayly in 1801, she already knew William Wirt very well. Indeed, she had already rejected his proposal once. William's first proposal came after less than a year of acquaintance. In July 1800, he wrote to his closest friend, Dabney Carr, "I have struck, and—have been stricken down . . . alas me!"[12]

Nineteenth-century courtship was a time for prospective couples to get to know each other. This was especially important for women, for whom marriage was the most important (and, for a few, nearly the only) choice of their adult life. Romantic love was becoming the most important factor in marriage choice. It was not the only factor, however. Although parents were less likely to arrange marriages for financial connections, they did occasionally veto matches. Perhaps more important, especially in the South, matches were formed within a pool of prospective mates which was defined by parents, relatives, and neighbors. Some parents in the southern seaboard insisted on providing their daughters with chaperons, but the Gambles followed the custom in the North—and adopted by well-to-do families in the upper South as well—and left their daughters alone with their male visitors. This sort of courtship encouraged romantic love by allowing the women themselves to learn, through conversation, if a man offered a good prospect of mutual love, respect, and companionship. Parents' reduced—or at least disguised—role in mate selection also suggested that women would be permitted more freedom in the important choices in their life, rather than being guided, protected, and sometimes ruled by their fathers and husbands. William Wirt courted Elizabeth at large gatherings, such as balls, in small groups like that described by Elizabeth, and alone in the Gambles' "middle parlour." It was in the last place that couples could—and Elizabeth and William did—make and break engagements without parental knowledge. For those families who adopted the new ideal of romantic love and self-directed courtship, it was only when a couple had already decided to marry that they asked for parental consent; except in unusual circumstances, it was routinely given.[13]

Had it not been for a relaxation in standards of wealth for prospective suitors in the early nineteenth century, William Wirt might never had made it into the group of possible mates considered by Elizabeth Gamble and her parents. William was born in Bladensburg, Maryland, on November 8, 1772, the youngest of three sons and three daughters, to Jacob and Henrietta Wirt, immigrants from Switzerland and Germany, respectively. The Wirts operated a tavern where some of the South's most prosperous planters and merchants gathered. Although the Wirts were not as successful as the Gambles, the family's fortunes were on the rise. Lavishly decorated, the tavern brought the family contact with influential men as well as a comfortable income. The family's good fortune did not last, however. In 1774 Jacob Wirt died, leaving the tavern to Henrietta for use during her lifetime along with a half lot with a new house, a brick store in Bladensburg, two lots in Hamburg near Georgetown, and two women slaves with their children. The income from these properties allowed William to attend a series of day schools and classical academies until 1787, when his share of the inheritance (his mother had died in 1779) gave out.[14]

At fifteen, William was penniless and without a vocation. The experience impressed upon him the terrifying specter of poverty and gave him a lifelong drive for self-advancement. Fortunately for young William, his classmate Ninian Edwards' father, Benjamin, offered William a place as tutor to Ninian and two of his cousins in Montgomery County. Although officially an employee, William was treated as a son in the Edwards household, and it was under Benjamin Edwards' tutelage that he began to read law. William obtained his license in 1791 in Virginia after only a year of study, having moved to the Old Dominion to take advantage of openings and evading the requirement of residency "by a manoevre" that may have been facilitated by his patron Benjamin Edwards or by Peter Carnes, a Maryland lawyer and planter who had frequented the Wirt tavern and had married one of William's sisters.[15]

Although he retained close ties with the Edwards family, William thereafter identified himself as a Virginian. He had good reasons to do so. As one traveler in Virginia noted in 1796, "the profession of a lawyer is here, as in every other part of America, one of the most profitable." With other young, landless southern men, William Wirt found that law was the route to money and acceptance into gentry society. Practicing law in Culpeper and Albemarle Counties, William wasted no time in putting his useful skill of acquiring patrons to work, marrying the eldest child of revolutionary veteran, physician, and planter George Gilmer and thus gaining entry into the upper echelon of Virginia society as well as access to the Gilmer library at Pen Park, near Charlottesville. Little is known of Mildred Gilmer or of her relationship with William. When she died in 1799, the couple was childless. According to the terms of his father-in-law's will, William did not inherit any of Dr. Gilmer's substantial estate. Once again, William was alone and poverty-stricken. Apparently hoping to make a new start in life, William moved to Richmond, where he was quickly offered the clerkship of the Virginia House of Delegates.[16]

In Virginia's capital, fortune and gentry status seemed within William's grasp. The young widower soon earned enough to purchase a slave as a valet and coachman for his two-wheeled chair. Only twenty-seven when he moved to Richmond, William drew a lively circle of friends with his banter and dramatic eloquence, enhanced by his six-foot frame, intense blue eyes, and unkempt light-colored curls that fell forward onto his forehead and distracted the eye from his large nose. William's fondness for good food and drink already showed in his "general fullness of development," as one acquaintance delicately expressed it.[17]

William's move into wealth and visibility was almost disastrous. Richmond offered numerous diversions—not all of them as innocent as gluttony—to the new widower. Gambling was an especially popular activity for Virginia men, one that allowed them to make public displays of their wealth and assert their honor. Cast out from his comfortable home with one of Virginia's leading families, William may have turned to Richmond's nightlife to gain status as well as to subdue his sorrow over his first wife's death. Good-naturedness, fondness of society, and "the natural giddiness of [his] character," William later lamented, drew him away from the rigid principles he had imbibed under the tutelage of Presbyterian schoolmasters in his youth and into a "storm of dissipation." In later years, rumor had it that Colonel Gamble discovered William and several male friends still conducting their revels in the wee hours. Wearing a wash basin on his head and brandishing a poker, William was gesturing wildly while reciting Falstaff's lines in Shakespeare's play. Another story had it that Elizabeth recognized William "in a state of brutal intoxication in the street." Laying a handkerchief embroidered with her initials over his face, she "awakened him to a sense of self-respect." After that incident, so the story went, she made absolute abstinence a condition for marriage. Whether true or not, rumors like these must have been troubling for both Elizabeth and her parents. An especial point of concern for Elizabeth may have been the recognition that her suitor's rumored exploits indicated an allegiance to the culture of honor, a value system that upheld patriarchy.[18]

Even had William's reputation been spotless, Elizabeth might have rejected his first proposal in 1800. At the time, southern women rarely accepted an initial proposal. This was not mere coquetry. Marriage was not to be taken lightly when it would, in all likelihood, determine how a woman would spend the remainder of her life. Later advice books warned young women to winnow their suitors carefully and to make their choice only when they were mentally and physically mature. Elizabeth, at sixteen, may have considered herself too young to make a good choice when William first proposed to her in 1800. Furthermore, having known the Richmond newcomer less than a year, she may have felt they had not yet reached the level of intimacy necessary to a successful match. Later in the century it would become common for men and women to throw obstacles in the path of courtship to test the love of their romantic partners. Once married, a woman gave up all legal and economic rights. Romantic love was the only form of power women were likely to have in their marriage, and it was important to test and strengthen it.[19]

Another reason that Elizabeth may have turned her suitor down the first time was that her parents disapproved. Especially in the South, parents in the early nineteenth century continued to exercise considerable control over the pace of their daughters' courtships. This was particularly true in situations in which there were questions about a potential husband's suitability. For the Gambles, the persistent rumors of their prospective son-in-law's dissipation may have been a serious objection. Part of their concern was religious; the Gambles were devout, perhaps even rigid, Presbyterians. Another cause for worry was their recognition that, despite the rhetoric of romance which surrounded courtship, marriage remained an important financial decision. Although the Gambles did not demand wealth for their daughters' future husbands, they did expect that any son-in-law of theirs would apply himself to a respectable and reasonably profitable career. Habitual drunkenness was a vice only planters with land and slaves could afford. In addition, the Gambles probably knew that alcoholism was linked to domestic abuse, a burden they surely wished to spare their young daughter. Elizabeth's youth offered an additional complication. The tradition of marrying daughters off in birth order may have remained viable in the South after eighteenth- and nineteenth-century northerners abandoned the practice to allow their children more leeway in selecting a mate. Elizabeth's older sister, Nancy, was still unmarried, a circumstance that may have troubled the Gambles. Finally, Elizabeth's parents apparently favored another suitor.[20]

Whatever her own misgivings or her parents' reasons, Elizabeth chose to continue the courtship by phrasing her refusal in such a way that William was not without hope. Because courtship rituals, especially in the South, sometimes resembled a game of cat and mouse, Elizabeth probably knew that William would not take this initial rebuff seriously. He did not. Elizabeth, he reported to his friend Dabney Carr, turned him down "so gently, so sweetly, so angelically, with a countenance so every thing that I could wish, that I will strike again and again." In January 1802, William proposed again. By this time Elizabeth was convinced of William's love. He had proposed twice, had endured competition with another man, and had not courted another woman during her illness in the preceding months. All this was important evidence of romantic love by nineteenth-century standards. But, apparently in accordance with her parents' wishes, Elizabeth once again rejected William's suit. This time she was more decisive. William accepted a post as chancellor of a new court of chancery in Williamsburg, and Elizabeth and William commenced a "long separation, which was concluded to be final between the parties."[21]

During the "probation of lovers" which followed Elizabeth's second rejection of William's suit, both parties had time to reevaluate their feelings. Both concluded that romantic love outweighed all other factors when making a match. Although Elizabeth had summoned more resolve in her response to William's second proposal, her reason seems to have been her desire to please her parents. She herself was eager to make her own choice, and that choice was the widower from Maryland. All of Elizabeth Gamble's attempts to care for the man preferred by her parents, the wrapper of the Wirts' letters indicated, only "awakened her to a sense of the fervor and immoveable constancy of her sentiments for the only being capable of filling her imagination and her heart." Meanwhile, although he courted a Mrs. Ellis in Richmond in a half-hearted way and went "visiting at a high rate," William continued to inquire about Elizabeth. Writing to his Richmond friend Mrs. Lucy F. Jones in the spring of 1802, he chided her for failing to tell him how courtships went on there. In particular, he asked if "Miss E. G." had made a choice yet. He could not help his inquisitiveness: "her dark eyes Still haunt *my dreams*." Finally William could stand it no longer. He returned to Richmond to meet with Elizabeth privately. Sitting with her persistent suitor on the sofa in the "middle parlour" of the Gamble mansion, Elizabeth at last admitted that William had a place "deep in her secret heart" and promised to marry him.[22]

Elizabeth and William Wirt dated their engagement from that moment, but it still remained to receive the blessing of Elizabeth's parents. For some families this would have been a routine matter, but the Gambles had given several indications that although they accepted the new models of courtship and the new emphasis on romantic love to a certain degree, they also felt an older obligation to protect and guide their daughter in her choice of a husband. Richmonders apparently shared this heightened concern for young women's reputations. Despite the informality that gradually was replacing chaperonage, even a hint that couples had formed unauthorized attachments was enough to compromise a woman's future. In the Old South, a woman's sexual purity was essential; although men benefited from a sexual double standard that permitted males a degree of sexual experimentation, a fallen woman would be a social outcast. Therefore, Elizabeth and William resolved to keep their engagement a secret until they received paternal blessing. When William wrote to Colonel Gamble, he did not mention that Elizabeth already had accepted his proposal. He explained to Elizabeth, "I thought it my duty to you to conceal even from your father, the real state of affairs: since if I had been compelled to resign my pretension your dignity and happiness of your future life would have required that you should be considered on all hands as having entertained no prepossession for any individual."[23]

William's decision to petition Colonel Gamble for formal permission to address his daughter—and his concern for protecting Elizabeth's reputation in case of a negative response—revealed that despite their commitment to an ideal of romance, intimacy, and companionship, Elizabeth and William bowed to social conventions that placed women's futures in men's hands. In his letter to Colonel Gamble, William alternated between the older conventions and the new. William followed tradition when he conceded Gamble's right to decide the matter and promised to support Elizabeth and their future family from his own funds. Perhaps recognizing his less than favored status, however, William did not stop with such formalities. "I have too often forgotten my health and that character of systematic steadiness, so important to a professional man," wrote William, managing in one sentence to repent for his misdeeds and remind the colonel of his important post in Williamsburg. William vowed henceforth to exhibit "moral purity and the dignity of the office" he held, thus hopefully allaying the Gambles' fears about his character. By assuring the Gambles of his moral and material capital, William overcame the objections that parents typically raised. He realized, however, that other men would have more desirable credentials. "I do not forget how destitute I am of those advantages which the world seems to regard, exclusively, in connexions of this kind," he admitted. As a substitute for family name and wealth, William offered another kind of attraction more in keeping with the new emphasis on companionship: romantic love. His own intense emotions—"the peace of my mind, &, I fear, my utility to society are at stake," he exclaimed—entitled him to consideration, William argued. "You have been young—you know what it is to have loved," he appealed. William's ultimate argument, guaranteed to success in light of his agreement with Elizabeth, was also the one that owed the most to the considerations of companionate marriage. William asked Gamble to consult with Elizabeth herself on the matter. "Let this, however, be an obstacle for her own consideration," he begged.[24]

William's letter had the desired effect. Colonel Gamble was impressed by William's "frankness" about his past transgressions and his "sincerity" in resolving to reform. He also was favorably disposed to the young man's willingness to honor the tradition of paternal consent. "You have anticipated all!" he said of possible objections to the match. Once all potential obstacles such as character and income were resolved to his satisfaction, Gamble was more than willing to allow his daughter to make up her own mind. "It has been our wish as far as it can possibly comport with that *duty* as parents," he explained, "that [our daughters] should on mature consideration, make their own choice." "Thus, you see, you are the mistress of your own destiny," crowed William in his first letter to Elizabeth.[25]

There was a certain irony in William's words. If in any sense Elizabeth was mistress of her own destiny, it was only at the moment that she selected a husband. When Elizabeth Washington Gamble became Elizabeth Gamble Wirt, her identity, so far as the law was concerned, would be subsumed under her husband's. American women inherited English common law's tradition of "coverture," by which a married woman's legal identity was "covered" by her husband's. As a feme covert, a married woman could not testify in court, make contracts, or sue for damages. Women also surrendered all property rights when they wed. As William Wirt's friend and fellow lawyer St. George Tucker put it, "A woman's personal property, by marriage, becomes absolutely her husband's, which at his death he may leave entirely away from her"; the husband also had the right to any money she might earn in return for his obligation to support her and her children and provide a dower (usually one-third of their joint estate and personal property) for her support after his death.[26]

Although increasing numbers of women in such states as Virginia, South Carolina, and New York gained control of the property they brought to marriage through separate estates in the nineteenth century, Elizabeth and William did not plan to use this option. Separate estates were intended to protect family property from ne'er-do-well husbands, not to increase women's autonomy. Separate estates were based on the principle of equity, which differed from the principle of equality evidenced in a later drive for married women's property rights. Equity did not challenge men's legal dominance directly, although it did undermine the principle of marital unity and begin the process of ameliorating women's inferior legal status. By convincing the Gambles to accept him as a son-in-law, William apparently escaped this limitation of his formal legal authority over his bride-to-be. Commenting on the dilemma of an acquaintance, William regarded the request by the affianced woman's father that separate estates be established as inappropriate for a respectable man and even reason to call off the engagement. Because his own background was marred by irresponsible behavior, William suggested that had Colonel Gamble requested such legal safeguards, he would have consented, but apparently Gamble had yielded to William's powers of persuasion and had imposed no such condition.[27]

Women's legal and economic powerlessness was compounded by the fact that men usually outpaced their wives in age, education, knowledge of the world, and physical strength as well. William, like many southern husbands, was significantly older than his wife: when they married, he had reached the age of thirty, while Elizabeth was just eighteen years old. Furthermore, William was a widower, well acquainted with Richmond's stylish society, whereas Elizabeth planned to move directly from her parents' household to the house she would share with William. Elizabeth evidently felt herself at an educational disadvantage as well; initially she belittled her intellectual abilities, burning most of the letters she wrote during the first nine years of her marriage in the belief that they were inferior to her husband's.[28]

With all the advantages that accrued to men in American society at large and in marriage, it was not surprising that Elizabeth was "pensive" during her wedding preparations. Her letters from this period have not survived, but one of her bridegroom's letters may have succeeded in pinpointing her concerns. William's perceptive comments revealed the uncertainty of companionate marriage, especially for women. Companionate marriage promised to replace patriarchal authority with mutual love, but by raising expectations of marriage, the new ideal also increased the chances for disappointment. "Too many, indeed, are there, and particularly of your sex," William admitted, who felt "that life is a cheat, & that it is merely the business of maturity & age to detect the fallacy of the promises of youthful hope & fancy . . . who ground it on the bitterest experience—who have seen not only the brilliant promises, but the actual enjoyments of youth reversed, blasted and exchanged for misery and despair." William was determined that Elizabeth would not suffer this fate.

"No," he cried. "My Betsey shall long be happy in the faithful & affectionate bosom of her husband."[29]

William's letter also indicated his awareness that in a marriage for love, a man's affectionate bosom, rather than parental oversight, would restrain the exercise of men's superior legal, economic, and social power over women. In the densely knit kinship networks of the southern seaboard, parents and other relatives continued to supervise young married couples and to ensure that men honored their family responsibilities. However, life in the South's cities weakened these kinds of controls, and when Elizabeth moved with her husband-to-be from Richmond to Williamsburg, she would be far removed from her anxious parents. Because of women's legal powerlessness and parents' declining influence over son-in-laws, the degree of marital equality achieved largely depended on the man's acquiescence—acquiescence in William's case encouraged by romantic love. Quite possibly William had vowed to himself that, given the chance, he would at last realize the idyllic family situation the death first of his parents and then of his first wife had stolen from him. Sensitive to the imbalance of power in their relationship, William vowed to submit to the dictates of romantic love and to act in whatever manner would please Elizabeth. "I should be very miscrable if I thought you the prey of regret," he worried. "Remember—you are not the prisoner of an engagement . . . There shall be no compulsion, no fetters but such as Love shall forge shall bind you to the engagement," he promised.[30]

Apparently William's letters reassured his bride. For engaged couples, the months between courtship and marriage offered a final opportunity to investigate a potential spouse and to reconsider if necessary. Many women in the early nineteenth century insisted on lengthy engagements, sometimes postponing marriage for years. The short duration of the Wirts' engagement and William's responses to Elizabeth's early letters suggest that she was certain of her bridegroom's character and his feelings for her. Although, like other women in the early Republic, Elizabeth worried that her letters failed to express her true feelings, they revealed her affection for her fiancé. She described her letters as "barren, uninteresting and inelegant," but William, who was himself skilled at "the language of love," assured her that this was not the case. As long as Elizabeth's letters came "warm from my Betsey's heart," William assured her, form and style did not matter. "Ah! my dear," he replied to one of Elizabeth's letters, "regret not any imaginary incapacity, to do justice to the feelings and affections of your heart—You write in a language most intelligible to your Williams heart—Well can he discern in your letters the affections of your warm heart while his own vibrates every delicate & fervid sensation." Shortly after their marriage, William described his response to one of Elizabeth's burnt love letters. "Beloved of my soul! dearest, dearest Betsey! you cannot imagine how this letter affects me!" he exclaimed. "My eyes are swimming with tears," wrote William, "this is the delicious tumult which you inspire."[31]

Beneath the delicious tumult of the couple's enthusiastic embrace of the values of companionate marriage lay a quiet but persistent concern about the feasibility of the new ideal, particularly its compatibility with the traditional conceptions of family life and male honor which continued to draw allegiance from some southerners. Elizabeth's virtual absence from the documentation of the Wirts' courtship reflected her lack of real power in the process, even as William's letters celebrated the new ideal of romantic love that placed men and women at the center of courtship. The announcement of the couple's marriage published in the *Virginia Gazette* indicated the difference in the meaning of marriage for the partners. "The amiable and accomplished ELIZABETH WASHINGTON GAMBLE, daughter of Col. ROBERT GAMBLE, of this City, merchant," was defined in relation to men; her entire identity, her sense of purpose, and her hopes for happiness would depend on her status as the wife of "the Honorable WILLIAM WIRT, esq. Judge of the High Court of Chancery for Williamsburg District." William, however much he loved Elizabeth, was not dependent on her in the same way. He maintained his own separate identity as a southern gentleman, a legal professional, and a successful public servant. When Elizabeth and William Wirt were wed on September 7, 1802, they began a marriage partnership that was defined from the start in very contradictory terms. The Wirts' union was a loving one, but it also was unequal.[32]

The inequality of marriage partners, highlighted here in Elizabeth and William Wirt's courtship, engagement, and wedding announcement, was a serious obstacle to the achievement of companionate marriage in the early Republic. Nineteenth-century couples often proclaimed that it was only in love, not in earthly success, that women and men could find true happiness. Despite these glowing tributes to the ultimate power of love, men retained power of another sort in the public realm of work and politics. For men, love could be the ultimate source of satisfaction, but for women, it was often the only path to emotional fulfillment. The Wirts, like many other couples, shared an intense desire for a happy and loving marital relationship, but men's and women's different roles inside and outside marriage meant that love had a very different significance for husbands and wives.[33]

CHAPTER TWO

Going to Housekeeping

Early Years in Williamsburg
and Norfolk, 1803–1806

"You have taken to yourself an helpmate":
Domestic Economy

Upon learning of his friend's marriage, Dabney Carr dashed off a letter of "warmest congratulations" to William Wirt. Carr recognized that his friend, in accordance with the companionate ideal, had married for love. "You have gotten the girl of your heart," he rejoiced with his friend, "her whom you have lov[e]d so long & so well." But in the same letter, Carr noted, "You have taken to yourself an helpmate."[1] As the Wirts set up housekeeping, first in Williamsburg (1803) and then in Norfolk (1803–6), their ideals of marriage were complicated by the demands of their household and their rapidly growing family. For Elizabeth and William Wirt, these new responsibilities were both an arena in which to practice their commitment to sharing their lives and a persistent source of tension in their marriage. The Wirts were committed to a life partnership in which each would serve as the other's "helpmate" in three crucial ways—as partners in domestic economy, as parents, and as loving spouses. During the first few years of their marriage, it quickly became apparent that Elizabeth and William were unable to transcend all differences to become equal partners in marriage. The Wirts consoled themselves for this failure with the hope that, in a short while, their circumstances would change and they would be able to perfect their partnership. Thus, in the early years of their marriage, the Wirts extended and refined their high standards of companionship while recognizing the gulf between their ideal of mutuality in all things and their daily lives of divided responsibilities.

The Wirts' marriage was an economic partnership, but it was an unequal one. In the opening years of their marriage, Elizabeth and William agreed that going to housekeeping was a joint venture. Both husband and wife would contribute to the domestic economy, which was based both on household production and on a cash income. However, men's and women's unequal earning power in the early nineteenth century made William's work as a lawyer the focal point of the Wirts' domestic economy. In financial matters, Elizabeth was her husband's helpmate. Although William occasionally served as his wife's assistant in household work, the pattern that the Wirts established in the early years of their marriage was a partnership between a male wage earner and a female helpmate, rather than between two equal contributors to the household economy.

When they married, the Wirts expected to establish a cooperative domestic economy to which both would contribute. It was only natural that Elizabeth should take an active economic role as "mistress of her Williams household," as he expressed it in 1802.[2] In early America, economic cooperation between husbands and wives was commonplace. In colonial New England, wives brought in income in two different ways. Some wives conducted small-scale business transactions on their own account, participating in a female exchange network and contributing their earnings to the household. Others acted as "deputy husbands," filling in for their spouses when business, politics, or war called the men away from home. Women in the early Republic also played an important role in the family economy. Wives in the Middle Atlantic often were their husbands' "silent partners" in trade or manufacture. Unlike deputy husbands or petty businesswomen, these women "shared work roles and economic goals" with their husbands. By cooperating with their husbands in business matters, these wives made up a "hidden economic sector" of women who made significant, but not independent, contributions to their family's finances. As one recent study of Philadelphia concluded, women in the early national period were "hidden investments to their families."[3]

Elizabeth had a solid background in the sort of cooperative family economy which scholars have uncovered in other regions. The Scotch-Irish migrants to backcountry Virginia specialized in business ventures that used the family's house as a base. In the Augusta County community where Elizabeth lived until 1792, the traditional economic role women had filled in Scotland and Ireland was encouraged and reinforced by the circumstances in the New World, which often drew men away for politics, campaigns against Native Americans, and war with European powers. As a girl Catharine Grattan (Gamble), Elizabeth's mother, had accompanied her own mother on regular trips between Staunton and Pennsylvania which supplied John Grattan with the goods to run the store he operated in Staunton, possibly from within the Grattans' house. Marrying Catharine Grattan may have encouraged Robert Gamble to become a merchant rather than a planter. The official partnership he formed with his brother-in-law was no doubt backed up by an informal partnership with his wife, who had been trained in business by her mother. Political and military conditions in the revolutionary backcountry would have encouraged Robert Gamble to rely on his wife's expertise and experience. It is likely that during the Revolutionary War, while Colonel Gamble was distracted by military matters, Catharine Gamble kept the store going. Scotch-Irish women were often called on for assistance in the family business, as evidenced by the ease with which widows in both Ireland and British North America continued to operate their deceased husbands' shops or taverns.[4]

William's childhood experiences prepared him to expect an economic partnership with his wife. At his death, William's father, Jacob, had left his tavern, stables, counting house, and smith shop (all located on adjacent lots) to his wife, Henrietta, for her life use, secure in the knowledge that operating a tavern out of her home had familiarized her with the profitable operation of the tavern, at least, and perhaps the smith shop and counting house as well. As a child, William had observed his mother as a businesswoman, first in partnership with her husband and then as a widow. When he married Elizabeth, he expected to realize the same sort of economic partnership with her. William did not expect his income to fulfill all the couple's needs. As Elizabeth's father pointed out to his son-in-law, "With . . . a reliance on your Salary only . . . you never could expect to acquire wealth thereby—or Secure a Competency for exigencies which no human foresight could prevent."[5]

Much had changed since Elizabeth and William Wirt's childhoods. By the turn of the century, women's economic role in the household was in decline. The new emphasis on female education and romantic love, ironically, has been linked to women's waning status as valuable contributors to the household. As the daughters of upwardly mobile families like the Gambles became more educated in the classics and the fine arts, they also became less prepared to run shops or to advise their husbands on business matters. Elizabeth, however, displayed a lifelong zeal for financial management. With a keen mind for business, perhaps honed in her father's store, she soon made herself the acknowledged economist of the Wirts' household. Elizabeth took pride in her ability to manage money, and it was probably her enthusiasm and skill that led the Wirts, like other families in the first half of the nineteenth century, to adopt a "household mode of production," in which the husband and wife formed an economic partnership. Households in early national and antebellum America were "mixed economies" that depended on both paid and unpaid labor. In early-nineteenth-century Virginia, as elsewhere in the South and the nation, members of the household were jointly responsible for a wide array of productive activities, some geared to bring in income, others to avoid expenditures, but all necessary to the success of what William and his circle called going to housekeeping.[6]

The Wirts expected to establish a working household in which each would have an active economic role, but when the newlyweds established their first household, they assumed different roles in their family economy. William was eager to establish an economic partnership with Elizabeth, but he knew that his bride was not ready to undertake full-scale household production immediately following the Wirts' marriage. As the younger daughter in a household that contained several slaves, Elizabeth probably had participated only sporadically or as her mother's delegate in household production. In late 1802 William worried that his bride might feel "apprehension or inquietude" at the duties that awaited her as "mistress of her Williams household." It was not uncommon in the South for young new brides, particularly those married to professionals, to begin their housekeeping on a small scale, adding responsibilities gradually as they gained in confidence and skill. Like other city dwellers in the growing nation, the Wirts relied heavily on the local market to supply themselves with most of their basic needs in Williamsburg, including pork, ham, and bacon "ready cured & made" as well as milk, butter, eggs, and vegetables. Purchasing goods in this manner required cash, and William made it his responsibility to reduce his bride's trials by devoting himself to work. He vowed: "If your husbands fondest, tenderest, purest love can shield your bosom from care, . . . you will be as light hearted as in the happy days of infancy." To keep his promise, William left Elizabeth in Richmond in mid-October to resume his duties as chancellor in Williamsburg.[7] It was a pattern that was to repeat itself often throughout the Wirts' marriage.

The Wirts' correspondence in the first month of their marriage indicated both the growing importance of a cash income and the significant impact that the demand for cash would have on marriage and gender roles. The demand for cash made men's paid labor the focal point of the family economy. Women's work in the household could significantly reduce a household's dependence on purchased goods and thus on the cash brought in by their husbands' wages. Ultimately, however, household operations required cash.

Without a cash income, the household economy would collapse. Although women in the early nineteenth century continued to serve as financial assistants and advisors in their husbands' business, they were always invisible contributors to the family's cash income. At the same time that new ideals of marriage weakened the hold of patriarchy, the growing importance of cash gave men a new source of authority which threatened to upset the egalitarian relationships in the new nation.[8]

The importance of cash in the Wirts' domestic economy soon propelled William to define wage earning as an essential component of his responsibilities as a married man. Although families in the North and the Middle Atlantic—as well as some in the upper South—began first to count and then to limit the number of children in the nineteenth century, the Wirts did not join this group. In 1803, William told his friend Dabney Carr that he suspected that he and Elizabeth would soon experience "an increase of family." William's phrasing suggested that the Wirts did not consider controlling reproduction. Instead, they planned to respond to an inevitable and unending "increase of family," which, William pointed out, "would in a short time demand an increase of revenue." With the expectation of increased expenses and a continued delay in undertaking domestic production, William worried about the Wirts' economic situation. "For the first time in my life (and with shame I confess it)," he wrote to Carr, "I look forward . . . with a thoughtful mind, and a heart aching with uncertainty, to the years which lie before me." William resolved to search for additional employment to augment his salary as chancellor of the Williamsburg court.[9]

It was a poor time to earn extra cash in Williamsburg. By the time Elizabeth joined her husband there in late 1802, the city was experiencing a decline that had begun when the state capital was moved from Williamsburg to Richmond, in 1780. As a result, as William discovered to his chagrin, there were few opportunities for the young chancellor to augment his salary with fees drawn from legal business. Looking around him at Williamsburg's roughly two hundred houses, which William and Mary student William Barry described in 1804 as "daily crumbling into ruins," William was despondent at the prospects for supporting a family there. By the spring of 1803, William had determined that he must resign the chancellorship and seek better opportunities elsewhere.[10]

Deciding where to go after William's resignation as chancellor highlighted the centrality of men's ability to earn money and the decision-making authority that came with that ability. Like many other men in the southern seaboard, William initially considered migration westward to Kentucky as an alternative to legal practice in Virginia. By the time Elizabeth and William married, land was scarce in Tidewater Maryland and Virginia. The "disposition to emigrate" swept the Tidewater in the early nineteenth century, sending a steady stream of migrants to the south and west. The cheap lands to the west, William thought with many other young men in the economically declining seaboard, offered unparalleled opportunities for men of ambition. "Ten years of life would do but little here," William thought, "[but] in Kentucky they might and probably would make my family affluent." William wrote several letters asking his male friends to validate his optimistic assessment of the several ways to make and invest money in Kentucky: law practice, planting, and "commercial speculations."[11]

Although migration to the southwestern frontier was, as one historian expressed it, "a family venture," it was a venture that was directed by men. Although many men, including William Wirt, validated their desire to migrate in terms of their responsibilities to their families, migration also put a strain on relationships. Southern men who migrated to the frontier might earn money to support their families, but many placed more emphasis on the autonomy and independence of the frontier. There, freed from the restraints and demands of kinfolk, some southern men relished the opportunity to "live like fighting cocks." They gambled with their families' fortunes, and while some succeeded beyond their wildest dreams, others failed miserably. William, in consultation with other young men from the declining Tidewater region, was enthusiastic about the frontier's prospects for his own independence and financial success as well as the potential benefits to the Wirts' growing family. What he hoped to find in Kentucky, he told Dabney Carr, was "a support for [his] family independent of the world and of [his] own life." William's comments suggested that for some southern men, earning power—whether in business or planting—could provide the basis for a revived patriarchy in which men had both the responsibility for caring for their dependents (women, children, and slaves) and the right to control them.[12]

In the Wirts' case, however, the patriarchy of earning power was blunted both by William's commitment to pleasing his young wife and by Elizabeth's parents. Sometime during the preparations for his explorations, William discovered that Elizabeth did not share his excitement at the prospect of fabulous wealth in a faraway land. Like the majority of southern white women, Elizabeth preferred familiar surroundings, the support of relatives, and reasonable comfort to the mere possibility of financial rewards in strange and uncomfortable surroundings. Most southern women felt constrained to keep silent about their objections; others were overruled by their husbands or other male relatives. However, Elizabeth was more fortunate. One night during the planning stages,

William awoke and "found her in tears, and after much importunity drew from her an acknowledgement that her distress proceeded from the idea of such a distant and most probably final separation from her parents and family."[13]

Elizabeth's desire to be near her parents and family surely attested to the close kinship ties of Tidewater families, but the migration episode also demonstrated the ability of women's kin to check their son-in-law's financial authority with their own power of the purse. During the spring of 1803, Colonel Gamble wrote to the Wirts to invite Elizabeth to stay with her parents while William visited Kentucky to investigate possible settlement sites, allowing her to visit with her mother "during a possible eventual period"—her first childbirth. Possibly Elizabeth communicated to her father her unhappiness at the planned migration. Although Gamble had originally offered his cautious approval of William's plan, he now made it clear that he would not assist his son-in-law financially in the move, even in so small a way as allowing his name to be used as security on a loan to finance the trip. Crestfallen, William felt that "the details as well as the whole project" now had to be "suspended for some months at least, perhaps for some years." When Littleton Waller Tazewell, a Norfolk lawyer, urged William to move there and share the abundant practice with him, William made up his mind to move to Norfolk.[14]

Norfolk seemed the ideal location for the steady income William desired. Founded in 1680, it was early established as a port city dominated by merchants and mariners. By the early nineteenth century, Norfolk was a major point of transshipment between Virginia's wheat fields and the northern flour mills, leading to an increase in shipbuilding. In the opening decade of the nineteenth century it was a happy location for its growing professional and artisan classes, and William hoped that membership in this group would bring him an income more suited to his new responsibilities as a provider for a family.[15]

Although the Wirts abandoned the plan of migration to the frontier (it was never resurrected), William's earning power continued to be the most significant factor in their selection of a new home. Before moving to Norfolk, William traveled between Williamsburg, Norfolk, and Suffolk to explore the possibilities of making the circuit in the Norfolk area: traveling from court to court to pick up business, chiefly from businessmen involved in the shipping trades. For William, the success of this experiment was defined by its potential for supporting a growing family. Recounting the trip to his friend Dabney Carr, William gleefully wrote, "I am assured, and I have every reason to beleive [sic] it, that my annual income will be 1200£—on one half of which I can maintain my family, even were it much larger than it is."[16]

Although William often referred to maintaining his family in letters to his male friends, the Wirts' Norfolk home served as the headquarters of the newlyweds' first working partnership for their family's support. William conducted an extended search for a house that would accommodate his legal practice. The house that he selected, "altho built for a private family, ha[d] until lately been occupied by the bank of Norfolk." For William, this was ideal. "This house from having been the office of the bank, as well as from its convenience to the great throng & press of business, is sufficiently public for my profession; & that room in the house, which was originally used as the bank room, will do for my office," he concluded. In addition to providing space for William's legal practice, the Wirts' Norfolk house had ample space for household production. A full cellar was completely finished, divided into "six or seven apartments—among them two kitchens, a cellar for liquor, a room for coal, another for wood &c." Although initially William had worried that Elizabeth would object to the "inconvenience" of having the office within the Wirts' residence, in practice this location proved to be a physical manifestation of the Wirts' belief that William's legal practice was only one part of the complex of productive activities that kept the Wirts' household going.[17]

For the Wirts, housekeeping was a cooperative enterprise to which both men and women contributed. Until the mid- to late nineteenth century, housekeeping indicated a set of tasks directed toward the support of the family, rather than the maintenance of the home. This was a project in which both cash-earning and cash-saving activities were important. William's comments on keeping house indicated the cooperative nature of the Wirts' domestic economy. When the Wirts were settled in their Norfolk home in January 1804, William announced with satisfaction that he and Elizabeth had "just got to House Keeping once more" and hoped to do well.[18]

Elizabeth and William cooperated in keeping house in a variety of ways. One of the most significant ways in which they shared responsibility for their family economy was to exchange legal and household services. Although William assumed primary responsibility for legal work and Elizabeth was in charge of household work, these activities often were interwoven so closely that it was difficult to distinguish between them. Soon after they moved to Norfolk, the Wirts established a pattern of ongoing exchange of advice, information, cash, goods, and services. They exchanged letters filled with copious "memoranda" that revealed the interconnections between their work, even during their separations. While Elizabeth relied on her husband to supply her with cash for household purchases and with household assistance, William depended on her to keep his legal papers in order and to supervise his legal assistants. William's law clerks were paid in both professional services (legal training) and household ones (room and board). Although these young men were William's employees, they worked for the Wirts, not just for him, rendering both professional and household assistance. In 1804, when Elizabeth's brother John worked and lived in the Wirts' household, William asked her to direct "brother Jack" to have "the office clean'd out & the books arranged therein" and also to see about purchasing a straw mat for the floors for the warm summer months. Unrelated men who did not share a household with the Wirts were also expected to work for Elizabeth as well as for William. In 1806 William sent word for another clerk, Parker, to attend to a variety of legal tasks as well as to buy corn for the Wirts' horses and indeed to do whatever Elizabeth wanted. William's letters from the Wirts' years in Norfolk are a rare insight into the close cooperation that women's invisible partnerships with their husbands could produce between husbands and wives in the early nineteenth century. William recognized his wife's informal partnership by authorizing Elizabeth to manage the family finances. "Consider my money as being perfectly your own," he suggested.[19]

In urging Elizabeth to spend the money he earned in legal fees as she saw fit, William acknowledged that her contributions to the household economy were as necessary as his own, but he also indicated that cash, even when produced by a husband's and wife's joint efforts, was assumed to be men's property. Only by engaging in income-producing or expense-reducing activities on their own could women claim an interest in the family's cash earnings. Elizabeth's work as the mistress of her William's household was her most visible contribution to the family economy. During the Wirts' two years in Norfolk Elizabeth laid the groundwork for productive activities that would reduce their household's dependence on purchased goods and William's always uncertain wages. In the early nineteenth century, these activities remained vital to the domestic economy. One scholar estimated that, based on the cost to replace her services, a middle-class housewife's economic contributions to her household averaged seven hundred dollars annually. At a time when William earned an annual salary of fifteen hundred dollars as the Williamsburg chancellor and considered his legal fees good at five hundred dollars per season in the circuit courts, this was no small sum.[20]

Southern "ladies" were the directors of extensive household production in the antebellum South. As Norfolk resident Anne Ritson expressed it, "Such economists are they, / Money they spare in ev'ry way." The vast amount of labor necessary to run an urban household in the early-nineteenth-century South has yet to be fully appreciated. Life in the new Republic's cities was more rustic than most modern city dwellers can imagine. In the age before refrigeration, items such as milk, butter, eggs, and fresh produce had to be provided by a family's livestock and gardens or purchased daily at the local market. Meat had to be salted or smoked to prevent spoiling. In order to meet these needs, city lots were crowded with cows, chickens, and pigs that roamed between vegetable gardens, fruit trees, and the various outbuildings such as dairies and smokehouses which were used for processing and storing food. Although antebellum houses that have been preserved as museums are rarely accompanied by their outbuildings, historical archaeologists have suggested that until the twentieth century, residences were only one part of an "urban farmstead." As one woman from Petersburg, Virginia, expressed it, housekeeping in Virginia's cities was "a sort of half farming life."[21]

Despite the growing availability of consumer goods, many well-to-do families continued to maintain urban farmsteads in nineteenth-century cities, especially in the South. Indeed, wealthier individuals tended to produce more of their own goods than their less fortunate neighbors. In part this was due to the capital investment needed to build outbuildings, buy and feed livestock, and purchase the tools of household production, such as spinning wheels and looms. In the South, a major investment was purchasing slaves to provide much of the day-to-day labor that a productive household demanded.[22]

Slave labor was essential to the domestic economy of southern households. From the start of their marriage the Wirts had been slaveholders, commencing housekeeping in Williamsburg in 1802 with only one slave. Once assured that his daughter and son-in-law would remain close to home, however, Colonel Gamble expressed his willingness to "give a fatherly assistance" in providing "Necessaries to wards housekeeping." One of these necessities, in his mind, was slave labor; even before the Norfolk house was selected, he encouraged William "to look out . . . for a Boy & a girl fit for Betsys chamber & a driver of her carriage & waiter—and if possible a good Cook also—& I will endeavor to remit you the needful or honor your drafts." With Colonel Gamble's generous assistance, the Wirts assembled a labor force for their Norfolk household which, at its peak in 1806, consisted of five adult slaves and an unspecified number of slave children.[23]

In southern cities, the mistress, rather than the master, was responsible for the day-to-day supervision of slaves. In the Wirt household, thanks to Colonel Gamble's intervention, Elizabeth's needs played a central role in the purchase of slaves as well as the practice of slave ownership. One of the Wirts' three slaves in 1805 had probably been purchased for Elizabeth's particular use following Gamble's 1804 proposal that William collect an old debt due to his father-in-law in the form of "a negro boy or a girl for Betsy." Elizabeth's requirements continued to dictate slave purchases. In 1805 she asked William to "be on the look out for a nurse cook & laundress, in the same woman." In April 1806 her father purchased two new slave women for her use. In 1806, the Wirts' slave force consisted of five adult slaves, two men and three women. The three women were probably the slaves that the tax assessor credited to Elizabeth "Wert," while her husband claimed the two men. In directing William to take a slave "for Betsy" in payment for a debt owed to her father, as well as in purchasing slaves for his daughter directly, Gamble may have intended that his daughter would have official property rights in the slave women who would work most closely with her in household operations.[24]

Slaveholding women in the upper South's cities used slave labor to increase the productiveness and profitability of their household. Slave women supplied most of the skilled and unskilled labor for the Wirts' household operations in Norfolk. Mattresses and carpets, as well as linens and clothing, were produced by even the wealthiest southern women. Typically mistresses and slaves worked side by side at spinning, weaving, and sewing. Particularly in the spring and fall, Elizabeth rallied her captive assistants—sometimes assisted by free white seamstresses hired for the purpose—to transform bolts of material into curtains, linens, carpets, clothing, and bedding appropriate to the season. Although in a less constant way, slave men also shared responsibility for household production. As coachmen, the Wirts' slave men were probably responsible for caring for the Wirts' livestock, an important part of the half-farming life in antebellum cities. While William complained that his two horses were a tremendous expense, the Wirts' other livestock—cows and chickens—provided milk, butter, and eggs for daily consumption as early as 1805. Slave men and women often performed complementary tasks in the household economy. Slave men may have fed the Wirts' animals and cleaned their stalls and pens, but women probably churned the butter and may have done the milking and egg collecting as well. Slave men and women also cooperated in garden-related work. Slave men probably broke in the soil and harvested ripe vegetables, and they would later become the Wirts' chief gardeners, although in Norfolk it was a slave woman who had charge of the garden in 1805. Slave men may have harvested the peas, lettuce, radishes, and other items grown in the Wirts' garden which contributed to year-round consumption as well as fresh produce in the summer. More durable items such as potatoes, carrots, and turnips could be stored in cool dirt cellars dug by slave men. Other fruits and vegetables could be canned, made into preserves, or pickled by Elizabeth and her female slaves.[25]

Overseeing these activities with slaves she held in her own name and often directed in her husband's absence, Elizabeth Wirt enjoyed a greater degree of autonomy than her husband's legal superiority and his description of his wife as mistress of his household suggested. Some studies of slaveholding women in the plantation South have indicated that these mistresses had very limited authority over the slaves and the tasks that were their responsibility. However, the Wirts exhibited a different pattern that may have owed much to their urban lifestyle. While planter men typically directed all the plantation's work—in both the house and the fields—professional men like William spent a great deal of time away from home, which reduced both their authority over and their assistance in the domestic routine. In the Northeast, which was highly urbanized by the antebellum period, the household was considered women's special domain. However, this development was accompanied by what one scholar termed the "pastoralization of housework," in which the reality of domestic production was obscured by romanticized depictions of "woman's sphere" in the home, which was supposedly distinct from men's world of competitiveness and money making. None of these models accurately describe the Wirts' domestic economy. For the Wirts, the household was an arena of production. Elizabeth was the principal director of all household activities, with the authority to make decisions about production and consumption. Occasionally, just as Elizabeth assisted William with his legal work, he assisted her with housework. Elizabeth might be mistress of her husband's household, but William was Elizabeth's helpmate in household production.[26]

William's letters to Elizabeth in October 1804 indicated that he bowed to her judgment on matters pertaining to their household economy. William shuttled back and forth between courts in Williamsburg and Suffolk while Elizabeth visited her parents in Richmond, but he made time to ready the Norfolk house for winter and Elizabeth's second parturition. "I wish," William explained to Elizabeth in late October, "to have every thing so fixed, as that when you come down to Norfolk, you may have nothing to do but to amuse yourself with Miss Laura [the Wirts' first child] and your books; so as that, for a month or two, your mind may be perfectly at ease." With this goal in mind, he set about the many tasks of preparing a household for winter. Consulting Elizabeth frequently for advice, William made arrangements to buy a dairy cow, stockpiled firewood and coal, made some improvements on the house, and stipulated to supply the household with meat for the upcoming year. In all these matters William requested his wife's opinion of his actions and kept her abreast of the minutest details, requesting Elizabeth to give directions and express preferences in her next letter to him. William indicated his wife's dominance over the Wirt household when he summed up his activities: "I hope you will have your home in better trim than it was when you left it."[27]

Although he ceded authority over household operations to Elizabeth, William did not expect her to have sole responsibility for them. In his eagerness to please his bride, he early established a pattern of acting as her assistant in housekeeping, just as she acted as his assistant in his legal work. In the spring of 1805, Elizabeth again stayed with her parents in Richmond while William attended to spring housecleaning in Norfolk. "The house shall be all put in sweet order, from the garret to the cellar, so as to render your return [to Norfolk] as tolerable as possible," he promised. In May he proudly informed Elizabeth, "Our house looks quite sweet—the floors have been well rub'd—the carpets removed up stairs—the furniture in good order & shining"; in short, all was ready for Elizabeth's return.[28]

Despite the advances the Wirts had made in establishing a working household in Norfolk, William continued to emphasize the household's dependence on his wages. Since the move to Norfolk, however, his earnings had been limited by the need to leave town during the lucrative fall courts. The Wirts, like most well-to-do southerners in coastal cities, vacationed inland and upland during the summer and autumn months, which brought mosquitoes, yellow fever, and malaria to the southern seaboard. After one summer in Richmond, however, William was reluctant to lose another season's wages. He was unwilling, he wrote to his mentor, Benjamin Edwards, to be "driv[en] . . . from [his] business into annual exile." In the summer of 1805, William decided not to accompany Elizabeth and the children to Montevideo, the Amherst County, Virginia, plantation of Elizabeth's sister, Nancy, and her husband, William H. Cabell. Instead, he returned to Norfolk to attend to business matters. For William, legal practice was both his priority and his prerogative. Despite Elizabeth's argument that the possible "recompense" did not justify the danger to William's health, he refused to join her in the countryside. Although he left Norfolk when Elizabeth's advice was echoed by his physician, he refused to go farther than Richmond on the grounds that he was awaiting a letter from a prospective client.[29]

Disappointed in her inability to deter her husband from viewing his legal career as the pivot upon which all major decisions were based, the following year Elizabeth convinced him that the couple should leave Norfolk and move to Richmond. Her enthusiasm may have been attributable in part to her hope that, with her father's help, she would be able to expand her role in the Wirts' domestic economy to complement her husband's local law practice. For William, Elizabeth's assurances that his legal business would not suffer by the move were no doubt given extra weight by Colonel Gamble's hints that he thought of "building a house and improving a very beautiful lot" for the couple in Richmond. Both Elizabeth and William hoped to improve their economic situation; furthermore, there was a possibility that their new home would offer them a new opportunity to realize a more equal partnership in which both marriage partners would serve as each other's helpmate. By July 1806 the Wirts were readying themselves for the move to Richmond, where they would live for the next eleven years.[30]

"The untumultuous joys of domestic life": Home and Family

Although Elizabeth's letters before and immediately after the Wirts' marriage have not survived, William maintained that they were an "impressive model of conjugal love," and he told his bride that he was "charmed" to read of her eagerness to join him in "the untumultuous joys of domestic life."[31] Home and family life were important aspects of conjugal love for the Wirts, but while both were committed to what William called the untumultuous joys of domestic life, they experienced that life differently. Elizabeth and William failed to establish a true partnership as parents during their time in Norfolk. William's frequent absences from home on business and the constant demands of childbearing and child care—including breast-feeding—made Elizabeth the primary parent. Different parenting responsibilities caused the Wirts to view home and family in different ways. Elizabeth, who bore most of the responsibility for home and family life, rarely waxed poetic on the untumultuous joys of motherhood. William made attempts to share the joys of domestic life equally, but he did not bear his share of the burdens of domestic responsibility.

Elizabeth and William Wirt expected to begin a family soon after their marriage. They married at a time when ideas about reproduction and child rearing were shifting. One of the hallmarks of the modern family, which had its origins in the United States in this period, was to treasure children as the physical manifestation of a couple's mutual love and affection. Some families who adopted these attitudes toward children also began to restrict family size, a development that scholars have linked to the new ideals of an affectionate family which paralleled the rise of companionate marriage. Because controlling the number of children in a family liberated women from a constant state of pregnancy, some scholars have interpreted this shift as a significant gain for women. One historian, investigating women's success in convincing their husbands to cooperate with them in controlling reproduction, coined the phrase "domestic feminism" to describe women's growing influence over the bedroom. Elizabeth's thoughts on fertility and family size do not survive, but William's letters indicate that the Wirts did not discuss birth control. Instead, like colonial Americans, William referred to the Wirts' growing family in vague terms such as "a little groupe" or the "dear little children." Although some well-to-do Virginians—including some in the Wirts' social circle—joined their counterparts in the Northeast and the Middle Atlantic in limiting or spacing childbirths, the Wirts' expectations of a large family may have been especially common in the South. The demographic transition, in which the fertility of white women fell by half between 1800 and 1900, was delayed in the South, where birthrates exceeded the national birthrate. In this context, identifying children as pledges of love increased the emotional significance of childbearing without reducing women's demands of pregnancy and childbirth.[32]

By June 1803, William and Elizabeth were expecting their first child. Elizabeth's letters from this time have not been preserved. Her husband's letters clearly demonstrated that he fully embraced sentimental notions of the family. "Blessed as I am at present," he wrote to Elizabeth, "I look forward with confidence to scenes of stronger, or at least of more diversified bliss—when we shall have another object to share our caresses and, if possible, to make us still dearer to each other." Even though modern ideals of family life celebrated the arrival of children as a significant event in a companionate couple's marriage, childbearing remained a female ritual in nineteenth-century America. Women were the chief actors in the childbearing experience; the woman in labor called female relatives, friends, neighbors, and midwives to her bedside to provide physical and emotional support. Although male doctors gained influence in the birthing room in the first half of the nineteenth century, female attendants continued to fill the room where a laboring woman was confined. Elizabeth followed this practice when she traveled to Richmond to be with her mother while she awaited her first childbirth. On September 3, 1803, the Wirts welcomed their first child, a daughter they named Laura Henrietta, into the world. The contrast between William's idyllic vision of conjugal and parental bliss and Elizabeth's experience of childbearing as a female ritual and responsibility would grow along with the Wirts' family.[33]

Traditional women's celebrations of childbearing placed the pregnant woman and the new mother at the center, but the modern notion of children as proof of a couple's love focused on the future or newborn infant and on the married couple. When William described children as "the sweet pledges of our love," he revealed just how much his ideas of companionship depended on a large family. New ideas about the significance of childbearing integrated men into family life, but they also made a woman's childbirth an event that her husband could claim as a token of her love. Some historians have suggested that southern men expected the arrival of heirs at frequent intervals as a validation of their manhood and as a source of future economic security. At the same time that companionate marriage and family invested the arrival of children with sentimentality, childbirth also had significance as a wife's gift to her husband. Whether as tokens of love or tributes to a patriarch, children were vital to nineteenth-century southern families. When William told Dabney Carr that the Wirts' "sweet" infant gratified him "most exquisitely," he revealed his attachment to the modern, sentimental family, but he also hinted that, with so much resting on the regular arrival of children, limiting family size would not be a priority for the new parents.[34]

Elizabeth had primary responsibility for caring for the sweet infant that William found so exquisitely gratifying. One important task that fathers could not share with mothers in nineteenth-century America was breast-feeding. Bottle-feeding was an undesirable alternative to breast-feeding in the antebellum South. There was no refrigeration to keep substitutes for breast milk fresh and free from disease. Furthermore, medical journals and female-authored advice books for mothers printed throughout the United States urged mothers to breast-feed their infants for their own happiness as well as for their children's health. All of these experts adopted a new idea that would become popular in nineteenth-century America: women were not simply the primary parents of young children, as had been true since colonial times, but they were also the best parents, for whom there was no adequate substitute. For all these reasons, and contrary to popular myths of slave mammies, most slave-owning women reserved the task of nursing for themselves where possible.[35]

The close mother-child bond that was fostered by breast-feeding excluded and excused men from caring for newborns. Breast-feeding demanded mothers' constant attention. Elizabeth habitually shared her bed with the Wirts' younger children to be available to them around the clock. Meanwhile, only days after Laura's birth, William was called away to Williamsburg on legal business. Writing home, he wondered: "How is my Betsey at this moment employed? Is she not sitting up in her bed quite cheery and pressing our precious babe to her breast?" Probably William correctly deduced his wife's activities, although it is doubtful that Elizabeth was as cheery as she had been before her husband departed.[36]

Laura's birth heightened the Wirts' attachment to the untumultuous joys of domestic life. It also sharpened the distinction between Elizabeth's maternal duties and William's responsibilities as a father. While Elizabeth held the Wirts' precious baby to her breast, William intensified his efforts to earn cash for the little family's support during the early years of the Wirts' marriage. In 1803, he resolved that his prominent position as chancellor in Williamsburg was worthless if it did not guarantee "blessed independence" for his family. "Although a man be full of honor," he remarked to Carr, "his stomach may be Empty." William's contemplations indicated that he was ready to renounce the lure of public fame so important to older definitions of southern manhood in favor of a new definition of masculinity which centered on providing for a family. The importance William attached to providing for his family was the key to what one scholar called a nineteenth-century "trend toward limited fatherhood." While in the seventeenth and eighteenth centuries the father was the family authority, "now, being fully a father meant being separated from one's children for a considerable part of every working day."[37]

William recognized the strain placed on him by attempting both to provide for his family and to care for the Wirts' children, and he attempted to reconcile these contradictory impulses with hopes and plans for the future. He would be required to "go to the Bar, and bend all the powers of [his] soul and body to the profession for fifteen years," he predicted, before he could devote the "latter days" of his "old age" to preparing the Wirts' children for "the theatre of life." This was all the more reason to hasten his accumulation of wealth, he thought, calling rapid economic advancement his most "weighty consideration." "Ten years of life would do but little here," he wrote to Carr, but "in Kentucky they might and probably would make my family affluent." After the Kentucky scheme was abandoned, William persisted in his vision of reconciling breadwinning with active parenting through early retirement. "O! my dear," he exclaimed in a letter to Elizabeth, "how sweet it will be, ten [or] fifteen years hence to retire with our children . . . How sweet to sit in a little groupe . . . and read to each other, first ourselves, then our children, by turns— or else to talk of virtue, religion, innocence, peace and happiness, while our dear little children listen, & feel their minds & hearts open." William hoped to share the joys and duties of family life with Elizabeth, but for him, this could only be achieved after he had attained "blessed independence" through his labor away from home. In the meantime, home and family would mean very different things for Elizabeth and William Wirt.[38]

During their Norfolk residence, Elizabeth's repeated and difficult pregnancies highlighted the Wirts' eagerness to share in these most intimate moments and their fundamental inability to do so. On January 31, 1805, Elizabeth delivered her first son, named Robert Gamble after his grandfather. This time Elizabeth remained in Norfolk for parturition, but once again she relied on "the ladies" in the neighborhood to assist her. William, like some men in the antebellum North, remained nearby, postponing a planned trip to Washington, D.C. Perhaps, like some middle-class northern fathers, he sent for the midwife or doctor and escorted the female attendants into the birthing room; he may have been present there himself. However, although William did not intentionally distance himself from childbirth, he felt helpless to aid Elizabeth, who was "very sick" and in danger of dying. The only way he could show his love was to await news of her health before his departure; "I may never see her again," he worried.[39]

The painful realities of domestic life in the early-nineteenth-century South threatened to drive a wedge between Elizabeth and William Wirt. In some Virginia families, crises like Elizabeth's nearly fatal illness in early 1805 inspired husbands and wives to cooperate in abstinence or another form of birth control to prevent further threats to the woman's health. For some reason, however, William appeared insensitive to the dangers pregnancy posed to his wife's well-being once the immediate danger had passed. On September 17, 1805—less than eight months after Robert's birth—she was confined again, giving birth to "a healthy, sprightly & beautiful child," a girl the Wirts called Emily. The timing indicated that, despite Elizabeth's fragile health, the Wirts resumed sexual activity almost immediately following Robert's birth. Three pregnancies in less than three years seriously compromised twenty-one-year-old Elizabeth's health. Despite going to her parents' house for the fall, she experienced another difficult childbirth. "Mrs. W. has been more indisposed this fall than she has ever before been for the same length of time," William worried, admitting he had feared for her life. Elizabeth survived, but Emily died shortly after her birth. Like other nineteenth-century women, Elizabeth was sustained by female rituals in this crisis. Women in early and antebellum America commonly were in charge of bathing, clothing, and mourning for stillborn children and those who died as young infants. Meanwhile, William again left Elizabeth to attend the Williamsburg courts. His letter of consolation in early October was an effort to ease his wife's grief and to hold out a promise of better times to come, times in which the Wirts could share the sorrows as well as the joys of domestic life. "I fear my Betsey you are too much depressed and dispirited," worried William. "Let us endeavour, . . . my love, to kiss the rod with a good grace; relying with firm trust that brighter & sweeter hours are at hand."[40]

Although pregnancy, childbirth, and breast-feeding were activities that Elizabeth and William could not share, children's health care was a potential arena for the Wirts to enjoy mutuality. During the summer of 1804, for example, William joined his wife and daughter in Richmond, where Laura had been taken in the hope that the healthier surroundings would speed her recovery from whooping cough. Apparently Elizabeth, several months into her second pregnancy, was unable to breast-feed Laura. Instead, several slave nurses assisted with Laura's care. It was common for slave and slaveholding women to exchange such services in the Old South. Some scholars have suggested that black and white women's mutual responsibility to care for children helped to bridge the hierarchical divisions of southern society. However, this sort of female interracial cooperation ran counter to the precepts of affectionate family life which the Wirts prized. As nineteenth-century families became more child-centered and the malleability of children became doctrine, many well-to-do families became reluctant to leave child care to servants. Child care manuals proclaimed that servants could not be trusted with the important tasks of caring for the health, morality, and education of impressionable children; instead, parents—primarily mothers—should be the ones entrusted with the care of young children. Although advice books in New England emphasized maternal care, the ideals of companionate marriage and affectionate family life led some men to expand their role in infant care. Fathers in the Old South often valued their role as caretakers of children's health, and many men considered themselves skilled domestic physicians. The Wirts' conscious attempt to limit their children's contact with slaves and to emphasize their own role in child care sometimes prompted William to become involved in family health care. During the summer, William accused one of Laura's slave "nurses" with endangering her charge's health by "contriv[ing] to spoil her milk . . . so that every time the poor girl sucked the milk was *regurgitated* and brought with it whatever medicine or aliment had been previously administered." This had brought a return of Laura's illness, which had required William "to sit up with her all night for several nights passed." William's outrage and his response— to spend many "solitary hour[s]" at his daughter's bedside—indicated the high value that new notions of proper family life could place on fathers' close involvement in parenthood.[41]

William's business travels usually prevented him from participating fully in family life, however. Caring for the children's health, like nursing, was primarily Elizabeth's responsibility. During the fall of 1803, one-month-old Laura suffered serious gastric distress, requiring Elizabeth's around-the-clock attention. "Ah! my dear; you begin already to feel the inquietudes of a mother," William noted, "those drawbacks on the pure bliss of a parent." William's letter indicated that only women were exposed to the inquietudes of caring for small children; men could enjoy the pure bliss of parenthood. Although William wrote anxious letters to Elizabeth to guide her through Robert's teething (a time antebellum southerners viewed as critical in a child's health, in part because it coincided with weaning) and to commiserate with Elizabeth over Laura's "dry feverish lips" during the fall of 1805, the responsibility for administering the heroic remedies recommended by nineteenth-century medical practitioners fell to Elizabeth during her husband's protracted absences. William tried to share his wife's concern, but he often succeeded only in adding to her workload as he filled his letters with recommendations that she dose Robert with "a little calomel [a poisonous mercury extract], for worms," and keep him updated on the minutest details of the children's health.[42]

The Wirts attempted to surmount the obstacle his work away from home posed to involvement in family affairs through their copious correspondence. Elizabeth gave William detailed descriptions of the children's health, appearance, first words, and activities. Such exchanges allowed William to return to his family in his imagination when it was not possible to do so in person. "The picture which you draw of yourself and our sweet babe riding out together and alternately kissing my letter," he wrote in response to a letter he received from Elizabeth in 1804, "is to me more lovely and affecting than any which painters or poets can draw." Elizabeth's pictures of family life strengthened William's desire for family togetherness. Her descriptions of their "little charmer," Laura, were especially affecting, combining idyllic, romanticized descriptions of family life with an emphasis on the void created by William's absence. "That other picture so simple, so natural, so tender, of our infant talking of my being 'gone' with her little head upraised, and her expressive countenance how does it awaken all the parent within me," William declared. Diverted from his legal work by Elizabeth's moving prose, William resolved to strive harder to meet the expectations of family togetherness he shared with his wife. Upon his reunion with Elizabeth, William hoped to take a more active role in being a parent to Laura, who would soon stop breast-feeding and would thus be less dependent on her mother. "Kiss her dear little mouth for me," he directed in November, "and learn her to walk and talk as fast as possible, that she may be out of the way by Christmass [sic], so as that her papa can nurse her."[43]

William continued to find it difficult to nurse the Wirts' children, but as they grew, he found that he was able to establish a role for himself encouraging them to walk and talk. The Wirts' frequent separations meant that childhood education would be the most significant way in which they could cooperate in child rearing. William's parenting activities—writing letters, sending kisses, and bringing presents home—were long distance and sporadic. However, these tokens of affection were destined to become the linchpin of the Wirts' child-rearing strategy. The Wirts' preferred methods of child rearing were clearly influenced by John Locke's 1693 book on the subject, *Some Thoughts Concerning Education.* Lockean thinking, which urged parents to treasure childhood as a time to impress virtue, industry, and reason on the receptive minds of the young, was central to the concept of modern child rearing which many well-to-do families embraced throughout the nation in the revolutionary and postrevolutionary years. Balancing love and guilt, the Wirts would attempt to produce autonomous yet self-controlled adults by making parental approval their chief reward—or, when withheld, their harshest punishment.[44]

Modern child rearing placed a premium on lavish displays of affection to motivate children to please their parents and on careful, methodical lessons that nurtured children's inherent rationality. William's love for letter writing and Elizabeth's constant presence at home were the ideal combination for the joint enterprise of modern child rearing. The Wirts followed Locke's advice to begin to mold their children as soon as possible. In 1805, William suggested, "As our Laura can talk so plain, suppose you begin to teach her the alphabet." While William offered advice on textbook selection and method, Elizabeth worked closely with Laura to help her learn the lessons that would earn her father's praise. When Robert was born, William evinced the optimistic attitude toward infancy and childhood which was typical of modern child rearing. Even while still a baby, Robert seemed a budding genius to his proud papa. Robert, wrote William to Benjamin Edwards, "is certainly a *very* handsome child, and if there be any truth in physiognomy, a fellow whose native sheet of intellectual paper, is of as fine a texture and as lustrous a white as the fond heart even of a parent can desire." The way to take advantage of such native talents was to foster a strong and affectionate relationship between parents and children. Once this connection was established, according to the theory of modern child rearing, children would willingly obey their parents out of love (or guilt). Unreserved love was a vital part of the Wirts' parenting, and in this part of child nurture, at least, William's letters offered ample scope for long-distance parenthood. "Kiss them for me three times a piece," he wrote in one typical letter in 1805, "and make them sensible if you can that they have a father who loves them beyond all the earth except their angel mother."[45]

Despite the Wirts' conviction that they both were integral members of the affectionate family circle, they participated in domestic life in different ways. Their perceptions of home were also different. For William, correspondence with Elizabeth and their children and visits home were occasional breaks from his labors in court. William's intermittent and limited involvement in family matters allowed him to identify the home with leisure. Domestic life, for William, promised a total cessation of work. He confided to Carr, "It would be my study so to unite my dignity with my interest as, in my old age, . . . [to] have amassed a sufficiency of wealth, to enable me to retire into the lap of my family, and give up my latter days to ease, to quiet, [and] to conjugal and parental bliss." Dreams like these reaffirmed William's commitment to fatherhood, but they also relegated an equal role in child rearing to the distant future. For the time being, such dreams served to increase William's commitment to work away from home. Only wealth and retirement would permit him to enjoy "the beloved circle of his family" on a permanent basis.[46]

When William wrote with relief of the prospect of retiring from his legal practice to join Elizabeth and their children, he anticipated the attitudes of future generations of urban Americans who would draw a strict line of demarcation between the male-dominated workplace, where marketplace competitiveness ruled supreme, and the home, supposedly protected from the incursion of selfishness and presided over primarily by a loving wife and mother. For William, being with Elizabeth and their children was an opportunity to retreat from the company of the "villains" and "the common hord [sic] of men" who inhabited the world beyond the walls of the home and to enter "the beloved circle of his family" and join those who were "fair" and "dear" to him.[47]

Elizabeth experienced family life in a different way. Because her own labor was located in the household, the ease and retirement that her husband identified with being at home were in short supply for her. Elizabeth suffered the pangs of childbirth, recovered from her pregnancies with difficulty, breast-fed the children despite her own weakened condition, and dosed the children with medicine—all of which William, by virtue of his sex and his absences from home, was spared. As the children's primary caregiver during her husband's absences, Elizabeth rarely echoed her husband's praises for the virtues of the untumultuous joys of domestic life. When she did express sentiments in accord with her husband's idyllic view of family life, Elizabeth idealized family togetherness, not leisure. Elizabeth wrote "picturesque" letters to her husband about the children designed to "bring [him] thereby in person, back to the white house," as he characterized a letter she wrote in 1805. "Believe me I feel all its force," he wrote in response. In the letters in which she echoed her husband's sentimental views on domestic bliss, Elizabeth clearly indicated that she wished to share the responsibilities, as well as the joys, of parenting with her husband.[48]

Elizabeth and William's disagreement over his decision to remain in Nor-folk during the summer of 1805 brought their fundamentally different under-standings of home and family into sharp relief. William insisted that he was deeply attached to the family group, but he also recognized that his claim to parenthood was tenuous. "Kiss my dear Children for me half a dozen times a piece," he requested, "and don't let Laura forget that she has a father—How much I long to see you & her & my little mouth-spreading boy, it is not in my power to describe. I think I love you all ten thousand times more than I ever did in my life." Despite his claim that he longed to be with Elizabeth and their children, William refused to join them. Elizabeth criticized her husband for this seeming contradiction. She argued that William's most important duty as a father was active involvement in the children's lives. Responding to her husband's explanation that his legal practice did not permit him to leave Nor-folk, she demanded: "You say your clients expect it of you—but my husband, will they provide for your children—guide, instruct, and raise them to hap-piness and virtue?" William, who thought of home as a delightful retreat from his more important responsibilities as a provider, rebuffed his wife's claim. Joining Elizabeth at the expense of a legal fee "wd. be acting very little like a man who wished to do his duty in providing for his children," he reasoned, adding, "And after a thousand heart breaking sigh[s] I have determined to do my duty in spi[te] of my feelings."[49]

When the Wirts moved to Richmond in the spring of 1806, they hoped that their new situation would allow them to reconcile duty with feelings. Elizabeth urged her husband to consider the advantages of both health and business in Richmond. Although her emphasis on business partially validated William's preoccupation with earning money, her motivation may also have been to find lucrative employment closer to home for her husband. After the move, she would use financial incentives to urge her husband to spend more time at home with her and the children. William hoped that Richmond might offer him another way to reconcile his responsibilities as a provider with his dreams of domestic bliss. After a year or two, he hoped to be able to provide for the family with a local law practice. As they prepared for the move, both Elizabeth and William looked forward with renewed enthusiasm to family togetherness and to sharing the duties and pleasures of domestic life. As William expressed it, "Home is still the place for happiness."[50]

"Domestic joys . . . encircle me": Love and Marriage

"But for the domestic joys which encircle me," William often proclaimed, he would be wretched.[51] Despite William's praise for domesticity, domestic life was imbued with profoundly different meanings for the Wirts. Domestic responsibilities truly encircled Elizabeth, who devoted her entire life to her husband, children, and home, but domestic joys merely supported William, whose life extended beyond the relationship he shared with Elizabeth to courts and boardinghouses in distant cities. The Wirts recognized that these circumstances imperiled their hopes of mutual companionship and love in marriage. During their years in Norfolk, Elizabeth and William expressed discontent with their present situation and made plans to bring their household, family, and marriage into closer conformity with their ideals of companionship.

From the very beginning of their marriage, Elizabeth and William found it difficult to reconcile their high ideals of mutual companionship with the prolonged separations created by William's career as an itinerant lawyer. Only a little more than a month after the wedding ceremony, William left Elizabeth with her parents in Richmond to return to his duties in Williamsburg. He assured his bride that this early separation, far from being a harbinger of things to come, was to be the last time that the newlyweds would be apart for an extended period of time. "I confidently hope that when we meet again we shall part no more on this side of eternity—at least, not for such an awful length of time . . . I fear not that my duties will ever again tear me from my Betsey's arms," William wrote hopefully. "Altho' sweet is the consciousness of discharging our duties, yet sweet too ah! how sweet was the embrace from which those duties tore me!"[52]

By identifying his sweet duties as companionate marriage and a respectable income, William expressed common aspirations for Virginians in the early Republic. But, in the course of the nineteenth century, these twin goals became increasingly opposed to each other. The ideal of companionate marriage required men to value affectionate family relationships and share domestic concerns with their wives, yet bringing in cash dictated lengthy daily or periodic absences from home and consequent isolation from the women and children who remained there. William Wirt was one of a new generation of men who experienced what one scholar termed the "dual nature of nineteenth-century manhood" in which men had conflicting duties associated with work and home.[53]

William was eager to reconcile these divergent claims. At first, he attempted to use his correspondence to conceal the gap between his daily life away from home and his commitment to sharing his life with Elizabeth. While his actions attested to the primacy of his legal career, his letters emphasized that Elizabeth's claim was stronger than that of worldly rewards. William's letters to Elizabeth in the early years of their marriage repeatedly contrasted the sweet rewards of love and marriage with the demanding duties of wage earning. Awaiting Elizabeth's arrival in Williamsburg in the fall of 1802, he showered his wife with flowery declarations of love and promised that they would soon be together forever. "My Betsey! O! my Betsey! how does your letter penetrate me!" he cried. "Ah! heaven! why is she not now in my arms, in my bosom? Am I forever doom'd to grasp only a shadow?—but no, dearest love—that is my comfort; we shall meet to part no more," he sighed happily. William assured his bride that he valued his relationship with her more highly than anything else. "While at home with you where else shall I ever think of going to look for happiness?" he demanded. "You fill all my wishes, all my desires all my hopes and affections so compleatly that, with you, it seems a matter of almost indifference with me whether I ever again see another face upon earth."[54]

Despite his assurances that Elizabeth fulfilled all his dreams completely, William was not indifferent to other matters. Her company, he wrote, was his reward for fulfilling his official duties. "After groping through the dark and disgusting mazes of human fraud and villainy, how delightful to change the scene and turn to the fairest, the dearest object of the creation . . . my Betsey." Despite the contrast that William often drew between his dark and disgusting law practice and his fairest and dearest wife, he began to identify his commitment to her with his ability to earn wages. This permitted him to pursue remuneration away from home and sanctified his lifelong preoccupation with money by redefining it as proof of his devotion to Elizabeth. "The most towering glory becomes dust in the balance when poised against the happiness of my beloved girl," he wrote in explanation of his decision to renounce the Williamsburg chancellorship in 1803. William's definition of his wife's happiness was economic; he believed that only by providing for Elizabeth's financial welfare could he demonstrate his love for her. When he laid plans for migration to Kentucky in early 1803, William again made rapid material advancement a prerequisite for blissful married life. Migration, he told Elizabeth, would allow him to retire at a young age to "the sweet arms and bosom of his Betsey." He added, "Until that period arrives my dear, . . . we should be resigned to the will of providence" and to the separations created by his own "professional carreer [sic]."[55]

Because she burned her early letters, Elizabeth's feelings in the opening years of her marriage were filtered through her husband's enthusiasm. However, William's correspondence indicates that she did not accept her husband's rationalizations. Even William's ebullient attitude toward migration could not obscure his wife's despair at the proposed removal to Kentucky. Elizabeth, who already had experienced one prolonged separation from her new husband, may have anticipated that his new plans—which involved ten to fifteen years of intense labor—would take him away from her for an even longer period. Her objections to the move indicate that she did not agree with her husband that a decade or more of hardship was the best way to attain conjugal and parental bliss. In the midst of his preparations for westward migration, William discovered that Elizabeth privately was opposed to his plans. Although in her discussions of the matter with William she "had consented to do it from the dictates of reason and judgment, . . . her heart and affections secretly revolted against the measure," he told Benjamin Edwards years later. William insisted that concern for his wife's feelings was the most important factor in his decision to remain in Virginia. "This discovery," he recalled, "and the manner of it would have been decisive with me against the removal." William's emphasis on the manner of his discovery suggested that his wife's initial unwillingness to reveal her true feelings to him affected him deeply. Nineteenth-century courting couples commonly conceived of their union as a spiritual one in which their very souls mingled. For newlyweds to conceal their feelings from each other, therefore, was a sign that something was seriously wrong. Upset by the suggestion that he had failed to respect or even to learn Elizabeth's preferences, William resolved to make her happiness his priority. "Fortune and Fame are indeed considerations of great weight with me," he exclaimed, "but they are light, compared with the happiness of the best of wives."[56]

Following the migration incident, William attempted to assure Elizabeth that he shared her conviction that companionship and love—not financial gain—were the desiderata of marriage. A relationship of love, he insisted, was a surer source of happiness than wealth. "Let other married persons seek happiness in splendor & ostentation," he scoffed. "Silently locked in the arms of my angel wife, and hearing nought but the softly breathed and thrilling voice of her love, I envy not the gorgeous pomp of wealth and the clamor and bustle of the gay—envy! I look on them with pity." While the Wirts laid plans to move to Norfolk and Elizabeth traveled to Richmond to prepare for Laura's birth, William declared his intention to live up to the highest ideals of companionate marriage. "Now *all alone and aloney*, I draw out my writing desk and sit down to pour out my heart to you," he began. "Ah! my dear—I do indeed love you, even more than I had myself supposed—you are all in all to me—I cannot endure this absence—a whole fortnight!" William urged Elizabeth to recall that this trial was merely temporary. "For my own part," he concluded, "I am inspired with the most delightful presentiment of success."[57]

Although William hoped for success in his marriage, he also desired success in his legal career. "I now live for *you* only my dear," he declared in the spring of 1803. But despite this vow, William devoted most of his time to work. He justified his seemingly contradictory words and actions with the argument that paid labor was an essential component of his commitment to Elizabeth. As he explained: "I consider my duty as a lawyer, as being the same thing as my duty to my Betsey and her children." William's letters placed the highest value on his relationship with Elizabeth, but he gave business the preference when faced with a conflict between love and law. "My heart is yours and yours only," he assured her. "No object of ambition, no pursuits of whatever nature can shake the temple of love which you have raised in your Williams heart." But although William claimed to "look to no other source of temporal happiness," he reminded Elizabeth, "There are times when my profession must supersede even you in my thoughts—the image of my Betsey and the soft recollection of her pure endearments and caresses, must sometimes give way to dusty piles of superannuated chancery papers." William explained that while love had the firmest grasp on his heart, it was dusty piles of legal paperwork that had the most immediate claim on his thoughts and his presence. "Nothing less than business should restrain him from flying to the heavenly circle of his Betsey's arms," he assured her, "that circle which bounds up all his hopes, wishes and affections, & consummates his happiness."[58]

William's strategy of maintaining business in far-flung courts while assuring Elizabeth that it was her company alone that consummated his happiness was unsatisfactory for both marriage partners. Elizabeth, who remained alone at home for long stretches while her husband traveled, suffered from insecurity. Repeatedly, she prompted William to reassure her that she could never "be driven by business or amusement entirely from [his] thoughts," as she worried in the fall of 1803. When such letters failed to arrive regularly, Elizabeth's doubts turned into resentment. Later that year, when William missed one of the biweekly mails, Elizabeth wrote him "a reproach" that required him to remind her that only "the inevitable pressure of business" could prevent him from putting his thoughts of her on paper. Elizabeth's letters to her husband forced him to concede that his travels were incompatible with the couple's ideal of companionship. He ruefully admitted, "My duty seems to take a cruelly capricious delight in calling me, to & fro, everywhere throughout the country, except to the place where my soul's rich treasure lies."[59]

William's legal practice exacerbated the dual nature of nineteenth-century manhood. Lawyers in the early nineteenth century got their start by riding the circuit. Young lawyers typically traveled from court to court, hoping to pick up clients along the way, rather than waiting for clients to come to an attorney's office. Once a lawyer built up a reputation, he could set up an office of his own, or he could secure a position as a judge or chancellor. These options allowed men to remain close to their families for all or most of the year, but they could be less lucrative than riding the circuit. Although judges and chancellors received a salary, only men with other sources of income, such as a plantation, felt that they could live on it. William rejected this option when he left his post in Williamsburg. In Norfolk, he planned to use his home office as a base of operations, but he intended to augment his Norfolk practice by making the circuit of other courts throughout Virginia as well. During their residence in Norfolk, the Wirts established a pattern of seasonal separations. Elizabeth and William spent five or six months together at their home during each winter (between November and May). For at least part of each summer and fall, they were either reunited at home or escaped to the cooler climes of their relatives' homes in Richmond or in the Virginia mountains. Spring and fall were the seasons when the Wirts were separated for months at a time, with either or both of them away from their shared residence. In all, the Wirts spent eleven of their twenty-nine months in Norfolk apart.[60]

Despite the time he devoted to it, William initially found little intrinsic satisfaction in his work. His disappointment in the daily practice of the law and his attachment to the ideals of companionate marriage helped to limit his devotion to his career in the early years of his marriage to Elizabeth. Lawyers had long been regarded with suspicion in Virginia, and the early nineteenth century saw a revival of antilawyer sentiment. Looking around him during the opening decade of the century, William saw little to recommend the profession of law. In the hiatus between law as a gentleman's occupation and a profession of the intellectual elite, the law was open to almost anyone. "To have to scuffle at the bar with the common hord[e] of men," William commented to Elizabeth, was "offensive." Furthermore, a lawyer's daily tasks had little resemblance to the nation building of a previous generation. William recoiled from "the pressure of employments so uncongenial with [his] spirit—this indiscriminate defence of right & wrong": "O! it is sickening even to death." His sentimental nature also curbed his interest in law. Moving to Norfolk, where not only legal practice but a good deal of polite conversation revolved around the unfamiliar and, to William, uninteresting "commercial controversies" related to the shipping industry, made law even less appealing. "How can men toil as I see them doing here," William demanded in a letter to fellow attorney Dabney Carr; "business in their heads, business in their hearts, business, forever in their faces, without one palpitation to tell them what love and friendship mean." By expressing the need for love and friendship, William resisted a wholehearted commitment to the law, a masculine profession that was in the forefront of developing an ideal of manhood which defined men's role in contrast to women and divorced from domestic life.[61]

Rather than defining himself solely in terms of his career, William repeatedly described legal practice as a means to achieve happiness at home. "I cannot say that I am indifferent to professional fame," he remarked to his friend and former pupil Ninian Edwards, "but I can truly say that I love it less, for itself, than as the means of attaining my *sunnum bonum*: competence for my family." The thought of sitting with Elizabeth and their "little prattlers" was William's source of motivation even while it kept him away from her: "O! what a spring does it give to my heart!" he exclaimed. "How does it animate me in the discharge of my present duties—to this period, beloved of my soul, let us look for consolation, Whenever present cares and inconveniences shall press upon us."[62]

In return for these lavish declarations of love, William expected Elizabeth to dismiss present cares and inconveniences. His own absences, he reasoned, were beyond his control. Although he accepted the responsibility of supplying his wife with lengthy, loving letters—except when "the inevitable pressure of business" prevented him—William expected Elizabeth to make herself happy for the sake of their marriage. His replies to his bride's early letters indicate that she was deeply unhappy. William frequently exerted himself to remind her to "be as cheerful and happy" as possible in the absence of "her William," and on one occasion he sternly admonished her: "You will not have the hysterics, my Betsey." William expected Elizabeth to display love and happiness in her letters to him, rather than express her dissatisfaction with his absence. While Elizabeth stayed with her parents in anticipation of Laura's birth, William urged her to "exert herself . . . to dispel all gloom and despondency from her mind, and permit only pleasing emotions to agitate her heart." Their future happiness, he suggested, depended on her. "Serenity and cheerfulness . . . may give a dicisive [*sic*] and a happy cast to the temper and character of you know who," he alluded to the expected childbirth. William's closing words linked Elizabeth's compliance with their reunion. "Once more, my dearest dear Be gay, & happy," he directed; "your Willm. will see you on sunday Morng." A letter Elizabeth wrote to her husband shortly before Christmas in 1803 contrasted pleasantly with her plaintive letters that fall. "A sweet, dear girl you have been, for writing to me so regularly and so pleasingly . . . Continue, my

sweet Betsey, thus to love me—& O! how happy we shall be!" The following
year, William praised Elizabeth: "You are a good wife to write to me so regularly and so very pleasingly."[63]

The link that William drew between Elizabeth's correspondence and the
couple's future happiness suggested that she bore primary responsibility for
the success of their marriage. Furthermore, his definition of a good wife suggested that husbands and wives had different responsibilities in marriage. Men
were expected to pledge allegiance to love and marriage while devoting themselves to paid work; women were expected to accept their husband's assurances
in good faith, to conceal their own unhappiness, and to ensure the couple's
future by joining their husbands in regular and pleasing correspondence.

Elizabeth found it difficult to accept this definition of love and marriage.
Particularly in her early letters, she complained that she lacked facility in "the
language of love." Other women in the early nineteenth century experienced
a similar inability to match their lovers' florid prose. Women tended to write
short, hasty letters that were more concerned with local gossip, daily news,
and concern for their correspondents' health than with the romantic fantasies
that filled men's letters. In the context of the Wirts' marriage, Elizabeth's complaints that her letters were "barren, uninteresting and inelegant" and that she
was "a poor letter-writer at best" suggest that she struggled to conform to her
husband's definition of a good wife but found this division of responsibilities
incompatible with the relationship of reciprocity and mutuality which her
courtship with William had idealized.[64]

Elizabeth attempted to substitute the support of her female kin for her
husband's companionship. Even when the Wirts were together, they spent a
great deal of time with the Gambles. From July to October 1804, for example,
while Elizabeth awaited her first childbirth, she and William stayed with her
parents in Richmond. When William left to go to court, Elizabeth remained
at the Gamble residence. Her lengthy stays with her mother in Richmond and
with her sister at the Amherst County plantation, Montevideo, where she had
moved with her husband, William H. Cabell, were closely tied to William's
circuit courts. In 1805 William spent April, June, and July in Williamsburg and
Suffolk; Elizabeth passed these months with her parents in Richmond. After
the Wirts spent August together at the Cabell plantation, William departed for
his autumnal round of courts in September 1805. While he attended courts in
Moorfield, Williamsburg, and Suffolk, Elizabeth returned to her parents'
home. They were not reunited until November, at their Norfolk residence. In
these circumstances, it was not surprising that Elizabeth found her family to
be a vital support system. Families in the southern seaboard enjoyed closely

knit kinship networks that provided their members with economic assistance and business contacts as well as affection. Nineteenth-century American women commonly participated in what one scholar termed a "female world of love and ritual," sharing the joys and the heartaches of the lives that they often lived apart from men. In the South, this world was composed around a central core of female kin, especially mothers, sisters, and cousins. The time Elizabeth spent with her relations suggests that she depended on her mother and sister for emotional support and practical assistance during her husband's extended travels.[65]

However, Elizabeth did not consider the bonds of kinship to be an adequate replacement for the shared love of companionate marriage. By accepting the new ideals of romantic love so completely, she left herself vulnerable to her husband's power to prolong their separations. During the summer of 1804, while Elizabeth waited for William to rejoin her in Richmond, she wrote a letter that made him worry that she was "unhappy." "My mind has been kept in such a state of expectation hope, anxiety & fear," she wrote to William, "that I would wish to have you as soon as possible to sooth[e] & cheer me." William responded with a lengthy letter in which he attempted to account for his wife's feelings. Marriage, he feared, had proved a disappointment for Elizabeth. "I cannot repress an apprehension that . . . you will be drawing comparisons between the liberty you once enjoyed . . . & the confinement to which you now submit; between the high bounding hopes of your young heart . . . , and the reality which has put an end to those hopes," he worried. "It is not very difficult for me to concieve [sic] what were the exulting promises of . . . your young heart . . . 'and now' do you not say to yourself 'all this is over—I am a wife and a mother.' "[66]

William's "philosophy" may have pinpointed Elizabeth's frustration. The sharp contrast between the exulting promises of romantic love and the sense that the promise of companionship was over after marriage contributed to a series of emotional crises for nineteenth-century women, from what one scholar labeled a "marriage trauma" to a lingering depression that contemporary physicians diagnosed as hysteria. These serious threats to women's emotional health were intimately linked to their rising expectations of marriage and men's inability or unwillingness to live up to those expectations. William, although devoted to his young wife and concerned for her feelings, could explain Elizabeth's feelings of unhappiness, but he would not relieve them. Rather than attributing her seeming despair to his own absences, he reasoned that "the fairy promises of [her] youth" were not intended to be realized in "actual life." "Was it the nature of things for you to continue a girl forever?" he queried. Although William offered to console her with the "ten-derest, fondest love," the solution he proposed was for Elizabeth to reconcile herself to her new situation without complaint. "O! my Betsey," he counseled, "let me trust . . . that you will bear with composure the lot of mortality."[67]

William found it difficult to comprehend his wife's growing discontent. His romantic vision of home life led him to make his relationship with Elizabeth a priority, but it also made it impossible for him to grasp the source of her unhappiness. Elizabeth, William wrote, was his "richest, . . . only treasure": "For you only will I live," he declared, "to you only can I look for happiness." Yet by viewing her as the source of his own happiness, and by defining his present striving for "prosperity" in contrast to the "more prosperous days" with "leave to toy away all the halcyon days with his beloved Betsey," William found it inconceivable that Elizabeth, who seemingly already enjoyed the hal-cyon days that he only could dream of, could be unhappy.[68]

William's romantic fantasies of love assumed a division between his own life and Elizabeth's even as they affirmed his commitment to companionship. In 1804, he wrote a letter to Elizabeth wishing her "happy" as his "fond heart" would have her. Perfect happiness, wrote William, would never be interrupted, not even by the "transient shadow" of a single "cloud of care." Such happiness, in his mind, was reserved for those who remained at home: women and chil-dren. The following year, William described Elizabeth and their two children as "blessed innocents," far removed from the strife of the world beyond the family circle. He alone knew difficulty, he wrote. "Far from your bosoms be the canker of care—in mine alone let it riot, since every family must have it's canker." In another letter, William confidently assured his wife that she could not understand what a "luxury" he found her letters, because she had not experienced "the contrast of previous trouble and vexation" which gave that luxury "its highest zest."[69]

By equating his own life with trouble and vexation and Elizabeth's with luxury, William suggested that men and women, by virtue of their different positions in society, should make different contributions within marriage. In the summer of 1804 he wrote that it was "sweet" to receive news of Elizabeth's "tears . . . of purest love" but he felt it was improper to admit that his "own heart sobs" and his eyes were "dim with tears." Elizabeth's tears, he explained, "were the effusions of a bosom enriched with love and sensibility," but as a man, he was obliged to check his emotional displays. He wrote, "But come; I must not indulge this love & sensibility (all divine as they are) too far—the points at which a man & woman should stop in this luxurious feeling are wide asunder, according to the maxims of the world; and the softness that would grace the woman would disgrace the man." William did not feel altogether comfortable with these strict definitions of masculinity and femininity, which conflicted with the ideal of companionate marriage as a union of equals. "My own nature . . . is a very rebel against this maxim," he confessed, "but 'so the law is written.' "[70]

William did not exclude himself entirely from love and sensibility, but he did define men's and women's responsibilities in marriage differently. Elizabeth lived her whole life in the luxury of domesticity, he wrote, whereas the maxims of the world required him to spend much of his time away from home. For himself, William defined a distinctively masculine domesticity that allowed him to retain a role in marriage without limiting his activity in his career. Indeed, male domesticity, by relegating such happiness to rare interludes or the distant future, actually increased men's commitment to work by invigorating and inspiring them. As William explained in the fall of 1804, while he looked forward to a winter at home in Norfolk: "I long to be settled at home again, before a good warm fire, with you and our dear child by my side—it will be so snug & comfortable—we can read, converse, & listen to the prattle of our Laura, and pass away the evenings so entirely to ourselves, so much at ease, so sweetly and interestingly. Will it not be delightful?" No matter how delightful, however, William reminded Elizabeth that togetherness would always be fleeting and that they should bless, rather than curse, the circumstances that made it so. "O! my Betsey that such happiness should ever be interrupted by the calls of business—but perhaps it is this business which gives a zest to the moments of ease and love—while ease and love refit us again for business . . . Thus love and business reciprocally aid each other. Business enables us to live and love; and love stimulates us to exertion in business. Instead, therefore, of wrangling of business, let us bless it as the father of life and love."[71]

The life and love that were spawned by men's preoccupation with wage earning placed more demands on women than on men. Men, William told Elizabeth, did not have the same leisure for correspondence which women did. When she chided him for a "single omission," he urged her to commend him instead, "considering how punctually and faithfully [he] corresponded through all the month . . . , and considering too that a man's time is broken in upon and consumed" by the demands of his business associates and clients. William did not consider the possibility that Elizabeth's life might also be "consumed" by the demands of those around her. "You cannot justify yourself by my example," he admonished. "No omission, then, on your part My Betsey."[72]

As their third wedding anniversary approached, it was apparent that the Wirts held divergent opinions on their success in attaining the relationship they had idealized during their courtship. For William, marriage was unalloyed bliss. Admitting to extravagant expectations, he told Elizabeth that he had not been disappointed. "I have found them all more than fulfilled, & love you, from experiment and conviction, more tenderly and more firmly than when I used to love the creature of my fancy," he enthused. William was confident of his wife's love, which was an important source of strength and support for him. "But for the domestic joys which encircle me," he often declared, "I should be the poorest wretch for business that ever groaned upon the Earth." In contrast, Elizabeth felt disappointment and unhappiness in her relationship with her husband. Following William's departure for the spring courts in 1805, she told him that she was "dejected." Elizabeth remained uncertain of her husband's feelings for her, and her anxiety prevented her from enjoying even his most affectionate letters. She worried that he might "find it tiresome and unpleasant to tell his wife he thinks of her every day and that she is as dear to him as her fond heart could wish."[73]

The rifts in the Wirts' marriage were exposed in 1805 when William resolved to remain in Norfolk rather than joining Elizabeth in Amherst County for the summer. William's decision demonstrated his "defiance" of his wife's wishes as well as the unhealthy climate, and his explanation highlighted the primacy he attached to "the business of providing." In her first preserved letter, Elizabeth expostulated with William, revealing the serious difficulties that his concern for his career created in their relationship. "Can your stay in Norfolk, in the most fortunate event yield a sufficient recompense for the misery it will, it has already occasioned me?" she demanded. "I am, and must continue to be exceedingly unhappy." Elizabeth's strong language left no doubt that the Wirts' marriage was in serious jeopardy and that she held William responsible. "Not for any earthly consideration would I make you so unhappy, as this step of yours has made me," she accused, reminding her husband that she would not bear sole responsibility for making their marriage work. "Do not delay," she begged, "but fly from the dreadful precipice on which you stand—and down which you are so near dashing all our hopes of happiness." Although William stopped short of the dreadful precipice by hastening to Richmond, he refused to concede the validity of Elizabeth's claims and fly to her side. Business prevented him from proceeding to the plantation, he appealed; his most important "duty" to "his better half" was to remain in town and seek legal fees. Instead of joining Elizabeth, William proposed that she come down to Richmond. The responsibility for maintaining the Wirts' relationship remained Elizabeth's.[74]

Despite his refusal to consider Elizabeth's complaints seriously, William continued to affirm his commitment to her. "My heart wears an elastic chain," he told her that fall, "which pulls me the stronger, the farther I go." As Elizabeth's letters continued to lament their separation, William sought desperately for ways to comfort her. When Elizabeth informed her husband of little Emily's death, William counseled submission. "Your favor of yesterday, my dear love, is just handed to me," he wrote. "I fear my Betsey you are too much depressed and dispirited—Pray do not give way to these feelings—in this world, my dear, whatever may be our mutual love and whatever our pecuniary prosperity, yet still our happiness cannot be perfect."[75]

Throughout 1805 and 1806, the Wirts searched for a way to achieve the perfect happiness they both desired. During the their tenure in Norfolk, the couple had discussed the merits of moving to Richmond and abandoning the circuit. "I amuse myself," William wrote, "in planning . . . fairy visions of futurity—I imagine that we have laid by, money enough to build a house in Richm[on]d—that we are living at it and I practising in the superior courts there & among the van of the profession—making my twelve hundred a year without once leaving the town—no more exiles from My dear Betsey . . . Would this not be delightful?" With the memory of Elizabeth's unhappiness the previous summer still vivid, by 1806 William had resolved to take whatever steps might be compatible with his duties as a breadwinner to forward his wife's happiness. "What are fees and what the summit of prosperity's proudest billow, unless my Betsey continues to love me and to believe that I love her beyond every other object of creation," he declared. "You are dear to my heart's inmost core," William asserted, backing up his claim by asking Elizabeth to "decide the measure."[76]

As they prepared to move to Richmond, Elizabeth and William made their new home the focal point of "a thousand plans of future happiness." The blissful, but distant, future that William had dreamed of now seemed within reach. "Yes, my own Betsey my hearts richest treasure we will be happy," he promised. "We will be good & love each other." In Richmond, the Wirts hoped to achieve the loving union that so far had eluded them.[77]

Elizabeth and William's early years of marriage suggest the different content of nineteenth-century domesticity for men and women. In antebellum America, a flood of popular magazines, sermons, and advice books directed at well-to-do, white Americans like the Wirts charged "true women" with creating and maintaining the domestic environment, which served as men's "haven in a heartless world." In these literary invocations of what later scholars termed "separate spheres," women reigned over the home, where they wielded influence over the family by virtue of their superior morality; men claimed the world beyond the walls of the home, where they demonstrated their power in competition for money, political pull, and honor. The home became women's kingdom and their prison, while men became shadowy presences with no real role in "woman's sphere." Such prescriptions celebrated and naturalized the divergent experiences of love and marriage which the Wirts found so troublesome and heightened the contradictions of companionate marriage in the early American Republic.[78]

∼

CHAPTER THREE

Betwixt Duty and Love

Conflicts in Richmond, 1806–1817

"A splendid debut *in the metropolis": Domestic Economy*

Elizabeth and William Wirt moved to Richmond with renewed hopes to realize a successful marriage partnership. Domestic economy was an important arena for the Wirts to put their ideals into practice. As he anticipated the move to Richmond, William wrote that he hoped to make "a splendid *debut* in the metropolis" with a highly publicized legal case; he added, "It will be my wish, unless I find you opposed to it, to go directly to housekeeping."[1] In Richmond, the Wirts' splendid debut would depend on Elizabeth and William's close co-operation. During their decade in Virginia's capital city, they cooperated closely in financial matters. Elizabeth expanded her role as William's informal assistant and as the director of a productive household, and William shouldered much of the responsibility for supervising household production. Despite this splendid debut, the Wirts did not achieve a satisfactory balance between household production and wage earning. William's forays into politics and writing, while initially strengthening his distaste for the legal profession, served to increase his commitment to the law and to the male prerogatives of profession and politics. What William once called the bitter "conflict 'twixt duty and love" became a lasting issue in the Wirts' marriage.[2]

The Wirts reaffirmed their commitment to a cooperative domestic economy in Richmond, but it was a cooperation in which William's work and the cash income it produced were central. Elizabeth and William continued to work in tandem in his home law office. Shortly after the Wirts' move, William wrote to Elizabeth to request advice on his legal career. She advised him on what cases to accept and on what to charge his clients. She assisted her husband in his legal practice in other ways as well, copying his letters, delivering legal documents, sorting paperwork, paying bills, or passing along information to William's business associates. By midsummer, William gleefully announced, he and Elizabeth would be "the masters & mistresses of $6000 cash." William's choice of words reflected the Wirts' practice of working together in business matters. However, it also indicated that cash would be William's measure of financial success. The Wirts' new home also indicated that cash-producing activities would continue to drive their household economy. William selected the couple's first Richmond residence, a rented row house located in the industrial district west of the capitol. Elizabeth expressed some dissatisfaction with the house and yard, noting that there was little room for household production. Despite the commodious interior of the Wirts' new home, there were no outbuildings for domestic labor, and Elizabeth complained about "the bad arrangements of the lower apartments" of the house.[3]

Despite their current bad arrangements, the Wirts planned to resume or even expand household production in Richmond. Elizabeth supervised the complete overhauling of their new residence. "I wish, when you get well rested, you would cast an eye at the house & enclosure," William wrote, "& see what changes you would choose to have." Shortly thereafter, William repeated his request. "I hope you will tax your mind, at this moment of ease & projection and before the cares of house-keeping come to engross us, to omit no improvement which will add to our convenience," he counseled, "and (if you find it probable that we shall occupy the house the full term of five years) no embellishment within the reach of our purse." William's remarks indicated that he and Elizabeth realized that an investment in their house could pay off in increased household production and that William, as well as Elizabeth, was eager to make their family economy rest on both partners' efforts.[4]

Shortly after the Wirts' move, however, William's interest in the law was sparked by the new possibility that he could make the law a steppingstone to public eminence and, perhaps, political office. William had been interested in politics for some time, but he had resisted the impulse. Shortly before the Wirts' move to Richmond, he told Benjamin Edwards that "the rocks and shoals of poverty and bankruptcy" made "the stormy Baltic of politics" too dangerous for a man who had the responsibility for supporting a family. Politics "might be the road to distinction," he admitted, "but not to independence either for myself or my children." However, William's entry into Richmond's circle of leading lawyers opened up the possibility that he could combine business and politics. The turning point was the trial of Aaron Burr, the revolutionary officer, New York politician, and former vice president whose career ended in disaster with his arrest and trial for treason in 1807. Burr's trial was the nation's first major treason case, and it caused a sensation. For William, who was employed on the side of the prosecution, it was a chance to prove himself. "Every question, capable of being raised," noted William's 1849 biographer, "was presented and contested with scrupulous pertinacity and with abundance of acrimony." William's arguments, which the defense attorney ridiculed as full of "flounces" and "furbelows," failed to convict Burr of treason, but William gained a reputation as a master of rhetoric and more public attention than he had ever garnered in Williamsburg or Norfolk. He also earned about two thousand dollars, a sum that easily paid the Wirts' living expenses for the entire year.[5]

Fame and fortune fired William's enthusiasm for other public displays. Always keenly aware of his outsider origins, William was eager to prove himself in the terms set down by Virginia's established planter families, including the ideas of manly self-sufficiency and dominance—demonstrated in combat or competition before an audience of one's peers—which historians have termed "honor." William admitted that he found it difficult to relinquish his early hopes of eminence in exchange for a modest revenue. "The idea has been always very dismal to me, of dropping into the grave like a stone into the water," he mused, "and letting the waves of Time close over me, so as to leave no trace of the spot on which I fall." The best-known example of southern men's defense of their honor is the duel, which was proscribed by evangelical religion. But other opportunities to prove one's courage, independence, and strength—qualities of mastery greatly valued by many men in the nineteenth-century South—also existed. Legal argumentation, in its fierce combat rigidly controlled by accepted forms, closely paralleled the *code duello*. Military service, competition for public office, and political letter writing could also affirm a man's honor in the eyes of his neighbors. William demonstrated a keen awareness of others' opinions and the need to announce his honor in his flirtation with all of these alternatives to the duel during the Wirts' residence in Richmond.[6]

Despite his growing attraction to politics, William continued to make his responsibilities as a provider his top priority. The *Chesapeake-Leopard* affair of June 22, 1807, touched off a series of events that pushed the Wirts to define William's breadwinning responsibilities as more suitable for a family man than a selfish desire for public acclaim. The *Chesapeake*, a U.S. frigate, was accosted by a British frigate, the *Leopard*, which demanded the surrender of three men, purportedly British subjects, thought to be aboard the *Chesapeake*. Four of the *Chesapeake*'s crew were forcibly removed and impressed by the British ship. The incident occurred in an atmosphere of resentment against the British search of American ships and impressment of American seamen, and emotions ran high. President Jefferson declared the waters of the United States off limits to armed British vessels and dispatched a message to the British ambassador "to demand the satisfaction and security which the recent outrage rendered necessary." Jefferson's action was solidly in the tradition of the duel, which required seconds to obtain apologies or, in their absence, deliver challenges. As William remarked to his kinsman Peachy Gilmer, "Between the alternatives of war & dishonorable submission, our countrymen will not long hesitate." William was thrilled at his fellow Richmonders' exuberant displays of patriotism as they passed resolutions, readied weapons, and drilled in newly formed militia companies. He proposed a visionary scheme of creating an all-officer brigade from volunteer regiments and offering its service to the president. The four regiments would be commanded by William himself, his friend Dabney Carr, and two others, all of whom would be commissioned as colonels. The first commissioned colonel would have the title of brigadier general conferred on him, and William happily noted that his fellow hopeful colonels had insisted that he take the first commission.[7]

The Wirts' disagreement over William's proposed brigade highlighted the importance that each attached to his duties as a provider. Elizabeth was extremely distraught at her husband's plans to increase his claims to honor. She drew a clear line between "private interests, And domestic claims" and "the sparingly bestowed applause of a thankless World." Elizabeth did not succeed in dissuading her husband from his plan, but the president's hesitation, the hostile response of the state militia, and the sluggish volunteer rate forced William to give up the legion as hopeless. William's enthusiasm for public display was temporarily dampened by the experience, and he concluded that domestic claims were more important than "militia glory." When in January 1808 President Jefferson suggested to William that he consider running for Congress, William admitted that in his eagerness for military service he had "overlooked domestic inconveniences" that now loomed large in his mind.[8]

Despite his resolutions, William continued to flirt with politics. Jefferson's term as president was drawing to a close, and James Madison, then secretary of state, was his designated successor as the Democratic Republicans' candidate. A reactionary faction of the Republican party, the Tertium Quids, led by John Randolph, opposed Madison's nomination and published a paper, titled

"A Protest," criticizing the proceedings of the caucus that had nominated Madison. William, an ardent Republican, flung himself into the fray, writing three letters signed by "One of the People" and published in the *Richmond Enquirer*. William's political letter writing again brought him into the public eye, and he was elected to the Virginia House of Delegates. Once again actual experience in politics cooled his enthusiasm, however. John Randolph responded to William's well-known authorship of the "One of the People" letters with what William called "scurrilous" personal attacks. William concluded that politics was a dirty business: "All, all is rancour, abuse, hostility and hatred, confusion and ruin."[9]

As William looked forward to the end of his term in office, the Wirts were poised to achieve unprecedented success in their domestic economy. In 1808 Elizabeth and William, with the Gambles' generous assistance, moved from their rented quarters to a home of their own. The house was the ideal location for the Wirts to expand household production. An 1805 advertisement described the frame house, located at the northwest corner of Sixth and Grace on Shockoe Hill, as "large and commodious . . . amply sufficient for the accommodation of a genteel family, with a garden, out houses, &c." Like many other houses constructed in the late eighteenth century, the residence consisted of a central block, or main house, flanked by smaller wings on either side. The main house was two stories high. The property also included a small building designated a dairy in later records.[10]

Although the house was technically William's property, Elizabeth took the lead in renovating it. William's acquiescence in Elizabeth's plans was based in part on his awareness that his in-laws were keeping a close eye on how their son-in-law used the property that they helped him acquire for their daughter's comfort. Well-to-do southern families demonstrated a concern for protecting the family property that went to their daughters from the mismanagement or debts of their husbands. This may have been especially true for the members of distinctive ethnic groups, who sometimes fostered greater female assertiveness within the bounds of family, kin, and ethnicity than was tolerated by the wider society in which they lived. To all appearances, Colonel Gamble did not, like a growing number of well-to-do Virginians, file an antenuptial agreement to protect his second daughter's property from her husband's use or misuse. (When he died unexpectedly in 1810, Gamble left his property to his wife, and when she died in 1832, she did leave a separate estate to Elizabeth.) Instead, Gamble provided in a less formal way for Elizabeth to have the management of what property he chose to settle on her before his death. Elizabeth and William Wirt treated the property they received from Gamble as Elizabeth's, to manage or dispose of as she pleased, even though it was not legally designated as such. Other couples in early America did likewise, and judges generally looked favorably on such informal arrangements and upheld them when contested in court.[11]

In planning the renovation of the Wirts' home, Elizabeth acted with the confidence that her father intended the house and lot and any improvements "for her," as William had described the purchase. She supervised the workers, made the necessary executive decisions to keep the work running smoothly, and gave William detailed descriptions of the work in progress. Although the couple seem to have been in concert regarding most of the improvements, Elizabeth did not hesitate to override her husband's directions on occasion. At least once she canceled the orders William had left for the workmen and gave her own instructions. "The operations within the House, are progressing," she commented in 1809, "but will in some measure be retarded by a *counter order* of *Mine* but which I am sure you would approve of were you here."[12]

Elizabeth's orders were designed to maximize household production. Like farm women in nineteenth-century America, Elizabeth gave special attention to the space that would be devoted to an expanded range of productive household activities. In October 1809 she informed her husband: "I have gone through all the intricacies of my *lumber room, store-room*, & closets, &c&c&c." With the slaves' assistance, Elizabeth saw that the "meat house" and the cellar were prepared for preserving and storing meat for the winter. Elizabeth designed the interior of the main house to allow for easy supervision of domestic work. Rather than locating the Wirts' chamber on the second floor of the central block, as was customary, she renovated the western wing in order to create an oversized bedchamber. The chamber was some distance away from the kitchen, which was located in the east wing, but its proximity to the cellar of the main building, which was probably subdivided into the Wirts' "*lumber room, store-room*, & closets, &c&c&c,*" allowed her to keep an eye on household goods. The "wooden covered way" that connected the wing to the main house would have eased the task of overseeing the dispensing of household goods as needed. Finally, the windows Elizabeth installed in the western wing allowed her to oversee the slaves at work in the yard, a utilitarian area used to butcher livestock, pluck chickens, milk cows, and so forth.[13]

The Wirts cooperated in their domestic economy with renewed vigor in their new home. Elizabeth successfully claimed a leading role in the Wirts' second Richmond household. Always the more practical partner, she encouraged her husband to supply her with "a full statement of all [his] transactions & affairs" so that she could keep "a Book of accompts [*sic*]." Elizabeth was

Fig. 1. In 1808 the Wirts purchased their first home, located at the corner of Sixth and Grace in Richmond's Shockoe Hill neighborhood. Elizabeth filled her letters with details of her plans for renovating the house. She was particularly pleased that the new house, unlike those the Wirts had rented in the past, had ample space for household production. Photo courtesy of the Library of Virginia.

sure that William would rely on her skills and welcome her help with the household finances. "Your own interest would surely prompt you to a fulfilment of this promise," she wrote, "and I will hope to see it accomplished." William conceded his wife's business skills, and by the following year, both Elizabeth and William made regular entries in what she called "our account Book."[14]

While he bowed to his wife's judgment in financial matters, William expanded his role as household assistant in Richmond. Slave labor enabled William to continue household production even in Elizabeth's absence. The Wirts increased their adult slave force during the seven years they lived at the Shockoe Hill location. From 1809 to 1811 the number of adult slaves (though not the composition of the slave group) held steady. In 1812 the Wirts were credited with eight slaves. After a slight decline to seven slaves in 1813 and 1814, the Wirts again owned eight slaves in 1815. William took an especially active role in supervising meat processing and preserving, a task for which male slaves were responsible. In the autumn, William routinely divided his time between his legal practice and pickling, sunning, and smoking bacon and beef. In the summertime, he supervised slave men at work in the garden. In September 1810, while Elizabeth stayed with her sister at her Virginia plantation, William directed preparations for the winter. "I will have some briskets of beef nicely corned for you," he promised Elizabeth, "& turnips will, by that time, be in fine order." Household assistance, William whimsically noted, was more valuable than romanticism in a husband. The practical partnership he offered, William noted, was a solid example of his commitment to a truly companionate marriage. "I cannot help smiling at the thought of the different attractions by which my brother Poets & myself woo our mistresses to see us," he commented with amusement. "Shinstone tells his—'My banks they are furnish'd with bees &c.' and Moore sings 'Will you come to the bower I have shaded for you' and I—'Will you come to the corn'd beef & turnips so nice'— Mine, however, is the most solid invitation," he concluded.[15]

Although women were customarily in charge of textile production and dairy work, slave ownership, a close-knit kin group, and the sporadic assistance of white servants enabled Elizabeth to share the supervision of these tasks with her husband as well. She often asked William to purchase raw materials such as flannel, thread, bobbins, and pins. She also directed him to rally her other helpers to begin work on clothing and other cloth goods. During the Wirts' time at the Shockoe Hill house, Elizabeth sent word for Celia and Marinda, two slave women, to sew winter clothing under the joint supervision of William, Elizabeth's mother, and a hired white woman. Slave women also spun under William's and housekeeper Ann Perry's direction. In addition to serving as his wife's proxy by conveying her directions to the black and white women workers, William kept Elizabeth apprised of household production, which sometimes brought in a cash income. In 1810, William wrote from Richmond, "Miss Ann has laid up a good smart pots of butter—hereafter she will send it to mother's to be sold with her's at market."[16]

Elizabeth enjoyed her cooperation with her husband in the joint project of housekeeping, and she was confident of her ability to make valuable contributions to the Wirts' family finances. In 1810 she initiated a new series of renovations designed to simplify household production. "Among other considerations, is my desire to revolutionise our dwelling so as to enable me to superintend our domestic oeconomy with perfect ease to myself, And I am sure with great benefit to the family," she explained. Elizabeth's renovations preserved and expanded the Wirt household's capacity for household production. She installed a staircase to connect the family room to the cellar, part of which was converted into a kitchen. Elizabeth proposed changes in the main building as well. The new "family eating room" that Elizabeth planned on the second floor of the main house, she pointed out, would be adjacent to the "upper store room," which would make the room "the most convenient one in the town." Elizabeth's changes made movement between family rooms and productive space easier, concentrating household production under her own—and William's—immediate supervision. Elizabeth also expanded her involvement in the local market. In 1811, she spent several weeks negotiating with a potential purchaser for the family's horse and carriage. William encouraged his wife to take the initiative in these dealings. "If he can treat with you," he assured her, "the treaty will be satisfactory with me."[17]

Although William appeared satisfied with Elizabeth's management and approved of her plans for a cooperative household economy with great benefit to the family, his superior ability to earn wages detracted from the Wirts' financial partnership. In 1812, Elizabeth and William disagreed over the best location of his office. Their discussion of the matter highlighted their different understandings of their domestic economy. As long as men's workplace was located within the household, women could contribute to the family economy as their husband's invisible partner. Elizabeth was eager to make the Wirts' domestic economy a true partnership between husband and wife. She shared her husband's legal work, and she welcomed his assistance in household production. By designing the Wirts' houses with home offices for William, Elizabeth created a space in which the boundaries between work geared toward producing goods and services and work oriented to the cash economy were flexible. After six years in Richmond, however, William proposed vacating his home office and leasing an office away from home. His plan indicated that he considered his professional career to be the family's mainstay. It would be advantageous, from this viewpoint, to locate his legal offices "nearer the capitol." Furthermore, William's proposal suggested that he saw his legal work as part of a male world that should be kept distant from women's domain at home. "How will it do for my dirty clients & your visiting ladies to be jostling each other," he demanded, "and how will it do for your ladies who wish to go to your chamber to be passing through an office full of the dirt of clients shoes; rubbish paper, tobacco spit &c. &c."[18]

William's eagerness to rent office space away from home, coupled with the contrast he emphasized between his visitors ("dirty clients") and Elizabeth's ("visiting ladies"), suggests that the connection between household work and wage work was clouded by his focus on the work that he performed as a lawyer. At the same time, William was demonstrating his acceptance of the notion that men and women occupied very different positions in the family economy. Men sought self-advancement in a competitive marketplace; women eschewed productive and paid activities. Elizabeth may have hoped to deter this development when she vetoed her husband's plan. "I do not think it would be advisable for you to rent an office away from home," she replied. "It would be very troublesome both to your clients, & self—and might be a loosing [sic] business." Although she succeeded in keeping William's workplace in the household, Elizabeth bowed to her husband's desire to separate his work from household work, assigning him an upstairs room in the main house for his office.[19]

William's continued involvement in politics, as well as his legal career, threatened the economic partnership that Elizabeth envisioned. Military glory was William's first step on the path to political eminence. In 1811, William had hoped to be tapped for the vacant position of U.S. attorney general. He laughingly admitted to a "light and weather-cock versatility" in his commitment to a quiet life. "It was, I think, only last winter that I told you, in all the Sincerity and Solemnity of friendly confidence, that I had resolved on a plan of life, from which I would not depart," he wrote to Carr that summer, "to follow with ardour the pursuit of my profession, . . . and thus keep myself clear, by many a league, . . . of those dark and rough storms which are perpetually scourging and lashing into foam the political Baltic." In the fall of 1811, however, William questioned that "sensible" but "perhaps a little too timorous" plan. His own "inconsistency" forced him to reexamine his aims, and he wondered if he had been consoling himself for the prospect of "political obscurity." Perhaps, he mused, there was "a fund of dormant ambition in [his] breast" which could not be silenced by "discreet, rational, philosophic talk." Although the expected offer did not come, William increasingly was disposed to heed the call of political ambition.[20]

During the summer of 1813 Richmond was besieged by persistent rumors of imminent invasion, and in the midst of rumors of "heart-sickening" British invasion, William raised an artillery company. His decision was shaped by his desire to prove his honor. Any other action, he explained to Elizabeth, would have made him seem guilty "of indifference or cowardice." Elizabeth resented what she saw as her husband's selfish obsession with personal fame. "You will have your career," she acknowledged bitterly.[21]

When William defended his actions, he outlined the potential connections between his public reputation and his success as a lawyer. He chose to understand Elizabeth's opposition to his military company as a criticism of his failure to devote himself to providing for their economic well-being. He told his friend Dabney Carr that Elizabeth was "down-hearted because of the Flying Artillery," which she considered "a boyish freak unfit for the father of six unprovided children." In response to this perceived objection, William defended his military service in the same way he justified his legal career away from home: as a duty he owed as a husband and a father. "Remember, dearest Betsey, what I owe not only to my country, but to *such a wife* and *such children* as Heaven has bestowed on me," he appealed. William's letter emphasized the dependence of the Wirt family on his income. "I know how entirely you, my most excellent wife, and our dear children depend on me—have I a heart, think you, to break these ties, in chase of the shadow of military glory—do you believe me so poor in understanding and so selfish in spirit, as to think that I should advance my own fame by the ruin and misery of my family?" William assured Elizabeth that, far from forgetting "profession & family, in chase of the phantom, military honor," he had that very day accepted a legal client. The War of 1812 prompted William to link his profession and family with his public reputation as a man of honor, who proved himself in combat and held himself ready for public office.[22]

During the Wirts' years in Richmond, William increasingly defined himself in accordance with standards of masculinity which scholars often describe in contrast to each other: the northern model of the professional breadwinner, and the southern ideal of the man of honor. In 1813, he continued to believe that these ideals were difficult to reconcile with each other, contrasting the phantom of military glory with his duties as a wage earner. However, by identifying both ideals of masculinity as the way to live up to his duties to his family, William pointed the way toward a standard of husbandly behavior which rejected the joint domestic economy for separate roles for men and women inside and outside the family. Court business, as well as military drill, kept William in Richmond during the summer of 1813 while Elizabeth and the children stayed in the countryside with the Cabells. "Professional duties & character," not a need for cash, directed William's actions. Increasingly, William defined himself in terms of his work. Like other professional men—particularly those who lived in the North—William was adopting a view of himself in which wage earning was integral to his sense of himself. "I will be the man of labour and of business," he vowed.[23]

Although William still considered Elizabeth to be his economic partner, the significance he attached to the male prerogative of wage earning made her not only an invisible partner but an inferior one. "I will press hard upon my profession," he promised. "I will cast about and miss no opportunity of turning a penny without doors—while my dear help-mate is turning many by oeconomy within." Following the disarmament of his local militia group in late 1814, William directed his energies toward business with renewed vigor. During the alarm in Richmond following the *Chesapeake-Leopard* incident in 1807, William had been impressed with the idea that law practice was an uncertain source of income in the event of war with England. "A national calamity will destroy the means of paying debts," he predicted, "and I suspect a suspension of all law process in civil cases will be the result." While tensions between the United States and England escalated, William cast about for other means of making money. By the early 1800s, Richmond had grown from a colonial trading post into a major industrial city. Coal production and related industries were particularly lucrative. Coalfields in neighboring Chesterfield County were first exploited in the mid-eighteenth century, and Virginia was the leading source of coal in the United States until the 1830s. During the War of 1812, work began on a U.S. government arsenal and foundry in Chesterfield County for cannon casting. The Bellona Arsenal, completed in 1817, was moved to Fort Monroe, but founder John Clarke continued to make cannon for the U.S. government. William entered a partnership with Clarke in late 1813, and in 1814 he traveled to Washington in a successful attempt to secure governmental contracts. Elizabeth's contacts and business experience were valuable assets in this new project. Her brother, John Gamble, was involved in powder mills in 1814 and may well have provided the Wirts with the necessary introduction to Clarke. In addition, Elizabeth conducted an extensive correspondence with her husband and Clarke regarding the enterprise. She forwarded her husband paperwork and made arrangements for shipping coal between cities. But although Elizabeth functioned as William's partner in this endeavor, only he received the rewards and the recognition due him as a "man of consequence," as he wrote from Washington early in 1816.[24]

In their ten years in Richmond, the Wirts had made substantial progress in establishing a working economic partnership. At the same time, however, the delight that William found in being a man of consequence in business and in politics threatened to undermine the Wirts' cooperation in their domestic economy. As the Wirts looked forward to the future, they expressed different goals. Elizabeth hoped to build on their splendid debut in Richmond with more extensive sharing of work roles. William, inspired by his successes as a public figure, made plans to unite his interests in politics and the law and to widen the distance between his work and the household.

In early 1816, Elizabeth engineered the Wirts' move to a new, larger home, located on the northwest corner of Main and Fifth Streets, midway between the Gamble residence and the Wirts' house on Shockoe Hill. Elizabeth's actions indicated her confidence in her business acumen and the economic power she retained in the Wirts' family finances. She researched the price and terms of the house she wanted and negotiated with the owner, Mr. Marx. William went along with his wife's arrangements, noting that the sale of the lots that the couple had been given by the Gambles would permit the purchase. The property that Elizabeth brought to the Wirts' marriage, although she had no legal claim to it, apparently bolstered her claims to the status of an economic partner. Elizabeth relied on male acquaintances to make the transactions she proposed, but she viewed her role as paramount. "Here I am talking of buying and selling—and actually doing it too, just like one of you gentlemen folks," she exclaimed.[25]

Elizabeth intended for the new house to allow her to expand her ability to engage in buying and selling. The large house, Elizabeth informed William, promised "comfort and convenience." Part of Elizabeth's pleasure with the new residence stemmed from the scope it offered for increased household production. By 1816, the Wirt household included nine adult slaves. The Wirts' new house included "servants rooms" in the main house and several outbuildings: a two-story attached brick kitchen, a one-story brick "Summerhouse," a stable, "The Necessary," also of brick, and a long building behind the kitchen to be used as William's office and as an icehouse. Elizabeth connected the kitchen and coal house with a covered passageway to the long building that took up the rest of the block on Main Street. Divided into an icehouse (nearest the kitchen and coal house) and offices, this building formed part of a complex of productive space for the Wirts' domestic economy. Elizabeth intended for the new house to enable the Wirts to continue their business partnership. An on-site office building, with a separate entrance on Main Street, satisfied William's desire for professional space set apart from the rest of the family. Yet by locating the coal house in the office and by connecting the office building to the kitchen with a covered passageway, Elizabeth demonstrated the connection between housework and wage work in a highly visible way that also facilitated continued role sharing by husband and wife.[26]

The Wirts' new home seemed the ideal place for them to expand their cooperation in their domestic economy. But by the time Elizabeth was negotiating the purchase and planning the renovation of the Wirts' third Richmond home, William had found a way to combine his renewed commitment to law with his dormant ambition for fame. Following the War of 1812, public law,

Fig. 2. In 1816, the Wirts purchased the Hancock-Wirt-Caskie House at the corner of Main and Fifth in Richmond. Elizabeth hoped that she and William would share work roles with "comfort and convenience" in their new residence. Photo courtesy of the Library of Virginia.

which combined wage earning with honor, replaced military glory as his great ambition. After the conclusion of the hostilities, William returned with renewed vigor to a project he had begun in 1805: a biography of Patrick Henry. In *Sketches of the Life and Character of Patrick Henry*, William elaborated a wholehearted defense of the law and its practitioners. *Sketches* described the rising new men of the nineteenth-century legal profession as possessed of both natural abilities and superior training—a pairing of qualities which, not coincidentally, William ascribed to both himself and Patrick Henry. In his earlier literary endeavors, William had criticized lawyers and viewed writing as an alternative to the law, but by the time he finished Henry's biography, literature had became a way for him to explore and finally to strengthen his commitment to the law.[27]

William had an opportunity to further his career as an honorable lawyer when in March 1816 he appeared for the first time before the U.S. Supreme

Court. The case required William to oppose his old rival for the attorney generalship, William Pinkney. Anticipating the prospect, William claimed to prefer "a life of literary ease" but soon recanted, telling Carr that, as the old saying went, " 'the blood more stirs to rouse the lion than to hunt the hare.' " When the time came, William was eager "to try the tug of war with the renowned Pinkney." William was warmly praised for his oratory in the case, and he found the experience exhilarating. Describing the encounter to Elizabeth, he used the terminology of knightly chivalry. "I had the honor to break a lance with Mr. Pinkney," he reported, noting with pride that his rival "gained nothing." William was encouraged to aim for distinction in the courtroom. "I will try my luck at Washington as soon as I can get a cause or two," he decided. The following February, William had another chance to try a case in the nation's highest court. He made the most of the opportunity, speaking without a break for four and one-half hours before a "thronged" courtroom. The speech was well received, and William could not resist boasting, "I . . . covered myself *with reputation and glory*."[28]

William's interests in law and politics converged as he realized that public law practice could bring him reputation and glory as well as cash. Reveling in the praise that was heaped on him for his appearances in the Supreme Court, William was ready to redirect his talents. In October 1817, a month prior to the publication of the Henry biography, his chance came in the form of an invitation from President James Madison to serve as U.S. attorney general. Elizabeth, who had been an unenthusiastic supporter of her husband's activities on the court circuit, at war, and in politics, was dubious. The position, she thought, offered "no solid profit or advantage" for the family and only "a little more gain" for the Wirts' finances. William did not wait to hear his wife's opinion, however. In a letter that crossed Elizabeth's in the mail, he informed her, "The die is cast—I have accepted the office." With this letter, William turned away from a domestic economy in which Elizabeth served as his helpmate and advisor and expressed eagerness to devote himself to his profession. The outcome of William's gamble would become clearer in Washington, where the Wirts lived for the next eleven years.[29]

"Happiness is nowhere but in private life": Home and Family

During the Wirts' years in Richmond, William often proclaimed, "Happiness is nowhere but in private life," in the bosom of his "beloved family."[30]

As their family grew, the Wirts stepped up their efforts to share in home and family life. Both Elizabeth and William devoted an overwhelming portion of their correspondence to the health and education of their children. As the children matured, William's enthusiasm for parenthood increased, and he took a leading role as their tutor and as the director of their studies with local instructors. Elizabeth, however, was in charge of implementing her husband's plans of instruction during his lengthy absences, a task she often found difficult. She also was responsible for the health care of the family, a never-ending list of chores made the more burdensome by her own frequent parturitions. Even when the Wirts were together, they played different roles in home and family life, and they were apart frequently. While Elizabeth struggled to maintain the Wirts' high standards of private life, William often left the bosom of his beloved family in search of public acclaim in work and politics.

Children were a focal point of Elizabeth and William's relationship. As the Wirts laid plans to move to Richmond, William looked forward to being united with his "beloved Betsey" and "her two little cherubs." He rhapsodized on the pleasures of home and family: "Heaven bless you all three—ye are the props and stays of my life—the fountains of all my earthly felicity—Heaven bless you here & hereafter—Kiss the sweet pledges of our love—& believe me ever your own devoted William." Already William was looking forward to a larger supply of earthly felicity. In April 1806, the Wirts were sure that Elizabeth was again pregnant. Elizabeth's thoughts on bearing four children in four years do not survive, but William was enthusiastic at the prospect of a large family. When he suspected that Elizabeth's pregnancy was a false one, he wrote: " 'Whatever is, is right,' . . . And I can well afford to give you a year or two farther of indulgence without departing from my determined number."[31]

William's comments, although teasing, indicated that he, not Elizabeth, would determine their childbearing patterns. "The political economy of fertility decisions," as feminist historians have noted, is an important index of changing roles in the family. Although Elizabeth's thoughts on childbearing have not been recorded, it cannot be assumed that she agreed with her husband on the desirability of a large family. Fertility patterns offer insights into marital relationships. Revealing men's and women's different agendas is crucial to an understanding of the repeated renegotiation of gender roles and relations between men and women. A close look at the Wirts' decisions about fertility reveals that William's romantic notions of family, although consistent with the ideals of companionate marriage in theory, tended to reinforce patriarchy in practice. While William had the power to determine family size, Elizabeth bore the burdens of childbearing and child rearing.[32]

The distribution of power in the family and men's and women's attitudes toward childbearing governed fertility decisions in the early Republic. The technology of birth control did not change substantially until the twentieth century, but a variety of options, including periodic abstinence and withdrawal, were available to and used by couples in eighteenth- and nineteenth-century America. With the exception of abortion, however, all of the available methods required husband-wife cooperation. There is no evidence that the Wirts ever attempted to limit the size of their family. In an 1811 letter in response to William's teasing inquiry as to whether she was yet again pregnant, Elizabeth replied in the negative, remarking: "Nor indeed am I in any haste upon this subject. The *curse* which alighted upon poor *Eve*—is too alarming to the most fortunate of us miserable *Females*—to permit any of us to be anxious upon this subject." Elizabeth's response indicated that she disagreed with her husband about the desirability of a large family. Frequent pregnancies, she opined, were a "*curse*" upon "miserable" womankind. However, Elizabeth came to the conclusion that there was no option for women but "cheerful submission" to the dictates of their husbands and of God. "With me—as there is no prospect of escape—I only wish that when it *must* come—I might have some choice in the affair," she continued, perhaps hinting to her husband that with his assistance, she might exercise more "choice" in the pacing, if not the number, of her pregnancies. Before closing her letter, however, Elizabeth backed down from even this gentle rebuke. "These things are overruled by Providence," she concluded, "And our part, is cheerful submission." The Wirts' correspondence contains few references to birth control, and this may have been their last discussion of the matter. Many years later, Elizabeth admitted to her mother that she was relieved at the thought that her childbearing years were over, but she seems to have acquiesced in her husband's wishes until she reached menopause. William's idyllic vision of family life, ironically, prevented him from desiring to cooperate with his wife in fertility decisions. William indicated that he knew that the number of children could be determined, but he showed no interest in limiting births, writing that " 'whatever is, is right.' " Although William displayed little knowledge of fertility limitation, he did express a desire to control childbirth by encouraging Elizabeth to produce the determined number of his choosing. While some men in antebellum America favored limiting family size to place more emphasis on the husband-wife relationship, for William, children, "the sweet pledges of . . . love," were the happy evidence of the ties that bound his "beloved Betsey" to her "devoted William."[33]

Although Elizabeth bore the responsibility of demonstrating her love by making sweet pledges of her love to her husband, William's sentimental regard for children meant that he shared the responsibility for making their family the source of all earthly felicity. William's work away from home often interfered with happiness at home and prompted him to reflect on his ideal, family togetherness. By October 1806 Elizabeth had settled into the Wirts' new home in Richmond, but her husband did not accompany her. From the inn where he stayed on his way to Williamsburg for the fall courts, William thought longingly of the house where his wife and children—including newborn Emily (the second)—stayed behind. William consoled himself by thinking of the family group formed by himself, Elizabeth, and their children. "Tell me, my love," he wrote to Elizabeth, "do you, with me, find a pure and calm delight in the idea of our growing old together—of seeing our children established, one after another, independently and happily in the world—of our 'tottering down the hill hand in hand and sleeping together at the foot?' " Despite William's legal career, it was important for the Wirts to share the responsibilities of seeing their children established.[34]

Caring for young children was a project the Wirts shared, but mother and father performed different tasks. William, who was often away on legal business, used a mixture of gifts and praise to maximize the effectiveness of long-distance child rearing. In April 1806 he wrote that he was bringing a present for Laura, on condition that she be "a good girl" and do "every thing her ma tells her." When Laura sent word the following year that she had stopped fighting with Robert, William felt that his approach was vindicated. "God bless my little Laura," he wrote to Elizabeth. "Her little message about her brother's fall & hurt & her kissing it is too sweet to pass without notice so kiss her for her father & tell her he will bring her a present." Elizabeth, who remained at home, showed her affection for the children by monitoring their health closely. In letters she wrote at the same time that William sent kisses and presents to Laura, she reported on every change in Robert's health. "Robert has just awakened from a long sleep, in a very fretful humour—and a fever," she wrote. Elizabeth kept a detailed accounting of Robert's symptoms, possible causes, and the treatments she administered. "Once or twice he evinced an inclination to vomit; which may proceed from worms," she speculated. "I have just prepared some Sulphur," she closed her letter, "& shall give it him, as soon as this letter is dispatched."[35]

While Elizabeth attuned herself to the children's needs, William regarded accounts of the children's days as entertainment. He asked Elizabeth to "be particular even *minute*" about the children: "My happiness consists in being with you & them; in knowing every thing that happens to you, in seeing all you do & hearing all you say—supply these enjoyments to me by giving a minute recital of these things in your letters." Elizabeth sometimes reminded her husband that she did not share his enjoyments. The constant attention that modern child rearing demanded was difficult to reconcile with William's frequent absences from home, and Elizabeth occasionally quoted the children to their father to make this point. In 1807, she quoted Robert's response to learning that his father had again left Richmond for business. Robert, then two, shook his head vigorously in solemn disappointment. "Bad Fader," he pronounced, "gone leave you and Me."[36]

Childbearing and nursing increased the strain on Elizabeth's health and on the Wirts' cooperation in home and family life. Apparently Elizabeth bore a fourth child, a daughter, sometime in the summer or fall of 1806. The Wirts named the baby Emily for the infant they had lost the previous year, and despite her own uncertain health, Elizabeth insisted on nursing her. She wrote that the baby was thriving "surprisingly—[despite] the feebleness of her nurse." Breast-feeding could give women a way to protect themselves against conception. Possibly this strengthened Elizabeth's commitment to nursing the children. In the spring, however, Elizabeth searched for a wet nurse for Emily, who had been "very sick." The timing of Elizabeth's next childbirth indicated that she, too, was very sick. Elizabeth bore Betsey Gamble on October 25, 1807. Emily died shortly before her mother's fifth—and probably premature—parturition. Elizabeth, who was told by her mother and other women that she experienced unusually easy childbirths and brief recovery periods, "had . . . a very bad week of it" after Betsey's birth. "My nipples have been very sore," she told William, "and I was longer troubled with other pains, than usual." Despite her discomfort, only nine days after Betsey was born, Elizabeth wrote, "I have been setting up these two days—and hope to make a good Nurse for our little Babe: who, subsists altogether on my milk, and appears to be in a thriving way." Both Elizabeth and William drew comfort from Betsey's thriving appearance. "How beneficent is Heaven so soon to replace our loss," William wrote thankfully from Williamsburg. The news that Elizabeth was able to nurse was a source of additional hope. "O! how fortunate how happy will it be," wrote William, "if the continued bounty of Heaven shall enable you to nurse her for a year without injury to your own health." Despite the Wirts' high hopes, the "little stranger" died on November 22, 1807.[37]

Even though they had different experiences of childbearing and child care, the Wirts shared a sentimental view of their family which helped them to envision a future in which both would share in the joys and sorrows of home life. Elizabeth frequently appealed to her husband's sentimental visions of family togetherness. Her letters to her husband made it clear that the family circle was incomplete without him. Having spent a day in the garden with Laura, age four, and little Robert, age two, Elizabeth "was perfectly attuned to harmony and love," she recounted for William's benefit. "My little prattlers too—skipping around me, made me to sigh, and wish, and sigh again—for their Father's approving eye, o'er their frolic's." William's presence was necessary to complete this scene, and Elizabeth prodded her husband to join his wife and children. "Hasten, my beloved William," she urged, "the time when you may sit happily and undisturb[ed], in the bosom of your family." Elizabeth knew that William responded with enthusiasm to this sort of letter. Writing from the Williamsburg court in November 1807, he told Elizabeth that he was "tired of Williamsburg" and eager to return to his "beloved [wife] and her cherub circle."[38]

Notwithstanding their mutual affection for the cherub circle, the Wirts were frequently separated when William embarked on "the political highway." Fortunately for the Wirts' shared attraction to home and family, William's flirtations with public politics at first reaffirmed his preference for private life. When he laid plans to head up a brigade against the British in 1807, Elizabeth begged him to reconsider "for the sake of [his] dear little children." Although William initially was unresponsive to Elizabeth's plea, once his hopes of military glory were dashed, he renewed his commitment to a loving family group, writing, "It is into our own hearts that we are, at last, to look for happiness." During his 1808–9 term in the Virginia House of Delegates, William complained that politics was nothing but "the merciless massacre of public and private character, of social and domestic peace and happiness." At the end of his term, he concluded, "Political power is not happiness, and . . . my happiness is nowhere but in private life and in the bosom of my beloved family."[39]

While William expended his enthusiasm for politics, Elizabeth bore the burden of private life alone. In July 1808 William wrote with concern of "the delicacy" of his wife's health. Despite Elizabeth's weakened condition, the Wirts had not suspended sexual activity, and their sixth child, Liz, was born on January 5, 1809. Like many other privileged southern women, Elizabeth used her slaves' labor to reserve the most rewarding or most skilled tasks for herself, especially those relating to child care. When she renovated the Shockoe Hill house in 1809, she designed her chamber with sufficient space for a cradle for Liz and trundle beds for the older children. More and more, Elizabeth lived her life surrounded by children for whom she bore almost sole responsibility. As one scholar noted, men's "patriarchal control over women" allows fathers "to shift a significant proportion of the cost of children to individual mothers."

Elizabeth's acerbic comments indicate that she resented her husband's shifting of the burden of family life onto her but that she felt powerless to change the situation. Although some nineteenth-century women found that female invalidism spared them from household and family responsibilities, even Elizabeth's failing health did not rescue her from the seemingly insupportable burden of maintaining home and family in her husband's absence. As she had in the years that the Wirts resided in Williamsburg and Norfolk, Elizabeth made frequent visits to her parents' house during her husband's "truely irksome & disappointing" absences from home.[40]

Although Elizabeth continued to take responsibility for child care for the younger children, William's share of parenting increased as the older children matured and began home schooling. A crucial aspect of modern child rearing was loving encouragement, a responsibility that William could share even when he was away from home. Indeed, William's sojourns from home may have heightened his influence over the Wirt children, who were deeply attached to their father and eager to gain his approval. Elizabeth and William capitalized on these sentiments. "Kiss my dear children for me six times a piece," he wrote home in 1809, "and tell them if they are good children and learn their books as mamma bids them, father will bring each of them something pretty." Such letters home were an inspiration for the children, according to a letter Elizabeth sent to William that fall. "The children are delighted with your letters & for the moment they are a fine stimulus to their learning," she reported. "Laura has got into syllables & is beginning to make 'pot-hooks & hangers'— Robert too learns with more facility & willingness than formerly."[41]

William's keen interest in home education helped the Wirts to share the responsibilities of parenthood, at least for the older children. By December 1809, when Laura was six and her brother was four, William was enthusiastic about parenthood. "I'll tell you what, sir, I begin to feel like somebody in this world," he confided to his friend Dabney Carr. "My son is beginning to read, and my daughter writes her name very smartly; and it gives me I can tell you, no small consequence in my own eyes, to be the parent of two such children." Early signs of intelligence inspired William to hope for more rapid advancement, and he made correspondence with the older children an indispensable part of his routine during his absences from home. By 1810 Laura was beginning to write her own letters to her father. William was delighted, and he made sure his daughter was aware of the joy he took in her correspondence. Although he was very busy, he responded to one of her letters, "It would not be right for me to recieve [sic] such a pretty letter from my daughter without answering it." William's letters were an important part of the Wirts' child-rearing strategy, which used love to motivate the children to please their parents. In July 1810 he wrote to Laura that she was receiving a letter instead of a gift. "A letter from an affectionate father ought to be far more precious in a daughters eyes than jewels and diamonds," he explained, "for jewels and diamonds cannot make you happy, but the love of your parents can always do it." Love was associated with proper behavior. "I hope to hear from your mother that you are a fine, sweet girl and are very industrious in your studies," William wrote to Laura; "that is the only way to make your parents happy and to make them love you dearly."[42]

While William succeeded admirably in motivating the children to learn, it was up to Elizabeth to administer the lessons. Because of William's frequent trips away from home, only Elizabeth could provide the constant presence necessary for the intense parent-child involvement that modern child rearing necessitated. Shortly before her seventh birthday, Laura was learning composition from tales of classical Greece and Rome. Elizabeth's description of these lessons indicated the close interaction and constant monitoring the Wirts considered an essential part of child rearing. Elizabeth took great pains to make the stories comprehensible to her daughter. In 1810, she dictated classical tales to Laura, noting that although the book from which the story was taken was written in "a comprehensible style, yet it must be simplified still more if a child has to repeat them." Elizabeth also showed Laura a map of the ancient world, pointing out the places featured in the tales they read. "I beleive [this] made the story doubly interesting to her," she remarked. Although Elizabeth was responsible for this sort of day-to-day supervision, she drew on William's influence as well as her own to discipline the children. As punishment for telling a fib, she once denied Robert the privilege of writing to his father. The apparent effectiveness of this ploy indicated the degree to which the Wirts, even when apart, cooperated in child rearing.[43]

The Wirts hoped to make family life a truly shared experience. When Elizabeth renovated their home in 1810, she planned to make "a snug little family room, or morning parlour" in the connecting way between her chamber and the main house. The new room would offer the Wirts a space in which to share parenting responsibilities. Elizabeth also planned a new "family eating room" on the second floor of the main house. Changes like these, she probably hoped, would encourage the Wirts to spend more time together with their children. Childhood education was a particularly promising arena for the Wirts' cooperation. Elizabeth urged William to expand his involvement in home instruction. She directed him to purchase an atlas, a telescope, field glasses, an orrery, and "Arrowsmiths map of the world" for use in the children's lessons during the winter months, when he would remain at home. William was enthusiastic about his role as instructor. He wrote often to Laura, the oldest, to prime her for the course of moral and mental instruction he planned for her, urging her, "Always try your best."[44]

Despite their often different roles as parents, Elizabeth and William shared the same ideas about modern child rearing. During the summer of 1812, they traveled together to several hot springs resorts, leaving Laura and Robert with Elizabeth's sister, Nancy Cabell, and her family. The Wirts wrote joint letters home to the children in which they echoed each other's themes of parental love and filial duty. "We both love you dearly, and pray for blessings on you every day," Elizabeth reminded them. "Be mighty good children," she advised. "Pray to your *good Father in heaven* to take care of you, & bless you, and make you good and amiable, that every body may love you and your Parents feel proud of you." William echoed his wife's sentiments. "I hope you are making good use of your time," he added, signing himself "your affectionate father." For both Elizabeth and William, parent-child love was the basis of modern child rearing. "I have received two letters from your uncle in which he says that you and Robert are both very good children, which makes your mother & me very happy," William praised.[45]

The Wirts' similar views on child rearing meant that they viewed William's absences from home—rather than a fundamental difference between men and women—as the chief obstacle to truly shared parenting. Elizabeth usually acted as the primary parent while William traveled around the countryside, but the couple could reverse roles, at least where the older children were concerned. In late 1812, Elizabeth made an extended visit to her sister's plantation, where she busied herself with one-year-old Catharine, who had been born in 1811, and awaited the birth of twin girls, Ellen and Rosa, on November 22, 1812. Elizabeth continued to take responsibility for the youngest children. When she returned to Richmond, she planned to have a cradle on each side of her bed for the twins. The older children, however, could be entrusted to William's care. Laura, Robert, and Liz remained in Richmond with their father for several months. Elizabeth wrote often to impress upon William the seriousness of his charge. She asked him to take daily strolls with Robert and to supervise the children closely. "My dear Husband, let me intreat of you—to devote yourself to them," she urged. "Be a Father & Mother to them—until I can take a part of the burthen [*sic*] off you."[46]

With twin infant daughters demanding her care, Elizabeth was eager to extend her cooperation with her husband in child-rearing matters. When she returned to Richmond, she would take only a part of the burden, she informed

William. When she undertook a fresh series of home renovations in 1812, she planned to remove William from his office in the main house, proposing that he could "go to the *antichamber* [*sic*] for the winter." The antechamber, or family room, would allow William to devote himself equally to legal work and the older children's lessons. William should exercise "self denial" and spend time at home with the children, she wrote, which was, she reminded her husband, "a good cause." Perhaps anticipating obstacles arising from William's social engagements, she encouraged him to spend as much time as possible at home, commenting, "You will not be much the looser, [*sic*] in the end. It will give you more time for study, and for business."[47]

As the older children advanced in their lessons, Elizabeth depended on William to provide them with guidance. Although the Wirts experimented with local schoolmasters, they concluded that home schooling was more effective. Work and politics sometimes made it difficult for William to fulfill his responsibilities as the children's tutor, however. In 1813, when William remained in Richmond to drill with his artillery company, Elizabeth wrote from the Cabell plantation to complain that the children were "not advancing one single step in their educations" without their father's attendance. Elizabeth appealed to William's commitment to his home and family. "May Heaven watch over & protect you, my beloved Husband. Oh, may he spare you to your helpless little family—so altogether necessary as you are to them."[48]

Although William tried to assure the children that his new role as a military captain did not detract from his interest in their lessons, his effectiveness as a loving parent was hindered by his activities. During a brief visit to Montevideo in late July or early August 1813, William attempted to assist Robert with his lessons. He had difficulty concealing his impatience with his son's slow progress. After his departure, he repented "every harsh word" he had uttered to "little Robert." William's brief visit had lasting repercussions. "Poor Robert did not want to write, for fear as he said that you would scold at him again," Elizabeth informed William. On his next visit, William took care to exercise more patience. He wrote a friend, "The education of my children keeps me continually engaged, from breakfast 'till dinner." When William again returned to Richmond, however, the children's education once more came to a standstill. "Laura & Robert have done scarcely any thing at their books," worried Elizabeth in September. During William's latest visit, Elizabeth had made it clear to her husband that she preferred to have him at her side, assisting her in child care. William admitted to his friend Dabney Carr that Elizabeth considered his military activities "unfit for the father of six unprovided children." William, too, recognized that his relationship with the children suffered thanks to his latest duty. "Kiss my beloved children for me," he instructed Elizabeth. "I wish you would convince Laura & Robert how much I love them for I fear they doubt it." To bolster his role in the children's lives from afar, William relied on his role as economic provider. "Father is working day & night to get money to provide for his children and pay for their educations," he reminded Robert, "and they ought not to make their father throw away money, earned so hardly, which they will do, if they neglect the education he has to pay for."[49]

William's absence made Elizabeth's responsibilities more arduous. He filled his letters with directions for her as well as assurances of his eagerness to see the children. "Kiss [our] sweet ones for me," he urged. "Don't fail to write every mail—and our sweet Laura too—also Robert if he can bear it—Make them perfect in their grammar." With Elizabeth to take up the slack at home, William resolved to stay at camp until he was convinced that the danger was past: "I shall bear up with a firm mind and discharge my duty with a steady hand." Meanwhile, he expected Elizabeth to expand her own role to fill the void. "You I hope, my beloved, are by this time composed," he remarked, "and our dear thoughtless little children happy—they know not the want of a father, and will never know it while they have such a mother." Elizabeth found single parenting a difficult and often overwhelming task. "It is no trifling matter to break up our Family root & Branch," she commented in 1814. In William's absence, Elizabeth had to force herself to carry on despite her own worry and depression. She closed one letter in tense, jagged phrases: "I go— to perform my duty to my children,—to foster & cherish them—For their Fathers sake,—so long as the Almighty disposer of all things is pleased to continue me with them—May almighty God . . . spare you to us—! Oh My Husband! My Husband!"[50]

William's absences from home continued to interfere with his cooperation with Elizabeth in child rearing. By early 1814, his perception of fatherhood was no longer one of unmixed bliss. "It is indeed a dread responsibility which we fathers have," he confided to his friend Dabney Carr. Letters from home forced William to admit the difficulty he faced in reconciling his fatherly role with his activities away from the family. In September 1814, Laura plaintively wrote, "My dear father I wish that you would come here and attend to my Caesar." Writing from military camp, William could only send his prayers and his hopes for the future. "Assure my dear children one by one of their father's tender love & blessing," he wrote to Elizabeth. "May God bless & protect them & preserve their father to shelter their childhood & see them safe to maturity," he fervently prayed. By this time, unpleasant camp conditions and the difficult responsibility of maintaining discipline and fostering morale among the enlisted men had begun to wear away William's romantic ideas of soldiering, and he sighed, "O! how I wish that I were with you, our dear children and beloved friends."[51]

William's prayers were granted. He returned home in October 1814, but business meetings in Washington continued to call him away from the family. William idealized the family but took very little responsibility for parenting as he expanded the Wirts' coal interests and attended court. During breaks in court, he told Elizabeth, "You visit me in my dreams and . . . play before my waking fancy surrounded by your sweet & beloved groupe of children." While her husband daydreamed of her play, Elizabeth struggled to replace her husband's tutelage with other instruction. Laura took French lessons from a local teacher, but she scolded her father for his long business trips to Washington, lest she forget her Latin during his absence. Robert attended a school taught in a house just next door to the Wirts. For the younger children, the Wirts hired a governess sometime in 1815 or 1816. Away from home, William had to rely on Elizabeth to be his proxy in child rearing. "Will you give my love & kisses one by one to our children[?]" he requested from Washington in 1816. The "pressure of business" did not even give William the time to send personal letters to each of the Wirts' children. "[I] wd. send a particular message to each, but I have really not time," he apologized.[52]

Elizabeth was eager to restore William to his role as family tutor. In the new home the Wirts purchased in early 1816, she expressed the family relationships she envisioned. For the first time, Elizabeth banished slaves from the main house, which was now the exclusive province of the family. Inside the main house, she planned space for family togetherness. "There are 3 excellent chambers above," Elizabeth enthused. "A very large and handsome chamber" occupied all of one side of the house; on the other side of the hall, on Main Street, were two chambers, "communicating by the means of a dressing room & closet." Elizabeth and William probably occupied the large room, with the children just across the hall in one of the two communicating rooms. Elizabeth converted part of the master chamber into a sitting room. This room, like the breakfast room, or family parlor, in the Shockoe Hill house, gave the Wirts a convenient space to spend time with each other and the children.[53]

Unfortunately for Elizabeth's plans, William's career was approaching a turning point at which he was at last able to combine the work of providing for the family with the personal satisfaction of public office. When he informed Elizabeth of the opportunity to take over the office of U.S. attorney general, she used every weapon at her disposal to dampen her husband's evident enthusiasm. While William traveled to Washington to discuss the office with the president, she enlisted the family's minister, John Holt Rice, on her side. Elizabeth appealed to her husband's keen sense of responsibility to home and family by reporting that Rice was "not at all in favour" of the prospect. Moving to the capital, she summarized the clergyman's objections, would "be taking [their] children to a bad theatre for morals & religion . . . for perhaps a little more gain—and no solid profit or advantage." Elizabeth's appeal to William's dual sense of responsibilities as a provider and as an active father was weakened, however, by the potential advantage that William saw in his new opportunity to join political eminence and financial profit. Having ascertained that his duties as attorney general would not necessitate giving up private practice or his investments in the Virginia coalfields, he wrote, "I have no doubt of bettering the situation of our dear children by the move." Like Elizabeth, William appealed to the welfare of their children, but his claims to bettering their situation rested on the argument that his post would bring the Wirts increased wealth and status. When he accepted the attorney generalship, William also accepted a new definition of fatherhood which rested on his efforts away from home for his family's benefit, rather than on his personal involvement in home and family life. The ramifications of this decision for the Wirts' home and family would become more clear following the family's move to Washington, D.C., in late 1817.[54]

"How could you have the heart to serve me so?": Love and Marriage

Elizabeth and William Wirt made significant advances in their marriage partnership during their residence in Richmond, but they also discovered that the problems they faced were difficult to eradicate. The Wirts agreed that what William once called the bitter "conflict 'twixt duty and love" was a serious obstacle to their goal of companionate marriage.[55] However, their definitions of love and duty were different. Elizabeth maintained that true love was impossible in her husband's absence, while William made love letters the mainstay of the Wirts' relationship. Elizabeth maintained that William had a duty to demonstrate his love for her by spending more time at home, but William defined his duty to his legal clients and his country as part of his responsibilities as a husband. By describing work and politics as a duty that he owed to Elizabeth, and by making the fulfillment of duty evidence of his love, William hoped to contain the tensions in their marriage. However, Elizabeth did not accept her husband's justifications. Although she sometimes admitted that William had multiple duties, when his pursuits led him away from her for extended periods of time, she was wont to demand, "How could you have the heart to serve me so[?]"[56] William, who anxiously strove to meet his wife's expectations—without surrendering the rewards of public life—often responded in kind to his wife's recriminations, defending his actions and overriding her objections. During the Wirts' years in Richmond, a series of short but sharp disagreements highlighted their different expectations of love and marriage.

William's commitment to his legal career during these years in Richmond posed a serious challenge to the couple's vision of companionate marriage. The Wirts had hoped that the move to Richmond would permit them to spend more time together, but William continued to take cases in far-flung courts which took him away from home for long stretches of time. When Elizabeth moved into the Wirts' new house in the fall of 1806, her husband set out to Williamsburg for the fall courts. William found it difficult to reconcile his responsibilities at distant courts with his responsibilities at home. "I am constantly resolving to be the best husband, father, and man in the world," he reflected. "O! that I had no other occupation on this ball of dirt, but contriving and executing schemes for the happiness of my blessed girl and her babes," he exclaimed. "Yet how often am I necessarily torn from them—how often am I forced to forget them entirely and devote myself, soul & body to some courts." William's long trips pushed him to reflect on the different claims to his soul and body. He frequently noted that he had to "snatch these moments from business" in order to give Elizabeth "any token of her William's affection." However, while he gave his body to his career, he maintained, "I am, in heart & soul, forever yours."[57]

By drawing a distinction between his physical separation from Elizabeth and his spiritual union with her, William attempted to be both the best husband in the world, which meant a loving companion, and the best man, a breadwinner. To bolster his assertion that Elizabeth had the best claim to his heart and soul, William relied on correspondence. In his letters, if not in person, William could be "Your own ever fond & faithful Wm Wirt." William used his letters to assure his wife that despite his preoccupation with legal business, he thought of her every day. "Short as this scroll is," he closed one note, "you are most sweet & dear to my heart." Elizabeth also made correspondence an important symbol of the Wirts' commitment to mutual love, routinely closing her letters with blessings on her "dearest husband" and signing herself "your Betsey." In their correspondence, the Wirts shared a language that celebrated their love for each other. However, while William's use of the language of love accepted and attempted to atone for his periodic stays from home, Elizabeth used the same rhetorical strategies to criticize her husband's absences. Assuring William that she had "a heart of the truest, and warmest affection" for her absentee husband, she added, "I begin to think I may look for you to morrow evening."[58]

. While William considered letters a substitute for togetherness, Elizabeth saw the couple's correspondence as a promise of future marital bliss. William could be made happy through correspondence, he indicated. "[I] should have been perfectly happy this evening if the Richmond mail had brought me one of your accustomed sweet favors," he noted in April. For William, Elizabeth's letters from home were "precious gratifications." But for Elizabeth, only William's return would be a "thrilling gratification": "Hasten, my beloved William," she urged, "the time when you may sit happily and undisturb[ed], in the bosom of your family, giving such an increase, & constant flow of happiness, as my heart now pants for, and which never will be perfect, while these tedious & distant courts so much engross you." William responded: "I wish, indeed, the time was gone by, when my duty to you and my dear children would force me no more to distant courts." Although the Wirts agreed on the goal of togetherness, by identifying his legal work with his duty to Elizabeth, William justified his continued absences.[59]

The Wirts' correspondence revealed the conflicts in their relationship as well as their shared ideals. In late April 1807 Elizabeth and William had a disagreement over who had less time to write. Elizabeth held that she—burdened with a migraine, the task of finding a wet nurse for Emily, and the care of Robert, who was ill—deserved the dubious distinction. "I insist that my William be not displeased at my omissions as a correspondent," she wrote, adding, "I much fear you will not gratify me with a letter this evening—if you do not, I shall be disappointed & a good deal hurt." Elizabeth's letter indicated that her own commitment to the marriage was clear in her daily activities and that the onus of responsibility for correspondence fell on her husband, who was away from home. But William insisted that his legal work was a better excuse for lapses in correspondence. "I am perpetually engaged here, in the dark and entangled mazes of ancient chancery suits," he wrote in explanation of his silence. "I have scarcely time for the refreshments and exercise which health demands—much less that kind of tranquility in which I would ever chuse to be, to address my Betsey . . . But while the unfrequency & brevity of *my* letters is thus easily explained, what has my Betsey to say in explanation of her silence," he demanded. To write this letter, he added, "I have stolen this morning from my duties." William's response to Elizabeth's letter indicated that he felt that his work away from home was evidence of his commitment to his wife, and that while rendering his services to his clients, he could still be "Your own & yours only."[60]

Differences like these sometimes caused both marriage partners to doubt the other's love and to suffer emotionally. "I am very anxious to read the effusions of your love," William wrote in the spring of 1807, fearing that he had "lost it." William wrote following a break in the Wirts' correspondence, and upon receipt of a "dear & most pleasing favor by the mail," he was "on the house-top" with joy. However, Elizabeth's fears were not so easily dispelled. She longed to "always feel assured of [William's] love," adding, "To doubt, as I am sometimes half inclined—Is a feeling, beyond endurance, or discription [sic]." Even when reassured, Elizabeth indicated, she was not happy in her husband's absence. She had decided not to attend a spring party, she remarked in 1807. "My enjoyment would be very little and unsatisfactory without you." In two successive letters, Elizabeth attempted to convince her husband to give up the circuit. "I wish you would not take any more business, in those distant courts," she wrote. "But as soon as possible wind [up] your old causes in them—And settle yourself at home." Until then, she reminded William, she would have "a melancholy heart."[61]

The *Chesapeake-Leopard* affair of June 22, 1807, touched off Elizabeth and William's most serious disagreement since his refusal to leave Norfolk in 1805. In the event of a "national calamity," William confided to his friend Dabney Carr, he would "not sit idly at home . . . like a granny." Instead, he determined, "I shall yield back my wife to her Father . . . and I shall march." William's enthusiasm for "a display of heroism" not only separated him from Elizabeth but propelled him toward a definition of manly resolve which took little notice of women's feelings. By planning to yield back his wife to her father, William indicated that women were men's property, not their life companions. Elizabeth felt this keenly. "I never in my life felt so Widowed," she cried, noting that her tears prevented her from writing further. "O! heaven restore me to my husband!"[62]

William's work on the legal circuit also widowed Elizabeth. "Will it not be possible to conclude your business there [in Williamsburg] this time so as not to go again?" she queried. "I am so sick of it." But William's stays in court were more often prolonged than curtailed. In November 1807, Elizabeth wrote, "I was counting the hours, half hours, and minutes, that must still pass away before I should see my William; when his letter was handed me." The letter, Elizabeth remarked, was a great disappointment. "I cannot say I gave it a very hearty welcome," she admitted. "Tender and affectionate as it is, it was still but a letter and not enough to satisfy the high raised hopes of a Wife Just (as

she thought) on the eve of being pressed to the bosom of her Husband."
William assured Elizabeth that he, too, felt their separations keenly. "Believe
me my dear Betsey that I already sigh to be with you," he wrote from Williamsburg in late 1807. Elizabeth, William reiterated frequently, was more important to him than anything else. As the election for the Virginia House of
Delegates, to which William had been nominated, approached the following
year, he assured her that he watched the proceedings with "total indifference."
Anticipating a visit from Elizabeth, he wrote: "Come then, my beloved, to my
arms & let me fold you into my heart of hearts—in your sweet & pure bosom
I shall forget every care 'and envy no mortal his splendor & state.[']"[63]

Although Elizabeth and William frequently expressed dissatisfaction with
the long stretches of time they spent apart, the family's dependence on William's wages gave him the prerogative—or, as William saw it, the positive
duty—to remain away from home to pursue his career. In late 1807, Elizabeth
indicated that she accepted her husband's explanation of his necessary absences, resolving that she would be "resigned" to William's "duties to others":
"All this I will agree is as it should be—dificult [sic] as it is to be reconciled
to it:—But, I will not complain." William's duties to others gave him the power
to decide when and for how long the Wirts would be together, as his jocular
signature to an 1808 letter indicated. "God bless you my dear Betsey," he
closed, "your ever faithful & affectionate—lord & master." In a similar vein,
Elizabeth thanked her husband effusively for his "poetic epistle," noting, "I
had made up my mind to be entirely forgotten by you." Emphasizing her
submission to her husband's schedule, Elizabeth hoped she was "not mistaken
as to the time of [his] return" but yielded to his "superior Judgment." She
closed: "Your dutiful & obedient Slave." This exchange, while atypical of the
Wirts' correspondence, suggested that their relationship, far from an equal
partnership, resembled that of a benevolent master and a doting slave.[64]

Elizabeth continued to rely on her relatives to help her cope with her husband's failings, but she was unwilling to replace marital intimacy with her circle
of kin. Instead, she attempted to enforce her own standards of companionship,
sometimes drawing from her husband a confession that he had failed to live
up to his responsibilities as a loving husband. While William was distracted
by his term in the Virginia House of Burgesses, Elizabeth visited her parents
frequently. Her letters to her husband chided him for his absences. "This
prolonged stay of yours my dearest Husband, is truely irksome & disappointing," she wrote to Williamsburg in October 1808. William promised to do
better. "You are too good and affectionate to experience aught from your
husband, but happiness un-alloyed," he wrote. "How I resolve & re-resolve!

Alas! poor human nature—Yet indeed my beloved, sole centre of my happiness and my hopes, I will be hereafter the best of boys—I have begun my reformation . . . and you shall see whether after all my abortive resolutions, I am not at last capable of making the girl of my heart happy."[65]

William's activities away from Elizabeth continued to postpone his reformation. He frequently worried that "the bright bright prospects of fame & wealth" which then surrounded him might "be reversed." William's concern for the future made him all the more anxious to make the most of the present. "Now that I am as yet on *terra firma* and favored with the smiles of fortune," he reflected, "what remains for me but to resolve, with the decisive energy of a man to deserve those smiles by my assiduity and my virtue[?]" William's definition of a man—a decisive, hardworking professional—had an impact on his definition of a husband. If he followed the course he had laid out for himself, he thought, he would ensure "the approving & cheering smiles" of his wife. For William, devotion to his career was intimately linked to love and marriage. "I cannot tell you with what a fervid glow of heart, my Betsey & the pledges of our love mingled in my reflexions," he told Elizabeth. "O! I do love you—with all my soul, my best & sweetest girl, do I love you—and well I may—for have you not been every thing to me—Are you not every thing to me—A cross of glory around my waking brows and a pillow of roses to my sleep."[66]

While William found that love and marriage helped to spur him on in his career, Elizabeth got less out of the relationship. Although Elizabeth assured William that he was "the best of Husbands," even the best of husbands in most nineteenth-century families allowed the major responsibility for happiness in marriage to devolve on their wives. For William, love heightened his enjoyment of good times and helped him endure bad times. "How doubly, quadruply sweet will fame & prosperity be, enjoyed with my dear Betsey and the precious pledges of our love!" he exclaimed. "And if adversity come, how will it be softened by the same causes!" However, the fame and prosperity that William hoped for and the adversity that he feared were his own; while he looked to Elizabeth as a steady source of support, he sometimes wondered what she got in return. "While you are thus blessing me," he pondered, "what can I do for you? love you?" When he attempted to think of ways in which he could offer more substantial rewards, evidence of his own success was all that came to mind. Following a major legal case that kept him in Richmond while Elizabeth went to the countryside in the summer of 1810, William speculated, "The heart of my wife is now anxious about the figure her husband made in this affair." William was aware that he did not fulfill his wife's expectations, but he chose to misunderstand her desires. Despite Elizabeth's repeated pleas that he give up his itinerant career and return to her side, he determined that the best way he could please his wife was to increase his own success.[67]

Elizabeth and William continued to disagree about his proper role in marriage. Despite his evident eagerness to keep his wife's love, William refused to relinquish his career abroad. William's letter to Elizabeth after he left Richmond for the fall circuit in 1810 indicated that the couple had quarreled, and had left their dispute unresolved, during the brief time he spent with her. "I do not know when I have felt your separation from me, . . . so much as on this last occasion," he mourned. "I feel as if you were gone from me for ever, and as if through my own folly, I had let slip the only opportunity I shall ever have of convincing you how dear you are to my affections." Despite this serious problem, William left for the fall courts for a stay of uncertain duration. "Our courts . . . have now begun," he wrote in early September, "and we have no more intermission from labor, not even during the Sabbath, until about Christmas." The intermission would be brief; "the few last days of December, and the month of January belong to us," continued William, "and then from the first of February to the first of July we are slaves again."[68]

William's prolonged stays at court not only deprived Elizabeth of his company but subjected her to serious doubts about his commitment to her. Occasionally she teased her husband about leaving home to visit his "other sweethearts." Elizabeth's lighthearted comment was a reference to the sexual double standard in antebellum southern society which allowed men (but not women) to engage in illicit sexual activity. In 1811, however, Elizabeth's remarks took on a new, foreboding quality when the serious possibility was raised that William had been unfaithful.[69]

William's legal work and his political visibility combined to make the Wirts the targets of a rumor that William had used the sexual double standard to his advantage during his lengthy spells in the Williamsburg courts. When the attorney generalship was vacant in 1811, William was a serious candidate for the position. Political visibility in the intensely partisan atmosphere of the early nineteenth century inevitably led to public scrutiny. That scrutiny, and the defamation of character which sometimes followed, was one of William's motivations for avoiding politics. "I saw by the experience of others," he explained to Carr, "the treatment which I should experience, and could anticipate, almost with certainty, the topics of abuse and vilification with which I should be regaled."[70]

William probably was thinking of the excesses in which he had indulged prior to the Wirts' marriage, but the scandal that erupted was far more damaging. In his business trips to Williamsburg, William frequently visited a friend, William Russell, whose house was across from the Raleigh Tavern, where William often boarded. Russell had an unmarried daughter, Catherine, known as Kitty. In late 1811, it became obvious that Kitty Russell was pregnant—and rumors named William the father. While women bore the brunt of their society's disapprobation in such circumstances, men, too, were affected. Men's liaisons with supposed inferiors—slaves, poor whites, and prostitutes—were tolerated if they were discreet, but an affair between an older married man and a younger unmarried woman from the middle or upper classes, if exposed, was unforgivable. "There is not a crime in the whole catalogue of guilt that I regard with more horror than . . . the seduction of an innocent girl," William exclaimed. His neighbors would react similarly; if public opinion deemed him a seducer, William's "reputation as a Man of honor" would be tarnished forever. Paths to attaining public office would be closed. Legal clients would be lost. And, of course, William's anxious attempts to behave as a loyal and loving husband would be sabotaged.[71]

William first heard of the rumors on a trip to Williamsburg in early November. To his "amazement and horror," William found that he had been named, along with several other men who frequented the Russell residence, as the possible seducer. Although William had not been in Williamsburg during the critical time period, the rumors did not die out. On his return to Richmond, William continued, "It was told to me first by one friend and then by another; that the report was in full blast here and in the surrounding country." Although gossipmongers conceded that it was "physically impossible" that William was responsible for Kitty Russell's pregnancy, even more vicious rumors then accused him of being her "original seducer," by whom she bore a child that she abandoned and allowed to die of exposure and starvation several years previously. William acted quickly to defend himself, writing to his friend Anthony Robinson of Williamsburg to assist him in obtaining "the means of repelling the calumny." Robinson rallied to his old friend's aid. He visited both the troubled Kitty Russell and her father, who was on his deathbed, to obtain affidavits, witnessed by the mayor and the alderman of Williamsburg, testifying to William's innocence. Kitty Russell declared "on oath" that William had "never at any time committed an act, or uttered a sentiment to [her] incompatible with the *purest* virtue, and *strictest* honour." William Russell's affidavit also testified to William's innocence. William was a true gentleman, the dying man wrote, and Russell had "never heard him utter an improper expression derogatory to the Character of a Gentleman." William's reputation as a man of honor was rescued by these measures. Another seducer—the "villainous"

W. Irvine, who had left Williamsburg and reneged on his pledge to marry Kitty Russell—was named, and the rumors dissipated (though not before damaging William's chances at the attorney generalship; he was passed over in favor of William Pinkney).[72]

The circumstances of Kitty Russell's difficulties were so mysterious, and the available evidence so tantalizingly limited, that it is difficult to ascertain how much blame William bore in this affair. The reputation that William had earned as an irresponsible widower following his first wife's death probably had something to do with the persistence of the rumors. In addition, the rumors may have owed something to Mrs. Mary Ellis, with whom William had a brief and tumultuous relationship following his rejection by Elizabeth. It is unclear whether William was courting Mrs. Ellis, a Richmond matron, or her daughter, eighteen-year-old Caroline Lewis. In either event, when William decided to end his courtship, Mrs. Ellis responded with bitter recriminations. William's response to her demand that he return her letters to him quoted her: "O! inestimable privilege! you are *a man*—and consequently not accountable to any one for your actions." The frequency of William's visits to Mrs. Ellis's home had inspired "idle reports" about their "most romantic friendship," and she probably assumed that an engagement was imminent, perhaps even in place, when William took back his "liberty" in order to renew his attentions to Elizabeth. Mrs. Ellis's "mingled resentment and contempt" indicated that she considered herself, or her daughter, a wronged party. Although William returned her letters, she retained his. Possibly she planned to use them as ammunition against him at some point in the future. Indeed, the letters that William wrote to Mary Ellis may have been those rumored to exist which showed "a criminal intercourse did once exist" between William and Kitty Russell.[73]

The real truth of the matter is obscured, more than revealed, by William's single preserved letter to Mrs. Ellis and by the few letters in the Wirt papers regarding "The Unfortunate Kitty Russell," as Elizabeth labeled the collection. It is clear, however, that the women in William's life, including Elizabeth, recognized a sexual double standard that not only freed men from accountability for their sexual or simply misleading relationships with women but denied women the right to openly accuse men of misconduct. Elizabeth's response to the Kitty Russell affair is as ambiguous as the records pertaining to William's fidelity. It was Elizabeth who gathered and preserved the affidavits and other letters that contributed to the "exculpating of [her] beloved WW." Whether Elizabeth was convinced of her husband's faithfulness or whether, like other southern women in similar situations, she chose to overlook his transgressions cannot be determined with any certainty. However, if any doubts were placed in Elizabeth's mind by the incident, they probably exacerbated her unhappiness with her husband's continued work in the circuit courts.[74]

William's commitment to his legal practice and his reputation as a gentleman created more significant and lasting problems for the Wirts than the Russell affair. By making wage earning a central component of his husbandly duties, William hoped to demonstrate his commitment to Elizabeth even during their separations. In 1813, he wrote to Elizabeth to inform her of a further delay in rejoining her at their summer home. Although William pretended to ask Elizabeth's opinion on whether he "ought in discretion to go up" during a week's hiatus in the court's business, he had made his decision already. "An oppressive load of duties" awaited him, he commented. "How should I act? I must not sacrifice my professional duties & character to my own indulgence," he reasoned; "this would be injustice to you and our dear children. Yet Heaven support me!—You know what a struggle it is—I sigh and groan—'Can a lover do more?'" William clung to the thought that Elizabeth would support his decision. "I am consol'd and upheld by imagining that I can hear you say, 'husband *I* am proud to see that you have self command enough to subject your feelings to your reason & duty—persevere in this and we shall do well.'" William convinced himself that Elizabeth would prefer that he remain at work and that he could best serve and please her by remaining away from her. "You may reproach me and trample me if I don't now stick to and tug at the oar," he vowed. "With such a wife! . . . what would I not do—to what point would I not persevere."[75]

William used the same reasoning to justify his actions in the War of 1812, which Elizabeth opposed. Perhaps recalling Elizabeth's unhappiness with his military excitement in 1807, in 1813 William framed his participation in the war as a duty he owed to her. "I promise you that your husband shall not disgrace you," he wrote. Elizabeth, who learned of her husband's activities from the newspaper before receiving his letter, did not prove receptive to his explanation of his decision. "How could you have the heart to serve me so, my Husband," she protested. "No doubt I have taken leave of you for the remainder of the Summer," she complained, signing herself "your unhappy Wife." William rejoined with more specific appeals to the danger the war posed to women. "My dear wife, had you been here at the time of the alarm, you would have applauded the step which I have taken. The alarm was accompanied by the news of the sack of Hampton and the rape of our women." William was convinced that such details would convince Elizabeth of the propriety of his actions as a concerned husband. "How would you have had your husband to have acted under the circumstances?" demanded William, "to have hung his head like a coward . . . had I acted so would you, could you have even respected, much less loved me again? Your heart says no—and, therefore, I am sure you forgive me nay that you applaud me and love me more than ever." By describing his military service as a duty he owed as a husband, William hoped to regain Elizabeth's approval. "I call Heaven to witness that I am anxious only to do my duty to my country in that way which alone is worthy of the man who has the honor of calling a woman, like you, his wife." Despite his evident excitement at the prospect of "military glory," William attempted to assure Elizabeth that his true allegiance was to her: "My happiness, dearest Betsey, is only at home."[76]

William's military responsibilities called him away from Elizabeth during the summer and early fall—the very months that the couple usually spent together at the Cabell plantation in the Virginia countryside. These separations put an additional strain on the Wirts' relationship. During the summer and fall of 1813 and 1814, William remained in military camp while Elizabeth made lengthy visits to her sister's plantation, Montevideo. While Elizabeth consoled herself with her sister's company, William wrestled with the competing claims of military masculinity and loving companionship. Letters from home, he confessed, touched him deeply, but he found his sentiments inappropriate for a military man. "Mr. Gilmer handed me your letter," he began one letter home, "which I read with a heart too swelling and eyes too over-flowing for a soldier—Let us bid adieu to this subject—it is too tender for me." Demands on William's time also curbed his tendency to sentimental love letters. "I am continually engaged—occupied—hurried," he explained his brief notes, "yet not so much so as not to dedicate many delicious moments to the recollection of my beloved, most affectionate & most tenderly attentive of wives." Indeed, by the fall of 1814, William was ready to trade the rigors of camp life for the rewards of companionship. "O! how I love & adore you, best, dearest of wives," he exclaimed. "My heart choaks me and my eyes are swimming: But these times will pass away and you will be again restored to my arms."[77]

While her husband pondered the relative value of manly honor and his wife's company, Elizabeth was frantic with loneliness and concern for him. "I have been very low in spirits ever since we parted," she wrote in 1813. "Indeed I do not know that I ever felt a seperation [sic], more painfully, more full of anxiety and disquietude . . . Hasten," she pleaded, "to the bosom of your affectionate (blue devil'd) I had like to have said—Wife." Even William's most effusive letters were no substitute for his presence. "Since it has been Heavens will to separate us," Elizabeth wrote, "language is poor and barren." Often Elizabeth feared that the Wirts' separation might prove permanent. "My heart was bursting full of agony," she wrote in 1814. "I have to struggle hard to keep alive my hope in Providence—But in despite of all my efforts—despair at times gets almost complete possession of me."[78]

When the Wirts were reunited in late 1814, it was on William's terms, and it was clear that his activities would continue to tear the Wirts apart. In October, William's company was disbanded, and he returned to Richmond. He immediately wrote to Elizabeth to urge her to join him there. He was her "commander in chief," he wrote, and as "a wife," Elizabeth should "immediately return home." "Here is your home," he pronounced, "your husband, [and] your duties." William's role would be quite different. He already was immersed in legal business, he remarked, but was eager for Elizabeth's supportive presence: "The courts are going on—fees coming in—my business all alive—and nothing remaining but to have my beloved wife & children once more fixed down snugly & comfortably around me." Despite his own continuing calls away from home, William indicated, Elizabeth's "duties" required her to return home immediately. "Think of the *unnecessary* anguish of heart which this seperation is inflicting on us both," he wrote, suggesting that while the separations induced by his own absences were necessary, his wife could offer no such excuse. Elizabeth did not have the same control over the Wirts' time apart that her husband claimed as her "commander in chief." "I shall take it for granted that you will come," William wrote.[79]

Although he expected Elizabeth to return home when he summoned her, William intended to continue his own travels unabated. His attachment to paid work was increased by his decision to relinquish "the giant phantom honor" in exchange for law work. "I will be a private citizen as long as I can see that by being so I shall be of any use towards maintaining you & our children," he vowed. For William, the separations required by his work as a private citizen, because they were directed toward the family's support, were necessary and proper, as perhaps (as he sometimes admitted) the difficulties posed by his political career were not. "My beloved dear, you are no doubt censuring me severely for apparent neglect," he wrote in 1815, defending himself with the claim that his work in court left him "neither time nor temper" to give Elizabeth "the offerings of a husband's heart." The following year, apologizing for his short letters, William attributed their brevity to "the pressure of business" and advised Elizabeth, "Console yourself by remembering that any hour which I take from you to devote to business, contributes, so far to hasten my return to your arms."[80]

William considered the pressure of business an acceptable excuse for denying Elizabeth the offerings of a husband's heart, but she considered her husband's work-related absences a serious obstacle to marital satisfaction. Their different perspectives were shaped by their unequal positions inside and outside marriage; while William could find satisfaction in business, Elizabeth based her entire happiness on the Wirts' marriage. "Here, we are shut out from all the world," she lamented. "You are all the world, to me." The thought of "a protracted seperation," she mourned in late 1814, had thrown "a gloom" over her "whole soul." Elizabeth was torn between conceding "the necessity" of her husband's work and resenting the unhappiness it caused her. "I cannot but assent—however reluctantly," she wrote, adding, "If it is right—and if it must be so—I will endeavour to act my part as well as I can—and submit with all the resignation I can command." Elizabeth's repeated references to her own reluctant submission, her subtle hint that the situation was not right, and her keen awareness that she was acting a part all indicated that she understood that her husband's decisions constructed a marriage relationship in which the marriage partners had different roles and unequal power. The script that William wrote required Elizabeth to support and love him without reserve but permitted him to deny her his company. Elizabeth found it difficult to play her assigned role as a resigned, submissive, yet affectionate wife. For her, companionship required both partners to devote themselves to the other. Husbands and wives should owe each other reciprocal love and respect.[81]

Elizabeth struggled to meet her husband's definition of wifely love without abandoning her own expectations of her husband as a loving companion. In 1815, she was eager for William to conclude his time on the circuit and return home. "When are you coming home?" she demanded in January. However, she almost immediately retracted her claim to William's company, quickly adding, "I do not wish to hurry you on my account . . . I am pleased . . . that you should be seen, and known, in the world." Elizabeth soon became still more weary of her husband's travels. "Your neglect," she wrote, "shuts me up in solitude." However, Elizabeth knew that William would justify his actions with the claim that he had to devote himself wholly to "the harry of business" in order to hasten back home. If such was the case, "I must admit your excuse," she added. Despite her apparent resignation, Elizabeth closed by telling her husband, "Come home, and behave yourself like a gentleman."[82]

Elizabeth's dissatisfaction with the Wirts' relationship resurfaced in early 1816 when she wrote to convince him to approve her proposal to purchase a new home for the family. "I have experienced so much inconvenience in this house," she declared. "I tell you I can live no longer here—but if you will not hearken to me—I may wish to *die* in it . . . I *must* have a more commodious dwelling." Elizabeth implied that William, so often away from home, did not appreciate her difficulties. "I think you ought to give more weight to the consideration of my comfort," she charged, "and the vexations & uneasiness that I have to struggle through." Elizabeth's pent-up disappointment and anger flowed forth. "So it is with merit in this bad world," she declared. "It is always slighted, and made to bear more than others—when your next wife comes, she'll make you know how a woman ought to be treated, who has half as much to recommend her as your humble servant." Although focused on the house, Elizabeth's expostulations revealed her deep dissatisfaction with the Wirts' relationship. "If you do not take care," she warned, "I shall wish . . . that I had a 'gooderer Husband.' " William did not see the broader implications of Elizabeth's tirade, however. Bewildered by the onslaught, he promptly replied, "There is nothing in my power to do to make you happy that I would not cheerfully do." What was in his power, of course, was financing a new house, and William added that his current case in Washington would delay his return home "for a week or ten days longer."[83]

William's definition of a good husband increasingly revolved around his own success in his career. The following year, when he was offered the post of U.S. attorney general, he did not hesitate. Love and career, for William, were closely linked, but love was losing ground. "I will love you all & be as happy as the day is long if my profession succeeds," he anticipated. While William cleared away pressing matters in the attorney general's office and made arrangements to buy a new home for the family, Elizabeth again expressed doubt about his commitment to her, suggesting that his devotion to her was secondary to his interest in business affairs. "I did not suppose you would care to hear from us every day," she began one letter. "I expected you would be so engrossed by your new cares, and novel situation, as not to be often troubled by thoughts of home." In contrast, Elizabeth reminded her absent husband, "Here you are so much missed, by us all, as to make us feel and lament your absence *in every passing moment.*" Although he did not hasten his return home, William did his best to assuage Elizabeth's fears. He demanded daily letters and responded immediately to all those he received, offering in each a variant on the sentiment "I am quite as anxious to see you all as you can be to see me—I do not know when I have felt a seperation more cruelly." William assured Elizabeth that he needed her quite as much as she needed him. To Elizabeth's announcement that she could not exist without her husband— "who is all the world to me, and without whom I am but as a dead lifeless Branch"—William responded, "I cannot have any peace of mind 'till I get you, here. I am quite moped and melancholy without you." Even in the midst of such sentiments, however, William connected love and companionship with his ability to perform his professional duties. "I am very sure that I should not be worth a cent without you," he finished. When the Wirts moved to Washington in late 1817, their contrasting definitions of their marriage partnership would come into even sharper relief.[84]

The Wirts created their marriage, home, and family during what one scholar termed "the golden age of domesticity." Both women and men subscribed to the domestic ideal, praising the home as a "haven in a heartless world." However, the division of responsibility for maintaining this oasis, as we have seen, meant that women and men experienced home life in different ways. Men and women's different roles inside and outside marriage meant that the conflict between duty and love could become, as it was for the Wirts, a conflict between husbands and wives as well.[85]

~

CHAPTER FOUR

An Almost Complete Divorce

Living Apart in Washington, 1817–1829

"New and pressing duties": Domestic Economy

Elizabeth and William Wirt, who had established a tenuous partnership in Norfolk and Richmond, were wrenched apart by the move to Washington. Their cooperation in their domestic economy, already under strain, crumbled rapidly under the pressure of their "new and pressing duties" in the capital city.[1] Both Elizabeth and William spoke often of doing their duty during their years in Washington. Increasingly, however, the Wirts found that they had separate duties. For William, the attorney generalship brought new satisfaction in his legal work. He expanded his legal practice still more during the Wirts' years in Washington, spending up to ten months of the year traveling to courts in Baltimore, Annapolis, Richmond, Philadelphia, and even Boston. Left alone at home for the majority of each year, Elizabeth struggled with increasing difficulty to maintain her authority over her staff of rebellious slaves and proud servants. Her new responsibilities as a Washington hostess also detracted from her productive activities within the household. The Panic of 1819 meant immense losses for the Wirts. Elizabeth attempted to retrench the Wirts' expenses and resurrect her role as an economic partner, but William, confident of his earning ability, believed that there was no need to curb extravagant spending. In the capital city, Elizabeth and William redefined their roles, adopting a new set of duties. William claimed a position as the primary breadwinner, and Elizabeth—after many protests—abandoned her role as a domestic producer to become a consumer. The Wirts' family economy was transformed by these new and pressing duties from a domestic partnership to a relationship between a male provider and a dependent woman.

Elizabeth and William spent November and December 1817 in a flurry of preparation for their move to Washington. The discussions they held about the move hinted at the new lifestyle they anticipated in Washington and the changes their new circumstances would mean for their domestic economy and their roles within it. William eagerly catalogued the financial advantages of his new office as attorney general. "There was no kind of necessity to give up my connexion with Clarke," he noted with satisfaction, "and they all assure me that there is nothing in the duties of the office to prevent the general practise of my profession in this place and attending occasional calls to Baltimore, Philad[elphi]a. Annapolis, or Rich[mon]d." William's post, by unifying his desire for a steady income and his ambition for public recognition, increased his commitment to his own career, rather than to a shared domestic economy. Elizabeth's responsibilities in Washington also took a new turn. Initially, she hoped to continue the household production she had established in Norfolk and Richmond. She vetoed her husband's plans to rent or board, saying that she preferred keeping house. Located on the south side of G Street near the intersection with Eighteenth—just off Pennsylvania Avenue and a short walk to the Executive Mansion—the fine brick dwelling that the Wirts purchased from Tobias Lear would allow them to resume housekeeping without inter-ruption. However, the purpose of the house, as far as William was concerned, was public display, not domestic economy. "Lear's is a truly beautiful place," enthused William, "fine grounds, open all around—a fine gravel paved street before the door—and a nice, clean paved footway."[2]

The Wirts' new home would be the family's footway into genteel Washing-ton society, and as such, it would be the focus of their increasingly different household responsibilities. William financed the Wirts' entry into Washington with cash; Elizabeth prepared the home to serve as a forum for socializing, rather than for domestic production. William borrowed heavily to pay $13,800 for the $12,000 house and the two lots that made up the rest of the block, making Elizabeth, as he remarked, "the mistress of a whole square." Most of Elizabeth's letters as the mistress of a whole square revolved around socializing. Washington society demanded a level of entertainment the Wirts had not experienced in Norfolk or Richmond. Politics inevitably permeated social gatherings in the nation's capital. Indeed, political rivalries and ambitions were played out in family homes. The Wirt house's location on President's Hill, rather than in the separate community centered on Capitol Hill, announced that the Wirts were connected with the authority of the executive branch, rather than with the increasingly popular dictates of the legislative. Washington's leading families, especially those connected with the president, were expected to follow the president and first lady's example and to entertain in high style. As an important figure in the presidential administration, William Wirt would be expected to participate in the dizzying whirl of Washington's social life during the winter season. "Every one is highly pleased with the appointment of Mr. Wirt," commented Washington resident and novelist Margaret Bayard Smith, adding that she hoped that he and his family would "be most agreeable additions to our society." William had his first taste of the social aspect of political leadership in mid-November, when he made his first "round of official and ceremonious visits." However, the bulk of responsibility for socializing fell to women. "How do you think you will stand all this?" William asked Elizabeth. "And yet you will have to go through it all—aye & more, too."[3]

Even before the move to Washington, Elizabeth began to prepare for her first season as a Washington hostess. She determined to sell three of the Wirts' six slaves, replacing their labor with that of white hired servants. Possibly Elizabeth felt that her new labor force, a mix of slave and free domestics, better reflected the atmosphere of the city, a national capital located in the South. Certainly she was concerned with the first impression the Wirts would make in Washington. "If we purchase the house of Lears," she mused in late November, "we will require new carpets for the two lower rooms. our old ones will do for the chambers this winter. new Tables for Dining room & parlour— new chairs for one or the other of the rooms." Elizabeth's memoranda for her husband's approval and purchase suggested the new role as a consumer which she would fill in the Wirts' Washington home. Meeting "the Presidential standard," not managing the family's finances, would increasingly occupy her during the coming years.[4]

In the Wirts' first years in Washington, William enthusiastically devoted himself to his new career, but Elizabeth made every effort to maintain the Wirts' household as a center of production. William found that his new post demanded his unremitting labor. In January 1818, he wrote to his friend William Pope. "Since I have been here I have had to work 'till midnight, every night," he reported, simply "to keep the channel of my office from being blocked up by drift-wood." William worked hard to reduce the demands on his time in Washington by imposing a strict interpretation of his duties in office, but he used the time gained to practice law more broadly, not to share household tasks with Elizabeth. Convinced that it was necessary to augment his $3,500 annual salary (raised, at his insistence, from $1,500), William expanded his private practice during his tenure as U.S. attorney general. With fees starting at $500 for cases in the Supreme Court and appellate courts, small fees of up to $100 for written opinions for the government, and an average of $1,000 in each term of the Federal District Court at Baltimore and the Maryland Court of Appeals at Annapolis, he earned an average of $10,000 annually. William emphasized the monetary gains of his new position above all else. "As to the office which I have received," he assured Pope, "it was not, trust me, either the supposed honor attached to it nor any ulterior promotion to which it might be supposed to lead that induced my acceptance.—No; as there is a God in Heaven, who knows the secrets of my heart, it was the single object of bettering the fortunes of my children, by pursuing my profession on more advantageous ground—nor would I have accepted any other office under the government, even the *highest*—for any other would have been utterly incompatible with what I deem my first duty—which is to provide for my household." William gave himself the full credit—and the full responsibility—for providing for the Wirts' household.[5]

Elizabeth shared her husband's determination to provide for her household. Eager to maintain her role as a household producer and a careful consumer, she urged William, "Take care how you embark in new speculations, or purchases, that may embarrass you at this time—give me but little—if that little can be enjoyed in peace and quiet." To conserve funds, Elizabeth planned to sew curtains and carpets for the Wirts' new residence and to bring as much furniture as possible from the Richmond house. "I passed yesterday, until candle light, in cutting out work," she commented in May.[6]

Elizabeth found it difficult to direct household activities during William's extended absences, however. The "uneasiness" that she expressed at giving slaves directions without her husband's support suggests that white women had trouble managing slaves without their husband's assistance. Although urban mistresses may have confronted this problem more frequently than plantation mistresses, studies of white women in the rural South also argue that elite southern women had problems exercising authority over their slaves. Elizabeth found it difficult to manage both her slaves and the housekeeper, Mrs. Lane, whom she hired to assist her in household supervision. "I have made a formal transfer of the keys," she reported in September 1818, "but there has not as yet been one movement towards making a *personal* use of them—Mary [a slave] continues to act, only giving *her* the keys at night, in place of Bringing them to me." Despite the housekeeper's presence, the other household workers frequently played truant. Two slave women, Celia and Hannah, were "laid up," Elizabeth complained, and Stephen, a hired manservant, "refused to have any thing to do with" his assigned tasks in the cellar. From Richmond, where he had gone to consult with his armory partner John Clarke, William could offer only advice and stern warnings to the servants and slaves. He suggested hiring another "hand" to work "about the cellar," suspecting that without a man's direction, Stephen would prove unmanageable. "Order all the servants, in my name and at their peril," he advised. William's attempts to assist his wife in household matters revealed just how tenuous her claims to authority were.[7]

By reasserting her control over her household workers, Elizabeth hoped to regain her pivotal role in the Wirts' domestic economy. She sold the slave woman Mary, discharged the "young English girl" whose duties were unspecified, and "held a *talk*, or *consultation* with Mrs L. as to the division of labour" among the household workers. With her newly reorganized staff, Elizabeth engaged in a frenzy of cleaning and other preparation in the autumn of 1818. The entire house was cleaned from top to bottom in preparation for winter. "I shall be buried all the week in cleaning and whitewashing," Elizabeth wrote. By November Elizabeth was ready to embark on a new project. She withdrew money from William's bank account to purchase "a Barrel of Herrings," a cow, flour, and "a side of Beef." Elizabeth's early winter purchases, though costly, were designed to allow her to use her own and her slaves' and servants' labor for preservation and production. Bulk purchases of raw materials, Elizabeth hoped, would save money in the long run. In the spirit of an economic partner, she did not hesitate to claim funds from William's practice. "I shall want money next week," she informed William. "Make Turner [William's client] pay the money to me." Elizabeth used William's legal fees to engage in household production on an impressive scale. In December, she purchased ten freshly slaughtered hogs to be cut up and preserved for the winter. Elizabeth negotiated the price and supervised the cutting up; she requested William to make the payment.[8]

Having reinstated housekeeping as an economic concern, Elizabeth expected William to recognize it as such and to assist her at home. Only a high fee would justify William's absence for Elizabeth. Informing her husband of a prospect in Delaware that offered "250$ as a fee and a thousand in case of success," Elizabeth recommended that William decline the case; "I am sure you will not stir for such a petty sum," she explained. William's presence at home was more precious than wages, she argued. Household supervision was particularly difficult for Elizabeth because of the composition of the Wirts' household. As free and slave workers jostled for position in the servants' internal hierarchy, Elizabeth complained that their uncooperativeness made it difficult for her to maintain "the proper dignity of the Mistress of a House." When one hired servant refused to work in the garden unless he was given a better room and a slave to clean it, Elizabeth expostulated, "I am completely out of *conceit* with white servants." By December 1818, Elizabeth was frantic. The Wirts' slave man, she wrote, had subverted her own authority: "He has the complete mastery of the House Mrs & all." Determined to maintain her authority at home, Elizabeth realized that her standing was weakened by her husband's absence. "I tell you man," Elizabeth pronounced, "you are wanting at home—so shorten your holiday . . . *I* want you every minute."[9]

The double rewards of wealth and reputation made it difficult for William to accede to his wife's wishes, however. In late 1818, a near duel with William's keenest competitor for clients, William Pinkney, demonstrated the close link between William's reputation as a man of honor and the demand for his legal services. Pinkney insulted William in front of the assembled court, and William asserted that his reputation as a man of honor was essential to his responsibilities as a provider. "I have a character to bear to my family, the richest inheritance, I hope to make it, that I can leave them," he argued. "I had no alternatives before me, none on earth," he exclaimed, "but to wander, at large, a despised and contemptable [*sic*] *coward*, to be kicked from the bar and to be kicked thro the earth, scorned by every eye." The duel was averted (Pinkney apologized), but the highly publicized contest sealed William's position as a leader in the Baltimore court scene. "Pinkney has injured his personal popularity very much by his treatment of me," he informed Elizabeth, "and my conduct has raised mine to it's summit." Despite his talk of duty to his family, William admitted to a thrill at the thought of undertaking more and challenging cases. "My spirits rise at the expected tug of war," he wrote in reference to the next stage of his legal battle with Pinkney, "and make me feel my strength." William continued to find himself busily engaged in legal business. "Every day has brought new and pressing duties," he wrote in early 1819, "and the moment of leisure has never yet come."[10]

William's increasingly lengthy absences exacerbated Elizabeth's difficulty in coping with household management. While William sought out the new and pressing duties he complained of, Elizabeth noted the "many demands upon [her] time just now." In early 1819 the Wirts lost both their housekeeper and Henry's nurse, and the new nurse distressed Elizabeth with her "wild courses." Elizabeth's greatest problems, however, stemmed from her inability to command authority over her male slaves in her husband's absence. In April, what began as what William optimistically (and condescendingly) termed "a truant frolick" became a full-fledged slave revolt. Frederick, one of the Wirts' slaves, armed himself with a pistol and a knife, joined forces with two other slave men belonging to the Wirts' neighbors, Mr. Lear and Mr. Dorris, and escaped to Baltimore, where the three runaways were apprehended, jailed, and recovered by Mr. Lear. Frederick's actions were all the more troublesome because of several indications that a widespread slave rebellion might be under way. Reports of arson came from as far away as Winchester and Norfolk, and rumors of a planned massacre flourished. "No one know what to think—or what to do," fretted Elizabeth, "and from a few circumstances I have heard related—*my old fears are aroused*—and I am too defenceless to rest at ease—in such times—and for you to be away too—when so much [is] required at home!" From Richmond, William could offer little in the way of concrete support. His own days were filled with anxiety about the early signs of bank failure that began the Panic of 1819. A nationwide enthusiasm for speculation, financed by dubious paper currency, ended abruptly when in early 1819 the entire country watched in horror as the inflated values collapsed. "The suffering for the want of money, here, is dreadful," William worried. Preoccupied with his own difficulties in Richmond, he had little sympathy to spare for his wife's "series of vexations." He would hurry home, he cautiously promised, only if he could "do no law business." William remained in Richmond for more than a week longer to settle the Wirts' accounts there and to attend to "business in the court." "This I must do, or I shall consider myself as neglecting a most important duty to my family," he explained.[11]

The financial difficulties of the 1820s exacerbated the Wirts' difficulties in balancing their budget and their roles in household economy. Their debts were heavy. William had borrowed money to finance the cannon foundry in Virginia as well as to move to Washington, and in the economic downturn that followed the panic, both real estate and industry proved to be a drain on the Wirts' funds, rather than a profitable investment. When the state banks collapsed, the Wirts were forced to default on a note for twelve thousand dollars to the Farmer's Bank of Richmond.[12]

Elizabeth and William responded differently to the economic crisis posed by the Panic of 1819. William, bemoaning the Wirts' "pecuniary distress," trusted in his legal fees—not in curbing expenses—to extricate the family from debt. He began a pattern of overwork that frequently threatened his health. During the winter 1820–21 session of the Supreme Court, William suffered a recurrence of the dizziness and fainting spells that had plagued him in his youth. "During the last Supreme Court," he explained to his fellow lawyer Dabney Carr, "I was very much engaged. I was forced to lose my wonted sleep, and had not a moment for exercise: The Court kept me constantly engaged till four o'clock; I had then to hasten home to dinner, and, immediately afterwards, to sit down to my papers till ten, eleven, and twelve at night—Then up again at three or four in the morning, and, with merely time enough to take breakfast, off, as rapidly as my carriage could drive me, to the capitol, at eleven." This breakneck pace continued for six weeks, at which point, "exhausted by past toils and want of sleep, . . . the symptoms of the vertigo returned." Despite his failing health, including temporary "dimness and blindness of sight," William refused to slow his pace. His goal, he wrote to Elizabeth, was to become "prosperous" with his "new plan of a more extended practise."[13]

William hoped that becoming prosperous would render unnecessary the "radical cure" of a "retrenchment of those habits of extravagance which seem[ed] to have become universal." Elizabeth, however, responded to the crisis with redoubled efforts to renew her economic partnership with her husband. "It is time to be at work," she announced. While William argued court cases in Baltimore, Elizabeth assisted him quietly from Washington by copying, addressing, and mailing his official letters "in good order." Elizabeth also tried to revive her role as financial manager and advisor. Receiving a hundred dollars from her husband, she pondered whether she should "lay it aside" to save or use the money to buy oats at a depressed price "before it took a rise." Elizabeth left the decision up to William but added her own counsel: "It is clear, that you *must retrench*—and even then, you can not get clear of the Banks—unless you would endeavour to sell out in the Bellona Furnace—That is the only expedient that I can fix upon to clear you of present debt."[14]

In addition to increasing her involvement in business and financial matters, Elizabeth also increased her household workload. Through hard work and careful purchasing, she hoped to avoid going further into debt. "I do now almost all the housekeeping," she remarked; "it is in that alone that we can practice oeconomy." For Elizabeth, housekeeping included a wide array of activities. Spring of 1820 found her copying letters and opinions for William, preparing papers for settling accounts, negotiating for the plowing and planting of an oat field on the Wirts' square, and supervising "Billy & Frederick in the garden . . . Omai & James in the garret scouring & taking down bed steads—Celia, & Mary, 'in the garden hanging out the clothes'—sunning the blankets & woolens & put[t]ing them away in linen bags from the moth[s]." Other letters informed William of Elizabeth's progress in cutting, piecing, and sewing clothing for the children, altering her own clothes to serve another season, gathering vegetables from the garden, preserving fruit and other household staples, and stocking up on well-priced hay, corn, and oats for the Wirts' horses. Elizabeth repeatedly reminded her husband of the value of her labor and encouraged him to regard her as his partner in domestic economy. "I will not attempt to pass these off for letters," she referred to her bulletins of progress. "They are merely hasty memorandums of Business."[15]

Despite William's thanks to his "dear wife" for her "clerical labors" and her "resignation" to "any sacrafice [sic] that prudence dictate[d]," the Wirts soon found that it was difficult to abandon habits of extravagance. With prospects of improved business, William looked forward to abandoning the resolution he and Elizabeth had made of avoiding unnecessary expenses, particularly where the children were concerned. "How are our dear little boys?" William asked in 1822. "What must I get for the twins—what for Elizabeth & Catharine?" Laura, too, should have something special, William resolved, proposing an expensive watch. "I know the debts," he wrote Elizabeth, anticipating her disapproval, "but this will not be a feather in the scale." In vain, Elizabeth cautioned her husband against unnecessary expense. "This 'feather in the scale'—is what we have been in the habit of saying all our lives," she noted wryly. "But it is not what *true oeconomists* either say or do." Elizabeth repeatedly wrote to urge her husband to learn economy. "Pray my Husband be moderate," she pleaded. "Let me pray of you, if you have made any money—to endeavour to learn the art of keeping it," she advised. " 'Tis time we had gained some such knowledge."[16]

Although William shared Elizabeth's concerns about finances, his views of extricating himself from debt were different. William opined that his income was the family's only sustenance. "We have curtails and bank debts to pay," he worried, "and *no* resources *save only these fees*—Our feelings must keep the peace while we are pressed by this necessity." With brighter prospects in law, William tended to overlook Elizabeth's contributions to the household economy. Preoccupied with his fees, he did not assist with work at home. The workers often stalled in their tasks, and Elizabeth's remonstrations were to no avail. "It is enough to fret a saint," she exclaimed. "May I not hope to see you to Morrow—or the next day at farthest[?]" William, busy with legal work, refused. "This cause will take I fear till saturday night to finish it," he explained, "and perhaps, even later—We must do our duty." While he refused to return from Baltimore himself, William confessed to "some faint expectation" that Elizabeth would leave home to visit him. She responded with a sharp reminder that she, too, had duties that could not be abandoned. "As to my going to Baltimore—it would not be right that I should do so," she remonstrated. "My gardens & house, require my constant attention to put them in order."[17]

Successes in court and a steady stream of fees encouraged William to abandon the more cautious strategy of domestic economy for a reliance on his increasingly rewarding career. "Do you not want money[?]" he inquired in May. "You have but to say so—and the deed is done the die is cast." Although he promised not to purchase luxuries without Elizabeth's consent, William soon began to agitate for permission to purchase gifts for the children. His growing income, he implied, could bear the additional expense. "I have done very well here," he crowed. "I mean that I am satisfied with my professional exertions . . . We must have Patience . . . and get along in *money matters* as well as we can." Crises in money matters only increased William's delight in the income his career brought. In 1822, upon receiving a demand for the prompt repayment of a loan for nearly two thousand dollars, William was smug. "Is it not fortunate that I have turned in to this Baltimore practise?" he asked Elizabeth with a hint of I-told-you-so satisfaction. "How should I have been able to meet these Bank:runs without it? Suppose now that we had had for this summer and for these Bank-calls no dependence but our salary!—Only suppose it! Is it not then Heaven-directed that I have been able to leap into a practise which I beleive will enable me to laugh at their demands?" The opportunity offered the next day seemed a divine answer to the Wirts' dilemma. William was offered the chance to replace his old archrival, Pinkney, as the representative for all of the insurance companies making claims to the recently established Commission on Spanish Claims, which was charged with providing citizens with redress for maritime losses incurred during the Napoleonic War and the War of 1812. "It is such a case as does not occur more than once in the course of a mans professional life," rejoiced William. The position would be worth twenty thousand dollars over the course of a few years, he estimated confidently. "Let us, therefore, agree to pursue our plans of oeconomy as closely as gentility and the character & standing of our children will permit," he recommended.[18]

The Wirts' letters in the years following the Panic of 1819 reflected their uncertain yet decided shift away from a joint domestic economy to a total dependence on William's wages. Although William still spoke of "our" salary, indicating his recognition of Elizabeth's assistance with his work in the attorney general's office, his official salary faded into insignificance with the fantastic profits that could be realized by "a mans" professional work. With less enthusiasm than her husband, Elizabeth also conceded at least a temporary dependence on her husband's earning power. "Am very sorry you can not be with us tomorrow," she stated in one letter, "but it would be a great folly to throw away fees or put aside business, to be with us a day or two sooner."[19]

Throughout the mid-1820s, Elizabeth and William struggled to redefine their domestic economy. Elizabeth hoped to resurrect the financial partnership the couple had established during their years in Virginia, but William's cash contributions and his professional duty remained absolutely essential. Elizabeth focused on keeping the family's expenses down. "I have gone to no expense that could be avoided," she assured William. Throughout the mid-1820s, Elizabeth took steps to economize. She arranged for the children's summer clothing through a combination of thrifty purchases, mending, and altering hand-me-downs; planned to bake, rather than buy, bread for the winter; and did the gardening herself. In 1824, she sold her home-cured ham and bacon to a local merchant. Elizabeth hoped that her husband would acknowledge the value of her efforts. "I have been exceedingly busy too *in my way*," she reminded him. Although William acknowledged Elizabeth's role, he viewed his own work as more important. While Elizabeth made plans to scrimp and save, William dreamed instead of earning his way out of debt. "I have turned into the practice of the law, might and main," William told Pope in June, "as a refuge both from poverty and low spirits."[20]

William's ascendancy, although spurred to an extent by economic urgency, threatened the Wirts' domestic economy by encouraging him to rely on his own efforts, rather than to cooperate with Elizabeth in family finances. If his hopes were realized, he informed Elizabeth in November 1823, he would reduce the debt by three thousand dollars by the end of the year. Confident of his earning ability, William undermined Elizabeth's thriftiness by purchasing jewelry for the girls, provoking Elizabeth to worry, "Where are we to economise—?" "What a difficult matter it is to economise, with a family used to indulgences," she observed. "It is much easier to become luxurious, than self denying."[21]

Gradually, Elizabeth relinquished her role as a producer and arrived at a grudging acceptance of her husband's role as the primary financial support of the family. Without her husband's cooperation and assistance, she concluded, she could not make housekeeping a successful proposition. As Elizabeth aged, her responsibilities weighed more heavily on her at the same time that William reduced his involvement in household work. In an attempt to reduce the family's expenses, Elizabeth cut down the Wirts' retinue of servants in 1823. Fewer household assistants, she soon found, placed a still heavier burden on the mistress. "I am perfectly *done-up* by stooping," she groaned after completing her work in the garden in 1824. "Really, I can not bear fatigue as I used to do," complained Elizabeth, "before I became so *heavy & stout*—my feet can scarcely perform their office at the close of every day." "I am more worsted by my labours than usual," she admitted in late April. Her declining energy prompted Elizabeth to reconsider her decision to keep her household staff small. If there was someone to see that the Wirts' slave man Omai "was made to clean himself of an evening to wait [on table] . . . instead of spending this time abroad," he could easily act as waiter and butler as well as coachman, Elizabeth thought. "But who is to make him do that?" she cried. Recollections of her past difficulties managing slave men must have led Elizabeth to doubt the practicality of her plan without her husband's constant assistance. Although William promised, "When I return Omai shall do his duty either voluntarily or by force," Elizabeth may have decided that the disadvantages of such a sporadic mastery would prevent her from achieving her purposes with only one male servant. She soon abandoned her plan and searched instead for an additional manservant.[22]

Simply adding workers did not resolve Elizabeth's dilemma, however. The difficulties of supervising "disorganized discontented spirits among the domestics" on her own, she wrote in telling exaggeration, made her "a perfect slave." A housekeeper was indispensable, Elizabeth decided, to spare her from the difficulties of managing an unruly group of slaves. "I have come to the resolution that if we can once meet with a good one that we had better give extravagant wages to ensure their staying with us," she concluded in 1824. By the following year, Elizabeth was still in search of a housekeeper, and she also hoped to purchase a slave cook. "But where is all the money to come from—!" she demanded. "That is a consideration, not to be put aside too easily."[23]

Exhausted and frustrated, by the mid-1820s Elizabeth had reached the conclusion that, however unpleasant she found William's itinerant career, it was necessary to provide for the family's comfort. William repeatedly sent money to Elizabeth to permit her to hire more household help. Elizabeth's reliance on her husband's wages made it difficult for her to oppose his career plans. When he asked her if she would prefer to leave Washington for New York or Baltimore, she reluctantly voted to stay in Washington. "*If* we can be ensured our present salary—& your practise in Balti[more]," she conceded, "I dare say we would do better to continue as we are."[24]

Where Elizabeth was reluctant, her husband was enthusiastic. William felt more strongly than ever that his legal work would be his most important life work. "The official questions which are propounded to me," he told his friend Dabney Carr, "are all out of the usual walks of my profession and call upon me to explore new paths and frequently to chop out an original trace with my own hands through the wilderness. My opinion books are full of this labor and will save much trouble to my successor. If they were published," William predicted, "they would do me more honor than any thing else I have ever done." To Elizabeth, William described his legal work in less glowing terms but maintained his centrality in ensuring the family's welfare. "I hope to be at home by the last of next week," he remarked in July 1825, "but the court talk of even sitting longer than then—Let them sit as long as they may—I must sit with them while they have any thing to do . . . for I must be known to be in quest of business—and I must be so too—for out of debt I am resolved, with the blessing of God, to be, next year—and O! what a relief will it be to us all!"[25]

As Elizabeth's financial partnership with her husband waned, a new domestic responsibility demanded her attention and William's cash: genteel socializing. In 1820, the Wirts decided to add a room to their house to prepare it for Laura's official debut into Washington society. To outfit the new room, Elizabeth ordered new furniture, including a mahogany sofa "of superior beauty," black marble mantelpieces, and yellow material and fringe for window coverings. She also attended estate sales for additional decorative touches. A comment she made to Laura on the purchase of a music stool and stand and a pair of silverplated candlesticks following one such sale might have applied to all the expenses incurred that year for construction and other home improvements. "As your Father says," Elizabeth wrote, "this is all for you Laura— an expense we should have dispensed with, but for your sake."[26]

The Wirts' attempts to maintain and even advance their standing in Washington society increased the gap between Elizabeth's goal of domestic economy and William's professional life. In 1825 the Wirts planned the details of a grand season. New carpets, grates, plastering, and paint were decreed necessary to ready their eastern room for the Wirt daughters to entertain their suitors. Although Elizabeth complained about the "monstrous charge" of these preparations, she and William agreed that it was a necessary expense. "If the room can be handsomely painted it will be worth the carpet," William ruminated, "and we might, I think, consult our own and our daughter's advantage by enabling her to make her parties as genteel as possible." Every day brought new expenses. "I have indeed been quite melancholy at the expenses that we have encountered this fall," Elizabeth worried, "and yet to be genteel it could not be helped—yet even this plea of *necessity* does not reconcile me to it." Only a week later, however, she was forced to write to William again to request more money, this time to purchase trunks, bureaus, and lamps to replace the "shabby" ones at home. "There is no end to our expenses," she wailed. "The expenses of the fall have almost crazed me already." The Wirts consoled themselves with the thought that their investment would not be wasted but would facilitate their daughters' marriage to eligible wealthy bachelors and the entire family's move into the upper ranks of Washington society. "I have a strong notion that Laura will get married before another winter," opined William, and Elizabeth commented, "There is no doubt but that Eli: [Liz] will come on, as soon as L. [Laura] is off [and] at all events, next winter."[27]

Preparation for the girls' debuts cast Elizabeth and William in a relationship of female consumer and male provider, a situation that contrasted strongly with their earlier attempts to realize a family economy to which each contributed. In 1826, Elizabeth was outfitting the girls with expensive Paris fashions, and the house was undergoing yet another renovation for the upcoming season. "Buy enough to put your own mind at ease on the score of gentility— and fear not," William advised Elizabeth with benevolent authority. While Elizabeth used William's fees to purchase the luxuries that gentility demanded, he devoted himself to making "a good fee." "I shall hardly be settled at home 'til February [1826]," he predicted in November 1825. "Work—work—work— money—money—money—wife and children—children—children," sighed William at the responsibilities that burdened him.[28]

In Washington, Elizabeth and William were divided, rather than united, by "the faithful & conscientious discharge of [their] duties."[29] William traveled to make speeches; Elizabeth remained at home, dependent on her husband's wages. However, the near future would give them an opportunity to resurrect their lost domestic partnership. Expecting to be summarily dismissed by the newly elected president, Andrew Jackson, William prepared to leave the capital for greener pastures.

The Wirts' discussions of the move indicated both how attenuated their partnership in their domestic economy had become and how it might be restored. In evaluating their future home, William indicated that he intended to continue in his by then accustomed role as breadwinner. "What remains of my life," he resolved, "must be devoted to the solid interests of yourself and our dear children—and in choosing the theater for my labours we should look *primarily to profit*." However, by consulting his wife about the approaching move, William gave her an opportunity to reclaim her role as his economic partner. She responded with alacrity. Elizabeth hinted that her husband had forced her into a new status as a consumer in the capital city by placing the family in a situation in which lavish entertaining was an indispensable requirement. "We entertain less than any other family with whom we associate," she reported to her mother, "and yet it takes a great deal to keep us in comfort and gentility. I do not beleive that there is any one else who aims with more perseverance than I do, at making the most of every thing," she assured herself, "yet if we cared not for appearance—there are many little things that might be dispensed with—But not while we move in the circle in which we now are—with a family to set off to advantage." Elizabeth indicated that abandoning her current responsibilities as a hostess—responsibilities that made the family dependent on her husband's wages—would be a relief. If they moved away from Washington, she remarked to William, they could dispense with "luxuries" in "a new administration of things." In the new administration, Elizabeth hoped to pare down her household staff and reintegrate William into her household routine. "If we remain where we are," she predicted, "we shall have to keep on in the old way, of spending faster than we can make it.—As a matter of *oeconomy*," she concluded, "it would I doubt not be advisable to make a move—I do not see how matters can be mended where we are." She had done all she could, Elizabeth insisted, to keep expenses down, and if she was to do more, she must have her husband's cooperation. "If you expect more from me," she concluded, "you will have to throw me on a new theatre—where you may have it in your power to superintend in person all your affairs—and assist by your council."[30]

"Our cares multiply upon us": Home and Family

"Alas!" cried Elizabeth in 1824. " 'The cares that do environ' the parent of a numerous offspring. . . . Ah me! Ah me! our cares multiply upon us—we have only to turn from one to the other, for variety, but not releif [*sic*]!"[31] During Elizabeth and William Wirt's time in Washington, their cares as parents diverged as well as multiplied. By the mid-1820s, Elizabeth had begun to explore a new identity for herself based on the very circumstances she had originally deplored: the waning significance of her economic contributions to the household, William's almost constant absence from home, and her close confinement to the unshared duties of parenting. William withdrew from active parenting, and his authority as a provider and as an academic mentor faded as Elizabeth claimed her role as the primary parent. William made sporadic efforts to regain his earlier importance as his children's beloved father, but his efforts failed. Having reoriented her life to adjust to her husband's distance from home, Elizabeth was unwilling to allow William to step in and out of the new domestic routines that she had established. The cares of parenthood, which formerly had united the Wirts, now pushed them apart.

The Wirts' family correspondence as they anticipated the move to Washington hinted at changes in their delineation of their responsibilities as parents. William's letters indicated that he planned to redefine his role in the children's education. He would reduce his active involvement in child rearing. His time, as Robert wistfully observed, "would be employed more usefully in executing [his] lately appointed office of *Attorney general to the united States*." Although William did not have time to devote personal attention to the children—he sent "love to all the dear little ones" in his letters to Elizabeth, directing her, "Say something to each one for me"—he would maintain a parental role by financing the children's schooling in the capital. Elizabeth proposed that the Wirts bring the children's governess with them to Washington to continue the children's home instruction—and, presumably, William's participation in the children's education and discipline. William, however, had different ideas. "Tell your dear mother that she shall do as she pleases, in every thing," he wrote to Laura, "except the school arrangements for her children"; on that subject, William continued, he expected Elizabeth to bow to his judgment. William planned instead to send the older children to local academies for instruction.[32]

As William reduced his direct participation in child rearing, Elizabeth struggled with the tasks of maintaining the Wirts' family life on her own. During the Wirts' years in Washington, the family included ten children, ranging in age from baby Henry, born June 20, 1818, to Laura, fifteen years older than her youngest sibling. Elizabeth pleaded with William to come home and help her with child care. Often, her letters took on a desperate tone as she cried: "Master Henry *will not sleep*[!]" From distant courts, William insisted that he felt the pull of duties at home, especially parenting, acutely. "You think I was not made to live at home among children," he accused Elizabeth, "and I think I was not made to live from them—My dear Agnes for example, just now," he asserted. "One look, one smile, one kiss of her's wd. be worth all Baltimore to me."[33]

Yet William's lengthy absences from home continued to detract from his declarations of devotion. In vain, Elizabeth sought to remind her husband of the important tasks that he neglected in his pursuit of fame and fortune—and of her own heavy burden as the sole family caretaker. When William nearly dueled with Pinkney in December 1818, Elizabeth was distraught: "Can it be that you the Father of ten children could have forsaken them . . . for a rash word spoken by reptile man[?]" William continued to think fondly of home while forsaking those who remained there. "The more I see of this villainous world," he proclaimed in 1818, "the more do I love the innocence and natural affection of my own fireside.—O! what a haven of peace after such a storm as I have been engaged in, here." William's extravagant praise for home was no substitute for his presence. In late 1818, Elizabeth informed William that four-year-old Agnes had issued an ultimatum. "She says 'tell him, tell him he must tome [i.e., come] today—if he dont, I'll twy [i.e., cry] every day—and wont love him.' "[34]

Home was only one arena for the Wirts' family life, however. As their family grew, they relied more and more on day schools and academies to supplement or to replace home instruction. During the Wirts' time in Washington, all the children attended school. The older children—Laura, Robert, Liz, and Catharine—attended day schools and boarding academies. The younger children—Ellen, Rosa, Agnes, Will Jr., Dabney, and Henry—attended local schools. Initially, William maintained his role as academic advisor from afar. His letters, as during the Wirts' years in Richmond, guided the children in their studies and provided them with support and encouragement. As William increased his commitment to his career, however, Elizabeth became the children's chief correspondent, and William lost influence over the children.

William was the family's acknowledged instructor. When Laura planned to continue her studies in the nation's capital, she made her father her ally. William reveled in his role as academic advisor. He designed Laura's lessons and made other necessary "arrangements" for her continued study at home. In December 1818 he counseled Laura: "Estimate properly the value of youthful study . . . and apply it to yourself." However, as Laura neared the conclusion of her studies, William passed responsibility to Elizabeth. When Laura went to the Cabells' in 1820 to help her cousin Louisa in preparations for her wedding, Elizabeth took the leading role in correspondence with her oldest daughter. Elizabeth's letters to her daughter were peppered with comments designed to prepare Laura for courtship and marriage. "Tell me . . . every thing about yourself," Elizabeth urged Laura. "At what hour you arose in the morning—how you arrayed yourself for the day—who helped you to make up your ruffs, &c &c?" Elizabeth also expressed concern that her daughter had not been properly trained for the housekeeping duties that would follow marriage. Although Laura intended to return quickly to Washington and her studies there, her mother had other plans. It was time, she wrote, for Laura to acquaint herself with "the minutia of housekeeping." While Elizabeth pushed her daughter to abandon her studies for finery and housewifery, William relinquished his role as his oldest daughter's personal tutor and academic advisor.

By 1820, William's letters to Laura were infrequent. "My love to Father," wrote Laura from Richmond. "I wish he wd. write to me—he promised to do so often when I took leave of him—I do not think I merit such neglect."[35]

The Wirts' oldest son also had reason to complain of his father's neglect. When Robert departed for West Point in 1820, Elizabeth and William adopted very different attitudes toward him. Elizabeth continued to guide her son through affectionate concern, but William replaced his former model of a loving father with the stance of a stern authoritarian. Robert wrote chiefly to his mother, whom he evidently viewed as more nurturing and supportive than his demanding father. "Dearest Mother," he began one letter, "I received your letters about the middle of last week—In a strange place, among strange people, cut off from all my connexions, you may conceive how much pleasure I received from perusing lines couched in the well known language of affection, that had so often addressed me from the lips of a Mother." Elizabeth responded with affectionate and regular letters, and Robert's communications with his father dwindled. In October 1820, Robert wrote a distraught letter to William in which he begged for his father's encouragement and approval. "Lowspirited" after a disastrous class recitation, Robert begged, "Advise me my father." But William, away in Richmond, did not respond to his son's urgent plea for assurance and love, and it was Elizabeth who cheered her son: "I have no fear of your doing honor to your Parents, and being a blessing to your friends, and to your Country."[36]

While Elizabeth sought to comfort and reassure her oldest son, William's letters to him were "written in a tone of displeasure" which he had never assumed toward his son before, according to Robert, and he was "very much hurt" by his father's stern "commands." In December 1821, the effects of William's waning influence over the children became horrifyingly clear when the Wirts learned that Robert had been the "ringleader" of a student rebellion at West Point. Elizabeth asked William to "make haste home" to assist her; "I know not what to say to him," she worried. However, William was unable to wield his wonted influence over his son. "[Robert] decline[d] my offer to finish his education by a college course," William told Elizabeth in the spring of 1822, adding with some bitterness, "He had better take the advice of some judicious friend in whom he *can* have confidence . . . He may otherwise live to repent his rashness."[37]

When Robert returned home, it was his mother who was his judicious friend. Robert was plagued by an unidentified illness (some physicians pointed to the liver, others to the lungs as the source of the disease); in addition, he was so severely depressed that his parents feared mental illness. By December

1822, the situation had become so desperate that William resolved to accompany Robert to Philadelphia for a consultation with the renowned physician Philip S. Physick. Robert responded to his father's ministrations with pathetic gratitude. "He is exceedingly fond of my nursing," commented William, "and expresses his gratitude most tenderly—calls me to suffer him to grasp my hand—will have no hand on his forehead but mine—and thanks me in a manner which proves that his original affectionate heart is all alive." Physick hopefully reported that Robert's mind was sound, only affected by "sympathy" with an unidentified physical ailment, and William hoped for a speedy recovery. Yet his eagerness to return to Washington and to the Supreme Court undermined the progress made. "Robert came in to see me," noted William; "[he] said he could not do without me . . . He is affectionately fond of me." Two days later, William returned to Washington, leaving Robert in a boardinghouse.[38]

The Wirts' descriptions of home, like their correspondence with their adolescent children, resonated with the growing distinction between their roles. Left alone at home for most of the year, Elizabeth tended the family with "a mothers watchfull care." In 1822, she described herself as "surrounded by the children." As a father, William related a very different set of duties. In 1823, he wrote that he was "intensely engaged morning, noon and night" in preparations for court. "If I can finish all I have to do on tomorrow I will go home the next day—but don't expect this for fear of a disappointment," he added. Increasingly, William's definition of fatherhood narrowed to encompass only the task of providing for the children economically—a responsibility that made it impossible for him to engage in the many other aspects of parenting. No longer actively involved in the children's lives, William replaced paternal guidance with gifts. Particularly during holidays, William was determined to give the children the material evidence of his love for them. In mid-December 1823, still away at court, William invested Christmas with immense significance. His extended stay away from home, he reasoned, would allow him to earn enough money to make Christmas a happy day. "What is the use of making their young blood stagnate in their veins by constantly prosing about oeconomy, and marring all their little enjoyments by gloomy complaints about the cost of them," he demanded. "For my own part I think every dollar well spent that gives their poor little hearts throb of happiness." While William made earning money central to his definition of fatherhood, Elizabeth described motherhood as a duty that bound her to her home and her children. "It is not possible for me to leave home," she noted, for that would be leaving her children "without either Father or Mother."[39]

Increasingly, the children relied on their mother for all their needs. Elizabeth shepherded Laura into the marriage market and took the leading role in guiding her in making a choice of a husband. "There are parties . . . every 3 or 4 days," she noted in January 1823, and on most evenings, the family entertained "a few Beaux." Anticipating Laura's engagement, Elizabeth also began to prepare Liz and Catharine for courtship and marriage, directing them away from classical education and toward more domestic pursuits: "housekeeping," baking, and "a sewing club." Health care also was Elizabeth's responsibility. In 1824, Elizabeth was Robert's only nurse. Robert was reluctant even to mention his "feeble" health to his father. "He objects to my making any mention of him to you," noted Elizabeth, "except that he is well."[40]

Robert's illness was a matter of deep concern for both Elizabeth and William, but they displayed their love in different ways that reflected how differently they defined their family duties. By late June it was decided that Robert's condition—now thought to be an infection of the lungs—demanded a sea voyage to the Mediterranean. William intended to accompany his son as far as New York, but despite his assertion that his "poor dear Son" was "the subject uppermost in [his] mind," he decided that legal business prevented him from making the trip. The unexpected expenses of a sea voyage ("There is such a heavy demand upon our purse in providing for our son," worried Elizabeth) gave additional weight to William's claims that his work demanded that he remain in Annapolis. Once aboard ship, Robert addressed his correspondence exclusively to his mother. Sadly, William admitted that his son had good reason to overlook his father in his missives home. "It makes me a little sad at heart that he should not . . . [have] even alluded to his father," he sighed, "yet all things considered it is not very surprizing [sic]." Despite his unhappiness at his alienation from his son, William did not write to him. Robert's voyage was costly—William estimated the expense at one thousand dollars—at a time when the amount of individual fees was disappointingly small, and William omitted personal involvement in favor of wage earning. "I have made a good speech to.day," he congratulated himself in mid-November. "It is a good day's work altho the fee is not very great—not more than 100 or 150 dollars for I see it will not do to refuse small fees and wait for large ones only, which are getting . . . few and far between." Though William did not know it, his preoccupation with work in Annapolis had denied him his final opportunity to reconcile with his son. The Wirts received word of Robert's death in late December 1824.[41]

The Wirts' loss made it still more obvious that mother and father had very different responsibilities at home. William's role was focused so closely on wage earning that Laura worried that it would be "improper" to ask him to comfort her grieving mother. Elizabeth, too, was unwilling to ask William to return home to lend her his support. "She did not wish me even to say any thing about it," Laura told William. William comforted Elizabeth, but he also assigned her the responsibility for the family. "May the Father of Mercies support and comfort you," William prayed. "May he pour into your bosom the rich consolations of his grace, and preserve and strengthen you for your husband and your children." William indicated that it was his grieving wife's duty to submerge her grief so that she could offer comfort to the rest of the family. "What could we do without you—and what can we do if you suffer yourself to sink under the sorrow that now afflicts you," he demanded. "Let us bear up, dearest love, and endeavour to fulfil our duty to our surviving children so long as we shall be spared to them." Although William proposed that both he and Elizabeth should do their duty to their remaining children, it was clear that the responsibility for keeping home life afloat was Elizabeth's.[42]

By the mid-1820s, the Wirts had come to describe their divided lives as necessary and unavoidable. "I am *very very tired* of these long seperations," admitted William. "I was trying to day to rally my whole family groupe before my mind's eyes and it seemed so like an effort to produce a resurrection of those who have left me forever, that it made my heart sink." Elizabeth felt hopeless to change the situation. "We are all . . . quite tired of your rambling," she sighed. "But when will it be any better—never, I fear."[43]

William made several attempts to regain his former importance in family activities following Robert's death. Liz and Catharine wrote often to their father to request his opinion of their ambitious plans for home study, including chemistry, Italian, history, arithmetic, physics, logic, grammar, geography, and music. "We want you to chalk out a course of history for us," Liz wrote in 1826, urging her father to reply immediately. "Do not forget that we await the word of command from you to begin our march of science," she prompted her father. "We wont'[sic] take a single step 'till we hear from you." William was "well pleased" with his daughters' plans. "I am very willing to take advantage of a stray inclination of this sort in my children," he told Catharine. However, William found time for correspondence with the children only during "the rare intervals of [his] toils." "I have come to a stand in my historical course for want of your presence and advice," Liz wrote in 1826. "Will you write to me directly, my dear Father, and tell me what to do?" Although William offered hasty advice in a letter to Elizabeth, he did not reply directly to his daughter's request. "I have a most monstrous record of 600 folio pages to prepare an argument on tonight," he explained; "[the children] must be content to be my creditors 'till I can pay them."[44]

William's interest in his older daughters waned as their schooling drew to a close. In 1826, he accompanied Liz, Laura, and Rosa to the Virginia Springs. Although he was pleased with Liz's and Rosa's deportment—Rosa was "a great favorite," William remarked, and Liz's "free, vivacious and natural manner" was very "pleasing"—William found the duty of supervising his daughters wearisome. It took constant effort, he discovered, to prevent them from crossing the invisible but all-important boundaries on young ladies' behavior. "They are very glad to get clear of my supervision . . . that they may not fall under the criticism of my eye," he commented. "I have not had to scold them much," he summed up, "that is—not a very great deal—that is—not continually." The tasks of chaperoning young ladies were very different from those of supervising girls' educations, William discovered to his chagrin, and he did not welcome the change. "I do not understand them," he said of the girls, "and their whims plague me infinitely more than they do you." Disappointed in his efforts at fatherhood, by the end of August, William was eager to relinquish to Elizabeth his temporary role as primary parent. "If you were with me," he wrote to her, "you wd. take all this off my hands and would give me our room to myself as soon as it was cleaned up, passing your morning and evenings in the girls' rooms—But without you," determined William, "I cannot get along with girls—and this is the last time that I will attempt it."[45]

By the end of the summer, William was eager to abandon the duties of parenthood for those of his profession. He had been chosen to deliver an oration in honor of former presidents Thomas Jefferson and John Adams, which he hoped would increase his "reputation" and thus his list of clients. He had only "broke ground," he groaned in mid-September, and he was making all haste to return to Washington in order to complete the work without the constant interruptions of parenthood. "It is nonsense to attempt so vain a thing as to compose such an affair, here, with the constant anxiety of these three girls on my hands," he concluded. "I find myself constrained to give it up 'till I can get home and lock myself up from all the world." Rather than a retirement from his labors, home now had become a place for William to prepare for greater success in the world. After spending a month in Washington, William departed for Annapolis secure in the knowledge that his oration had been a success. "I have concluded . . . my argument in this great Ringgold cause," he rejoiced. "They call it here one of the greatest, if not the very greatest, argument, I have ever made in any cause."[46]

As he retreated from active fatherhood, William attempted to fulfill his responsibilities as a parent through his work away from home. Urging Henry to work on the alphabet and his catechism, William enclosed a coin. "I send you one more fip," he wrote, "but this must be the last—for father must not spoil you . . . You must love father and his letters for there [sic] own sake—not for the money," he closed on a plaintive note. William's admonition fell on deaf ears. "The boys were . . . very much delighted with their letters," reported Catharine; "thier [sic] fip's added not a little to their delight." Despite his recognition of his waning influence over the children, William continued to consider financial support the most important duty of fatherhood. In the 1820s, he began to invest in Florida on his own behalf, hoping to establish a fund for the future needs of the family. The plan made William's legal work, rather than his presence and advice, central to his responsibilities as a father. If all went well, he calculated in 1826, he should be able to earn up to eleven thousand dollars that year. "If we get all this we shall be able to buy land enough in Florida for all our wants and all our childrens, in the course of the coming year."[47]

While William busied himself with the family's financial wants, Elizabeth developed new parenting strategies that left little place for her husband. Elizabeth's direction of Liz's and Catharine's daily regimens in preparation for courtship and marriage shut William out of the aspect of child rearing he valued the most. Although Elizabeth wrote to William to procure the latest Paris fashions for Liz's debut in the winter season of 1826–27, he found that searching the shops for hats, cloaks, and other finery was no substitute for exchanging letters on academic subjects with his daughters. "All this is hebrew to me," he complained to Elizabeth. "I feel that I am entirely out of my element in all this matter," he despaired. "I wish I had you here for a few days." Elizabeth's criticism of her husband's selections discouraged him from further attempts to participate in the girls' coming-of-age rituals. "Altho' I am most willing to do any thing I am always afraid of doing wrong," he excused himself. "Elizabeth's white dress is given up on your decision," he concluded, "and you must equip her according to your own taste."[48]

Earning money was William's chief fatherly duty in the mid-1820s, and it was a duty that drew him farther out of the orbit of family affairs. In December 1826, William was peripheral to the family's preparations for Christmas. Elizabeth informed him that she had already provided for the girls. "For the Boys—I have made no provision," she added, "supposing that you would—But should you not I shall put money into their stockings, which will do just as well." Elizabeth's discussion of the seasonal celebration made it clear that

William's role in the family had been concentrated entirely on wage earning; a few cents could substitute for his personal involvement in the children's holiday. William's work in court prevented him from giving the children more personal attention. "I owe Lizzy and Catharine a letter," he commented in 1827, "but they must trust me yet a little longer—My cases will detain me I fear much longer than I anticipated." Once again, William replaced letters with gifts. "We are in the midst of our trials," he wrote, "and I shall be too busy to write to the children . . . I think Lizzy ought to have a coral necklace, bracelets and buckle," he added, "and perhaps a cross to match her comb." William felt compelled to remind his family that his work away from home was his way of showing his love for his family. "It is his love for those at home that force him on these excursions," he reminded Catharine when she complained of her father's absence and sparse correspondence, "and it is *their* business rather than *his own* which disables him from writing to his children—will you remember this another time."[49]

While his love for those at home took William away from them, Elizabeth consolidated her control over the Wirts' family life. By the late 1820s, their household production levels had decreased enough that Elizabeth's domestic work consisted primarily of child rearing. In her husband's absence, Elizabeth focused more attention on the children than ever before, making motherhood a full-time occupation. One of Elizabeth's maternal duties, as she defined them, consisted of giving the children religious training. While the older children—Laura, Robert, Liz, and Catharine—had received moral instruction from both parents, the younger children's souls were Elizabeth's responsibility. As the century progressed, more and more ministers and women became convinced that women, whose responsibilities as economic producers were reduced or ignored, should undertake the sacred duty of religious guidance. In the context of what one scholar termed the "feminization of religion," Elizabeth demanded greater recognition of her role as moral instructress, and William readily accepted her suggestions. Elizabeth's religious reading led her to the conclusion that she should expand her duties as a mother to include attempts to prepare her children for early conversion. "I wish them all to prepare, without delay, to make a public confession of their faith & dependance upon the Savior, in obedience to his command," she wrote in 1827. Elizabeth determined that her own methods, utilizing the gentle guidance and maternal explanations that had worked well with the older children, were preferable to the "pompous style" of the family's Presbyterian clergyman, Dr. Laurie. "I feel an aversion . . . to their being received into his church, under his teaching," she concluded. "And have the vanity to think, that I would make a better instructor of youth myself—in practical religion, and in the duties that infirm, weak, human nature is equal to." Elizabeth would become the chief instructor of youth in the Wirt family, as William, from his distant posts, resisted her efforts to involve him. "You can not shake off the responsibility, under which Providence has placed you," insisted Elizabeth. "You will have to give in your account, willing or not. Oh think of it, before it be too late." William did shake off the responsibility, however. Although he approved of his wife's activities, he saw no role for himself in the plan. "I have no time to pursue this subject," he explained. "You view it rightly—and consider me as consenting to all you propose."[50]

By the late 1820s, Elizabeth and William had reorganized their responsibilities at home to accommodate William's career. Elizabeth took steps to make her role even more central. In 1827, she withdrew the girls from school after deciding that the teacher was not "a proper teacher for girls of any delicacy or refinement." The girls' education, as well as their preparation for marriage and their moral development, would henceforward be Elizabeth's sole responsibility. Removed from school, the younger girls—Ellen, Rosa, and Agnes— joined Catharine and Liz under their mother's guidance. Morality was one of Elizabeth's chief concerns; she proscribed novels and fairy tales, encouraged the girls to join local benevolent societies, and escorted them to religiously affiliated charity events, such as a Catholic fair to benefit a school for orphans. Elizabeth also made supervising the girls' health and exercise "*a sacred and indispensable duty*," as William noted in 1827. In addition, she acted as the girls' social director and occasional hostess. "We are to have a large dining party tomorrow," Elizabeth told Laura in early 1828. "I have had the Jellies Blanc manges, custards &c prepared."[51]

William, meanwhile, attempted to regain a role for himself by taking an interest in the boys' education. His plan, however, was to send them away to school, rather than to instruct them himself. In 1828, William was thrilled at the prospect of sending the boys to a school near Northampton. The Round Hill school, he enthused, inculcated "systematic habits of study" in its student body. "There they learn every thing *radically*," he raved. "Their physical as well as intellectual powers are completely developed." William and Dabney, if not Henry as well, should go immediately to Round Hill, William proposed. William's role would be to provide the funds and to select the school. "As to the expence," he remarked, "our sons must be educated—I shall probably be able to do little or nothing else for them—and that ought to be done as well as it can be done . . . It is an afflicting case—but our duty must be done."[52]

Despite William's references to "our duty," he was marginalized from the

Wirts' home and family in the late 1820s. William made a few attempts to reintegrate himself into the domestic routines established in his absence, but he soon discovered that it was difficult to regain the role that he had relinquished so readily. William initially withdrew from the older girls' lives when they left school for their debuts. He had little respect for his wife's social management. "When I am from home," he told Liz, "I am always really *busy* with *business*—whereas you are busy only with dissipation." A brief experiment with supervising Liz at a party in Baltimore in the spring of 1828 left William with no desire to learn more about his daughters' dissipation. Detailing the round of dances and other parties to Elizabeth, he declared, "I am excessively sick and tired of it all—and heartily wish my self at home." But after returning home with Liz, William promptly departed for Philadelphia "for the remainder of the season," leaving Elizabeth again in charge of the festivities. By the summer, both Liz and Catharine had serious suitors. While William observed the girls' "swains" from afar, it was up to Elizabeth to supervise this "critical and most interesting Epoche" in their daughters' development.[53]

William's periodic attempts at involvement in the girls' entry into society had soured his perceptions of fatherhood. "I have no great opinion of the virtue of my lectures," he wrote. Liz had treated his advice in Baltimore with "contempt," he complained. "The time has been when she attached some consequence to my advice," he sighed, "but unfortunately for her as well as me, but more unfortunate for herself, it seems to have passed away . . . It grieves me to say this and still more to know it to be true," William concluded sadly. When William had an opinion or advice to offer, he made Elizabeth his conduit. "I wish you would give your girls a lecture on that line in Popes Rape of the Lock," he once suggested, " '*oft* she *rejects*, but *never once offends*' . . . But you can instruct them better on this subject than I can."[54]

Elizabeth responded by taking control of all aspects of her daughters' courtships. She made inquiries about the girls' suitors and received their appeals for permission to propose. When Elizabeth asked her husband's opinion of her idea of allowing Catharine's suitor to take away a miniature of Catharine with him to France, William refused to participate in the decision. "As to the affair of the miniature dispose of it as you please," he wrote. "You are prudent & wise & I shall be satisfied with your decision." When William recanted and belatedly attempted to slow the progress of Catharine's romance, Elizabeth laughed at his untimely gesture, calling attention to the handicap to parenting which William's legal career created. "It is diverting enough to hear you off at a distance saying 'thus far shalt thou go'—you shall care just so much, & no more, for each other," she smiled. "Did you really expect that human passions were to be thus controlled, & measured out, by a third person." Although she actively intervened in the girls' courtships, Elizabeth suggested that such supervision was a parental prerogative reserved for one on the scene; from his courts, William could neither judge nor advise his daughters on their romances. Chagrined, William admitted his failings and entrusted the matter to Elizabeth. When a suitor proposed to Liz in late June, William held himself aloof. His own "*flashing* views" might assist Elizabeth, he wrote, but her decision was final: "I confide in what I sincerely affirm, *your own superior wisdom*, to take the proper course."[55]

During the summer of 1828, Liz's and Catharine's poor health gave William another opportunity to regain his former close relationship with his daughters. In August William took both girls on a trip through the northern states en route to Round Hill, where Will Jr. was enrolled for the first time. Initially William found the trip rewarding. He consulted with several doctors along the way and reported with satisfaction, "Catharine, we think, improves already in health," as well as, "I never saw her in better spirits." "Father is quite as *Motherly* & careful in his dear attentions as you yourself would be," Catharine reported. But Elizabeth could not so easily relinquish her by then accustomed role as chief parent. She urged William to slow the pace of the journey and gave specific instructions about both the quantity and the variety of drugs that Catharine was to be treated with. Elizabeth was justifiably concerned about the heroic remedies the medical men William consulted might prescribe for Catharine, and when she learned that William had deviated from her recommendations, she discouraged further experiments. "It would be impossible to tell you the distress which your letter of today has given me," she cried. "Rub that dear childs chest with *tartar emetic ointment*!!—shocking! You know nothing of the effect of it," she accused, "or you never would have consented to try such an experiment during a journey." If William's confidence in his ability to care for his daughter survived Elizabeth's criticisms, it crumbled a month later, when Catharine's health refused to respond to his ministrations. "I am now anxious for her to be under your care," he concluded.[56]

By 1829, the Wirts had adopted a model of home and family which assigned men and women very different roles. Elizabeth was the family's "dear Mother," William remarked, and she was the best possible parent for the children. "She is all wisdom and goodness," he told Liz. "Her opinions are infinitely better than mine, and she will advise you tenderly as well as wisely." Although William was thankful for his "happy, innocent and most affectionate family," rather than enjoying their company, he was preoccupied above all with "placing them in independent if not affluent circumstances." In Baltimore, however, William hoped to attain this goal in only "a few years." Describing himself as "bright and buoyant with hope," he looked forward to finding "gaiety and cheerfulness" at home in Baltimore.[57]

"Vexatious drawbacks to happiness": Love and Marriage

As the Wirts prepared for their move to the nation's capital, Elizabeth admitted that she found herself "exceedingly low in spirits." She had serious misgivings about the move to Washington. "I have realized the apprehension of an almost compleat divorcement, untill I can scarcely bring myself to beleive that, we shall perhaps in a few weeks, be living together as quietly and happily as ever," she wrote. Elizabeth referred only to the time that the Wirts spent apart while William located a new home for the family in Washington and she made preparations to leave Richmond. Yet her apprehensions of an almost complete divorce were realized in a much more profound and enduring way than she had anticipated. Elizabeth and William Wirt's changed circumstances in Washington, especially their endorsement of separate roles in which William was primarily responsible for bringing in money while Elizabeth was left with a revised list of domestic duties that no longer included household production, shattered their hopes of realizing an economic partnership. The new roles that Elizabeth and William adopted in parenting, which endorsed separate expectations for men and women, exacerbated the psychological rift between husband and wife. Finally, William's work in widely scattered courts kept him away from home for up to ten months each year, widening the gap between him and Elizabeth. "These separations, so long protracted, are vexatious drawbacks to happiness, my dear Husband," she noted soberly. During their years in Washington, under the stress of these vexatious drawbacks to happiness, Elizabeth and William turned away from their hopes of shared bliss and succumbed to an almost complete divorce.[58]

Elizabeth and William's correspondence in late 1817, as they anticipated their move to Washington, forecast the changes that the move would mean in their relationship. Although William insisted that Elizabeth and the children should move to Washington as soon as possible—"as to our living asunder I would die first," he proclaimed—Elizabeth gloomily prophesied that, even after the move was accomplished, her hopes of a more perfect union of shared love and duty would be postponed. "How I long to have you home again," she mused from Richmond. "But alas I may bid farewell to the hope of ever more possessing this happiness permanently for some years to come. I expect you will be less at home than abroad, if you find it necessary to extend your practice as you suppose." Elizabeth highlighted the divisions between husband and wife which William's decision dictated: "I am quite melancholy at the prospect before *me*—but for you I feel gratified and pleased." She anticipated—rightly—that the Wirts' relationship would not resume its former character, even once the couple was reunited. William's new duties as attorney general and the Wirts' new responsibilities in Washington society would mean significant changes that would interfere with their efforts to find mutual companionship in marriage. They would not live, Elizabeth predicted, as quietly as they once did: "I fear we shall not be allowed to do altogether as we please in that respect."[59]

Duty, not pleasure, was the hallmark of the Wirts' years in Washington, and duty increasingly was defined in highly gender-specific ways. From the start, their letters to each other indicated that they were preparing to yield their vision of a life of shared love and duty to undertake a life of separation and different duties. As Elizabeth sighed in 1818, "Pleasure must give way to duty." William agreed, remarking, "It is our business, in all situations, painful or otherwise, to do our duty." For most of the Wirts' tenure in Washington, William's practice followed a regular pattern: January through March were spent in Washington at the Supreme Court; April at the federal district court in Baltimore; and June and July at the Maryland Court of Appeals at Annapolis. After a vacation in August, William returned to Baltimore for the district court for the months of September, October, and November. He divided December between the Maryland Court of Appeals at Annapolis, the federal district court at Baltimore, and preparing for the upcoming session of the Supreme Court in Washington. During many years, William spent only about two months out of each year at home. His eagerness to establish himself in his extended practice as well as in the attorney general's office caused frequent delays in his plans to return home. Writing from Baltimore in August 1818, William warned his wife that his decision to enter the county court there meant that he would prolong his stay in Maryland. It was necessary, he reminded her: "for I am here on a new theatre and must do my duty *manfully*." William's emphasis on his duty as a man indicated that the Wirts would devote their years in Washington to duties that pushed them apart, rather than to seeking the mutual pleasure of companionate marriage.[60]

With greater consistency than she had demonstrated in Virginia, Elizabeth acquiesced in her husband's conviction that his first duty was to provide, rather than to participate in the daily rhythms of family life. To accommodate the male role that William had marked out for himself, Elizabeth made it her duty to support him. In May 1818, William made the first of many sojourns to Maryland to try his luck in the circuit court of the United States, which held its session in Baltimore. Informed that her husband's stay would be prolonged, Elizabeth responded with unaccustomed resignation. "I thank you for your very acceptable letter," she wrote to William. "And although it gives me a certainty of lengthened absence—*that* is what I had made up my mind to expect, and am therefore the more easily reconciled to it." Elizabeth joined her husband in giving him credit for the sole support of the family, even excusing him for his brief letters. "I have to thank you for your two sweet favours," she replied, "short and sweet, as they are. But indeed I would not wish them to be longer, in consideration of your poor hands, and the demands upon your (I will *not* say *poor*) head. I did look for you on Sunday with such a certainty—that I could not help being greviously disappointed—but you were not to blame—and there is consolation in that—and what is more, you have my perfect and entire aprovation, and I may add congratulation—to your prolonged stay. However painful is your absence—it is for the best—and what I must count upon enduring."[61]

Elizabeth and William had different feelings about the new roles they had adopted in their marriage. Elizabeth found her role as faithful supporter difficult to endure. By midsummer of 1818, she was weary of her husband's extended absences from home. "How vexatious, and disappointing this prolonged absence," she scolded in late July, "and I *do* want to see you so bad—for all *you* are not half so good as you used to be, in writing to me every day . . . The fact is you must make haste home and then we shall all go right—and be so happy! so no more of your delays, if you please!" Two weeks later, when William still had not returned, she stepped up her pleas. "Do you think you will indeed stay longer than this week?" she asked. "Oh, surely not . . . It seems to me as if you had already been away half a year—Time drags on so heavily." While Elizabeth mourned her own disappointment, William was enthusiastic about his new activities. "I am gaining honor," he told Elizabeth; "Heaven blesses me at every step."[62]

The Wirts' different attitudes toward their marital responsibilities caused friction in their marriage. "Here is a gloomy, dark, rainy day," Elizabeth told William in September 1818, "and I am just as *sombre* and gloomy myself . . . My spirits are completely prostrated." In "wretched spirits," she begged him to hasten his return: "Do not make a long stay from us!" Although William attempted to reassure Elizabeth of his love, his reply clearly showed the happiness he felt at his burgeoning career away from her. "Think not, blessed dear, that [my] duties, severe as they are, have excluded my own dear fireside from my heart's core," he soothed, emphasizing that his severe duties were less important to him than his dear fireside. However, in contrast to the Wirts' years in Richmond, William's attempt to phrase his work in terms of his love for Elizabeth was followed immediately by evidence that he enjoyed his duties for their own sake. "There is great excitement, here, and the whole world around us looks to me as the only vindicator of the injured honor of the nation," he puffed. Offering to take a recess and come home if she wanted him to, William urged Elizabeth not to ask it of him. "With all your love for me," he assured himself, "and all your anxiety for my company I know you value more the honorable & conscientious discharge of my public duties and my official fame." Having established the overwhelming importance of his legal work to his own satisfaction, William attempted to satisfy Elizabeth with the promise of two hundred dollars and dismissed her claims, adjuring Elizabeth and the children to "make yourselves all as happy as you can" and not to fail to write to him. Perhaps offended by her husband's condescending tone, Elizabeth refused to be pacified. "I must bring you to confess yourself in the wrong," she replied, "[before] I shall be again, your loving and dutiful Wife." William did not admit the justice of Elizabeth's demands. "Since the days of Aaron Burr I have never been engaged in such a scene of litigation as has been witness here," he wrote, comparing the case to the one that first brought him acclaim. "I have been conscious all the while of my apparent neglect of your kind attentions," he admitted, referring to his sketchy correspondence, "but I have relied on your candid construction and affectionate indulgence." Elizabeth's affectionate indulgence was strained in her reply. "The sound of your return would be cheering," she remarked, "if I could allow the hope to spring up in my heart that you would indeed come—But I feel as if you had been gone from me so very, very long a time, and been estranged from me so completely—that I dare scarcely expect such a happiness."[63]

Elizabeth and William became even more estranged before his return. In his publications, his political maneuverings, and in his enthusiastic participation in the War of 1812, William had flirted with the convention of the duel, which, more than anything else, marked a southern man as possessed of honor and deserving of leadership. Despite his heated rhetoric, he avoided an actual duel until December 1818. Then, William's first and only duel was touched off by "a collision" with Pinkney in court. The occasion was the commencement of the Baltimore piracy trials, which opened in late November 1818 at the federal circuit court. The trial was the first confrontation between William and his archnemesis on Pinkney's own turf, and both parties—as well as the roomful of spectators—were primed for a dramatic altercation. They were not disappointed. As William described the classic steps of the duel: "He insulted me by a rude remark which was generally beleived here to have been premeditated—I resented it in court—and words ensued . . . His language was such as left me no alternative but resentment out of court, giving him a day after the thing occurred to see if he would not, of himself, offer a voluntary apology on the scene where the insult was given. He failed to do so and I was driven to the unchristian necessity of exacting from him the reparation due to my honor." Pinkney, confronted by a formal challenge to a duel, backed down. "He has made the necessary explanations," concluded William, "and we meet tomorrow at breakfast at Mr Upton Heath's, his friend, in company with Mr. John Patterson . . . who was mine." The entire episode had occurred the previous week, and William had done his utmost to keep Elizabeth ignorant of the entire affair. "You will not be surprised that I have not mentioned it to you before," he told her after the conclusion of the clash, "but I have been extremely afraid all the while that you would hear of it—and am very glad you have not—You will see some reason why I have not found time all this while to write to you."[64]

It was small wonder that William was extremely afraid that Elizabeth would learn of his activities, for the duel touched off another serious disagreement that revealed the major shifts under way in the Wirts' relationship. When Elizabeth received the news, she was beside herself. Opposed to duels on religious grounds, she was still more concerned with the prospect of being "forsaken" by her husband. "Oh my Husband, my Husband, what shall I say or do," she wailed. "Oh thought of horror and frenzy! Have I been so near to being desolate[?]" William refused to apologize for his actions. Invoking his authority as a man and the public actor for the family, he told Elizabeth, "You are not a judge of these things, my love.—Your husband's honor should be left in his own hands." Had he not proved his honor, William argued, he would have proven himself undeserving of his "beloved wife." "Think my dearest love of this," he urged, "and then say if I have not acted worthily both of you, my highest object, and of myself." Although he dismissed Elizabeth's objections, William could not help worrying about his reception at home. "Do not reproach me when I come home," he pleaded, "for this is, now, my only terror—All is peace here and I am told on all hands that I am perfectly understood.—I hope I may be, *by you*—Enough of this now, love.—Think of it no more," he counseled, effectively closing the discussion.[65]

The Wirts' exchange indicated the marital tensions created by men's and women's unequal positions in society in nineteenth-century America. True to the model of companionate marriage, William was anxious for Elizabeth's approval. He hoped that she would understand his decision, accept his argument that he did it out of love for her, and commend his actions. At the same time, however, he knew that one of the prerogatives of a wife in a companionate marriage was to reproach her husband for actions that left her desolate. To defend himself, therefore, he used the language of manly honor and patriarchal authority to prevent his loving wife from acting as a judge of his actions. His acts as a man of honor, he indicated, did not fall under her proper supervision, and she should think of it no more. The duel indicated that although the Wirts continued to idealize romantic love, William was prepared to use his authority as a public actor to enforce his wife's compliance. The Wirts' marriage was no longer a union of two individuals but the uneven joining of a male superior and a female subordinate, the division between them clumsily papered over by the language of dearest love.

William never again participated in a duel, but his work as U.S. attorney general and as a lawyer with a national reputation gave him the same power to dictate the terms of marriage. In December 1818, after being separated from her husband almost constantly since April, Elizabeth wrote "with a heavy heart" on "the certainty" of his continued absence. "I am really heart-sick at the prospect—Is there to be no end to it?" William's reply offered no consolation. Rather than assuring his wife of his love, he directed her to support his decisions, whatever the emotional cost. "Do not, in addition to my own low health & spirits, oppress me, dearest love, by the knowledge that *your* spirits are low.—It is our business, in all situations, painful or otherwise, to do our duty," he reflected. "And I shall and must do mine in this cause." While William made it his duty to prolong his absences from home, Elizabeth struggled to comply with his expectations of her. "What can be done?" she asked in the spring of 1819. "Nothing—*But submission*—This *same sub[mission]:*— requires no little exertion of fortitude & resolution."[66]

Elizabeth and William's determination to submit to their duties forestalled discussion of alternative arrangements. William, determined to fulfill his responsibilities to his public office, discounted his own longings for Elizabeth's company. When he wrote from court, he sent all his love to his "dearest and best of wives" but continued to emphasize that his first duty was to the courts. "My soul sinks under this long absence," he admitted, "but I must do my duty and see this cause through . . . I hear you sigh. but my dearest love I must either resign my commission or do my duty under it." Elizabeth, too, cloaked her desire to be with her husband with her determination to adopt the new role he had assigned to her. "How glad I am to hear that you will soon be with us," she wrote, adding, "I would submit to your longer stay." Elizabeth made it clear, however, that she was constantly on the lookout for an opportunity to change the Wirts' situation. "I hope this is the last letter you will receive from me, this year at least," she pondered wistfully shortly before Christmas 1821. "These separations, so long protracted, are vexatious drawbacks to happiness, my dear Husband," she wrote, "and if I knew how to better my self, I would not submit to them, so I wouldent." William, however, suppressed all his desires to endow the Wirts' marriage with its former intimacy. "Do you know that I *heartily* wish I were with you?" he asked Elizabeth the following spring. "That is to say my *heart* wishes it—while my *head* says I should be here . . . Out of debt! *Once* out of debt!—to that my labours shall be turned—and I must submit to privations of all sorts, to emancipate myself and my family."[67]

Although William argued that he, too, experienced the Wirts' separations as privations, by the early 1820s it was obvious that he relished his work and the rewards it brought. In 1821, despite his poor health, William spoke for twice as long as he had intended (four hours instead of two) and still was "halfway only" in his speech. Although "much exhausted," William was happy with his exertions. "*I satisfied myself,*" he concluded with pleasure, and he looked forward to the remainder of the case, despite its uncertain duration. Flushed with pride at acquitting himself well, William attempted to justify his prolonged stay to Elizabeth in less glowing terms. "This is a *duty* my dear love," he wrote. "I have contracted to go thro' with it—and I must keep my engagement."[68]

The Wirts' different views of their new lifestyle, as much as William's prolonged absences, placed a serious strain on their relationship. In 1822, Elizabeth lamented their growing separation. "This itinerant life, which he feels it necessary to lead, is very unpleasant to me," she wrote. Elizabeth's phrasing indicated that she did not share her husband's view that their unpleasant separations were entirely necessary. Furthermore, Elizabeth suspected that William felt differently about the couple's itinerant life. "I beleive he is very well pleased with it," she confessed to Laura, "and he improves upon it certainly, in health, & spirits." Elizabeth repeatedly charged her husband with deserting her emotionally as well as physically. "You say nothing about coming home," she prodded. "*I* really am somewhat embarrassed when asked about you nowadays," she chided, "and hear the people say—'Why I beleive Mr W has left you altogether—or, Mr W—is scarce ever at home now a days &c &c[']—which I frequently hear said." By the following year, Elizabeth spoke not of abandonment but of divorce, indicating the increasing seriousness of the couple's physical and emotional distance. "Nancy joins me in love to you," she wrote, "and says she does not see that it is worth your while to live in our state of divorce, for all you are making by it."[69]

Although William continued to pay tribute to future happiness as a reward for present sacrifice, Elizabeth no longer found his explanations convincing. "Independence is the prize we play for," he reminded her in 1823, "and to achieve it, we must not regard privation and self.denial." Elizabeth recognized that her husband found satisfaction in the work that he justified, to her, in terms of his responsibility to earn his way out of debt. She wryly noted that William's promise to call a halt to his absences after relieving the Wirts' debts was destined to be an empty one. "So you are 'resolved to discontinue this out practice! as soon as you are out of debt, & can afford it!' " she mimicked him in 1824. "There can be but little difficulty in promising that much, upon such terms, I think. Would to heaven you could afford it!" she added with heartfelt sincerity. "*Two months in the year*—and not always that either—is too bad a life to lead."[70]

Despite William's growing attraction to the rewards of public life and Elizabeth's increasing unhappiness with her marriage, the Wirts continued to identify love and marriage as the surest sources of happiness. Robert's death inspired the Wirts to reaffirm their commitment to each other. "Our ranks are getting thinner," William mourned, "and we must cherish each other the more tenderly." Preoccupied with her own grief, Elizabeth neglected writing to William for most of January. "I have not loved you less!" she assured him. "No, my dear husband:—whenever even the idea of happiness is present— my heart reverts to you—and to you alone—with any certainty of happiness: —over all things else there rests a cloud of obscurity, and fearful uncertainty."[71]

William's commitment to his breadwinner role continued to cast a shadow of fearful uncertainty over the Wirts' relationship, however. By the mid-1820s, Elizabeth and William no longer resisted their separate destinies. In 1825, Elizabeth reluctantly seconded her husband's decision to remain away for the holidays. "This is a sad hearing indeed," she sighed, "that you are not to be with us even on Xmass.—After such a long separation, to be denied that day of all days . . . It is a hard fate indeed. And yet," she conceded, "our expenses have been so great—that we can not choose between labour, & rest—but must drudge on whether we will or no." William's reply echoed Elizabeth's resignation to the couple's long separation: "It is decreed that I cannot go down." Although William indicated that he had no hand in the matter, in fact it was he who decided that his cases in court were more important than returning home to make amends to Elizabeth. His letter the next day indicated that he regretted the effect he knew this would have on his relationship with his wife but that his commitment to his career was stronger than his grief. "My heart sinks and my eyes feel like filling at the thought of not being able to see you even at Xmass—But I am in the track of my duty and must not quit it however much I may groan in the spirit."[72]

Although both of the Wirts described their division as a duty, they experienced their new relationship differently. Whereas Elizabeth wrote of her difficulty in summoning the resolve to "march on with resignation, in the path of duty," William described duty as a kind of pleasure. "Do you think this is pleasure to me?" he demanded in 1827. "No—no—no," he answered, "at least no other pleasure than that which arises from the consciousness of doing our duty." It was increasingly evident that William did indeed derive a positive pleasure from his own duties. Preparing for "a most exciting" case in Baltimore in May, he chided Elizabeth for her complaints at his neglect of their correspondence. "You have no conception of the excitement—nor what is expected from me tomorrow," he wrote condescendingly. "Bless your heart— you did not know this or I am sure you would not have thrown this damper on me." The case drew an impressive audience—150 "ladies" crammed the balconies, and "the hall . . . [was] crowded with gentlemen"—and William spoke for nearly five hours to the "intensely interested" assembly. "When I closed there was a clapping of hands as loud as you ever heard in a theatre," he swelled with pride, "ladies & all even one of the Judges joining in it—In short," William concluded, "it was the proudest triumph that I have ever had in my whole professional career—*it was the proudest day of my life*." William's declaration that the proudest day of his life was a successful court case negated his stated commitment to Elizabeth above all else. "Were I to cease to love you," he had told her the previous month, "I sh[oul]d lose the whole stimulus that gives life and this world an interest in my eyes." In courtroom displays, however, William found another stimulus that threatened to overshadow his commitment to his wife. While William found satisfaction in his itinerant career, Elizabeth mourned the loss of her previous close relationship with her husband. William's letters, she complained, were unusually short. "It is too much trouble, to say how you prosper &c while there is so much of novelty, & interest to take up your time [and] attention," she speculated. "But we shall hear it some time or other. And some time or other your heart will turn with interest, & affection to your own E W Wirt."[73]

"We are not & cannot be, so *gay & happy*, as while you are with us," Elizabeth remarked in 1827. "But we try to busy ourselves in our duties." As the years passed with no indication that William's work pace would slacken, the Wirts devoted themselves to finding pleasure in their different duties. In letters to Laura and Thomas Randall, who married in the summer of 1827, Elizabeth and William demonstrated how wide the gap between them had become. It was their responsibility, William reminded Elizabeth, to guide the Randalls in their life together. "They are a little foolish at first like all unbroken colts," he remarked, "but they will soon get used to the gear." The Wirts, who had embarked on their own marriage with anticipations of mutual love and respect and total reciprocity, wrote letters of advice to Laura and her new husband which recommended much more rigid guidelines for conjugal relationships and which urged the newlyweds to find happiness in filling their respective roles, not in their love for each other.[74]

The Wirts' letters to Laura and her husband indicated that men's proper role in marriage was to make money and decisions; women were expected to follow their husband's lead and make themselves happy in the circumstances that men dictated. William wrote rarely to his daughter, instead devoting his infrequent letters to the Randalls to his son-in-law. As he propounded the necessity of hard work and savings to his son-in-law, William affirmed the new role he had marked out for himself during his marriage as a provider, not a companion. "We must inculcate oeconomy on the Judge," declared William, and do their part to assist their daughter's husband to "be easy and in a few years affluent in his circumstances." William's infrequent but lengthy letters offered Randall extensive advice on his duties as a husband: earning money in planting and the law and providing Laura with a comfortable home. Randall's responsibilities, the Wirts indicated, would guide the family's future. Laura was desperately unhappy at the prospect of moving to Florida with her new husband and hoped to remain in Washington while he attended his first court in order to give her more time to prepare. Elizabeth, however, advised her daughter to "yield to circumstances." "The Colonel [Randall] takes this in the morning," she wrote to William. "I have told him that you & he must arrange the business part of the subject, & that *we* [women] must be guided by that."[75]

As she urged Laura to undertake her new duties as a wife with resolution, Elizabeth indicated how much her expectations of marriage had changed since her own marriage a quarter century earlier. "May you be supported, & enabled to discharge cheerfully the duties which you have taken upon yourself," she prayed. "Let us both labour to the same end," proposed Elizabeth, "to the faithful & conscientious discharge of our duties." "The everyday duties of life," not "personal gratification," defined a woman's life, she reminded her daughter, and the wisest action was to hew to the course of duty no matter how unpleasant or difficult. Although women's daily tasks might be "irksome," she noted, she herself experienced "relief," if not pleasure, when she successfully fulfilled her role as "a female." Elizabeth indicated that a woman's duty, however unpleasant, was to devote herself to housework and other domestic duties without complaining. In particular, Elizabeth admonished her daughter, a good wife would not ask her husband to share or sympathize with her tasks and tribulations. "He has his trials to bear, almost as it were alone," she characterized a man's work. "To throw all our burthen upon him in addition to his own makes *his* a hard fate." In her advice to Laura, Elizabeth expressed her own resolution to negate her own claims on her husband in order to further his happiness, looking for her own happiness in her own, distinct duties. "We must at last make our happiness to consist *in the performance of duties*," she urged. Women should dismiss their "petty cares" and seek happiness not in the "respect and affection" of their husbands, who were preoccupied with their own problems, but "in the conscientious discharge of the duties of [their] situations, what ever they might be."[76]

Elizabeth's letters indicated that she had adopted her husband's dictum that happiness could only be found in the conscientious discharge of the duties of their situations, situations that were dramatically different for women and men. Rather than seeking happiness in her marriage, by the 1820s, Elizabeth found personal satisfaction in the everyday duties of life, devoting herself to the "*trifles*" of housework and child care. Elizabeth rarely left home during the Wirts' years in Washington. When her relatives in Virginia urged her to visit, she turned them down, pleading domestic responsibilities in the capital city. As Elizabeth withdrew from her female kin, she also retreated from the company of other women. As the Wirts' neighbor Margaret Bayard Smith observed, "She is ... a domestic woman, visiting as little as her situation will allow." During the Wirts' years in Virginia, despite the couple's difficulties, Elizabeth had taken pride in her ability to manage their finances and had enjoyed her cooperation with her husband in child rearing. In Washington, however, she relinquished her role as an economic partner and claimed a central position as the family caretaker. Elizabeth's fierce resistance to William's belated attempts to restore his place at home indicated how thoroughly she had invested herself in her domestic duties in Washington. "Surrounded by the children," as she described herself in 1822, Elizabeth insulated herself from her relatives, her neighbors, and her husband.[77]

William was not oblivious to his wife's emotional withdrawal, but his preoccupation with his own professional success prevented him from taking action to regain her love. In 1828, at the urgings of his physician, William insisted that he would reduce his workload for the winter. "I promise you I will not kill myself at the supreme court," he assured Elizabeth, "but will rather make a little free with my professional repute than to do so." Repeatedly, however, fame and fortune impelled him to break his promise. With strong anticipations of a transfer of the presidency from the stately Monroe to the rabble-rousing Andrew Jackson, William, a Jeffersonian Democrat, knew that his tenure as attorney general was drawing to a close, and he was determined to make the most of his remaining time in office. "I am anxious to make every blow tell," he confided to his son-in-law. The plaudits of the Baltimoreans—"I have heard my argument exceedingly trumpeted," William told Elizabeth—made William's task more bearable. Elizabeth displayed her knowledge of her husband's devotion to and pride in his work when she predicted that he would not reduce his workload voluntarily. "He promises me, that he will not labour his causes so profoundly this winter," Elizabeth remarked to Laura. "But I know him too well, to beleive this—He can not bear to make a slight examination of a cause—or to rest, while there is possibly any new turn to be given to it." When William left for court in the spring, Elizabeth predicted: "We shall not have much of his company, until midsummer . . . A hard fate this," she sighed, "but it cannot be otherwise—and we must bear it as well as we can."[78]

By the late 1820s, Elizabeth and William Wirt seemingly had resigned themselves to the hard fate of an almost complete divorce. Baltimore, however, held out hope for a renewed commitment to mutual love and companionship in marriage. Retiring from the attorney generalship, Elizabeth noted with relief, would allow William to claim a more "equitable compensation" for his labor. "I feel almost assured that it would prolong my Husbands life to give it up," she wrote to her mother. "He does so slave himself & labour so incessantly without a moments respite or time to say his *souls his own* . . . There is not one moments pause from the commencement, to the end of the court, for him—but work, work, work until midnight & after—and that every night." Elizabeth hoped that in their new situation, his labor would "be greatly lightened, & his pay better for his labour"; best of all, she thought, "We shall have too so much his society at home." William also looked to Baltimore as an escape from overwork, exhaustion, and illness. Recovering from a violent attack of vertigo in February 1829, he assured his friend Dabney Carr that he welcomed the change. "Pinkney and Emmet both died 'with harness on their back,' " he observed soberly, "and if I were to continue to bear the conjoint burthen of duties of Attorney General and private practitioner I should probably do the same. I am therefore frankly relieved by getting rid of one half of the burthen," he rejoiced. By mid-April 1829, the Wirts were packed and ready to undertake their new life in a rented house in Baltimore. The new home would provide a final testing ground for their ideal of companionate marriage.[79]

As Elizabeth and William Wirt's estrangement in Washington demonstrates, men's and women's desire and need for each other existed within very different contexts in nineteenth-century America. Men's emotional dependence on their wives curbed their social, economic, and political dominance; women's reliance on their husbands as their chief source of happiness reinforced their status as dependents. Moreover, the responsibility for creating and sustaining companionship was unevenly divided. Wives, with the most invested in marriage, were assigned the task of ensuring the couple's success; husbands, who enjoyed outlets outside marriage, set the terms of the relationship. Ironically, women had little power to realize the perfect love for which they bore primary responsibility and on which they, more than men, depended for happiness. For the Wirts, as for other couples in the early national period, the demands and the joys of love and marriage were apportioned unevenly.

༠

Building Castles in the Air

Planning for the Future in Baltimore, 1829–1834

As they looked around them at the first signs of spring in Baltimore in 1829, Elizabeth and William Wirt drew a sigh of relief at their escape from the corrosive atmosphere of Washington, where their separate duties had threatened to create an unbridgeable rift between them. The move to Baltimore marked another shift in Elizabeth and William's relationship. During the Wirts' years in Baltimore, economic distress, disappointments in William's political and professional endeavors, repeated bouts of illness, and family tragedy combined to bring both Elizabeth and William to a rejection of "the storms, the trials, and the temptations of this sinful & miserable world." Turning away from the miseries of the world, they devoted their years in Baltimore to an attempt to regain their lost intimacy. "It seems & feels as if we are *doing* something, instead of *dreaming*, merely, of Castles in the air," William rejoiced in 1833. With a shared mission to create a shelter from the uncertainties and vices that surrounded them, Elizabeth and William made a final attempt to renew their commitment to a true marriage partnership.[1]

The Wirts' decision to leave Washington had a dramatic effect on their relationship. The circumstances of their departure from the capital—the ascendancy of Jackson and of a new style of popular politics which struck the Wirts as demagogic—weakened William's commitment to the law and the political role that was so closely connected to the legal profession. Like many other Americans who had come to maturity during the early republican era, William Wirt viewed with mistrust the nation's turn away from refined leadership to popular representation. His own loss of office as a result of Jackson's spoils system ensured his continued loyalty to a mythical past to which the present was a poor successor. Politics had once been disinterested public service by gentlemen of principle, William believed, but it was now "so dirty and disreputable a business" that he "loath[ed the] thought of it." With the onset of the nullification crisis, William's despair deepened. "God help us," he prayed. "I still hope there is a resurrection for our once glorious and still beloved country—If not, I will bide myself in some mountain cave or turn shepherd in the wilds of Florida—Say my prayers—and hope for Heaven."[2]

William's unfavorable view of the current political situation cast a pall over his continuing business in the courts. One of his most important cases in the 1830s was *Cherokee Nation v. Georgia*. A series of cases beginning in 1830 sought to prevent the eviction of the Cherokees as provided for by the Indian Removal Bill, which Jackson favored. William, employed on behalf of the Cherokees to protect their rights to their ancestral lands against the claims of the white settlers, saw the issue as central to the new preeminence of Jacksonian-style faction and self-interest.[3] Like the rest of "the people," complained William, the Georgia settlers had been infected by the madness of Jacksonian democracy. "The Indian question is the chord of their insanity," he remarked to Carr. "They are hardly responsible for what they do or say under the influence of the *mania* which has seized them. Heaven knows to what lengths they will carry it," he noted pointedly, "supported as they are at Washington." The Cherokees' attempts to have their status as a foreign nation recognized, and an injunction against Georgia's policy of removal instituted, failed. The case was symbolic of William's disappointment in the dispassionate hand of justice. In the current atmosphere, complained William, "madness and injustice in the public mind" foiled all his attempts to defend injured clients.[4]

William began to criticize his profession with more vigor than he had since the publication of his life of Patrick Henry in 1817. "I believe I shall be able to live if Vice continues," he remarked grimly in 1829. "The Parsons and Lawyers depend entirely on vice for their living," he added. "Old Nic[k] is their best professional friend." Gone were the days when William clothed his legal duties in the trappings of chivalry. Instead, he dwelled on the rigors of preparation. "[This] is one of the [most] entangled causes I have ever had to do with," he wrote during his professional debut in Boston in 1829. "The counsel have been poring with me over the papers all day till I am quite stupid & the whole case is as clear as mud." Although William carried off the case with aplomb, he dismissed the plaudits of those who witnessed his performance; "I feel far more deeply and exquisitely the happiness reflected from the bosoms of my beloved family," he declared.[5]

In the 1830s, as they had during their courtship, Elizabeth and William shared a world-view that valued personal relationships above money and reputation. The criticism that William and other Whiggish politicians and writers leveled at the ascendance of self-interest and vice shared a common language with the many voices in the 1830s which lauded the home as a haven from the sinfulness and materialism of the world beyond the home's walls. Literature of the 1830s criticized the rise of corrupt pursuit of profits in the nation's booming cities. Evangelical religion, too, was blazing a new path of reform, determined to reawaken Americans to piety. Central to these various proposals for renewal was an idealized home, where women, presumably protected from the selfish materialism of the workplace and the sordid self-interest of politics, would cast a benevolent influence over the home and the family that gathered there. In the 1830s, this emerging ideal of the home included men in its blissful depictions of harmonious family life. Men like William, who had experienced for themselves the stress of politics and business, could find a refuge at home with their wives and children.[6]

When William wearied of the stresses of politics and the law, he looked to the "sweet pure circle of innocence, intelligence, and love" that made up his family. Like many others in nineteenth-century America, he often equated love and religion. Not only was family life more tranquil than the world beyond, noted William, but it was more virtuous as well, a consideration that meant more to him as he aged and began to consider his approaching demise. Women writers of the 1830s worked hard to convince their reading public that women, and the homes they reigned over, were uniquely situated to promote religion, and ministers allied with them to publicize the virtues of domestic piety. William joined in this celebration of family religion. "There is something of Heaven, methinks, in these feelings between parents and children," he wrote to Catharine. "They are a faint type of that pure and holy Love which subsists between our Heavenly Father and the spiritual children which surround his throne." As the earthly echo of heaven, William concluded, family ties outranked all "earthly possession[s]." "Fame, Fortune, prosperity in every shape would be poor and indifferent but for the hearts that are touched and the eyes that are brightened at home by hearing of it," he declared.[7]

While William's difficulties and disappointments directed him away from fame, fortune, and prosperity toward the pure and holy love of his family and of heaven, Elizabeth also abandoned her efforts to advance the family's status for the enjoyment of family life. Her encounters with "the gentlemen" of

Baltimore convinced her that relationships within the bounds of the family were more rewarding than public entertaining. At one party early in 1830 she declared herself "completely disgusted with parties." Several of the young men attending the party became quite intoxicated. They proceeded to use vulgar language and stagger about the rooms, and they finally had to be removed "for fear of disgracing themselves." "It is shocking to be obliged to allow your daughters to associate with such characters," remarked Elizabeth disapprovingly, "and I feel strongly tempted to withdraw from it *in toto*."[8]

Elizabeth and William's uncertain health also encouraged them to withdraw from public life to enjoy the heavenly peace and affection of their family circle. William's repeated illnesses detracted from his attachment to the activities that had taken him from home so often during the Wirts' tenure in the capital city and pushed him to rearrange his priorities. His health, never reliable, had taken another turn for the worse following the Wirts' move to Baltimore. Elizabeth described her husband's health as "*uncertain*" and "very delicate" when he left for Annapolis in July 1829, and she urged William to make haste home. She was positively "wretched" in his absence, she wrote. "Oh, would that you were done with this cause," she worried, "and could return home to be nursed." William no longer disregarded his wife's concern for his health. "I continue well," he assured Elizabeth in August, "but exceedingly tired and worne out with this endless work down here—for endless it really seems to be . . . No one thinks of employing me in a plain case," he complained, "they give me only hard cases—and as I have been constantly at it now ever since last fall I begin to feel the want of a little rest," he admitted. "This I hope will be my last hard cause for some time to come," he added, "and rest will be very sweet to me." At the conclusion of the fall court in 1829, William was very happy to return home. "I am overdone," he confided to Elizabeth. "My back is almost broke—and my strength quite exhausted." William cheered himself not with news of his successes but with the thought of concluding his responsibilities for the season. "I can assure you that I have no pleasure in being here—and will get away the very moment I can do so with propriety."[9]

William's failing health reinforced his disillusionment with law and politics. Public life had lost its charm for him, he confided to his closest friends. "I find that there is much more trouble and less pleasure in supporting a reputation than in gaining it," he reflected in a letter to Dabney Carr. "I am more tired of work than I was in the beginning," he mused, and as he felt himself aging, the pull of his "own beloved wife and children" grew stronger. He "never had any political aspirations," William reaffirmed in an 1830 letter to William Pope, and he found legal study laborious. True happiness, he concluded, could be found only in the company of Elizabeth and their children, and his happiest moments were during family meals, when, despite his sixty years, he was "boyish," "foolish," and "as frolicksome as a kitten." William looked forward with pleasure to the thought of complete retirement. Four more years, he calculated in 1830, would provide him with enough to make arrangements for his family's support. "I shall quit as soon as I can," he determined, "for the work is too severe at my time of life—and will precipitate my trial at another bar, I fear, before I am ready to meet it."[10]

For Elizabeth, as for William, poor health provided another impetus for renewed commitment to marriage and family. In the spring of 1830 the entire family was ill. "Ma is engaged in nursing the sick," wrote Rosa, taking up the pen on her mother's behalf, "for we have a house full of them." Throughout the spring and summer, nearly every member of the family suffered from "constant uneasiness," gave Elizabeth "a great alarm," or was pronounced "seriously ill." "With so much sickness continually occurring in the family," Elizabeth confided to her mother, she labored under "great anxiety." In July William gave the family "a great alarm" with an attack of pain and swelling "in the region of the kidneys." As Elizabeth hovered anxiously by his side, she recalled: "It appeared to me that he must certainly expire under the torture he suffered." On the same day, little Dabney's pony returned home riderless, and Elizabeth feared that he had been thrown and killed. Worn out by nursing the family and under the pressure of so much fear for her husband and child, Elizabeth declared, "It was an evening of trials for me."[11]

Elizabeth also suffered from health problems. In August and September the entire family traveled to the springs in Bath, Virginia (now Berkely Springs, West Virginia), in the hope of regaining their full health. There Elizabeth joined the sick list. Drinking the waters brought on "severe *dysentery*," followed by "an attack of piles." "The sickness Etc have laid me on my back ever since," she wrote in mid-September. In addition, Elizabeth was suffering from other agonies: "I have had some affection of the womb," she wrote in confidence to her mother, "*a bearing down feeling* . . . and have been obliged to bolster myself up on *pillows*, my weight on the lower part of my back, being to[o] much for those parts."[12]

Difficulties in their separate duties primed both William and Elizabeth to turn away from other things in order to concentrate on their love for each other and their children. Constant reminders of the nearness of death led them to a renewed appreciation of religion and of the promise of eternal life and a joyous reunion with loved ones in heaven. "Our dear Catharine joined the church the Sunday before last," Elizabeth noted happily in August 1830. "I hope God will make them all his own, in his good time—and that we all may meet around the throne of mercy in a happy eternity!" Disappointments in fulfilling the sharply differentiated roles that they had defined during their sojourn in Washington also renewed the Wirts' interest in the dream of unity they had cherished when they first wed. Tragedy quickened Elizabeth and William's tentative steps toward a renewed partnership.[13]

Christmas of 1830 found William at court in Washington. "This has been the dullest and most anxious Xmass to me that I have ever passed," he sighed. Homesick and heartsick at the "torrent of prejudice" against his client, William declared that the pressure of his professional difficulties made him almost physically ill. The worst was yet to come, however. Two days later he was called home to sit by Agnes's deathbed. Sixteen years old and the family's acknowledged favorite, Agnes died of what doctors diagnosed as dysentery on December 30, 1830.[14]

Agnes's death would have a major impact on Elizabeth and William's life together. Like many families in the early-nineteenth-century South, the Wirts described death in highly sentimental terms. A child's death was a crushing blow that reminded parents what they considered truly important. The importance of religious conviction and the power of earthly love were typical themes that tended to blend and to reinforce each other. Before her death, Agnes had exhibited a degree of piety which was a source of melancholy pleasure for her family. "Mr Nevins [the Wirts' pastor] was here this evening to see us," Ellen informed her father soon after Agnes's death. "He talked of our beloved Agnes, & mother shewed him some of her dear little books, containing her recollections of Mr Nevin's sermons, her thoughts & feelings on the subject of religion, which he pronounced to be excellent & extraordinary for a child of her age." Agnes's personal religious writings convinced the family's pastor, as well as her siblings and parents, that "the dear had early commenced to think seriously & deeply on t[he] subject of Religion," and in the months following their loss, the Wirts resolved to follow their departed daughter's example.[15]

Following Agnes's death, Elizabeth and William turned away from their separate responsibilities to a shared concern with religious duties and the hope that their family would be reunited in heaven. The Wirts interpreted their loss in religious terms. The child's premature death, they decided, was a reminder from God that earthly ties and rewards were insubstantial compared with the promise of salvation. "The selection of the victim is too striking to be misunderstood," William told his friend Dabney Carr. "There is a better world of which I have thought too little—to that world she is gone—and thither my affections have followed her. This was Heaven's design—I see and feel it as distinctly as if an Angel had revealed it—as if my Angel daughter had been permitted to reveal it." In the last years of his life, William Wirt increasingly turned his attention away from his hitherto almost all-consuming legal career toward religious matters. From Washington, to which he returned soon after Agnes's death, William wrote that his "nervous system" and his "intellect" were "prostrated" by the blow. "And how are you my own beloved dear?" he inquired of Elizabeth. "Alas," he cried, "I know too well how your mind and spirits are—but, dearest, I have come to this conclusion—that there is no way to save our hearts from a repetition of these dreadful blows, but by preparing ourselves, with God's assistance, to live as it were above this world and the evils that here betide." Out of her grief Elizabeth also drew the lesson that she should devote herself to religious matters with more zeal and constancy. " 'I knew my duty, but I did [it] not,' " she lamented. "I slighted it, and put it aside . . . I thought it enough to give God a portion of our time, & of our hearts, and beleived that the vain empty world had a claim to the rest." Elizabeth resolved to follow the example of their "dear Angel" and to reject the worldly "cares, vexations, and vanities" to seek "higher things."[16]

Shared grief and a common resolution to turn away from the vain empty world to religion brought Elizabeth and William closer. Their daily correspondence was filled with reflections on their loss, and both came to the same conclusion. "It is utterly impossible that either of us should ever again feel the same interest in the things of this world," mused Elizabeth. William's letter of the same day echoed her sentiments. "May the Lord sanctify and bless this dispensation to us all," he wrote; "it has certainly broken one of the strongest cords that bound me to this earth and reduced the passing time & scene to insignificance." In their reactions to the "dreadful blow" of Agnes's sudden death, Elizabeth and William were united.[17]

The change was most dramatic for William, who had been drawn away from spiritual contemplation in his prolonged struggle to attain fame and fortune. In Baltimore, however, his work faded in significance compared with "the paramount love" he felt he "ought to bear to the Saviour." Accepting Agnes's death as the chastisement of a loving God, he hoped to make up for past transgressions by reorienting his life away from "*earthly treasures*" toward heaven. "Dear Saviour let me never forget this lesson," he prayed, "O let me never forget . . . that the all.absorbing object of all our souls should be to meet in Heaven, however we may be separated here." William's intense concern for his soul in the aftermath of the family's tragedy gave new meaning to the doubts he had entertained about the value of his labor. "I have no taste now

for worldly business," he told Elizabeth. "The strife and contention and em-
ulation of the bar—the strife of victory" had lost their charm for William.
"Alas what are such victories," he demanded. "What is their worth—snares,
snares, all, for immortal spirits—the tempter's snares."[18]

William did not immediately abandon his profession, for all his disen-
chantment with the public recognition and acclaim he now identified as the
tempter's snares. After Agnes's death, however, he described his work in a new
way. Work remained an unquestioned duty and a necessary burden for the
family's financial support. After repeated disappointments and losses, however,
William no longer viewed his profession as a field for proving himself. He had
lost his "relish" for "earthly distinction," he told Elizabeth, but he would
persist in his work as a duty to God. "Here the Almighty has cast my lot,"
concluded William, "and here He orders me to stay for the performance of
such duties as he is pleased to assign me." The language of duty was not a
novelty for William. What was new in his descriptions of his work duties was
his assignment of credit for success not to his own efforts but to divine support.
William knew from his religious background that he was helpless to achieve
his own salvation. Complete dependence on God was a hallmark of evangelical
Protestantism. "I know that there is no salvation but through him," he wrote
in this tradition. "Without his pardon and acceptance I am lost. I think that
I am wholly willing, heart & soul, to cast myself upon him and trust to Him
alone—O that I may at last find favor and acceptance with him." In the final
stage of his professional career, William extended the theme of human help-
lessness to his work in the courts as well as his hopes for eternal life. "I rest
upon my gracious Lord," he wrote, "to give me strength for my duties."[19]

Relinquishing the responsibility for success or failure in court to God did
not reduce William's time commitments to his legal work immediately, but it
permanently reduced the degree to which he measured himself by his work.
He became more apt to express dissatisfaction with his work. "Tho it is Saturday night," he wrote in the midst of the Cherokee case, "still I have no rest
but am run off my legs by business . . . O I am so so weary—altho I have now
only a few more days of court, I dread them—for I am so exhausted that I
feel as if I cd. stand no more." Neither visions of glory nor a fat fee occurred
to William to cheer his labors; instead, he declared his absolute dependence
on a higher power. "Still let me trust in the mercy of my God," he closed. "O
He is good and able to support me." Although his income remained the main
source of support for the Wirt family, William ceased to think of himself as
the provider; God, he reiterated, would sustain both him and his wife and
children. Following an important argument in 1831, William held fast to his

conviction that God deserved what credit was due. "I have, thank Heaven, discharged my duty . . . in a manner satisfactory to myself and it is said to the public," he observed, adding, "I feel no vanity about it . . . I feel grateful to the mercy of Heaven that in my state of my mind and heart & body, I have been so far strengthened as to be able to do decent justice to my cause . . . That I shall not suffer by the comparison with others is of but little consequence for earthly glory—for what is earthly glory!—it is of no farther consequence than that it enables me to keep my place in my profession so as, with the farther blessing of Heaven, to make it a means of support for you and our dear children," he wrote to Elizabeth.[20]

By making God the arbiter of duties and the sustainer of strength, William offered Elizabeth the opportunity to reaffirm their shared responsibilities. Although his duties included an additional component—legal work—Elizabeth and William assumed that in a larger sense, their duties were identical. Like many Virginians of the time, the Wirts' attachment to religion often privileged family reunion over individual salvation. "For this," vowed William, "let us all strive and never rest 'till we have secured it . . . that joyous re-union in Heaven for which I have so often prayed while our charmer still knelt with us in our circle of love." From this time forward, both Wirts resolved, they should live for each other, for their children, and for God. "*Happiness* can never again be ours," mourned Elizabeth, "yet we have dear dependant [*sic*] beings left to us, who look to us for comfort & cherishing—we have many duties yet to perform—and God will in his mercy to them I hope spare us to them, yet a little longer." For as long as they were spared, Elizabeth counseled, she and William should act as "the instruments of good" for their children: "When finally reunited, at the throne of mercy, we may be enabled to say 'here are we Lord, & those children which thou gavest us.' " William, too, described the remainder of his life as consecrated to God and the loved ones entrusted to him by heaven. "All my sweet ones demand my care—my sweet, faithful, best of wives & mothers—My sweet, affectionate, intelligent, lovely, devoted children—For your sake and theirs, and as a duty to my God," he resolved, "I am preparing to brace myself for the duties of the profession in which it has been his pleasure that we should depend for the earthly means of support."[21]

Although William continued to travel in order to attend to his legal work, phrasing that work in terms so similar to those Elizabeth used to describe her own tasks reduced the division between them. "I have nothing to care for now in this [world]," he declared, "but my wife and remaining children—[how they are] faring, how they do and what they are doing; and preparing my self, under God, and, so far as I can, promoting their preparation for a better world—this [world] has no longer any allurement for me, out of my own family circle." In late January Elizabeth called attention both to the Wirts' physical separation and to their spiritual reunion. "It is indeed a severe trial to be so seperated, at such a time," she wrote. "But our spirits meet and mingle at the throne of grace, often, often."[22]

By describing William's legal career as a moral imperative of parenthood, the Wirts incorporated his work into their marriage partnership. William's final attempt to win political eminence was similarly absorbed into their partnership. While William's previous forays into politics had filled Elizabeth with dismay and had created tension in the Wirts' relationship, his most dramatic entrance into politics became a project that he and Elizabeth shared. In February 1831 William regarded politics with fear and loathing. As men jockeyed for position in the upcoming presidential election, he held himself aloof from the proceedings. "How I long to be able to lock myself up in the bosom of my family and devote myself to them and Heaven—Sweet refuge from this turbulent world," he sighed. "There is so much dirty work, unprincipled intrigue, and villainous faction that I have no confidence in any of them," he declared. "I have no hopes from man to save our country—My trust is in God Alone whose it is to will & do."[23]

Although William recognized "nothing short of Almighty power" was sufficient to divert disaster in politics—as in his own legal career—he assumed that a "mortal man" would be selected "to be His agent." When in late September the Anti-Masonic party made its surprise nomination for president—William Wirt—William remarked that it was "as if a thunderbolt had dropped at [his] feet in a clear day." Considering the circumstances, however, he soon decided that the thunderbolt was God's way of selecting him as a divine agent of moral and political regeneration. The Anti-Masonic movement, which had its origins in opposition to Masonry after the murder of a Mason for revealing the fraternity's secrets, rose from the tumult of the Jacksonian years to begin a party devoted to returning the nation to its lost purity and harmony. In essence this was a commitment to defeating Jackson in the next election—a mission William could heartily approve. William was ready to be convinced that both patriotism and religion demanded him to accept the nomination. "If the opposition choose to rally upon me," he imagined, "I may become an instrument in the hands of Providence of rescuing the country from it's present fallen condition."[24]

Elizabeth had opposed William's earlier ventures into politics, criticizing his political enthusiasm, which, she charged, led him to neglect his family responsibilities. Sanctified as God's will, however, William's political maneuverings took on a new and different aspect. Three decades earlier, when William and Elizabeth had married, she had demonstrated political acumen and a strong bent for the genteel style of politics which was threatened by Jacksonian democracy. When William accepted the Anti-Masons' nomination, Elizabeth became a willing collaborator. She encouraged William to publish "the Jefferson letter," perhaps a letter from the former president which seemed to offer a benediction to a likely successor, "to give an impetus, & direction to public sentiment." When William's friends Dabney Carr and James Meredith prepared a brief sketch of William's life, Elizabeth took it on herself to revise the work before it was circulated. "I sent it to Mr Meredith, with my pencil marks," she reported in mid-October 1831. Elizabeth assumed that her role as publicist would be accepted, and she scoffed at Meredith's initial hesitation to accept her aid; "he did not seem to be in a very communicative, or a very good humour, as I thought," she remarked. "And I suppose thinks that *a woman* has nothing to do with such things." Elizabeth proved Meredith wrong. She zealously read the newspapers for reports of William's nomination and discussed public sentiment with her husband. Elizabeth also culled William's papers for the works that might reflect most favorably on him, including his eulogy for Jefferson and Adams, with plans to publish a set of collected writings to forward her husband's candidacy.[25]

As 1831 drew to a close, it became clear that the Anti-Masons' estimates of their voting strength had been vastly overrated. William's good spirits in the face of defeat supported his claims that "disinterested patriotism," and not a desire to be president, had motivated his final political involvement. "God knows that I have had no desire but to do what I supposed to be my duty to my Country," he wrote. "So far as personal feelings and motives are concerned," he confided to Carr, "I would infinitely rather have avoided the situation. My desires, my wishes are all for private life; I can find no happiness in political strife." Even before the election, William set aside all hopes of the presidency without apparent regret. "With a good house, my wife and children and a few friends around me," he mused, "how happy would I be 'to doff the world aside and let it pass.' "[26]

William's attitude was fortunate, for his final foray into politics soon proved to be disastrous. When Henry Clay was nominated as the National Republican candidate for president, William feared that his candidacy would divide, rather than unite, the opposition to Jackson, and he worried that, although he was committed to "the single patriotic and honorable purpose of Union," he might be cast in a "false light" as "an instrument of *disunion*." "In truth my dear friend, I am very weary and sick of public life and it's affairs," William admitted. "We have become a nation of fools and blackguards," he charged, "so much faction, corruption, intrigue, and impenetrable and imperturbable stupidity and infatuation . . . a prospect of things becoming worse and worse, 'till the scene winds up with a *protectorate* or a dissolution of the Union." The election results—William gained only 7 out of 286 electoral votes, all from Vermont—ended William's hopes of returning national politics to a golden age of virtuous public service, and he at last relinquished all interest in the path of law and politics he had followed for so long.[27]

The election of 1832, coming on the heels of the Wirts' expulsion from Washington and their family's serious illnesses, strengthened Elizabeth and William's disappointment in public life and their commitment to each other and to their children. The early 1830s were important years for Elizabeth and William Wirt as parents. By the spring of 1831, both Liz and Catharine were engaged—Liz to navy lieutenant Louis Malesherbes Goldsborough, and Catharine to a Mr. Farley. The engagements were postponed as the family mourned for Agnes. With the prospect of separating from their two oldest daughters, and the memory of their most recent loss still fresh, Elizabeth and William concentrated on cementing their ties to their remaining children. Religion was central to their efforts. "We shall meet again, I trust in the redeeming mercy of my Saviour, to part no more," William assured Elizabeth. "Yes I shall meet her [Agnes] in Heaven and she will fly again to my arms—And there with Gods blessing we shall all be joined, where instead of the varied miseries of this life we shall enjoy ever varied and never ceasing happiness." Elizabeth also placed her hopes in a heavenly reunion. "Surely the holy tie of Parent & child, will be acknowledged in a happy Eternity," she thought. "I can form no idea of a Heaven that could obliterate such sweet affection."[28]

"Family prayers" became an important part of the Wirts' daily routine in Baltimore. Elizabeth probably continued to direct these sessions as she had in Washington. Yet, even in his absence, William shared the task with his wife. Catharine described her father's fresh enthusiasm for religious instruction in a letter to her grandmother. "It would do your heart good," she rejoiced, "to see the sweet spirit of christian resignation & ardent love to God and his Saviour which breathes through all our dear Father's letters—This severe affliction has through the tender mercies of our God been blessed to his everlasting good." William plunged into parenthood with fresh enthusiasm, devoting himself to religious training with an intensity he had not exhibited since accepting the attorney generalship. "Love and blessings and kisses to all our precious dears," he wrote from Washington in February 1831. "I commend you and them to the gracious protection and love of our God and Saviour."[29]

William joined Elizabeth in her campaign to see all the children become members of the church. "I thank God that my children here are beginning to make a proper estimate of the comparative value of time and Eternity," he wrote to his son-in-law Thomas Randall. "It is my prayer to Heaven, night and morning, that not one of my dear ones may miss the way—but that we may all meet each other at least in that brighter world where all tears shall be wiped away and we shall part no more." William accepted what he called "a father's privilege and . . . a father's duty" in calling his children "to the serious consideration of this subject."[30]

Elizabeth and William's renewed cooperation in parenting eased them through the difficult decisions that confronted them in Baltimore. In early November Liz married Louis Goldsborough, and the newlyweds moved to the Wirts' Washington house. Catharine, however, had discovered that her fiancé was *"a confirmed deist,"* and had broken off her longstanding engagement. The Wirts gave Catharine their united support, even encouraging her to follow her own inclinations in the rejection of two other proposals in 1832 and 1833, despite the marriage of her younger sister Rosa in early July 1832. The Wirts joined ranks to give their daughter their combined counsel. "Consult your own heart," recommended William. "Let it speak freely & for itself. The affair is pre.eminently your own my beloved child—& your own affections must decide the case." "I concur in your dear Fathers views entirely," agreed Elizabeth. "I certainly do not desire to see you married unless you are thereby greatly to increase your happiness & your comfort."[31]

The united front that Elizabeth and William presented during their years in Baltimore was underpinned by a strong desire to achieve at last the perfect union they had dreamed of when they first married, a shared life that they would devote to each other's happiness, to their children, and to their own spiritual growth. Although Elizabeth had regained her strength, William's poor health—attributed by his doctors and his family to his long years of unremitting labors in court—sharpened the Wirts' desire to establish a secure plan for William's retirement. As the Wirt daughters married and moved away with their husbands and as the Wirt sons passed from childhood to adolescence, Elizabeth and William also cast about them for a plan that would provide both a central gathering place for the scattered family members and a source of livelihood for those who remained. Elizabeth's brothers Robert and John Gamble and their families had already settled in Florida, and her mother died in 1832. William's miserable performance in the presidential election had severed the Wirts' last tie to the upper South. The Wirts' lands in Florida soon became central to their final scheme for family togetherness and financial security.

There at last, William hoped, he would find the harmony and pure affection he had envisioned from the start of their married life. "With Gods blessing, I am securing a quiet retreat for the evening of our days in this same Florida project," he mused in a letter to Elizabeth in 1833. "I feel snug & comfortable in the anticipation," he added happily.[32]

The alarms of the early 1830s gave the Wirts good reason to seek refuge. In December 1831 William suffered an attack of fever, cough, nausea, and "a sort of *suffocation*," which the family feared was "the forruner [sic] of *death*." Between gasps for breath, William expressed the belief that he would not survive the night and asked for his favorite Psalm to be read aloud to him. Although he survived, his health did not improve significantly. In March 1832, Elizabeth wrote anxious letters to Rosa, who had accompanied her father to the Supreme Court in Washington. "Your dear Father's threatening symptoms still continued," she worried. "If I could bear *healing under my wings*," longed Elizabeth, "how swiftly would I fly to his releif—but I could do nothing," she pronounced; "my going could do him no good, in his present situation—[as] he would still be obliged to study—No," she concluded, "nothing but a release from this pressure of business can benefit him." A month's visit to the springs in Pennsylvania and western Virginia failed to rejuvenate William's failing health. He reported that he was plagued by diarrhea and "spasmodic" cramps in his extremities upon his arrival at Pennsylvania's Bedford Springs in mid-August. Although "the mountain air" and "the Bedford water" effected a "cure," it was only a temporary one. "I find," remarked William, "that I have a natural alacrity at relapsing." When he returned to work in Annapolis in November, Elizabeth's frantic letters indicated that her husband had not yet recovered his health. "Hasten home my beloved," she urged. "Oh do not linger from us—do not kill your self for the sake [of] one fee.—If you are not speedily much better—return—oh return quickly," she repeated. "We all continue well," Elizabeth added, "but you are sick my beloved—And oh, my heart is sick therefor [sic]—Do not stay away from us ... [but] come home and be nursed by your own faithful heart sick Wife."[33]

Despite William's determination to continue at his practice, his faith in his ability to sustain the family on the proceeds was at a low ebb. In 1832, he told his brother-in-law William Cabell he had earned nearly ten thousand dollars but added, "What my practice may be worth next year no one knows. The business is getting worse & worse," William noted gloomily, "and, at my time of life, is not very likely to grow better." His concerns for his family's future weighed on his mind, perhaps undermining his recovery. During the hiatus between courts, he had resumed responsibility for supervising the boys' edu-

cations, and he was "grieved to find how little they [knew]." The schools in
Baltimore were "good for nothing," William declared. The Wirts' hopes of
establishing their sons in the professions through training in northern schools
had been dashed years before with Robert's disastrous career at West Point,
and the other alternative William identified—"a planting life"—required
hands-on training on a plantation and a tremendous investment in land and
slaves. But the Wirt boys were still too young to leave home for Florida; William Jr., the oldest, was just sixteen in 1832, and his brothers Dabney and Henry
were fourteen and thirteen, respectively. "What shall I do about this?" worried
William.[34]

As their prospects in Baltimore dimmed, the Wirts identified their Florida
lands as an oasis in a troubled world. "I wish I had a *villa* in Florida or
somewhere else, to retire to," William mused in a letter to his friend Dabney
Carr. "Out of the bosom of my own sweet family and the small circle of dear
friends that is yet left me, I have no enjoyment connected with this earth." It
was time, he decided, to make Florida his way station to heaven. There, he
told Carr, he "would settle a plantation for the support of [his] family and
beat out a retreat from the gaze of public life and public men." He proposed
to Elizabeth that they should "hide . . . in some nook" and share "a '*quiet
life.*'"[35]

Unlike William's earlier plans for migration and future success, the Florida
scheme met with Elizabeth's enthusiastic endorsement. This was a necessary
prerequisite for William. "At my time of life," he explained to his son-in-law
Louis Goldsborough, "and in my state of health, I consider myself as acting
for my wife & children, rather than myself; and I will, therefore, take no step
in which they are so much more interested than myself, without consulting
them." Thus, when William began to write to his Florida son-in-law, Thomas
Randall, to ask his aid in locating and purchasing a "very good gang of negroes" to clear and plant the Wirts' Florida holdings, he consulted Elizabeth
about the best way to raise funds for the project. She responded without hesitation. "Your dear Father asks if I am willing to embark my interest in the
Richmond property in Florida speculations," she mentioned to Catharine.
"Yes—surely if he thinks it best," she concluded, consenting to the sale of the
lots and James River stock she had inherited from her mother. William estimated the value of the Wirts' Richmond property at ten thousand dollars;
added to the ten thousand that Elizabeth's brothers Robert and John Gamble
owed her, Elizabeth's separate estate would provide twenty thousand dollars
for the settlement of the Wirts' Florida lands. To this William would add the
proceeds from the sale of his surplus lands in Florida—about three thousand

acres in Jackson, Gadsden, and Leon Counties valued at five dollars an acre—
and the Wirts' Washington property, worth perhaps ten thousand dollars after
payment of the five-thousand-dollar mortgage. This would leave the Wirts with
"200 acres of splendid land" on the south end of Lake Miccosukee, which the
Wirts planned to work with approximately fifty slaves.[36]

In 1832 the Wirts moved slowly. William wrote letter after letter to his
friends and relatives requesting their opinions and advice about the project he
had in mind. He had already made commitments to the Supreme Court for
the winter of 1832–33, he explained, so that he could not make a move before
the conclusion of that Court. Besides, he wished to move cautiously and "prepare, *leisurely*, for the object." He filled his correspondence with demands for
detailed information about slaves for sale in Florida and elsewhere, the precise
profits that might be expected, and the additional expenses he should count
on for tools, stock, and "*this, that,* & the other." The project was also delayed
for want of funds; the Wirts were unable to "get any thing like a decent price"
for their properties, William complained.[37]

A final reason for delay was the Wirts' desire to make their property in
Florida not only a profitable source of income but an idyllic refuge. William's
requests for information on plantation management were less concerned with
learning the details of directing a large force of slaves than with obtaining
reassurances that profits would flow freely. He preferred to think of the Florida
scheme as an escape from the mundane concerns of daily life. "I am not
surprized that you love the Country," he remarked to Catharine in 1831. "I
have always loved it all my life and for your reasons—Its purity, and quiet,
and innocence, and its grand expanse, and the contemplation of the Creator
to which it so strongly invites us—It is the place for religion," he concluded,
"and O if we ever get to Florida how sweet will it be there among the flowers
and oranges and under these genial skies to converse with our God & Saviour,
as Adam and Eve, in their primitive state of innocence, conversed with Him
in Paradise." Like some other southerners from the declining seaboard, William idealized the plantation as an escape from both the grasping materialism
of the city and the exuberant egalitarianism of the frontier. Antebellum literature celebrated the plantation, like the home, as the site where the harmony
and virtue of a past age could be regained. But how to reconcile the purity,
quiet, and innocence that the Wirts identified with a family group set apart
and protected from others—especially black slaves—with the day-to-day management of a plantation?[38]

In early 1833 it seemed that the Wirts had discovered the solution to their
dilemma. Together with his son-in-law Louis Goldsborough, William proposed

a visionary scheme: settling a plantation not with slaves but with a "German Colony." Several shiploads of Germans from Wirtemberg, William explained, had arrived in Baltimore's and Alexandria's ports. Chiefly farmers but with a smattering of artisans among them, the Wirtembergers were led by their Protestant clergyman, Reverend Mohl. William's plan was to "get fifty or sixty *select families*" to migrate to Florida under Goldsborough's direction. Their destination would be the land that William owned near Monticello, which he christened Wirtland. In exchange for their transportation costs and the supplies necessary for building a village, complete with a church and a school supervised by Reverend Mohl, the Germans would be required to sign contracts for five years. (The children would be bound until they reached their majority at age twenty-one.) In return, they would receive one-third of the profits from the cotton they planted, over and above the corn, vegetables, and proceeds from family gardens they succeeded in raising for their own sustenance. "My risk," rejoiced William, "is only in the expense of transportation of this *northern hive*"; all investments in cabins, stock, and other plantation improvements, he surmised, would not be lost even if the Germans violated their agreement. The total cost of all these preparations would be only six thousand dollars. Best of all, William remarked, "There is not to be *a black* on the place, even among my servants . . . My wife never liked the idea of Florida *with negroes*," he explained, "but she is so delighted with this project— as my daughters are too . . . that they can write and talk to me of nothing else." William's plan met with universal acclaim at home. "I am quite *charmed*, with this German plan, and impatient to begin," exclaimed Elizabeth. "I am all impatience to hear more of the German affair—and full of anticipations, and hopes of ease & comfort for your old age." The German plan gave Elizabeth the chance to renew her economic partnership with her husband. She accepted William's commission to use her years of expertise as the family's bookkeeper in the service of the project, purchasing a book for recording the contracts with the German apprentices and accounts of the Wirts' "Florida expenditures—outlay & income."[39]

Despite the Wirts' enthusiasm, the "German affair" almost immediately encountered difficulties. Thomas Randall, who had not yet learned of the new plan, purchased forty slaves at an estate sale in Florida on William's authority at a cost of nearly eleven thousand dollars. "We are all . . . very sorry of brother Thomas's purchase," wrote Catharine. "Mother says that instead of . . . incurring this great debt, she wishes you wd. have the negroes sold again as soon as possible . . . She says . . . she hates the idea of having such a plantation of *negroes*, as every body else has—she so greatly prefers the white Germans—."

Elizabeth repeated her recommendation in a postscript: "Oh! I do so wish to have nothing more to do with such property," reminding William of her dislike for managing even household slaves. "One great comfort to which I looked in our removal, was the getting rid of the few we already have. I would authorise the Judge, at once, to dispose of them *if possible*." Although William replied that he shared Elizabeth's "repugnance" to becoming slaveholders on a grand scale, he soon told Randall that, rather than choosing between the free labor and slave plans, "the negroes might be made auxiliary to the main plan of German colonization, and would form a good *corps de reserve*, in case the Germans should prove faithless, or unable to stand the climate." He quickly revised his plan: he would rent another plantation and keep the two forces separate. Wirtland would be reserved for the German colony; the slaves would work on the Miccosukee property and on Dulce Domain, a plantation William hired from his brother-in-law John Gamble, executor for the estate of another of Elizabeth's relatives, Abram Cabell. "[The slaves] will not be near you nor the Germans," William assured Elizabeth. "You shall never see them unless you choose it." The loan he obtained from the U.S. Bank for the purchase— $10,750—was cosigned by a member of the board of directors, William noted, and was safe from hasty calls for repayment. "I anticipate no difficulty from the debt," he reassured his wife.[40]

In February 1833, the Wirts' hopes were buoyant. If Goldsborough's expedition was successful, William wrote to Elizabeth, they would have "a place of refuge" that was not contingent on "professional business." With his cases in court falling off, William was unconcerned at the prospect that rumors of his imminent departure would cause his business to decline still further. "The idea I am going to Florida will soon become general," he anticipated. "This report of itself will, I apprehend, drive me there *next year*—and I shall, I assure you be very willing to be so driven." The plan soon ran into further difficulties, however. Louis Goldsborough had to delay his plans repeatedly as a consequence of the rough February weather. Days, then weeks, slipped by, and William was forced to make repeated "advances" to the immigrants. Under their enforced inactivity, the Germans soon became restless. "Murmurings, & discontent" soon flared into open rebellion as the Germans split into two groups, one loyal to Reverend Mohl, the Wirts' liaison with their settlers, and one determined to "displace" the clergyman. By March 22, when the "colony" finally set sail, there were only "150 souls," rather than the 200 to 250 William had counted on.[41]

While the Wirts impatiently awaited news from Florida, their hopes for the future were weakened by signs that William's illness had returned. "It is a sad hearing this of your having a cold & cough," Elizabeth wrote in March 1833. Upon William's return home the following month it was apparent that his condition was far more serious than he had let on. Elizabeth demanded that her husband travel to Philadelphia to be examined by the renowned Dr. Physick, and William's physician concurred. "I do not think myself in any extremity," William protested. "I have no diarrhea . . . and yet," he admitted, "*without any apparent cause*, my muscles are wasting—and I am quite weak." William's physician repeated his diagnosis of the previous year; he insisted that William "*must* discontinue the practice for some months," or he would literally "kill [him]self at work." "Now this I am persuaded is nonsense," scoffed William. "For first I am not killing myself at work." More important, however, with the success or failure of the costly Florida venture in the balance, William felt the pressure of his debts more than ever. "The *resuscitation of mind & spirits*, which he says is indispensible [*sic*] to my restoration, could never be enjoyed by me, while I was sacrificing my property, day after day, to gain a daily meal, and saw poverty & ruin just ahead," William agonized. "It is certainly a critical time for me, both as to fortune & health—& all seems to hang on the eventual success of the Florida project."[42]

The repeated delays and setbacks put William in an agony of uncertainty. "My whole fortune, with all the temporal hopes and expectations of my family, are embarked in the Florida project," William reminded Goldsborough. "It is not unnatural that it should occupy my thoughts almost continually, pondering and trying to anticipate what may prevent miscarriage, and help to ensure success." The stakes were high. Rumors of astronomical profits in Florida— William heard tales of planters making from three hundred to six hundred dollars per worker—had roused his hopes of extricating himself from his debts in only a year. The combined costs of the two Florida plantations—about seventeen thousand dollars—together with the five-thousand-dollar mortgage on the Washington house left the Wirts with a debt of twenty-two thousand dollars after the sale of Elizabeth's stocks and the Wirts' Richmond house (the lots remained on the market). Despite his reduced force, William urged Thomas Randall to look out for other plantations for hire. For the first year, he thought, he might abandon the plan of a cohesive German village in favor of "a tremendous planting." All his lands, owned and rented, should "be wholly devoted to cotton," recommended William; he would rely on his relatives in Florida to provide his slaves and German apprentices with corn "*on account.*" "Now *only think*," he exclaimed, "what a *glorious deliverance* it wd. be to me *from debt, from the toils of the bar, and the rigors of two more northern winters,* if, by renting fields or by any other honest means, I could be sent out to you, a *free man, next year*—and *600* bales of cotton would do it—*If it can be done, let it be done.*"[43]

As a free man, William hoped to be able to quit his legal practice at once and live the quiet domestic life of his daydreams. However, his ambitious plans did not bear fruit. On their arrival in Florida, the German settlers were in poor condition to work even on the Wirts' lands. "Enervated by the heat of the climate & disordered by the water," the settlers may also have been disgruntled at the prospect of being expected to devote themselves exclusively to clearing land for planting cotton, rather than being allowed to cultivate their own provision crops. Caterpillars in the cotton must have made the unaccustomed work even more unpleasant. The one person with influence over the group, Reverend Mohl, was ill, perhaps with malaria. One German had died. "The Destroyer" found Louis Goldsborough as well; for weeks in July and August he was confined with "a pretty sharp fever," unable even to sit up to write letters. Overworked, sickly, and alarmed by the disastrous beginning, many of the Germans fled soon after their arrival. Desperate to salvage the operation, William abandoned his plan of keeping the white and black workers apart and began to make arrangements to exchange the Wirts' remaining Richmond property for twenty to thirty more slaves. He had repeatedly violated his end of the bargain with his northern hive, and the remnant soon joined the exodus. "Never mind the affair," sighed William. "It is only one of our castles in the air come down."[44]

Together, the Wirts attempted to rebuild their castles in the air. William's facade of resignation barely concealed his anxiety about the debts he had incurred and his strong presentiments of death. Despite his insistence that he was not really ill, in April he admitted to his brother-in-law William Cabell, "There is another question which I have been meditating with some anxiety . . . what is to become of my family if I shd. die immediately[?]" Still William hoped to be able to send Elizabeth and the children to Florida by the following year. He did not include himself in the expedition to Florida he still hoped would be possible in the near future. In May he embarked on a much shorter journey with Elizabeth, Ellen, and Henry to the Virginia Springs. William and Elizabeth held long conversations about the debts due him, and he gave her a power of attorney to act in his name. When they reached Richmond, William took a sudden turn for the worse. "Your dear Father gave us all a great alarm last night," Elizabeth wrote to Catharine, "and indeed *I* beleive the Physician thought at one time that he was sinking fast—just as he was undressing for bed he was seized with a weakness & dizziness that disabled him." After putting him to bed, Elizabeth called for a doctor, who gave him a dose of "*chalk julep.*"

Apparently the dose was prepared with pure opium, rather than the diluted form of the drug that was called for, and William spent the night in a "delirium." Rest and a cessation of all medicine restored him, however, and by late September Elizabeth pronounced him "decidedly better."[45]

Cautiously, Elizabeth and William Wirt made plans for what they anticipated would be his final term in the Supreme Court. William fought with difficulty to keep up his spirits. Everywhere he looked, loans were being called. In 1833, he anticipated calls for the immediate repayment of loans and bills totaling more than two thousand dollars. "To meet all these demands," he worried, "I have in hand not more than about $1500 . . . I have just got home from the Springs & know not what business awaits me or whether any does. I am now trying one of my old causes—and have, as yet, heard of no new ones—This is a gloomy prospect," he sighed, "& I feel it, sometimes, more oppressively than I ought. At others again I recover some buoyance, and have golden dreams and build castles in the air." By the next year William hoped to secure an additional force of slaves to send to Florida. Thomas Randall wrote with the good news that both corn and cotton were thriving on the Wirts' plantation, and William located a New York merchant who, as a personal favor, agreed to advance the Wirts forty dollars per bale of cotton for the entire crop.[46]

By December 1833, gloom had again descended. "We have *bloody times*, at hand, for all debtors," pronounced William. Although the Wirts had succeeded in selling a downtown lot in Richmond for $1,500 and Elizabeth's James River Canal shares for $2,800, William had been forced to borrow more than $8,000 to buy the twenty-five slaves he had sent to Florida that month. William expressed no concern for the remaining debt of $4,370—"It is lent to me for as long a time as I please," he explained—but the $17,000 borrowed from the U.S. Bank gnawed at him. "It is impossible to be at ease considering the situation of the Banks of the U.S. and the necessity it must be under to press all its debtors," cried William, "and if they press me, I fear I am gone." The Richmond property already sold and Elizabeth's remaining half square, offered at $1,200, had been more than absorbed by the purchase of the additional slaves and by other "contingent expenses" for the plantation. Still, the Wirts' assets were considerable: Elizabeth's half interest in the Gamble mansion in Richmond (estimated at $4,000) and the Washington house (worth perhaps $10,000, although it had cost the Wirts $12,000). Furthermore, John and Robert Gamble owed Elizabeth $10,000 between them. "But I fear it cannot be at all counted on," worried William; "[though] I have property & debts enough (*without touching an atom of my Florida property*) to pay off this debt . . . I fear it will *all* have to go."[47]

In this extremity the Wirts gave up their house to move into a boarding-house. "Our means are now so curtailed," worried Elizabeth, "your Father's health so delicate & uncertain, that it would be madness to spend our little lightly." While Elizabeth, William, and the three girls, Catharine, Ellen, and Rosa, took rooms in Baltimore, Dabney and Henry were sent to live with Elizabeth's sister Nancy and her husband, William Cabell, in Richmond. Will Jr. left for Florida with Liz and Louis Goldsborough. Upon their arrival, they wrote to the Wirts with the sad news that Laura had died of tuberculosis. The Wirts felt their separation and their losses keenly. "We have to struggle hard against melancholy—in this breaking up of all our family circle & home comforts," wrote Elizabeth.[48]

Still, the Wirts hoped to follow their difficulties with golden dreams. At Christmastime William rallied his strength for his last appearance in the Supreme Court. "We go down,—that is my dear wife, my two daughters and myself, on the 11th of next month," he reported to Dabney Carr. "My health is so good that I hope to be able to bear all the labors of the winter without flinching," William predicted hopefully, "and to meet you . . . *next* summer in better plight than I did *this*." Once in Washington, William continued to hope for the best. "I am now very anxious to hear from you, dear Louis, about *plantation matters*," he wrote in February. William peppered Goldsborough with questions about his progress in clearing, his plans for building, and the health of the slaves. Florida, he still hoped, would be the family's earthly refuge from worry and care.[49]

It was not to be. On February 9, 1834, William walked to church in a cold drizzle. The sermon affected him deeply, and he sobbed aloud during the service. Afterward, he returned home and went to bed with a fever. Over the next few days his fever increased, and he alternated between delirium and lethargy. On February 17, "the eye that had been so long closed opened suddenly," and Catharine, who had been at her father's side, called Elizabeth to him. "She approached the bedside," Catharine related the scene. "He looked fixedly at her and said: '*Wife, I am going before you!*' I feared this would upset her, but God upheld her, and she answered meekly: 'Yes my beloved you *are* going before me, and you will see our dear angels in Heaven sooner than I shall . . . It will only be for a little while, and we too shall come and join you.' " On the morning of the 18th William drew his last breath. "At that instant," recalled Catharine, "the Sun which had been all the morning veiled in clouds burst into the room with full meridian splendor, and the . . . [mocking] bird, which had been . . . hanging silent and unobserved in his cage, struck up a requiem note so subdued and so sweet that it might well nigh be mistaken for the rustling of an angel's wing. My poor dear Mother threw herself into our arms and exclaimed 'The seal of happiness to him, but of Misery to us'—" The deathbed scene, as Catharine described it, partook of the conventions of sentimental death which were common in the early-nineteenth-century South. The agonies of death were obscured by reflections on the state of the dying family member's mind and soul, the departed was described as leaving a troubled world for the glory of heaven, and those left behind gave way to overwhelming grief. Elizabeth's misery had special significance. When she surrendered to her sorrow, she surely mourned not only for her husband but for herself as well, knowing that William's untimely death had denied the Wirts their final opportunity to realize their vision of married bliss.[50]

With the end of the Wirts' marriage came the end of the early national period, an era that scholars have come to identify as one of especial promise for egalitarian, loving relationships between men and women.[51] During the 1830s, the divisions between men's and women's lives hardened, taking on the recognizable outlines of what scholars have termed separate spheres in the North and domestic patriarchy in the South. Both consigned men and women to clearly demarcated roles and assigned husbands and wives very different responsibilities for marriage. Elizabeth and William Wirt's life together helps explain how the promise of companionship within a marriage partnership of mutuality, reciprocity, and symmetry proved false for them and for other men and women in the early American Republic.

~

A Contested Legacy

For more than three decades, Elizabeth and William Wirt had struggled to attain the high standards they held for their marriage and family. Catharine, the Wirts' oldest unwed daughter, summed up her parents' relationship in a brief poem: "How link'd, how blessed we might have been," she mused, "had fate not frown'd so dark between!"[1] Certainly the Wirts never fully achieved the blessed link they had longed for. They spent a significant proportion of their married life apart, and more important, at many points their expectations and their experiences of marriage sharply diverged. Even during their best times, the Wirts never fully succeeded in realizing their ideal of mutuality, equality, and reciprocity.

Elizabeth spent the months following William's death establishing a lasting memorial to her husband as he had been in the Wirts' happiest moments: a loving and committed husband and father. Perhaps, like other southern women who found that their marriages did not live up to their higher expectations, Elizabeth remade her husband in the image of her own beau ideal once he was gone. Elizabeth worked hard to demonstrate to others—and perhaps to convince herself as well—that it was only William's death that truly destroyed the Wirts' hopes for a true marriage partnership. "*This last most desolating bereavement*," she wrote in 1834, "has forever extinguished the flickering flame of happiness that still illuminated my path."[2]

Elizabeth took an active role in establishing and preserving William's "idolized memory." She offered his memorialists hints and even made "a few corrections" to their eulogies, and she wrote to William's many prominent acquaintances to acquire "copies of His numerous and widely dispersed letters," which she intended to incorporate into "His Biography." In death, Elizabeth was determined, William would live on in memory, spreading his influence as a husband and father—arbiter of morality, gifted storyteller, and wise advisor—beyond the bounds of his own family. Out of all the memorials of her husband's death, Elizabeth singled out one for special attention. The obituary, marked "For dear William," described William's "unflinching patriotism" and his standing "as the ornament of [the legal] profession." But the opening words captured the aspect of William's life which he had shared with Elizabeth. "In him," began the notice, "his family have lost all that can be lost, in one among the most tender, devoted, and enlightened of husbands and fathers." Elizabeth may well have had a hand in writing or revising this notice. She wrote numerous letters to William's friends, thanking them for their condolences and for the eulogies they delivered on William's behalf. "My heart warms toward you for the glowing and living portrait you have given of my beloved," she praised Samuel Southard. "Let me thank you from my heart Dear Sir, for the kind and honorable mention here made of *his* once happy, but now bereaved and heart-broken *wife*—and of the dear Children of our affection. To be associated with him in this commemoration, is grateful to our bleeding hearts, which are forever cut off in this world, from the intimate communion with him, which made our earthly happiness."[3]

Despite the Wirts' many difficulties during their life together, it was fitting that Elizabeth emphasized her intimate communion with her husband, rather than his worldly success. Ironically, despite his endless pursuit for wealth and an economic safety net for his wife and children after his death, William died leaving little more than debts to his family. The Florida lands had not yet realized their promise. As a widow, Elizabeth found herself in possession of a vast quantity of uncleared, unproductive lands—and a debt in excess of twenty thousand dollars, a truly astronomical sum at the time. After William's death, local creditors exerted pressure that forced Elizabeth to flee Baltimore only a few months after the family's loss. In March, Elizabeth prevailed upon a friend, Henry Didier, to allow her to use his house to display the Wirts' belongings for auction. Miserable and poverty-stricken, the Wirts left Baltimore immediately following the auction for Richmond, where they crowded into the former Gamble residence with Nancy Cabell and her family. The quarters were cramped. Elizabeth, Catharine, and Ellen slept in one chamber, and Henry and Dabney occupied another. A third room was Elizabeth's sitting room. Will Jr. remained in Florida as Louis Goldsborough's informal apprentice in planting. Watching her "dear ones being scattered abroad over the face of the earth" was difficult for Elizabeth. "The chords which so sweetly bound together" their family circle had been "severed."[4]

Elizabeth devoted the remaining years of her life to repairing the cords that held the family together. William had entrusted his widow with full responsibility for the family's finances following his death. In his will, he appointed Elizabeth to be the "sole executrix" of his estate. She was also his only heir, and William's will granted his widow all his property unconditionally. "I give, devise and bequest unto my excellent and beloved wife Elizabeth W. Wirt, all of my estate of every nature, kind and description whatsoever," his will stated, "in perfect reliance upon her judgment, prudence and maternal affection, to manage, use and dispose of the same to the best advantage for her own maintenance and comfort, and for the support, education and happiness of our dear children and their advancement in life as they shall arrive at legal age or marry."[5]

Elizabeth's vigorous actions following her husband's death demonstrated that he had not misplaced his trust in her judgment, prudence, and maternal affection. While he lived, William had been the family's sole legal representative. Only he was legally qualified to sue for payment of sums due him or to negotiate for terms on the debts he owed. As a widow, Elizabeth was once again a feme sole, a single woman capable of acting on her own behalf. Combining her native acumen, her new legal status, and the sympathy she evoked as a widow, she set about rebuilding the family's finances. She pressured her husband's debtors (including the federal government) for payment, arranged for favorable repayment schedules for the Wirts' loans, used the funds she had inherited from her mother to finance the boys' educations, and moved to Wirtland to direct the plantation during the difficult years following the Panic of 1837. The next few years were arduous ones. Prices remained low following the Panic of 1837, and it was with great difficulty that Elizabeth paid the regular sums due for repayment of her debts. In 1840 Ellen reported that Elizabeth had been forced to sell personal articles "that she might raise money to buy ... bread"; bank failures had been so severe, she explained, that merchants would not extend credit even for bare necessities.[6]

Somehow Elizabeth not only survived these hard times but managed to protect her children from the ravages of poverty. Dabney went to the University of Virginia in 1838. Henry followed him there in 1840, and in 1842 Will Jr. left Florida to pursue medical training in Baltimore. Elizabeth also supervised her remaining daughters' welfare. For them, marriage was the avenue to financial security, if not wealth. After a lengthy courtship, Catharine married Thomas Randall's brother, Alexander, in 1842 and moved to Annapolis, where her husband was engaged in a small but growing medical practice. Ellen married a Florida planter, Edmund B. Vass, who owned a plantation of more than six hundred acres, sometime during the depression that followed the Panic of 1837. In 1839 Vass died, leaving Ellen mistress of his plantation, Lequan. In 1841 she settled his estate by auctioning off his slaves. With a sizable inheritance, Ellen soon married again, this time to Dr. Charles McCormick, who had attended her during an illness in 1840. Dr. McCormick was an army physician, and his work took the couple to Arkansas in 1843.[7]

Elizabeth held out during the worst of the depression, refusing to sacrifice her potential assets in stock, land, or slaves. By the end of her fifth year in Florida, she had withstood calls for the full amounts of her various debts, supervised the clearing of the plantation, and given both her sons and her daughters a start in life. Now fifty-eight years old, Elizabeth decided that her work in Florida was done. In 1842 she entrusted her brother, Robert Gamble, with the management of the plantation and went to live with Catharine and Alexander Randall in Annapolis. From Annapolis, Elizabeth continued to oversee the plantation and to use the proceeds to assist her children and grandchildren. But Elizabeth's family circle was shrinking. Liz and her husband lived an itinerant life in successive boardinghouses along the east coast. In 1843, Liz moved to Portsmouth, New Hampshire. Rosa died at her husband's residence in Baltimore in 1849, and Henry died of a bronchial complaint in 1850. After a sojourn in Oklahoma, Ellen moved with her husband to New Orleans, where she died in 1853. Catharine, after a botched operation for breast cancer, also died in 1853. Elizabeth remained at the Randall household in Annapolis, taking over the care of both Laura's and Catharine's children. As she approached her seventieth birthday, Elizabeth found herself once again acting as the mistress of a house. "There is a house full of Lady relatives here to dinner to day," she wrote in 1854, "and I have been so often interrupted by seamstresses, servants and Children, that I must have written rather incoherently."[8]

There was nothing incoherent, however, about Elizabeth Wirt's last will and testament, which she initially wrote in 1851 and revised repeatedly, first in 1852 and again in 1854. Elizabeth claimed the right to dispose of her husband's estate as she saw fit. "Having been appointed sole executrix of the last will and testament of [her] dear husband, William Wirt, and by him invested with power to manage, use and dispose of all his estate of every nature, kind and description whatever," she stated, she was empowered to make whatever arrangements she considered "just and equitable." Elizabeth may have seen a need to remind her heirs of William's decision to leave his property to her without restrictions because her will, like other women's wills in the antebellum upper South, exhibited a particular definition of equitable treatment. Men generally divided their inheritance equally among their children. But women often made their decisions based on more personal factors, including gender, need, and the decedent's judgment of fairness. Elizabeth Wirt exhibited this sort of "personalism" in her will and codicils. She directed that Laura's husband and children and Henry's children, who had received significant support already, would receive reduced portions of the estate. Elizabeth also provided her one surviving daughter, Liz, with a separate estate and with an extra bequest to allow her to purchase a home of her own. Elizabeth must have known that her many omissions, special bequests, and conditions would provoke protests. Her will, with its many personalistic touches, differed from men's wills, and she was aware that it might be contested on the grounds that William had an equal, not an equitable, division of his estate in mind when he gave his widow license "to manage, use and dispose" of his estate for their children's "support, education and happiness."[9]

William's estate—consisting of the encumbered Florida property, slaves, and equipment—had been purchased with funds from the sale of the stocks and real estate that Elizabeth had inherited from her parents. Although no official record of a separate estate for Elizabeth has been preserved, the Wirts clearly considered the property that Elizabeth was given outright by her father and willed by her mother to be her own. After Catharine Gamble's death in 1832, William promised William H. Cabell, Elizabeth's brother-in-law: "My wife shall have her rights if any effort of mine can secure them." Elizabeth retained control of the property she inherited from the Gambles, designating Cabell her representative on occasion. Since William's death, Elizabeth had drawn on her personal property to tide the family over during the hard years following the Panic of 1837, to cultivate the Florida estate, and to enable Wirtland to realize a profit during the cotton boom that followed the depression. She used these facts to buttress her claim to the right to distribute the united property from William's estate and her own as she pleased.[10]

Three years after her final disposition of her property, in 1857, Elizabeth Wirt died after a lengthy and painful illness. At her death, the joint estate of Elizabeth and William Wirt was estimated at seventy thousand dollars. With such a sum involved, it is not surprising that, despite Elizabeth's care in drawing up her will, the heirs promptly took sides for a legal battle. Alexander Randall, who was coexecutor with Will Jr., and Liz, the principal beneficiary, supported the will. But other family members expressed disappointment and anger at Elizabeth's provisions. Henry's widow, Harriet Louisa (Wirt) Girardeau, and Laura's husband, Thomas Randall, led the protest. Having consulted with Randall, Girardeau commented, "he expressed himself much surprized at the disposition Mrs W had made of her property & added that the rest of the family agreed with him in opinion."[11]

In 1859 a special judge for the circuit court in Anne Arundel County, Maryland, delivered his opinion. Although a review of William's will convinced him that it conferred "on Mrs. Wirt a fee simple and absolute estate," a codicil that William had added at the request of one of his creditors created ambiguity. Although William "ratified & confirmed" his original will, his recollection of the will was that he had "devised & bequested" his entire estate to Elizabeth "during her natural life for the support of herself & for the support & education of [their] children." The phrasing of the legal document introduced the possibility that William had intended to create a trust for the children, granting Elizabeth only the use of his property during her own lifetime, rather than owning it outright. The wording of the codicil was "a serious difficulty," noted the judge; if William had thereby created a trust for the Wirt children, then Elizabeth was not empowered to exclude any descendants from his portion of the estate. In particular, because Elizabeth specified that she revoked the portion of her will that gave any portion of her own estate to Henry's two children, the judge concluded that Elizabeth did not mean to disinherit the Girardeau girls entirely, but only from her portion of the joint estate.[12]

The case was forwarded to the auditor, whose task was to ascertain the respective value of the estate of William Wirt and the estate of Elizabeth Wirt. It was not a simple matter. "These Estates are now and have been for upwards of twenty years so intermingled," complained Alexander Randall, "that he is a better accountant than I am who would undertake . . . to decide these various questions touching the respective rights of these Estates." For more than two months the case dragged on. Finally, however, it became clear that "it was a grave question in the case whether *there was any* Estate of Mr. Wirt." "After his death," one of the Wirts' descendants explained the details of the case more than thirty years later, "my grandmother carried on for many years the Florida plantations paid large amounts of his debts out of her own property, educated the children &c &c and on these accounts had very large claims individually against his estate, which was also largely indebted to her at the time of his death." Alarmed at the prospect of losing any claim to the estate, the representatives for Henry's daughters compromised, taking five thousand dollars for each Girardeau girl, to be held in trust and invested for them, estimating the sum of the two trust funds (ten thousand dollars) to be equivalent to one-seventh of the combined estate. With that compromise, "an agreement of all the parties," it was hoped that it would be possible "to settle amicably that family suit."[13]

But the ugly family quarrel continued to resurface. Henry's two daughters, Elizabeth and Letitia, who received interest from their trust funds to support them during their childhood, demanded immediate surrender of their trusts in 1873. Robert Gamble, who had been appointed the young women's guardian, was in financial difficulties, and he was unable to pay the full amount until 1878. Family squabbles over money again erupted following Elizabeth Wirt Goldsborough's death in 1885. Liz had survived her husband (he died in 1877), and her death once again posed the problem of where to draw the line between a widow's separate estate and the money she inherited from her husband. Liz had died childless, and under the terms of Elizabeth Wirt's will, her separate estate from her mother reverted to the Wirt estate for distribution among the heirs Elizabeth named—a list that did not include Letitia Wirt Dupont and Elizabeth Wirt Baker, Henry's children. Despite their demands for equal treatment, the two women received only a few hundred dollars from their aunt (from the small estate she had received from her husband). When Dabney died in 1893, he also left no children, and his share of the estate was also returned to the Wirt inheritance for distribution among the surviving heirs. William Wirt Jr. did not enjoy his share for long; he died six years later. According to the terms laid down by Elizabeth, the Wirts' joint estate passed down to her grandchildren, excluding Henry's daughters. The will proved to be a lasting source of discontent. In the 1890s, Lizzie Baker, as she was known, mounted yet another unsuccessful attempt to contest Elizabeth Wirt's will.[14]

Lizzie Baker was a journalist, an amateur historian, and a member of the Daughters of the American Revolution. A genealogical enthusiast, she compiled numerous newspaper clippings, birth, marriage, and death certificates, and other family records for her never completed magnum opus: a biography of "my Grand Father," William Wirt. Embittered by her exclusion from the Wirt estate, Lizzie had little use for the grandmother for whom she was named. William was her "*beau ideal*," she told her daughter, and "one of the grandest exponents of pure patriotism this country ever knew." But in Lizzie's assorted biographical sketches and genealogical disquisitions, Elizabeth Wirt was a shadowy figure at best, useful only insofar as she connected Lizzie to "Col. Robert Gamble a faithful soldier of the Revolutionary war." William was the epitome of manly individualism and worldly achievement; Elizabeth was a nonentity, carelessly classified as "the angel of his home."[15]

Lizzie Baker's summation of Elizabeth and William Wirt's life contrasted sharply with Margaret Smith's observations nearly seven decades earlier. While both Smith and Baker greatly admired William Wirt, they offered very different analyses of Elizabeth and William Wirt's marriage. Margaret Smith, the Wirts' contemporary, described them as a happy, loving couple; Lizzie Baker described her grandparents as a strong, successful man backed by a quiet, submissive woman. These different descriptions of the beau ideal suggest the dynamic dialogue about marital relationships in nineteenth-century America—a dialogue that historians continue today, particularly with reference to the South. Margaret Smith, a domestic novelist whose career helped to create the ideal of companionate marriage, celebrated the Wirts' union as an example of a successful marriage that lived up to the high standards of mutual love and respect that many scholars argue flourished in the early-nineteenth-century United States. Lizzie Baker, who never forgave her grandmother for denying her what she believed was her rightful heritage, accepted and even glorified an unequal relationship between a strong patriarch and a submissive wife which several studies describe as characteristic of the Old South. Neither assessment fully captures the essence of the Wirts' relationship, an extended attempt to negotiate the meaning of marriage and to achieve true companionship. The Wirts' story indicates that interpretations of marriage and family life in the past—like Elizabeth's will—demand repeated testing to yield a more complete understanding of the legacy of Elizabeth and William Wirt and others like them.

Elizabeth and William Wirt left an enduring legacy as well as a contested one. Their lifelong negotiations on their marriage and their roles within it illuminate marital relations at a crucial juncture for women and men in America. The Wirts' marriage spanned the first three decades of the nineteenth century, the same years in which women and men in the new nation adopted the new ideal of companionate marriage and also complicated the achievement of that ideal by developing rigid definitions of men's and women's positions in separate spheres and patriarchal households. Women and men in the early Republic set patterns for gender relations in marriage which would prove both enduring and resilient. Companionate marriage, complete with its contradictions, would become a hallmark of the modern American family. Today, women and men continue to strive for the companionate ideal.

~

Notes

Introduction

1. [Margaret Bayard Smith], *The First Forty Years of Washington Society, Portrayed by the Family Letters of Mrs. Samuel Harrison Smith (Margaret Bayard)*, ed. Gaillard Hunt (1906; reprint, New York, 1965), 244, 316–17.

2. For an introduction to companionate marriage, see Carl N. Degler, *At Odds: Women and the Family in America from the Revolution to the Present* (New York, 1980), chap. 1, and Robert L. Griswold, *Family and Divorce in California, 1850–1890: Victorian Illusions and Everyday Realities* (Albany, N.Y., 1982), chap. 1. On the early national period, see especially Linda K. Kerber et al., "Beyond Roles, Beyond Spheres: Thinking about Gender in the Early Republic," *William and Mary Quarterly*, 3d ser., 46 (July 1989): 565–85, and Jan Lewis, "The Republican Wife: Virtue and Seduction in the Early Republic," *William and Mary Quarterly*, 3d ser., 44 (October 1987): 689–721.

3. Illustrative works in women's history include Barbara Berg, *The Remembered Gate: Origins of American Feminism: The Woman and the City, 1800–1860* (New York, 1978); Nancy F. Cott, *The Bonds of Womanhood: "Woman's Sphere" in New England, 1780–1835* (New Haven, Conn., 1977); Ann Douglas, *The Feminization of American Culture* (New York, 1977); Kathryn Kish Sklar, *Catharine Beecher: A Study in American Domesticity* (New York, 1973); and Barbara Welter, "The Cult of True Womanhood, 1820–1860," *American Quarterly* 17 (Summer 1966): 151–74. For a critical appraisal of these frameworks, see Linda K. Kerber, "Separate Spheres, Female Worlds, Woman's Place: The Rhetoric of Women's History," *Journal of American History* 75 (June 1988): 9–39. For the new male studies, see especially Ronald Preston Byars, "The Making of the Self-Made Man: The Development of Masculine Roles and Images in Ante-Bellum America" (Ph.D. diss., Michigan State University, 1979); Peter G. Filene, *Him/Her/Self: Sex Roles in Modern America*, rev. ed. (Baltimore, 1986); Anthony Rotundo, *American Manhood: Transformations in Masculinity from the Revolution to the Modern Era* (New York, 1993); and Peter N. Stearns, *Be a Man! Males in Modern Society* (New York, 1979).

4. For companionship in the South, see especially Russell Lindley Blake, "Ties of Intimacy: Social Values and Personal Relationships of Antebellum Slaveholders" (Ph.D. diss., University of Michigan, 1978); Ann Williams Boucher, "Wealthy Planter Families in Nineteenth-Century Alabama," (Ph.D. diss., University of Connecticut, 1978); Mel-

inda S. Buza, " 'Pledges of Our Love': Friendship, Love, and Marriage among the Virginia Gentry, 1800–1825," in *The Edge of the South: Life in Nineteenth-Century Virginia*, ed. Edward L. Ayers and John C. Willis (Charlottesville, Va., 1991), 9–36; Jane Turner Censer, *North Carolina Planters and Their Children, 1800–1860* (Baton Rouge, La., 1984), 72–73; Jan Lewis, *The Pursuit of Happiness: Family and Values in Jefferson's Virginia* (New York, 1983), chap. 5; and Daniel Blake Smith, *Inside the Great House: Planter Family Life in Eighteenth-Century Chespeake Society* (Ithaca, N.Y., 1980).

Works that argue that southerners continued to evince patriarchal family life include Joan E. Cashin, *A Family Venture: Men and Women on the Southern Frontier* (New York, 1991); Catherine Clinton, *The Plantation Mistress: Woman's World in the Old South* (New York, 1982), and Bertram Wyatt-Brown, *Southern Honor: Ethics and Behavior in the Old South* (New York, 1982).

Several scholars have noted the conflict between these two patterns in the Old South. See especially Drew Gilpin Faust's epilogue to Carol Bleser, ed., *In Joy and in Sorrow: Women, Family, and Marriage in the Victorian South, 1830–1900* (New York, 1991), 253-59, esp. 253–55; Suzanne Lebsock, *The Free Women of Petersburg: Status and Culture in a Southern Town, 1784–1860* (New York, 1984), chap. 2; and Steven M. Stowe's review essay "Private Emotions and a Public Man in Early Nineteenth-Century Virginia," *History of Education Quarterly* 27 (Spring 1987): 75–81.

5. For quotations, see William Wirt to Elizabeth Wirt, August 31, 1811, William Wirt Papers, MS 1011, Manuscripts Department, Maryland Historical Society Library, Baltimore, on microfilm at Rice University, Houston, Texas (hereafter WW, EW, and MHS). On the importance of correspondence for well-to-do southerners, see especially Steven M. Stowe, "Rhetoric of Authority: The Making of Social Values in Planter Family Correspondence," *Journal of American History* 73 (March 1987): 916–33, and "Singleton's Tooth: Thoughts on the Form and Meaning of Antebellum Southern Family Correspondence," *Southern Review* 25 (Spring 1989): 323–33.

6. WW to EW, May 2, 1817, MHS; on Virginians and love, see especially Lewis, *Pursuit of Happiness*, chap. 5.

7. [Smith], *First Forty Years*, 317–18; EW to WW, July 18, 1810, MHS. On women's love letters in early America, see Ellen K. Rothman, *Hands and Hearts: A History of Courtship in America* (New York, 1984), 11.

8. [Smith], *First Forty Years*, 316; WW to EW, August 31, 1811, MHS. On men's letter writing in early America, see Konstantin Dierks, "The Feminization of Letter Writing in Early America, 1750–1800" (paper delivered at the Second Annual Conference of the Institute of Early American History and Culture, Boulder, Colo., June 1, 1996).

9. For quotation, see [Smith], *First Forty Years*, 239. On "masculine domesticity," see especially Margaret Marsh, "Suburban Men and Masculine Domesticity, 1870–1915," in *Meanings for Manhood: Constructions of Masculinity in Victorian America*, ed. Mark C. Carnes and Clyde Griffen (Chicago, 1990), 111–27.

10. For quotation, see [Smith], *First Forty Years*, 317–18. On the supreme importance of love and the different meaning for men and women, see especially Lewis, *Pursuit of Happiness*, chap. 5.

11. WW to Dabney Carr, September 9, 1810, and EW to WW, December 20, 1821, MHS. For men's and women's different views of men's travels for political reasons, see

Steven M. Stowe, *Intimacy and Power in the Old South: Ritual in the Lives of the Planters* (Baltimore, 1987), 77–89. For women's isolation, see Clinton, *Plantation Mistress,* chap. 9.

Chapter One ⌒ Forming a Life Partnership

1. WW to EW, December 6, 1803, William Wirt Papers, MHS.

2. On companionate marriage in England, see Lawrence Stone, *The Family, Sex and Marriage in England, 1500–1800* (London, 1977). For an overview of companionate marriage in the United States, see Degler, *At Odds,* 8–9.

3. On the era, see especially Kerber et al., "Beyond Roles, Beyond Spheres." For literary treatments of marriage, see Jay Fliegelman, *Prodigals and Pilgrims: The American Revolution against Patriarchal Authority, 1750–1800* (Cambridge, 1982), chap. 5; Jan Lewis, "Republican Wife"; Jan Lewis, "Motherhood and the Construction of the Male Citizen in the United States, 1750–1850," in *Constructions of the Self,* ed. George Levine (New Brunswick, N.J., 1992), 143–63; and Shirley Samuels, "The Family, the State, and the Novel in the Early Republic," *American Quarterly* 38, no. 3 (1986): 33–88.

4. On southern evangelicalism, see Donald G. Mathews, *Religion in the Old South* (Chicago, 1977). On the South's wave of religious awakenings about 1800, see John B. Boles, *The Great Revival, 1787–1805: The Origins of the Southern Evangelical Mind* (Lexington, Ky., 1972). On the connection between evangelicalism and affectionate family life, see especially Lewis, *Pursuit of Happiness,* esp. chap. 5.

5. On "domestic patriarchy," see Alan Kulikoff, *Tobacco and Slaves: The Development of Southern Cultures in the Chesapeake, 1680–1800* (Chapel Hill, N.C., 1986), chap. 5. For the "revolution against patriarchy," see Fliegelman, *Prodigals and Pilgrims,* esp. chap. 6; and on new ideals of marriage and family, see Lewis, "Republican Wife," and Samuels, "Family, the State, and the Novel." Literature on the revolutionary era reassessment of women's role and status is voluminous. See especially Ruth Bloch, "American Feminine Ideals in Transition," *Feminist Studies* 4 (June 1978): 101–26; Linda Kerber, *Women of the Republic: Intellect and Ideology in Revolutionary America* (Chapel Hill, N.C., 1980); Patricia Jewell McAlexander, "The Creation of the American Eve: The Cultural Dialogue on the Nature and Role of Women in Late-Eighteenth-Century America," *Early American Literature* 9 (Winter 1975): 252–66; and Mary Beth Norton, *Liberty's Daughters: The Revolutionary Experience of American Women, 1750–1800* (Boston, 1980). For a critical assessment of the effect of the revolutionary conflict on women, see Joan Hoff Wilson, "The Illusion of Change: Women and the American Revolution," in *Our American Sisters: Women in American Life and Thought,* ed. Jean E. Friedman and William G. Shade (Lexington, Mass., 1982), 117–36.

6. On evangelical manhood, see Philip Greven, *The Protestant Temperament: Patterns of Child-Rearing, Religious Experience, and the Self in Early America* (New York, 1977), esp. 124–40, and Mathews, *Religion in the Old South,* 119–22. On the "man of sensibility," see especially G. J. Barker-Benfield, *The Culture of Sensibility: Sex and Society in Eighteenth-Century Britain* (Chicago, 1992).

7. For the first quotation, see WW to EW, May 19, 1805, MHS. On the Gambles, see Lyman Chalkley, *Chronicles of the Scotch-Irish Settlement in Virginia Extracted from the Original Court Records of Augusta County, 1745–1800,* 3 vols. (Baltimore, 1966), 1:

300, 3:159; Nell McNish Gambill, *The Kith and Kin of Captain James Leeper and Susan Draker, His Wife* (New York, 1946), 116–18 (second and third quotations); George R. Gilmer, *Sketches of Some of the First Settlers of Upper Georgia, of the Cherokees, and the Author* (Baltimore, 1965), 26–30; and John P. Kennedy, *Memoirs of the Life of William Wirt, Attorney-General of the United States*, 2 vols. (1849; rev. ed., Philadelphia, 1850), 1:89–91, 257–58 (first quotation). On the Gamble mansion, see Mary Wingfield Scott, *Old Richmond Neighborhoods* (Richmond, Va., 1950), 186–88.

8. For quotation, see WW to Lucy F. Ford, July 11, 1802, MHS. William referred to the Gamble sisters' popularity in another letter to Ford in May (n.d.) 1802: "Pray are the Miss G's as terrible in the beau monde, and as obdurate as ever?" he inquired. Elizabeth's portrait is reproduced in Fillmore Norfleet, *Saint-Memin in Virginia: Portraits and Biographies* (Richmond, Va., 1942).

9. On the gains for women's education on a national scale, see Kerber, *Women of the Republic*, chap. 7; and Norton, *Liberty's Daughters*, chaps. 6 and 7. For the South in the same era, see Clinton, *Plantation Mistress*, chap. 7. For William's thoughts on education, see [William Wirt et al.], *The Rainbow* (Richmond, Va., 1804), 10–15; and [William Wirt], *The Old Bachelor*, 3d ed. (Baltimore, 1818), 70–71, 98.

10. On Elizabeth's education, see George Wythe Munford, *The Two Parsons* (Richmond, Va., 1884), 265–75 (all quotations on 270); Virginius Dabney, *Richmond: The Story of a City*, rev. ed. (Charlottesville, Va., 1990), 77–78; Norfleet, *Saint-Memin in Virginia*; and Sarah P. Stetson, "Mrs. Wirt and the Language of Flowers," *Virginia Magazine of History and Biography* 57 (October 1949): 379–89. For women's colleges in the South, see Christie Anne Farnham, *The Education of the Southern Belle: Higher Education and Student Socialization in the Antebellum South* (New York, 1994).

11. WW to EW, November 6, 1805, MHS; Clinton, *Plantation Mistress*, 61–62.

12. EW to Thomas [Monteagle] Bayly, March 11, 1801, Virginia Historical Society, Richmond; and WW to Dabney Carr, July 14, 1800, MHS.

13. On parents' reduced or disguised role in marriage choice, see Censer, *North Carolina Planters*, 65–68, 78–95; Rothman, *Hands and Hearts*; Daniel Scott Smith, "Parental Power and Marriage Patterns: An Analysis of Historical Trends in Hingham, Massachusetts," *Journal of Marriage and the Family* 35 (August 1973): 419–28. For the Wirts' courting arenas, see WW to Dabney Carr, December 12, 1800, and WW to EW, May 22, 1805, MHS.

14. Kennedy, *Memoirs*, 1:16–49. For a description of the tavern, see Kulikoff, *Tobacco and Slaves*, 221–24.

15. Kennedy, *Memoirs*, 1:49–55 (quotation).

16. For quotation, see Maurice Duke and Daniel P. Jordan, eds., *A Richmond Reader, 1733–1983* (Chapel Hill, N.C., 1983), 27. On William's connection with the Gilmers, see Kennedy, *Memoirs*, 1:63–76, and Will of George Gilmer, Will Book No. 3, with Inventories and Accounts, 1785–98, p. 265, Albemarle County, Virginia, microfilm at Clayton Genealogical Library, Houston, Texas.

17. For quotation, see Kennedy, *Memoirs*, 1:15. For William's finances, see Joseph Clarke Robert, "William Wirt, Virginian," *Virginia Magazine of History and Biography* 81 (October 1972): 398–401.

18. For stories of William's conduct, see WW to EW, September 27, 1803 (first quotation); WW to Benjamin Edwards, December 22, 1809 (second quotation), MHS;

Kennedy, *Memoirs*, 1:91–92; and William Wirt Jr. and Dabney Carr Wirt, "Draft of a letter from Oak Grove to Episcopal Recorder," December 28, 1854, (last quotation), William and Elizabeth Wirt Papers, 1810–54, Department of Manuscripts, Perkins Library, Duke University, Durham, N.C. (hereafter Duke). For William's Presbyterian upbringing, see S. A. Link, "William Wirt, the Christian Lawyer," *Methodist Quarterly Review* 57 (October 1908): 731–32, 736–37; on gambling and honor, see T. H. Breen, "Horses and Gentlemen: The Cultural Significance of Gambling among the Gentry of Virginia," in *The American Man*, ed. Joseph H. Pleck and Elizabeth H. Pleck (Englewood Cliffs, N.J., 1980), 77–106.

19. On courtship rituals, see Clinton, *Plantation Mistress*, 63–64; on courtship guides, see Frances B. Cogan, *All-American Girl: The Ideal of Womanhood in Mid-Nineteenth-Century America* (Athens, Ga., 1989), chap. 3; and on the romantic test, see Karen Lystra, *Searching the Heart: Women, Men, and Romantic Love in Nineteenth-Century America* (New York, 1989), chap. 6.

20. An account of the Wirts' courtship written nine years after their marriage revealed that the Gambles "had been anxiously endeavoring to forward the suit of another." See the introduction to engagement letters, 1811, preceding 1802 letters in MHS. It is unclear if Elizabeth, William, or one of their children wrote this account. On parents' continuing control over courtship, see Clinton, *Plantation Mistress*, 59–65. On northern courtship and birth order, see Smith, "Parental Power and Marriage Patterns."

21. WW to Dabney Carr, July 14, 1800, and introduction to engagement letters, MHS.

22. WW to Elizabeth Gamble, August 3, 1802; WW to Mrs. Lucy F. Jones, March 20, May (n.d.), 1802; WW to EW, May 22, 1805; introduction to engagement letters; and WW to EW, August 31, 1811, MHS.

23. WW to Elizabeth Gamble, June 26, 1802, MHS (draft).

24. "Rough Draft of Wm Wirt's letter to Colo. Gamble soliciting permission to address his daughter," June 16, 1802, MHS; on such letters, see Clinton, *Plantation Mistress*, 65.

25. Robert Gamble to WW, June 21, 1802, and WW to EW, June 26, 1802, MHS.

26. St. George Tucker, *Blackstone's Commentaries: With Notes of Reference to the Constitution and Laws, of the Federal Government of the United States, and of the Commonwealth of Virginia*, 5 vols. (Philadelphia, 1803), 441–46 (quotation on 445); see also Norma Basch, *In the Eyes of the Law: Women, Marriage, and Property in Nineteenth-Century New York* (Ithaca, N.Y., 1982), 15–19, 22–26, 42–69; Joan R. Gundersen and Gwen Victor Gampel, "Married Women's Legal Status in Eighteenth-Century New York and Virginia," *William and Mary Quarterly*, 3d ser., 39 (January 1982): 114–34; Lebsock, *Free Women of Petersburg*, chap. 2.

27. WW to EW, October 30, 1806, MHS. On separate estates in Virginia, see Lebsock, *Free Women of Petersburg*, chap. 3. On separate estates elsewhere in the nation, see Basch, *In the Eyes of the Law*, 72–88, and Marylynn Salmon, "Women and Property in South Carolina: The Evidence from Marriage Settlements, 1730–1830," *William and Mary Quarterly*, 3d ser., 39 (October 1982): 655–95. On equity law, see Basch, "Equity vs. Equality: Emerging Concepts of Women's Political Status in the Age of Jackson," *Journal of the Early Republic* 3 (Fall 1983): 297–318.

28. Clinton, *Plantation Mistress*, 60, 78, app. A, tables 1 and 3 (pp. 232–33), and app.

B, tables 1 and 2 (p. 240); Lebsock, *Free Women of Petersburg*, chap. 2; and WW to EW, August 31, 1811, MHS.

29. WW to EW, August 3, 1802, and May 15, 1804, MHS.

30. For quotation, see WW to Elizabeth Gamble, August 3, 1802, MHS. On romantic love, see Lystra, *Searching the Heart*, 9. On kinship and parental oversight, see Joan E. Cashin, "The Structure of Antebellum Planter Families: 'The Ties That Bound Us Was Strong,'" *Journal of Southern History* 56 (February 1990): 55–70.

31. Elizabeth's letters were destroyed, but William frequently quoted her comments in his replies, as in these letters. For quotations, see WW to EW, October 16, 26, 28, 1802, and October 16 and December 13, 1803, MHS. On love letters, see Lystra, *Searching the Heart*, chap. 1. On engagement, see Cogan, *All-American Girl*, chap. 5. On women's fear of commitment, see Rothman, *Hands and Hearts*, 157. According to Rothman, it was not uncommon between 1770 and 1840 for women's letters to be short, hasty, or delayed (11).

32. *Virginia Gazette*, September 11, 1802 (quotations), and Anne Waller Reddy and Andrew Lewis Riffe IV, *Virginia Marriage Bonds: Richmond City* (Staunton, Va., [1939]), 1:2.

33. On the different meaning of love for men and women, see Lewis, *Pursuit of Happiness*, chap. 5.

Chapter Two ～ Going to Housekeeping

1. Dabney Carr to WW, October 16, 1802, William Wirt Papers, MHS.

2. WW to EW, October 31, 1802, MHS.

3. On "deputy husbands" and colonial businesswomen in New England, see Laurel Thatcher Ulrich, "'A Friendly Neighbor': Social Dimensions of Daily Work in Northern Colonial New England," in *Women and Power in American History: A Reader*, 2 vols., ed. Kathryn Kish Sklar and Thomas Dublin (Englewood Cliffs, N.J., 1991), vol. 1:37–50; *Good Wives: Image and Reality in the Lives of Women in Northern New England, 1650–1750* (New York, 1982), chap. 2; "Housewife and Gadder: Themes of Self-Sufficiency and Community in Eighteenth-Century New England," in *"To Toil the Livelong Day": America's Women at Work, 1780–1980*, ed. Carol Groneman and Mary Beth Norton (Ithaca, N.Y., 1987), 21–34. For the South, see Julia Cherry Spruill, *Women's Life and Work in the Southern Colonies* (Chapel Hill, N.C., 1938). On women as "silent partners," see Lisa Wilson, *Life after Death: Widows in Pennsylvania, 1750–1850* (Philadelphia, 1992), 115. All other quotations are taken from Susan Branson, "Women and the Family Economy in the Early Republic: The Case of Elizabeth Meredith," *Journal of the Early Republic* 16 (Spring 1996): 47–71, quotations on 48, 53.

4. On Catharine Grattan Gamble, see Gilmer, *Sketches of Some of the First Settlers*, 27–29. On the Gambles, see Chalkley, *Chronicles of the Scotch-Irish Settlement*, 3:254; and Gambill, *Kith and Kin*, 117. For other examples of Scotch-Irish women's economic activity in Virginia's interior during the colonial and revolutionary periods, see Gail S. Terry, "Women and Public Life: The Cultural Boundaries of Home and Family among a Western Virginia Elite" (paper presented at the Third Southern Conference on Women's History, sponsored by the Southern Association for Women's Historians, Houston, Tex., June 4, 1994). On Scotch-Irish women's economic activity more gen-

erally, including their activities as widows and needlewomen, see L. A. Clarkson and E. Margaret Crawford, "Life after Death: Widows in Carrick-on-Suir, 1799," in *Women in Modern Ireland,* ed. Margaret MacCurtain and Mary O'Dowd (Edinburgh, 1991), 236–54; W. H. Crawford, "Women in the Domestic Linen Industry," in ibid., 255–64; Nancy J. Curtin, "Women and Eighteenth-Century Irish Republicanism," in ibid., 141-42; Hasia R. Diner, *Erin's Daughters in America: Irish Immigrant Women in the Nineteenth Century* (Baltimore, 1983), 25–27; and R. A. Houston, "Women in the Economy and Society of Scotland, 1500–1800," in *Scottish Society, 1500–1800,* ed. R. A. Houston and I. D. Whyte (Cambridge, 1989), 120–26. On widows, see Wilson, *Life after Death*; and Lisa Wilson Waciega, "A 'Man of Business': The Widow of Means in Southeastern Pennsylvania, 1750–1850," *William and Mary Quarterly,* 3d ser., 44 (January 1987): 40-64. Wilson, *Life after Death*, includes a significant number of Scotch-Irish in her sample (see 6, 8).

5. For quotation, see Robert Gamble to WW, December 11, 1802, MHS. On William's mother, see Kennedy, *Memoirs,* 1:16.

6. See especially Jeanne Boydston, *Home and Work: Housework, Wages, and the Ideology of Labor in the Early Republic* (New York, 1990), quotation p. 123 ("mixed economies"); Branson, "Women and the Family Economy," 69; and Michael Merrill, "Cash Is Good to Eat: Self-Sufficiency and Exchange in the Rural Economy of the United States," *Radical History Review* 4 (Winter 1977): 42–71 ("household mode of production" quotation on 57).

7. For quotations, see WW to EW, October 31, 1802, MHS. The 1800 census for Virginia has been destroyed. According to the 1787 tax list, Robert Gamble had one slave over age sixteen and two below that age; provided none of these were sold or died, there would have been at least three adult slaves in the Gamble household by the time of Elizabeth's marriage. By 1810 Gamble had four slaves. See Netti Schreiner-Yantis and Florence Speakman Love, comps., *The 1787 Census of Virginia* (Springfield, Va., 1987), 1:110; and Manuscript Federal Census, 1810, Richmond City, Henrico County, Virginia, microfilm at Clayton Genealogical Library. On women's lack of preparation for their duties as housekeepers, see Clinton, *Plantation Mistress,* 19; Fox-Genovese, *Within the Plantation Household,* 110–14; and Anne Firor Scott, *The Southern Lady: From Pedestal to Politics, 1830–1930* (Chicago, 1970), 27–28. On women's small start in house-keeping, see Fox-Genovese, *Within the Plantation Household,* 113-14. On purchasing bacon and butter, see WW to EW, October 21, 1804, and April 12, 1806, MHS. On Williamsburg's town market, see "George Tucker's Description of Williamsburg in 1796," reprinted in *William and Mary Quarterly,* 2d ser., 19 (April 1939): 193.

8. See especially Boydston, *Home and Work,* esp. chap. 6; and Lebsock, *Free Women of Petersburg,* 164–94.

9. WW to Dabney Carr, March 28, 1803, William Wirt Letters to Dabney Carr, Archives, the Library of Virginia, Richmond (hereafter LOV).

10. On Williamsburg, see Jane Carson, *We Were There: Descriptions of Williamsburg, 1699–1859, Compiled from Contemporary Sources and Arranged Chronologically* (Williamsburg, 1965), quotation on 94.

11. WW to Dabney Carr, February 13 and March 28, 1803, MHS; see also WW to Ninian Edwards, January 10, December 16, 1802, March 2, 1803, published in Ninian W. Edwards, *History of Illinois, from 1778 to 1833; and Life and Times of Ninian Edwards*

(Springfield, 1870), 12–14, 404–11. On the difficulty of obtaining land in Jeffersonian Virginia and Maryland, see Kulikoff, *Tobacco and Slaves*, 131–61; and Lewis, *Pursuit of Happiness*, chap. 4. On migration, see Cashin, *Family Venture*; and Jane Turner Censer, "Southwestern Migration among North Carolina Planter Families: 'The Disposition to Emigrate,' " *Journal of Southern History* 57 (August 1991): 407–26.

12. WW to Dabney Carr, March 28, 1803, LOV; and Cashin, *Family Venture* ("fighting cocks" quotation chap. 5).

13. WW to Benjamin Edwards, March 17, 1805, MHS.

14. For quotations, see Robert Gamble to WW, April 2, 1803, and WW to Robert Gamble, April 9, 1803, MHS. See also WW to Benjamin Edwards, March 17, 1805; Robert Gamble to WW, April 8, 1803; and WW to Robert Gamble, April 9, 1803, MHS; and WW to Dabney Carr, June 6, 1803, William Wirt Papers, Library of Congress, Washington, D.C. (hereafter LC). On kinship ties and their financial content, see especially Cashin, *Family Venture*, chap. 1, and Cashin, "Structure of Antebellum Planter Families," 55–70.

15. On Norfolk, see Thomas J. Wertenbaker, *Norfolk: Historic Southern Port*, 2d ed. (Durham, N.C., 1962).

16. WW to Dabney Carr, June 6, 1803, LC. See also Robert Gamble to WW, May 2, 1803; WW to EW, May 10, 1803; and WW to William Pope, August 5, 1803, MHS. For a discussion of the practice of traveling the circuit, see Maxwell Bloomfield, *American Lawyers in a Changing Society, 1776–1876* (Cambridge, Mass., 1976), 242, 248–49.

17. WW to EW, November 30 and December 6, 1803, MHS.

18. For quotation, see WW to Peachy Gilmer, January 17, 1804, William Wirt Letterbook to Peachy Gilmer, MHS. See also Ruth Schwartz Cowan, *More Work for Mother: The Ironies of Household Technology from the Open Hearth to the Microwave* (New York, 1983), 16–18.

19. For quotations, see WW to EW, May 22, 1804, March 30, 1806, and April 18, 1805, MHS. See also WW to EW, October 2, 1803, and April 7, 1806, MHS. Boydston, *Home and Work*, 131–39, calculates that the income produced by taking in a boarder (and thus saved by providing a worker with board in lieu of or as part of his or her wages) was $130 a year.

20. On women's contributions, see Boydston, *Home and Work*, 131–39. For William's earnings, see Robert, "William Wirt, Virginian," 402; WW to Dabney Carr, June 6, 1803, LC.

21. For the "urban farmstead" concept, see Leslie C. Stewart Abernathy, "Urban Farmsteads: Household Responsibilities in the City," *Historical Archaeology* 20, no. 2 (1986): 5–15. For quotations, see A Lady [Anne Ritson], *A Poetical Picture of America, Being Observations Made, During a Residence of Several Years, at Alexandria, and Norfolk, in Virginia; Illustrative of the manners and Customs of the Inhabitants: And Interspersed with Anecdotes, Arising from a General Intercourse with Society in that Country, from the Year 1799 to 1807* (London, 1809), 104, 106; and Lebsock, *Free Women of Petersburg*, 149.

22. On wealth and household production, see Richard L. Bushman, "Family Security in the Transition from Farm to City, 1750–1850," *Journal of Family History* 6 (Fall 1981): 238–56, esp. 239. On slave labor, see Fox-Genovese, *Within the Plantation Household*, 137–39; Lebsock, *Free Women of Petersburg*, 153–61.

23. For quotations, see Robert Gamble to WW, April 25 and May 2, 1803, MHS. On

the Wirts' slaves before their move to Norfolk, see WW to EW, May 10, December 13, 1803, and Robert Gamble to WW, July 25, 1803, MHS; WW to Peachy Gilmer, August 4, 1804, LC. On their holdings in Norfolk, see Norfolk Borough Land and Personal Property Books, 1804, 1805, and 1806, LOV, microfilm at Clayton Genealogical Library.

24. For quotations, see Robert Gamble to WW, March 30, 1804, and WW to EW, October 3, 1805, MHS. For Gamble's purchase, see Robert Gamble to EW, April 6, 1806, MHS. On the Wirts' human property, see Norfolk Borough Land and Personal Property Book, 1806, LOV, microfilm at Clayton Genealogical Library.

25. On textile production in the South, see Clinton, *Plantation Mistress*, 24; Fox-Genovese, *Within the Plantation Household*, 120–28; and Lebsock, *Free Women of Petersburg*, 152–53. For the Wirts' comments on textile production, see WW to EW, October 21, 1804, April 18, May 16, 1805, MHS. On chickens, see WW to EW, May 12, 1805; on cows, see WW to EW, July 12, 1804, March 30, 1806, MHS. William complained of the expense of his horses in WW to Benjamin Edwards, March 17, 1805, MHS. On slave gardeners, see WW to EW, May 10, 1805, MHS. On garden produce, see EW to WW, June 19, 1810, and WW to EW, May 10, 1805, MHS. Elizabeth asked William for sugar to preserve peaches in 1812. See EW to WW, July 9, 1812, MHS.

26. For descriptions of divisions of household authority and perceptions of the domestic economy, see especially Fox-Genovese, *Within the Plantation Household*, chap. 1; Cott, *Bonds of Womanhood*; and Boydston, *Home and Work*, esp. chaps. 6 and 7.

27. WW to EW, October 13, 21 (all quotations), 1804, MHS.

28. WW to EW, May 12 and 22, 1805, MHS.

29. WW to Dabney Carr, June 24, 1803, William Wirt Letters to Dabney Carr, LOV; WW to Benjamin Edwards, March 17, 1805 (first quotation); WW to EW, August 9, 1805; EW to WW, August 5, 1805 (second quotation), MHS.

30. WW to Ninian Edwards, September 17, 1805, in Edwards, *History of Illinois*, 413.

31. WW to EW, October 26, 1802, MHS.

32. For quotation, see WW to EW, October 11, 1803, MHS. On the demographic transition, see Degler, *At Odds*, chap. 8; on domestic feminism, see Daniel Scott Smith, "Family Limitation, Sexual Control, and Domestic Feminism in Victorian America," in *A Heritage of Her Own: Toward a New Social History of American Women*, ed. Nancy F. Cott and Elizabeth H. Pleck (New York, 1979), 222–45. Important discussions of changing reproduction attitudes and practices include Richard A. Easterlin, "Factors in the Decline of Farm Family Fertility in the United States: Some Preliminary Research Results," *Journal of American History* 63 (December 1976): 600–612; Susan E. Klepp, "Revolutionary Bodies: Mid-Atlantic Women and the Fertility Transition, 1760–1820" (paper presented at the Second Annual Conference of the Institute of Early American History and Culture, Boulder, Colo., June 1, 1996); Jan Lewis and Kenneth Lockridge, " 'Sally Has Been Sick': Pregnancy and Family Limitation among Virginia Gentry Women, 1780–1830," *Journal of Social History* 22 (Fall 1988): 5–19; and Sally G. McMillen, *Motherhood in the Old South: Pregnancy, Childbirth, and Infant Rearing* (Baton Rouge, La., 1990), 32–35, 107–8.

33. For quotation, see WW to EW, June 30, 1803, MHS. On Elizabeth's parturition, see Robert Gamble to WW, April 2, 1803; WW to EW, September 6, 1803; WW to Dabney Carr, January 10, 1804, MHS. On female support during pregnancy and childbirth, see McMillen, *Motherhood in the Old South*, chap. 3, and Carroll Smith-

Rosenberg, "The Female World of Love and Ritual: Relations between Women in Nineteenth-Century America," in her *Disorderly Conduct: Visions of Gender in Victorian America* (New York, 1985), 53–76.

34. For quotations, see WW to EW, October 14, 1805, MHS, and WW to Dabney Carr, January 16, 1804, William Wirt Letters to Dabney Carr, LOV. On the meaning of childbirth to men, see especially Clinton, *Plantation Mistress*, 153; Klepp, "Revolutionary Bodies."

35. See especially McMillen, *Motherhood in the Old South*, chap. 5.

36. For quotation, see WW to EW, September 6, 1803, MHS. See also WW to EW, October 28, 1813; EW to WW, December 13, 1812, MHS.

37. WW to Dabney Carr, February 13, 1803, MHS, and John Demos, *Past, Present, and Personal: The Family and the Life Course in American History* (New York, 1986), chap. 3 (quotations on 57, 52).

38. WW to Dabney Carr, February 13, 1803, MHS; WW to Dabney Carr, March 28, 1803, William Wirt Letters to Dabney Carr, LOV; WW to EW, October 11, 1803, MHS.

39. WW to Peachy Gilmer, February 9, 1805, LC. For men's involvement in birth, see Shawn Johansen, "Before the Waiting Room: Northern Middle-Class Men, Pregnancy, and Birth in Antebellum America," *Gender and History* 7 (August 1995): 183–200.

40. For quotations, see WW to Peachy Gilmer, January 5, 1806, LC; and WW to EW, October 3, 1805, MHS. For discussions of maternal health and birth control in Virginia gentry families, see Buza, " 'Pledges of Our Love,' " 23–25, and Lewis and Lockridge, " 'Sally Has Been Sick.' "

41. For quotations, see WW to Peachy Gilmer, August 4, 1804, LC. On black and white women's cooperation in nursing, see Sally G. McMillen, *Southern Women: Black and White in the Old South* (Arlington Heights, Ill., 1992), 66, and Joan Rezner Gundersen, "The Double Bonds of Race and Sex: Black and White Women in a Colonial Virginia Parish," *Journal of Southern History* 52 (August 1986): 351–72. On warnings against leaving children with servants, see especially Barbara Finkelstein, "Casting Networks of Good Influence: The Reconstruction of Childhood in the United States, 1790–1870," in *American Childhood: A Research Guide and Historical Handbook*, ed. Joseph M. Hawes and N. Ray Hiner (Westport, Conn., 1985), 123–27. On southern men as domestic physicians, see Sally G. McMillen, "Antebellum Southern Fathers and the Health Care of Children," *Journal of Southern History* 60 (August 1994): 513–32.

42. For first quotation, see WW to EW, October 4, 1803, MHS; on health care, see, for example, WW to EW, October 17 (on Robert), 24 (on Laura), 1805, MHS. On infant health care, see McMillen, *Motherhood in the Old South*, chap. 6; Blake, "Ties of Intimacy," chap. 5, esp. 157–65.

43. WW to EW, November 1, 1804, MHS.

44. See especially Bernard Wishy, *The Child and the Republic: The Dawn of Modern American Child Nurture* (Philadelphia, 1968). For William's comments on Locke, see WW to Benjamin Edwards, February 26, 1809, MHS.

45. For Laura's early childhood, see WW to EW, July 26, 1805, MHS. See also WW to EW, October 13, November 1, 1804, and November 3, 1806, MHS. On Robert's capacities, see WW to Benjamin Edwards, March 17, 1805, MHS. For the final quotation, see WW to EW, July 21, 1805, MHS.

46. WW to Dabney Carr, February 13, 1803, and WW to EW, June 28, 1803, MHS.

47. WW to EW, April 16, 1805, and October 16, 1802, MHS.

48. WW to EW, April 30, 1805, MHS.

49. WW to EW, July 26 and August 9, 1805; EW to WW, August 5, 1805, MHS.

50. WW to EW, March 30, 1806, MHS. See also EW to WW, April 28, 1807, MHS, and WW to EW, April 2 and July 8, 1806, MHS.

51. WW to Dabney Carr, January 16, 1804, LC.

52. WW to EW, October 16, 1802, MHS.

53. Lewis, *Pursuit of Happiness*, chaps. 4 and 5, and Griswold, *Family and Divorce in California*, chaps. 5 and 6 (quotation on 92).

54. WW to EW, October 26, 1802, MHS.

55. WW to EW, October 16, 1802, and June 28, 1803, MHS.

56. WW to Benjamin Edwards, March 17, 1805, MHS. See also Lystra, *Searching the Heart*, 9, 42–46.

57. WW to EW, May 10 and June 30, 1803, MHS.

58. WW to EW, May 17, June 30, and October 4, 1803, and July 12, 1804, MHS.

59. Elizabeth's letters from this period are not extant, but William's replies quoted portions of them. For her anxieties, see WW to EW, September 29, 1803; for William's replies, see WW to EW, October 20 and 23, 1803, MHS.

60. Bloomfield, *American Lawyers*, 242, 248–49.

61. For quotations, see WW to EW, October 22, 1802, and April 16, 1805, MHS, and WW to Dabney Carr, January 16, 1804, William Wirt Letters to Dabney Carr, LOV. On antilawyer feeling, see Bloomfield, *American Lawyers*, chap. 2; A. G. Roeber, *Faithful Magistrates and Republican Lawyers: Creators of Virginia Legal Culture, 1680–1810* (Chapel Hill, N.C., 1981), chap. 7. On law as a masculine profession, see Michael Grossberg, "Institutionalizing Masculinity: The Law as a Masculine Profession," in *Meanings for Manhood: Constructions of Masculinity in Victorian America*, ed. Mark C. Carnes and Clyde Griffen (Chicago, 1990), 133–51.

62. WW to Ninian Edwards, September 17, 1805, in Edwards, *History of Illinois*, 415, and WW to EW, June 28, 1803, MHS.

63. WW to EW, June 30, September 27, October 20, and December 13, 1803, and July 7, 1804, MHS.

64. Elizabeth is quoted in WW to EW, October 16 and 28, 1802; for the phrase "language of love," see WW to EW, October 16, 1803, MHS. On women's letters compared with men's letters, see Rothman, *Hands and Hearts*, 11.

65. Buza, " 'Pledges of Our Love,' " 11–13; Cashin, "Structure of Planter Families"; Smith-Rosenberg, "Female World of Love and Ritual."

66. William quoted Elizabeth's letter in his own; see WW to EW, July 17, 1804, MHS.

67. Ibid. On "marriage trauma," see Cott, *Bonds of Womanhood*, 80–83; on "hysteria," see Carroll Smith-Rosenberg, "The Hysterical Woman: Sex Roles and Role Conflict in Nineteenth-Century America," in *Disorderly Conduct*, 197–216.

68. WW to EW, June 30 and September 27, 1803, MHS.

69. WW to EW, May 14, 1804; April 28 and May 5, 1805, MHS.

70. WW to EW, July 17, 1804, MHS.

71. WW to EW, October 21, 1804, MHS. For the concept of "masculine domesticity," see Marsh, "Suburban Men and Masculine Domesticity," 111–27.

72. WW to EW, May 5, 1805, MHS.

73. For William's views, see WW to EW, April 7, 1805, MHS, and WW to Dabney Carr, January 16, 1804, LC; William quoted Elizabeth's letter in WW to EW, May 9, 1805, MHS.

74. For William's rationale, see WW to EW, July 26 and August 9, 1805, MHS; for Elizabeth's remarks, see EW to WW, August 5, 1805, MHS.

75. WW to EW, [September 2, 1805] and October 3, 1805, MHS.

76. WW to EW, April 16, 1805, and April 2 and 7, 1806, MHS.

77. WW to EW, October 14, 1805, MHS.

78. See especially Cott, *Bonds of Womanhood*; Christopher Lasch, *Haven in a Heartless World: The Family Besieged* (New York, 1977); and Welter, "Cult of True Womanhood," 151–74.

Chapter Three ⌇ Betwixt Duty and Love

1. WW to EW, July 13 and 16, 1806, MHS.

2. WW to EW, September 22, 1809, MHS.

3. For quotations, see WW to EW, July 11 and 17, 1806, MHS. For examples of Elizabeth's activities, see WW to EW, July 13, 17, and 23, 1806; October 21, 1806; October 28, 1808; and October 17, 1813, MHS. For the Wirts' residence, see WW to EW, July 8, 1806, MHS and WW to David Bullock, April 4, 1809, in William Wirt Letterbook, William Wirt Papers, MHS; *Virginia Gazette*, October 23, 1805, November 28, 1809; Richmond City Land Book, 1809, in LOV, microfilm in Clayton Genealogical Library; "A Plan of the City of Richmond," 1809–10, in Alexander Wilbourne Weddell, *Richmond, Virginia, in Old Prints, 1737–1887* (Richmond, Va., 1932); and "Old Richmond Neighborhoods," map in Scott, *Old Richmond Neighborhoods*.

4. WW to EW, July 8, July 16, 1806, MHS.

5. For William's comments, see WW to Benjamin Edwards, May 6, 1806, MHS. For the Burr conspiracy and excerpts from the trial, see Kennedy, *Memoirs*, 1:149–90 (quotations on 165 and 169), and V. B. Reed and J. D. Williams, eds., *The Case of Aaron Burr* (Boston, 1960). On his fee, see WW to Benjamin Edwards, July 2, 1808, MHS.

6. For quotation, see WW to EW, quoted in Kennedy, *Memoirs*, 1:133. On honor, see especially Ayers, *Vengeance and Justice*, chap. 1, and Wyatt-Brown, *Southern Honor*. On the duel, see Stowe, *Intimacy and Power*, chap. 1; on alternatives to the duel, see Robert Wiebe, *The Opening of American Society: From the Adoption of the Constitution to the Eve of Disunion* (New York, 1984), 98–104, 181–91.

7. For quotations, see Kennedy, *Memoirs*, 1:192; WW to Peachy Gilmer, July 18, 1807, William Wirt Letterbook, MHS. See also WW to Dabney Carr, July 6, 19, and 28, August 4 and 12, 1807, MHS, and Kennedy, *Memoirs*, 1:191–206.

8. EW to WW, July 12, 1807 (first quotation); WW to Dabney Carr, July 28, September 1, 8, 14, 22, 1807, MHS; Thomas Jefferson to WW, January 10, 1808, and WW to Thomas Jefferson, January 14, 1808 (second quotation), reprinted in Kennedy, *Memoirs*, 1:208–10.

9. Kennedy, *Memoirs*, 1:225–26; WW to Dabney Carr, May 23, 1808; and WW to Benjamin Edwards, July 2, 1808, MHS.

10. On Gamble's help, see WW to Benjamin Edwards, July 2, 1808, MHS, and WW

to Peachy Gilmer, June 29, 1808, LC. For quotations, see *Virginia Gazette and General Advertiser*, March 23, 1805 (first quotation), and Mutual Assurance Society Fire Insurance Policy #1721, October 13, 1815 (renewal), LOV (second quotation). On the house and Shockoe Hill, see [Samuel Mordecai], *Richmond in By-Gone Days: Being Reminiscences of an Old Citizen* (Richmond, Va., 1856), 63, 79; Scott, *Old Richmond Neighborhoods*, 145; and Richmond City Land Book, 1810, 1811, 1812, 1813, 1814, 1815, 1816, 1817, LOV, microfilm at Clayton Genealogical Library.

11. I am indebted to Gail S. Terry for bringing my attention to the significance of ethnicity and for sharing with me her paper "Women and Public Life." On women's use of separate estates in Virginia, see Lebsock, *Free Women of Petersburg*, chap. 3. References to the Wirts' use of property deeded to them by the Gambles may be found in WW to William H. Cabell, December 3, 8, 1832, MHS; EW to Robert Gwathney, December 8, 1832, William Wirt Letterbook, MHS; and Will of Elizabeth Washington Wirt, Will Book I, p. 158, Richmond Circuit Court, Richmond, Va. On the courts' support of separate estates, see Lebsock, *Free Women of Petersburg*, 79–86, and Salmon, "Women and Property in South Carolina," 674–75. On informal separate estates, see Wilson, *Life after Death*, 41–42.

12. WW to Benjamin Edwards, July 2, 1808, and EW to WW, April 9, 1809, MHS.

13. For Elizabeth's review of the house's productive areas and her renovations of the west wing, see EW to WW, October [28], April [6], 9, and 11, 1809; WW to EW, April 9, MHS. On the cellar and its contents, see EW to WW, April 11, October 28, 1809; WW to EW, September 17, 1809, MHS. The location of the kitchen has been surmised from William's letter discussing the arrangement of walkways in the backyard; see WW to EW, September 17, 1809, MHS. The "wooden covered way" is noted in the 1815 insurance policy (a renewal). For a discussion of similar revisions proposed by rural housewives, see Sally McMurry, *Families and Farmhouses in Nineteenth-Century America: Vernacular Design and Social Change* (New York, 1988).

14. EW to WW, September 26, 1809, September 4, 1810, MHS.

15. For quotation, see WW to EW, September 9, 1810, MHS. For other examples of William's activities in slave supervision, see WW to EW, June 15, 19, September 9, 1810; August 28, September 20, 27, 1811; October 30, 1813, MHS. For the Wirts' slave holdings, see Richmond City Personal Property Books, 1809, 1810, 1811, 1812, 1813, 1814, 1815, LOV, microfilm at Clayton Genealogical Library.

16. For quotation, see WW to EW, July 16, 1810, MHS. On textile production during Elizabeth's absences, see EW to WW, September 26, 1809, December [13], 1812, and November 6, 1814; WW to EW, September 8, 17, October 4, 13, 1809; and EW to Laura Wirt, July 23, 1812, MHS.

17. For quotations, see EW to WW, July 18, 1810, and WW to EW, September 20, 1811, MHS; see also WW to EW, September 17, 27, and 28 and October 4, 1811; EW to WW, September 13, 15, and 22, 1811, MHS.

18. WW to EW, December 10, 1812, MHS.

19. EW to WW, December [13?], 1812, MHS. On the "pastoralization of housework," see Boydston, *Home and Work*, esp. chap. 5.

20. WW to Dabney Carr, August 11, 1811, MHS; see also Kennedy, *Memoirs*, 1:285-89.

21. WW to EW, June 29, 1813, and EW to WW, July 4, 1813, MHS.

22. WW to Dabney Carr, August 23, 1813, and WW to EW, July 15, 1813, MHS.

23. WW to EW, October 28, 1813, MHS. For standards of masculinity, see especially Byars, "Making of the Self-Made Man"; Rotundo, *American Manhood*; and Wyatt-Brown, *Southern Honor*.

24. For quotations, see WW to EW, October 30, 1813, and January 1, 1816, and WW to Dabney Carr, July 19, 1807, MHS. For the Wirts' investments, see EW to WW, December 29, 1815, MHS, and Dabney, *Richmond*, 20, 93–94.

25. WW to EW, January 10, 1816, and EW to WW, January 13, 1816, MHS. For the house and its purchase, see Scott, *Houses of Old Richmond*, 84–88; Richmond City Land Books, 1816, 1817, LOV, microfilm at Clayton Genealogical Library; and EW to WW, January 7, 11, and 12, 1816, MHS.

26. On the house, see EW to WW, January 13, 1816, MHS; Mutual Assurance Society Fire Insurance Policy #810, April 4, 1817, LOV; and plans of the Hancock-Wirt-Caskie House, drawings by Frank Fields, courtesy of Aubrey R. Bowles III, Richmond, Virginia. On slave ownership, see Richmond City Personal Property Book, 1816, LOV, microfilm at Clayton Genealogical Library.

27. Bloomfield, *American Lawyers*, 173–75; Roeber, *Faithful Magistrates*, 241–48; William R. Taylor, *Cavalier and Yankee: The Old South and American National Character* (New York, 1961), 73–89.

28. WW to Francis W. Gilmer, April 1, 1816, and WW to Dabney Carr, April 7, 1816, printed in Kennedy, *Memoirs*, 1:353–54, 358–60; WW to EW, March 3, 1816, MHS; and WW to Dabney Carr, February 27 and March 24, 1817, printed in Kennedy, *Memoirs*, 2:18, 21.

29. For the offer, see James Monroe to WW, October 29, 1817, MHS. For Elizabeth's reaction, see EW to WW, contained in Laura Wirt to WW, November 12, 1817, MHS. For William's response, see WW to EW, November 13, 1817, MHS.

30. WW to Benjamin Edwards, February 26, 1809, MHS.

31. For William's views of the family circle, see WW to EW, April 1, 1806, MHS. For Elizabeth's suspected pregnancy, see WW to EW, April 2 and 7, 1806, MHS.

32. Nancy Folbre, "Of Patriarchy Born: The Political Economy of Fertility Decisions," *Feminist Studies* 9 (Summer 1983): 261–84, and Allison MacKinnon, "Were Women Present at the Demographic Transition? Questions from a Feminist Historian to Historical Demographers," *Gender and History* 7 (August 1995): 222–40.

33. For Elizabeth's comments, see EW to WW, September 6, 1811, MHS. On fertility decisions in the early Republic, see Buza, " 'Pledges of Our Love' "; Johansen, "Before the Waiting Room"; Susan E. Klepp, "Lost, Hidden, Obstructed, and Repressed: Contraceptive and Abortive Technology in the Early Delaware Valley," in *Early American Technology: Making and Doing Things from the Colonial Era to 1850*, ed. Judith A. McGaw (Chapel Hill, N.C., 1994), 68–113; Lewis and Lockridge, " 'Sally Has Been Sick.' " Elizabeth admitted her feelings to her mother when her last child was seven months old and she was not yet pregnant. "I almost begin to hope that I have had my number," she confided; "would not that be glorious!" See EW to Catharine Gamble, [February 1, 1819], MHS.

34. WW to EW, October 21, 27 (quotation), 1806; on Emily, see EW to WW, October 22, 1806, March 27, April 15, 26, and November 3, 1807, MHS.

35. WW to EW, April 7 and May 3, 1806, April 24, 1807; EW to WW, April [23; misdated 24], and 24, 1807, MHS.

36. WW to EW, April 9, 1805, and EW to WW, April 15, 1807, MHS.

37. "A Sketch of William Wirt Compiled by his loving granddaughter Elizabeth Wirt Baker," February 22, 1899, Wirt Family Papers, MS #1704, Southern Historical Collection, Library of the University of North Carolina at Chapel Hill (hereafter SHC); EW to WW, October 22, 1806, March 27, April 15, 26, and November 3, 1807; and WW to EW, November 4, 1807, MHS.

38. EW to WW, April 26, 1807, and WW to EW, November 4, 1807, MHS.

39. WW to Benjamin Edwards, May 6, 1806, July 2, 1808; WW to Dabney Carr, September 14, 1807; and EW to WW, July 12, 1807, MHS.

40. For quotations, see WW to Benjamin Edwards, July 2, 1808, and EW to WW, October 30, 1808, MHS; Folbre, "Of Patriarchy Born," 263. See also WW to EW, September 8, 1809, and EW to WW, April 26, 1807, October 2, 1808, MHS. On the connection between women's health problems and the release from household work (including childbearing), see Sklar, *Catharine Beecher*, 204–9; Smith-Rosenberg, "Hysterical Woman," 197–216, esp. 208–9.

41. WW to EW, June 20, 1809, and EW to WW, September 26, 1809, MHS.

42. For quotations, see WW to Dabney Carr, December 21, 1809; WW to Laura Wirt, July 14 and 22, 1810, MHS. For other examples of correspondence with the children, see WW to EW, September 8, 11, and 22, 1809, and WW to Laura Wirt, July 14, 17, 22, and 28, 1810, MHS.

43. For Laura, see EW to WW, July 18, 1810; and for Robert, see EW to WW, September 4, 1810, MHS.

44. EW to WW, July 18, 1810; WW to EW, July 22, 1810; and WW to Laura Wirt, July 14, 1810, MHS.

45. EW to Laura Wirt, July 17, 1812; WW and EW to Laura Wirt, July 28, 1812; and WW to Laura Wirt, August 20, 1812, MHS.

46. For quotation, see EW to WW, December 6, 1812, MHS. See also WW to EW, January 6, 1813, and EW to WW, November 1, 1812, and January 10, 1813, MHS.

47. EW to WW, December 6, 1812, MHS.

48. EW to WW, July 11, 1813, MHS. For experiments with teachers, see EW to WW, October 30, 1811; WW to EW, January 6, 1813; Leroy Anderson to WW, February 7, 1813, April 7, 8, 13, May 1, 1813, MHS.

49. WW to EW, August 6 and September 10, 1813; EW to WW, August 8 and September 12, 1813; WW to William Pope, August 22, 1813; WW to Dabney Carr, August 23, 1813; and WW to Robert Wirt, October 28, 1813, MHS.

50. WW to EW, September 19 and 24, 1814, and EW to WW, September 10 and 17, 1814, MHS.

51. WW to Dabney Carr, February 15, 1814; Laura Wirt to WW, September 7, 1814; WW to EW, September 16 and 24, 1814, MHS.

52. For quotations, see WW to EW, May 9, 1815, and January 6, 1816, MHS. For the children's lessons, see EW to WW, September 10, 1814, and January 13, 1816; Laura Wirt to WW, January 16, 1815; and Robert Wirt to WW, January 5, 1815, MHS.

53. EW to WW, January 13, 1816, MHS (quotation); Mutual Assurance Society Fire

Insurance Policy #810, April 4, 1817, LOV; and Plans of the Hancock-Wirt-Caskie House, drawings by Frank Fields, courtesy of Aubrey R. Bowles III.

54. EW to WW, contained in Laura Wirt to WW, November 12, 1817; and WW to EW, November 13, 1817, MHS.

55. WW to EW, September 22, 1809, MHS.

56. EW to WW, July 4, 1813, MHS.

57. WW to EW, October 27, November 3 and 20, 1806, MHS.

58. WW to EW, April 15 and 21, 1807, and EW to WW, March 27 and April 24, 1807, MHS.

59. WW to EW, April 21, 24, and 26, 1807, and EW to WW, April 24 and 26, 1807, MHS.

60. EW to WW, April [23; misdated 24] (quotation), 24, 1807, and WW to EW, April 24, 1807, MHS.

61. WW to EW, April 24, 1807, and EW to WW, April 29 [misdated 28], 30 [misdated 28], 1807, MHS.

62. WW to Dabney Carr, July 19, 1807, and EW to WW, July 12, 1807, MHS.

63. EW to WW, July 12 and November 3, 1807, and WW to EW, October 29, 1807, and April 11, 1808, MHS.

64. EW to WW, November 3, 1807, and July 9, 1808, and WW to EW, July 8, 1808, MHS.

65. EW to WW, October 30, 1808, and WW to EW, October 28, 1808, MHS. See also EW to WW, April 26, 1807, October 2, 1808, MHS.

66. WW to EW, July 15, 1810, MHS.

67. EW to WW, June 19, 1810, and WW to EW, June 27 and July 20, 1810, MHS.

68. WW to EW, September 9, 1810, and WW to Dabney Carr, September 9, 1810, MHS.

69. For quotation, see EW to WW, July 9, 1808, MHS. On the ideal of female chastity in the South and the consequences for women who violated this prescription, see Clinton, *Plantation Mistress*, chap. 6; Clinton, " 'Southern Dishonor': Flesh, Blood, Race, and Bondage," in Bleser, ed., *In Joy and in Sorrow*, 52–68, esp. 58–59; Scott, *Southern Lady*, 52–56; and Wyatt-Brown, *Southern Honor*, 298–307.

70. WW to Dabney Carr, August 11, 1811, MHS; see also Kennedy, *Memoirs*, 1:285-89.

71. WW to [Anthony] Robinson, November 23, 1811; William Russell to WW, February 2, 1812, MHS. All correspondence pertaining to Kitty Russell is misfiled in 1813 in the microfilm edition. For an example of another prominent southern man whose reputation was endangered by reports that he had engaged in inappropriate sexual behavior with his four nieces, see Drew Gilpin Faust, *James Henry Hammond and the Old South: A Design for Mastery* (Baton Rouge, La., 1982), 241–45, 254, 287–91, 302. As Peter Bardaglio effectively argues, isolating a few southern men for flagrant disregard for sexual mores, as in incest cases where force was used, actually protected them from legal or social consequences for less blatant sexual coercion. See " 'An Outrage upon Nature': Incest and the Law in the Nineteenth-Century South," in Bleser, ed., *In Joy and in Sorrow*, 32–51.

72. WW to [Anthony] Robinson, November 23, 1811; A. Robinson to WW, January

6, 1812; statement of Catherine Russell, January 6, 1812; William Russell to WW, February 2, 1812; and W. Irvine to William Russell, n.d., MHS.

73. WW to Mrs. Mary Ellis, August 3, 1802; WW to [Anthony] Robinson, November 23, 1811, MHS. See also Robert, "William Wirt, Virginian," 402–3.

74. See the cover sheet for WW to [Anthony] Robinson, November 23, 1811, MHS. For another example of a southern woman who publicly stood by her husband during the revelations that he had had incestuous relations with their nieces, see Carol Bleser's discussion of Catherine and James Henry Hammond in Bleser, ed., *The Hammonds of Redcliffe* (New York, 1981), 10.

75. WW to EW, October 28, 1813, MHS.

76. WW to EW, June 29, July 8 and 15, 1813, and EW to WW, July 4, 1813, MHS.

77. WW to EW, September 7, 9, and 12, 1814, MHS.

78. EW to WW, June 29, 1813, and September 5 and 17, 1814, MHS.

79. WW to EW, October 10, 1814, MHS.

80. WW to EW, October 19, 1814, January 16, 1815, and January 6, 1816, MHS.

81. EW to WW, October 16 and 28, 1814, MHS.

82. EW, postscript to WW, Robert Wirt to WW, January 5, 1815; and EW, postscript to WW, Laura Wirt to WW, January 16, 1815, MHS.

83. EW to WW, January 7, 1816, and WW to EW, January 10, 1816, MHS.

84. WW to EW, November 17 and 28, 1817; EW to WW, November 5 and 23, 1817; and WW to Laura Wirt, November 26, 1817, MHS.

85. See Lasch, *Haven in a Heartless World*, and Glenna Matthews, *"Just a Housewife": The Rise and Fall of Domesticity in America* (New York, 1987), chap. 2.

Chapter Four 〜 An Almost Complete Divorce

1. WW to Henry Thompson, January 28, 1819, William Wirt Papers, MHS.

2. For quotations, see WW to EW, November 13 and 22, 1817, MHS. See also EW to WW, November 18, 1817, MHS, and Federal Writers' Project, *Washington: City and Capital* (Washington, D.C., 1937), 154–55.

3. For quotations, see WW to EW, November 17 and 23, 1817, MHS, and [Smith], *First Forty Years*, 142. On the Washington social scene, see James Sterling Young, *The Washington Community, 1800–1828* (New York, 1966), chaps. 4 and 5, and Anne Hollingsworth Wharton, *Social Life in the Early Republic* (Philadelphia, 1902).

4. For quotations, see EW to WW, November 25, 1817, and WW to EW, December 3, 1817, MHS. See also EW to WW, November 25, 26, 29, December 1, 1817, MHS. For changes in the Wirts' labor force, see WW to EW, November 16, December 3, 1817; EW to WW, November 21, 23, 25, 26, 1817, December 1, 1817, MHS; and Richmond City Personal Property Book, 1817, LOV, microfilm at Clayton Genealogical Library.

5. WW to William Pope, January 18, 1818, MHS. On William's sources of income, see Joseph Charles Burke, "William Wirt: Attorney General and Constitutional Lawyer" (Ph.D. diss., Indiana University, 1965), chap. 3, esp. 84–85.

6. EW to WW, May 8 and 11, 1818, MHS. See also EW to WW, November 25, 26, 29, December 1, 1817; EW to Catharine Gamble, postscript to Laura Wirt to Catharine Gamble, May 24, 1818, MHS.

7. EW to WW, November 21, 1817 (first quotation), August 11, September 17 (second quotation), 1818, and WW to EW, September 18, 1818 (third quotation), MHS. On mistress-slave relationships, see especially Fox-Genovese, *Within the Plantation Household*, 22–23, 97, 207.

8. EW to WW, September 20 and 22, November 17, 1818, and EW to WW, postscript to Robert Wirt to WW, November 21, 1818, MHS. See also EW to WW, December 3, 4, 1818, MHS.

9. EW to WW, August 24, September 22, and December 2 and 9, 1818, MHS.

10. For quotations, see WW to EW, December 3, 5, and 14, 1818, and WW to Henry Thompson, January 28, 1819, MHS. On Wirt's competition with Pinkney, see Burke, "William Wirt," 97–100.

11. For quotations, see EW to Catharine Gamble, [February 1, 1819]; EW to WW, April 11, 1819, and WW to EW, April 10, 12, and [14], 1819, MHS. On the escaped slave and slave uprisings in the capital city, see WW to EW, April 10, 1819, MHS, and Constance Green, *Washington: Village and Capital, 1800–1876* (Princeton, N.J., 1962), 58–59, 63, 141.

12. William did not extract himself from the armory partnership until 1825. See Burke, "William Wirt," 170.

13. WW to EW, April 17, 1819, and March 31, 1822; WW to Dabney Carr, May 14, 1821, MHS.

14. WW to EW, April 17, 1819, and EW to WW, April 19 and November 18 and 23, 1819, MHS.

15. For quotations, see EW to Laura Wirt, May 26, 1820, and EW to WW, April 26, 1820, MHS. For examples of Elizabeth's work at home, see EW to WW, April 12, 14, 15, 16, 20, 1819; April 25 and 27 and September 1, 1820, and EW to WW, postscript to Robert Wirt to WW, August [n.d.], 1820, MHS.

16. WW to EW, November 20 and 24, 1819, April 17 and 18, 1822, and EW to WW, April 18 and 19, 1822, MHS.

17. WW to EW, November 21, 1820, and April 14 and May 5, 1822; EW to WW, November 21, 1820, and [April 15, 1822], MHS.

18. WW to EW, May 8, 9, 30, and 31, 1822, MHS. Pinkney died on February 25, 1822. See Robert M. Ireland, *The Legal Career of William Pinkney, 1764–1822* (New York, 1986), 221–25.

19. EW to WW, May 17, 1822, MHS.

20. EW to WW, May 20 (first quotation), 21, and 22 and November 15, 1823 (second quotation), April 28, 1824; WW to William Pope, June 5, 1823 (third quotation), MHS. To Elizabeth, William wrote: "I am sure that you have incurred no unnecessary expense," adding that getting out of debt would require him to pursue "another and a better harvest" in the circuit courts. See WW to EW, May 21, 1823, MHS.

21. WW to EW, November 11, 1823, and EW to WW, November 5 and 7, 1823, MHS.

22. For quotations, see EW to WW, November 5, 1823, April 27 and 28, and May 9, 1824, and WW to EW, November 7, 1823, MHS. For changes in the Wirts' labor force, see EW to WW, November 16, December 7, 1823, MHS.

23. EW to WW, May 9 and 27, 1824, May 6 and 16, 1825, MHS.

24. EW to WW, May 25, 1824, MHS. For examples of William's financial contributions, see WW to EW, May 8, 1822, May 21, 1823, and July 2, 1825, MHS.

25. WW to Dabney Carr, February 1, 1824, and WW to EW, July 8, 1825, MHS.

26. For quotations, see EW to Laura Wirt, May 10, 1820, and EW to WW, September 1, 1820, MHS. See also EW to WW, April 6, September 2, October 28, November 18 and 21, 1820; WW to EW, August 31, 1820, MHS.

27. EW to WW, November 17 and 19 and December 20 and 26, 1825; WW to EW, November 9 and 18, 1825; see also WW to EW, October 21, 23, 1825; EW to WW, November 10, 11, 15, 18, 21, 22, 1825, MHS.

28. For quotations, see WW to EW, November 23 and 25 and December 26, 1825, MHS. See, for examples of Elizabeth's shopping, EW to Catharine Gamble, December 10, 1826; WW to EW, December 11, 17, 1826, MHS.

29. EW to Laura Wirt Randall, September 9, 1827, MHS.

30. WW to EW, November 30, 1828; EW to Catharine Gamble, October 18, 1828; and EW to WW, November 29, 1828, MHS.

31. EW to WW, November 12, 1824, MHS.

32. Robert Wirt to WW, November [n.d.], 1817; WW to EW, November 16, 1817; and WW to Laura Wirt, November 26, 1817, MHS.

33. EW to WW, September 22, 1818, and WW to EW, August 12, 1818, MHS. On the Wirts' children, see Elizabeth Wirt Baker, "A Sketch of William Wirt," February 22, 1899, Wirt Family Papers, SHC.

34. EW to WW, November 26 and December 3, 1818; WW to EW, December 13, 1818, MHS.

35. EW to WW, September 22, 23, 1818; WW to Laura Wirt, December [n.d.], 1818; EW to Laura Wirt, May 10 and 26, 1820; and Laura Wirt to EW, June 7, 1820, MHS.

36. Robert Wirt to EW, October 15, 1820; Robert Wirt to WW, October 25, 1820; and EW to Robert Wirt, October 28, 1820, MHS.

37. Robert Wirt to EW, June 13, 1821; EW to WW, December 11 and 13, 1821; and WW to EW, April 13, 1822, MHS.

38. For quotations, see WW to EW, December 18 and 23, 1822, MHS. For Robert's illness, see WW to EW, April 17, July 5, December 18 and 22, 1822; Laura Wirt to WW, April 19, 1822; and WW to Robert Wirt, December 4, 16, 1822, MHS.

39. WW to EW, October 11, 1822, and December 16, 1823; EW to WW, [April 15, 1822], October 10, 1822, and May 16, 1825, MHS.

40. EW to WW, January 5 and 12, 1823, and May 3 and 13, 1824; Elizabeth G. Wirt to WW, postscript to Catharine G. Wirt to WW, November 9, 1824, MHS.

41. For quotations, see WW to EW, June 25, October 20, and November 16, 1824, and EW to Nancy Cabell, June 26, 1824, MHS. On Robert's health and the voyage, see William H. Cabell to WW, June 20, 1824; WW to EW, June 22 and November 13, 1824; Agnes Sarah Bell (Nancy) Cabell to EW, June 24, 1824; EW to Nancy Cabell, June 26, 1824, MHS. On his death, see Laura Wirt to WW, December 21, 1824, MHS.

42. Laura Wirt to WW, December 21, 1824, and WW to EW, December 27, 1824, MHS.

43. WW to EW, May 23, 1825, and EW to WW, July 7, 1825, MHS.

44. Elizabeth G. Wirt to WW, May 27 and October 24, 1826; WW to EW, October 25 and November 18, 1826; WW to Catharine Wirt, November 12 and 18, 1826; see also Catharine Wirt to WW, September 1, 1826, MHS. For other examples of the girls' letters

to their father, see Elizabeth G. Wirt to WW, November 15, 1826, and Catharine Wirt to WW, November 13, 23, 1826, MHS.

45. WW to EW, August 31 and September 3, 1826, MHS.

46. WW to EW, August 31, September 13, and October 29, 1826, MHS. See also EW to WW, October 22, 1826; WW to EW, October 25, 1826, MHS.

47. For quotations, see WW to Henry Wirt, November 19, 1826; Catharine Wirt to WW, November [n.d.], 1826; WW to EW, November 9, 1826, MHS. For William's Florida investments, see Jerrell H. Shofner, *History of Jefferson County* (Tallahassee, Fla., 1976), 17, 21.

48. WW to EW, December 12 and 19, 1826; see also EW to WW, December 18, 1826, MHS.

49. EW to WW, December 22, 1826; WW to EW, April 15 and 24, 1827; and WW to Catharine Wirt, May 21, 1827, MHS.

50. EW to WW, October 14, 20, and 21, 1827, and WW to EW, October 17, 1827, MHS. See also Douglas, *Feminization of American Culture*, esp. chaps. 2 and 3.

51. For quotations, see EW to WW, November 7, 1827; WW to EW, October 6, 1827; and EW to Laura Wirt Randall, January 25, 1828, MHS. For the girls' withdrawal from school and subsequent activities, see EW to WW, October 9, 18, and 24, November 7 and 15, 1827, January 5, 1828; EW to Laura Wirt Randall, March 14 and April 19, 1828; Ellen Wirt to Catharine Gamble, January 3, 1828; Rosa Wirt to WW, May 5, 9, 1828; WW to EW, May 7, 1828; and Elizabeth G. Wirt to WW, May 8, 1828, MHS.

52. WW to EW, May 5 and 29, 1828, MHS. See also EW to WW, May 6, 1828; WW to EW, May 7, 1828, MHS.

53. WW to Elizabeth G. Wirt, April 11, 1828; WW to EW, March 28, 1828; EW to Laura Wirt Randall, April 26, 1828; WW to Laura Wirt Randall, May 2, 1828; and EW to WW, May 15, 1828, MHS.

54. WW to EW, April 27 and May 11, 1828, MHS.

55. For quotations see WW to EW, June [n.d.], and June 1, 1828, and EW to WW, June 2, 1828, MHS. See for examples of Elizabeth's control of the girls' courtships, EW to WW, May 6, 15, 26, June 29, [n.d.], 1828, MHS.

56. For quotations, see WW to EW, August 10 and 18 and October 3, 1828; Catharine Wirt to EW, postscript to WW to EW, September 6, 1828; and EW to WW, August 24, 1828, MHS. On Liz's ailments, see EW to WW, January 2, 4, 1828; WW to EW, March 30, 1828, MHS. On Catharine, see EW to WW, July 8, 1828; WW to EW, August 10, 1828, MHS. On the trip, see Catharine Wirt to EW, August 28, 1828; Elizabeth G. Wirt to EW, August 28, 1828, MHS.

57. WW to Elizabeth G. Wirt, January 3, 1829, and WW to Dabney Carr, February 28, 1829, MHS.

58. EW to WW, postscript to Laura Wirt to WW, November 12, 1817, and EW to WW, November 23, 1817, and December 20, 1821, MHS.

59. WW to EW, November 20, 1817; EW to WW, postscript to Laura Wirt to WW, November 17, 1817; and EW to WW, November 23, 1817, MHS.

60. For quotations, see EW to WW, September 22, 1818, and WW to EW, August 8, December [9], 1818, MHS. On William's work schedule, see Burke, "William Wirt," 79; Kennedy, *Memoirs*, 2:70, 73.

61. EW to WW, May 8 and 11, 1818, MHS.

62. EW to WW, July 30 and August 11, 1818, and WW to EW, May 9, 1818, MHS.

63. EW to WW, September 17, November 26, and December 2, 1818; WW to EW, November 25 and 30, 1818, MHS.

64. WW to EW, December 2, 1818, MHS. See also Kennedy, *Memoirs*, 2:76–77; and Ireland, *Legal Career of William Pinkney*, 164–70. On the duel, manhood, and honor, see Kenneth S. Greenberg, *Masters and Statesmen: The Political Culture of American Slavery* (Baltimore, 1985), chap. 2; Stowe, *Intimacy and Power*, chap. 1; and Wyatt-Brown, *Southern Honor*, 350–61. On the mechanics of the duel, which did not necessarily include actual combat, see Jack K. Williams, *Dueling in the Old South: Vignettes of Social History* (College Station, Tex., 1980).

65. EW to WW, December 3, 1818, and WW to EW, December 5, 1818, MHS.

66. EW to WW, December 7, 1818, and April 11, 1819, and WW to EW, December [9], 1818, MHS.

67. WW to EW, December 10, 1818, and May 1, 1822; EW to WW, November 24, 1819, and December 20, 1821, MHS.

68. WW to EW, April 2, 1821, MHS.

69. EW to Laura Wirt, July 6, 1822; EW to WW, July 10, 1822, and December 20, 1823, MHS.

70. WW to EW, December 4, 1823, and EW to WW, December 20, 1824, MHS.

71. WW to Laura Wirt, January 8, 1825, and EW to WW, January 16, 1825, MHS.

72. EW to WW, December 20, 1825, and WW to EW, December 23 and 24, 1825, MHS.

73. EW to WW, April 9 and 15, 1827; WW to EW, April 21, May 18 and 20, and December 17, 1827, MHS.

74. EW to WW, October 6, 1827, MHS (misdated October 7), and WW to EW, January 4, 1828, MHS. Hints about Elizabeth's true feelings are contradictory. During the Wirts' Williamsburg residence, William made comments that suggested that Elizabeth's manner toward Kitty Russell was cold, perhaps indicating that she suspected her husband had at one time had a relationship with the other woman. See, for example, WW to EW, April 9, 14, and 18, 1805, MHS. However, at the time of the rumors, Elizabeth wrote to her husband: "My well founded confidence in the best, and most faithful of husbands is not to be shaken by trifles." Nine years of marriage had strengthened, not weakened, Elizabeth's faith in her husband's fidelity. See EW to WW, September 6, 1811, MHS.

75. For quotations, see WW to EW, December 30, 1827, and EW to WW, July 10, 1827, MHS; see also Laura Wirt to WW, postscript to EW to WW, July 12, 1827, MHS. Examples of William's letters to his son-in-law include WW to Thomas Randall, November 29, December 21, 1827, January 17, July 4, November 22, 1828, MHS.

76. EW to Laura Wirt Randall, September 9, October 12, and October 15–18, 1827, MHS.

77. For quotations, see EW to Laura Wirt Randall, October 15–18, 1827; EW to WW, October 10, 1822, MHS; and [Smith], *First Forty Years*, 239, 318. See also William H. Cabell to EW, June 28, 1824, MHS.

78. WW to EW, January 11, 1828; WW to Thomas Randall, February 1, 1828; EW to Laura Wirt Randall, January 10 and April 26, 1828; see also EW to WW, April 25, 1828, MHS.

79. For quotations, see EW to Catharine Gamble, postscript to Rosa Wirt to

Catharine Gamble, January 17–18, 1829; and WW to Dabney Carr, February 28, 1829, MHS. On the move, see EW to Catharine Gamble, January 25, 1829; Rosa Wirt to Catharine Gamble, March 19, 1829; and WW to Catharine Wirt, April 13, 1829, MHS.

Chapter Five ⁓ Building Castles in the Air

1. WW to Nancy Cabell, March 28, 1831, and WW to EW, February 26, 1833, MHS.

2. For quotations, see WW to Thomas Swann, September 13, 1830, and WW to William Pope, May 3, 1830, MHS. For the political context, see especially Daniel Walker Howe, *The Political Culture of the American Whigs* (Chicago, 1979), and Robert P. Sutton, "Nostalgia, Pessimism, and Malaise: The Doomed Aristocrat in Late-Jeffersonian Virginia," *Virginia Magazine of History and Biography* 76 (January 1968): 41–55.

3. See, for example, WW to Thomas Swann, October 4, 8, 1830; WW to Thomas Randall, October 7, 1830; WW to Dabney Carr, September 29, October 9, 1830, MHS.

4. WW to Dabney Carr, September 29, 1830, and WW to EW, December 25, 1830, MHS. In his letter to Elizabeth, William referred to the impeachment of James H. Peck, judge of the Missouri District Court.

5. WW to William H. Cabell, May 18, 1829; WW to EW, June 13, 1829; and WW to Thomas Randall, August 3, 1829, MHS.

6. Daniel Walker Howe describes the writings of domestic authors Sarah Josepha Hale and Catharine Beecher as "feminine versions of Whiggery." See *Political Culture of the American Whigs*, 4. On literary and religious denunciations of contemporary ills, see especially Curtis Dahl, "The American School of Catastrophe," *American Quarterly* 11 (Fall 1959): 380–90. On evangelical religion in the cities and the zeal for reform in the 1830s, see Terry D. Bilhartz, *Urban Religion and the Second Great Awakening: Church and Society in Early National Baltimore* (Rutherford, N.J., 1986); Fred J. Hood, *Reformed America: The Middle and Southern States, 1783–1837* (University, Ala., 1980); Paul E. Johnson, *A Shopkeeper's Millennium: Society and Revivals in Rochester, New York, 1815–1837* (New York, 1978); and Mary P. Ryan, *Cradle of the Middle Class: The Family in Oneida County, New York, 1790–1865* (Cambridge, 1981), chap. 3. On women writers and the cult of domesticity, see especially Nina Baym, *Woman's Fiction: A Guide to Novels by and about Women in America, 1820–1870* (Ithaca, N.Y., 1978); Mary Kelley, *Private Woman, Public Stage: Literary Domesticity in Nineteenth-Century America* (New York, 1984); and Matthews, *"Just a Housewife,"* chaps. 1 and 2. On the celebration of the home more generally, see Kirk Jeffrey, "The Family as Utopian Retreat from the City: The Nineteenth-Century Contribution," *Soundings* 55 (Spring 1972): 21–41, and Maxine van de Wetering, "The Popular Concept of 'Home' in Nineteenth-Century America," *Journal of American Studies* 18 (April 1984): 5–28.

7. WW to Catharine G. Wirt, August 5, 1829, MHS. On religion and domesticity, see especially Douglas, *Feminization of American Culture*, chap. 2; Colleen McDannell, *The Christian Home in Victorian America, 1840–1900* (Bloomington, Ind., 1986); and A. Gregory Schneider, *The Way of the Cross Leads Home: The Domestication of American Methodism* (Bloomington, Ind., 1993). For Virginia, see Lewis, *Pursuit of Happiness*, chap. 2.

8. EW to WW, postscript to Ellen Wirt to WW, January 21, 1830, MHS.

9. EW to WW, postscript to Rosa Wirt to WW, July 21, 1829; EW to WW, July 26, 1829; and WW to EW, August 7 and 12, 1829, MHS.

10. WW to Dabney Carr, August 3, 1829; WW to William Pope, June 25, 1830; and WW to Thomas Swann, April 16, 1830, MHS.

11. Rosa Wirt to Laura Wirt Randall, May 27, 1830; EW to Catharine Gamble, June 27, July 6, 1830; Catharine G. Wirt to Catharine Gamble, July 17, 1830, MHS.

12. For quotations, see EW to Catharine Gamble, postscript to Rosa Wirt to Catharine Gamble, September 13, 1830; see also WW to EW, July 22, 26, 29, August 1, 11, 15, 16, 18, 19, 20, 21, 22, 1830, and Catharine G. Wirt to Catharine Gamble, September 3, 1830, MHS.

13. EW to Catharine Gamble, August 16, 1830, MHS.

14. WW to EW, December 25, 1830, MHS; see also Elizabeth Wirt Baker, "A Sketch of William Wirt," February 22, 1899, Wirt Family Papers, SHC.

15. Ellen Wirt to WW, January 5, 1831, MHS. On sentimental views of death, see Censer, *North Carolina Planters*, 16–17, and Lewis, *Pursuit of Happiness*, chap. 3.

16. WW to Dabney Carr, March 23, 1831; WW to EW, January 3, 1831; and EW to WW, January 6, 1831, MHS.

17. EW to WW, January 29, 1831; WW to EW, January 29, 1831, MHS.

18. WW to EW, January 6, 1831, MHS.

19. WW to EW, January 13, 29, 1831, MHS.

20. WW to EW, January 27 and March 12, 1831, MHS.

21. WW to EW, January 3 and 13, 1831; EW to WW, January 27 and 29, 1831, MHS; and Lewis, *Pursuit of Happiness*, chaps. 2, 3, and 5.

22. WW to EW, February 14, 1831, and EW to WW, January 27, 1831, MHS.

23. William's musings on the subject were prompted by his nomination to the National Republican Convention, scheduled for December, which would select the national Republican candidate for president. For quotation, see WW to EW, February 25, 1831, MHS. See also WW to Dabney Carr, May 22, June 16, September 30, 1831, MHS.

24. WW to EW, February 18, 1831, and WW to Dabney Carr, September 30, 1831; see also WW to Dabney Carr, October 5, 1831, MHS. On the Anti-Masonic party, see David Brion Davis, "Some Themes of Counter-Subversion: An Analysis of Anti-Masonic, Anti-Catholic, and Anti-Mormon Literature," *Mississippi Valley Historical Review* 47 (September 1960): 205–24.

25. For quotations, see EW to WW, postscript to Catharine G. Wirt to WW, October 6, 1831, and EW to WW, October 13, 1831, MHS. See also EW to WW, October 17, 18, and 20, 1831, and EW to Catharine G. Wirt, postscript to Ellen Wirt to Catharine G. Wirt, February 9, 1832, MHS.

26. WW to Dabney Carr, November 27 and December 5, 1831, MHS; see also WW to Thomas Randall, December 7, 1831, and WW to Dabney Carr, January 12 and February 11, 1832, MHS.

27. WW to Dabney Carr, January 12 and May 23, 1832, MHS. On the election, see Kennedy, *Memoirs*, 2:327–34.

28. WW to EW, March 1, 1831, and EW to WW, February 3, 1831, MHS.

29. Catharine G. Wirt to WW, January 13, 1831; Catharine G. Wirt to Catharine

Gamble, January 7, 1831; and WW to EW, February 2, 1831, MHS; see also Elizabeth G. Wirt to WW, January 7, 19, 1831; Ellen Wirt to WW, January 9, 1831; and WW to EW, January 29, 1831, MHS.

30. WW to Thomas Randall, April 21, 1831, MHS.

31. For quotations, see Marcia Ouseley to Catharine G. Wirt, August 20, 1832; WW to Catharine G. Wirt, August 20 and October 3, 1833; and EW to Catharine G. Wirt, August 23, 1833, MHS. See also Rosa Wirt to EW, November 3, 1831; Catharine G. Wirt to EW, November 4, 1831, August 14, 1832; Ellen Wirt to Catharine Gamble, November 5, 1831; WW to Thomas Randall, May 31, 1832; and Catharine G. Wirt to Laura Wirt Randall[?], July 5, 1832, MHS.

32. WW to EW, February 26, 1833, MHS.

33. Ellen Wirt to Catharine G. Wirt, December 18, 1831; EW to Rosa Wirt, March 14, 1832; WW to Dabney Carr, August 22, 1832; and EW to WW, November 5, 1832, MHS.

34. For quotations, see WW to William H. Cabell, December 14, 1832, William Wirt Letterbook, 1832–34, MHS; WW to Dabney Carr, September 6, 1832; and WW to Thomas Randall, December 7, 1831, MHS. See also WW to Thomas Randall, October 26, 1832, MHS.

35. WW to Dabney Carr, May 23, 1832, and WW to EW, November 11, 1832, MHS.

36. For quotations, see WW to L. M. Goldsborough, December 12, 1832, William Wirt Letterbook, 1832–34, MHS; Thomas Randall to WW, January 10, 1832, MHS; EW to Catharine G. Wirt, postscript to Rosa Wirt to Catharine G. Wirt, January 31, 1832, MHS; and WW to William H. Cabell, December 14, 1832, William Wirt Letterbook, 1832–34, MHS. See also EW to WW, February 1, 1832, and WW to EW, February 11, 1832, MHS; and see WW to Robert Gwathney, December 3, 1832; EW to Robert Gwathney, December 8, 1832; WW to William H. Cabell, December 8, 1832; WW to Thomas Randall, December 12, 1832; and WW to L. M. Goldsborough, December 12, 1832, William Wirt Letterbook, 1832–34, MHS.

37. WW to Thomas Randall, December 7, 1831, MHS, and WW to William H. Cabell, December 14, 1832, William Wirt Letterbook, 1832–34, MHS; and WW to Dabney Carr, May 23, 1832, MHS. See also WW to Thomas Randall, December 12, 1832, January 3, 1833; WW to L. M. Goldsborough, December 12, 1832; and Thomas Randall to WW, April 4, October 20, 1832, MHS.

38. WW to Catharine G. Wirt, March 5, 1831, MHS. See also Taylor, *Cavalier and Yankee*.

39. WW to Thomas Randall, February 4, 1833; EW to WW, February 1, 3, 1833; and WW to EW, February 14, 1833, MHS. See also WW to EW, February 2, 1833, MHS; WW to Thomas Randall, February 8, 10, 1833, William Wirt Letterbook, 1832–34, MHS. For the costs of the German expedition, see WW to John Glenn, February 7, 1833, and WW to Thomas Randall, February 10, 1833, William Wirt Letterbook, 1832–34, MHS.

40. For quotations, see Catharine G. Wirt to WW, February 9, 1833, and Elizabeth's postcript, MHS; WW to Thomas Randall, February 8, 1833, William Wirt Letterbook, 1832–34, MHS; and WW to EW, February 10, 1833, MHS. See also WW to John White, February 19, 1833; WW to Thomas Randall, December 10, 1833, MHS; and WW to John Glenn, February 10, 1833, and WW to Thomas Randall, February 10, 1833, William Wirt Letterbook, 1832–34, MHS. The plantation William rented was about the same size as his own, 150 to 200 acres.

41. WW to EW, February 12, March 6 and 9, 1833; WW to L. M. Goldsborough, February 28, 1833; EW to WW, March 11, 1833; and WW to Thomas Randall, March 22, 1833, MHS. On factionalism among the settlers, see EW to WW, March 5, 8, 10, 11, 1833, MHS. For William's earlier estimates, see WW to EW, February 12, 1833; WW to Thomas Randall, February 8, 10, 1833, William Wirt Letterbook, 1832–34, MHS.

42. EW to WW, March 8, 1833, and WW to William H. Cabell, April 10, 1833, MHS.

43. For quotations, see WW to L. M. Goldsborough, February 16, 1833, MHS, and WW to Thomas Randall, February 10, 1833, William Wirt Letterbook, 1832–34, MHS. For estimates of profits, see WW to Thomas Randall, March 8, 1833, MHS; WW to William H. Cabell, December 14, 1832, William Wirt Letterbook, 1832–34, MHS.

44. WW to EW, June 5, 1833; WW to L. M. Goldsborough, July 18, 1833; Thomas Randall to WW, August 14 and 17, 1833, MHS; and WW to L. M. Goldsborough, May 16, 1833, William Wirt Letterbook, 1832–34, MHS.

45. For quotations, see WW to William H. Cabell, April 10, 1833; EW to Catharine G. Wirt, June 17 and September 25, 1833, MHS. See also WW to EW, June 2 and 5, 1833, and EW to Catharine G. Wirt, June 18, September 25, 1833, MHS.

46. For quotations, see WW to L. M. Goldsborough, October 27, 1833, MHS. See also Thomas Randall to WW, May 11, 1833, MHS.

47. WW to Thomas Randall, December 10, 1833, MHS.

48. For quotations, see EW to Catharine G. Wirt, September 25, 1833, and EW to Henry Wirt, December 9, 1833, MHS. See also WW to Catharine G. Wirt, October 4, 6, 1833; WW to Dabney C. Wirt, November 26, December 11, 1833; Elizabeth W. Goldsborough to WW, January 20, 1834; Ellen Wirt to Henry Wirt, February 3, 1834; WW to L.M. Goldsborough, February 6, 1834, MHS.

49. WW to Dabney Carr, December 25, 1833, and WW to L. M. Goldsborough, February 6, 1834, MHS.

50. Catharine G. Wirt to [Eliza Clayton, February 1834], Elizabeth Wirt Letterbook, 1834–41, Wirt Family Papers, SHC. On sentimental death in the Old South, see Censer, *North Carolina Planters*, 16–17; Lewis, *Pursuit of Happiness*, 81–96.

51. See especially Kerber et al., "Beyond Roles, Beyond Spheres."

Epilogue

1. Unsigned poem, March [n.d.], 1833, William Wirt Papers, MHS.

2. EW to William Nevins, September 23, 1834, Elizabeth Wirt Letterbook, 1834–40, Wirt Family Papers, SHC. For other examples of women reshaping their husbands' image, see Bleser, ed., *Hammonds of Redcliffe*, 12; Carol Bleser, "The Perrys of Greenville: A Nineteenth-Century Marriage," in *The Web of Southern Social Relations: Women, Family, and Education*, ed. Walter J. Fraser Jr., R. Frank Saunders Jr., and Jon L. Wakelyn (Athens, Ga., 1985), 72; Mary Elizabeth Glade, "Private Lives and Public Myths: The Bagbys of Virginia" (Ph.D. diss., University of Colorado at Boulder, 1996).

3. EW to John P. Kennedy, July 1, 1834; EW to Samuel L. Southard, April 7, July 1, and September 18, 1834; EW to Salmon P. Chase, July 11, 1837; and EW to John Q. Adams, August 8, 1837, Elizabeth Wirt Letterbook, 1834–40, SHC; and *Daily National Intelligencer*, February 19, 1834, MHS. Elizabeth selected those letters that demonstrated "moral sentiment, graphic description, and didactic excellence" as the basis for her

husband's biography. See EW to Samuel L. Southard, September 18, 1834, Elizabeth Wirt Letterbook, 1834–40, SHC.

4. For quotation, see EW to James Hagarty, July 31, 1835, Elizabeth Wirt Letterbook, 1834–41, SHC. See also EW to Henry Didier, March 22, 1834, Elizabeth Wirt Letterbook, 1834–41, SHC; Catharine G. Wirt to Elizabeth W. Goldsborough, May 6, 1834; William C. Wirt to EW, July 7, 1834; William C. Wirt to Dabney C. Wirt, August 1, December 10, 1835, Wirt Family Papers, SHC; and Catharine G. Wirt to Elizabeth W. Goldsborough, March 20, 1834, Goldsborough Papers, Duke.

5. Will of William Wirt, Will Book 1, p. 544, Richmond Circuit Court, Richmond, Virginia. The will was dated December 18, 1831, and proven in Anne Arundel County, Maryland, March 5, 1834.

6. Ellen Wirt to Elizabeth W. Goldsborough, March 4, 1840, Elizabeth Wirt Letterbook, 1834–41, SHC.

7. On the boys, see Catharine Wirt to Dabney C. Wirt, April 11, 1838; EW to Henry Wirt, February 25, 1840; Henry Wirt to William C. Wirt, February 4, 1843, Wirt Family Papers, SHC; William C. Wirt to EW, September 27, 1841; Henry Wirt to William C. Wirt, September 30, 1842, William and Elizabeth Wirt Papers, Duke. On Catharine's extended courtship, see Catharine G. Wirt to Elizabeth W. Goldsborough, July 28, 1835, Goldsborough Papers, Duke. For her marriage and move, see Catharine W. Randall to Elizabeth W. Goldsborough, August 25, 1842, Wirt Family Papers, SHC. On Ellen's first marriage, see Shofner, *History of Jefferson County*, 31, 40, 128, 135. See also Catharine Wirt to Dabney C. Wirt, January 12, June 8, 29, 1839, Wirt Family Papers, SHC. On Ellen's second marriage and move, see Shofner, *History of Jefferson County*, 40; Ellen Wirt to Henry Wirt, postscript to EW to Henry Wirt, February 25, 1840; Henry Wirt to William C. Wirt, February 4, 1843; EW to William C. Wirt, March 19, 1843; Ellen W. McCormick to Henry Wirt, February 14, 1844, Wirt Family Papers, SHC.

8. For quotation, see EW to Dabney C. Wirt, September 21, 1854, William and Elizabeth Wirt Papers, Duke. On Elizabeth's last years at the plantation, see Shofner, *History of Jefferson County*, 109–17; Catharine W. Randall, August 25, 1842, Wirt Family Papers, SHC. On Elizabeth's continued interest in plantation matters, see Shofner, *History of Jefferson County*, 202–3. On Elizabeth's continuing financial support for the family, see also Henry Wirt to William C. Wirt, February 4, 1843; Catharine W. Randall to Elizabeth W. Goldsborough, January 5, 1844; William C. Wirt to Henry Wirt, February 4, 1844; Ellen W. McCormick to Henry Wirt, February 14, 1844; EW to Henry Wirt, April 8, 1844; and EW to Louisa A. Wirt, February 5, 1846, Wirt Family Papers, SHC; Dabney C. Wirt to EW, August 24 and September 9, 1854; and William C. Wirt to EW, February 20, 1854, William and Elizabeth Wirt Papers, Duke. On Liz's move to New Hampshire, see EW to William C. Wirt, March 19, 1843, Wirt Family Papers, SHC; L. M. Goldsborough to Elizabeth W. Goldsborough, March 3, 1843, Goldsborough Papers, Duke. For Rosa and Catharine's deaths, see Elizabeth W. Goldsborough to "Sister" [?], December 8, 16, 19, 24, 1852; and Elizabeth Wirt Baker, "Sketch of William Wirt," February 22, 1899, Wirt Family Papers, SHC; Shofner, *History of Jefferson County*, 40, 202–3.

9. Will of Elizabeth Washington Wirt, Will Book 1, p. 158, Richmond Circuit Court, Richmond, Virginia; and Will of William Wirt. See also Lebsock, *Free Women of Petersburg*, chap. 5.

10. For quotation, see WW to William H. Cabell, December 3, 1832; see also EW to Robert Gwathney, December 8, 1832, William Wirt Letterbook, MHS. For a discussion of the financing of the estate, see, for example, the copy of the opinion rendered "In the matter of the Estates of Wm Wirt & Elizabeth W. Wirt decreed in the Circuit Court for Anne Arundel County of Maryland in Equity," [June 1859]; J. Wirt Randall to Elizabeth Wirt Baker, August 28, 1893, Wirt Family Papers, SHC; and Will of Elizabeth Wirt.

11. H. L. Girardeau to [W. O. Girardeau], February 22, 1857; see also Alexander Randall to Elizabeth W. Goldsborough, November 11, 1857; Frank H. Stockett to William O. Girardeau, July 7, 1859; Elizabeth W. Goldsborough to Thomas Donalson, March 4, 1859; Mr. Carlisle to Elizabeth W. Goldsborough, March 11, 1859, Wirt Family Papers, SHC; Alexander Randall to Louis Malesherbes Goldsborough, September 4, 1858; Alexander Randall to Elizabeth W. Goldsborough, November 12, 1858, Alexander Randall Letters, LOV. For Elizabeth's obituary, see *Maryland Republican*, February 14, 1857, copy in Carrington Family Papers, Virginia Historical Society, Richmond. Elizabeth became ill in September 1856; she died on January 24, 1857.

12. Copy of opinion, "In the matter of the Estates of Wm Wirt & Elizabeth W. Wirt" [June 1859], Wirt Family Papers, SHC; Will of William Wirt; Will of Elizabeth Wirt.

13. Alexander Randall to Louis M. Goldsborough, September 4, 1858, Alexander Randall Letters, LOV; and J. Wirt Randall to Elizabeth Wirt Baker, August 28, 1893, Wirt Family Papers, SHC. See also Frank H. Stockett to William O. Girardeau, July 7, 1859; W. O. Girardeau to Frank Stuckett, July 12, 1859, Wirt Family Papers, SHC.

14. On Gamble's guardianship, see J. Wirt Randall to Elizabeth Wirt Baker, March 25, June 4, [June or July] 20, 1873; Elizabeth Wirt Baker to J. Wirt Randall, July 4, 1873; Robert H. Gamble to J. Wirt Randall, May 24, 1873; Robert H. Gamble to Elizabeth Wirt Baker, November 13, 1873, December 1, 1874; George P. Ramsey to Elizabeth Wirt Baker, December 2, 1875; J. W. Gamble to Elizabeth Wirt Baker, August 24, 1874; Elizabeth Wirt Baker to James Baker, April 26, 1878; and "Settled Account between Col. R. H. Gamble & Elizabeth Wirt Baker," [May 15, 1878], Wirt Family Papers, SHC. On continuing legal squabbles, see WW to Elizabeth Wirt Baker, February 26, December 24, 27, 1886, [n.d.], 1886; J. Wirt Randall to Elizabeth Wirt Baker, August 28, 1893, Wirt Family Papers, SHC. See also Memoriam of Dr. William Wirt, [1899], Carrington Family Papers, Virginia Historical Society, Richmond.

15. Elizabeth Wirt Baker to Cora Baker, June 7, 1895; "Sketch of William Wirt," February 22, 1899; and "Application for membership [in] United States Daughters," n.d., Wirt Family Papers, SHC.

Essay on Sources

Manuscript collections of the many letters written by and to Elizabeth and William Wirt and their family are the major source for this study. By far the richest collection for a study of the Wirts' marriage is the William Wirt Papers (MS 1011) held by the Maryland Historical Society Library in Baltimore, available in a twenty-four-reel microfilm set at Rice University, Houston, Texas. In addition to regular correspondence, the Maryland Historical Society collection contains rough drafts of some of William Wirt's literary efforts; the William Wirt Letterbooks, 1806–16 and 1832–34, which contain copies of William Wirt's letters to business acquaintances and correspondence relevant to the Florida experiment, respectively; the William Wirt Letterbook to Peachy Gilmer, 1802–33, and the William Wirt Letterbook to Francis W. Gilmer, 1813–22, containing copies of William's letters to his relatives from his first marriage; a journal and notebooks by Robert Wirt; and a diary by Catharine Wirt. All of these items are filed separately at the end of the correspondence and are designated in the footnotes.

Other collections are useful primarily for documenting specific time periods or topics. For Laura Wirt's adolescence, courtship, and early marriage, for instance, the Laura Wirt Randall Papers at the Virginia Historical Society in Richmond are a valuable supplement to the letters written by her parents. This collection, in typescript form, also contains excerpts from Elizabeth's and William's wills and some helpful family background. For Elizabeth Wirt's widowhood, an especially useful set of papers is the Wirt Family Papers (#1704), held by the Southern Historical Collection at the Library of the University of North Carolina at Chapel Hill, which contain the Elizabeth Wirt Letterbooks, 1834–40 and 1834–41. This collection also contains useful biographical and genealogical information compiled by Elizabeth Wirt Baker.

The Wirts were prolific correspondents, and these collections, while the most extensive, did not exhaust their enthusiasm for letter writing. Other Wirt letters used for this study can be found in the William Wirt Papers at the Library of Congress in Washington, D.C., especially valuable for William's correspondence with the Wirt children; in the Elizabeth and William Wirt Papers, 1810–54, in Special Collections at the Perkins Library of Duke University in Durham, North Carolina, with several interesting letters between the Wirt sons and their mother after William's death; and in the Louis Malesherbes Goldsborough Papers, 1830–73 (Personal Letters), also in Special Collections at the Perkins Library at Duke University, containing useful information on the Wirts' daughter Elizabeth G. Wirt. The Alexander Randall Letters in the Archives at the

Library of Virginia in Richmond contain some letters regarding the execution of Elizabeth Wirt's estate. Copies of William Wirt's letters to and from his male friends and business associates may be found in microfilm form at the Library of Virginia: William Wirt Letters to Dabney Carr, 1803–31; Francis Walker Gilmer Letters to William Wirt, 1812–25; and William Wirt Letters to Littleton W. Tazewell, 1803–27. The originals are held in the Archives at the Library of Virginia. Letters to, from, and about the Wirts may be found at the Virginia Historical Society in the Breckinridge Family Papers, the Carrington Family Papers, and the Abraham Joseph Cabell Papers. In the same repository, there are several scattered items of interest: the Elizabeth Wirt Letter, March 11–12, 1801, to Thomas [Monteagle] Bayly; several letters from William Wirt to Francis Walker Gilmer and John Holt Rice; and an obituary of Agnes Wirt in the Henrietta (Ogle) Tayloe Scrapbook.

~

To study a couple, biographical information and sources on local history are indispensable. Several sources illuminate William Wirt's career as a lawyer, author, civil servant, and politician. John P. Kennedy's two-volume *Memoirs of the Life of William Wirt, Attorney-General of the United States* (1849; rev. ed., Philadelphia, 1850) offers a rags-to-riches interpretation of Wirt's life and includes many of his letters, although many of these, particularly those pertaining to his domestic life, have been extensively edited. William Wirt's career as an author and his contributions to the myth of the Old South are discussed by William R. Taylor in "William Wirt and the Legend of the Old South," *William and Mary Quarterly*, 3d ser., 14 (October 1957): 477–93, and *Cavalier and Yankee: The Old South and American National Character* (New York, 1961). Articles that illuminate William's early years and his entry into law are S. A. Link, "William Wirt, the Christian Lawyer," *Methodist Quarterly Review* 57 (October 1908): 730–43, and Joseph Clarke Robert, "William Wirt, Virginian," *Virginia Magazine of History and Biography* 81 (October 1972): 398–401. Joseph Charles Burke, "William Wirt: Attorney General and Constitutional Lawyer" (Ph.D. diss., Indiana University, 1965), offers a detailed account of William Wirt's career in Washington, D.C. His political views are discussed in Michael L. Oberg, "William Wirt and the Trials of Republicanism," *Virginia Magazine of History and Biography* 99 (July 1991): 305–26. The Anti-Masonic nomination and presidential campaign are discussed by Marvin R. Cain, "William Wirt against Andrew Jackson: Reflection on an Era," *Mid-America: An Historical Quarterly* 47 (April 1965): 113–38. William's Florida venture is discussed at length in Jerrell H. Shofner's *History of Jefferson County* (Tallahassee, Fla., 1976). William Wirt's own extensive published writings include *Letters of a British Spy*, published in the local papers in 1803; *The Rainbow* (Richmond, Va., 1804); *The Old Bachelor*, 3d ed. (Richmond, Va., 1818); and *Sketches of the Life and Character of Patrick Henry* (Philadelphia, 1817). A few letters to and from William Wirt are included in Ninian W. Edwards, *History of Illinois, from 1778 to 1833; and Life and Times of Ninian Edwards* (Springfield, 1870).

Information on Elizabeth Gamble Wirt is rather limited. Sarah P. Stetson's article "Mrs. Wirt and the Language of Flowers," *Virginia Magazine of History and Biography* 57 (October 1949): 376–89, is the only published work that focuses on her. However, extensive information is available on the Gamble family. For background on the Gambles' settlement and kinship networks, I found Lyman Chalkley's three-volume *Chron-*

icles of the Scotch-Irish Settlement in Virginia Extracted from the Original Court Records of Augusta County, 1745–1800 (Baltimore, 1966); Nell McNish Gambill, The Kith and Kin of Captain James Leeper and Susan Draker, His Wife (New York, 1946); and George R. Gilmer, Sketches of Some of the First Settlers of Upper Georgia, of the Cherokees, and the Author (Baltimore, 1965), valuable. George Wythe Munford, The Two Parsons (Richmond, Va., 1884), discusses Elizabeth's school; Salmon P. Chase, a great admirer of Elizabeth Wirt and her daughters, comments on Elizabeth's personality in John Niven et al., eds., The Salmon P. Chase Papers, vol. 1, Journals, 1829–1872 (Kent, Ohio, 1993). Elizabeth Wirt's own book, Flora's Dictionary (Baltimore, 1829), was republished several times and can be found at the Virginia Historical Society. Elizabeth's and William's wills are filed in the Will Books of the Richmond Circuit Court, Richmond, Virginia.

Because the Wirts moved from place to place, several sources were consulted for local context. Jane Carson's We Were There: Descriptions of Williamsburg, 1699–1859, Compiled from Contemporary Sources and Arranged Chronologically (Williamsburg, 1965) contains detailed firsthand accounts of the Wirts' first home. On Norfolk, I used Thomas J. Wertenbaker, Norfolk: Historic Southern Port, 2d ed. (Durham, N.C., 1962). Primary accounts published in Maurice Duke and Daniel P. Jordan, eds., A Richmond Reader: 1733–1983 (Chapel Hill, N.C., 1983), supplemented Virginius Dabney's Richmond: The Story of a City, rev. ed. (Charlottesville, Va., 1990). For Washington, Constance Green, Washington: Village and Capital, 1800–1876 (Princeton, N.J., 1962), and James Sterling Young, The Washington Community, 1800–1828 (New York, 1966), were useful for background, while Margaret Bayard Smith's published correspondence, The First Forty Years of Washington Society, Portrayed by the Family Letters of Mrs. Samuel Harrison Smith (Margaret Bayard), ed. Gaillard Hunt (1906; reprint, New York, 1965), offered details on social life in the capital city. For the Wirts' last years, I found Terry D. Bilhartz, Urban Religion and the Second Great Awakening: Church and Society in Early National Baltimore (Rutherford, N.J., 1986), and Gary Lawson Browne, Baltimore in the Nation, 1784–1861 (Chapel Hill, N.C., 1980), helpful.

~

My reading of these sources has benefited enormously from the large and growing body of literature on the history of men, women, and their gender relations in marriage and the family. Scholars of women's experiences in the past first drew attention to the importance of gender in American history. Nancy F. Cott, The Bonds of Womanhood: "Woman's Sphere" in New England, 1780–1835 (New Haven, Conn., 1977), and Barbara Welter, "The Cult of True Womanhood, 1820–1860," American Quarterly 17 (Summer 1966): 151–74, offered two very different assessments of ideals of femininity which, nonetheless, both inspired investigation of female culture and the domestic ideology of "woman's sphere" in antebellum America. Illustrative work in this area includes Kathryn Kish Sklar's careful exploration of one woman's promotion of women's role in the home, Catharine Beecher: A Study in American Domesticity (New York, 1973), and Carroll Smith-Rosenberg's richly detailed essay on women's friendships, "The Female World of Love and Ritual: Relations between Women in Nineteenth-Century America," in her Disorderly Conduct: Visions of Gender in Victorian America (New York, 1985), 53–76. Other classic views of woman's sphere and the "feminization" of American Protestantism are contained in Barbara Berg, The Remembered Gate: Origins of American

Feminism: The Woman and the City, 1800–1860 (New York, 1978), and Ann Douglas, *The Feminization of American Culture* (New York, 1977). For a critical appraisal of these frameworks, see Linda K. Kerber, "Separate Spheres, Female Worlds, Woman's Place: The Rhetoric of Women's History," *Journal of American History* 75 (June 1988): 9–39.

Following in their footsteps, the new men's studies scholars have begun to inquire into men's experiences as inhabitants of the separate sphere of the workplace. The groundwork was laid by Peter G. Filene, *Him/Her/Self: Sex Roles in Modern America*, rev. ed. (Baltimore, 1986), and Peter N. Stearns, *Be a Man! Males in Modern Society* (New York, 1979). Ronald Preston Byars' Ph.D. dissertation, "The Making of the Self-Made Man: The Development of Masculine Roles and Images in Ante-Bellum America" (Michigan State University, 1979), is a valuable source on new ideals of manhood in the nineteenth century which anticipated several of Anthony Rotundo's conclusions in his recent book *American Manhood: Transformations in Masculinity from the Revolution to the Modern Era* (New York, 1993). Much of the recent and ongoing research is included in collections of essays. See for some examples Harry Brod, ed., *The Making of Masculinities: The New Men's Studies* (Boston, 1987); Mark C. Carnes and Clyde Griffen, eds., *Meanings for Manhood: Constructions of Masculinity in Victorian America* (Chicago, 1990) ; and J. A. Mangan and James Walvin, eds., *Manliness and Morality: Middle-Class Masculinity in Britain and America, 1800–1940* (Manchester, England, 1987).

Recently, historians have begun to challenge the construction of separate spheres. Some studies have suggested that the ideology of separate spheres and its corollaries, "true womanhood" and the "cult of domesticity," competed with other ideals of womanhood in the mid-nineteenth century. See Frances B. Cogan, *All-American Girl: The Ideal of Real Womanhood in Mid-Nineteenth-Century America* (Athens, Ga., 1989), and Laura McCall, " 'The Reign of Brute Force Is Now Over': A Content Analysis of *Godey's Lady's Book*, 1830–1860," *Journal of the Early Republic* 9 (Summer 1989): 217–36. Others have dug beneath the surface acceptance of separate spheres to reveal that, even while clinging to the tenets of separate spheres, men and women throughout the nineteenth century often set aside the restrictions of separate spheres within the context of marital relationships and family duties. See the excellent work done on Victorian love by Karen Lystra, *Searching the Heart: Women, Men, and Romantic Love in Nineteenth-Century America* (New York, 1989), and on women's ventures into the commercial arena as widows by Lisa Wilson, *Life after Death: Widows in Pennsylvania, 1750–1850* (Philadelphia, 1992). Recent articles on the early national period have suggested that this era offered especial promise for men and women to share their lives. See the series of short articles in Linda K. Kerber et al., "Beyond Roles, Beyond Spheres: Thinking about Gender in the Early Republic," *William and Mary Quarterly*, 3d ser., 46 (July 1989): 565–85, and Jan Lewis's study of ideals of marriage in early national periodicals, "The Republican Wife: Virtue and Seduction in the Early Republic," *William and Mary Quarterly*, 3d ser., 44 (October 1987): 689–721. Glenda Mathews, in her book *"Just a Housewife": The Rise and Fall of Domesticity in America* (New York, 1987), suggests that the early nineteenth century was a "golden age of domesticity," in which men and women alike looked to marriage, family, and the home as the surest source of happiness. New work in the history of gender challenges scholars to view masculinity and femininity in relation to each other. See, for example, the essays in Laura McCall and Donald Yacovone, eds., *A Shared Experience: Men, Women, and the History of Gender* (New York, 1998).

Southern women's historians also have challenged the dominant interpretations of "woman's sphere" and have suggested that patriarchy's hold was stronger in the South. Catherine Clinton, *The Plantation Mistress: Woman's World in the Old South* (New York, 1982), and Elizabeth Fox-Genovese, *Within the Plantation Household: Black and White Women of the Old South* (Chapel Hill, N.C., 1989), both protest the "New Englandization" of women's history and argue that white plantation women, isolated from other women on far-flung plantations and subjected to the dominance of their husbands, did not experience the "bonds of womanhood" which northeastern white women shared. Suzanne Lebsock's study of urban southern women, *The Free Women of Petersburg: Status and Culture in a Southern Town, 1784–1860* (New York, 1984), contends that southern women were able to develop an autonomous female culture in upper South cities which revolved around "personalism."

Studies of masculinity in the South also suggest that patriarchy persisted longer there than in the North. On the male culture of honor, see especially Kenneth S. Greenberg, *Masters and Statesmen: The Political Culture of American Slavery* (Baltimore, 1985); Steven M. Stowe, *Intimacy and Power in the Old South: Ritual in the Lives of the Planters* (Baltimore, 1987); and Bertram Wyatt-Brown, *Southern Honor: Ethics and Behavior in the Old South* (New York, 1982). Studies of the conflict between evangelicalism and honor in the South include Edward L. Ayers, *Vengeance and Justice: Crime and Punishment in the Nineteenth-Century American South* (New York, 1984), and Ted Ownby, *Subduing Satan: Religion, Recreation, and Manhood in the Rural South, 1865–1920* (Chapel Hill, N.C., 1990).

Studies of the history of the family, looking at the same time period in which these historians have pondered separate spheres and its alternatives, have discerned a trend from authoritarian, patriarchal households to affectionate, nuclear families. Robert L. Griswold, *Family and Divorce in California, 1850–1890: Victorian Illusions and Everyday Realities* (Albany, N.Y., 1982), provides a useful discussion of the trajectory "from patriarchy to companionship." See also Lawrence Stone, "Family History in the 1980s: Past Achievements and Future Trends," *Journal of Interdisciplinary History* 12 (Summer 1981): 51–88, and Carl N. Degler, *At Odds: Women and the Family in America from the Revolution to the Present* (New York, 1980).

The impact of the rise of companionship on the Old South is a matter of some debate. While some scholars argue that what Allan Kulikoff, in his *Tobacco and Slaves: The Development of Southern Cultures in the Chesapeake, 1680–1800* (Chapel Hill, N.C., 1986), terms "domestic patriarchy" was preserved in the antebellum South, the overwhelming bulk of scholarship offers evidence of "modern," "companionate," or "affectionate" family life in the Old South. These studies include Russell Lindley Blake, "Ties of Intimacy: Social Values and Personal Relationships of Antebellum Slaveholders" (Ph.D. diss., University of Michigan, 1978); Anne Williams Boucher, "Wealthy Planter Families in Nineteenth-Century Alabama" (Ph.D. diss., University of Connecticut, 1978); Melinda S. Buza, " 'Pledges of Our Love': Friendship, Love, and Marriage among the Virginia Gentry, 1800–1825," in *The Edge of the South: Life in Nineteenth-Century Virginia*, ed. Edward L. Ayers and John C. Willis (Charlottesville,

Va., 1991), 9–36; Jane Turner Censer, *North Carolina Planters and Their Children, 1800-1860* (Baton Rouge, La., 1984); Jan Lewis, *The Pursuit of Happiness: Family and Values in Jefferson's Virginia* (New York, 1983); Sally G. McMillen, *Motherhood in the Old South: Pregnancy, Childbirth, and Infant Rearing* (Baton Rouge, La., 1990); and Daniel Blake Smith, *Inside the Great House: Planter Family Life in Eighteenth-Century Chesapeake Society* (Ithaca, N.Y., 1980). Joan E. Cashin's *A Family Venture: Men and Women on the Southern Frontier* (New York, 1991) is the most recent and compelling interpretation of southern families as authoritarian networks of extended kinship. A recent collection of essays reveals that southern families often combined patriarchal and affectionate relations. See Carol Bleser, ed., *In Joy and in Sorrow: Women, Family, and Marriage in the Victorian South, 1830–1900* (New York, 1991).

～

Work on women, men, and families is closely related to scholarship on the nature of the household economy and men's and women's roles in it. Recent research has challenged the notion that women existed in a separate, nonproductive, "woman's sphere." Jeanne Boydston, in her book *Home and Work: Housework, Wages, and the Ideology of Labor in the Early Republic* (New York, 1990), convincingly argues that the ideology of separate spheres hid the reality of continued household production. A number of local studies have demonstrated women's significant contributions to the household economy through domestic production. In the mid-Atlantic, Joan Jensen's *Loosening the Bonds: Mid-Atlantic Farm Women, 1750–1850* (New Haven, Conn., 1986) and Nancy Grey Osterud's *Bonds of Community: The Lives of Farm Women in Nineteenth-Century New York* (Ithaca, N.Y., 1991) both demonstrate women's participation in dairy production and sale; in New England, Laurel Thatcher Ulrich's research suggests the importance of women's textile production and petty exchange networks in the colonial and early national eras. See Ulrich, " 'A Friendly Neighbor': Social Dimensions of Daily Work in Northern Colonial New England," in *Women and Power in American History: A Reader*, ed. Kathryn Kish Sklar and Thomas Dublin (Englewood Cliffs, N.J., 1991), vol. 1, *To 1880*, 37–50; *Good Wives: Image and Reality in the Lives of Women in Northern New England, 1650–1750* (New York, 1982); and "Housewife and Gadder: Themes of Self-Sufficiency and Community in Eighteenth-Century New England," in *"To Toil the Livelong Day": America's Women at Work, 1780–1980*, ed. Carol Groneman and Mary Beth Norton (Ithaca, N.Y., 1987), 21–34.

Historians of southern women, beginning with Anne Firor Scott's classic work, *The Southern Lady: From Pedestal to Politics, 1830–1930* (Chicago, 1970), have long contended that even the most elite white women in the antebellum South engaged in extensive household production, from textile production to meat preservation to candle making. See Clinton, *Plantation Mistress*; Fox-Genovese, *Within the Plantation Household*; and Lebsock, *Free Women of Petersburg*. Julia Cherry Spruill's pioneering book *Women's Life and Work in the Southern Colonies* (Chapel Hill, N.C., 1938) remains the best source on colonial southern women's paid and unpaid labor.

The division of responsibility and authority in the household has been the topic of provocative study. Cott's study of urban northeastern women, *Bonds of Womanhood*, asserts that the removal of many productive tasks from the household to a male-dominated workplace allowed women to assert their influence over the home, popularly conceived of as woman's sphere. Studying the plantation South, Fox-Genovese has argued in her *Within the Plantation Household* that continuing household production in the rural South allowed planter-class men to retain control over the household and its members and that women had little authority over the household functions for which they were responsible. In contrast to both of these interpretations, Laurel Thatcher Ulrich suggests that New England men and women in the early national period pursued separate productive activities that sometimes were interwoven. See *A Midwife's Tale: The Life of Martha Ballard, Based on Her Diary, 1785–1812* (New York, 1990). In a recent essay, Susan Branson illuminates the ways in which women acted as invisible contributors to the family economy. See her "Women and the Family Economy in the Early Republic: The Case of Elizabeth Meredith," *Journal of the Early Republic* 16 (Spring 1996): 47–71.

The physical space in which household production took place is illuminated by Leslie C. Stewart Abernathy, "Urban Farmsteads: Household Responsibilities in the City," *Historical Archaeology* 20, no. 2 (1986): 5–15. On women's role in vernacular house design, see Sally McMurry, "Women in the American Vernacular Landscape," *Material Culture* 20, no. 1 (1989): 33–49; Rebecca Sample Bernstein and Carolyn Torma, "Exploring the Role of Women in the Creation of Vernacular Architecture," in *Perspectives in Vernacular Architecture*, ed. Thomas Carter and Bernard L. Herman (Columbia, Mo., 1991), 4:64–72; and Jan Jennings, "Drawing on the Vernacular Interior," *Winterthur Portfolio* 27 (Winter 1992): 255–79. On women, vernacular architecture, and household production, see Sally McMurry's fascinating book *Families and Farmhouses in Nineteenth-Century America: Vernacular Design and Social Change* (New York, 1988).

The physical setting for the Wirts' domestic economy is revealed through a variety of local records. Local newspapers offer details on each of the Wirts' houses and on the products sold by local merchants. See, for example, the *Norfolk Commercial Register* and the *Virginia Gazette and General Advertiser*. Local inhabitants' accounts of daily life also record interesting information. On Williamsburg's town market, see "George Tucker's Description of Williamsburg in 1796," reprinted in *William and Mary Quarterly*, 2d ser., 19 (April 1939): 192–96; for Norfolk household production, see A Lady [Anne Ritson], *A Poetical Picture of America, Being Observations Made, During a Residence of Several Years, at Alexandria, and Norfolk, in Virginia; Illustrative of the manners and Customs of the Inhabitants: And Interspersed with Anecdotes, Arising from a General Intercourse with Society in that Country, from the Year 1799 to 1807* (London, 1809); and A. G. Roeber, ed., "A New England Woman's Perspective on Norfolk, Virginia, 1801-1802: Excerpts from the Diary of Ruth Henshaw Bascom," *Proceedings of the American Antiquarian Society* 88 (1978): 277–325; and for Richmond, see [Samuel Mordecai], *Richmond in By-Gone Days: Being Reminiscences of an Old Citizen* (Richmond, Va., 1856).

The Wirts' residences are also revealed in local records. For Norfolk, see the Norfolk Borough Land and Personal Property Books at the Library of Virginia (microfilm available at Clayton Genealogical Library, Houston, Texas). The Richmond City Land Books, the Library of Virginia (microfilm at Clayton Genealogical Library); "A Plan of the City of Richmond," 1809–10, in Alexander Wilbourne Weddell, *Richmond, Virginia, in Old Prints, 1737–1887* (Richmond, Va., 1932); and Mary Wingfield Scott, *Old Richmond Neighborhoods* (Richmond, Va., 1950), reveal the location of the Wirts' property in Richmond. Their Mutual Assurance Society Fire Insurance Policies in the Library of

Virginia's Business Records Collection offer bird's-eye views of the houses and their outbuildings. For a description of the Washington, D.C., residence, see Federal Writers' Project, *Washington: City and Capital* (Washington, D.C., 1937).

Slave ownership as well as the location and layout of the Wirts' homes helped to shape their family economy. The difficulties that Elizabeth Wirt confronted in Washington are illuminated by Fox-Genovese's *Within the Plantation Household*. Fox-Genovese argues that southern slaveholding women were only their husbands' deputies; their authority was derivative, and when their husbands were absent, they had difficulty managing slaves and even feared for their own safety. The especial difficulties created in the urban environment, where free and slave, black and white workers came together in the household, are suggested by Stephanie Cole, "Servants and Slaves: Domestic Service in the Border Cities, 1800–1850" (Ph.D. diss., University of Florida, 1994). During their residence in Norfolk and Richmond, the Wirts' slaveholdings were recorded each year in the Norfolk Borough Land and Personal Property Books and the Richmond City Personal Property Books at the Library of Virginia. The Wirts' decennial slaveholdings in Richmond, Washington, D.C., and Baltimore are recorded in the manuscript federal censuses for 1810, 1820, and 1830. Both the property books and the census records are available on microfilm at the Clayton Genealogical Library.

⁓

Married couples were the center of an affectionate family. As feminist scholars have pointed out, understanding the fertility strategies in those families is essential to reaching a more complete view of marriage and gender roles. See Nancy Folbre, "Of Patriarchy Born: The Political Economy of Fertility Decisions," *Feminist Studies* 9 (Summer 1983): 261–84, and Allison MacKinnon, "Were Women Present at the Demographic Transition? Questions from a Feminist Historian to Historical Demographers," *Gender and History* 7 (August 1995): 222–40.

Historians have proposed a variety of interpretations of the "demographic transition" in the United States, in which the fertility of white women declined by one-half from 1800 to 1900. Daniel Scott Smith contends that women's success in influencing their husbands to cooperate in birth control accounts for the change; see his article "Family Limitation, Sexual Control, and Domestic Feminism in Victorian America," in *A Heritage of Her Own: Toward a New Social History of American Women*, ed. Nancy F. Cott and Elizabeth H. Pleck (New York, 1979), 222–45. In contrast, Richard A. Easterlin, in "Factors in the Decline of Farm Family Fertility in the United States: Some Preliminary Research Results," *Journal of American History* 63 (December 1976): 600–612, argues that men's economic interests were more important, as they searched for a way to provide local land for their children. Sally G. McMillen accounts for the well-known higher birthrates in the South by reference to a combination of factors, including the persistence of patriarchy, high infant mortality rates, and the availability of land, in her study *Motherhood in the Old South*.

Recent studies of the Middle Atlantic and the Upper South have provided new evidence about the link between marital felicity and fertility control. Susan E. Klepp's work on Pennsylvania women suggests that conjugal love was a significant factor in the growing interest in limiting fertility in the revolutionary era in her paper presented at the Second Annual Conference of the Institute of Early American History and Culture, "Revolutionary Bodies: Mid-Atlantic Women and the Fertility Transition, 1760–1820" (Boulder, Colo., June 1, 1996). Jan Lewis and Kenneth Lockridge's generational analysis of Virginia gentry's fertility rates and Melinda Buza's research in these families' personal papers suggest that some southern women successfully used "domestic feminism" to convince their concerned husbands to cooperate in birth control in late-eighteenth- and early-nineteenth-century Virginia families. See Lewis and Lockridge, " 'Sally Has Been Sick': Pregnancy and Family Limitation among Virginia Gentry Women, 1780–1830," *Journal of Social History* 22 (Fall 1988): 5–19, and Buza, " 'Pledges of Our Love.' "

The subject of modern or affectionate child rearing has been a rich topic for historical research. The pathbreaking work on modern child rearing in the United States is Bernard Wishy's *The Child and the Republic: The Dawn of Modern American Child Nurture* (Philadelphia, 1968). Philip Greven, *The Protestant Temperament: Patterns of Child-Rearing, Religious Experience, and the Self in Early America* (New York, 1977), provides the fullest discussion of the effect of religion on child rearing. Other useful studies include Anne Boylan, "Sunday Schools and Changing Evangelical Views of Children in the 1820s," *Church History* 48 (September 1979): 320–33; Monica Kiefer, *American Children through Their Books, 1700–1835* (Philadelphia, 1948); Anne Scott MacLeod, "Children's Literature for a New Nation, 1820–1860" and "Child and Conscience," in her *American Childhood: Essays on Children's Literature of the Nineteenth and Twentieth Centuries* (Athens, Ga., 1994), 87–98, 99–113; MacLeod, *A Moral Tale: Children's Fiction and American Culture, 1820–1860* (Hamden, Conn., 1975); Gail S. Murray, "Rational Thought and Republican Virtues: Children's Literature, 1789–1820," *Journal of the Early Republic* 8 (Summer 1988): 159–77; and Robert Sunley, "Early Nineteenth-Century American Literature on Child Rearing," in *Childhood in Contemporary Cultures*, ed. Margaret Mead and Martha Wolfenstein (Chicago, 1955), 150–67. An excellent new synthesis of modern child rearing is Jacqueline S. Reinier, *From Virtue to Character: American Childhood, 1775–1850* (New York, 1996). On modern child rearing in the South, see especially Censer, *North Carolina Planters and Their Children*; Lewis, *Pursuit of Happiness*; and Smith, *Inside the Great House*.

Most of these works also address the new centrality of motherhood as the primary influence over young children. For a discussion of women's growing importance as caretakers and child rearers, see the classic work on the subject, Anne L. Kuhn, *The Mother's Role in Childhood Education: New England Concepts, 1830–1860* (New Haven, Conn., 1947). In the South, McMillen's *Motherhood in the Old South* demonstrates that southern women fully accepted the nineteenth-century cult of the mother and contests the myth that black mammies took primary charge of white children.

The role of fathers in child rearing is an important new area of study. The South's reverence for fatherhood may have led men there to take a more active role in child care and child rearing. An important recent study of the former is Sally G. McMillen, "Antebellum Southern Fathers and the Health Care of Children," *Journal of Southern History* 60 (August 1994): 513–32. Case studies of southern fathers who were actively involved in modern child rearing include Philip Hamilton, "Education in the St. George Tucker Household: Change and Continuity in Jeffersonian Virginia," *Virginia Magazine of History and Biography*, 102 (April 1994): 167–92, and Sarah Woolfolk Wiggins, "A Victorian Father: Josiah Gorgas and His Family," in Bleser, *In Joy and in Sorrow*, 233–

52. James Morton's new article on Civil War soldier-fathers suggests that war both increased fathers' interest in parenting and interfered with personal care. See "Fatherhood in the Confederacy: Southern Soldiers and Their Children," *Journal of Southern History* 63 (May 1997): 269–92.

While these studies document men's activities as parents, other studies suggest the ways that gender shaped fatherhood. John Demos, *Past, Present, and Personal: The Family and the Life Course in American History* (New York, 1986), discusses the "trend toward limited fatherhood" in nineteenth-century America, while Robert Griswold eloquently describes the tension in the male role and the resulting views of fathers by their children in a series of studies on the nineteenth- and twentieth-century United States. See Griswold, *Family and Divorce in California*; " 'Ties That Bind and Bonds that Break': Children's Attitudes toward Fathers, 1900–1930," in *Small Worlds: Children and Adolescents in America, 1850–1890*, ed. Elliott West and Paula Petrik (Lawrence, Kans., 1992), 255–74; and *Fatherhood in America: A History* (New York, 1993). Studies of men in twentieth-century America similarly illuminate the different quality of domestic life for men. See Kathleen Gerson, *No Man's Land: Men's Changing Commitments to Family and Work* (New York, 1993), and Margaret Marsh, "Suburban Men and Masculine Domesticity, 1870–1915," in Carnes and Griffen, *Meanings for Manhood*, 111–27. A detailed and insightful examination of one father's attempts to balance affectionate fatherhood with paternal wage earning is Charles Strickland, "A Transcendentalist Father: The Child-Rearing Practices of Bronson Alcott," *Perspectives in American History* 3 (1969): 5–73.

Family relationships and men's and women's different roles in domestic life were often expressed in domestic architecture. Literature on the meaning of "home" and the structure of domestic life in the nineteenth century is extensive. See especially Clifford Edward Clark Jr., *The American Family Home, 1800–1960* (Chapel Hill, N.C., 1986); Clark, "Domestic Architecture as an Index to Social History," *Journal of Interdisciplinary History* 7 (Summer 1976): 35–56; Colleen McDannell, *The Christian Home in Victorian America, 1840–1900* (Bloomington, Ind., 1986); Jane C. Nylander, *Our Own Snug Fireside: Images of the New England Home, 1760–1860* (New York, 1993); Norma Prendergast, "The Sense of Home: Nineteenth-Century Domestic Architectural Reform" (Ph.D. diss., Cornell University, 1981); and Maxine van de Wetering, "The Popular Concept of 'Home' in Nineteenth-Century America," *Journal of American Studies* 18 (April 1984): 5–28. For the slave South, an excellent source is John Michael Vlach's *Back of the Big House: The Architecture of Plantation Slavery* (Chapel Hill, N.C., 1993). A beautifully illustrated volume with interpretive essays on both the home and the surrounding space in a southern city is Dorothy Knox Howe Houghton, Barrie M. Scardino, Sadie Gwin Blackburn, and Katherine S. Howe, *Houston's Forgotten Heritage: Landscape, Houses, Interiors, 1824–1914* (Houston, 1991).

~

Marriage and family began with courtship. In the nineteenth-century United States, parents reduced or disguised their role in marriage choice to allow couples to form matches based on romantic love and sexual attraction. On this shift, the classic essay is Daniel Scott Smith, "Parental Power and Marriage Patterns: An Analysis of Historical Trends in Hingham, Massachusetts," *Journal of Marriage and the Family* 35 (August

1973): 419–28, which suggests a link between a decline in the practice of marrying daughters off in birth order and the rise of companionate marriage. Ellen K. Rothman's study *Hands and Hearts: A History of Courtship in America* (New York, 1984) expands on these conclusions but addresses only northern couples.

Studies of southern women and families disagree on the nature of courtship in the antebellum South. Censer's excellent study of elite parents in the upper South demonstrates that these families adopted the new ideals of romantic love and the new practices of relaxed courtship; see *North Carolina Planters and Their Children*. By contrast, other studies suggest that while southern families adopted the ideal of mutual compatibility, the ritualistic nature of courtship and the continuing emphasis on money in marriage precluded this desired result for elite couples in the South. See Clinton, *Plantation Mistress*, and Stowe, *Intimacy and Power in the Old South*. Stowe's close case study of one southern woman's courtship, " 'The *Thing*, Not Its Vision': A Woman's Courtship and Her Sphere in the Southern Planter Class," *Feminist Studies* 9 (Spring 1983): 113–30, is a compelling example of how one courtship failed to produce intimacy. Several examples of marriages in which parental advice was selectively taken and parental opposition to a match was overcome in favor of romantic love in the early republican South are discussed in Wylma Wates, "Precursor to the Victorian Age: The Concept of Marriage and Family as Revealed in the Correspondence of the Izard Family of South Carolina," in Bleser, *In Joy and in Sorrow*, 3–14.

With the exception of Lystra's *Searching the Heart*, few studies take marriage and gender roles as their primary focus. Case studies offer the most insight into men's and women's intimate relationships. One study of several northern abolitionist couples is Blanche Glassman Hersh, " 'A Partnership of Equals': Feminist Marriages in Nineteenth-Century America," in *The American Man*, ed. Joseph H. Pleck and Elizabeth H. Pleck (Englewood Cliffs, N.J., 1980), 183–215. Southern historians have made the most progress in examining the dynamics of marriage, although most of these studies are brief or unpublished. Articles that reveal the persistent differences between southern men's and women's experiences of marriage are Carol K. Bleser, "The Perrys of Greenville: A Nineteenth-Century Marriage," in *The Web of Southern Social Relations: Women, Family, and Education*, ed. Walter J. Fraser Jr., R. Frank Saunders Jr., and Jon L. Wakelyn (Athens, Ga., 1985), 72–89, and Steven M. Stowe, "Intimacy in the Planter Class Culture," *Psychohistory Review* 10 (Spring–Summer 1982): 141–64. Essays that suggest the importance of changing gender roles within marriage in the nineteenth-century South include Carol Bleser and Frederick Heath, "The Clays of Alabama: The Impact of the Civil War on a Southern Marriage," and Virginia I. Burr, "A Woman Made to Suffer and Be Strong: Ella Gertrude Clanton Thomas, 1834–1907," both in Bleser, *In Joy and in Sorrow*, 135–53 and 215–32. Carol Bleser offers some reflections on marriage in her introduction to the Hammond family correspondence, *The Hammonds of Redcliffe* (New York, 1981). Book-length studies of southern couples who experienced tensions due to men's career-related absences are Mary Elizabeth Glade, "Private Lives and Public Myths: The Bagbys of Virginia" (Ph.D. diss., University of Colorado at Boulder, 1996), and Madge Thornall Roberts, *Star of Destiny: The Private Life of Sam and Margaret Houston* (Denton, Tex., 1993).

In addition to these works, several others have been instrumental in shaping my interpretation of the Wirts' marriage. Drew Gilpin Faust and Steven Stowe, both offering reflections on recent studies of women, men, and the family, have noted the conflict between patriarchy and companionship in the Old South. See Faust's epilogue to Bleser, *In Joy and in Sorrow*, 253–59, and Stowe's review essay "Private Emotions and a Public Man in Early Nineteenth-Century Virginia," *History of Education Quarterly* 27 (Spring 1987): 75–81. Studies of Virginia women and families offer valuable insights into the Wirts' marriage. Lebsock has suggested that southern women's higher expectations of marriage in the first half of the nineteenth century may have led to disappointment when their marriages did not live up to the high standards of companionship; see *Free Women of Petersburg*. Lewis's *Pursuit of Happiness* discusses the different meanings of love for men and women. A study of twentieth-century domestic life which vividly reveals discrepancies between men's satisfaction with their marriages and women's unhappiness is Elaine Tyler May's *Homeward Bound: American Families in the Cold War Era* (New York, 1988).

Index

Library of Congress Cataloging-in-Publication Data

Jabour, Anya.
    Marriage in the early republic : Elizabeth and William Wirt and
the companionate ideal / Anya Jabour.
        p.   cm.—(Gender relations in the American experience)
    Includes bibliographical references and index.
    ISBN 0-8018-5877-1 (alk. paper)
    1. Wirt, E. W. (Elizabeth Washington), 1784–1857.   2. Wirt, Wil-
liam, 1772–1834.   3. Marriage—United States—History—19th century—Case studies.   4. Sex role—United States—History—19th
century—Case studies.   5. United States—Social life and customs—1783–1865.   I. Title.   II. Series.
HQ535.J28 1998
306.81'0973'09034—dc21   97-52180
                                                                CIP